Macmillan Interdisciplinary Handbooks

# Philosophy

## *Medical Ethics*

Macmillan Interdisciplinary Handbooks
# Philosophy
*Donald M. Borchert,* SERIES EDITOR
*James Petrik and Arthur Zucker,* ASSOCIATE EDITORS


Philosophy: Sources, Perspectives, and Methodologies
*Donald M. Borchert, editor*

Philosophy: Education
*Lynda Stone and Bryan Warnick, editors*

Philosophy: Environmental Ethics
*David Schmidtz, editor*

Philosophy: Feminism
*Carol Hay, editor*

Philosophy: Medical Ethics
*Craig M. Klugman, editor*

Philosophy: Mind
*Brian P. McLaughlin, editor*

Philosophy: Religion
*Donald M. Borchert, editor*

Philosophy: Sex and Love
*James Petrik and Arthur Zucker, editors*

Philosophy: Sport
*R. Scott Kretchmar, editor*

Philosophy: Technology
*Anthony F. Beavers, editor*


*Other Macmillan Interdisciplinary Handbooks series:*
# Gender
*renée c. hoogland,* SERIES EDITOR
*Nicole R. Fleetwood and Iris van der Tuin,* ASSOCIATE EDITORS

# Religion
*Jeffrey J. Kripal,* SERIES EDITOR
*April D. DeConick and Anthony B. Pinn,* ASSOCIATE EDITORS

Macmillan Interdisciplinary Handbooks

# Philosophy

## *Medical Ethics*

*Craig M. Klugman*

EDITOR

**MACMILLAN REFERENCE USA**
*A part of Gale, Cengage Learning*

Farmington Hills, Mich • San Francisco • New York • Waterville, Maine
Meriden, Conn • Mason, Ohio • Chicago

**Philosophy: Medical Ethics**

Craig M. Klugman, *Editor in Chief*

Carol A. Schwartz, *Project Editor*
Hélène Potter, *Associate Publisher*
Kristine Julien, *Graphic Design Specialist*

For product information and technology assistance, contact us at
**Gale Customer Support, 1-800-877-4253.**
For permission to use material from this text or product,
submit all requests online at **www.cengage.com/permissions.**
Further permissions questions can be emailed to
**permissionrequest@cengage.com.**

Cover image: Alberto Ruggieri/Illustration Works/Getty Images.

While every effort has been made to ensure the reliability of the information presented in this publication, Gale, a part of Cengage Learning, does not guarantee the accuracy of the data contained herein. Gale accepts no payment for listing; and inclusion in the publication of any organization, agency, institution, publication, service, or individual does not imply endorsement of the editors or publisher. Errors brought to the attention of the publisher and verified to the satisfaction of the publisher will be corrected in future editions.

LIBRARY OF CONGRESS CATALOGING-IN-PUBLICATION DATA

Names: Klugman, Craig M., 1969- editor.
Title: Philosophy : medical ethics / Craig M. Klugman, editor in chief.
Other titles: Medical ethics
Description: Farmington Hills : Macmillan Reference USA, a part of Gale, Cengage Learning, 2016. | Series: Macmillan interdisciplinary handbooks | Includes bibliographical references and index.
Identifiers: LCCN 2016011059 | ISBN 9780028663333 (hardcover) | ISBN 9780028663425 (ebook)
Subjects: LCSH: Medical ethics.
Classification: LCC R724 .P49 2016 | DDC 174.2--dc23
LC record available at http://lccn.loc.gov/2016011059

*Gale, a part of Cengage Learning*
27500 Drake Rd.
Farmington Hills, MI 48331-3535

ISBN 978-0-02-866333-3 (this volume)
ISBN 978-0-02-866331-9 (Macmillan Interdisciplinary Handbooks: Philosophy set)

This title is also available as an e-book.
ISBN 978-0-02-866342-5
Contact your Gale sales representative for ordering information.

Printed in Mexico
1 2 3 4 5 6 7 20 19 18 17 16

*so what do you decide to do?*

# Contents

*Preface to Series*                                                      xi

*Introduction*                                                           xiii

**Chapter 1: Primer on Ethical Theories in Medical Ethics** ..................... 1

> Rebecca Feinberg
> *Teaching Assistant, Professor of Health Law, Policy and Bioethics*
> *DePaul University, Chicago, IL*
>
> Craig M. Klugman
> *Professor of Bioethics and Health Sciences*
> *DePaul University, Chicago, IL*

**PART ONE: LIFE SPAN—FIDUCIARY RELATIONSHIP** ..................... 13

**Chapter 2: Reproductive Technologies** ..................... 15

> L. Syd M Johnson
> *Professor, Department of Humanities*
> *Michigan Technological University, Houghton*

**Chapter 3: A Conversation on the Ethics of Abortion** ..................... 41

> Bertha Alvarez Manninen
> *Associate Professor of Philosophy, School of Humanities, Arts, and Cultural*
>   *Studies*
> *Arizona State University–West Campus, Tempe*

**Chapter 4: Genetic Testing: Ethical, Legal, and Social Issues** ..................... 69

> Cheryl J. Erwin
> *Director of the Center for Ethics, Humanities, and Spirituality*
> *Texas Tech University Health Sciences Center, Lubbock*

**Chapter 5: Genetic Interventions: Therapy and Enhancement** ..................... 97

> Keisha Ray
> *Postdoctoral Fellow, McGovern Center for Humanities and Ethics*
> *University of Texas Health Science Center at Houston*

**Chapter 6: Neuroethics** ..................... 121

> Karen S. Rommelfanger
> *Director, Center for Ethics Neuroethics Program; Assistant Professor, Department of Neurology*
>   *(School of Medicine) and Department of Psychiatry and Behavioral Sciences*
> *Emory University, Atlanta, GA*

Julia Marshall
*Graduate Student, Department of Psychology*
*Yale University, New Haven, CT*

Paul Root Wolpe
*Director, Center for Ethics; Professor, Departments of Medicine and Pediatrics (School of Medicine) and Department of Sociology*
*Emory University, Atlanta, GA*

**Chapter 7: Preparing for the End of Life** ............................................................... 153
Nicole M. Tolwin
*Graduate Nursing Student*
*University of Illinois, Chicago*

Craig M. Klugman
*Professor of Bioethics and Health Sciences*
*DePaul University, Chicago, IL*

**Chapter 8: Physician-Assisted Suicide and Euthanasia: Death as Treatment?** ...................... 181
Lois Snyder Sulmasy
*Director, American College of Physicians Center for Ethics and Professionalism*
*Philadelphia, PA*

**PART TWO: PROFESSIONALISM—FIDUCIARY RELATIONSHIP** ......................................... 205

**Chapter 9: Truth and Deception in Health Care** .............................................................. 207
Julija Kelecevic
*Regional Ethicist*
*Hamilton Health Sciences, ON, Canada*

Andrea Frolic
*Director, Office of Clinical and Organizational Ethics*
*Hamilton Health Sciences, ON, Canada*

**Chapter 10: Confidentiality** ....................................................................................... 223
Robert S. Olick
*Professor, Bioethics and Humanities*
*SUNY Upstate Medical University, Syracuse, NY*

**Chapter 11: Consent** .................................................................................................. 243
Stephen S. Hanson
*Associate Professor, Department of Philosophy*
*University of Louisville, KY*

**Chapter 12: Conflicts of Interest** ............................................................................... 261
Howard Brody
*Independent Scholar*
*Galveston, TX*

**Chapter 13: Clinical Ethics Consultation** .................................................................... 279
D. Micah Hester
*Chief and Professor of Medical Humanities*
*University of Arkansas for Medical Sciences, Little Rock*

**PART THREE: SOCIAL JUSTICE** ...................................................................................... 301

**Chapter 14: Organ Transplants** ........................................................................ 303

Aviva M. Goldberg
*Associate Professor, Department of Pediatrics and Child Health, Faculty of Health Sciences*
*University of Manitoba, Winnipeg, Canada*

**Chapter 15: Modern Research Ethics: A Historical Perspective** ........................... 331

Sean Philpott-Jones
*Chair, Department of Bioethics*
*Clarkson University, Capital Region Campus, Schenectady, NY*

**Chapter 16: Public Health Ethics** ..................................................................... 361

Daniel Goldberg
*Assistant Professor, Department of Bioethics and Interdisciplinary Studies*
*Brody School of Medicine, East Carolina University, Greenville, NC*

Craig M. Klugman
*Professor of Bioethics and Health Sciences*
*DePaul University, Chicago, IL*

*Glossary* ..................................................................................................... 385

*Index* .......................................................................................................... 395

# Preface to Series

This volume is part of a ten-volume series of interdisciplinary philosophy handbooks prepared especially for undergraduate college students. The publisher of the series is Cengage Learning, Inc., which holds the Macmillan Reference USA imprint under which the award-winning second edition of the ten-volume *Encyclopedia of Philosophy* was published in 2006. I had the privilege of serving as editor in chief for that edition. Now I have the honor of serving as editor in chief of this handbook series. Furthermore, I have the added delight of collaborating once again with Hélène Potter, Cengage's associate publisher for reference works, who played a major role in the production of the *Encyclopedia* and is the person Cengage called upon to develop this new series of interdisciplinary philosophy handbooks.

When Hélène Potter invited me to join her in this new publishing adventure, she described two features that would make these new philosophy handbooks truly innovative.

First, philosophy handbooks are usually written for an audience already knowledgeable about philosophy: philosophy majors, graduate students, and professors. In contrast, the people for whom these handbooks have been prepared are undergraduate college students who have had little or no exposure to philosophy. Each handbook provides an introduction to a subfield of philosophy, an exploration of fifteen to twenty-five topics in that subfield, and bibliographies to encourage students to explore the topics further. In other words, each handbook combines some features of an introductory textbook with some features of a reference resource. The teacher-scholars who wrote the chapters in these volumes have worked diligently to make their discussions comprehensible to philosophical novices and at the same time respectable in the eyes of philosophy scholars.

Second, the word *interdisciplinary* in the title for the project signals the other innovative aspect. Our project is interdisciplinary because it uses material from nonphilosophy disciplines—such as anthropology, film, history, literature, and other fields—to present illustrations of human experiences that raise the crucial questions philosophers try to address. These illustrations from nonphilosophy disciplines are used to initiate philosophical analysis.

This strategy seems to have been used by the ancient Greek philosopher Plato (427–347 BCE). For example, through the lens of the trial of Socrates, Plato masterfully explored vital philosophical questions. Socrates (470–399 BCE) engaged many leading citizens in public discourses in which he cleverly questioned their claims to possess important knowledge that enabled them to judge human affairs and guide society appropriately. His relentless questioning that exposed in public the flawed nature of the knowledge that these prominent citizens claimed to possess fomented increasing hostility toward Socrates.

Eventually, Socrates was put on trial in 399 BCE and charged with impiety toward the gods, turning moral values upside down, and teaching his socially disruptive ideas to others for money. Despite his eloquent defense, Socrates was found guilty by a citizen jury and was given a death sentence that required him to drink a cup of poisonous hemlock.

Plato's account of the defense Socrates presented to the jury not only displayed Socrates's wisdom and verbal eloquence but also painted a verbal portrait of how Socrates practiced philosophy and what questions were of vital concern to him. Socrates appears as someone who pursued the examined life, cost what it may, and who encouraged others to pursue the examined life as well. Such a pursuit involves using one's reasoning capacity to explore and understand all facets of human life and experience. And such a pursuit can lead a person to know and practice the virtues or skills that can promote human flourishing and happiness.

In the first volume of the series, which serves as a primer on philosophy, portions of the trial of Socrates as reported by Plato in his *Apology* are displayed and discussed to expose the thoughts and passion of a model philosopher, Socrates. In addition, the primer volume discusses some of the challenges from various forms of skepticism that philosophers have faced when, in the footsteps of Socrates, they have tried to gain knowledge. The primer also provides a sample of the diverse philosophical traditions that have developed through the centuries in different parts of the world. Finally, the primer volume provides introductions to nine contemporary subfields of philosophy. To each of these nine subfields one of the nine volumes following the primer volume is devoted. Those subfields include environmental ethics, medical ethics, philosophy of education, philosophy of feminism, philosophy of mind, philosophy of religion, philosophy of sex and love, philosophy of sport, and philosophy of technology.

Allow me to encourage philosophical novices and their teachers to read those introductions to nine subfields in this primer. I daresay that one or two or perhaps even more of those introductions will generate a spark of interest and an eagerness to explore more fully those subfields presented in the individual volumes dedicated to them.

Please remember that numerous other subfields of philosophy are exciting and important—such as the philosophy of art, of science, of history, of language, of logic, and of metaphysics—for which additional interdisciplinary philosophy handbooks may be developed.

I am confident that I speak for the more than 150 teacher-scholars who have contributed chapters to this ten-volume series when I say, "We wish you an exciting and enlightening adventure as you pursue the examined life with the help of the words that we have written for you."

It is important that I indicate my appreciation to Macmillan/Cengage for allowing me to invite two of my fine colleagues from the Philosophy Department at Ohio University to serve as associate editors for the series: James Petrik and Arthur Zucker. Both are excellent teacher-scholars who have given generously and joyfully of their time and talent to this project.

Professors Petrik and Zucker wish to join me in acknowledging with gratitude the steadfast and skilled support we have received from Cengage's senior editor for our project, Carol Schwartz, who, like Hélène Potter, was also an extraordinary colleague in the production of the *Encyclopedia of Philosophy* several years ago.

*Donald M. Borchert*

*Editor in Chief, Macmillan Interdisciplinary Handbooks: Philosophy*
*Editor in Chief, Macmillan's* Encyclopedia of Philosophy
*Emeritus Professor of Philosophy, Ohio University, Athens*

# Introduction

In the 1947 novel *The Plague* by existential writer Albert Camus (1913–1960), Dr. Bernard Rieux discovers a dead rat. This remarkable finding is the harbinger of an outbreak of bubonic plague in Oran, Algeria, in the 1940s. Over the ten months that this novel follows, Dr. Rieux and the community face this deadly epidemic. Those with wealth flee the city until the city gates are closed, and all citizens are quarantined inside its gates. Dr. Castel is the senior physician in the town and finds himself embittered by the relentless dying of his patients. Eventually, he discovers an antiplague serum and then must decide who receives the very few doses that have been produced. Dr. Rieux is an outsider in the medical community and not taken seriously. When he identifies the disease, his words are initially lost on the city leaders and senior physicians.

Rieux focuses on treating the poor rather than those with means, and he struggles with his duties as a doctor to provide care for patients when most of them die of the plague. To survive both psychologically and existentially, Rieux cuts himself off from his emotions to avoid being depressed by the suffering he sees around him. At the end of the novel, the reader learns that Rieux is the narrator of the tale. He does his job because it is his duty to relieve suffering and to struggle against disease, even when faced with seemingly impossible odds. A vacationer who becomes trapped in the quarantined city states, "I've learned modesty. All I maintain is that on this earth there are pestilences and there are victims, and it's up to us, so far as possible, not to join forces with the pestilences" (Camus [1948] 1991, 253–254).

Camus presents physician characters who are toiling in extraordinary circumstances. Drs. Rieux and Castel work to fulfill their duties to a sick populace while trying to maintain their own humanity and a grasp on the meaning of their work. Their journey is similar to that of every medical and health-care student: the amount of knowledge they must master and the volume of sickness and need in the world can be overwhelming. The student, like Dr. Rieux, sacrifices much of a personal life in service to others and tries to do the right thing.

Camus's novel highlights issues of medical practice, professionalism, and balancing the rights of individual patients with the needs of the community. Philosopher Donald Borchert explains that "philosophers have been pushing their philosophical inquiries into more and more areas of human experience" (2016, 257). One of these areas of examination is medicine in the form of medical ethics.

Medical ethics is the examination and application of morality and ethical decision making in the practice of medicine. The focus is on "what one ought to do" in general practice and in particular (sometimes unique) situations. This is the oldest and most developed of the subfields that comprise the modern field of bioethics. Bioethics is "the broad terrain of the moral problems of the life sciences, ordinarily taken to encompass medicine, biology, and some important aspects of the environmental, population and social sciences" (Reich 1995, 250). As a broader umbrella term, bioethics is a field that incorporates not only medical ethics but also nursing ethics, research ethics, clinical ethics, and public health ethics. Bioethics, according to Craig Klugman, "is about examining actions, behaviors and duties between health-care professionals, patients, and society" (2016, 274).

# A BRIEF HISTORY OF MEDICAL ETHICS

The 2013 film *The Physician* is about Rob Cole, a young boy in the eleventh century who tries futilely to prevent his mother's death. While wandering England, he connects with a traveling barber surgeon and learns to crudely treat a number of medical conditions. Rather than being satisfied with simply doing procedures, he has a desire to know how the body works and why those procedures are effective. When he comes across a skilled and educated surgeon trained in Persia, Cole decides to make his way to a famed medical school. The problem is that the institution is located in a part of the world where Christians are not permitted to study. Dressing as a Jew, he makes his way across the known world to not only learn the skills and knowledge of medicine but also to understand the ethical choices that come with such abilities.

The history of medical ethics may not be as exciting as this film, but the risks Rob Cole takes to study and the decisions he has to make go back even further than the days portrayed in the film. For example, during the Renaissance in Europe, anatomy was beginning to be taught through dissection, whereas previously one would read the classical authorities, Aristotle or Galen (both of whom had it very wrong), to learn this subject. For the medical student of the Renaissance, fear of and laws against desecrating a corpse, as well as religious precepts regarding respect for the dead, made it nearly impossible to get access to a cadaver. The enterprising medical student would have to bring his own body to school, often by stealing it from a recent grave. Thus, for most medical students, their training began with an act of theft, justified by the future benefit this would—they hoped—provide to their patients.

Medicine as a practice evolved hand in hand with ethics to help provide guidance to physicians in determining the right thing to do. One of the earliest medical ethics writings comes from the Hippocratic Corpus, a collection of treatises on health and disease from the Pythagorean physicians in the fourth and fifth centuries BCE. One of the most famous of these works is the Hippocratic Oath, which provides moral guidance for the physician:

I swear by Apollo Physician and Asclepius and Hygieia and Panaceia and all the gods and goddesses, making them my witnesses, that I will fulfil according to my ability and judgment this oath and this covenant:

To hold him who has taught me this art as equal to my parents and to live my life in partnership with him, and if he is in need of money to give him a share of mine, and to regard his offspring as equal to my brothers in male lineage and to teach them this art—if they desire to learn it—without fee and covenant; to give a share of precepts and oral instruction and all the other learning to my sons and to the sons of him who has instructed me and to pupils who have signed the covenant and have taken an oath according to the medical law, but no one else.

I will apply dietetic measures for the benefit of the sick according to my ability and judgment; I will keep them from harm and injustice.

I will neither give a deadly drug to anybody who asked for it, nor will I make a suggestion to this effect. Similarly I will not give to a woman an abortive remedy. In purity and holiness I will guard my life and my art.

I will not use the knife, not even on sufferers from stone, but will withdraw in favor of such men as are engaged in this work.

Whatever houses I may visit, I will come for the benefit of the sick, remaining free of all intentional injustice, of all mischief and in particular of sexual relations with both female and male persons, be they free or slaves.

What I may see or hear in the course of the treatment or even outside of the treatment in regard to the life of men, which on no account one must spread abroad, I will keep to myself, holding such things shameful to be spoken about.

If I fulfil this oath and do not violate it, may it be granted to me to enjoy life and art, being honored with fame among all men for all time to come; if I transgress it and swear falsely, may the opposite of all this be my lot. (Edelstein 1943, 5)

This oath is called a covenant because it represents a sacred bond between a physician and that physician's peers and that physician's god. The Hippocratic Oath is a call to support a profession and to practice professional behavior. For example, the doctor is supposed to put the patient first, preserve privacy, maintain relationship boundaries, and support both current and future peers. The physician must be competent and know the limits of his skills and must never harm others. According to historian of medicine Ludwig Edelstein, although abortion and euthanasia were legal acts in ancient Greece, for the Hippocratic physician, such acts were ethically proscribed. These same issues are still controversial after millennia of philosophical analysis. As you will read in the pages of these volumes, the Hippocratic Oath's ideals are upheld in the practice of medicine and healing today.

Medical ethics holds its mythical beginning to this Hippocratic Corpus. From this starting point, medical ethics has influenced many physicians in waxing philosophically about the nature of their profession and the limited power doctors have over life and death. For example, the Roman physician Galen (129–c. 216 CE), author of *The Best Doctor Is Also a Philosopher*, believed that physicians must study philosophy to learn virtues, reason well, and have an understanding of how a body functions.

With the fall of Rome, the Middle Ages descended upon Europe, but medicine and science continued to progress in the Arab world. One of the most famous medical ethics works from this era is *Practical Ethics*, written by Ishaq ibn Ali al-Ruhawi. He extolls physicians to be patient with others, temper their desires, attend the sick, and be generous to the poor.

The Arab world extended into Spain, where physician Mosheh ben Maimon, or Moses Maimonides (1135–1204 CE), lived. In his *Guide for the Perplexed*, Maimonides presents a theological text that explores ethical conflicts, including in medicine. This work explores the ethical dilemma of abortion by focusing on the relationship between the pregnant woman and her fetus. He is credited with writing both an oath and a prayer for healers.

In the oath, Maimonides tells the physician to be humble because the practice of medicine is a calling, not an opportunity for fame and fortune. He reminds the physician to always view the patient as a fellow human being who suffers and that one should always be improving one's craft. The prayers add a hope that the physician will be a model of virtue in medicine and will always be deserving of a patient's confidence. Maimonides tells the physician to always be learning and that serving patients and the profession is doing divine work (Maimonides 1917).

With the Renaissance, Europeans discovered the lost writings of the ancient philosophers and developed an interest in knowing how the world worked. The Enlightenment saw the development of the scientific method, which led to new understandings of nature and to technological progress. Physicians John Gregory (1723–1773) and Thomas Percival (1740–1804) are considered the parents of modern secular medical ethics. Gregory focused on physicians' duties to patients and professionalism. Percival was interested in physician self-regulation and integrity—the belief that one works within one's own competency and scope of practice.

In the United States, medical ethics took root in 1847 in the newly founded American Medical Association (AMA). As one of its first acts, the AMA wrote a code of medical ethics, which served to cement Percival's idea that the medical profession should be regulated from within rather than from without, as well as to give patients confidence in the medical profession.

## TRANSFORMATION INTO BIOETHICS

Historically, medical ethics had been the purview of physicians, not philosophers. Few in philosophy in the mid-twentieth century were concerned with applied ethics and decision making. Applied ethics was viewed as belonging to religion—making determinations about right and wrong. Beginning in the 1960s, scholars in philosophy, religion, and law became interested in ethical questions raised in the practice of medicine and its role in society. Christian ethicist Paul Ramsey (1913–1988) wrote on just war, reproductive technology, fetal research, and objectification of patients. Catholic theologian Richard McCormick (1922–2000) was interested in in vitro fertilization, gestational surrogates, euthanasia, and access to medical care. Philosopher and Episcopal priest Joseph Fletcher (1905–1991) expounded upon abortion, infanticide, euthanasia, eugenics, and cloning. Physician and philosopher Edmund Pellegrino (1920–2013) worked on the physician-patient relationship, assisted suicide, artificial reproduction, abortion, genetic engineering, and managed care.

Although from different disciplines, these individuals and many others found themselves studying similar topics—patient autonomy, research abuses, and powerful new technologies. This convergence of medicine, religion, philosophy, and law gave rise to bioethics. According to bioethicist Arthur Caplan, bioethics is the child that overshadowed its parents (2015, 25).

The term *bioethics* comes from the work of German theologian Fritz Jahr (1895–1953), who coined the term *Bio-Ethik* in 1927 to refer to moral obligations between humans and all living things. In 1970, biochemist Van Rensselaer Potter (1911–2001) popularized the term in his article "Bioethics, the Science of Survival" and in his 1971 book, *Bioethics: Bridge to the Future*. Potter called for biosphere ethics, a new discipline to link ethics and the environment. Only after the establishment of the Joseph and Rose Kennedy Institute for the Study of Human Reproduction and Bioethics (later the Kennedy Institute of Ethics) in 1970 and the Institute of Society, Ethics, and the Life Sciences (now known as the Hastings Center) in 1969 did the term *bioethics* become synonymous with health care and medical ethics.

Bioethics appeared at this time in history because of four societal trends in the late 1960s and early 1970s: reports of abuse of human subjects in research, the rise of medical technology, the social/civil rights movement, and public engagement on the part of scholars.

The first trend was bringing reports about abuse of human subjects in research experiments into the public light. Dr. Henry Beecher, an anesthesiologist at Harvard Medical School, published "Ethics and Clinical Research" in the *New England Journal of Medicine* (1966). In this groundbreaking article, Beecher describes twenty-two studies involving human subjects that he considered unethical. The violations included withholding treatment, lack of patient consent, and physicians deliberately infecting patients with disease. In 1972, reporter Jean Heller of the Associated Press wrote a story that publicly revealed the Tuskegee Study of Untreated Syphilis in the Negro Male (today more commonly called the "Tuskegee Study"). Heller's exposé showed that from 1932 on, a group of 600 men (399 infected with syphilis and 201 in a control group) were enrolled in this US Public Health Service study of a disease in nature. This meant observing the progression of syphilis in a body without medical interference. The subjects were poor, African American men from a rural county in Alabama. Study personnel lied to the men about their disease and about the nature of the procedures to which they were subjected. Beginning in 1942, study personnel prevented the subjects from receiving the new cure, penicillin. In that year, the drug became available to military personnel and recruits; consequently, study personnel prevented the men from enlisting. Even once penicillin became available to the public, study personnel prevented the men from receiving it; their names were printed on lists distributed to doctors and clinics throughout the region to be sure that no one gave them penicillin.

The second trend was the growth of new technologies. The 1960s saw the development of chronic kidney dialysis, as well as organ transplants (pancreas, liver, and heart). The US Supreme Court ruling on abortion (*Roe v. Wade*) and the first human born from in vitro fertilization followed in the 1970s. These technologies gave physicians the ability to extend life, treat disease, and change how humans reproduced. With new technology came new responsibilities and a need to examine how and when these tools were used.

The social and civil rights movements were the third trend. This was a period when people who had formerly been denied a political and social voice demanded to be heard. Vietnam War protests, the 1963 March on Washington, and the counterculture movement were all attempts to bring power to the people and take it away from those who had always hoarded it. The idea of paternalism—that someone in authority knows what is best for others and makes their decisions—was strongly challenged. People wanted autonomy—the right to self-governance, which required access to education and health, the redefinition of gender roles, and voting rights. Similarly, medicine had been paternalistic. Patients often were not informed of their diagnosis or even the nature of their treatment. Doctors expected patients to simply comply with medical orders. Similar to the calls for equal participation and self-control in public life, patients demanded to be partners in health-care decisions and not simply objects on which physicians practiced. According to Larry McCullough, "the view that physicians for centuries had been engaging in systematic medical paternalism became not just a central claim but, perhaps, the defining claim of American bioethics in its origins and throughout its history to date" (2013, 219).

The fourth trend was that scholars in the new field of bioethics were willing to participate in public life. As a result of the Tuskegee Study, the US Congress called for a national commission to develop ethical guidelines for research using human subjects. This first public bioethics commission included several scholars who identified themselves as working in bioethics. They wrote the 1979 *Belmont Report*, which spelled out the three principles of respect for persons, beneficence, and justice. This work also laid the foundation for informed consent in research and clinical medicine. Since 1974 there have been six national bioethics commissions, and the last three US presidents (starting with Bill Clinton) all established bioethics groups to provide guidance on public policy issues in medicine and health. Besides working with the government, bioethicists have engaged with hospitals, pharmaceutical companies, and medical device manufacturers.

Scholars in bioethics were also willing to speak with reporters. From its beginning, the Hastings Center worked with journalists (in part to gain recognition for the new field and fledgling center) to educate reporters about new technologies. For the reporter, bioethics stories sell—people are interested in the moral implications of medical decisions. Along with being experts for news articles, bioethicists today write their own blogs, produce podcasts, and contribute to social media.

## THIS VOLUME

This book is geared toward the undergraduate student (in school or in life) who is interested in the field of medical ethics and bioethics but who may not have a strong background in philosophy (though those with such a background will also be engaged). After all, everyone eventually becomes involved with medicine at some point, whether one chooses to study medical ethics, work in the health professions, or seek treatment as a patient.

Whether studying for a course or for personal interest, this volume provides an interdisciplinary experience by incorporating films, books, and art to explore bioethical topics. This volume on medical ethics is organized around three distinct themes: (1) ethics across the life span; (2) ethical issues in health and medical professionalism; and (3) bioethics in social justice. The focus moves from the individual patient-provider relationship to those of the greater community.

The first chapter is a primer on the ethical theories used in modern biomedical ethics. For readers who have a strong background in moral philosophy, this chapter may not be necessary, but for those who are novices to the study of medical ethics, this review should provide some tools for examining the ethical issues raised in future chapters. Rebecca Feinberg and Craig Klugman explore deontology (rules-based reasoning), ethics of care (relationship focus), natural law (specifically double effect), principlism (autonomy, beneficence, nonmaleficence, and justice), utilitarianism (consequences for a population), and virtue ethics (character, case-based reasoning, and narrative ethics).

**Part One** of this book looks at bioethical issues across the human life span. Spanning from the production of new life to genetics, the brain, and death, this section examines specific issues that apply at different life stages.

**Chapter 2** surveys the creation of human life in a laboratory through artificial reproductive technologies. L. Syd M Johnson uses the 2008 movie *Baby Mama* to look at whether infertility is a disease and to examine the ethical implications of creating and destroying embryos in search of parenthood. Technologies such as egg and sperm donation and gestational surrogacy allow single people, same-sex couples, and those struggling with infertility to become biological parents through science. Dr. Johnson looks at whether gametes are commodified in a society that uses technology (such as egg freezing) to mold life events (such as having children around the social norms of building a career during reproductive years rather than changing work expectations to accommodate biology).

Finally, Dr. Johnson uses the concept of procreative liberty and the nonidentity problem to show questions of autonomy and the potential harms that such processes may pose to children who would not exist without those technologies.

In **Chapter 3**, Bertha Manninen begins by looking at the foundational Supreme Court cases that have established the legal framework of abortion in the United States. Presenting an objective viewpoint, Dr. Manninen explores both pro-life and pro-choice positions as to whether the human embryo is a moral being in its own right or holds the status of potential moral human. From Pope John Paul II's view that the unborn are vulnerable and need to be protected to Judith Jarvis Thomson's analogy of the fetus being an interloper on a woman's body, Dr. Manninen explores the moral status of the embryo through legal, cognitive, and interest approaches. Dr. Manninen examines when fetal and maternal rights conflict and the complicated and special relationship between a woman and her not-yet-born offspring. Last, she explores common grounds between the political sides in regard to economic disparity and respect for fetal life.

**Chapter 4,** which discusses ethical, legal, and social issues in genetic testing, opens with the discovery of genetics and testing. Given that genetic data are highly identifiable, Cheryl Erwin discusses the ethical and legal challenges of conducting research with genes and stem cells. She discusses ownership of genetic material and how the law allows DNA to be patented and commodified. This chapter also looks at issues of testing across the life span— from embryos in a laboratory to newborns, children, adolescents, and adults. This new technology has changed the physician-patient relationship because, although medical genetic testing happens through a doctor's office, direct-to-consumer testing means that medical assessments are available for the first time without a health-care professional. Because a person shares similar DNA with family members, one person's DNA information gives knowledge to others, irrespective of whether they want to know. For example, if a daughter tests positive for the *BRCA 1* or *2* genes (specific breast cancer genes), that result also means at least one of her parents carries the gene(s) and her siblings may be at risk as well. What happens when a DNA test shows that the people one thought were one's parents are not actually one's genetic parents? Or when DNA is used to convict (and free) people of crimes? Dr. Erwin suggests that there are privacy, confidentiality, and discrimination issues raised in genetic testing to which the law has not yet caught up.

Another aspect of genetics that raises ethical questions is the manipulation of DNA to cure disease and even to enhance human functioning. While it is currently possible to select among a number of embryos to give birth to a child that lacks a gene that codes for a disease, it may soon be possible to change the DNA of an embryo. Science may be able to replace damaged DNA or to insert DNA that offers a certain eye color or even enhanced strength. In **Chapter 5**, Keisha Ray explores the difference between somatic cell (adult cells in a single body) and germ-line cell (the eggs and sperm that are passed to future generations) engineering. She asks whether having the technology to custom design children obligates us to use it in order to give our children the best tools for a chance at a successful life. Should we genetically engineer a future humanity that is more adaptable to a world beset with climate change? As Veronica Roth's *Divergent* trilogy (2011–2013) asks, what happens to humanity once we have genetically engineered children who are born with expert tendencies in very narrow areas of human experience? Dr. Ray examines whether such technologies would make social and economic injustices worse or whether they can potentially decrease such disparities.

**Chapter 6** explores the newly emerging field of neuroethics. As explained by Karen Rommelfanger, Julia Marshall, and Paul Root Wolpe, neuroethics is (1) the ethics of neuroscience and (2) the neuroscience of ethics. The first area looks at issues of coercion and consent in research and clinical care among patients where manipulation of the brain may be a goal. Other tools, such as deep brain stimulation, cosmetic neurology and enhancement, neuromarketing, brain training, and downloaded learning, may provide opportunities to manipulate the brain to alter how we think and perhaps even who we believe we are. The second area includes questions of whether we have free will or if there is an ethics center of the brain that makes decisions before we are aware of our choices. Some research even suggests that there is a God-center to the brain and that religion may be preprogrammed into our biology. If tools are developed that allow us to peer inside and manipulate human brains, what are the implications of mind reading or of inserting suggestions and even commands directly into a brain?

Our human life spans end in dying and death, which are the topics of Chapters 7 and 8. Craig Klugman and Nicole Tolwin offer various definitions and criteria for death in **Chapter 7**. Differentiating between social, medical, and biological deaths, they explore how these different types of deaths have functioned and interacted through various eras of human history. They discuss how death today often occurs in the highly technological environment of the hospital, whereas new models such as hospice and palliative care provide more focus on human dignity and control than on the prolongation of dying. Patient control of dying comes from a long legal and ethical history that focuses on patient autonomy and a right to refuse unwanted medical treatment. Documents such as advance directives and advance-care-planning conversational tools allow patients to have more control over their final days and future medical care that they may need. The authors also look at the philosophical distinction of withdrawing and withholding care, as well as the challenging notion of futility.

Lois Snyder Sulmasy in **Chapter 8** explores the ultimate in patient control at the end of life: physician-assisted suicide, euthanasia, and voluntary cessation of eating and drinking. Drawing on law and ethics, Dr. Snyder Sulmasy shows the philosophical, causal, and legal distinctions of these actions. This chapter examines—in a critical fashion—the arguments both for and against assisted suicide and euthanasia, as well as debates over pain control that may shorten life, the limits of autonomy, and the dangers of the slippery slope. Dr. Snyder Sulmasy calls for a change in end-of-life care policy in the United States—one that focuses more on controlling pain and providing comfort care rather than freedoms of ending one's life.

**Part Two** analyzes issues of professionalism in health care. These topics look at virtues of the practicing health-care provider, including tools that ensure patient autonomy so that providers and patients are equal partners in pursuing health. Chapters 9 through 13 explore truth-telling, confidentiality, patient consent, conflicts of interest, and clinical ethics consultation.

In **Chapter 9**, Andrea Frolic and Julija Kelecevic describe the virtue of truth-telling, a general precept of medical practice that a physician and most health-care providers always tell the truth. This tendency to be truthful is a recent addition to medicine. Deception and obfuscation were once common toward patients with terminal illnesses or disease. Despite this normative rule of truth-telling, there are times when doctors tend to lie—in securing health insurance coverage for treatment, in giving treatment to individuals with disorders that affect their thinking, and in talking to children. Similarly, patients sometimes lie to their doctors out of embarrassment or fear of stigmatization or abandonment. Lastly, Drs. Frolic and Kelecevic show that norms of truth are culturally bound and that legal requirements can interfere with a physician's duty to tell the truth. Some laws actually require a doctor to tell scientific lies.

Robert S. Olick explores the virtue of confidentiality in **Chapter 10**. In the realm of the fiduciary relationship between a physician/health-care provider and a patient, confidentiality is an agreement to keep secrets that a physician needs to know in order to help diagnose and heal. Patients need to trust that this vulnerability will be protected. Confidentiality has a basis in both ethics (such as the Hippocratic Oath) and in law (such as the 1990 Patient Self-Determination Act and the 1996 Health Insurance Portability and Accountability Act). As a *prima facie* duty, breaches of confidentiality are sometimes required by the law, such as when a third party is threatened, or when a patient's condition poses a potential harm to others. For example, diagnoses of infectious diseases or epilepsy (which can pose a hazard to a person's ability to drive) often require reporting the patient to public authorities. Confidentiality also presents challenges when working with children, adolescents, and suspected victims of abuse. Lastly, Dr. Olick suggests what confidentiality looks like in a world of electronic health records and social media.

In **Chapter 11,** Stephen S. Hanson writes about consent, a backbone of the American medical system whereby patients and potential research subjects must give their permission before they are examined, diagnosed, treated, or even seen by a health-care professional. The highest standard of consent is informed consent—the written documentation of an autonomous person's considered decision. Consent means that, in most circumstances, a competent and capacitated patient has the right to decide what happens to that patient's body. Special challenges occur when treating children who legally lack the competency to make their decisions because of their status as minors. While their parents give consent, children are asked to assent—give their agreement—according to their age and intellectual capacity to understand. In emergency situations where the patient is unconscious or lacks capacity to give consent, then under the reasonable person standard, doctors may use the implied or presumed standards of consent—that a person in need of help would want that help.

A conflict of interest occurs when an individual owes a duty to more than one party and those interests may collide. An example is when a physician prescribes a particular drug because the physician gets a small payment for every prescription written for that medication. Howard Brody in **Chapter 12** offers a variety of definitions for such conflicts, the places where they occur, and the boundaries that are often crossed as a result of these situations. He offers examples of conflicts, such as physicians accepting free meals from drug sales representatives, taking paid trips to give talks, and accepting consulting fees from companies that also pay for their research, as well as medical technology companies that write articles for publication and pay physicians to use their names as bylines. Some solutions, Dr. Brody says, include disclosure of the conflict, removing oneself from the situation, and accommodation to the situation.

Micah Hester introduces clinical ethics consultation in **Chapter 13**. He explains why and how philosophers entered the clinical setting, offering consultation on complicated moral issues. Such interests quickly became formalized in the forms of ethics committees and clinical ethics consultants—individuals trained in philosophy and facilitation/mediation, with an understanding of relevant law and institutional policy. Consultants and committees serve as a mechanism for the resolution of ethical issues in medical care through service, education, and case consultation. Dr. Hester describes one model of consultation and demonstrates how it works through a sample case.

**Part Three** deals with issues of social justice, mainly the equitable distribution of benefits and burdens within society. The topics of organ transplants, research ethics, and crisis ethics in public health address population-level ethical issues rather than those that involve a specific patient and provider.

In **Chapter 14,** Aviva Goldberg analyzes the process of organ transplantation, including procuring organs and selecting who receives them. Traditionally, organs came from the recently deceased, but new procedures allow controlled deaths to maximize the chances of a successful transplant. This chapter also looks at using organs from living donors, prisoners, and children. Dr. Goldberg assesses different systems of signing people up for donation, including opt-in volunteer programs and systems in which all citizens of a nation are presumed to be donors. Among other ethical challenges are paired exchanges (a patient and a relative willing to donate but who is not a match are paired with another couple in a similar situation and put together in a chain until everyone has a matched donor); biologically compatible donors who do not wish to donate and request that the physician lie and say they were not a match (to avoid any social pressure or damaged relationships); patients advertising that they need an organ; and medical tourism, where people from wealthier countries travel to poorer ones and buy organs from people who desperately need the money.

Modern research ethics builds on the research abuses discussed earlier to ensure that patients are not forced into participating in a study and are not injured or killed in being part of one. Sean Philpott-Jones takes a historical approach in looking at the checkered past of human-subjects research in **Chapter 15**. He evaluates the ethical principles, laws, and review boards that we have developed to oversee such work and limit the risk to human participants. For example, the Nuremberg Code was created after World War II as a set of rules to be used in charging and trying doctors who conducted abusive human-subjects experiments on unwilling participants in Nazi Germany. This code is the basis for the principle of informed consent not only in research but also in medical practice. As mentioned earlier, in the United States, the *Belmont Report*'s three ethical principles of respect for persons, beneficence, and justice underlie the "Common Rule" (the federal law that protects human research subjects), which created the system of institutional review board (IRB) approvals for proposed research.

Daniel Goldberg and Craig Klugman propose the need for population-level public health ethics in **Chapter 16**. The authors explain how public health differs from medical care and how these different goals of upstream (preventive) action suggest a need for adopting utilitarian, communitarian, and contractarian foundations of ethics. Public health is concerned with reducing aggregate morbidity and mortality in populations. At its most simplistic, public health ethics is a balancing of community needs and individual rights. Unlike medical ethics, which are only normative in nature, public health has police powers—rules regarding quarantine are legally enforceable regardless of the consent of any particular person. The framework of public health principlism (solidarity, efficacy, integrity, and dignity) is then applied to public health challenges such as disaster and crisis management; surveillance, quarantine, and stigma; health behavior change; smoking; and nutrition.

## INTERDISCIPLINARITY

By its very nature, bioethics is an interdisciplinary field. In the years after religion, law, philosophy, and medicine came together in this endeavor, arts, literature, sociology, history, anthropology, and health communications have all contributed to bioethics. Even the national bioethics professional organization is called the American Society for Bioethics and Humanities. In undergraduate programs, medical schools, residency programs, and nursing schools, bioethics uses art and literature to teach patient experiences of illness. Teachers of medical ethics use films and television to demonstrate ethical conflicts in medical practice.

The humanities have value in their own right and should be pursued for their own inherent worth. For bioethics, however, the humanities also offer a base for a shared experience, which allows us to examine, understand, and reflect on ethical issues displayed. Not every student has experienced a death, but we can watch the 1995 play *Wit* by Margaret Edson as a class and discuss the fictional patient's experience, research on dying patients, advance directives, and professionalism as portrayed on stage. Bioethics and the humanities work hand in hand to give us insight into the lived reality of illness and health from the perspective of both patients and health-care providers.

As with the other volumes in this series, each chapter in this book refers to the humanities and the arts to provide a deeper understanding and context for the issues discussed. Chapter 9 introduces truth-telling with an excerpt from *The Death of Ivan Ilych* (1886), a novella by Leo Tolstoy that explores, in part, the deception of not telling someone that he is dying and the pretenses that a family goes through to deny that impending death. In Chapter 13, clinical ethics consultation is likened to a design consultant on an HGTV show who works to bring together the design styles of people with very different tastes and values. Chapter 15, which examines modern research ethics, begins with *The Constant Gardener* (2005), a film that investigates medical research by companies located in wealthy countries working in resource-poor countries to conduct studies that would not pass human-subjects review at home.

Even if the reader has no intention of joining a health profession, the sad truth is that we will all be consumers of health, public health, and medical care, whether as a patient, family member, or a friend. We will all be faced with ethical decisions in medicine and health. If readers are familiar with the arts discussed, that exposure will help enhance and provide understanding of a chapter's topics. If readers are not familiar with a work, then I invite them to read or watch it as a way to gain a fuller understanding of the topic and its portrayal of human experience. The list of literature, film, art, theater, and television in this volume is extensive. Besides being educational, engagement with this material is entertaining and fun. For every science-fiction movie discussed, there is a real-life debate occurring on a similar technology that is—or will become—available.

For example, consider the lessons in history, culture, and scientific knowledge offered by a single painting. In *The Anatomy Lesson of Dr. Nicolaes Tulp (1632)*, the Dutch painter Rembrandt presents a scene of medical learning: a public dissection of a criminal, Adriaen het Kint. Public dissection after execution was a more severe punishment than execution alone. Wearing dark gowns and frilly collars, the students gather around the praelector (reader and teacher), who is dressed in black and wearing a hat. The instructor has a pointer that is pulling back the skin on a dissected arm. The cadaver rests in a position that could be taken as his simply being asleep. In a corner of the frame sits an ancient book on a pedestal, most likely Galen's treatise on anatomy. The students' eyes rest not on the actual body in front of them, but on the text—which differed significantly from the real body but whose authority was rarely questioned. The names of the students appear on a sheet of parchment held by a student who gazes directly at the viewer.

Like the students gathered around the corpse to learn from the praelector, you are invited to dissect the major issues that occupy bioethicists today through this volume.

*Craig M. Klugman*

*Professor of Bioethics and Health Sciences*
*DePaul University, Chicago, IL*

## BIBLIOGRAPHY

Beecher, Henry K. "Ethics and Clinical Research." *New England Journal of Medicine* 274, no. 24 (1966): 1354–1360. doi: 10.1056/NEJM196606162742405.

Borchert, Donald M. "Subfields of Philosophy." In *Philosophy: Sources, Perspectives, and Methodologies*, edited by Donald M. Borchert, 257. Farmington Hills, MI: Macmillan Reference USA, a part of Gale, Cengage Learning, 2016.

Caplan, Arthur L. "Done Good." *Journal of Medical Ethics* 41 (2015): 25–27. doi: 10.1136/medethics-2014-102290.

Edelstein, Ludwig. *The Hippocratic Oath: Text, Translation, and Interpretation.* Baltimore: Johns Hopkins University Press, 1943.

Klugman, Craig M. "Medical Ethics." In *Philosophy: Sources, Perspectives, and Methodologies*, edited by Donald M. Borchert, 276–287. Farmington Hills, MI: Macmillan Reference USA, a part of Gale, Cengage Learning, 2016.

Maimonides, Moses. "The Oath of Maimonides." *Bulletin of Johns Hopkins Hospital* 28 (1917): 260–261. Translated by Harry Friedenwald.

McCullough, Larry B. "The Role of an Ideology of Anti-paternalism in the Development of American Bioethics." In *The Development of Bioethics in the United States*, edited by Jeremy R. Garrett, Fabrice Jotterand, and D. Christopher Ralston, 207–220. New York: Springer, 2013.

Potter, Van Rensselaer. *Bioethics: Bridge to the Future.* Englewood Cliffs, NJ: Prentice-Hall, 1971.

Potter, Van Rensselaer. "Bioethics, the Science of Survival." *Perspectives in Biology and Medicine* 14, no. 1 (1970): 127–153.

Reich, Warren T. "Bioethics." In *Encyclopedia of Bioethics*, 2nd ed., edited by Warren T. Reich, 250. New York: Macmillan, 1995.

Sass, Hans-Martin. "Fritz Jahr's 1927 Concept of Bioethics." *Kennedy Institute of Ethics Journal* 17, no. 4 (2007): 279–295.

## FILM

*The Physician.* Dir. Philipp Stölzl. 2013.

## NOVELS

Camus, Albert. *The Plague.* Translated by Stuart Gilbert. New York: Vintage International, 1991. First published in French in 1947 and in English in 1948.

Roth, Veronica. *Divergent* Trilogy. New York: Katherine Tegen Books, 2011–2013.

## FINE ART

Rembrandt van Rijn. *The Anatomy Lesson of Dr. Nicolaes Tulp*, oil on canvas, 1632 (Mauritshuis), The Hague, Netherlands.

# CHAPTER 1

# Primer on Ethical Theories in Medical Ethics

**Rebecca Feinberg**
*Teaching Assistant, Professor of Health Law, Policy and Bioethics*
*DePaul University, Chicago, IL*

**Craig M. Klugman**
*Professor of Bioethics and Health Sciences*
*DePaul University, Chicago, IL*

Medical ethics and bioethics are, by their nature, interdisciplinary pursuits. As the field of bioethics has evolved, it has drawn from philosophy, law, medicine, religious studies, literature, sociology, anthropology, art, film, and more. At its core, all of the disciplines are focused on the human experience of illness and health.

As an applied philosophical practice, bioethics has both empirical and normative approaches. In the empirical approach, bioethics is descriptive. That is, bioethics looks at what people's experiences are in being patients, healers, and decision makers. Another empirical approach is polling what health-care providers and the public consider to be important health-care issues. Drawing on the arts and social sciences, these critical examinations look at "what is" (as opposed to "what ought to be"). An example is current bioethics studies that are looking at magnetic resonance imaging (MRI) scans to see what parts of the brain are working when people make ethical decisions, examine the values inherent in a code of ethics, or even draw lessons from the characters in a novel.

Reflecting its philosophical origins, bioethics can also be normative—making a claim about how things ought to be. These are statements about what ought to be, and what ought not to be permitted. For example, bioethics looks at whether human embryos should be created solely for research (or whether researchers should use only those left over from in vitro fertilization techniques) or whether people ought to be permitted to have medically assisted suicide. In normative bioethics, one examines cases and arguments, takes them apart for criticism, and builds arguments that support other perspectives and points of view.

Normative bioethics primarily draws from logical argumentation, but it also relies on moral philosophy and other ethical theories. In this chapter, we introduce you to the major theories used in modern biomedical ethics: ethics of care, deontology, natural law, principlism, utilitarianism, and virtue ethics (role modeling, casuistry, and narrative ethics). Together, these theories are like a bioethics toolkit. When examining a case or a policy proposal, one can use these tools to gain insight, different perspectives, and potential recommendations. It is rare that a single theory will provide the full answer, and in most cases a good analysis employs two or more of these theoretical approaches.

In studying these theories, it is helpful to look at how each one would examine a similar case. For this purpose, we will draw on the discussion of trolleyology in Chapter 6, "Neuroethics." In the novel *The Fault in Our Stars* (Green 2012), the character Van Houten talks to the main characters about the Trolley Car Dilemma. There are many variations of the problem, but for our purposes let us say that there is a sealed trolley car with eight passengers. The car is approaching a bridge that has been washed away in a recent storm. The resulting crash will kill all eight passengers. However, there is a switch that will redirect the car on a spur line and save the passengers, but an innocent person has been tied to those tracks and will die if the train is redirected.

The question in the Trolley Car Dilemma is whether or not to pull the switch. The following discussion examines how each of the ethical theories just mentioned would approach this question.

## ETHICS OF CARE

*"The central focus of the ethics of care is on the compelling moral salience of attending to and meeting the needs of the particular others for whom we take responsibility … the ethics of care values emotion rather than rejects it"* (Held 2006, 10).

The philosophical theory titled "ethics of care" is based on the psychological work of Carol Gilligan (1936–), who differentiated two forms of moral reasoning in the process. The first form is concerned with rights and justice, and the second form is primarily concerned with caring through emotional connections with others. She attributes rights and justice to traditionally male thinking and care to traditionally female thinking (Gilligan [1982] 1993). The ethics of care is often confused with feminist ethics because both theories take a critical analysis stance toward traditional moral philosophy. Men and women are capable of both forms of moral reasoning and use one or the other depending on the given situation. Feminist philosopher Nel Noddings (1929–) believes that we are guided by caring itself and that our focus should be to create conditions in which caring can flourish. Noddings (1984) specifically addresses caring, compassion, concern, and sensitivity as components in the application of ethics of care.

When analyzing a situation using ethics of care, one looks for context-specific details that are unique to the case. The highest priority is given to maintaining relationships and seeking options through the tools of communication and collaboration. The solution to any problem within ethics of care should ideally avoid harm (if unable to avoid harm entirely, seek to minimize harm) to nurture the relationship. Ultimately, ethics of care promotes caring among all involved.

Because ethics of care is so situationally dependent, it is difficult to apply to scenarios. One must be emotionally invested in the players and involved in the situation as it unfolds. When engrossed in the situation, a person can use one's intuitive sense of correctness in analyzing the human relationships of those involved. When utilizing ethics of care, impartiality should be avoided. Instead, the foundation of this theory's application is investment in the characters and immersion in the situation.

The ethics of care is the basis of the ethics of nursing, a field of health care known for its compassion. In the American Nurses Association Code of Ethics (2015), the first provision states, "The nurse, in all professional relationships, practices with compassion and respect." Provision 2 states, "The nurse's primary commitment is to the patient, whether an individual, family, group, or community." The nursing code is patient-centric and emphasizes relationships.

Despite the challenges in applying ethics of care to a situation in which one is not actually participating, one can attempt to analyze the trolley case. In the trolley scenario the choice is between allowing the trolley to crash, killing all eight people on board, or pulling a switch and killing the person tethered to the track.

Assuming we are one of the eight people on the train car, then we will pull the switch. As a person on the train car, we have developed relationships with the other seven occupants of the trolley and are invested in their welfare. As philosophers who subscribe to the ethics of care philosophy, we also seek to minimize the harm. Saving eight people, despite the loss of the person tethered to the tracks who will inevitably die, ultimately causes less harm. The problem with this analysis arises if the scenario is twisted slightly.

Let's say that you are external to the train car and watching the events unfold. The eight people in the train car are strangers with whom you have no relationship, but the person tied to the tracks is your beloved father, the grandfather to your children and family patriarch. In this case, your relationships and emotional investment will prevent you from pulling the switch. The greatest harm from your perspective would be the damage to your family if your father is killed and thus allowing the trolley to continue on its way, killing the eight strangers, is less harmful from your relationship perspective.

## DEONTOLOGY

*"I would express thus Duty is the necessity of acting from respect for the law.... A maxim is the subjective principle of volition. The objective principle (i.e. that which would also serve subjectively as a practical principle to all rational beings if reason had full power over the faculty of desire) is the practical law" (Kant [1785] 2013, 16–17).*

Deontology is derived from the Greek terms *deon*, meaning "obligation" or "duty," and *logos*, meaning "science" or "study of." Deontological ethical theories focus on the rightness or wrongness of the action itself rather than the consequences or the character of the actor. An ethical act in deontology is one that adheres to a moral or natural law, standard, or rule. Since the measure of rightness of an action is external to the actor, these are universalist theories, meaning that the morality of an action is independent of the context of the situation, individual, time, or place. If something is wrong, then it is always wrong, will always be wrong, and has always been wrong.

The major thinker of deontology for medical ethics is Immanuel Kant (1724–1804). Kant states that an action is moral if, and only if, it is done out of a sense of duty. "Duty is the necessity of acting from respect for the law." By this he means "moral law," not civil law. An action could be legal by following civil law but unethical by not following moral law.

A moral law must be followed out of absolute necessity. It is not bound to a specific set of circumstances, or to a desired aim of action. As Kant states, "Act only according to that maxim whereby you can at the same time will that it should become a universal law without contradiction" (Kant [1785] 1993, 30). That is a universal law—applying to all people, in all places, in all times. It is absolute, unconditional, is an end itself (not a means to an end), and must be obeyed. A maxim is "the subjective principle of volition" (13). For example, let us propose a maxim that a person can tell lies to protect the feelings of others. The universalizability test would ask if that is always true. If people can lie, then we would never be able to know whether someone was telling the truth. We would never be able to trust anyone, which would lead to an inability for people to live together, do business together, enter into contracts or relationships, and society would collapse. Kant considers telling the truth to be an inviolable moral law.

As you can see, finding the moral law requires reasoning. Kant believed our capacity to reason yields *autonomy*, that is, an ability for self-regulation and governance. Once you have discerned the moral law for an action or a choice, you use your autonomy to decide whether to follow the law. Kant says that a rational person would choose to follow the law, but you have the autonomy to make a different choice, even though realizing that choice would be immoral and irrational.

Consider the trolley car example. Should we throw the switch that speeds up the train to derail, or should we let the larger group die? Kant tells us that it is wrong to kill a person because it is irrational to end a rational mind: it is a moral law not to kill. Thus, a deontological perspective would find that we should not throw the switch because it is our action of throwing the switch that would kill the person tied to the tracks. Not throwing the switch is inaction. Since a deontologist is concerned with intent, neither consequences nor feelings are relevant. So the fact that eight people die because of our inaction is not important.

## DEONTOLOGY IN BIOETHICS

In bioethics, deontological theories are sometimes called *Kantian ethics* or *duty-based ethics*. The notion is that right and wrong are determined by an external standard. This can be the moral law, but it can also be the civil law, institutional policy, or professional standards.

Consider an example from Chapter 9 on truth-telling. Say a patient comes to a physician's office and is diagnosed with tuberculosis. The patient does not want anyone to know and asks the physician to keep this a secret. What the patient does not know is that there is a state and federal law that requires physicians to report infectious diseases to the state health department. As seen earlier, there is a moral law to which one must adhere. Therefore, a health-care provider also cannot lie. Using deontology, the physician would report the disease and its details in full.

# NATURAL LAW AND DOUBLE EFFECT

*"Now the object of the theological virtues is God Himself, Who is the last end of all, as surpassing the knowledge of our reason. On the other hand, the object of the intellectual and moral virtues is something comprehensible to human reason. Wherefore the theological virtues are specifically distinct from the moral and intellectual virtues." (Thomas Aquinas [1265–1274] 1947, Q54, Art 52)*

According to natural law theory, God created the universe. Within that he created humans with the ability to reason and an overall plan that includes natural law—notions of right and wrong, good and evil. As humans we have some intrinsic awareness of this nature, and we have the capacity to reason and to discover the natural law. It is part of human nature to want to follow the natural law.

Thomas Aquinas (1225–1274) is perhaps the best-known moral philosopher of this ethical theory. He believed that all things that help humans to refine their rational capacities are good, and anything that inhibits this process is bad. When someone makes an argument that something is wrong because it is "not natural," that person is making a natural law argument. The other implication of this theory is that all people have equal moral worth because their creator equally endows all with the capacity to reason.

## NATURAL LAW IN BIOETHICS

Thomas Aquinas also developed the principle of double effect. This concept applies when one is contemplating an action that leads to two outcomes: one outcome is good and one outcome is bad. If (1) the good outcome outweighs the bad and (2) the intended outcome is the good one, then the action is permissible. Looking at the trolley car example, the potential action is pulling the switch. The good outcome is saving eight lives. The bad outcome is one death. The good of saving eight lives outweighs the bad of unintentionally leading to a single death, and the intention is to save the eight lives. Therefore, by the principle of double effect, the action of pulling the switch would be permissible because the intent is to save eight lives.

In bioethics, a common example of double effect is the use of morphine at the end of life. Morphine has two results: it diminishes pain and suppresses respirations. In a terminal patient who is suffering from intractable pain, a person may justify increasing the morphine to potentially lethal doses. The good outcome is the diminished pain; the bad outcome is the suppressed respiration that may lead to death. The intention is to relieve the patient's pain, not to stop the breathing, though this may occur. Since the good action (pain control) outweighs the bad (respiration suppression) and the outcome is a good one (pain control), the act of administering increasing doses of morphine is morally permissible.

# PRINCIPLISM

*"A set of principles in a moral account should function as an analytical framework that expresses the general values underlying rules in the common morality. The principles ... function as guidelines for professional ethics"* (Beauchamp and Childress 2001, 12).

Philosopher Thomas Beauchamp (1939–) and theologian James Childress (1940–) hold that, in solving an ethical dilemma, most people would agree on how to address it. However, they feel that ethicists would not get to the dilemma because they would expend too much time and energy trying to decide on which ethical theory to base the analysis. To save time, Beauchamp and Childress looked at the common elements that people examined in coming to similar recommendations for a given situation. The result is what they call *principlism*, a set of four guidelines to moral deliberation. The principles are nonhierarchical, and each one is a *prima facie* duty that must be balanced with the others. In other words, no one principle is absolute; all must be weighed in tandem for a full analysis.

Beauchamp and Childress offer the principles of autonomy, beneficence, nonmaleficence, and justice. Each of these will be defined and then examined in the following sections.

## AUTONOMY

The principle of autonomy suggests that an individual, possessing knowledge and understanding with the capacity to deliberate and communicate, has the right to arrive at the ideal decision for himself or herself. Autonomy is compromised when any exterior entity influences the outcome of that decision (as in coercion). A frequently used example in bioethics is paternalism, in which a doctor, who possesses additional knowledge and power, influences the decision of the patient. In brief, autonomy means "self-governance."

## BENEFICENCE

The principle of beneficence is seeking to promote good. An analysis of a situation using beneficence as the guiding principle will result in the action that fulfills the obligation of yielding the most benefit. This obligation also includes a requirement to take action to protect others from harm. Beneficence is an inherent part of bioethics because health-care workers have a fundamental directive to serve the good of the patient. Recognize that the most benefit can be a complex outcome. For example, a terminal cancer patient who is suffering in intractable pain with no hope of relief or recovery may be best served by terminal sedation rather than aggressive chemotherapy. The goals of terminal sedation—to end pain—and chemotherapy—to treat cancer—are both beneficial. Though the end result of terminal sedation is loss of life, beneficence also recognizes the end of pain and suffering.

## NONMALEFICENCE

The principle of nonmaleficence is the application of "do no harm," including avoiding risk of harm. Nonmaleficence is judged on the result of the action (i.e., did harm occur?), not on the intentions of the actor. This principle is a major tenet of bioethics and, therefore, medical care, appearing in the Hippocratic Corpus *Of the Epidemics* ("Do No Harm"; Adams 2009) and the Hippocratic Oath as "I will do no harm or injustice to them" (North 2002). Since many forms of productive medical care, such as surgery, are harming in order to heal, it is impossible to examine nonmaleficence independent of beneficence. The ultimate goal is not to avoid every possible harm but rather that the balance of harm should be proportionally minimal to the benefit.

For example, an individual with an inflamed appendix is becoming progressively more ill. It is clear that appendicitis is progressing and without intervention the appendix will rupture, spilling its contents into the abdomen, leading to sepsis and eventual death for the patient. To prevent this sequence of events, the patient must receive an operation to remove the appendix. An operation, by its very nature, is a harm (i.e., cutting into a human being), but balancing the harm from the surgical incisions with the benefit of removing the appendix results in a clear, positive outcome. Thus, the harm of the surgical procedure is justifiable when viewed in the context of the resulting benefit.

## JUSTICE

The principle of justice utilizes the concepts of equity and fairness in its analysis. An application of justice seeks to balance burdens and benefits and to fairly distribute scarce resources. Inherent in the principle of justice is the avoidance of bias from any assessment (bias can be racism, sexism, classism, or any other arbitrary discriminatory classification). A determination of action based on justice will seek to equally distribute shares of both the positive and negative.

In bioethics, the distribution of organs for transplant is a good example of justice. The United Network for Organ Sharing (UNOS) keeps a running list of recipients based on date of registration and medical need. UNOS does not consider race, wealth, sexual orientation, or any other nonmedical classification when allocating organs for transplant. This practice ensures justice in the distribution of this limited resource.

### THE TROLLEY DILEMMA

In the trolley car example, we would use the four principles to guide our analysis. If it were possible, we would ask all nine people—the eight passengers inside the car and the one person tethered to the tracks—what they think about the situation and what they desire for an outcome (assuming there was no way for all nine to live). But because there is no communication system, we would be making a decision on their behalf. There is no autonomy in this case.

Under beneficence, the best benefit would be to save their lives. We can save eight lives and lose one, or save one life and lose eight. Nonmaleficence looks at whether our actions may cause harm. If we pull the switch, then one person dies; if we do not pull the switch, then eight people die. Either way, harm is done, but pulling the switch results in less harm (i.e., one dead person tethered to the track versus eight dead passengers). In using justice, we are looking at equity and fairness. We might say that the entire scenario is not "fair." We also want to be sure that we are not choosing to allow the one person to die because of some characteristic or group he or she belongs to (or allowing the eight passengers to live for some characteristic or group membership). Justice would suggest that saving more lives is better. Since autonomy and nonmaleficence offer little guidance, beneficence and justice will influence any choice. The greater benefit can be gained by flipping the switch.

## UTILITARIANISM

*"Happiness is the sole end of human action, the promotion of it the test by which to judge all human conduct"* (Mill [1861] 1985, 237).

Utilitarian theory, credited to philosophers Jeremy Bentham (1748–1832) and John Stuart Mill (1806–1873), is based on the principle of utility, often referred to as the greatest happiness principle. The philosophy is outcome oriented, focused solely on the outcome of the decision and its subsequent ramifications. Utilitarians seek the solution that will result in the greatest happiness for the greatest number of people. Thus, the unit of analysis is populations, not individuals. The definition of happiness in this case encompasses more than pleasure but includes all intrinsic goods such as love, knowledge, success, and friendship.

When performing a utilitarian analysis, one must consider a broad range of factors to determine the balance of results. Each potential action will have a cascade of implications that must be assessed and added to the decision scale. Ultimately, each decision is a form of moral cost-benefit analysis that seeks to determine which act produces the greatest happiness and the least pain. In each determination, some pain will result, but the goal is overall happiness that outweighs the unhappiness (also called pain).

As a guide for determining what consequences each action will produce, Bentham offers seven tests of utility, commonly called the Hedonistic Calculus.

- Intensity: How intense is the pleasure?
- Duration: How long does it last?
- Certainty: How sure are you that it will occur?

- Promixity: How soon will it occur?

- Fecundity: How many more pleasures will it spawn?

- Purity: How free from pain is the pleasure?

- Extent: How many people experience the pleasure? (Bentham [1781] 1907)

The philosophical analysis is concerned with the happiness that results from the outcome. Thus, actions themselves are not judged to be moral or not moral; rather, the results of those actions are judged. Motives are insignificant in a utilitarian analysis. It matters not what the actor intended to have happen; it matters only what resulting happiness occurs from the action.

Utilitarianism is one of the foundational theories of public health ethics (see Chapter 16, "Public Health Ethics"). When there is a high demand for a limited resource, such as antiretroviral therapy (ART) in Africa (where ARTs are not widely available), resource allocation is discussed. If there are only enough ARTs to treat three out of every ten HIV-infected patients, who should receive the medication? A utilitarian would choose the individuals in society whose treatment has additional ramifications beyond the patient taking the pills. This list would include expectant mothers, who may be able to prevent transmission of the virus to their unborn child with ARTs; sex workers, who are less likely to transmit the disease to their clients when their viral load is lowered by ARTs; and health-care workers, who must be kept as healthy as possible to continue to treat the rest of the population. These additional benefits would create greater happiness and would tip the scales of a utilitarian's analysis.

Another example of utilitarian theory in bioethics is the case of a public health mandate that overrides an individual's autonomy, specifically mandated vaccines. Though vaccines are eminently safe and considered beneficial to the individual receiving them, they serve a greater purpose as well. There are many in every community who, for medical reasons, cannot get vaccinated for communicable diseases and rely on the majority of the population being immunized (herd immunity) for protection. There are also some who object to vaccination on the grounds of autonomy. A utilitarian would weigh overriding an individual's autonomy and taking the minor risks involved in vaccination (i.e., small amount of pain from the actual injection and loss of autonomous liberty) against protecting the entire population by achieving herd immunity (i.e., large amount of happiness). This perspective would mandate that the vaccine be given to all who can medically receive it.

When using utilitarian theory to analyze the trolleyology case, one seeks the outcome that serves the greatest happiness. The greatest good is served by saving eight people and allowing only one to die: you pull the switch, saving the eight people aboard the trolley and killing the track worker. This results in eight times the happiness for those trapped in the car, their loved ones, their as-yet-to-be-born children, and so forth. The purity of this happiness is diminished by the one death, but the saving of eight lives means the decision to flip the switch is the correct one.

In philosophical application (not necessarily in bioethics), utilitarian analysis can be further differentiated into act utilitarianism and rule utilitarianism. Act utilitarianism looks at the consequences of a specific act, allowing one to tailor the philosophical theory to individual circumstances. Rule utilitarianism looks at universalizable rules that produce the greatest happiness and can be applied to all situations.

A philosophical analysis would take the trolley scenario one step further and alter the facts enough to alter the outcome. For example, the eight people aboard the trolley might be convicted murderers bound for life in prison and the one person on the track is a brilliant scientist who is on the cusp of a scientific breakthrough that will cure all forms of cancer. In this new scenario, a utilitarian will not flip the switch. Though eight people will die, the greatest happiness for society as a whole comes from curing cancer and not from saving eight convicted inmates.

This second scenario helps to demonstrate the difference between act and rule utilitarianism. Act utilitarians would alter their behavior in the second scenario and not flip the switch because the assessment of the act results in the greatest happiness (saving the scientist who will cure cancer for all). But rule utilitarians would not alter their behavior and would still flip the switch because they would adhere to the rule of saving eight people over one individual.

# VIRTUE ETHICS

*"That moral virtue is a mean, then, and in what sense it is so, and that it is a mean between two vices, the one involving excess, the other deficiency, and that it is such because its character is to aim as what is intermediate in passions and in action"* (Aristotle 350 BCE, Book 2, Section 9).

For Aristotle, the good or the aim of all action is *eudaimōnia*, or happiness, which he defines as "living a fully satisfying, contemplative life." He says that all humans are uniquely born of all creatures with the capacity to reason. Thus, it is our purpose in life to develop and use our reason. We develop this capacity so that we may discover the virtues and, by practicing them, make them a habit that becomes part of our character. For Aristotle, virtue is a quality of good character—it is about being a good person. He also says that it is not enough to know the virtuous action; we must actually act on it.

Aristotle's philosophy is a form of situationism—for every situation there is a single right action, and every situation is somewhat different. We use our reason to determine what virtue should be employed to make a choice. A virtue is the mean between the extremes of excess and deficiency. For example, Aristotle says that when it comes to charity, the excess is extravagance: we give away everything we have. The deficiency is stinginess: we give away nothing. The mean between those extremes is liberality or generosity: we give away some but not all. Another example, courage, is the mean between cowardice and foolhardiness. Aristotle also includes fidelity (faithfulness or loyalty), honesty (telling the truth in most circumstances), and temperance (controlling one's desires).

Because Aristotle is interested in character, these virtues reflect one's use of reason and one's ability to be one's authentic self. An action must fulfill three requirements before it is virtuous:

(1) *A deliberate awareness of the quality of the act.* One has to know what one is doing, why, and what the consequences of the action will be.

(2) *A voluntary choice.* One needs to make the choice of one's own volition; one cannot be forced into it.

(3) *A consistent and established character.* A single act of virtue in a lifetime of unvirtuous choices does not make an action virtuous. Aristotle is interested in character, so the choice must reflect one's authentic self. This can change over time so that an unvirtuous person becomes virtuous, but it must become an established pattern.

## VIRTUE ETHICS IN BIOETHICS

Virtue ethics has made its way to modern bioethics through three theories: role modeling, casuistry, and narrative ethics. Each of these is discussed in the following paragraphs.

**Role Modeling.** In role modeling, when making a decision, one looks at a person who embodies virtue and then asks what a virtuous person would do. Then one makes a similar kind of choice. In the trolley car scenario, one would look at a paragon of virtue and decide what that person would do. Of course, the path determined by following a model depends on the person one chooses. If it is Superman, perhaps he would find a way to save everyone. Someone more human might choose to save everyone or to not kill the one (and lose the eight). Without a defined role model for this scenario, virtue ethics provides little guidance.

**Casuistry.** Casuistry is also known as "case-based reasoning." The right answer is found by looking at similar cases one has faced in the past. This is often used in the US judicial system when judges decide on a current case by looking at precedence—similar cases in the past. When an abortion case comes before the US Supreme Court, the justices look at previous abortion cases, examine how the current and past ones differ, and then use the previous decisions to guide the current one. In this way, a decision is informed by the past but can take new knowledge and situations into account.

One of the challenges of casuistry is knowing which cases to choose and how many cases should be considered for comparison. For use in medicine, philosophers Albert Jonsen (1931–) and Stephen Toulmin (1922–2009) suggest that one should have 100 cases of personal experience to draw upon when making medical ethics choices (1988).

In the trolley car example, casuistry would ask us to look at how we have personally dealt with similar cases in the past, or absent that, how others have dealt with similar cases. A real-life application is found in the programming of driverless cars. For example, programmers have to decide if the car should be programmed to sacrifice a pedestrian crossing the street in order to save the lives of four passengers inside the vehicle. Alternatively, if the car were about to hit four pedestrians walking along a blind curve in the road, would the car be programmed to sacrifice the driver to save the pedestrians? No solution has yet been found, and there are too few real-life examples to have a series of cases to examine.

**Narrative Ethics.** Rather than focusing merely on the logic of decision making, narrative ethics puts more focus on character issues, such as identity, motivation, and specificity. Philosopher Hilde Lindemann Nelson suggests that narrative ethics can "(1) teach us our duties, (2) guide morally good action, (3) motivate morally good action, (4) justify action on moral grounds, (5) cultivate our moral sensibilities, (6) enhance our moral perception, (7) make actions of persons morally intelligible, and (8) reinvent ourselves as better persons" (Nelson 2001, 36).

Thus, narrative ethics provides a deeper and richer understanding of the case than a simple set of facts does. It also suggests that the ethical response is to help write a good narrative—one that is authentic to the characters and true to the story. One of the challenges of narrative ethics is that although it provides a way to widen understanding, it does not provide a method for making the decision.

In the trolley scenario, narrative ethics would want to ask who the people in the trolley are, who the person on the tracks is, and how they got there. Narrative ethics would also ask who is flipping the switch and what is in their past that brought them to this place. If the eight people in the car are all invading space aliens about to enslave the planet and the person on the track is an innocent human victim, then not flipping the switch might have more narrative integrity than flipping it. On the other hand, if the eight people are six-year-old preschoolers and the person on the track is a serial murderer, flipping the switch may make more sense narratively. A simple trolley car scenario does not provide enough information to reach a satisfactory choice.

## Summary

Modern medical ethics, as part of bioethics, draws on traditional theories of moral philosophy as well as adding a few of its own. Deontological ethics defines right decisions as those that follow moral laws and rules. Ethics of care takes the emotional connections we have in our relationships and acknowledges their importance. Natural law provides the principle of double effect to help make decisions when choices provide both a good and a bad outcome. Principlism introduces the mid-level principles of moral deliberation: autonomy, beneficence, nonmaleficence, and justice. Utilitarianism answers dilemmas by looking at the consequences and asking what choice provides the greatest good for the greatest number. And virtue ethics, which is interested in good character, has led to role modeling, casuistry, and narrative ethics in the modern pantheon of bioethical theories.

When solving any particular case, most likely no one theory will provide a good solution. In bioethics, these theories are used as tools, often in tandem, to help us look at a case from different perspectives. As we discovered with the trolley car example, some theories are not helpful while others provided quite divergent views. The bioethicist uses these as tools of moral deliberation—one factor to consider when looking at a particular case. Other factors include medical facts, law, professional practice, standards of care, institutional policy, and family and social dynamics. This interplay of factors will come together in the rest of the book as we explore various topics in medical ethics/bioethics.

## Bibliography

Adams, Francis, trans. "Of the Epidemics, by Hippocrates." The Internet Classics Archive. 2009. Retrieved February 28, 2016, from http://classics.mit.edu/Hippocrates/epidemics.1.i.html.

American Medical Association House of Delegates. "Principles of Medical Ethics." 2001. Retrieved February 25, 2015, from http://www.ama-assn.org/ama/pub/physician-resources/medical-ethics/code-medical-ethics/principles-medical-ethics.page.

American Nurses Association. "Code of Ethics." 2015. Retrieved February 25, 2015, from http://www.nursingworld.org/DocumentVault/Ethics_1/Code-of-Ethics-for-Nurses.html.

Beauchamp, Tom L., and James F. Childress. *Principles of Biomedical Ethics*. 5th ed. New York: Oxford University Press, 2001.

Bentham, Jeremy. *An Introduction to the Principles of Morals and Legislation*. 1907. First published 1789. Retrieved February 25, 2015, from http://www.econlib.org/library/Bentham/bnthPML.html.

Gilligan, Carol. *In a Different Voice: Psychological Theory and Women's Development*. Cambridge, MA: Harvard University Press, 1993. First published 1982.

Green, John. *The Fault in Our Stars*. New York: Dutton, 2012.

Held, Virginia. *The Ethics of Care: Personal, Political, and Global*. Oxford: Oxford University Press, 2006.

Jonsen, Albert R., and Stephen Toulmin. *The Abuse of Casuistry: A History of Moral Reasoning*. Berkeley: University of California Press, 1988.

Kant, Immanuel. *Fundamental Principles of the Metaphysics of Morals*. Translated by T. K. Abbott. Hazleton: Pennsylvania State University Press, 2013. First published 1785.

Kant, Immanuel. *Grounding for the Metaphysics of Morals*. 3rd ed. Translated by J. W. Ellington. Indianapolis, IN: Hackett, 1993. First published 1785.

Mill, John Stuart. *The Collected Works of John Stuart Mill*, Vol. 10: *Essays on Ethics, Religion, and Society*. Edited by John M. Robson. Toronto: University of Toronto Press, 1985. First published 1861.

Nelson, Hilde Lindemann. *Damaged Identities, Narrative Repair*. Ithaca, NY: Cornell University Press, 2001.

Noddings, Nel. "An Ethic of Caring." In *Caring, a Feminine Approach to Ethics and Moral Education*, 79–103. Berkeley: University of California Press, 1984.

North, Michael, trans. "Greek Medicine." US National Library of Medicine. 2002. http://www.nlm.nih.gov/hmd/greek/greek_oath.html.

Thomas Aquinas. *Summa Theologica*. Translated by the Fathers of the English Dominican Province. New York: Benziger Bros., 1947. First printed 1265–1274.

# Part One:
# Life Span—Fiduciary Relationship

The first part of this volume looks at bioethical issues across the human life span from conception to death. The ethical issues raised here are a result of changing medical technologies that challenge historical notions of human life. This section deals with the concept of the technological imperative: the human drive to understand our world, to develop tools to control the world (including ourselves), and, once such tools and knowledge exist, to use them to better ourselves. Once the genie is out of the bottle, it can be difficult to put it back again. These chapters examine the implications for technologies that we have used for decades and those that are on the cusp of transforming aspects of human experience.

Consider Chapter 2, which looks at the concept of reproduction. For most of human history, procreation was an organic process between a man and a woman. With the development of in vitro fertilization technology in the late 1970s, egg and sperm can be procured from humans and fertilization is assisted by scientists in a laboratory. The produced embryo can then be transferred into the mother or into a gestational surrogate. The egg may come from the person who will raise the child, the gestational surrogate, or an egg donor.

Chapter 3 looks at the controversy surrounding abortion and the question of when an embryo or fetus gains moral status that outweighs the decisional rights of the mother.

Chapters 4 and 5 investigate the possibilities of *genethics*, or the ethics of genetic technologies. Chapter 4 offers a look into genetic testing and implications in the prenatal, natal, newborn, child, and adult stages of life. Chapter 5 analyzes the possibilities for genetically engineering humanity—from eliminating certain diseases to shaping the look of a human being.

Similarly, Chapter 6 examines *neuroethics*, which can be understood as (1) the ethics of neuroscience and (2) the neuroscience of ethics. What does it mean for personal identity and privacy when we can read people's minds or insert messages directly into the brain? Are ethics and morality preprogrammed into the human brain or, as many philosophers hold, a habit that must be cultivated?

Chapters 7 and 8 explore the implications of technology at the end of life—from mechanisms that can maintain a body's function long after the person's brain has died to techniques that might allow physicians to help terminally ill patients die. These chapters ask what the proper role of the physician is.

# CHAPTER 2

# *Reproductive Technologies*

**L. Syd M Johnson**

*Professor, Department of Humanities*
*Michigan Technological University, Houghton*

People have been making babies for as long as there have been people. For most of human history, there was only one way to create new people (through sexual reproduction) and only one way to gestate a baby (in the womb of the woman who conceived it). But not every couple can successfully create offspring the old-fashioned way, for a variety of reasons. Although people have long used folk remedies, prayer, and social means such as adoption to have children, since the late twentieth century assisted reproductive technologies (ARTs) have proliferated, bringing new hope, and sometimes hardship, to those trying to procreate. Along with medical advances have come numerous ethical questions, as ARTs force us to consider the nature of family and parenthood, the role of sex in reproduction, the role of third parties in family building, the obligations and duties would-be parents have when they create children, as well as the limits of parental procreative liberty, and the potential for destroying life in the form of human embryos, in the effort to create new life. This chapter will consider these bioethical questions by looking at several forms of ART: in vitro fertilization, sperm and egg donation, and surrogacy.

Many of the ethical questions and concerns raised by ARTs are illustrated by two films: *Baby Mama* (2008), about a successful business executive who turns to a surrogate to have a baby, and *Starbuck* (2011), about a forty-something slacker who learns he has fathered hundreds of children as a sperm donor.

"I want a baby now!" —Kate (*Baby Mama*)

*Baby Mama* is a goofy comedy about serious matters. Kate (played by Tina Fey) is a successful executive, but at thirty-seven she is a woman of advanced reproductive age, and she hears her biological clock ticking loudly. She has pursued her career and put off having children, only to find that her successful career came at a cost. "Some women got pregnant," she laments, "and I got promotions." She undergoes nine failed attempts to get pregnant via ART. Kate's story is a familiar one; in Western societies, the increasing level of gender equality and importance of women in the workforce has led to the prevalence of delayed motherhood. Many women defer childbearing to pursue education and careers, or marry and start their families later in life, but pregnancy rates by sexual reproduction or by using ART decline precipitously after women reach thirty-six years of age.

In *Starbuck*, a man discovers that he has exactly the opposite problem: he has reproduced not too little but too much, albeit without his knowledge, when his donated sperm is used to create 533 children.

# ASSISTED REPRODUCTIVE TECHNOLOGY

For as long as people have been making babies, some have found themselves without the children they desire. In the seventeenth century, few people would have sought medical treatment for infertility. Doing so could have been viewed as defiance of the Lord's will. The childless were expected to cope with their condition through social means, such as adoption and helping to rear the children of others. Two centuries later, however, the medicalization of infertility had begun, and physicians were attempting to surgically restore fertility, unsuccessfully for the most part. By the mid-twentieth century, infertility clinics were multiplying across America, along with public faith in the power of science and technology to cure what ailed them, but effective treatments for most causes of infertility were still lacking.

In unassisted sexual reproduction a man's sperm cell makes its way through a woman's cervix and uterus, and into one of the fallopian tubes, where it can penetrate an egg and fertilize it, producing an embryo. That embryo must then make its way through the fallopian tube and into the uterus, where it implants in the uterine lining, marking the beginning of pregnancy. Infertility occurs when anything involved in that complex process goes awry. When the causes of infertility cannot be treated through conventional medical means such as surgery and medication, would-be parents can turn to ARTs.

# IN VITRO FERTILIZATION

The first reported instance of human eggs being fertilized outside the body occurred in 1944, when Harvard Medical School physician John Rock and his lab assistant Miriam Menkin succeeded in fertilizing four eggs in vitro. Their groundbreaking work would eventually help usher in a new age of procreation, one in which the intimate link between sex and reproduction could be severed. *In vitro* is Latin for "in glass" and is used to describe experiments or procedures in which biological processes that normally occur in the body are performed with cells outside the body. It contrasts with *in vivo*, meaning "in the body," and *in utero*, for "in the uterus." *In vitro fertilization* (IVF) is the fertilization of human eggs by human sperm outside the body in a petri dish. IVF involves transferring a fertilized embryo from a petri dish into a woman's uterus. It is a technically complex procedure involving several steps.

A woman's ovaries typically produce and release a single egg once per menstrual cycle. IVF requires the retrieval of several eggs at once, so a woman preparing for IVF takes hormonal fertility drugs that stimulate her ovaries to superovulate and produce multiple eggs. When the eggs are ready, they must be surgically extracted from the follicles of the ovaries. The retrieved eggs are microscopically inspected and those of the highest quality are inseminated by mixing them with sperm. If sperm cells successfully fertilize an egg, an embryo will result. Sometimes a technique called intracytoplasmic sperm injection (ICSI) is needed to increase the chances of fertilization. ICSI uses an extremely fine needle to pierce the egg and inject a single sperm cell into it.

Once fertilization has occurred, the embryos are left to grow in a culture medium for a few days, until the single-cell embryos develop into multicellular blastocysts, and the embryos are ready to be transferred to a woman's body. A thin, straw-like catheter is inserted through the vagina and cervix and guided into the uterus to transfer the embryos. If all goes

***Louise Brown, born in 1978 as the world's first "test-tube baby," with her son Cameron, mother Lesley, and in vitro fertilization (IVF) pioneer Robert Edwards.*** *Millions of infertile couples worldwide have children today because of IVF, and some of the children born with the assistance of this procedure, like Louise Brown, have now become parents themselves. Nevertheless, IVF and other assisted reproductive technologies have spawned genuine bioethical concerns, many of them scarcely imagined when Louise Brown emerged into the world.* **67PHOTO/ALAMY.**

as planned, the embryos will implant in the uterine lining. To increase the chances of pregnancy, two embryos are often transferred at once. The entire IVF process, from retrieval to transfer, is known as a cycle and typically takes about two weeks.

## A REVOLUTIONARY BIRTH

Before the development of IVF, little could be done to help women who were unable to become pregnant. The birth of a baby girl in 1978 changed everything. Her name is Louise Brown, and she was the first baby born via IVF. Because of her origins, Louise Brown was called a test-tube baby, and newspaper headlines around the world announced her birth. Her mother, Lesley Brown, was the first woman to become pregnant and give birth following the revolutionary IVF procedure pioneered by Patrick Steptoe and Robert Edwards.

Although Louise Brown was a perfectly normal baby, her birth prompted much handwringing and consternation, with critics invoking visions of a future in which massive factories grew test-tube babies to order, as envisioned in Aldous Huxley's 1932 novel *Brave New World*. Needless to say, such dystopian nightmares never came to pass. Millions of infertile couples worldwide have children today because of IVF, and millions of people who would not exist without IVF do exist. Some of them, such as Louise Brown, have become parents themselves. If the early concerns about IVF and so-called test-tube babies amounted to little more than hyperventilating informed more by science fiction than science fact, IVF and other ARTs have spawned genuine bioethical concerns, many of them scarcely imagined when Louise Brown emerged into the world.

## TREATING INFERTILITY: WHAT IS THE DISEASE?

Many issues cause infertility in both women and men. When a woman has blocked fallopian tubes, her eggs cannot travel along the tubes to be fertilized or through the tubes to implant in the uterus. Some women experience premature ovarian failure and are unable to produce eggs. This problem is sometimes caused by illness or by gonadotoxic therapies, which are medical treatments that are toxic to the organs that produce gametes (sperm and eggs). Cancer treatments are among the most common gonadotoxic therapies for both women and men and can result in partial or total loss of fertility. Men may have too few sperm cells, or sperm that are poor in quality, sometimes as a result of disease. In all of these cases, infertility can be attributed to medical causes—it results from naturally occurring physiological abnormalities, or from disease, or as a side effect of therapies used to treat disease. In these cases, ART can be considered a treatment that addresses a medical condition. Lesley Brown was unable to become pregnant because of blocked fallopian tubes. Before IVF, women like her were generally considered sterile and unless surgery could repair the blockage, they had no effective options for becoming pregnant.

Much has changed in the decades since Louise Brown was born. The majority of women who now use IVF do so not because of physiological factors such as premature ovarian failure or blocked fallopian tubes, but because of advanced reproductive age. More women, like Kate in *Baby Mama*, are delaying childbearing to pursue education and careers. Couples often marry later in life, divorce and remarriage are more common, and the use of effective methods of contraception have eliminated many unintended pregnancies, allowing both women and men more control over the timing of reproduction. As a result of these social developments, many women want to have children later in life, when achieving pregnancy without ART can be difficult or impossible.

Some critics argue that infertility caused by advanced age is not a medical condition or an illness but simply nature taking its course. As a result, the argument goes, the use of ART is inappropriate because it is unnatural and disrupts the natural order. Such an argument has serious limitations. Humans defy nature in many ways. Any time we treat illness (e.g., treating cancer in children, which may result in infertility in adulthood), we are disrupting a natural process. When we use antibiotics to fight bacterial infections, we use human-made, artificial means to defeat natural processes. The argument that ART is inappropriate or unethical because it is unnatural does not hold up when one considers the many ways that we use medicine and medical technology to make our lives better and longer.

Nonetheless, it could be said that ART merely circumvents biology in order to satisfy the desires of would-be parents, and thus should not be considered a medical treatment for infertility. After all, being unable to naturally conceive is neither a life-threatening condition nor a disease when it occurs due to advanced age. Furthermore, conception, pregnancy, then childbirth is not the only way to become a parent. Many happy families are created through adoption. Before IVF, couples who could not have biologically related children sometimes adopted children. The medicalization of reproduction seems to have created both a demand for ART services and a social perception that biological parenthood is superior, even necessary.

Should medical technology be harnessed to fulfill desires that might be satisfied in other ways? If the problem solved by IVF is choosing to have children later in life, might this problem be better solved by other means, such as changing societal attitudes about natural parenthood and adoption or providing social support to women with jobs and careers so that they are not held back by becoming parents when they are younger?

Because infertility is not always considered a disease, and because of the high cost of ART, health insurance does not always cover the procedure. A single cycle of IVF—all the procedures involved in a single attempt to achieve pregnancy—costs on average about US$16,000. But a live birth is the outcome in only about 30 percent of IVF cycles. The older the woman, the lower the chances of a live birth become. In most cases, more than one cycle of IVF is required to achieve pregnancy and live birth, meaning couples can spend tens of thousands of dollars getting the baby of their dreams. And sometimes, the cradle remains empty.

Aside from the cost, which can make IVF accessible only to those with the means to pay for it, IVF has potential health risks for both mother and baby. The risks to children born via ART are not well understood, but scientific evidence shows that a significantly higher percentage of chromosomal abnormalities and major birth defects occur in children conceived through IVF and ICSI, compared to children conceived naturally. Because so many steps and processes are involved in IVF, and IVF with ICSI, it is not known specifically what causes these abnormalities or whether they result from the same factors that caused subfertility or infertility in the parents. Nonetheless, with many millions of children born worldwide with the help of ART, the potential for harm to those children raises important ethical questions, and they will be discussed in the section "Procreative Liberty and Harm to Offspring" later in this chapter.

## CREATING AND DESTROYING EMBRYOS

Because egg retrieval for use in IVF is costly and onerous, and because pregnancy rates using IVF remain relatively low, many eggs are extracted during a single IVF or egg donation cycle. The eggs are fertilized, and some of the resulting embryos are then cryopreserved for use in additional IVF attempts. The number of embryos created is often in excess of the number of desired children, resulting in leftover embryos. The main ethical issue concerns the disposal of excess embryos. The destruction of embryos is controversial for those who view embryos as persons with a right to life.

The US Office of Population Affairs estimates that there are 600,000 cryopreserved embryos in the United States alone; frozen embryos might remain viable for a decade or more. In 2010, a Virginia fertility clinic reported that a healthy baby boy had been born from an embryo frozen for twenty years. Couples who no longer want to use their embryos can choose to have them thawed and disposed of, although many people find this option undesirable. Even couples who don't view their embryos as actual children may feel emotionally conflicted about destroying them, along with any possibility of having more children. Some opt to simply pay to keep their embryos frozen indefinitely. Another option is to donate the embryos for use in research, although this option is not widely available in the United States. A fourth option involves donating the embryos to another couple, a kind of embryo adoption known as "snowflake adoption." Many couples decline this option because they don't want someone else raising their children. Finally, some simply abandon their embryos, leaving fertility clinics to decide what to do with the orphaned embryos.

In 1991, a British law was enacted to deal with the large numbers of abandoned embryos left in storage. The law permitted embryos to be cryopreserved for five years, with an additional five years permitted at the request of both donors. In the summer of 1996, about 3,300 unclaimed human embryos were thawed and left to deteriorate and die by order of the government. The mass disposal stirred tremendous controversy around the world.

Many people believe that embryos are persons and that destroying them, or not transferring them, denies them their chance at life. Discarding unwanted embryos would be comparable to abortion or murder per this view. The Roman Catholic Church believes life begins at conception and considers the disposal of embryos to be murder. The Vatican denounced the mass destruction of British embryos as a prenatal massacre. The US President's Council on Bioethics (PCB) argued that in vitro embryos have the same status as embryos that have been implanted; that is, they are human organisms-on-the-way, deserving of equal respect and treatment. The PCB rejected the routinized creation, use, and destruction of nascent human life. Some proponents of the view that life begins at conception claim that the cells of an embryo derive their human status simply from having the requisite number of forty-six human chromosomes.

Not everyone shares this view of embryonic life. Unless they are transferred to a woman's uterus, embryonic cells are little different from other cells in the body, which also have the requisite forty-six human chromosomes. Advocates of disposal argue that days-old, extracorporeal (outside the body) embryos, with their undifferentiated cells, are not yet persons, and their destruction is not akin to murder. Moreover, it is argued, an extracorporeal embryo is unlikely to develop into a living infant and so should not be considered a person. (Technically, an extracorporeal embryo has zero chance of developing into a living infant.) For every one hundred frozen embryos, only about sixty-five will survive thawing, and only about ten will implant in a woman's uterus. Of those, only a handful will result in live births. The odds then are against some 95 percent of frozen embryos, even if they are wanted and used in an attempt to reproduce.

The large and growing stockpile of stored embryos necessitates that their disposal be addressed. When Louise Brown was conceived, Steptoe and Edwards retrieved a single egg from her mother. Extra embryos were not then a problem. Today, about 165,000 IVF procedures are performed annually in the United States alone, and dozens of eggs can be retrieved during a single cycle, which has the benefit of reducing the number of cycles and surgical procedures needed to acquire eggs for IVF, while also reducing the cost of IVF. Because the failure rate of IVF remains high, having extra embryos in the freezer is attractive for would-be parents who may require multiple cycles to achieve pregnancy. Stored embryos can also be used to give birth to siblings later.

Limiting the number of eggs retrieved per IVF cycle could reduce the embryo surplus, but the medical and financial costs would be significant. Women would have to undergo more egg retrieval cycles if they needed more eggs. The already prohibitive costs of IVF would increase, making it more difficult for infertile couples to procreate. Couples who believe that their embryos are babies-in-waiting would likely transfer all of their embryos or offer them for adoption to prevent their destruction. The primary benefit of reducing the number of stored eggs would be that other couples could avoid making difficult and uncomfortable decisions about what to do with their extra embryos. The risks and burdens of additional egg retrieval cycles would outweigh that small benefit.

## EGG AND SPERM DONATION

Couples who want to create a baby through IVF are not limited to using their own gametes. Donated eggs or sperm can be used to avoid transmitting a genetic disorder, or because one or both would-be parents have abnormal or absent gametes. Same-sex couples can use donated gametes, as can a single woman without a male partner, who can use donated sperm to become pregnant. The ethical concerns related to sperm and egg donation are quite different, owing in part to differences in the level of invasiveness, difficulty, and risk assumed by the donors.

***Patrick Huard stars as sperm donor David Wozniak in director Ken Scott's Canadian comedy*** **Starbuck, *2011.*** *Standing in a room full of young people he has fathered, forty-something slacker Wozniak realizes that the sperm donations he made 693 times under the alias "Starbuck" to raise cash decades earlier resulted in the births of hundreds of children.* Starbuck *offers a forum to explore bioethical debates about reproductive technologies within the broader context of philosophical questions about exploitation, liberty, identity, and the meaning of kinship and family.* PHOTOS 12/ALAMY.

## SPERM DONATION

Males can produce sperm continuously throughout their adult lives, so there is little risk to future fertility for sperm donors. For healthy male donors, sperm donation is a relatively easy and pleasant procedure that requires no medical intervention. The donor masturbates, and the ejaculate is collected in a plastic cup. The sperm can be cryopreserved, or frozen, for storage and future use. Sperm banks collect and store sperm from anonymous donors, paying a modest fee to the donor. In *Starbuck*, David Wozniak (played by Patrick Huard), using the alias Starbuck, donated sperm 693 times to a single Montreal sperm bank to make some extra cash.

Years later, David is a forty-something slacker who has never quite succeeded in life. When his girlfriend becomes pregnant, she would rather break up with him than allow him to father their child. Then David learns that his sperm were used to create 533 children; 142 of his offspring sue him to learn his identity, saying that they have been denied their human right to know their father and who they are. The revelation of his very extended family inspires David to think about parenthood and family, about the responsibilities of fatherhood, and his connection to all of his children. His best friend, a lawyer and father of four, tells him, "You are in no way capable of raising a child," exemplifying the lack of faith everyone seems to have in the father of 533.

David sets out to find out about his many children, and when he learns of the longing and sense of loss his offspring experience, he is moved to reveal himself and accept responsibility for his acts of unconscious procreation. Although Starbuck's story may seem farfetched, it is not far from the truth. An anonymous sperm donor in California has fathered more than 150 children, and counting. Some countries, including Britain, France, and Sweden, limit how many children can be fathered by a single sperm donor, but no such restrictions exist in the United States. When so many children are conceived from a single genetic father, the risk of spreading genes for rare inheritable diseases is greatly increased. When numerous children within a geographical region have been fathered by a single donor, it also increases the odds of accidental incest among half-siblings. When a single sperm donor can be the genetic father of literally hundreds of children, it raises questions about the meaning of family for those children. Like David's kids, they can have hundreds of genetic siblings born to different mothers, raised in different families.

The anonymity of sperm donors means that the offspring of those donors have no access to information about half their family medical history and ancestry. A case in Ontario, Canada, illustrates how this problem can have negative consequences for families. Angela Collins and Margaret Hanson selected a sperm donor from a US-based sperm bank. They thought that they had selected a donor who was highly educated, with an impressive health history. Years after the birth of their son, they received an e-mail from the sperm bank that accidentally identified the anonymous donor, and they learned that he was a college dropout with schizophrenia and a criminal history. The parents sued the sperm bank, alleging negligence, fraud, misrepresentation, and battery, and seeking damages as well as a medical monitoring fund for their child because he has an increased risk of developing schizophrenia. The same donor reportedly fathered thirty-six other children.

The ethical worries about sperm donation primarily concern the social, emotional, and health consequences for the offspring. There is no physical risk to sperm donors and no risk to the future fertility of men who donate. The same is not true of egg donors, so the ethical concerns about egg donation are different and primarily focus on risks to the donors.

## EGG DONATION

The first birth and pregnancy reported using donor eggs was in Australia in 1983. The donor was a woman who was undergoing IVF for tubal disease; the recipient was a woman with ovarian failure. The egg was fertilized with sperm from the recipient's husband and resulted in a healthy full-term birth. When egg donation was first introduced in the early 1980s, the donors were other women undergoing IVF, or friends or relatives of the recipient. When it became possible to cryopreserve embryos for future use, women undergoing IVF no longer had surplus eggs they could not use, thus eliminating one source for donated eggs. IVF is often more successful using donor eggs, particularly when the recipient is older. Thus, demand for donor eggs soon outpaced the supply, and commercial egg donation, and a market for donor eggs, came into being.

The process of creating embryos through IVF is essentially the same when gametes come from donors, except that when there is an egg donor, she undergoes the procedures for superovulation and egg retrieval, and following IVF the embryos are transferred into the recipient's uterus. Egg donation is time-consuming and rigorous. First, the prospective donor undergoes physical, gynecological, and psychological exams. If she is accepted and matched with a recipient, the process of inducing superovulation begins. The donor first takes hormones that suppress the normal egg maturation process, inducing an artificial menopause. She then has daily injections, for a period ranging from six to fourteen days, of follicle-stimulating hormones or gonadotropins that will encourage the development of multiple egg follicles. During the hyperstimulation period, every one to three days she must have blood tests and a transvaginal ultrasound to monitor the development of her eggs and adjust the dosage of hormones as needed. Once the eggs have matured, ovulation is triggered by an injection of human chorionic gonadotropin, and egg retrieval occurs about thirty-six hours later. The eggs are retrieved through transvaginal ultrasound aspiration, in which an ultrasound probe is used to guide a needle into each ovary to remove the mature eggs from the follicles. On average, fifteen to twenty-five eggs are produced and retrieved.

The most severe side effect of superovulation is ovarian hyperstimulation syndrome, which occurs in 1 to 10 percent of donors. Ovarian hyperstimulation syndrome can result in dehydration, blood-clotting disorders, enlargement of the ovaries, kidney damage, and, in rare cases, death. A rare complication called ovarian torsion sometimes requires that ovaries be surgically removed, resulting in impaired fertility for the donor. The surgical egg retrieval procedure can also, rarely, result in injury and hospitalization for the donor.

The long-term risks of ovarian hyperstimulation are not well understood, but it may increase the risk of ovarian cancer. Additionally, because female humans are born with all the eggs they will ever have, the donation of dozens of those eggs might affect the future fertility of the egg donor. Because of the risks to the donor, there are important bioethical concerns about egg donation. When an infertile or subfertile woman undergoes egg retrieval in order to have a child, she stands to benefit from whatever risks and sacrifices she undertakes. For egg donors, those risks and potential sacrifices are made for someone else's benefit. Sometimes, the donor is motivated entirely by altruism: she may be donating eggs to a friend or a sister. Other times, she may receive financial compensation, ranging from several thousand to tens of thousands of dollars.

Compensation for egg donation is legal in the United States. Donors can be anonymous or non-anonymous, or they can be designated donors providing eggs to a specific recipient. The legal status of egg donation varies from country to country. Egg donation is completely illegal in Germany and Italy; in France, it is legal, but donors cannot be paid; Canada allows non-anonymous donation without payment, whereas the United Kingdom allows non-anonymous donation with payment. Because of the invasiveness, discomfort, risks, and the time-consuming nature of egg donation, few women are willing to undergo the procedure without compensation, and in countries where compensation is not permitted, few donors are available. Some countries that permit compensation limit the amount, typically in the range of US$1,000 to US$2,000. In the United States, the fertility industry is largely self-regulated, with no legal caps on payments to donors.

The ethics committee of the American Society for Reproductive Medicine (ASRM) endorses financial compensation of less than US$5,000 for egg donors. Compensation of more than that must be justified, but ASRM guidelines prohibit "putting a price on human gametes or selectively valuing particular human traits" and so do not allow compensation to vary according to the number or quality of eggs retrieved or the donor's ethnic or personal characteristics. Sums above US$10,000 are not appropriate, according to ASRM. Many fertility clinics adhere to those guidelines, but egg donors are sometimes paid significantly more when would-be parents are looking for a donor with particular characteristics.

A market for premium donor eggs exists, with egg brokers acting as go-betweens for donors and recipients. Advertisements offering payments of US$50,000 or more are common in the newspapers of Ivy League universities; some offer payments as high as US$100,000 for the right donor. The desired donors must typically meet strict physical standards and have high SAT scores. Online forums where potential egg donors advertise their services are used by women who have already successfully donated multiple times. Some list not only the number of times they have donated in the past, but also the number of eggs harvested and the number of successful pregnancies that resulted.

Compensation for the considerable time, inconvenience, and discomfort associated with egg donation is generally considered ethically permissible. Three main ethical concerns arise when payments to egg donors exceed what is considered reasonable compensation: coercion, undue inducement, and the commodification of eggs and children.

**Coercion.** One obvious type of coercion involves threatening an individual to force the person to comply with a demand. A classic example is the mugger who threatens someone with a gun to force the victim to hand over a wallet. This form of coercion involves a threat to make someone worse off, such as by physical harm. Potential egg donors are not coerced in this way when large sums of money are offered to them. The money might make them better off than they are, but they can turn down the money without being harmed or made worse off.

If large sums of money constitute coercive offers, they must be coercive in some other way. A woman in need of money to pay her rent or a large tuition bill, or to provide food for her family, may feel that she can't turn down a large offer to donate her eggs. However, even though she may benefit significantly from the money, that does not make the offer coercive, even if she has no better options. The women typically recruited as egg donors are not living in homeless shelters or struggling to feed their families. Rather, they are frequently very accomplished young college students and professionals. Such women might still be tempted by large sums of money—US$50,000 is a lot of green and a potentially life-changing sum. However, it is not coercive to offer someone a large sum of money, even if it is payment for something she would not otherwise do. Most people work in jobs for the money they earn and do things they would not otherwise do. We don't consider it coercive when a woman who dreams of being a folksinger instead becomes a corporate lawyer so she can make a lot of money. Offering her a large salary to work in a law firm is not coercive, even if she finds the offer tempting enough that she gives up her artistic dreams.

**Undue Inducement.** We might still criticize large payments offered to potential egg donors as being undue inducements. Undue inducement involves the offer of a reward so irresistible that it blinds individuals to the disadvantages of participating in the proposed activity. Undue inducements thus may be manipulative, and may exploit an individual's susceptibility to tempting offers in a way that undermines the individual's autonomy and ability to provide voluntary and informed consent. When life-changing sums of money are offered, potential egg donors may be more likely to discount the risks and burdens of donation, including the risk of impaired future fertility, as well as the psychological and legal consequences of their agreement to forgo parental rights and future contact with children who are their genetic offspring. They may make choices they will later regret.

What would be an ethical remedy for such irresistible offers? Payments to egg donors are intended to be inducements. Where payments are not allowed, the altruism of the donors must be relied upon instead, and few women are willing to donate to complete strangers without compensation. The exact amount that a particular individual may find irresistible, or an undue inducement, will vary. Some women might consider US$5,000 to be an amount of money worth the discomfort and risk of donation. For someone else, the amount will be much higher. No specific amount of money can be set as a threshold for undue inducements.

One of the concerns with undue inducements is that they might compromise the autonomous choices made by potential donors and encourage them to choose in a way that is against their own best interests. This claim is difficult to verify. People often make choices that, from an outsider's perspective, may seem foolish or irrational. That they may appear so to another does not mean they are actually foolish or irrational for the person making the choice. Interfering in a beneficial transaction between consenting adults is considered paternalistic. *Paternalism* is interference with the freedom of an individual, motivated by the desire to protect that person, often without the person's informed consent. To be paternalistic is to act as a parent toward children, to take the role of protector of people who are considered incapable of taking care of themselves.

The philosopher John Stuart Mill argued that paternalistic interference limits the liberty of individuals and is unwarranted when a person's actions will only harm the self. The bar for justifiably interfering with someone's decisions and actions is much higher: the decision or action must threaten harm or cause harm to others. Mill, in defending almost absolute liberty and freedom from state and social interference, invoked what he called the *harm principle*, which states that the only justification for interfering with individual liberty is harm to others. In other words, our personal liberties are rightfully limited if our actions can cause harm to someone else.

The fact that a woman does something she would not otherwise do, and does it only because a large amount of money is offered, does not mean that the inducement was undue or harmful. There is no good reason to think that the potential donors themselves are not capable of deciding whether it is worthwhile for them to undertake the risks and burdens of egg donation.

Finally, although there is concern about large payments being undue inducements, there has been little concern about payments that are too low. In many contexts, we think people are treated unfairly not because they are paid too much for their work, but because they are paid too little. If we can potentially exploit women by offering them too much money, it seems even more plausible that we can exploit them by offering too little for the risks and burdens they undertake as egg donors. Here again, the problem is determining exactly what would be the right amount to pay for egg donation.

**Compensation, or Buying Eggs?** It seems clear that offering a larger payment to a donor who is considered exceptional is in fact paying for her eggs, rather than compensating the donor for her time, inconvenience, and discomfort. After all, the Harvard coed who receives US$50,000 does not experience ten times the discomfort and inconvenience as the state university student who receives only US$5,000. Therefore, larger payments do not appear to be additional compensation but rather payment for eggs deemed to be of exceptional quality. This issue raises concerns about the commodification of eggs.

**Commodification.** Commodification occurs when something is turned into commercial property, when an item is offered for sale, and when a market price is attached to it. Generally, ethical concerns do not exist when selling objects such as cars, refrigerators, or works of art, nor are there worries about persons selling their services. It's not unethical for surgeons, carpenters, and violinists to sell their skills and to get paid more when their work is especially valued. However, concerns about commodification and commercial sale frequently arise in contexts involving certain services, such as prostitution, and with the sale of certain objects, such as eggs. The sale of blood and blood products, or hair, for example, is not considered ethically problematic. The question is why the selling of some body parts or products, or some services, is ethically worrisome, whereas others are not.

ASRM warns against the commodification or selling of human eggs, or turning eggs into commercial property, when it prohibits basing payment on the specific characteristics of the donor. Some critics of commercial gamete donation argue that market values are inappropriate, and even destructive in the family sphere. Thinking of children as property and of family life as essentially a series of commercial transactions would degrade and distort our view of families. That is undoubtedly true, although it is not clear that buying the gametes used to create a child—and perhaps viewing those purchased gametes as a kind of property—is tantamount to viewing the resulting child as property. Others have raised the concern that it could be psychologically damaging to children to learn that they were sold by their genetic parents. Like the children of Starbuck, they may grow up feeling that their conception was no more meaningful to their genetic father than selling a cup of coffee.

Gametes, of course, are not children, and buying gametes is not the same thing as buying a child, even if those gametes are used to produce a child. No evidence shows that children born from donated gametes are damaged psychologically by their origins in donated (or sold and purchased) cells. Furthermore, children created through IVF using donated gametes simply would not exist at all without those gametes and the interventions used to create the embryo that became the future child. Is the harm caused by having genetic origins in a commodified gamete so severe that those children would be better off never existing at all? That seems highly unlikely. (For more information, see "The Nonidentity Problem" later in this chapter.)

The story of Angela Collins and Margaret Hanson illustrates one way that real harm might come to families, and perhaps a child, when gametes are commodified and sold. It could create a financial incentive for the seller to deceive the buyer about the gametes being purchased. It is not hard to see how the incentive might increase as the financial stakes increase. A market for gametes, then, may create what are known as *perverse incentives*. Perverse incentives occur when individuals are given an incentive to do something they would not otherwise do, which has negative, unintended consequences that are contrary to the interests of the person offering the incentive. By paying for gametes, buyers may create an incentive for gamete donors to falsify their medical history or hide undesirable characteristics so that they appear to have the qualities desired by the buyers. The sperm donor in the Collins and Hanson case, for example, made false claims about his level of educational attainment, in addition to hiding his history of psychiatric illness and criminality.

## GENETIC DETERMINISM AND EUGENICS

A further concern relates to the practice of offering a premium price for the eggs of a donor who has specific desired characteristics, such as athleticism or high SAT scores. The willingness to pay more for the eggs of women who are measurably smarter, or have a more exclusive education, or who match some physical ideal evinces a belief in genetic determinism. Genetic determinism is the simplistic and false belief that DNA dictates all the characteristics a person will have. In fact, gene expression is complex and involves environmental as well as genetic factors. The type of family and home environment a child grows up in will have a greater influence on that child's intelligence, educational attainment, and psychological well-being than can be predicted by the phenotypic characteristics exhibited by an egg donor. Moreover, the precise combination that will occur when the donor egg's genes are combined with the genes of the sperm cannot be predicted. A false belief in genetic determinism on the part of parents could result in harm to the child, especially if the child fails to develop the superior qualities the parents strived to create.

Genetic determinism is also behind concerns about eugenics. Eugenics is the social practice that aims to improve the genetic quality of the human population. Modern eugenics began in the early twentieth century in Great Britain, as a social movement that advocated the improvement of human genetic traits through the promotion of reproduction among people with the desired traits (a practice known as positive eugenics) or through reduced reproduction or sterilization of people with undesired traits (known as negative eugenics). Negative eugenics was a national policy of Germany under Nazi rule; millions of people deemed undesirable were murdered under the Nazi racial hygiene program. The eugenics movement fell out of favor after World War II, but concerns about positive eugenics, or the selective breeding of people with the most desirable traits, have been revived as the use of ART has increased. In particular, placing higher value on gametes from donors seems like positive eugenics when such choices are based on characteristics such as SAT scores. Are these choices attempts to create genetically superior humans, while rejecting those humans who are deemed genetically inferior?

## SOCIAL EGG FREEZING

Cryopreservation has not been a reliable option for women who want to preserve their own eggs for use later. The large size and high water content, along with the location of chromosomes, in human eggs make them vulnerable to intracellular ice damage during the freezing and thawing process of cryopreservation. The success rate for achieving pregnancy using cryopreserved eggs has been less than 2 percent.

Women who might benefit from egg freezing include those who are undergoing gonadotoxic cancer treatment and women like Kate in *Baby Mama* who might use so-called elective or social egg freezing to delay childbearing for nonmedical reasons. Since 2002, advances in the cryopreservation process, and in particular a process called *vitrification*, have improved the survival of frozen eggs. Vitrification uses high concentrations of cryoprotectant chemicals to solidify the egg cell into a glass-like state that does not promote the formation of ice in the cell. In 2012 ASRM deemed human egg freezing to be no longer experimental, although it cautioned against its use for elective purposes, citing insufficient evidence concerning the safety, efficacy, cost-effectiveness, and emotional risks involved. Nonetheless, the prospect of being able to freeze one's own eggs for later use has led to the explosive growth of elective egg freezing and egg banking, particularly for women who hope to defer childbearing and stop their biological clocks. Egg freezing literally banks eggs for future use.

Social egg freezing has been praised as a means of promoting women's reproductive freedom and autonomy by allowing them to extend their natural reproductive cycle and choose motherhood at a time that is socially and financially appropriate for them. It can be

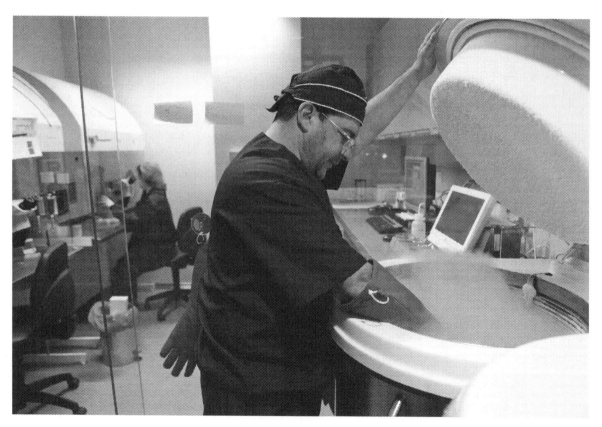

**Cryopreservation of embryos at a fertility clinic in Valencia, Spain.** *Because egg retrieval for use with in vitro fertilization (IVF) is costly and onerous, many eggs are extracted during a single IVF or egg donation cycle. The eggs are fertilized, and some of the resulting embryos are then cryopreserved for future use. The number of embryos created and stored in this manner, however, is often in excess of the number of desired children, resulting in leftover embryos—and ethical issues related to their disposal.* UNIVERSAL IMAGES GROUP/GETTY IMAGES.

viewed as a way of promoting gender equality, leveling the playing field by allowing women to delay parenthood in the same way that men can. However, egg freezing is an expensive option, costing US$12,000 to US$17,000 for the egg retrieval process, plus the annual cost of several hundred dollars to store the frozen eggs, as well as the later cost of IVF to fertilize the eggs and transfer the embryos. Although egg freezing may have some effect on leveling the playing field between men and women, the high cost introduces inequality between rich and poor women, who cannot access the expensive service equally.

Social egg freezing is a response to the tremendous social pressures on young women, who must choose between establishing a career and establishing a family. One criticism of social egg freezing is that it is an individual solution—one that puts the onus on women—to a social problem that might be better addressed by policies that allow women to choose motherhood at a more biologically appropriate time. Such policies include paid maternity and paternity leaves, subsidized child care, and family-friendly workplaces. Some high-tech companies, such as Apple and Facebook, include egg freezing in their employee benefits, which implies an endorsement of invasive and risky medical procedures, and a policy of rewarding women for not becoming pregnant, over corporate policies that would make motherhood an option for younger workers. Employer-subsidized egg freezing might actually serve to increase social injustice, by putting added pressure on women to choose to delay motherhood, without addressing the workplace inequalities that penalize women—but not men—for having families.

That women have a smaller biological window of opportunity than men to reproduce is a fact, but it is gender inequality, rather than biological inequality, that undermines the full exercise of women's reproductive autonomy. The elective use of egg freezing to address social, nonmedical limits on reproduction, rather than increasing women's reproductive freedom and autonomy, may allow society to defer confronting the inequality of social structures that make it difficult for women to combine childbearing and employment. Egg freezing does nothing to address the social injustices of gender inequality, and it may simply reinforce them while adding economic inequality between women to the mix.

## SURROGACY

No method of assisted reproduction highlights the socioeconomic inequalities between women more than surrogacy. In *Baby Mama*, Kate's adventures in surrogacy begin when her sister suggests that she try it. Kate replies that surrogacy is "for weirdos," but Chaffee Bicknell (played by Sigourney Weaver), a surrogacy broker, convinces her that surrogacy is just another form of outsourcing, not unlike hiring a nanny to provide child care. Kate meets Angie (played by Amy Poehler), a would-be surrogate who, together with her deadbeat boyfriend Carl (Dax Shepard), is looking to make some fast cash by renting out Angie's womb.

Surrogacy arrangements are common today, but they continue to provoke strong emotions, as well as ethical debate. The emotional responses are often negative. Like Kate, some people think surrogacy is weird, or repugnant, or unnatural. Others view the commercialization of surrogacy and the payment to the surrogate as a form of objectionable and unethical baby selling. Surrogacy, like other forms of ART, is expensive—the total costs of surrogacy can exceed US$100,000 (although only a fraction of that goes to the surrogate). Concerns about exploitation and undue inducement are commonly expressed, just as they are with payments to egg donors, especially given the socioeconomic differences between the contractual parents and the surrogate. As with Kate and Angie, contractual parents are typically quite wealthy, whereas the surrogate mother is frequently a woman of lesser means.

Surrogacy is an option for parents who have no other means of creating a family. Same-sex couples, for example, are not permitted to adopt in some places—for them, surrogacy is a way to have children. Heterosexual couples who are unable to adopt, or who find adoption to be undesirable, may view surrogacy as their only option to have a child or to have a child who is genetically related to one or both parents.

## BABY M

The first known pregnancy and birth by commercial surrogate in the United States was in 1976, when a surrogate mother was recruited through a newspaper ad, and was paid US$7,000. The first surrogacy case to land in a US court was the case of Baby M. In 1985, Mary Beth Whitehead entered into a surrogacy contract with William Stern to bear a child conceived of Whitehead's egg and Stern's sperm and then surrender her parental rights to the child. Stern's wife Elizabeth was not infertile, but she had multiple sclerosis, and the couple was concerned about the effects a pregnancy might have on her health. Whitehead was paid US$10,000 to be artificially inseminated with Stern's sperm and to gestate and give birth to a baby. Whitehead, who already had children of her own, had a change of heart after the baby girl was born. She gave up the money and kept the child. The Sterns sued. The police seized the child, known in court documents as Baby M, and after a long and emotional court battle, the New Jersey Supreme Court invalidated the surrogacy contract, calling it "illegal, perhaps criminal, and potentially degrading to women." In an unexpected turn, the court nonetheless awarded custody of Baby M to the Sterns, saying it was in the best interest of the child. Whitehead, who the court said was the baby's legal and natural mother, was granted visitation rights.

Mary Beth Whitehead was what is today called a traditional surrogate, meaning that she supplied the egg, making the child genetically related to her. IVF was not widely available at the time, but today it is the more common method of conception when a gestational surrogate is employed. The gametes may be supplied by the contractual parents or they may be from donors, but the gestational surrogate is not typically genetically related to the fetus in order to prevent emotionally fraught custody conflicts like the one in the Baby M case.

## COMMERCIAL SURROGACY

It is important to distinguish between two types of surrogacy arrangements: noncommercial and commercial surrogacy. Noncommercial (altruistic) surrogacy usually occurs between relatives or friends. There have been several highly publicized cases of mothers serving as surrogates for their infertile adult daughters, thus giving birth to their own grandchildren. Sisters and close friends sometimes act as altruistic surrogates as well. In a commercial surrogacy, the surrogate is paid for her services, which include undergoing medical interventions to transfer embryos to her womb, nine months of pregnancy, during which time she is usually required to submit to routine prenatal care, then labor and childbirth, and finally, giving up the child.

Surrogacy contracts can vary, but they frequently include clauses that prohibit the surrogate from engaging in risky activities such as smoking, drinking, or taking drugs. The medical expenses for the surrogate are paid for, and she typically receives a small stipend throughout pregnancy to cover her expenses, although most of her compensation comes in a lump sum payment after she gives birth and relinquishes the infant. More controversial provisions might allow the contractual parents to demand termination of the pregnancy if the fetus has an undesirable medical condition or disability, or to refuse to take custody of the infant following birth.

> "She's just an ignorant white trash woman that I paid to carry my kid."
> —Kate (*Baby Mama*)

*Baby Mama* depicts the pitfalls of surrogacy contracts that stem from the socioeconomic and class differences between parents and surrogate. Angie is pressured to be a surrogate by her unemployed boyfriend Carl, who views the baby-growing checks as a windfall. When Angie doesn't become pregnant as planned with Kate's baby, Carl schemes to deceive the desperate mom-to-be, a plan that starts to unravel when Angie leaves him and moves in with Kate. Meanwhile, controlling, nervous Kate takes on an awkward new role, acting like a surrogate mom to the immature and vulnerable Angie, and attempts to change her lifestyle and dietary choices for the benefit of the baby. When it turns out Angie is pregnant, it's not clear if the baby is her own or Kate's desperately wanted child. A DNA test and a court declare decisively that Kate is not the mother of the child, a simplistic gloss on the complex problem of defining family. Genetic kinship, after all, is not a requirement for motherhood, as is made obvious by adoption.

## BABY SELLING

Concerns about the possibility of baby selling are more relevant to surrogacy than to egg donation. Children are neither property nor things, and the objection to selling babies is that it is an affront to human dignity, a commodification and objectification of a human being, analogous to slavery. Surrogacy for hire seems to violate deeply held notions of the value of human life and the idea that human life has an intrinsic value that cannot be translated into a market value. Putting a price on a baby seems to devalue what is important and unique about human life. In the Baby M case, the court concluded that the baby was not sold because she was already Stern's biological child. A man cannot buy what is already his, according to the court. This decision ignored both that the baby was Whitehead's and that the surrender of parental rights to the child was the whole point of the surrogacy contract.

In commercial surrogacy, the question is whether the surrogate is selling a baby or selling a service by renting her womb and being paid for the risks and sacrifice, as well as the time, inconvenience, and discomfort associated with impregnation, pregnancy, and childbirth. However, because surrogates are not paid merely to produce a child but to surrender it suggests baby selling rather than the selling of a service alone. If the surrogate changes her mind and decides to keep the baby, she is not entitled to compensation, demonstrating that it is not merely the service of gestating and giving birth that she is paid for but rather handing over the baby. Surrogacy contracts sometimes contain clauses that state that in cases of stillbirth, surrogates will not be paid in full, even though they have performed their duties. The goal of contractual parents is not merely to have their progeny brought into the world, to be raised by just anyone, but rather to have a child in their possession to call their own.

The baby-selling objection to surrogacy, then, has some basis in fact. Intuitively, it seems correct to say that baby selling is wrong. It treats human beings as chattel, as things to which a price can be attached. If selling a baby is wrong, then surrogacy arrangements that pay women to gestate, give birth, and relinquish a baby are also apparently wrong. That is, even if we think there is nothing especially wrong about noncommercial surrogacy, commercial surrogacy is different: it is wrong because it involves selling a human being. Is there a way to make surrogacy ethically acceptable, by removing the taint of baby selling?

One way would be to simply prohibit commercial surrogacy. Surrogacy for purely altruistic reasons, to deliver children into the arms of loving parents, would not commodify or objectify human beings. But few women are interested in bearing children for complete strangers purely out of the goodness of their hearts, so altruistic surrogacy would benefit few people. Another possible solution would be to limit surrogate payments to nothing more than compensation for pregnancy-related medical expenses, as is permitted in some jurisdictions with adoptions. The same problem occurs: few women would be willing to bear children for strangers without compensation for their time, effort, and discomfort. If we think that the option of commercial surrogacy is a benefit not only to would-be parents and their children, but also to the surrogates who are able to make money, then limiting surrogacy to noncommercial agreements would greatly reduce the benefits available to all parties.

The fact that the overall benefits of surrogacy would be diminished by eliminating commercial surrogacy is not an effective argument in favor of retaining commercial surrogacy. After all, selling a baby, if it is wrong, is wrong for reasons similar to the ones that make selling other people, such as slaves, wrong. The fact that many people could benefit from slavery would not justify the practice. Likewise, even if many people benefit from commercial surrogacy, and far fewer people would benefit from noncommercial surrogacy, the loss of benefits is not by itself a strong enough justification to override the morally serious problem of selling babies.

## EXPLOITATION

> "This whole thing made you feel so happy, and it made me feel so important."
> —Angie (*Baby Mama*)

In *Baby Mama*, Angie and Carl were in it for the money, although Angie admits that having a child for Kate was fulfilling, and made her feel important. Indeed, Angie benefited from her friendship with Kate, which gave her a sense of self-worth and empowerment that enabled her to leave Carl. Arguably, she left one exploitative relationship for another, but many women who act as surrogates say that the experience of helping another couple have a family is personally fulfilling. It is also a source of income for women like Angie, whose lack of skills or education qualifies them only for low-wage work.

One feminist critique of commercial surrogacy is that it amounts to slavery and exploits women from lower socioeconomic classes. The claim is that surrogacy treats women like baby factories and objectifies them in a way that offends their human dignity. Unlike the baby-selling objection, which claims that surrogacy commodifies and objectifies babies, this objection to commercial surrogacy is that it commodifies, objectifies, and degrades women and fails to respect them as humans by putting a price on the use of their bodies. The poor women like Angie who have babies for rich women like Kate are thus exploited by commercial surrogacy.

It may well be the case that poor women are more susceptible to undue inducement when large amounts of money are offered in exchange for their services as a surrogate. But as with egg donation, offering money to people so that they will do something they otherwise wouldn't does not necessarily exploit them. Exploitation requires more than making a tempting offer. We exploit people when we use them as a means to our ends—as is undoubtedly the case with surrogacy. But the exploitation comes not from using people, which is something we all do, but rather from using them in ways that they do not agree to, or that are unfair or harmful. If women were not fairly compensated for their time, inconvenience, and labor as surrogates, we might say they were exploited because they were unfairly treated.

Although both sides of the surrogacy arrangement might benefit, if the benefits are unequally or unfairly distributed, we could claim that the surrogate is exploited. Likewise, if contractual parents took advantage of a woman's lack of education or her poverty, they might exploit her socioeconomic vulnerability when using her as a surrogate. If she had better options, she wouldn't agree to be a surrogate. Carl, who was himself unemployed, clearly manipulated and exploited Angie, using her ability to gestate a baby to serve his own ends in a way that did not fairly benefit Angie. Carl also manipulated and exploited Angie and Kate when he coerced Angie into deceiving Kate about the pregnancy. Kate's ignorance was taken advantage of and exploited, and she was used as a means to Carl's ends. Do contractual parents take advantage of the surrogate's socioeconomic status in a way that is exploitative? In some contexts, it seems quite possible that they do. Transnational surrogacy is one of those contexts.

## TRANSNATIONAL SURROGACY

Medical tourism is the practice of traveling to a foreign country to seek medical treatment. In many cases, patients from high-income countries, such as the United States, travel to lower-income countries that have high-quality health-care facilities. There, they can receive treatments that are experimental or unapproved in their home country; they may also obtain less expensive health care. The global spread of ART has led to the growth of a particularly controversial form of reproductive medical tourism: transnational gestational surrogacy.

One of the most common destinations for wealthy Americans, Europeans, and Asians seeking a transnational gestational surrogate is India, which has many established fertility clinics staffed by well-trained medical personnel. More importantly, India offers a large population of poor, uneducated women whose ability to make money is severely limited. Women in India earn about half the wages paid to men doing the same work, and the jobs available to unskilled, uneducated laborers are dangerous, with high rates of injury and illness. Additionally, for religious and cultural reasons, most Indian women do not smoke or drink alcohol. India's laws concerning custody of children produced through surrogacy strongly favor the contractual parents, and because the surrogates employed are frequently illiterate, they often do not know what their rights are, nor do they fully understand what they are agreeing to in surrogacy arrangements.

The circumstances of transnational surrogacy as practiced in a country such as India create legitimate concerns about exploitation, and vulnerability to exploitation, for the women who are recruited as surrogates. These concerns arise in part because of the extreme economic inequality between the contractual parents and the surrogate. However, although contractual parents often turn to transnational surrogacy in order to reduce costs, for the women who serve as surrogates the bargain-basement fee they receive can still be an extraordinary, life-changing sum. Typically, a surrogate in India is paid US$6,000 to US$10,000, about half what an American surrogate can receive. It's an amount an unskilled

Indian woman might not be able to earn working for a decade at a dangerous job. Such fees might well constitute an undue inducement given the circumstances of poor, working women in India. As was the case with egg donation, the ethical problem with an undue inducement is that it could manipulate a person, make her disregard the risks involved in the offer, and compromise her ability to protect her own interests. Yet, it is not clear that this manipulation happens to the surrogate in India, who might be quite capable of weighing the risks and benefits of surrogacy and making the choice that provides the most benefit for herself and her family. Rather than being exploitative, surrogacy payments in fact may be empowering for extremely poor women, who are presented with the means to pay for a child's education or start a business that can help pull her family up out of poverty.

It may still be the case that transnational surrogacy exploits women because poor women in low-income countries are paid far less than a surrogate in a wealthy Western country. That is, the payments to Indian surrogates may be unfair because the women are not paid the full value of their labor. Such payments may be unfair even though the surrogates benefit from them. This type of exploitation is potentially widespread in all areas of transnational commerce. Wages in low-income countries are much lower than they are in wealthy industrialized nations. A worker in a US garment factory might make minimum wage, whereas his or her counterpart in India, which has no set minimum wage, makes the equivalent of mere pennies for doing the same work. However, this by itself does not make the wages unfair. An important consideration when comparing wages is that the cost of living in India is significantly lower than it is in the United States. The unfairness and exploitation results when, taking into account the different costs of living, the real wage paid to Indian workers is far less. Real wages are the amount that the wages can buy in terms of goods and services. For example, if an American garment worker must work ten minutes to earn enough to buy five pounds of flour, and the Indian worker must labor all day to buy five pounds of flour, the Indian worker is paid far less in real wages. If the Indian garment worker is paid less in terms of real wages, we might say she is exploited.

According to this argument, to the extent that surrogates in low-income countries are not fairly compensated for their work, they are exploited. But as with other exploitative industries that do not fairly compensate workers, there is a dilemma: if workers are paid what would be considered a fair wage in a high-income country, there is less economic incentive for transnational corporations to locate their factories in low-income countries, and jobs may be lost. Potentially, this loss of jobs makes the workers even worse off than when they were working for unfair wages. Similarly, removing the financial incentives for transnational surrogacy could make potential surrogates worse off in the sense that they will lose some opportunities to earn what are for them extraordinary, life-changing, and empowering sums of money.

In transnational surrogacy, the costs of ART, prenatal and obstetric care, and broker fees are all lower than elsewhere. It may be possible to pay the surrogate a sum comparable to that earned by a surrogate in the United States and still make the total costs a relative bargain. In that case, paying a fair wage would not make potential surrogates worse off by removing a source of income. It would make them even better off. Additionally, some couples opt for transnational surrogacy because commercial surrogacy is outlawed in their home country. Australia, Canada, Israel, and many European countries, for example, have made commercial surrogacy illegal. Those couples are not seeking a bargain but rather a service they cannot get at home. They would not be deterred by the higher cost of paying transnational surrogates fair compensation. Thus, because transnational surrogates could be fairly compensated by paying them the equivalent of what their counterparts in wealthier countries receive, without threatening the practice or benefits of transnational surrogacy, the lower payments they currently receive are unfair and exploitative.

It can be concluded that transnational surrogacy is exploitative because it does not pay poor women in low-income countries a fair and equitable wage for their work. What is fair is judged by comparing transnational surrogacy fees to those paid to American surrogates who do the same work. The assumption is that the fees paid to American surrogates are not exploitative.

Surrogates also may be exploited if they have vulnerabilities that others could use to their advantage. In the case of transnational surrogates, it is obvious that poverty and a lack of education are vulnerabilities that could be exploited, but that a woman is poor and illiterate does not mean she is incapable of weighing her options and making an informed decision that benefits her.

## TAKING ADVANTAGE OF SURROGATES

Agencies that recruit surrogates in the United States stress the positive and altruistic aspects of being a surrogate and emphasize that surrogacy is about building families. They seek women who have already had children of their own, and understand the physical demands of pregnancy and childbirth, but they also place a lot of emphasis on psychological characteristics and seek women who want an opportunity to feel special and experience the joy of helping others and making a difference in someone's life. Surrogacy is referred to as a gift—the greatest gift humanly possible. It is clear that the women being sought as surrogates are not only capable of a healthy pregnancy and birth, but also empathetic, altruistic, and self-sacrificing, willing to give a child to a childless couple. They may be women like Angie, who are naive, vulnerable, and needy or who want to feel important and special. The women sought by surrogacy agencies might be especially vulnerable to emotional manipulation and exploitation of their altruistic natures. The question is whether they are exploited by surrogacy as a result.

Some critics of commercial surrogacy claim that the willingness to be altruistic limits the ability of potential surrogates to recognize that they are sacrificing more and giving more than they receive in return. Indeed, the very idea that they are giving someone the greatest gift possible would seem to make it impossible for surrogates to be compensated adequately with money alone. One criticism of commercial or altruistic surrogacy is that it exploits surrogates by taking advantage of their willingness to give. Surrogates allow themselves to be used—exploited—for someone else's benefit.

This charge of exploitation could be rejected as paternalistic. The claim that some surrogates are exploited because they can't look out for their own interests, control their own bodies, and exercise their reproductive freedom is paternalistic. It conflicts with the moral stance that women have both the ability and the right to make their own reproductive choices, even if those choices might seem weird or unsavory to others. Indeed, many of the concerns about surrogacy, as well as egg donation—coercion, undue inducement, and exploitation—are paternalistic, implying that women are incapable of making informed, rational choices about what will benefit them, are incapable of resisting emotional or financial pressures, and are incapable of protecting themselves against demeaning and degrading treatment. Consider the fact that the same concerns are not brought up in the context of men and sperm donation.

A final criticism of surrogacy, and of ART more generally, is that it is harmful to the children produced. This criticism will be addressed in the next section.

## PROCREATIVE LIBERTY AND HARM TO OFFSPRING

"There's no wrong way to make a family." —Chaffee Bicknell (*Baby Mama*)

Early opposition to IVF and ARTs centered on the possibility that these technological means of reproduction would result in unhealthy babies and children. Potential harm to the offspring produced through ART included physical, emotional, and social harm.

ART is not without risks to offspring. Some studies have shown a small increase in the risk of birth defects, neurological problems, and lower birth weight in children conceived via IVF. ICSI now occurs in about half of IVF treatments, and children conceived through ICSI have a higher risk of chromosomal and genomic disorders.

The most common risk of IVF is multiple gestation and birth, resulting in twins, triplets, or higher-order multiple births. Multiple births pose significantly higher risks of death, illness, birth injury, and permanent disability for both offspring and mothers. One-third of IVF procedures lead to multiple births, and the incidence of multiple births has increased dramatically since the early 1980s, largely as a result of ART. The birthrate for triplets and higher-order multiple births increased by 400 percent in the two decades after Louise Brown's birth. The risks of multiple-gestation pregnancies and births have prompted practice guidelines for fertility doctors to discourage the transfer of large numbers of embryos to avoid multiple births. Fetal reduction, also known as selective abortion, can be performed to reduce the number of fetuses *in utero*, but the procedure carries the risk of miscarriage and loss of the entire pregnancy. Additionally, some people object to abortion on moral or religious grounds, and opt for the risks of multiple-gestation pregnancies and births instead.

Infertility sometimes results from genetic abnormalities in a person's gametes; the use of ARTs may make it possible for those individuals to reproduce and pass genetic diseases on to their offspring. ART is increasingly used by individuals of advanced reproductive age, male and female, whose gametes may be affected by age. Those gametes, which would not result in a fertilized, viable embryo without assistance, may increase the risk of birth defects and disease in offspring. Some studies have shown that advanced paternal age increases the risk of schizophrenia and autism spectrum disorders.

Finally, some opponents of surrogacy and the use of donor gametes raise concerns about the psychological harm for children conceived and born through commercial arrangements. Children like Starbuck's could feel a sense of loss and longing because their genetic father masturbated into a plastic cup for money and then cared to contribute nothing more to their lives, their upbringing, and their well-being. All of these are concerns about the interests and welfare of children who result from assisted reproduction. Importantly, they are not exclusively concerns about children conceived or born through assisted reproduction. Naturally conceived children can experience the same illnesses and risks as the children of ART. Children who are adopted may experience the same sense of loss and abandonment as children conceived of donor gametes, or gestated by a surrogate.

Nevertheless, if ART can potentially harm offspring, that would be a reason to limit its use. Mill's harm principle provides a clear limit on the use of ART in cases where offspring might be harmed by it.

## THE NONIDENTITY PROBLEM

However, at the heart of all considerations about harms or the ill effects on welfare for children who result from ART is a philosophical paradox: the nonidentity problem, which concerns the possibility (or impossibility, thus the paradox) of a person being harmed by that which caused the person's birth. It appears that a child can be harmed by the method of conception or gestation or the social circumstances of the family the child is born into. But if the child is harmed, the harm is impossible to separate from the child's very existence. If the child benefits from existing—which we generally think is true—then it would seem impossible for the child to be harmed, to be made worse off, by whatever makes it possible for the child to exist. For example, if a child is conceived of donor gametes, that particular child, the one who resulted from the combination of specific donor gametes, does not have the option of being conceived without donor gametes. The only alternative for that child is nonexistence. If the child's parents had tried to conceive when they were younger, when they would not have needed ART, a different child would have existed at a different time, but not the child who we think has been harmed by ART.

Thus, given that each of us is conceived of a specific sperm and egg combination, at a specific time, and under the condition of being gestated by someone, and if it appears that a child has been harmed by ART, that apparent harm is in fact unavoidable. The only alternative to existence in the harmed condition is nonexistence. Because existence is a benefit—and better than never being born at all—we cannot actually say that the child has been harmed by being made worse off by the ART that caused him or her to exist.

The nonidentity problem makes it difficult to claim that ART results in harm to the offspring whose existence depends on it. The exception is children whose lives are so terrible that it really would have been better had they never been born at all. Undoubtedly such children exist—children who suffer terribly and live brief, painful lives—but the millions of children who have been born through ART have, by and large, rather ordinary lives that are well within the normal range. Indeed, because the same illnesses and disabilities, the same emotional and psychological adversities they experience are also experienced by children conceived and born without ART, there does not seem to be anything unique, or uniquely problematic, about the effects of ART on the offspring produced.

## PROCREATIVE AUTONOMY AND LIBERTY

Because it is difficult to coherently show that ART harms offspring, some defenders of procreative freedom claim that there should be no limits on the right of potential parents to use ART to produce children. Procreation is almost universally considered to be one of the most important and worthwhile of human activities, and the right to procreative autonomy is thus a fundamental right of human beings. Procreative autonomy is the right to choose when, how, and with whom to procreate—or when not to procreate. Procreative liberty is the right to be free from interference in the exercise of one's procreative activities. As a right against interference, procreative liberty does not guarantee that anyone can have access to ART or that ART must be provided. There is no obligation, for example, to provide someone with donor gametes just because an individual is unable to produce his or her own. If it should turn out that transnational surrogacy exploits and harms the surrogates, the procreative liberty of the contractual parents would not justify that exploitation. But just as people who can procreate without assistance should be free to do so if they choose, people who require ART to procreate should be free to do so if there is no significant harm to others that can result.

Critics of unlimited procreative liberty say that it takes too limited a view of the potential harms of ART and only considers individual rights and individual harms without looking at the broader social context in which ART is used. Some feminist critics, for example, are concerned that some forms of third-party reproduction, involving gamete donors or surrogates, might objectify children by treating them as a means to parental satisfaction, while also objectifying women and treating them as well as a means to satisfy procreative desires in a way that perpetuates oppression. Others are concerned that third-party reproduction damages notions of kinship and family, causing children to think of themselves as manufactured products, denied the sense of identity that comes from knowing their biological heritage. Still others question the strength of the moral foundation of procreative liberty, which is built on acceptance of the view that children cannot be harmed by ART if it causes them to exist.

If we accept that a child with a life that is worth living cannot be harmed by ART, and that procreative liberty thus gives license to procreate at will using ART, then almost anything would be permitted, and parents need give no consideration to the health or interests of their future children as long as those children would have a life worth living.

Critics of the argument for procreative liberty argue that it does allow almost anything, but only when one considers procreation after the fact. After the child exists, if he or she has a worthwhile life, it cannot be said that the child was harmed by creation. But before the fact, when the decision is made about whether to create a child who will predictably face hardships, it is not obvious that the parents' interests in procreating, and their procreative autonomy, justify creating the child just to satisfy their own needs and desires. Even if procreative autonomy and liberty are important values, comparable to the value of procreating, other important values and moral considerations bear on procreative choices.

Actions that affect others can never be completely free, and the possibility of causing harm to others is one widely acknowledged constraint on our liberties, including procreative liberty. A salient fact about procreating with the help of ART is that, unlike sexual reproduction, which sometimes results in unintended pregnancies, ART must be undertaken with intention and deliberation. Becoming a parent through ART is never accidental. It is a matter of choice, and those choices can affect others in ways that are unexpected and unintended.

## Summary

When Louise Brown was born, the staunchest critics of IVF hardly imagined the real and deeply divisive questions and problems reproductive technology would actually generate. The many and diverse bioethical issues raised through *Baby Mama* and *Starbuck* are pervasive with ARTs. These movies situate bioethical debates within broader philosophical questions about exploitation, coercion, harm, liberty, identity, personhood, and the value of life and the meaning of kinship and family.

Some of the bioethical concerns related to ARTs are deeply context-dependent. For example, payments for surrogacy and egg donation may be exploitative in some situations but not others. Was Angie exploited by Kate, by Carl, or by both? Possibly, she wasn't exploited at all. The availability of socially motivated reproductive technologies such as elective egg freezing might be advantageous and equalizing for some women, or they might only perpetuate existing unjust social structures that disadvantage and harm women. Children might be harmed in a variety of ways when they are created using ART, but identifying and weighing that harm requires wrestling with complex questions about our identity and origins, and coming to terms with the ways that families have changed in the last several decades.

The rapid growth and acceptance of ART has occurred simultaneously with many social changes, such as greater inclusion of women in the workforce, increasing rates of divorce and single parenthood, and expanding definitions of marriage and family. Long-settled notions of family and parenthood have been called into question as a result of these social upheavals and by new ways of making babies. What makes a group of people a family? Is it biology? Genetics? Social custom? The law? There is no simple answer, no single concept of *family* that can handle the myriad ways that families can now be created.

The very existence of ART testifies to the enduring and profound desire people have to procreate, and no amount of social change can alter that fundamental and most basic yearning. Both Kate and David, in their own nontraditional ways, show how the urge to procreate and parent—to make a family—takes shape in unexpected ways. For many people, as for Kate and David, what matters is not the plastic cup or the petri dish, but the happy ending, when a child, and a family, comes into being.

## Bibliography

Alpern, Kenneth D., ed. *The Ethics of Reproductive Technology.* Oxford: Oxford University Press, 1992.

American Society for Reproductive Medicine Ethics Committee. "Financial Compensation of Oocyte Donors." *Fertility and Sterility* 88, no. 2 (2007): 305–309.

Annas, George J. "Fairy Tales Surrogate Mothers Tell." *Law, Medicine and Health Care* 16, nos. 1–2 (1988): 27–33.

Buchanan, Allen, Dan W. Brock, Norman Daniels, and Daniel Wikler. *From Chance to Choice: Genetics and Justice.* Cambridge: Cambridge University Press, 2001.

Canadian Press. "Sperm Bank Allegedly Gives Couple Wrong Donor Info: Canadian Couple Sues U.S.-Based Sperm Bank, Xytex, after Accidentally Learning Donor Details." *CBC News.* 2015. http://www.cbc.ca/news/canada/sperm-bank-allegedly-gives-couple-wrong-donor-info-1.3022603.

Cohen, Cynthia B. "'Give Me Children or I Shall Die!' New Reproductive Technologies and Harm to Children." *The Hastings Center Report* 26, no. 2 (1996): 19–27.

Cohen, Cynthia B. *New Ways of Making Babies: The Case of Egg Donation.* Bloomington: Indiana University Press, 1996.

Forster, Heidi. "The Legal and Ethical Debate Surrounding the Storage and Destruction of Frozen Human Embryos: A Reaction to the Mass Disposal in Britain and the Lack of Law in the United States." *Washington University Law Review* 76, no. 2 (1998): 759–780.

Harris, John. "The Welfare of the Child." *Health Care Analysis* 8, no. 1 (2000): 27–34.

Harwood, Karey. "Egg Freezing: A Breakthrough for Reproductive Autonomy?" *Bioethics* 23, no. 1 (2009): 39–46.

Humbyrd, Casey. "Fair Trade International Surrogacy." *Developing World Bioethics* 9, no. 3 (2009): 111–118.

Huxley, Aldous. *Brave New World.* New York: Harper Perennial, 2006. First published in 1932.

Kavka, Gregory S. "The Paradox of Future Individuals." *Philosophy and Public Affairs* 11, no. 2 (1982): 93–112.

Kolata, Gina. "$50,000 Offered to Tall, Smart Egg Donor." *New York Times,* March 3, 1999. http://www.nytimes.com/1999/03/03/us/50000-offered-to-tall-smart-egg-donor.html.

Levine, Aaron D. "Self-Regulation, Compensation, and the Ethical Recruitment of Oocyte Donors." *The Hastings Center Report* 40, no. 2 (2010): 25–36.

Macklin, Ruth. "Is There Anything Wrong with Surrogate Motherhood? An Ethical Analysis." *Journal of Law, Medicine and Ethics* 16, nos. 1–2 (1988): 57–64.

Marietta, Cynthia S. "Birth of Healthy Baby from 20-Year-Old Frozen Embryo Raises Ethical Questions." *Health Law Perspectives* (January 2011). https://www.law.uh.edu/healthlaw/perspectives/2011/(CM)%20IVF.pdf.

Marsh, Margaret, and Wanda Ronner. *The Empty Cradle: Infertility in America from Colonial Times to the Present*. Baltimore: Johns Hopkins University Press, 1996.

*Matter of Baby M.*, 537 A.2d 1227, 109 N.J. 396, 109 N.J.2d 396 (1988).

Mill, John Stuart. *On Liberty*. 1859. https://www.gutenberg .org/files/34901/34901-h/34901-h.htm.

Mroz, Jacqueline. "One Sperm Donor, 150 Offspring." *New York Times*, September 5, 2011, D1.

Murray, Thomas H. "What Are Families For? Getting to an Ethics of Reproductive Technology." *The Hastings Center Report* 32, no. 3 (2002): 41–45.

Office of Population Affairs, US Department of Health and Human Services. "Embryo Adoption." http://www.hhs .gov/opa/about-opa-and-initiatives/embryo-adoption/.

Parfit, Derek. *Reasons and Persons*. Oxford: Oxford University Press, 1984.

President's Council on Bioethics. *Monitoring Stem Cell Research*. Washington, DC, 2004. https://repository.library .georgetown.edu/bitstream/handle/10822/559369/pcbe _final_version_monitoring_stem_cell_research.pdf?seq uence=1&isAllowed=y.

Roberts, Melinda A. *Child versus Childmaker: Future Persons and Present Duties in Ethics and the Law*. Lanham, MD: Rowman and Littlefield, 1998.

Robertson, John A. *Children of Choice: Freedom and the New Reproductive Technologies*. Princeton, NJ: Princeton University Press, 1994.

Robertson, John A. "Procreative Liberty and Harm to Offspring in Assisted Reproduction." *American Journal of Law and Medicine* 30, no. 1 (2004): 7–40.

Ryan, Maura A. "The Argument for Unlimited Procreative Liberty: A Feminist Critique." *The Hastings Center Report* 20, no. 4 (1990): 6–12.

Steinbock, Bonnie. *Life before Birth: The Moral and Legal Status of Embryos and Fetuses*. 2nd ed. Oxford: Oxford University Press, 2011.

Steinbock, Bonnie. "Payment for Egg Donation and Surrogacy." *Mount Sinai Journal of Medicine* 71, no. 4 (2004): 255–265.

Wang, Jeff, and Mark V. Sauer. "In Vitro Fertilization (IVF): A Review of Three Decades of Clinical Innovation and Technological Advancement." *Therapeutics and Clinical Risk Management* 2, no. 4 (2006): 355–364.

**FILM**

*Baby Mama*. Dir. Michael McCullers. 2008. A comedy about a successful career woman who hires a surrogate mother.

*Starbuck*. Dir. Ken Scott. 2011. A forty-something slacker finds out that the sperm donations he made decades earlier have resulted in hundreds of children.

CHAPTER 3

# A Conversation on the Ethics of Abortion

*Bertha Alvarez Manninen*
*Associate Professor of Philosophy, School of Humanities, Arts,*
*and Cultural Studies*
*Arizona State University–West Campus, Tempe*

On January 22, 1973, the US Supreme Court decided the controversial case *Roe v. Wade*. In a 7–2 vote, they ruled that the right to privacy guaranteed by the due process clause of the Fourteenth Amendment to the US Constitution secured for women the right to an abortion. Among the many defenses offered, an important one was that the government had no right to interfere in the lives of its citizens when it came to intimate and personal issues, such as procreative choices. The *Roe v. Wade* decision is best understood through a historical lens, as two important Supreme Court cases in the years prior emphasized the importance of reproductive liberty and privacy. In 1965, *Griswold v. Connecticut* reversed the ban on contraception for married couples, and in 1972, *Eisenstadt v. Baird* extended the *Griswold* decision to include unmarried persons. Justice William Brennan (1906–1997), writing the majority opinion for the latter case, stated that "if the right to privacy means anything, it is the right of the individual, married or single, to be free from unwarranted governmental intrusion into matters so fundamentally affecting a person as the decision whether to bear or beget a child."

The justices did not conclude that a woman's right to abortion was categorical; restrictions were built into the decision. The idea of breaking pregnancy up into trimesters originated with *Roe*. According to the justices, within the first trimester, no state can prohibit a woman from obtaining an abortion, and a state may do so in the second trimester only if the abortion is considered to be harmful to the woman's health. Within the third trimester, however, states can enact laws prohibiting or severely restricting abortion access. This is because, back in the 1970s, fetal viability, referring to the time that the fetus could survive outside of the womb, occurred within the third trimester. Given more sophisticated technology, however, fetuses are now able to survive outside the womb earlier in pregnancy. As of 2016, the youngest premature baby to survive was Amilia Taylor, who was born in 2006 at twenty-one weeks and six days toward the end of the second trimester. In response to the evolving state of fetal viability, the 1992 Supreme Court case *Planned Parenthood v. Casey* altered *Roe*'s decision and specified that a state could prohibit abortion at the onset of fetal viability whenever in pregnancy it occurs. Forty-two states have laws that prohibit later-term abortions, often after fetal viability, except when necessary to preserve the health of the pregnant woman (Guttmacher Institute 2015).

Although Supreme Court decisions regarding contraception have been, historically, relatively uncontroversial, the same cannot be said about the decision to legalize abortion. Even before *Roe*, abortion had been a topic of much debate in the United States—one that was agitated even more in the 1960s after it was discovered that the drug Thalidomide, which had been prescribed to pregnant women to lessen the symptoms of morning sickness, resulted in severe fetal abnormalities. In 1962, television actress Sherri Finkbine (1932–) sought, and was denied, a therapeutic abortion in Arizona upon discovering that her fetus had been adversely affected by Thalidomide. After much publicity and protest from the American public, she and her husband flew to Sweden to procure the abortion. The fetus was so deformed it was not possible to determine its sex by sight. The Finkbine incident is considered crucial in the resurgence of the fight for abortion rights, because abortions were not legal in all fifty states until *Roe*. Far from settling the debate, however, abortion continues to be a topic of extensive discussion in the United States. A 2012 Gallup poll revealed that 17 percent of US citizens would not vote for an elected official who did not share their views on abortion; 45 percent admitted that abortion is one of the most important social issues they consider when deciding whether to vote for a candidate (Saad 2012). Sometimes the debate has turned violent, resulting in the kidnapping, attempted murder, and murder of abortion providers, as well as of receptionists and security guards at abortion clinics. Abortion clinics are also often the target of arson, bombings, and vandalism.

The 2007 documentary *Unborn in the U.S.A.* follows various pro-life advocates as they work to spread their antiabortion message across the United States. In the film, Father Frank Pavone (1959–), a representative of Catholic Priests for Life, adamantly voices his disapproval of any kind of violence done to abortion doctors. The Reverend Don Spitz, however, a member of the extremist pro-life group Army of God, is asked to comment on the murder of Dr. Barnett Slepian (1946–1998), an abortion provider in Buffalo, New York, who was gunned down while in his house and in front of his children: "I have no sympathy for Mrs. Slepian or Barnett Slepian. He knew what he was doing. He was murdering children. So, you know, that's too bad. If he was killed in front of his family that's a little too bad" (*Unborn in the U.S.A.* 2007).

As is the case with most controversial issues, aggressive reactions often occur because of a lack of respectful and intelligent dialogue. The aim of this chapter is to provide the reader with an avenue for thinking about, and engaging the issue of, abortion in a more critical manner. Among the topics discussed are the following: What is the moral status of the human fetus; that is, should it be bestowed with the same rights as all other extrauterine human beings? In what ways have fetal rights come into conflict with maternal rights? Can the right to an abortion be defended even if the fetus is granted moral and legal rights? Is it possible to adjudicate between women's need for abortion access and a medical provider's right to act within the boundaries of his conscience if he opposes abortion? Could selective abortion be morally defensible if the goal is to preserve the life of some of the fetuses in a multiple pregnancy? Finally, this chapter will end by emphasizing some shared values between the pro-life and pro-choice perspectives in the hope that dialogue can be built on these commonalities.

# FETAL HUMANITY AND THE RIGHT TO LIFE

Many pro-choice advocates tend to portray pro-life advocates as essentially adversarial to women's rights and their welfare. Professor Marsha Vanderford, in her study of the mutual vilification that takes place in the abortion debate by individuals on both sides, notes that "pro-choice rhetoric cast a negative light on pro-lifers by describing their actions as entirely corrupt … [they are] focused on 'emotional issues which manipulate people into activism based on fear' and accomplished their goals in 'nasty way[s]'" (1989, 170). Although it is undoubtedly true that, as mentioned, pro-life extremism has led to much violence, it is unfair to paint the pro-life position as an intrinsically violent or irrational one.

When pro-life advocates look at a human embryo or fetus (the term *fetus* will be used to denote intrauterine life at all stages), they typically see a vulnerable human being that is, in their eyes, morally equivalent to a newborn infant. Just as most people typically recoil at the thought of killing an infant, pro-life advocates equally recoil at the thought of abortion. It is true that the fetus begins to resemble a human being early in pregnancy. By the fifth week of gestation, the fetus's brain, spinal cord, and heart begin to develop. The eyes and ears begin to form between the sixth and seventh week. The lungs begin to form around the eighth week. Although a fetus is, quite literally, a mass of cells during the blastocyst period (from conception until about two weeks postfertilization), it quickly surpasses this state to become a functioning organism most of us would likely recognize as a nascent human being.

This was portrayed rather humorously (yet also seriously) in the movie *Juno* (2007) when the lead character, sixteen-year-old Juno MacGuff, initially decides to get an abortion after an unplanned pregnancy. While entering the clinic, she runs into a lone protestor, one of her classmates. To deter Juno, her classmate yells out: "Your baby probably has a beating heart, you know. It can feel pain. And it's got fingernails!" At first Juno scoffs at the "fingernails" comment, but once inside, upon noticing many other people in the waiting room focusing on their nails, she decides to not abort. The implication here is that focusing on some aspect of the fetus's humanity—in this case, fingernails—is sufficient for illustrating that killing it is morally wrong.

In his encyclical *Evangelium Vitae*, Pope John Paul II (1920–2005) describes abortion as an attack on human life "at the time of its greatest frailty" (1995, 21). All human life, he argues, "is sacred and inviolable at every moment of existence, including the initial phase which precedes birth" (1995, 109). He empathetically acknowledges the social and economic pressures that lead to many women obtaining abortions: that "acute poverty, anxiety, or frustration in which the struggle to make ends meet, the presence of unbearable pain, or instances of violence, especially against women, make the choice to defend and promote life so demanding" (1995, 21). He argues, however, just as it isn't morally permissible to kill born children to alleviate economic or other social pressures, it is equally impermissible to destroy intrauterine life.

Because they equate abortion with murder, pro-life advocates see the quest to eliminate abortion as a moral imperative. This was an important motivation behind the Partial-Birth Abortion Ban Act of 2003, which prohibits a type of late-term abortion (officially referred to in the medical literature as "intact dilation and extraction") because it is deemed excessively cruel. In this procedure, the fetus is partially delivered and then its cranium is decompressed so that it can pass through the vaginal canal. The procedure is comparatively rare, accounting for less than 1 percent of later-term abortions, which themselves constitute about 10 percent of all abortion procedures in the United States (Guttmacher Institute 2014). The argument against the ban is that, when these kinds of abortions do happen, they often are performed in the interest of maternal health. Nevertheless, the point is that the pro-life impetus to prohibit abortion stems from the belief that it is a form of murder and, for later-term abortions, an excessively cruel form of murder.

The key premise pro-life advocates assume, and that many pro-choice advocates deny, is that the human fetus is morally equivalent to a born human being: that the fetus has the same moral status and moral rights, and therefore is worthy of the same legal rights, as any human person. Pro-choice advocates have often accused pro-life advocates of begging the question when it comes to fetal personhood, and the consequent belief that abortion is murder, because these are the very premises that require argumentation, rather than mere assumption. Because the issue of fetal personhood so often divides pro-life and pro-choice advocates, it is imperative to explore the issue further.

## IS THE HUMAN FETUS A HUMAN PERSON?

One theme that has been touched on repeatedly in science-fiction films concerns what kinds of beings are worthy of moral status. And, if there is one thing these films have illustrated, it is that a being need not be human to be a person. Fictional characters such as E.T., Data from *Star Trek: The Next Generation*, David from the movie *A.I.*, the replicants from *Blade Runner*, Samantha from the movie *Her*, and Ava from *Ex Machina* present to the audience examples of nonhuman beings who nevertheless have conscious minds, self-awareness, and moral agency. That is, despite that they are made from different material "stuff," these beings have minds (or, for the religiously inclined, they have souls). Such examples help us draw a conceptual distinction that will be key in our discussion of fetal moral status—biological humanity is separate from moral personhood. One may possess the latter without the former. But may one possess the former without the latter? Like most questions in philosophy, the answer here is: "It depends."

Often, many who are in favor of abortion rights will deny the fetus's humanity. When feminist writer Linda Bird Francke (1939–) and her husband decided to get an abortion in

***Alicia Vikander stars as android Ava in director Alex Garland's 2015 science-fiction thriller* Ex Machina.**
*Fictional characters like Ava, an attractive female humanoid robot who develops a relationship with the person hired to test her "humanity," offer audiences examples of nonhuman beings who nevertheless have conscious minds, self-awareness, and moral agency.* **MOVIESTORE COLLECTION LTD/ALAMY.**

response to an unplanned pregnancy, he attempted to comfort her by saying, "it's not a life … it's a bunch of cells smaller than my fingernail" (1978, 5). Clearly, however, he could not have literally meant that the fetus was not alive. Even early fetuses are, at the very least, biologically alive, and they are certainly members of our species (*Homo sapiens sapiens*).

Regardless of how they are worded, statements like these don't really mean to question fetuses' biological status, but rather their moral status—that is, it has to do with their personhood, rather than their biological humanity. The main question, then, is this: when does the fetus become the kind of being that is worthy of having moral (and, from a pro-life perspective, legal) rights? Three possible answers will be considered, along with some difficulties for each one.

## THE GENETIC APPROACH TO MORAL STATUS

The phrase "life begins at conception" is well-known among pro-life advocates. But such a phrase doesn't just mean that a new biological organism begins to exist at conception. People who are pro-life mean something much more than this; they mean that morally significant life begins at conception. According to this view, genetic humanity, being a member of the species *Homo sapiens sapiens,* is sufficient for being proscribed full moral status. This is the tacit implication in *Juno*—focusing on some aspect of the fetus's biological humanity was deemed sufficient for preserving its life. Pope John Paul II, in accordance with the accepted view of the Catholic Church, argues that "from the time that the ovum is fertilized, a life is begun which is neither the father nor the mother; it is, rather, the life of a human being with his own growth … [this new human being] is a person with his characteristic aspects well determined" (1995, 107). Consequently, he argues, it is as morally wrong to destroy a nascent human life as it is to destroy any other human life. The view that it is always morally wrong to destroy human life in any instance is called the "sanctity of life" view (and this extends beyond abortion to other moral issues as well, such as euthanasia, the death penalty, and the ethics of war).

Philosopher Don Marquis (1935–) holds a similar position in his essay "Why Abortion Is Immoral." From the time an individual human life has begun, this life has a future ahead of it that consists of "activities, projects, experiences, and enjoyments which would otherwise have constituted my personal life" (1989, 189). Depriving a fetus of its life is morally wrong, according to Marquis, for the same reason that it is morally wrong to deprive most of us of our lives, "since the loss of the future to a standard fetus, if killed, is, however, at least as great a loss as the loss of the future to a standard adult human being who is killed, abortion, like ordinary killing, could be justified only by the most compelling reasons" (1989, 194). It is imperative to note that there are substantial differences between Marquis's argument and typical sanctity of life arguments. Marquis is not opposed to some instances of voluntary euthanasia, for example, specifically in cases in which a human being's future is fraught with intense pain and suffering. In these cases, because killing human beings would not deprive them of meaningful or enjoyable life experiences, it would be permissible to euthanize them upon their request.

This aspect in Marquis's otherwise pro-life argument can have significant implications for abortions resulting from fetal disability or disease. Although some disabilities are not so severe as to render the resulting child's life devoid of positive life experiences, some undoubtedly are. For example, one of the most devastating genetic disorders is Tay-Sachs disease, which causes progressive degeneration of the child's nerve cells, resulting, eventually, in almost complete paralysis before death (usually by five years of age). In a heartbreaking account of her son's battle with Tay-Sachs, Emily Rapp (1974–) wrote that had she known about his condition she would have aborted him—not because she didn't want to care for him, but to spare him pain.

> If I had known Ronan had Tay-Sachs ... I would have found out what the disease meant for my then unborn child; I would have talked to parents who are raising (and burying) children with this disease, and then I would have had an abortion. Without question and without regret, although this would have been a different kind of loss to mourn and would by no means have been a cavalier or uncomplicated, heartless decision. I'm so grateful that Ronan is my child. I also wish he'd never been born; no person should suffer in this way—daily seizures, blindness, lack of movement, inability to swallow, a devastated brain—with no hope for a cure. Both of these statements are categorically true; neither one is mutually exclusive. (Rapp 2012)

Marquis's argument may allow for this instance of abortion to be classified as morally permissible because, arguably, Ronan did not have a future of sufficient value. In this case, abortion would have been more akin to euthanasia. Of course, things start to get tricky when discussing other possible disabilities or diseases that may have a varying impact on a child's quality of life (including who can best judge what counts as a sufficiently valuable quality of life). Nevertheless, the goal here is to emphasize how Marquis's argument may differ from traditional pro-life arguments (e.g., from the kind Pope John Paul II was espousing, because he would have categorically condemned the abortion of even a Tay-Sachs-stricken fetus).

Although Marquis's argument leaves room for concluding that in some (very rare) instances abortions would be permissible, he also argues that it would be impermissible to destroy nonhuman life if the being in question also has a life full of meaningful and enjoyable experiences (1989, 190–192). The fictional characters mentioned above—Data, David, E.T., the replicants from *Blade Runner*, Samantha, and Ava—all possess lives and futures of value, for their destruction would also result in them missing out on a life full of worthwhile activities and experiences. Many nonhuman animals, such as primates and dolphins, may also meet this criterion. So, although in general Marquis's argument may typically line up with many pro-life arguments, there are important areas where they may diverge. Nevertheless, it is true that, according to Marquis, being a healthy member of the species *Homo sapiens* is sufficient to render one worthy of moral status because it ensures that the individual in question, whether fetus, child, or adult, has a future of value. This renders the vast majority of abortions, even in the earliest stages of pregnancy, seriously immoral.

**Some Complications.** Despite that fact that many pro-life advocates often will make an exception for the impermissibility of abortion access in cases of sexual assault, it is difficult to argue in favor of this if one is really committed to the belief that fetuses have the same right to life as all human persons. This is because the right to life should not be compromised on the basis of someone's genesis, especially one for which the human being in question is not morally responsible. In his book *Defending Life: A Moral and Legal Case against Abortion*, pro-life philosopher Francis Beckwith (1960–) makes this point:

> If the unborn is fully human, then we must ask whether the relieving of the woman's mental suffering justifies the killing of an innocent human being. But homicide of another is never justified to relieve one of emotional distress ... the same innocent unborn entity that the career-oriented woman will abort to avoid interference with a job promotion is biologically and morally indistinguishable from the unborn entity that results from an act of rape or incest. (Beckwith 2007, 106)

Philosopher Christopher Kaczor (1969–), in his book *The Ethics of Abortion: Women's Rights, Human Life, and the Question of Justice*, also affirms this point: "the circumstances of one's conception, even if conception takes place because of rape, do not seem to make any difference in terms of personhood" (2011, 183). If the fetus is truly considered a person with all the full rights thereof, it is hard to make the case that this right should be forfeited because the fetus was the product of rape. The idea here is not at all to deny that rape is an act of horrific violence, but rather to question whether this act should compromise the fetus's right to life.

Another complication is that this view of personhood would render some functions of some forms of birth control morally equivalent to murder. Birth control primarily functions by preventing fertilization, either by inhibiting ovulation altogether or making it difficult for sperm to reach the ovum. A secondary function of some forms of birth control, however, is that it renders the endometrium in the uterus inhospitable for implantation if fertilization does happen to occur. If a fertilized egg fails to implant, this is not, strictly speaking, an abortion because women are only considered officially pregnant once implantation has successfully occurred. If one believes that life begins to matter morally at conception, then a form of birth control that may prevent a fertilized egg from implanting could be deemed morally problematic.

For example, in the 2014 case *Burwell v. Hobby Lobby*, the owners of the Hobby Lobby stores argued that they should not have to cover in their employees' medical insurance plans what they called "abortifacient" methods of birth control. Included in this list were emergency contraception pills, also known as the "morning-after pill," under the guise that it functions by preventing the implantation of a newly fertilized egg. However, the most recent evidence does not substantiate this claim. The International Federation of Gynecology and Obstetrics has officially stated that the pills work only to interfere with the process of ovulation, or prevent sperm and egg from meeting. The active chemical found in the pills, levonorgestrel, does not "prevent implantation of the fertilized egg in the endometrium" (International Federation of Gynecology and Obstetrics 2012).

One final consideration is what this view of moral status implies for women who experience miscarriages. In 2015, Carmen Guadalupe Vásquez Aldana (1989–) was released from prison in El Salvador after serving a seven-year sentence for miscarrying her third-trimester fetus. Her prison term was a consequence of Article 1 of the country's constitution, which "recognizes as a human person every human being since the moment of conception" (Constitution of the Republic of El Salvador 2003). Just as the death of any extrauterine person is investigated and the guilty parties responsible for the death often serve time in prison, the same would be the consequence for pregnant women if they were found "guilty" of causing the death of their fetus in the event of a miscarriage, even if very early in the pregnancy. The implications for this are concerning, because the causes for miscarriages are often unknown or multifaceted, and it would subject women who are grieving their loss to some sort of criminal investigation (see Manninen 2012).

## THE COGNITIVE APPROACH TO MORAL STATUS

The cognitive approach to moral status lies on the far opposite end of the genetic account. Advocates of the cognitive approach first seek to answer a more fundamental question: what is it that makes the typical human being morally significant, so that while it would be murder to kill him or her, it isn't considered murder to kill, say, a fish or an ant? In her article "On the Moral and Legal Status of Abortion," philosopher Mary Anne Warren

(1946–2010) argues that what makes a typical human being morally significant is his or her cognitive capacities: consciousness, sentience (the ability to feel pain and pleasure), reasoning abilities, moral agency, self-motivated activity, language capacities, and self-awareness (1973, 55). Even cognitively impaired human beings possess some of these traits. Data, David, E.T., Ava, Samantha, and the replicants, also, possess these cognitive capacities, even though they lack genetic humanity. According to the cognitive approach to moral status, all of these fictional characters would count as persons. Some nonhuman animals, while sentient and conscious, lack self-consciousness, language capacities, and moral agency, and so their moral status typically is considered inferior to that of a human being's status. Although Warren acknowledges that there can be genuine debate concerning to what degree an individual must possess these robust mental traits to count as a person, certainly, she holds, a being that lacks all of these traits cannot be a person, nor have moral status.

Early fetuses possess none of these cognitive abilities. In this sense, then, machines like Ava, David, and Data can claim personhood and moral status far more readily than a human fetus. Mid-gestation, fetuses do possess some degree of sentience, but no fetus, at any point of gestation, "is fully conscious … it cannot reason, or communicate messages … [it] does not engage in self-motivated activity, and has no self-awareness. Thus, in the relevant respects, a fetus, even a fully developed one, is considerably less personlike than is the average mammal, indeed the average fish" (Warren 1973, 58). As such, any moral status or rights one could bestow upon even a sentient fetus could never be strong enough to "override a woman's right to obtain an abortion, at any stage of her pregnancy" (Warren 1973, 58).

**Some Complications.** The most concerning consequence for this view is that its criteria for moral status do not just exclude fetuses—many other kinds of human beings also lack these cognitive traits. Some mental disabilities are so extreme that the individual never develops any cognitive capacities beyond basic sentience. Individuals with advanced dementia, also, may fail to meet many of these cognitive criteria. Every single human being begins life as an infant, and, although infants are sentient and conscious, a newborn isn't significantly more person-like than a late-term fetus. Indeed, it isn't really until the toddler stages at which human beings develop language capacities, self-awareness, or self-motivated activity. As such, this criterion of personhood entails that it is not intrinsically morally wrong to commit infanticide, even against perfectly healthy infants, or to kill people with extreme cognitive disabilities or the elderly in the advanced stages of dementia (for a similar view to Warren, see Singer 1993 and Tooley 1972; these philosophers do argue that it may be impermissible to kill such beings for extrinsic reasons, e.g., because it would harm the people who love them). As such, this view of moral status, while making room for the conclusion that abortion is permissible, precludes the most vulnerable kinds of human beings.

## THE INTEREST APPROACH TO MORAL STATUS

The interest view (as philosopher Bonnie Steinbock calls it in her 1992 book *Life before Birth: The Moral and Legal Status of Embryos and Fetuses*) offers a middle-ground approach. Take, as an example, a cell phone. Every few years, it is common to replace cell phones with newer models with no concern about what happens to the old ones. In general, it is not believed that cell phones suffer by being replaced or destroyed. When phones are equipped with sturdy protective cases, it is not to avoid suffering for the phone if it is dropped, but rather because the owners will suffer or be harmed if the phone is destroyed. The phone itself is simply not an object of moral concern.

If a person were to do the same with a dog (replace the dog every few years in exchange for a puppy), surely such behavior would be met with scorn. Pets are taken to the veterinarian to ensure their health and well-being, not simply for the owner's well-being. Neglecting to care for animals is a moral fault because animals are sentient and can be harmed (as opposed to cell phones). As Steinbock puts it, "so long as a being is sentient … it has an interest in not feeling pain, and its interest provides moral agents with *prima facie* reasons for acting. Sentience, then, is sufficient to give a being moral status" (1992, 24).

It is not necessary to be presently sentient, or presently conscious, to have interests. If this were the case, then sleeping human beings, or individuals in temporary comas, would lack interests and therefore moral status. It also is not necessary to be able to *take* an interest in something to *have* an interest in it. Infants and children may not be able to take an interest in receiving their vaccinations because they have a limited understanding of what is needed to secure their health (indeed, they may actively desire not to get them given they don't want to get pricked), but they certainly have an interest in getting vaccinated (for a more thorough discussion of this distinction between kinds of interests, see Steinbock 1992, 16–18). According to this view, what is necessary for having any interests at all, including an interest in continued existence, is whether the being in question, whether human or nonhuman, possesses the capacity for sentience and therefore conscious awareness: "Without conscious awareness, beings cannot care about anything. Conscious awareness is a prerequisite to desires, preferences, hopes, aims, and goals. Nothing matters to nonsentient, nonconscious beings. Whether they are preserved or destroyed, cherished or neglected, is of no concern to them" (1992, 14).

According to this view, then, there is a categorical difference between the kind of beings that possess the capacity for sentience (like infants, children, adult human beings, cats, dogs, and birds) and the kind of beings that do not possess this capacity (like computers, bicycles, skin cells, hair follicles, or clocks). Philosopher L. W. Sumner (1941–), in his book *Abortion and Moral Theory*, puts it this way: "if morality has to do with the promotion and protection of interests or welfare, morality can concern itself only with beings who are conscious or sentient. No other beings can be beneficiaries or victims in the morally relevant way" (1981, 136–137). According to this view, fetuses undergo a fundamental categorical change while *in utero*, from beings with no moral status (before they develop the capacity for consciousness) to beings with moral status, now with interests and a welfare that can be advanced or stunted.

When in gestation does the fetus develop the capacity for consciousness? Although brain waves can be detected in a fetus as young as eight weeks' gestation (see Kushner 1984, 5–8), this alone is insufficient for deeming the fetus sentient because not all instances of neural activity indicate consciousness. A human being can have brain waves in the parts of the brain that are responsible for reflexive, rather than conscious, reactions. It is almost unanimously held among neurologists that "an intact, normally functioning cerebral cortex is indispensable for human cognitive abilities" (Kuljis 1994, 49–50). Multiple studies indicate that the approximate time in gestation when the fetus attains such a functioning cerebral cortex is between eighteen and twenty-five weeks' gestational age (e.g., see Burgess and Tawia 1996).

Once the fetus develops the capacity for consciousness, the interest view acknowledges that late gestation fetuses, who are capable of experiencing and valuing their lives, have an interest in continued existence (Steinbock 1992, 109). Before approximately eighteen weeks' gestation, however, no harm befalls a fetus who has been aborted because the fetus is not yet the kind of entity that can be harmed at all. Because the vast majority of abortions take place within the first trimester, in the first twelve weeks of pregnancy (Guttmacher Institute 2014), these abortions would not be considered morally wrong under the interest view.

**Some Complications.** This view, also, is open to complications. Most notably is that such a view of moral status, while including sentient animals and humans, excludes from moral consideration some other kinds of human beings as well. For example, individuals in persistent vegetative states (PVSs), who no longer possess the capacity for any degree of conscious awareness, would lack moral status altogether under this view. Some fetuses develop a neural-tube defect known as anencephaly, which results in them being born without a forebrain or cerebrum. Such infants consequently lack the capacity for consciousness altogether. According to the interest view, these human beings, although technically alive in that they are not brain-dead (because brain death involves the death of the whole brain, not just the parts responsible for consciousness), nevertheless have no interests and as such no moral status. Consequentially, there would be no imperative to treat them or sustain their lives in any way. As Steinbock writes, "the biographical life [the mental life] of the PVS patient is over, even though he is not biologically dead. Sustaining his biological life is not something we can do for his sake or to benefit him" (1992, 29). On the same principle, it would be permissible to abort an anencephalic fetus, whose forebrain never develops, because it lacks the capacity for sentience altogether. Someone who has moral objections to such a consequence would likely have moral objections to the interest approach to moral status.

Other views concern the question of when a human being gains moral status, but these three are the most prevalent. Either one believes the human fetus is always a person (from the time it begins to exist), that it is never a person (at least not before it is born), or that it becomes a person sometime during gestation. None of these views is without complications. The upshot is that the question of what defines personhood and moral status is deeply complex.

One important consideration is whether the fetus's potential to eventually become a person (if one does not already believe that it is one) is sufficient for ascribing to it the rights of persons. Philosopher John T. Noonan (1926–) certainly believes so: "If a fetus is destroyed, one destroys a being already possessed of the genetic code, organs, and sensitivity to pain, and one which had an eighty percent chance of developing further into a baby outside the womb who, in time, would reason … once conceived, the being was recognized as man because he had man's potential" (1970, 51–59).

As many philosophers have pointed out, however, potentiality is not actuality—you cannot treat a potential *X* in the same way, and with the same rights, as an actual *X*. A child is a potential adult, but cannot be given the rights of an actual adult. As Peter Singer (1993) notes, Princes Charles (1948–) and William (1982–) are the potential kings of England, but they do not thereby have the same rights as the actual monarch. Therefore, the justification for ascribing to the fetus the rights of persons, including the right to life, solely based on its potential to become a person in the future, seems to stand on tenuous grounds. Other philosophers, however, have defended the view that the fetus's potential is morally relevant by arguing that realizing that potential creates an interest in continued existence for the fetus: one that the right to life may function to protect (see Stone 1987 and 1994, and Manninen 2007).

If fetuses are ascribed rights at some point during gestation, then inevitably fetal rights will come into conflict with pregnant women's rights. It is worth looking at some cases in which such conflicts have arisen to illustrate that the consequences of attributing moral status and moral rights to fetuses potentially extend beyond the issue of abortion.

## FETAL RIGHTS VERSUS MATERNAL RIGHTS

In the film *Grandma* (2015), a socially liberal and emotionally distant grandmother who takes her granddaughter to have an abortion confronts a mother and her very young daughter protesting at the clinic. Grandma says to the little protestor that she hopes the girl grows up to see beyond oppression and bigotry. The protestor responds by punching grandma. Such ugly rhetoric and reactionary behavior can be found on all sides of the abortion debate. Just as pro-choice advocates vilify pro-life advocates, pro-life advocates do the same to their ideological adversaries. Vanderford notes that those who support abortion choice are often accused of "bully[ing] reluctant communities to accept and implement unpopular abortion policies" (1989, 173). They are "motivated by bigotry" and their advocacy is equated to "racists plan[s] for sterilization" (1989, 174). Pro-choice supporters are also often painted as "antifamily" and, in general, as being "antichild" (McDonnell 1984, 68). Women who obtain abortions are also often accused of callousness and selfishness, of being willing to murder their "babies" out of mere "convenience."

Once again, the tendency toward vilification of those with opposing viewpoints obfuscates reality. Pro-choice advocates typically identify as such because they have genuine concerns over the treatment of women in society, about the economic disparities that contribute to the prevalence of abortion, and about the deep-seated assumptions concerning the proper role of women in society—one that cashes out their worth via their biological capacity for pregnancy (e.g., see Firestone 1970). Moreover, pro-choice advocates are disturbed by how quickly women's fundamental rights are compromised in the alleged interest of preserving fetal welfare, as was evident in Vásquez's miscarriage case.

In 2013, a picture circulated on the Internet of Nevaeh Atkins being born. Coming into the world via a cesarean section, Nevaeh reached out from *in utero* and grabbed Dr. Allan Sawyer's finger as he pulled her out (for the picture, see James 2013). While undoubtedly beautiful, the picture also serves as a reminder that fetuses do not exist in a physical, or cultural, vacuum. The fetus is surrounded by another human body—the pregnant woman. Anything that affects the fetus in any way, whether good or bad, has to go through another human being whose health and welfare are also at stake. Sociologist Monica Casper's (1966–) book *The Making of the Unborn Patient: A Social Anatomy of Fetal Surgery* chronicles the evolution of medical practices focused on fetal welfare, and the repercussions such practices have had on how pregnant women are perceived. When ascribing rights onto fetuses, the typical consequence, Casper argues, is that women are transformed "into environments or containers for the unborn patient" (1998, 89). Casper quotes a fetal surgeon who, perhaps unwittingly, makes his dehumanization of the pregnant woman apparent: "We tend to view the fetus as independent. We're not looking at the mother; we see her as a carrier for the fetus" (1998, 144).

Reproductive rights advocate Rachel Roth also notes the dehumanizing language proponents of fetal welfare often use to describe pregnant women. These women are referred to as "maternal hosts" or the "fetal environment." Their bodies are derided as the "maternal abdominal wall [that serves as a] fortress against fetal health care" (2000, 75). Roth also highlights how the alleged concern for fetal welfare has been used to adversely affect women's interests. For example, jobs have been denied to any woman of childbearing age regardless of whether she intends to get pregnant. This happened in 1982 when the company Johnson & Johnson refused to hire any potentially pregnant woman, up to the age of seventy, for any position that could result in lead exposure. As Roth emphasizes, however, it is difficult to believe that the company's concerns really were about fetal welfare, because they also refused to transfer men from those same jobs who were concerned about lead exposure and its effect on their sperm (2000, 77). When one takes into account that these jobs are often high paying, in contrast to the kind of jobs "approved" for fertile women, the cost that fetal welfare laws can have for women in the workplace is considerable.

In some instances, women have either been denied medical treatment or have been forced into a procedure, because precedence is given to fetal welfare. In 2012, a sixteen-year-old pregnant girl in the Dominican Republic died from complications with cancer after physicians first refused to administer chemotherapy on the grounds that it would terminate her thirteen-week pregnancy. After three weeks in the hospital, she was finally given treatment, but her body failed to respond to it. She died shortly thereafter (Romo 2012). In 1987, Angela Carder (1960–1987) was twenty-six weeks pregnant when her aggressive and recurring cancer metastasized into her lung. She had decided to undergo treatment, radiation and chemotherapy, while pregnant. Initially, her fetus was deemed nonviable; however, hospital administrators at the George Washington University (GWU) hospital sought a court hearing to decide whether an attempt should be made to deliver the fetus via cesarean section before commencing treatment. Carder's husband and family all spoke on her behalf (her condition had deteriorated so rapidly that she was unable to speak for herself) and all opposed the procedure on the grounds that she was unlikely to survive it. The hospital board nevertheless approved the cesarean section. Carder was later informed of the decision and, in a moment of lucidity, proclaimed that she did not want the procedure done. Against her and her family's wishes, the cesarean section was performed. Both Carder and the fetus died shortly thereafter. Her family sued the GWU hospital, and the American Civil Liberties Union requested the D.C. Court of Appeals to overturn the decision given the concern that the case would establish precedent. In 1990, the court ruled that Carder's rights had indeed been violated and that she had retained the right to make medical decisions both for herself and her fetus (*In re A.C.* 1990). Despite this case, physicians repeatedly have threatened to report women to child welfare authorities if they refuse to undergo a cesarean section (e.g., see Hartocollis 2014).

Many pro-life advocates assume that when maternal and fetal rights conflict, the latter trumps the former. Some philosophers, however, have called this into question, at least when it comes to abortion rights. In one of the most influential pro-choice essays ever written, philosopher Judith Jarvis Thomson (1929–) argues that granting fetuses full rights, including a right to life, does little to challenge a woman's right to an abortion.

## BODILY AUTONOMY AND ABORTION RIGHTS

Jodi Picoult's 2004 book *My Sister's Keeper* tells the story of Anna, a thirteen-year-old girl who was deliberately conceived to provide blood and bone marrow for her sister Kate, who continually battles leukemia. When Anna is informed that she is expected to donate a kidney to Kate, she sues her parents for medical emancipation. In Anna's narrative, one thing that repeatedly comes across is that, in being utilized for her body, she consistently feels ignored: "[my parents] don't really pay attention to me, except when they need my blood or something.… They don't listen to me" (2004, 22). The main moral dilemma in the book is whether one person can be compelled to sacrifice her body to save another person. Although the reader feels sympathy for the dying and struggling Kate, the exploitation of Anna's body, and therefore of Anna herself, is also a cause for deep moral concern.

## THE VIOLINIST EXAMPLE

In her seminal 1971 essay "A Defense of Abortion," Thomson argues that focusing on fetal personhood is a wrongheaded approach for dealing with the issue of abortion—from both the pro-choice and pro-life perspective. Although she does not think a newly fertilized ovum could be considered a person, she concedes that "it comes as a surprise when one first learns how early in [the fetus's] life it begins to acquire human characteristics. By the tenth week, for example, it already has a face, arms, and legs, fingers and toes; it has internal organs, and brain activity is detectable" (1971, 47–48). On the other hand, asserting that the fetus is indeed a person, as pro-life advocates tend to do, also comes up short—for granting that the fetus is a person with a right to life does not thereby entail that the fetus is entitled to whatever is necessary to preserve its life, especially if this means forcibly using someone else's body for sustenance. To make this point, Thomson offers the following thought experiment:

> You wake up in the morning and find yourself back to back in bed with an unconscious violinist. A famous unconscious violinist. He has been found to have a fatal kidney ailment, and the Society of Music Lovers has canvassed all the available medical records and found that you alone have the right blood type to help. They have therefore kidnapped you, and last night the violinist's circulatory system was plugged into yours, so that your kidneys can be used to extract poisons from his blood as well as your own. The director of the hospital now tells you, "Look, we're sorry the Society of Music Lovers did this to you—we would never have permitted it if we had known. But still, they did it, and the violinist now is plugged into you. To unplug you would be to kill him. But never mind, it's only for nine months. By then he will have recovered from his ailment, and can safely be unplugged from you." Is it morally incumbent on you to accede to this situation? No doubt it would be very nice of you if you did, a great kindness. But do you *have* to accede to it? (Thomson 1971, 48–49)

Thomson argues that it is clear here that the answer is no. No one can be compelled to stay connected to the violinist, even if unhooking him would result in his death. Although it would be awfully nice of someone to volunteer to preserve his life, it cannot be something that anyone is obligated to do: "nobody is morally required to make large sacrifices, of health, of all other interests and concerns, of all other duties and commitments … in order to keep another person alive" (1971, 61–62).

It is important to emphasize what Thomson is not arguing. In this example, she never denies that the violinist possesses rights, including the right to life. Neither his personhood nor his moral status is questioned. Rather, what she is arguing is that no person's right to life can entail that another person can be compelled to use her body to sustain that life: "I am not arguing that people do not have a right to life.… I am arguing only that having a right to life does not guarantee having either a right to be given the use of or the right to be allowed continued use of another person's body—even if one needs it for life itself" (1971, 56). If Thomson's argument is correct, granting that the fetus is a person with full rights and moral status, even from its earliest genesis, does little to challenge a woman's abortion right. Pro-life advocates assume that establishing fetal personhood is sufficient for illustrating that abortions are morally wrong, that it is an instance of murder, and that it should not be allowed. The violinist example is meant to illustrate that the right to life does not always take precedence over the right to bodily autonomy. Before seeing whether Thomson's argument successfully applies to abortion rights, it is worth exploring some actual cases that appear analogous to the violinist example.

## "REAL-LIFE" VIOLINIST EXAMPLES

A common scene across university campuses is a blood-donation truck attempting to coax students, faculty, and staff into giving blood. Often various tactics are used to try to attain willing donors: T-shirts are given away; donors can enter raffles or receive a free coupon for some fast-food treat; or they can be enticed simply by juice, cookies, and the knowledge that they helped someone who was sick. It remains a fact, however, that donors have to be willing participants. Even if there were a critical shortage of blood at hospitals and clinics, no one can be dragged in from the street and forced to give blood. The decision must always remain with the donors alone, and, moreover, they can stop the donation and walk away at any point they choose.

The contention that we cannot force individuals to donate their bodily fluids to save the lives of others was affirmed in the 1978 Pennsylvania court case *McFall v. Shimp*. Robert McFall (1939–1978) suffered from aplastic anemia, a disease that affects the patient's bone marrow because of damaged blood cells. The only effective treatment open to him was a bone marrow transplant, and it was determined that his cousin, David Shimp, was a compatible donor. Shimp, however, did not consent to the transplant. In a desperate attempt to secure the only thing that could save his life, McFall sued Shimp to compel him to donate. The judges of the Tenth Pennsylvania District Court admonished Shimp for not voluntarily conceding to the donation, but ultimately they decided that they could not force him to give his bone marrow even though it meant certain death for McFall (and, indeed, McFall died two weeks after the final decision). They wrote: "For our law to compel the defendant to submit to an intrusion of his body would change the very concept and principle upon which our society is founded. To do so would defeat the sanctity of the individual" (*McFall v. Shimp* 1978).

In 2007, Simon Pretty (1961–2007) also was in need of a bone marrow transplant to survive cancer, only this time it was his sister, Helen Pretty, who refused to donate. Unlike the *McFall v. Shimp* case, Pretty did not attempt to sue his sister, but his wife repeatedly pleaded with her to consent to the donation. She continuously refused, citing an earlier quarrel between the siblings. Pretty died in 2007, leaving behind his wife and four children (Halliwell 2009).

In all these cases, the life or health of people with full moral status and an uncontested right to life was dependent on other individuals donating their respective body in some capacity to save them. Arguably, Shimp and Helen Pretty acted in ways that were morally indefensible, although it need not always be the case that refusing to donate bodily fluids to others is morally contentious (the potential donor could have health reasons for refusing to donate). Nevertheless, Thomson's point is vindicated by these cases: no matter how in need a person may be, their right to life does not entail that someone else can be forced to use their body to sustain them.

## THE PHYSICAL DEMANDS OF PREGNANCY

The main reason David Shimp gave in defense of his decision against donating bone marrow was that "there's no guarantee when doctors stick more than 100 needles into my pelvis that something won't go wrong" (*Anemia Victim McFall Dies of Hemorrhage* 1978, 11). Although it is true that complications can arise from bone marrow donation, they mostly are related to the risks associated with the use of anesthesia during surgery; experts from the Mayo Clinic assure donors that they likely will "be able to get back to [their] routine within a couple of days" (Mayo Clinic Staff 2014).

Pregnancy, however, is far more physically dangerous and burdensome than a bone marrow transplant. Constitutional scholar Donald Regan describes it thusly:

> Carrying a fetus and giving birth are burdensome, disruptive, uncomfortable, and usually to some extent painful activities. Among complaints not merely uncomfortable but painful, some of which can be very painful indeed, we find: backache; costal-marginal pain (caused by the enlarged uterus pushing against the lower ribs); abdominal "round ligament" pain; abdominal muscle pain; pelvic ache; pelvic shooting pain (as the fetus bumps a nerve at the rim of the pelvis); foot and leg cramps; the different pain and leg cramps associated with varicose veins; hemorrhoids; pain and pins-and-needles in the wrist (carpal-tunnel syndrome); and mastitis. Finally, as a result of the general softening of ligaments during pregnancy, along with the extra weight and the loss of balance, there is an increased susceptibility to sprains and to aching feet. (Regan 1979, 1580–1581)

In addition, pregnancy can result in months of debilitating morning sickness, gestational diabetes (which raises the odds of becoming permanently diabetic), placental abruption (which can lead to excessive and fatal bleeding), urinary incontinence, hypertension, the potential for invasive abdominal surgery (if a cesarean section is needed), or the potential for perineal tearing. A 2014 study published in the *Lancet* found that the rates of maternal mortality had increased in the United States—approximately 18.5 women out of 100,000 die during childbirth.

The purpose of the violinist example is to test the reader's intuitions—is it morally permissible to be forced into a condition of considerable bodily burden to save the life of another person? The previous cases illustrate that the violinist example, although *prima facie* aberrant, has some real-world parallels, and in each case, it was affirmed that one human being cannot be forced to make such a sacrifice (just as Anna could not be forced to continue giving bodily fluids and her kidney to her sister). Because pregnancy involves a far greater risk than a blood or bone marrow donation, there is even more reason to conclude that women cannot be forced to do something that wasn't required of Shimp or of Helen Pretty, or of the average blood or bone marrow donor. Thomson's point appears vindicated: any instance of bodily sacrifice to sustain the life of another person must be voluntary. Therefore, even if the fetal right to life is granted (either morally, or even legally, as many pro-life advocates have attempted to do by lobbing in favor of personhood amendments to state constitutions), women cannot be forced to sustain a pregnancy.

## SOME OBJECTIONS TO THOMSON

Although philosophers have proposed a number of objections against Thomson's argument, two of the most prominent ones will be considered here. Both of these objections call into question the strength of Thomson's analogy between the violinist example and the typical cases of pregnancy.

**The Responsibility Objection.** In Thomson's example, the individual was kidnapped and forced into a connection with the violinist. She did nothing to contribute to the violinist's need for her body. This is also the case for Shimp and Helen Pretty—neither one incurred a moral obligation to save their respective family member because neither of them contributed to their medical state. The same, however, cannot be said about typical cases of pregnancy, in which the woman voluntarily engages in sexual intercourse. In this regard, she deliberately takes part in an action that she knows may result in the creation of a fetus that will need her body for survival. In a very real sense, then, the woman (and the man as well) has caused the fetus's need to be dependent on her body. Therefore, she incurs an obligation to help sustain the fetus by the only means available—the continued use of her womb (unless, of course, she has been raped, in which case her situation is far more analogous to the violinist example). Philosopher John T. Wilcox, in his essay "Nature as Demonic in Thomson's Defense of Abortion," has offered this objection among many others: "A woman voluntarily engages in sexual intercourse, knowing full well what the consequences may be. Might we say sensibly that in the ordinary case she *has* given the fetus special rights to her body?" (2001, 262).

The underlying principle at work here is something like this: "If one deliberately engages in action *X*, fully knowing that consequence *Y* may likely ensue, then one is morally responsible for the outcome of *Y* and must act to meet that responsibility." Thomson predicts this objection to her argument, and she responds with counterexamples that call into question the veracity of this principle. Suppose someone lives in a neighborhood where many of the houses have been broken into. She is aware that opening a window significantly raises the odds that a burglar will break in and, indeed, this is what happens. Has she relinquished her right to protest the invasion of her home? Thomson thinks not, calling such a reaction "absurd" (1971, 59). And the absurdity increases when one considers how many people deliberately put bars up so that they can open their windows while decreasing the odds of a burglar breaking in (a clear analogy to birth control).

Is Thomson's rebuttal a good one? On the one hand, it seems clear that one does not relinquish the right to not have intruders on one's property, even if one engaged in an action that one knew raised the odds of such intruders. Yet, on the other hand, the underlying principle stated previously does indeed capture our moral intuitions in some cases—for example, if someone drinks and drives knowing full well he may crash and hurt someone, he is very much responsible for the outcome of his action. This example illustrates that, in some cases, the conditional "If one deliberately engages in action *X*, fully knowing that consequence *Y* may likely ensue, then one is morally responsible for the outcome of *Y* and must act to meet that responsibility" is clearly true. Thomson's burglar example clearly illustrates that in some cases the principle is not true. Is pregnancy an instance of the former or latter? Thomson thinks it is more analogous to the burglar example, but she does not provide an argument in favor of this (although others have; see, e.g., Boonin 2002 and Manninen 2014).

**The Special Relationship Objection.** In Thomson's example, no relationships exist between the violinist and the individual. She did nothing to contribute to his ailment, and she also holds no special responsibilities for him—he is not her friend, parent, spouse, or child. Many philosophers argue that relationships form an important part of our ethical lives and that they establish moral obligations that we would not otherwise have to strangers (e.g., see Ross 1930). In this sense, the fetus is significantly different from the violinist; as Wilcox puts it: "the woman and her fetus are one flesh and blood, the child is her child … the violinist is a total stranger" (2001, 260; see also Beckwith 2007, 182–184). Because of this relationship between the woman and the fetus, she perhaps does have a moral obligation to sustain its life after all.

It is hard to deny the premise that family members have special moral obligations to each other in virtue of their relationship; it is even harder to deny that parents, in particular, have special and stringent moral obligations to their children. The key question, however, is whether solely having a genetic relationship with someone is sufficient to ground familial moral obligations. A fetus is typically a woman's genetic child (unless the pregnant woman used a donor egg or is functioning as a surrogate for another woman), but other than this, she has not yet formed a social relationship with it (although some pregnant women do begin to bond with the fetus *in utero*, this is not necessarily the case). Is this genetic relationship sufficient to ground moral obligations? Wilcox seems to think so, as he asserts that he has obligations to his "natural brother" (2001, 260). Kaczor agrees here, stating that "biological relationships are morally, humanly important" (2011, 166).

But this isn't very clear to others. Philosopher David Boonin, for example, maintains that "it seems to be utterly mysterious how the mere fact of biological relatedness could, in and of itself, generate such a difference in moral obligations" (2002, 229). If a man donates sperm, or a woman donates ova, to help another couple become parents, do they thereby incur moral obligations to the resulting offspring; or do the social parents, rather than the genetic ones, incur those responsibilities? If a woman uses a donor egg to get pregnant, would that mitigate the alleged moral obligations she has to the fetus, since in this case they wouldn't be related genetically at all? Moreover, even if we do grant that the woman's biological relationship to the fetus is sufficient for incurring some moral obligation to it, is she so morally obligated that she can be compelled to use her body for its continued gestation? This, also, is not clear. Someone who puts forth the special relationship objection to Thomson has to both show that a woman's genetic relationship to the fetus does establish some moral obligation toward it, and also that this obligation is so stringent that it could entail involuntary use of her womb. It is true that Thomson seems to assume that genetic ties are insufficient to incur certain moral obligations, and that assumption is indeed questionable. It isn't clear, however, that the contrary contention is true either. The upshot is that more argumentation is needed on either side.

## LINGERING ISSUES

Beyond the immediate issues that are part of the abortion debate, other related issues present complications for both the pro-choice and pro-life perspective. Two will be discussed in this section.

First, for those who are pro-choice, there is a question concerning whether physicians, particularly those in obstetrics and gynecology (ob-gyns), have a right to deny abortion services to women if this is something against which they have a serious moral objection. Although pro-choice advocates argue that women have a right to decide whether to use their body to sustain a fetus, would they be equally willing to apply a pro-choice perspective to physicians who may harbor serious moral objections to abortion?

Pro-life advocates often argue that, short of putting a woman's life in danger, no abortion is morally permissible because there can be no social reason (e.g., financial concerns) that justifies killing a fetus. But what about situations in which the pregnancy itself may compromise the health of some fetuses? Because of the increasing use of artificial reproductive technologies, the rates of higher-ordered multiple pregnancies (HOMPs, defined as pregnancies consisting of three or more fetuses) have increased in the past few years. If aborting one or more of the fetuses gives the remaining one(s) a better chance of living a healthy life, would abortion be permissible under those circumstances?

## ABORTION AND THE CONSCIENTIOUS OBJECTOR

Dr. Allan Sawyer is an ob-gyn in Phoenix, Arizona. As mentioned previously, he delivered Nevaeh Atkins. In 2003, he was a *Phoenix Business Journal* health-care finalist. In 1997 and 2010, he was voted one of *Phoenix Magazine*'s "Top Docs." His credentials and dedication to his patients are impeccable. He is also the president of the American Association of Pro-Life Obstetricians and Gynecologists. In 2009, he provided the Arizona Supreme Court a declaration for the case *Planned Parenthood of Arizona v. Terry Goddard*. In it, Dr. Sawyer wrote: "If I were forced to violate my conscience with regard to provision of abortion services, I would leave the practice of medicine in the United States" (Sawyer 2009).

Should Sawyer, and other practitioners in reproductive medicine who share his ethical ideals on abortion, have the right to refuse to perform the procedure? Some pro-choice advocates do not think so. In their article " 'Dishonourable Disobedience'—Why Refusal to Treat in Reproductive Healthcare Is Not Conscientious Objection," physician Christian Fiala and Joyce Arthur, founder and executive director of the Abortion Rights Coalition of Canada, argue that refusing to provide abortion services (or contraception services) under the guise of being a conscientious objector (or CO, as they call it) is harmful to women in a variety of ways:

> Women may be burdened with additional costs, such as for travel or daycare, and may need to take more time off work—if they can find and get to another doctor or clinic. Delayed access to abortion can also result in significant morbidity. Waiting extra weeks or even months for the procedure increases the medical risk of abortion and may require a more complicated method. … Low-income and rural women are hurt the most by the exercise of CO, because such women may not have the resources to seek services elsewhere. It also disproportionately affects women from ethnic minorities, and women who experience intimate partner violence or sexual violation, who are twice as likely to need abortion services than women who don't experience such violence. (Fiala and Arthur 2014, 16)

Although abortion access is a constitutionally protected right for women, state lawmakers have made it harder for women to obtain abortions by implementing certain policies—for example, twenty-four-hour waiting periods and parental consent laws. Also, there is such a negative stigma against abortion providers that even those who were once willing to provide abortions ultimately end up not doing so. Professor Lori Freedman (1973–) refers to these physicians as "willing and unable"—that is, although they otherwise would be willing to provide abortion services, concerns for their personal safety, the safety of their loved ones, and for the continuation of their practice prevent them from doing so. Freedman's research in *Willing and Unable: Doctors' Constraints in Abortion Care* (2010) illustrates that only 52 percent of ob-gyns who had intended preresidency to provide abortions as part of their practice ultimately end up doing so. According to Fiala and Arthur, allowing physicians to opt out of providing abortions as a CO "adds further to the already serious abrogation of patients' rights and medical ethics" (2014, 17).

On the other hand, some individuals, for example Dr. Edmund Pellegrino (1920–2013), have emphasized that "freedom of conscience is a moral right" (2002, 226). Forcing people to act in ways that they perceive to be gravely morally wrong is not only an insult to their personal integrity, but it also may result in "severe psychosocial and emotional sequelae" (2002, 228). Physicians are not exempt from these harms and, indeed, may even be more deeply affected given that they are directly dealing with significant life and death issues. Pellegrino also expresses concern with the attitude that someone should not go into medicine unless they are willing to provide all the legal services associated with their field, including abortion and contraception services. Such a stance "assumes that the [religious] physician and others who hold firm moral beliefs can separate their professional and personal lives when this means cooperation with what is morally objectionable. For a physician with deep religious commitments, a 'value free' stance on certain issues is simply unthinkable" (2002, 239).

In cases in which a patient and a physician have a disagreement because of a clash in religious or ethical views, Pellegrino argues that the physician is morally required to continue to care for the patient until she, or her family, are able to arrange an alternative means of attaining the desired care in question. The responsibility for attaining this care, however, must remain with the patient or her family or support system; physicians cannot be expected to arrange these alternative means because "to cooperate in an act which is regarded as inherently morally wrong, such as arranging for an abortion or assisted suicide, is to be a moral accomplice" (Pellegrino 2002, 239).

For a physician like Dr. Sawyer to be forced to conduct an abortion would be to force him to commit what is, in his eyes, murder. Certainly many would disagree with him, and physicians like him, that abortion is indeed murder, but that disagreement, as has been illustrated thus far, is a deeply complex and philosophical one. It is not unreasonable to believe that individuals should not be forced to violate their conscience when it comes to ethical issues, especially when it comes to the taking of human life. Pro-choice advocates often argue that no one can make pregnancy choices on behalf of a woman because she alone is entitled to make a decision that has such a personally deep impact on the rest of her life. Indeed, Fiala and Arthur themselves make this point: women's abortion decisions are often "well-thought out and based on personal circumstances only they can fully appreciate" (2014, 16). Pellegrino would argue that the same goes for physicians who have often chosen their profession for honorable reasons, and they have a right to act in that profession within the limits of their moral values and beliefs.

Conversely, it is true that many women already have a difficult enough time procuring safe and legal abortion, even in a post-*Roe* era, and allowing for the implementation of CO clauses would only exacerbate these difficulties. This consequence of restrictive abortion access is seen in the 1987 movie *Dirty Dancing*, in which one of the characters, Penny, elects to have an illegal abortion. Because the provider is an "underground" abortionist, with no medical training, Penny's abortion results in grave physical consequences and almost renders her permanently infertile. This example mirrors the reality of many women who sought illegal abortions during the pre-*Roe* era. To avoid these kinds of situations, a case can be made that competent physicians have a moral obligation to provide women with safe abortions. Therefore, although a strong argument can be made concerning the legitimacy of CO clauses when it comes to abortion, it is also not unreasonable to believe that CO clauses would violate women's health, autonomy, and constitutionally protected reproductive rights.

## THE ETHICS OF SELECTIVE ABORTION

Cable television channels showcase several shows about the everyday life of families with multiples. One of the most famous is *Jon and Kate Plus 8* (later *Kate Plus 8*), which chronicles the lives of the Gosselins, a family with a set of twins and a set of sextuplets. There has been a plethora of similar reality shows—for example, *Raising Sextuplets, Table for Twelve, Make Room for Multiples*, and *Quints by Surprise*. The purpose of these shows is rather uniform: to peek in on the lives of a family clearly overwhelmed by a large group of feisty, adorable, and healthy children.

The reality of having multiples is not often as rosy. HOMPs often result in infants with a host of health problems. Often these health problems are a result of prematurity and competition for finite resources within the womb. According to Bernard Guyer and his coauthors (1997), some studies have shown that children who result from HOMPs are seven times more likely to die in their first year than children from singleton pregnancies. Multiples often have a much lower birth weight than singletons, which "significantly impacts infant morbidity" (Elster et al. 2000). In "Multifetal Pregnancy Reduction" (1998), Karen Hammond writes that because of their prematurity, these infants can suffer from a plethora of physical impairments, such as cerebral palsy, strokes, blindness, anencephaly, hydrocephaly (an accumulation of fluid in the brain), mental retardation, respiratory distress syndrome, intracranial hemorrhage, hyaline membrane disease (a disease that prevents the lungs from properly expanding), bronchopulmonary dysplasia (chronic lung disease), and intraventricular hemorrhage. Hammond notes also that women who gestate a HOMP are also likely to suffer severe health problems, such as high blood pressure, blood clots, anemia, preterm labor, thrombophlebitis, and postpartum hemorrhage.

The incidences of HOMPs have almost quadrupled since 2006 because of the more pervasive use of artificial reproductive technologies aimed at helping otherwise-infertile couples to procreate. One of the most controversial cases of a HOMP occurred in 2009, when Nadya Suleman (1975–), derogatorily known in the media as "Octomom," gave birth to eight babies. Suleman already had six other children, all products of in vitro fertilization (when a woman's egg is fertilized outside the womb and then placed back into her body for implantation and gestation). Her physician, Michael Kamrava, was highly criticized, and his medical license was revoked in 2009 after it was discovered that he implanted all eight embryos in Suleman (at her request) and had routinely implanted a large number of embryos in other patients as well.

Suleman's children all appear to be in good health. In many cases, however, the outcomes are not as positive. In 1997, the McCaughey septuplets were born in Des Moines, Iowa, after their mother was prescribed the fertility drug Metrodin. Two of the children, Nathan and Alexis, suffer from cerebral palsy. In 1985, in Orange, California, because of the mother's use of Pergonal, the Frustaci septuplets were conceived. One baby was stillborn and three died shortly after birth due to hyaline membrane disease. The remaining children also have cerebral palsy. The Morrison sextuplets, born in 2007, were also products of fertility drugs and were born prematurely at twenty-three weeks' gestational age. Five of the six children died within two months of their birth. In 2009, the Stansel sextuplets were born as a result of ovulation induction and intrauterine insemination (a kind of artificial insemination when washed and concentrated sperm is inserted directly into a woman's uterus; this was the kind of procedure that produced the Gosselin children). Four of the six children died, and the two surviving girls have health problems.

In all of these cases, the family's respective physicians recommended that the parents undergo selective abortion. This means that one or more fetuses would be terminated in the womb, often the ones perceived to already be weaker than the others, for the purpose of reducing the pregnancy to a safer size. The procedure is not without risks; there is an approximate 8 percent chance of losing the pregnancy altogether. In these cases, however, abortion is viewed as a "'lifeboat' intervention, a procedure intended to increase the likelihood of survival of some of the fetuses to birth, rather than the death or significant pain and suffering of all fetuses" (Elster 2000, 619).

For those who already support abortion choice, there is likely no need for additional moral justification in cases of selective abortion. For those generally opposed to abortion, however, the ethics of selective abortion presents

*Nadya Suleman, surrounded by the octuplets she gave birth to (through in vitro fertilization) in January 2009.* *Because of the increasing use of artificial reproductive technologies, the rates of higher-ordered multiple pregnancies—with associated complications—have also increased, giving rise to new ethical dilemmas centering on the issue of selective abortion.* **RON SIDDLE/ANTELOPE VALLEY PRESS/AP IMAGES.**

some complications. Many would likely argue that it is still an instance of impermissible killing; that no matter what the outcome, it is wrong to sacrifice some lives to save others. This was the ethical perspective of the McCaughey parents: "To get rid of it, or selectively abort or whatever, is murder. It's the taking of a human life. That's God's job. He's the one who decides who's going to be born, who isn't" (Elster 2000, 619). This condemnation, however, may be mitigated by the possibility that all the fetuses may die or that some may die and the others' health would be severally compromised if the abortion does not occur.

Another factor that makes the ethics of selective abortion complicated is that its alleged moral permissibility is predicated upon incomplete information—there is never a guarantee that the resulting infants will suffer from medical problems, and, if they do, what the severity of those problems would be. Although the Stansels, Frustacis, and Morrisons each suffered a painful loss, the Gosselin and Suleman children are all healthy. Although two of the McCaughey children have some medical issues, none is so impeded that it prevents him or her from living a fruitful life. If the moral permissibility of selective abortion is going to be predicated upon what is best for the resulting children, it is sometimes difficult to make that assessment simply because we don't know what those results will be (although the evidence highly suggests that most children from HOMPs likely will suffer from some degree of medical difficulties).

At the same time, it is not only the children who are in danger—the pregnant woman is as well. Many pro-life advocates would concede that abortion is permissible in cases in which the woman's life is as stake—see, for example, Beckwith, who writes, "such a decision is the result of applying pro-life principles: it is *prima facie* a higher good that one human being should live rather than two die if one cannot save both" (2007, xiii)—and an argument can be made that one of the purposes of selective abortion is to help preserve the health of the mother. The success of this argument, however, may depend on the kind of danger the pregnant woman is in. Pro-life advocates may concede to the permissibility of abortion in these circumstances only if the alternative for the woman is death (which may not be known until the woman faces the actual situation).

# SHARED VALUES

Abortion provider and physician Susan Wicklund's (1954–) book *This Common Secret* tells about her years of experience as an abortion provider, including her various interactions with pro-life protesters. She writes about a conversation she once had with a young pro-life advocate and about the mutual esteem they gained for each other after hours of civil face-to-face dialogue, even though their respective views on abortion were unaffected:

> I gained respect for his convictions and earnest beliefs. He, I think, learned a few things about the realities of abortion and the tough life dilemmas women are faced with. Several times over the ensuing months we met and talked more. The last time we spoke was just before he was entering a seminary. At the end of the conversation, before we parted ways, he said, "You know, I can't hate you anymore." (Wicklund 2007, 238–239)

It is not often that abortion ethics is discussed within the context of shared values; however, both pro-choice and pro-life individuals have expressed sympathy to some of the concerns being raised by the other side. Focusing on these shared values may aid in establishing some path toward convergence and help dissipated the vitriolic attitude that often permeates this issue.

## RESPECT FOR FETAL LIFE

As mentioned, philosophers such as Warren, Singer, and Michael Tooley have argued in favor of abortion rights by denying that fetuses are people or have any significant degree of moral status. Not all pro-choice advocates agree with this perspective and, indeed, even Warren, although she always remained pro-choice, softened her view on fetal moral status in her later writings (see, e.g., Warren 2000). Frances Kissling (1943–), former president of Catholics for Free Choice, argues in her article "Is There Life after *Roe*?" that it is imperative that pro-choice advocates argue their perspective for women's rights while simultaneously acknowledging that fetal life has value simply in virtue of being nascent human life. Kissling is pro-choice because she feels that "nobody should be forced to carry a pregnancy to term without their consent" (Kissling 2005). This, however, does not preclude acknowledging that human life, at all stages, has value that is worth respecting: "The fetus is indeed a wondrous part of our humanity.... The precise moment when the fetus becomes a person is less important than a simple acknowledgment that whatever the category of human life the fetus is, it nonetheless has value, it is not nothing" (Kissling 2005).

Naomi Wolf (1962–), a pro-choice feminist, also implores other pro-choice advocates to "defend abortion rights within a moral framework that admits that the death of the fetus is a real death" (Wolf 1995). Ethicist and activist Leslie Cannold's (1965–) book

*The Abortion Myth* (1998) features commentary from several women who have procured abortions, and most thought that the termination of their pregnancy was a somber event and that the fetal life that was lost was one worthy of profound respect. The balance between defending abortion rights and displaying respect for fetal life is a delicate one (see Manninen 2014). The upshot is that this is one avenue in which pro-choice and pro-life advocates may begin to find some kind of agreement.

## POVERTY AND OTHER SOCIAL CONCERNS

In response to Kissling's call for pro-choice advocates to demonstrate more respect for fetal life, Rosalind Petchesky (1942–), a pro-choice scholar, wrote an e-mail to Kissling where she countered: "If and when those who dominate anti-abortion politics could for a minute take seriously the rights to a decent life and health of born children, maybe then we could start to talk about advancing respect for fetal life, early or late" (Lerner 2004). Steve Tracy, a pro-life theologian, agrees with the spirit of Petchesky's comment. In his article "Abortion, the Marginalized, and the Vulnerable," Tracy offers a critique of traditional pro-life philosophy for limiting their concern to only fetal life: "'Pro-life' means the valuing of all human life whatsoever, giving particular attention to the care and protection of the weak and marginalized. Yet all too often it means 'valuing only the lives I deem valuable'" (2010, 27). Tracy argues that far too often, pro-life rhetoric and antisocial justice rhetoric appear to go hand in hand: "all too often those of us in the pro-life movement are, at best, known for only being anti-abortion, and, at worst, for being anti-social justice. For instance, of the 113 members of Congress that the nonpartisan Children's Defense Fund identified as 'the worst' for children, all are pro-life" (2012, 27).

Pro-choice advocates have, for years, called attention to the economic and social disparities that influence so many women to seek abortions. In one study, 73 percent of women cited financial insecurity as one of the reasons they procured an abortion; 60 percent were below 200 percent of the federal poverty line (Finer et al. 2005). Tracy acknowledges this in his article, and calls for the pro-life community to support social programs aimed at providing material support, offering social support, and addressing physical and sexual abuse. Fellow pro-life advocate Joseph Wright emphasizes that legally prohibiting abortions will "likely affect 10% of abortion decisions in the United States" (Wright 2008), but that addressing the actual socioeconomic factors that lead to women choosing abortions would be far more effective. He offers as an example the findings of the US Conference of Catholic Bishops: "an effective effort to reduce abortions would 'include nutritional, prenatal, childbirth and postnatal care for the mother; nutritional and pediatric care for the child; adoption and foster care services; counseling and spiritual assistance; opportunities for teenage parents to continue their education during pregnancy and after childbirth; and support for victims of rape and other forms of abuse and violence'" (Wright 2008). Indeed, the top five countries with the fewest incidences of abortion per one thousand women provide a wide range of social and material support to all their citizens, including "the right to housing, healthcare, and a minimum income. ... Ironically, the very lack of such rights and high rates of childhood poverty in the U.S. contributes to high rates of births among teenagers. Without adequate support systems or education and job opportunities, young people are simply more likely to start parenthood early in life" (Schalet 2010, 7, 20).

This is one area, again, where pro-life and pro-choice advocates can find common ground—both sides can promote social and economic policies aimed at supporting pregnant women. For pro-life advocates, the previously mentioned points make the impetus for doing so obvious—it would possibly save a lot more fetuses than simply outlawing abortion. Tracy ends his article by highlighting the success story of the Teenage Parents Program in Louisville, Kentucky, which provided teenage mothers child care for their infants while they were in school, and required them to work in the nursery for one period a day to gain hands-on child-care education. In 1998, statistics illustrated that among pregnant teens in Louisville, 75 percent of those younger than fifteen procured abortions, whereas 39 percent of teens between the ages of fifteen to nineteen obtained them. This is a clear contrast to the 1 percent of teen girls in the Teenage Parents Program who obtained abortions (2010, 33). For pro-choice advocates, mitigating the social pressures that influence abortion decisions simultaneously increases women's reproductive freedom. Christian pro-choice feminist Kathy Rudy makes this point:

> I believe that no woman ought to bear a child against her will. I also believe, as a corollary, that no woman ought to be forced into having an abortion (or a sterilization) because she cannot organize enough social and economic resources to have her baby. ... Feminists ought to be striving against the things that make childrearing the exclusive burden of women and working toward ways in which raising children receive the support of the wider community ... [similarly] our churches could and should be working to alleviate the injustices that make abortion necessary. (Rudy 1996, 56, 108, 143)

## Summary

This chapter has covered a number of issues that surround the abortion debate and has hopefully illustrated that the topic is far more complicated than is typically acknowledged. Part of being a good critical thinker is being able to defend one's perspective on controversial issues, and to recognize the logical implications of one's views. Questions concerning fetal moral status, for example, are fundamentally philosophical ones, and no one position is devoid of difficulties. Although, ultimately, most people will settle on a particular criterion for moral status, one that may heavily influence their stance on abortion, it is important to recognize that this is a complicated issue that requires critical thought.

Another important issue highlighted in this chapter is that it is imperative to think about the implications and limits of our moral and legal rights. Even granting that fetuses are persons may not, by itself, be sufficient to conclude that abortions are morally wrong, or that they ought to be prohibited. But even if one does believe that abortions generally should be prohibited, this view may be challenged in cases of HOMPs, where both the lives and health of women and fetuses are at risk. It is also important to consider the implications of granting fetal rights for issues other than abortion, especially when women's welfare and rights may be compromised in disturbing ways (as both Vásquez's and Carder's cases illustrate). Yet, affirming that women have a right to an abortion may not necessarily entail that someone who has deep reservations about abortion should be obligated to provide one (though it may—the point is that we need to engage in deeper critical thinking to argue one perspective over the other).

Finally, the importance of dialogue and focusing on commonalities cannot be underestimated. A myopic view on abortion rights, from individuals on both sides of the question, typically results in dehumanizing one's opponents and assuming the worst of them, which sometimes leads to violence. It is possible to fundamentally disagree on whether abortion is morally permissible, and yet agree that valid points are brought up by members of the opposing side that are worth taking seriously. Just as the grandmother in the film *Grandma* is pro-choice and the ethics of abortion are never mentioned, she does tell her granddaughter that it is not a decision to be made lightly because she will think about this fetus and its potential life every single day. It is the focus on shared values that not only can temper the contempt that permeates the abortion debate but also can begin to create a path toward discourse that may result in very real and significant social changes.

## Bibliography

### ACADEMIC WRITINGS

"Anemia Victim McFall Dies of Hemorrhage." Michigan Daily. August 11, 1978, 11. Available at http://news.google.com/newspapers?nid=2706&dat=19780811&id=JdxJAAAAIBAJ&sjid=xx0NAAAAIBAJ&pg=1277,5656020.

Beckwith, Francis. *Defending Life: A Moral and Legal Case against Abortion*. New York: Cambridge University Press, 2007.

Boonin, David. *A Defense of Abortion*. New York: Cambridge University Press, 2002.

Burgess, J. A., and S. A. Tawia. "When Did You First Begin to Feel It?—Locating the Beginning of Human Consciousness." *Bioethics* 10, no. 1 (1996): 1–26.

Cannold, Leslie. *The Abortion Myth: Feminism, Morality, and the Hard Choices Women Make*. St. Leonards, New South Wales, Australia: Allen and Unwin, 1998.

Casper, Monica. *The Making of the Unborn Patient: A Social Anatomy of Fetal Surgery*. New Brunswick, NJ: Rutgers University Press, 1998.

Constitution of the Republic of El Salvador. 2003. http://confinder.richmond.edu/admin/docs/ElSalvador1983English.pdf.

District of Columbia Court of Appeals. *In Re A.C.*, 1990.

Elster, Nanette, et al. "Less Is More: The Risks of Multiple Births." *Fertility and Sterility* 74, no. 4 (2000): 617–623.

Fiala, Christian, and Joyce Arthur. "'Dishonourable Disobedience'—Why Refusal to Treat in Reproductive Healthcare Is Not Conscientious Objection." *Woman: Psychosomatic Gynecology and Obstetrics* 1 (2014): 12–23.

Finer, Lawrence, Lori Frohwirth, Lindsay Dauphinee, et al. "Reasons U.S. Women Have Abortions: Quantitative and Qualitative Perspectives." 2005. http://www.guttmacher.org/pubs/journals/3711005.pdf.

Firestone, Shulamith. *The Dialectic of Sex*. New York: Morrow, 1970.

Francke, Linda Bird. *The Ambivalence of Abortion*. New York: Random House, 1978.

Freedman, Lori. *Willing and Unable: Doctors' Constraints in Abortion Care*. Nashville, TN: Vanderbilt University Press, 2010.

Guttmacher Institute. "Facts on Induced Abortion." 2014. http://www.guttmacher.org/pubs/fb_induced_abortion.html.

Guttmacher Institute. "State Policies in Brief: An Overview of Abortion Laws." 2015. http://www.guttmacher.org/statecenter/spibs/spib_OAL.pdf.

Guyer, Bernard, Marian F. MacDorman, Joyce A. Martin, et al. "Annual Summary of Vital Statistics—1997." *Pediatrics* 102, no. 6 (1998): 1333–1349.

Halliwell, Rachel. "My Husband's Sister Could Have Saved Him from Leukemia; Instead She Sentences Him to Death." *Daily Mail* (London). 2009. http://www.dailymail.co.uk/femail/article-1159338/My-husbands-sister-saved-leukaemia---instead-sentenced-death.htm.

Hammond, Karen. "Multifetal Pregnancy Reduction." *Journal of Obstetric, Gynecologic, and Neonatal Nursing* 27, no. 3 (1998): 338–343.

Hartocollis, Anemona. "Mother Accuses Doctors of Forcing a C-Section and Files Suit." *New York Times*, May 17, 2014. http://www.nytimes.com/2014/05/17/nyregion/mother-accuses-doctors-of-forcing-a-c-section-and-files-suit.html?_r=0.

International Federation of Gynecology and Obstetrics. "Mechanism of Action: How Do Levonorgestrel-Only Emergency Contraceptive Pills (LNG ECPs) Prevent Pregnancy?" 2012. http://graphics8.nytimes.com/packages/pdf/health/contraception/ICEC_FIGO_MoA_Statement_March_2012.pdf.

James, Michael S. "Infant in Womb Shown Holding Doctor's Hand." ABC News. January 3, 2013. http://abcnews.go.com/blogs/headlines/2013/01/infant-in-womb-shown-holding-doctors-hand.

John Paul II, Pope. *Evangelium Vitae*. New York: Random House, 1995.

Kaczor, Christopher. *The Ethics of Abortion: Women's Rights, Human Life, and the Question of Justice*. New York: Random House, 2011.

Kassebaum, Nicholas, Amelia Bertozzi-Villa, Megan S. Coggeshall, et al. "Global, Regional, and National Levels and Causes of Maternal Mortality during 1990–2013: A Systematic Analysis for the Global Burden of Disease Study 2013." *Lancet* 384, no. 9947 (2014): 980–1004.

Kissling, Frances. "Is There Life after *Roe?* How to Think about the Fetus." 2005. http://www.abortionconversation.com/community/materials/ACP_Reading_week3.pdf.

Klotzko, A. J. "Miracle or Medical Mischief? The Saga of the McCaughey Septuplets." *The Hastings Center Report* 28, no. 3 (1998): 5–8.

Kuljis, Rodrigo O. "Development of the Human Brain; the Emergence of the Neural Substrate for Pain Perception and Conscious Experience." In *The Beginnings of Human Life*, edited by F. K. Beller and R. F. Weir, 49–56. Dordrecht, Netherlands: Kluwer Academic, 1994.

Kushner, Thomasine. "Having a Life versus Being Alive." *Journal of Medical Ethics* 10, no. 1 (1984): 5–8.

Lerner, Sharon. "The Fetal Frontier: Pro-Choice Advocates Wrestle with the Uncomfortable." 2004. http://www.villagevoice.com/2004-11-30/news/the-fetal-frontier/.

Manninen, Bertha Alvarez. "Beyond Abortion: The Implications of Human Life Amendments." *Journal of Social Philosophy* 43, no. 4 (2012): 140–160.

Manninen, Bertha Alvarez. *Pro-Life, Pro-Choice: Shared Values in the Abortion Debate*. Nashville, TN: Vanderbilt University Press, 2014.

Manninen, Bertha Alvarez. "Revisiting the Argument from Fetal Potential." *Philosophy, Ethics, and Humanities in Medicine* 2, no. 7 (2007). http://www.peh-med.com/content/2/1/7.

Marquis, Don. "Why Abortion Is Immoral." *Journal of Philosophy* 86, no. 4 (1989): 183–202.

Mayo Clinic Staff. "Risks of Blood and Bone Marrow Donation." 2014. http://www.mayoclinic.org/tests-procedures/bone-marrow/basics/risks/PRC-20020055.

McDonnell, Kathleen. *Not an Easy Choice: A Feminist Re-Examines Abortion*. Toronto, ON, Canada: Women's Press, 1984.

Noonan, John T. "An Almost Absolute Value in History." In *The Morality of Abortion: Legal and Historical Perspectives*, edited by John T. Noonan, 51–59. Cambridge, MA: Harvard University Press, 1970.

Pellegrino, Edmund. "The Physician's Conscience, Conscience Clauses, and Religious Belief: A Catholic Perspective." *Fordham Urban Law Journal* 30, no. 1 (2002): 221–244.

Pennsylvania District (10th), Allegheny County. *McFall vs. Shimp*. 1978. http://www.ucs.louisiana.edu/~ras2777/judpol/mcfall.html.

Rapp, Emily. "Rick Santorum, Meet My Son." *Slate*, February 27, 2012. http://www.slate.com/articles/double_x/doublex/2012/02/rick_santorum_and_prenatal_testing_i_would_have_saved_my_son_from_his_suffering_.html.

Regan, Donald. "Rewriting *Roe v. Wade*." *Michigan Law Review* 77 (1979): 1568–1646.

Romo, Rafael. "Pregnant Dominican Teen at Center of Abortion Debate Dies." 2012. http://edition.cnn.com/2012/08/17/world/americas/dominican-republic-abortion/index.htm.

Ross, W. D. *The Right and the Good*. New York: Oxford University Press, 1930.

Roth, Rachel. *Making Women Pay: The Hidden Costs of Fetal Rights*. Ithaca, NY: Cornell University, 2000.

Rudy, Kathy. *Beyond Pro-Life and Pro-Choice: Moral Diversity in the Abortion Debate*. Boston: Beacon Press, 1996.

Saad, Lydia. "Abortion Is Threshold Issue for One in Six U.S. Voters." Gallup Organization. 2012. http://www.gallup.com/poll/157886/abortiothreshold-issueone sixvoters.aspx.

Sawyer. Alla. "Declaration of Allan T. Sawyer, MD." *Planned Parenthood of Arizona v. Terry Goddard*. 2009. http://www.ethicalhealthcare.org/source/Sawyer_Decl.pdf.

Schalet, Amy. "Sex, Love, and Autonomy in the Teenage Sleepover." *Contexts* 9, no. 3 (2010): 16–21.

Singer, Peter. *Practical Ethics*. New York: Cambridge University Press, 1993.

Steinbock, Bonnie. *Life before Birth: The Moral and Legal Status of Embryos and Fetuses*. New York: Cambridge University Press, 1992.

Stone, Jim. "Why Potentiality Matters." *Canadian Journal of Philosophy* 17, no. 4 (1987): 815–829.

Stone, Jim. "Why Potentiality Still Matters." *Canadian Journal of Philosophy* 24, no. 2 (1994): 281–293.

Sumner, L. W. *Abortion and Moral Theory*. Princeton, NJ: Princeton University Press, 1981.

Thomson, Judith Jarvis. "A Defense of Abortion." *Philosophy and Public Affairs* 1, no. 1 (1971): 47–66.

Tooley, Michael. "Abortion and Infanticide." *Philosophy and Public Affairs* 2, no. 1 (1972): 37–65.

Tracy, Steven. "Abortion, the Marginalized, and the Vulnerable: A Social Justice Perspective for Reducing Abortion." *Cultural Encounters* 6, no. 2 (2010): 23–33.

Vanderford, Marsha. "Vilification and Social Movements: A Case Study of Pro-Life and Pro-Choice Rhetoric." *Quarterly Journal of Speech* 75, no. 2 (1989): 166–182.

Warren, Mary Anne. *Moral Status: Obligations to Persons and Other Living Things*. New York: Oxford University Press, 2000.

Warren, Mary Anne. "On the Moral and Legal Status of Abortion." *Monist* 57, no. 4 (1973): 43–61.

Wilcox, John T. "Nature as Demonic in Thomson's Defense of Abortion." In *The Ethics of Abortion*, edited by Robert

Baird and Stuart Rosenbaum, 257–271. Amherst, NY: Prometheus Books, 2001.

Wolf, Naomi. "Our Bodies, Our Souls: Rethinking Pro-Choice Rhetoric." *New Republic*, October 16, 1995. Available at http://www.priestsforlife.org/prochoice/ourbodiesoursouls .htm.

Wright, Joseph. "Reducing Abortion in America: Beyond *Roe v. Wade*." Catholics United. August 2008. Available at http://www3.nd.edu/~cdems/College_Democrats_of _Notre_Dame/College_Democrats_of_Notre_Dame /Issues_files/reducing-abortion-in-america.pdf.

## LITERATURE

Picoult, Jodi. *My Sister's Keeper*. New York: Atria, 2004.

Wicklund, Susan. *This Common Secret: My Journey as an Abortion Doctor*. New York: Public Affairs Press, 2007.

## FILM AND TELEVISION

*A.I.: Artificial Intelligence*. Dir. Steven Spielberg. 2001. David, a child-mecha designed to permanently love on whomever he imprints, searches for centuries for the "mother" who abandoned him.

*Blade Runner*. Dir. Ridley Scott. 1982. Deckard, a blade runner who specializes in destroying "replicants," searches for androids who have escaped.

*Dirty Dancing*. Dir. Emile Ardolino. 1987. Coming of age story set in the 1960s involving first romances against a backdrop of music and dancing.

*E.T.: The Extra-Terrestrial*. Dir. Steven Spielberg. 1982. Elliott, his siblings, and his friends set out to reunite an abandoned alien with his spaceship.

*Ex Machina*. Dir. Alex Garland. 2015. Ava, an attractive female android, develops a relationship with Caleb, a human hired to test whether he can be convinced of her "humanity."

*Grandma*. Dir. Paul Weitz. 2015. A comedy in which a young woman and her eccentric grandmother spend a day scrounging for money to pay for the granddaughter's abortion.

*Her*. Dir. Spike Jonze. 2014. Lonely writer Theodore Twombly falls in love with Samantha, his new operating system designed to meet his needs and evolve in intelligence and consciousness.

*Jon and Kate Plus 8* (*Kate Plus 8*). 2007–present. Television series airing on the Discovery Health Channel and then TLC that chronicles the lives of the Gosselins, a family with a set of twins and a set of sextuplets. One of many similar reality shows focusing on large families, including *Raising Sextuplets, Table for Twelve, Make Room for Multiples*, and *Quints by Surprise*.

*Juno*. Dir. Jason Reitman. 2007. Sixteen-year-old Juno MacGuff decides on adoption over abortion after facing an unplanned pregnancy, and has to deal with the emotional repercussions of that decision.

*Star Trek: The Next Generation*. Created by Gene Roddenberry. 1987–1994. Syndicated television series taking place one hundred years after the story line of the original *Star Trek* and following the adventures of the new crew of the USS *Enterprise*.

*Unborn in the U.S.A*. Dir. Stephen Fell and Will Thompson. 2007. Documentary focusing on pro-life advocates, their political goals, and their moral stances on abortion.

CHAPTER 4

# Genetic Testing: Ethical, Legal, and Social Issues

*Cheryl J. Erwin*
*Director of the Center for Ethics, Humanities, and Spirituality*
*Texas Tech University Health Sciences Center, Lubbock*

Genetic science began with the work of Gregor Mendel (1822–1884), who proposed that traits are passed from one generation to the next through a predictable process of pedigree patterns. Genetics is the study of the ways that DNA is structured in our cells and chromosomes, translated into RNA and from mRNA into proteins.

Genes are not simply inherited directly from one's parents; they also go through a process of recombinant assortment and have varying degrees of expression and penetrance. Genetics is also proving to be dauntingly complex. The field of personalized genetics is characterized in the twenty-first century by the subfields of genetics, proteomics, metabolomics, molecular medicine, and biomarkers.

We are also learning that the environment, which we used to refer to as a "black box," leads to changes in the inherited pattern of genetic information through the attachment of methyl groups that alter gene expression. The new science of epigenetics links genetics with the environment, diet, behavior, and other experiences to alter genes to have a "memory" of events, even the events of our grandparents. Although human beings are genetically 99 percent the same, the 1 percent difference between humans and our individual environmental exposures create important challenges to how we understand ourselves and interact with the world.

The ethical stance toward genetics historically has taken an individualistic philosophical position. Genetic information is intensely personal, intergenerational, and tied to the reproductive function of genetics. This has given rise to a clinical and professional ethos of nondirective counseling, autonomous decision making, and individual rights—the polar opposite of the approach taken by public health initiatives aimed at assessing the health of the community. This inherent tension between the coercive power of the state through public health powers and the right of individuals to be secure in their person underlies many of the ethical, legal, and social tensions in genetics. As Samuel Warren (1852–1910) and Justice Louis Brandeis (1856–1941) said in "The Right to Privacy" (1890) more than one hundred years ago, new conditions will often require us to define anew the exact nature and extent of the right of privacy in one's personal life.

Our collective fascination with genetics and genetic testing has been the subject of motion pictures for nearly one hundred years. Although some of the earliest films are unremarkable, the 1936 musical comedy *College Holiday*, starring Jack Benny (1894–1974), gives us an early glimpse into the notion we could use genetic information to create a better race of human beings. More modern films are briefly mentioned in this chapter and can be viewed to gain an understanding of how the popular media has portrayed genetics across different time periods. A common theme in these films is the danger of trying to create a perfect human. Another theme involves the need for privacy and confidentiality in genetic information as a way to control one's own identity. Other themes can be discerned through the stories of the people who played a part in the genetic revolution of the past century. The place to begin this discussion is with the beginnings of genetic science.

## HISTORICAL ASPECTS OF GENETIC TESTING

Francis Galton (1822–1911) was Charles Darwin's (1809–1882) cousin. When Darwin published his *On the Origin of Species* in 1859, Galton became interested in farmers' ability to obtain permanent breeds of plants and animals with specific characteristics through careful selection and mating. Galton wondered whether the human race could be similarly improved. In 1869, Galton published *Hereditary Genius*, in which he proposed that heredity dictated talent and character, as well as physical features. Galton used his rudimentary knowledge of genetics to make bold claims. For example, he claimed it would be possible to produce a highly gifted race of human beings through selective human breeding. To achieve this goal, he suggested the government could sponsor examinations of hereditary merit. The people with the highest hereditary merit would be recognized by the state and encouraged to mate. The lowest ranking could be segregated into monasteries and convents, where they could not propagate their inferior genetics.

Herbert Spencer (1820–1903) promoted the concept of "social Darwinism," which made eugenics seem to be progressive and tied eugenics to Darwin's theory of evolution by convincing people that the evolution of biological organisms also could be applied to the evolution of society. Competition was regarded as a necessity to social progress. The eugenic movement grew out of social Darwinism as both a political and moral crusade to rid society of individuals with inferior genetics. Such concepts are the basis of the film *Gattaca* (1997), in which one's social worth and place in society are determined solely by one's DNA. In one scene, a job interview consists of nothing more than a genetic test, suggesting that if an employer knows your genetic makeup, they know everything they need to understand about who you are.

However, not all social Darwin societies are fictional. After World War I (1914–1918), eugenics gained momentum as a political ideology based on "science." In Germany, Nazi eugenics was articulated in German ideology after the publication of *Release and Destruction of Lives Not Worth Living* in 1920 by Alfred Hoche (1865–1943), a professor of medicine, and Karl Binding (1846–1920), a professor of law. According to this ideology, "allowable killing" should be extended to the incurably sick. Physicians played an important role, with more than eleven thousand doctors in the National Socialist Physicians' League. As Henry Friedlander explains in *The Origins of Nazi Genocide* (1995), the participation of physicians has been ascribed to personal aspirations and the desire for career advancement. Political and economic motivations, combined with a strong sense of national pride, seem to have been enough to cause large numbers of doctors to abandon their commitment to healing and patient welfare.

In the United States, eugenicists campaigned for legislation designed to promote superiority based on race. In this manifestation it was not aimed at blacks, but at the new immigrants from the "inferior" regions of southern Europe. Kenneth Ludmerer writes in *Genetics and the American Society: A Historical Appraisal* (1972) that these anti-immigrant sentiments gained their greatest legislative power when the Eugenics Committee of the United States became the most influential lobbying group of the House Committee on Immigration and Naturalization. Although geneticists objected to eugenics principles, they were not effective in stopping the passage of eugenics laws in the United States, beginning with Indiana in 1907. Eventually a majority of states passed laws permitting the sterilization of certain individuals deemed "inferior." An investigation into North Carolina's sterilization laws, titled "Special Report: Against Their Will" by Kevin Begos (2002), suggests that race and punishment were often the goals of castration of boys and girls as young as fourteen years old. The experience in North Carolina was not unique in this country, as over thirty states enacted eugenics laws that allowed for sterilization of certain undesirable persons.

As discussed above, the movie *Gattaca* explores the ethical problems involved when science is used to justify social decisions. Science has been used, or misused, throughout history for political, social, and legal purposes. For example, "in 1798, Thomas Jefferson ordered the excavation of Native American burial grounds, claiming he had the right to remove the remains 'by virtue of a higher order called science'" (Nelkin 2002, 123). In the 1927 case of *Buck v. Bell*, the US Supreme Court famously upheld Virginia's compulsory sterilization saying, "the principle that sustains compulsory vaccination is broad enough to cover cutting the Fallopian tubes. Three generations of imbeciles are enough." We must be careful to represent science accurately, to apply it to social decisions wisely, and to use restraint generously because power is too easily misused, and science is too easy a justification for the misuse of power. It is important to keep in mind that the "power over nature turns out to be a power exercised by some men over other men with nature as its instrument" (Lewis 1943, 719). The big lesson of history is that ethical reflection is an important element in all applications of science in the social and cultural sphere.

## GENETICS RESEARCH AND THE HUMAN GENOME PROJECT

For medicine to harness genetic information to help patients, we must first understand how genes work to produce illness. This requires research, and testing of the human genome to locate individual genes, and then testing to understand how those genes interact with the environment to promote health or cause illness. According to US federal law, research is defined as systematic investigation, including research development, testing, and evaluation, designed to develop or contribute to generalizable knowledge. Before exploring the stories of research and the development of genetic testing, it is important to return to a brief historical explanation of research and how scientists often have failed to put ethical considerations foremost in the laboratory.

The Hippocratic Oath does not directly address research, saying only "I will use my power to help the sick to the best of my ability and judgment; I will abstain from harming or wronging any man by it" (Edelstein 1943). Thomas Percival's 1803 *Code of Ethics* does not mention experimentation, nor does the 1847 Code of Ethics of the American Medical Association. Perhaps the first mention of the ethics of research occurred when Claude Bernard (1818–1878) warned in 1865 against a failure to weigh the risks of experiments with human subjects. "It is immoral then, to make an experiment on man when it is dangerous to him, even though the result may be useful to others" (Bernard [1865] 1957, 102). Sir William Osler (1849–1919) cautioned his students in 1907 that physicians "have no right to use patients entrusted to our care for the purpose of experimentation unless direct benefit to the individual is likely to follow" (Bliss 1999, 353). Eugenics, the Nazi experiments, the Nuremberg Doctors' Trial, and the Tuskegee Syphilis Study all proceeded in a vacuum of research ethics. After Henry Beecher, in his 1966 article "Ethics and Clinical Research," summarized twenty-two studies from prestigious medical journals in which researchers provided no indication of having explained risks to patients, attention finally was paid to defining the field of research ethics. The National Commission for the Protection of Human Subjects of Biomedical and Behavioral Research (1974–1978) was established as part of the 1974 National Research Act. In 1979, the National Commission produced the *Belmont Report*, which identified fundamental principles for research involving human volunteers and was the basis of subsequent federal regulation in this area.

The Human Genome Project was established in 1990 to explore the sequence of the genetic code in humans. Because of the prior ethical lapses in research, the National Institutes of Health (NIH) required 3 to 5 percent of all funding toward genetic research be given to an examination of the ethical, legal, and social issues involved in genetic research. To learn about the sequence of genes in the human genetic code (the human genome), human beings had to allow their blood and other tissue samples to be genetically tested and in some cases grown in a laboratory as a cell culture to have more tissue for repeated genetic testing. This raised new ethical issues that the research community never before had to deal with. Because this continues to be new territory, research on genetics with human participants routinely involves heightened scrutiny because it raises a number of special concerns, which will be discussed next.

## GENETIC TESTING AND RESEARCH WITH STORED TISSUE SAMPLES

US law did not address ethical concerns about research on stored tissue samples before some early cases that were brought to the courts, but bioethicists have been discussing this ever since the first questions came to light. Can researchers use stored blood samples to conduct genetic research? What would stop them? The new science of genetic testing moved forward before an ethical consensus was reached, and the law was called upon to answer these questions.

The legal controversies of genetic testing and research with tissue samples started in 1976 when John Moore, a cancer patient, began seeing Dr. David Golde, a cancer researcher at the University of California, Los Angeles (UCLA) (*Moore v. Regents of the University of California, 1990*). Under Golde's supervision, UCLA performed a splenectomy to remove Moore's spleen. Rebecca Skloot reported in 2006 that Moore signed a consent form authorizing the hospital to dispose of any severed tissue or member by cremation. Moore, who lived in Seattle, was asked to, and did, travel to Los Angeles to receive treatment for cancer of the spleen. Golde realized the cells in Moore's spleen could be used to produce a potentially profitable protein, and he set about to develop a cell line. After Golde filed a patent application for the "Mo" cell line he had developed from Moore's cells, he then asked Moore to sign a consent form granting UCLA the rights to any profits. Moore knew he had given the right to dispose of the tissue, but when he was asked about profits he got suspicious. He started investigating what profits there might be and sought the help of a lawyer.

Moore eventually sued UCLA for his share of profits. Golde's patent was granted in 1984 and the Genetics Institute, a private firm, entered into a development agreement. By

1986, Golde's stock options in Genetics Institute were worth nearly $2,250,000. Moore claimed in his lawsuit that he did not know his cells would be used for research and commercial profit (*Moore v. Regents of the University of California*, 1990). Nobody had even raised this ethical and legal issue before. Did Moore have a right to consent to the research? On the issue of informed consent, the court held for Moore and said that Golde failed to disclose the potential for profit before operating on Moore. Moore also claimed a property right in the cells taken from his body, but the claim for a property interest in his own body was not allowed, the court said, because Moore had no right to property (his spleen) once it was removed from his body and transformed by research. The court looked at this issue as though Moore donated the tissue because, in the absence of an explicit contract for compensation, it is as though the patient had made a gift of the removed tissue. This was the beginning of categorizing body parts as "property."

As a result of the Moore case, medical researchers now routinely ask patients to agree that they understand their removed tissues become property to be sold or used in research. It is questionable, however, whether patients truly understand what will be done with their body tissues. One patient at the University of California, San Francisco (UCSF), described being asked to sign a form during routine medical care that stated, "I also understand that my medical information and tissues, fluids, cells and other specimens (collectively, 'Specimens') that UCSF may collect during the course of my treatment and care may be used and shared with researchers" (Reardon 2013). Although this may surprise patients, it allows them to ask questions or even refuse to have their tissue specimens used for research. Some patients want to know the purposes for the research with their tissues, but other patients may not even notice this language in their doctors' forms. Most consent forms now seek consent for a broad range of research purposes. Patients should be aware of this before granting any consent for research with their body tissues.

After we view body tissues as property that is owned once the tissue is donated, another question is raised: if someone owns human tissue, who is the rightful owner? In the case of *Washington University v. Catalona* (2007), the university and a researcher both claimed the right to a large specimen collection. William Catalona is a surgeon and researcher who worked at Washington University in St. Louis. He had assembled a large collection of tissue samples for use in his research on prostate issues. He asked all of his research participants to sign consent forms disclosing the uses he intended. When he decided to move to another university, the university refused to let him take the tissue samples, claiming that they owned the collection because it had been assembled while Catalona was on the faculty and had used federal grant funding. Catalona wanted to continue his research with these tissue samples at his new university, and he asked his research subjects to withdraw their consent and to sign a new consent. The court was asked who owned the tissue samples and ruled in favor of Washington University on all counts, saying that Washington University owns all the biological materials and that neither Catalona nor any research participant has any ownership interest in the banked specimens. This decision means that once patients have donated a tissue sample, they have no say in what is done to that tissue.

Many scientific advances can be attributed to research using stored tissue samples, but as Laura Rowe explains in "You Don't Own Me" (2009), it may come as a surprise that your tissue samples are likely stored in a biobank or repository. The National Bioethics Advisory Commission (1999) estimates that biobanks in the United States house more than 282 million specimens from more than 176 million individuals. In many cases, health-care providers obtain a patient's biological materials during the course of routine treatment. In many other cases, the health-care provider may seek a profit from these tissues by selling them to a biotechnology research firm.

### THE STORY OF HENRIETTA LACKS AND THE HELA CELL LINE

Nobody told Henrietta Lacks (1920–1951) that the cells being removed from her body would be turned into a cell line. Yet, perhaps nobody was more surprised to find out their mother's cells had been used around the world than her children. When Lacks went to Johns Hopkins University Medical Center in 1951, she did not know that her cancer cells would be turned into the HeLa cell line and multiplied so many times that the total volume of her cells would account for the mass of many human beings. As detailed in Rebecca Skloot's best-selling book *The Immortal Life of Henrietta Lacks*,

> One scientist estimates that if you could pile all HeLa cells ever grown onto a scale, they'd weigh more than 50 million metric tons—an inconceivable number, given that an individual cell weighs almost nothing. Another scientist calculated that if you could lay all HeLa cells ever grown end-to-end, they'd wrap around the Earth at least three times, spanning more than 350 million feet. In her prime, Henrietta herself stood only a bit over five feet tall. (Skloot 2010, 2)

Skloot's book about Lacks has become a standard text in schools across the country, yet many readers still do not grasp that their own tissues samples are being used in research without full understanding for most people. Even those who sign consent forms without reading thoroughly may not be aware of the uses to which their tissues are put. Some of the uses may be morally or ethically objectionable to the individuals who donated their tissues. The ethical issues still left unanswered by the legal cases include whether signing a consent form is enough to provide human subjects with an understanding of how their specimens will be used. Patients should be made aware of the potential for profit from their tissue specimens and be allowed to not be the subject of research. The *Report of the Public Responsibility in Medicine and Research (PRIM&R) Human Tissue/Specimen Banking Working Group* (2007) restates this position by insisting any research must be consistent with the original informed consent. Those who argue for researcher control over tissue samples point to the need to advance scientific inquiry, citing the *Catalona* case as an example. Some scholars, such as Henry Greely in "The Uneasy Ethical and Legal Underpinnings of Large-Scale Genomic Biobanks" (2007), have called for a revision of federal law to require reconsent for future uses. Although the law has taken a property rights approach to ownership of human tissues, the ethical questions about how best to conduct research with tissue samples emphasize the individuals who contributed the samples matter. Because the uses for tissue samples are so diverse, a one-size-fits-all solution is unlikely to be found.

### GROUP HARMS FROM GENETIC TESTING

Research with anonymous individuals is permitted by the federal regulations governing research, but ethicists will point out that this research inadvertently may lead to the stigmatization of identifiable groups. Litigation between Arizona State University (ASU) and the Havasupai Indian tribe illustrates the potential for group harm. In 1989, ASU genetics researchers approached the Havasupai for consent to conduct research on diabetes. The researchers collected more than two hundred blood samples from tribe members. The consent form signed by the participants described the research as a study of "the causes of behavioral/medical disorders," but tribal leaders said discussions focused on diabetes (Mello and Wolf 2010). In 1991, the ASU Institutional Review Board approved a study designed

***Havasupai Indian elder and spiritual leader Rex Tilousium, joined by other members of the Arizona tribe, speaks during a news conference in Phoenix, April 21, 2010.*** *A settlement ended litigation between the Havasupai tribe and Arizona State University (ASU), which had gathered blood samples from tribe members to conduct research on diabetes, according to the understanding of the Havasupai. When those samples were also used to study genetic evidence of schizophrenia and depression among the Havasupai, the group objected and filed a lawsuit for invasion of privacy. The case raises awareness of an important ethical issue: the consent process needs to adequately inform individuals of the possibility that their participation could lead to identification with (and stigmatization of) groups with a shared genetic heritage.* **ROSS D. FRANKLIN/AP IMAGES.**

to investigate diabetes, schizophrenia, and depression in the Havasupai. These additional studies undermined the tribe's trust in what they had been told about the purpose of the genetic study. In a letter from the tribe's legal counsel, the tribe asserted, "ASU conducted genetics experiments on the Havasupai blood samples or derivatives for purposes unrelated to diabetes without tribal members' consent." Additionally, "ASU's actions have invaded the personal privacy of Havasupai tribal members and the cultural and religious privacy of the Havasupai Tribe" (*Havasupai Tribe of Havasupai Reservation v. Arizona Board of Regents*, 2008). The different understandings of the tribe underscore the need for additional conversations between researchers and the groups they study.

The case raises important questions of noneconomic harm, such as dignitary harm, to groups characterized by a shared genetic heritage and identifiable in society through affiliation with the affected group. In such cases, there is no assurance that data will not be identifiable. The consent process needs to adequately inform individuals of the possibility their participation could lead to identification with the group, and the community, as well as individuals, should be asked to consent to the research project. The *Havasupai* case was settled in 2010 when the board of regents of ASU agreed to pay the tribe $700,000 for wrongs done, without specifying the nature of the harms. The *Havasupai* case has raised our awareness of the harms that may come to groups of individuals who may face stigmatization and suffer a loss of a sense of spiritual connection and group identity.

## GENETIC TESTING OF STEM CELLS

Personalized medicine (also known as precision medicine) uses genetic testing to gain knowledge of an individual's genetics to customize drug therapies for a particular disease or disorder. Personalized medicine has the potential to prevent the wasteful use of therapies that will not work with a particular genetic profile and to identify the best therapy for the patient's particular genetic condition. To realize the promise of this type of precision medicine, scientists need to test different treatments in the lab to understand the genetic mechanisms at work with various genes. To do this, researchers need to use living cells that have been isolated from humans and introduce genetic factors to see how they work to prevent or promote disease processes. Stem cells are used to perform the genetic testing behind much personalized medicine that benefits patients.

Embryonic stem cells have the ability to divide without limit and to give rise to specialized cells. Normal human development begins with a fertilized egg that has the potential to form an entire human being. This one cell is *totipotent*—meaning it has the ability to develop into any type of cell in a human body. This totipotent stem cell first divides into two cells, and each one of these cells is totipotent. In fact, identical twins form when these cells separate and create two identical human beings. Stem cells have the ability to renew themselves through a process known as *cell division*. Under certain conditions, stem cells may be induced to turn into specialized cells, including tissue and organ-specific cells. In some organs, such as the gut and bone marrow, stem cells regularly divide to repair and replace worn out or damaged tissues. According to the NIH in *Stem Cell Basics* (2015), in such organs as the pancreas and the heart, stem cells only divide under special conditions. To sum up the basics of stem cells: in humans, two types of stem cells are present: embryonic stem cells, such as fertilized eggs; and nonembryonic cells, called *somatic* or *adult* stem cells. However, these adult stem cells are not totipotent, and they have limited ability to renew themselves or turn into different kinds of cells. Because of this difference, it is much easier to work with embryonic stem cells, but ethical issues come up that do not present with adult stem cells. So the question becomes whether science or ethics should prevail.

In 2006, researchers identified a way to create a third type of cell. Kazutoshi Takahashi and others (2007) found a way to allow some specialized adult cells to be "reprogrammed" genetically to take on many of the properties of stem cells. This new type of stem cell, called an *induced pluripotent stem cell* (IPSC), was produced using human somatic cells in 2007. These pluripotent cells do not have all of the ability of totipotent cells to transform into any type of cell, but they offer the hope of avoiding the ethical issues involved in using embryonic stem cells.

Human embryonic stem cells retain a greater ability to differentiate into any of the types of cells a patient might need. They raise more ethical issues than their adult counterpart, the IPSC. Because of the ability of human embryonic stem cells to potentially give rise to a complete human being, they could be implanted in a woman's uterus and thus have the potential to become a fetus and, if carried to term, an infant. Various arguments have been provided by those who oppose human cloning for stem cell research. The first objection to using embryonic stem cells involves uncertainty about the moral status of embryos. The second argument disfavoring the use of embryonic stems cells involves how such moral status should be properly weighed against the claim of lives in being to health technologies. Some scholars resolve this dilemma by pointing to the "doomed" status of frozen embryos that are slated for destruction after a time. The opposite point of view posits that is it morally permissible to cause the destruction of a human embryo in cases where that act would help another living human being (Curzer 2004). In a variation of this argument, proponents of using embryonic stem cells for research say that because these embryos were slated for destruction in any event, the researcher does not cause their destruction but only causes the manner of their destruction. It is possible to respond that the premise of these arguments is flawed because the frozen embryos could be adopted and brought to term by couples who are unable to procreate using their own biological material. More embryos are created each year than could be adopted, and although the position may have appeal, it may be infeasible in practice.

Additional ethical issues raised by human embryonic stem cells include opposition to the use of human embryos as research subjects; a reduction of the gene pool; a fear of unscrupulous cloning applications, such as mixing human cells with eggs from various animals; and the possibility of a slippery slope created by the somatic cell nuclear transfer (SCNT) method because it is used for both therapeutic and reproductive cloning. All of the reasons in the debate over the ethics of stem cell research are important to understanding the full potential of stem cells to change what it means to be human. Particularly, because different people can hold different conceptions of what it means to be human, the question eventually becomes how we accommodate different viewpoints within a pluralistic society. The answer must come from the public arena through debate, and often the law is the means for this reconciliation. Researchers who utilize stem cells today are subject to institutionally based stem cell research oversight committees tasked with the job of reaching consensus on the ethical issues.

In the case of *Sherley v. Sebelius (2011)*, the District of Columbia Circuit Court held that fetal stem cell research, as protected by NIH guidelines, could move forward. The NIH Guidelines on Human Stem Cell Research (2009) currently remain in effect for all organizations that accept funding from the federal government. Although not everyone agrees on the ethical arguments for or against the use of stem cells in research, the ethical debate and legal cases have shaped the way our society addresses the lack of consensus.

## DISCLOSURE OF RESEARCH RESULTS TO PARTICIPANTS

Participants who undergo genetic testing as a part of research have a potential to find out important information about themselves, as well as their family members. The information gathered could be helpful to individuals who otherwise might not have access to genetic tests or other information about themselves. Similarly, genetic information has the potential to disrupt relationships, identify risk for genetic illness, or reveal unknown existing abnormalities. All genetic information implicates family members, so an additional concern involves how genetic information affects other family members.

The first question involved in sharing research results with participants is whether researchers have a duty to recontact participants, especially in cases in which the researchers might warn them of potential dangers. This issue was highlighted in the case of *Grimes v. Kennedy Krieger Institute* (2001) after a study was designed to identify an economical way to abate lead paint in public housing. Children in the research had varying degrees of abatement, with some children living in homes that never had lead paint. Parents sued because the researchers failed to warn them in a timely manner that they discovered elevated levels of lead in their homes through data collected in the study. The court held the researchers have a special duty to participants in research and found Kennedy Krieger Institute (KKI) liable in negligence for a failure to inform the parents of the lead contained in their homes. The court also held that informed consent forms may constitute a contract with participants, and federal law requires all risks be disclosed. Specifically, the court noted that KKI failed to inform the parents that it was possible or probable that lead might contaminate the blood of their children. The duty to inform participants of the risks discovered was referenced to the requirement to observe sound ethical principles, including respect for persons. It also bears noting in the KKI case that there was no question of the clinical relevance or the potential harm inherent in the children's exposure to lead-based paint.

The second question involved in sharing research results with participants pertains to whether clinical relevance is required before finding an ethical obligation to disclose. Some have argued that research findings lack the clinical reliability of standard-of-care medicine. This line of reasoning holds that research findings are not intended to be diagnostic in nature, and procedures used in research may lack the validity needed before participants are alarmed by results that may not indicate a personalized risk. Additionally, as John P. A. Ioannidis noted in "Why Most Published Research Findings Are False" (2005), some research may not be able to be replicated. The other point of view is that all participants in research have, as the KKI court noted, a relationship of trust with researchers. Because of that special relationship of trust, it is ethically incumbent upon researchers to disclose what they know. Even if certain findings are subject to an element of uncertainty, researchers have an ethical obligation to disclose that the information is given in a manner that makes clear that the accuracy and reliability may not be equal to clinical testing. The principle of respect for persons requires that researchers communicate clearly both the results of research and the limits of the research findings.

The controversy over disclosure may be most acute in cases in which research results in incidental findings. Incidental findings may occur in genetic studies when an analysis of the genetic information reveals something about the participant in research that was previously unknown. Misattributed paternity is one such incidental finding that is estimated to occur in approximately 10 percent of the population, although the actual numbers are difficult to determine conclusively. Some research may identify individuals who have a genetic trait of which they were not aware. In some cases, the trait may be the existence of a nondisease gene for which the participant was misdiagnosed as having the gene associated with the disease. In other cases, the presence of a deleterious allele may be detected where none was suspected. Susan M. Wolf and her coauthors summarized the legal and ethical literature on incidental findings by stating: "Researchers have an obligation to set up a process for recognizing [incidental findings], verifying whether there is indeed a suspicious finding of concern, and offering the finding to the research participant (or the guardian or representative of a minor or incompetent participant) for clinical evaluation and follow-up" (2008, 228). The literature cautions attention to the specific facts of each case, with a respect for participant preferences that includes the option not to know of incidental findings in cases in which no clinical treatment options exist.

Although case law and ethical scholarship point in the direction of an ethical duty to disclose research results, this has not developed into a standard practice for all research. Several reasons prove to be important exceptions. Investigators or scientists who have no clinical relationship with participants in research do not have the same type of relationship that physician-scientists have with participants, and the obligation to disclose does not necessarily extend to them. Additionally, some participants do not want results from genetic studies, such as studies of genetic conditions that affect family members but which may or may not affect them. These individuals have a right not to know their genetic fate, to live their life in the manner of their choosing. Finally, as Robert A. Philibert and his coauthors note in "Methylation Array Data Can Simultaneously Identify Individuals and Convey Protected Health Information: An Unrecognized Ethical Concern" (2014), research with biorepositories may allow investigators to identify risks to participants, but the researchers may have no way to get in contact with them or to convey the results.

# COMMERCIALIZATION AND INTELLECTUAL PROPERTY

Genetic tests for individual use and patient care may be substantially more expensive if patents allow companies to claim property ownership in a section of the human genetic code. One of the most important issues in genetic testing has been whether or not the law should protect ownership of genetic information with patents that create an exclusive right to use that information unless patients are willing to pay a premium price. This is the issue that the courts wrestled with for years before reaching a conclusion in 2013. Like most issues, it is important to understand the history behind the decision to understand how genetic information has challenged long-standing traditions.

The idea of patenting the genetic sequence of living organisms has been controversial since its beginnings. In 1980, the US Supreme Court ruled in *Diamond v. Chakrabarty* that living inventions and discoveries could be defined as "patentable subject matter" provided that the patent guideline criteria are met. The *Chakrabarty* decision spawned a wave of biotechnology patents, including simple genetic sequences (known as expressed sequence tags) and whole genes, as well as more complicated matter, including genetically modified mammals. For the purposes of this article, only gene patents will be discussed.

A patent is a legally recognized right to exclude others from use of the subject matter of the patent. Since the *Chakrabarty* decision, legal scholars have focused on two fundamental ethical and policy questions underlying the wisdom of granting patents to living organisms. The first concern is whether it is appropriate to grant exclusive control over knowledge and the building blocks of parts of the human body. The second concern is whether, if deemed appropriate, these patents might create a "patent thicket" that would slow down research into lifesaving medical treatments. Initially, the controversy, at least in the United States, was about access to care, but the issue became more intensely debated after public funding became increasingly involved with the passage of the Patient Protection and Affordable Care Act of 2010.

### BREAST CANCER PATENT LITIGATION

In the environment of increased emphasis on access and affordability, a lawsuit was brought against Myriad Genetics. Myriad was the owner of the patent for the *BRCA1* and *BRCA2* genes (breast cancer genes 1 and 2), granted after Myriad was the first to discover the precise location of these two human genes. A mutation in one or the other of the genes can substantially increase the risk of developing breast and ovarian cancer. The lawsuit culminated in a Supreme Court decision in 2013 (*Association for Molecular Pathology v. Myriad Genetics*).

The US Constitution grants Congress the power "to promote the progress of science and useful arts, by securing for limited times to authors and inventors the exclusive right to their respective writings and discoveries" (Art. 1, Sec. 8). At issue in the *Myriad Genetics* case were two competing views of what it means to promote this knowledge. Myriad argued that to promote innovation and research, patent protection is indispensable to incentivize investment in research and development. By contrast, academic scholars and researchers argued that innovation is most enabled with a free flow of information. The court, however, focused its attention primarily on the rules of patent law. The court explained it had "long held that this provision contains an important implicit exception[:] Laws of nature, natural phenomena, and abstract ideas are not patentable." Rather, "they are the basic tools of scientific and technological work" that lie beyond the domain of patent protection (*Association for Molecular Pathology v. Myriad Genetics*, 2013). The court went on to invalidate the Myriad patent because, although Myriad had gone to exhaustive effort to locate the gene, the naturally occurring DNA segment is a product of nature and not patent eligible merely because it has been isolated.

Following the *Myriad* decision, costs for genetic testing of patients have plummeted. Although the court let stand patents for cDNA (complementary DNA is a tool used in genetic research), testing for individual genes or gene sequences is likely to become more common and more affordable. DNA sequencing is also becoming more common in forensics and the determination of ancestry and families of origin.

# GENETIC TESTING FOR HEALTH-CARE DECISION MAKING

The documentary film *Do You Really Want to Know?* (2012) follows three families dealing with the decision of whether to be tested for the Huntington's disease gene (known as the *HTT* gene). A positive result is a death sentence—having the gene means you will have the disease. As the film shows, genetic testing can provide evidence of the presence of an individual gene, such as *BRCA1*, or a list of genes in a genome profile for a reasonable cost. According to the National Human Genome Research Institute, these tests can reveal important and private information about an individual, yet most genetic tests historically have not been regulated. The US Food and Drug Administration (FDA) announced draft guidelines for the regulation of some laboratory-developed tests in 2014 (Executive Order 13145, 2000), but controversy is lingering about whether the FDA has legal authority to regulate genetic tests developed by individual laboratories. This leaves the door open for widespread use of genetic testing at a reasonable cost.

Author Lisa Genova, whose earlier book, *Still Alice* (2007), was adapted into an Academy Award–winning film, has written about the psychological, ethical, and emotional difficulties of living with Huntington's disease (HD). Her 2015 novel *Inside the O'Briens* depicts the lives of family members who discover that deep family secrets have hidden the genetic condition that has been passed from mother to son. Joe discovers he is suffering from the condition while working as a police officer in Boston, and his children, one by one, face the prospect that they each have a 50 percent chance of carrying the lethal *HTT* gene as well. The story mirrors the lived reality of facing a deadly disease with no cure, and asking whether it is better to know how you will likely die, or better not to know.

## PRENATAL AND PREIMPLANTATION GENETIC TESTING

Prenatal genetic screening utilizes genetic testing performed with a sample of a pregnant woman's blood through a process of maternal fetal-cell sorting. Samples of fetal DNA are available through amniocentesis. Would-be parents may use preimplantation genetic diagnosis (PGD) to select embryos with specific genetic traits. For example, parents who carry the gene for Huntington's disease may wish to select to implant only those embryos that do not carry the autosomal dominant *HTT* gene, thus ensuring their child of a life without threat of developing this deadly disease. Other parents, however, may wish to select for genetic traits that enhance an otherwise normal embryo.

The use of PGD and other fetal screening technologies raises questions about how we value human life. The technology may be used to select embryos on the basis of sex or other traits desired by the parents. The American Society for Reproductive Medicine has issued an ethics statement warning about the potential for abuse of sex selection as a criterion for use of PGD. The American Society for Reproductive Medicine gives great weight to the reasons given by parents for use of these technologies, allowing that the selection of an embryo based on sex may be ethically appropriate in cases in which there is a sex-linked genetic illness that could be avoided. For couples wanting to select the sex of their child for nonmedical reasons, sex selection holds the risk of gender bias, social harm, and the diversion of medical resources.

A movie that portrays the difficult ethical and family issues that can come up in the process of genetic testing is *My Sister's Keeper* (2009), based on the book of the same name.

*Abigail Breslin stars as Anna Fitzgerald, pictured here with her gravely ill older sister Kate (Sofia Vassilieva) and her father Brian (Jason Patric), in* My Sister's Keeper, *2009. Conceived by her parents through in vitro fertilization and preimplantation genetic diagnosis as a marrow and tissue donor for Kate (who suffers from a form of leukemia), Anna endures countless surgeries and medical procedures to help keep her sister alive. Anna's refusal, at age thirteen, to donate a kidney to Kate, then suffering from renal failure, sets off a chain of events that illustrate a number of ethical and social issues centering on genetic testing and reproductive technologies.* AF ARCHIVE/ALAMY.

In this movie, the parents of Kate—a child with a form of leukemia—learn that it is possible to have a second child who would be a perfect genetic match for the older girl and to have the infant serve as a tissue donor to save the older child's life. Anna is brought into the world after using in vitro fertilization and PGD to select the embryo with the perfect genetic profile to become a savior to the older child. As Anna matures she rebels against being used as a source of spare parts for the older child. She files a lawsuit against her parents to allow her to refuse an operation that would once again save Kate's life. The themes developed in the story include the right to define one's own life even before legal adulthood, the nature of family and genetic relationships, the way in which the law must become involved in these cases to prevent egregious violations of human dignity, and the way in which new genetic technologies challenge our understanding of who we are.

The law has been the source of guidance in a number of genetic issues. One question the law has been asked to decide is whether genetic testing can be used to enhance otherwise normal children. The courts have refused to endorse such efforts. In the case of *Harnicher v. University of Utah Medical Center* (1998), the prospective parents unsuccessfully sued the medical center that performed the assisted reproductive treatment for failure to utilize sperm that would have produced children "better looking than her triplets and that in her mind, she was damaged by that fact." The court declined to find liability, saying that a normally constituted person would be able to adequately cope with three healthy, nondeficient children. The use of genetic technologies should be guided by sound judgment and well-thought-out reasons before undertaking these tests. As we will discuss, genetic counselors are now commonly used to help with these decisions before genetic testing.

## TESTING AND SCREENING OF CHILDREN, NEWBORNS, AND ADOLESCENTS

Genetic testing of children, newborns, and adolescents raises numerous issues of diagnosis, prediction, carrier status, histocompatibility testing, and testing for adoption. The American Academy of Pediatrics (2013) as well as the American College of Medical Genetics and Genomics (2013) have stated that decisions about whether to offer genetic testing and screening should be driven by the best interest of the child and should be accompanied by professional genetic counseling to interpret the results. Genetic testing of children should not deprive the child of the right to an open future, in which he or she is allowed to choose whether to know or not know genetic information. For example, the gene for Huntington's disease can be detected in a child but would not affect them until adulthood. Many adults thoughtfully choose not to know their genetic fate. For these reasons, the American Academy of Pediatrics recommends disclosing genetic test results at an age-appropriate time.

The departments of public health in all states collect blood samples from every newborn at the time of birth to screen for certain medical conditions, but the number of tests performed on the screening panel in each state varies. Newborn blood samples are used to evaluate the prevalence of disease in a state, such as HIV, and are useful to identify preventable conditions, such as phenylketonuria. Residual blood samples are saved as dried blood spots and retained by most states. The information that may be gained from research using these dried blood spots is a gold mine for researchers who could profit from the genetic information they contain, but this poses difficult ethical questions. The lack of parental consent for retention of these samples and their use in research was the subject of two separate lawsuits in Minnesota and Texas.

As a result of legal challenges in Minnesota, the courts held that keeping the dried blood spots did not violate privacy in the context of newborn screening (*Bearder et al. v. State of*

*Minnesota, et al.*, 2009). In Texas, parents brought a legal challenge claiming that retaining the blood samples was a violation of the Fourth Amendment protection against unreasonable searches and seizures by the government: the blood spots "contain deeply private medical and genetic information, and were expropriated without knowledge or consent." The court agreed that this was a case involving "bodily integrity" (*Beleno v. Lakey*, 2009), and the Texas legislature changed the law and authorized a settlement with the families. The new Texas law allows parents to withhold consent for genetic testing or for retention of dried blood spots after a certain period (Newborn Screening, 2016). Texas also agreed to destroy five million dried blood spots that were retained without parental consent before the new legislation took effect. State laws continue to vary, and many do not address issues of use and retention of dried blood spots in a consistent manner. More work needs to be done in this area of the legal environment to ensure that parental rights are protected and federal rules for research are consistent with state law.

## DIRECT-TO-CONSUMER GENETIC TESTING

For a modest amount of money, anyone can send off a sample of saliva, order the tests desired, and have his or her DNA analyzed by a number of companies that offer direct-to-consumer (DTC) genetic testing. Since 2008, when one company's DTC genetic test was hailed by *Time* magazine as the "invention of the year," the industry has been subject to intense scrutiny. In 2010, the US Government Accountability Office (GAO) issued a report questioning the validity of the test results obtained from DTC companies. The report contains examples of misleading and contradictory analyses of genetic tests, with identical saliva samples receiving different genetic profiles. Also, the use of DTC genetic testing of children is considered not ethically appropriate at this time because of the lack of adequate oversight on test accuracy, content, and interpretation.

The first ethical issue identified by the GAO report involves questionable claims that DTC genetic testing can accurately identify health conditions. The *New York Times* (Peikoff 2013) and *Forbes* (Munos 2013) have noted the limited usefulness of the genetic test results. Consumers who are not aware of the limited usefulness of these tests may be misled into believing their health is at risk, when in fact the information from DTC testing currently is subject to criticism from the government, as well as the media.

Ethicists have said the rhetoric of the websites advertising DTC genetic testing may lead potential customers to believe they will be able to learn about their identity through genetic testing. The idea of learning identity includes knowledge one may gain through paternity testing, ancestry identification through autosomal chromosomes, and maternal influences of mitochondrial genetics. Some companies claim to be able to identify what percentage of a person's DNA is "Neanderthal" (Scott 2011). Even if such a claim can be authenticated, it is not clear what significance the information would have for health-care decisions. It does demonstrate that personal identity is equally a socially constructed concept, and an individual's identity is formed by much more than the genetic code. Nonetheless, the idea that "who am I" could be answered by a simple spit test has great appeal to many people.

# GENETIC TESTING IN CLINICAL CARE

The relationship of doctor and patient can be challenged by new genetic technologies. In 1927, Francis W. Peabody (1881–1927) described the importance of the relationship between a doctor and patient saying, "The significance of the intimate personal relationship between physician and patient cannot be too strongly emphasized, for in an extraordinarily large number of cases both diagnosis and treatment are directly dependent on it" (Peabody 1927). Later in the twentieth century, Jay Katz (1922–2008) noted the decline of personal understanding in the doctor-patient relationship and the reliance on biomedical technology to provide answers to important questions of health and disease. The framework for biomedicine in the twenty-first century risks placing a reliance on genetic information above the time-consuming process of asking questions and listening to patient's concerns and fears. The public tends to view genetic information as much more determinative than it really is. Patients who are concerned about the implications of genetic conditions likely would desire much more conversation about their condition than typically occurs in an encounter with one's physician.

## THE DOCTOR-PATIENT RELATIONSHIP

Since the time of Hippocrates, confidentiality has been at the core of the doctor-patient relationship. There are several rationales for why confidentiality is so important, including a Kantian (from Immanuel Kant [1724–1804]) respect for individuals. Consider that medical information could be used to an individual's detriment if it were made public—for example, in employment decisions. From a consequences perspective, confidentiality serves to reassure patients that their information will not be divulged. This relation of confidentiality has been protected in statutes and case law (*Doe v. Marselle*, 1996). Some states take a strong stance toward confidentiality, whereas other states take a more nuanced approach, allowing for disclosure of otherwise confidential information to prevent harm to third parties. Genetic technologies challenge notions of confidentiality, as well as calling into question the duties of the physician to others who may be affected by that knowledge. Genetic testing has disrupted our social understanding of the duties of confidentiality and disclosure of genetic information in cases in which that knowledge may have profound implications for family members.

The Florida case of *Pate v. Threlkel* (1995) asked whether a physician owes a duty to the adult children of a patient to warn about a parent's genetically based condition because the genes could have been passed along to the daughter. The parent had been treated for medullary thyroid carcinoma in 1987, a genetic condition. The daughter claimed that the treating physicians knew or should have known of the genetic nature of this disease and should have warned her about the genetic risk. The legal duty to warn family members was found to be analogous to other legal duties that seek to prevent harm to others. The Florida court held that when there is "a duty that is obviously for the benefit of certain identified third parties and the physician knows of the existence of those third parties, then the physician's duty runs to those third parties." The court went on to say that the duty to warn of genetically transferable disease may be satisfied by warning the patient. The Florida court did not place on physicians a duty to contact family members, but it did find the physicians liable for failing to inform the patient, who could then relate the information to her children.

In New Jersey, the Superior Court was asked a similar question about a man who had been treated for colon cancer that eventually metastasized to the liver. The patient's daughter, who was ten years old at the time of her father's death, did not discover that her father had colon cancer until she began experiencing symptoms of the same disease herself twenty-seven years later. In *Safer v. Estate of Pack* (1996), the court was asked to determine whether Dr. George Pack had a duty to disclose to his patient's daughter. Pack had told the daughter he was treating a "blockage" or "infection" and that she should not worry. The court found "there is no essential difference between the type of genetic threat at issue here and the menace of infection, contagion or a threat of physical harm." The New Jersey court found a duty to warn family members of genetic risk.

In both of these cases, the issue of including family members in the sphere of duty owed by a physician turns traditional notions of confidentiality upside down by creating a duty to breach confidentiality because of the genetic risk of the patient's children. In Minnesota, the question was reversed: does a doctor have a duty to warn the parent of genetic risk if the child is found to carry the genetic disorder called fragile X syndrome? A physician was asked to perform genetic tests for the daughter of a couple, but failed to do a fragile X test. The doctor instead told the parents that the genetic tests were negative, but the doctor did not mention the failure to perform fragile X testing. Later, the parents asked a second physician about the possibility of having another child with the same developmental delay, and they were again told there was no genetic reason to worry. When the mother remarried and gave birth to a son, the second child had the same problem as his sister. Later, the second child's new physician ordered genetic testing and found the son tested positive for fragile X and that his half sister and mother tested positive for carrier status.

The mother and her second husband asked the court whether there is a duty to warn the parents about the first child's genetic condition because they might conceive another child. The court held "that a physician's duty regarding genetic testing and diagnosis extends beyond the patient to biological parents who foreseeably may be harmed by a breach of that duty" (*Molloy v. Meier*, 2003). The duty to warn parents that they may carry a genetic risk to a future child is based in the reality that genetic testing and diagnosis affects not only the patient but also the family. Again, the duty of confidentiality that dates back to Hippocrates was challenged because of the implications to others who may avoid harm if warned.

Together, these cases raise important questions about how genetics connects one generation to the next. Although physicians grapple with genetic technologies in the clinic, legal standards for how to best disclose and explain genetic risk are still emerging.

## GENETIC COUNSELING

Genetic services are complex and require knowledge of the genetic mechanisms of disease, as well as an evaluation of the patient's personal and family history for potential hereditary predisposition to genetic disorders. Plus, one has to consider how a patient may react to the results of such testing. Genetic counselors are trained to understand the different genetic expressions of such diseases as cancer, Huntington's disease, and fragile X syndrome, and they are able to make recommendations for genetic testing, surveillance, management, and prevention for at-risk relatives. When physicians lack the specialized knowledge of genetic risk, genetic counselors can serve as an appropriate resource for referral of patients who need more information. According to the American College of Medical Genetics and Genomics, genetic counseling includes "a discussion about the clinical and genetic aspects of a suspected diagnosis—including the mode of inheritance, identification of family members at risk, and discussion of the benefits, risks, and limitations of genetic testing and the alternative to not test—and helps patients make informed decisions about genetic testing considering their health-care needs, preferences, and values" (2015). The use of genetic counselors can be an important resource for physicians, patients, and families.

Few genetic diseases are simple to predict or rule out because few single genes cause disease without the presence of other genes or environmental factors (i.e., few genes have "full penetrance"). HD offers an example of one such disease that affects nearly 100 percent of individuals who carry one copy of the deleterious *HTT* allele. For most genetically predisposed diseases, genetic risk involves a complex of genetic factors combined with environmental effects. Numerous guidelines have been issued for counseling patients with regard to various genetic risks, including forms of cancer, Alzheimer's disease, and breast and ovarian cancer. Although these guidelines are intended to be clinically useful to trained experts, the law does not allow the guidelines to dictate the standard of care in particular negligence cases, but they may be used by qualified experts in forming their expert opinion (*Conn v. U.S.*, 2011). Courts are charged with making determinations of the facts in each case, and they do allow this authority to be usurped by professional guidelines.

# IMPLICATIONS OF GENETIC TESTING FOR PARENTAGE AND FAMILIES

New reproductive technologies are changing the legal and ethical landscape and are introducing new questions about what it means to be a mother or father. Is it genetics that makes you related to your parents or siblings, or something else? It is possible for three people—one surrogate and two genetic parents—to create an embryo gestated by a surrogate who wishes no parental involvement. And it is possible to leave behind a genetic road map that discloses genetic secrets the children would prefer to remain private. Additional questions are raised in other countries like Iceland, where nearly everyone's genetic information is in a public database. Although families for thousands of years have been adopting, remarrying, and using their own ways to form families, the law has been the means by which society officially answers questions about how much genetics shapes family relationships, and how much families are shaped instead by social agreements.

## CONTESTED PARENTAGE

To determine who is the parent of a child, the law traditionally has been traced to understandings of adoption. In the New Jersey case of *Matter of Baby M* (1988), the court was asked to decide the rights of a gestational mother inseminated with donor sperm. The court refused to honor a preconception, prebirth agreement to surrender a child. Such an agreement constitutes a "contractual system of termination and adoption designed to circumvent our statute." In cases in which the birth mother has no genetic relation to the child (such as when using an egg donor or the egg of a contracting couple), however, adoption laws have not been helpful. In the Massachusetts case of *Culliton v. Beth Israel Deaconess Hospital* (Greely 2001), the court held that adoption law is inapplicable to surrogacy arrangements and genetic parents are the legal parents of the child. In California, the courts agreed, finding genetic parents are the legal parents, not the birth mother who was not genetically related to the child (*Johnson v. Calvert*, 1993). The reliance on genetics to determine legal parentage can be problematic when the genetic parents decide to donate an embryo to another couple, or in cases in which a couple chooses to create an embryo from donated egg and sperm.

## FAMILIAL CONTROL OVER GENETIC INFORMATION

Some patients exert the right not to know their genetic risk. For example, a woman who wishes to have prenatal testing for Huntington's disease (the *HTT* gene) when one of her partner's parents have the manifest disease might reveal the man's genetic status as a carrier of the *HTT* mutation if the fetus tests positive. How can the man's right not to know be protected? The question eluded scholars early in the debate over family control over genetic information (Suter 1993). The technology has advanced to allow exclusion from prenatal genetic testing of chromosome 4 without examination of the *HTT* locus, or the woman may opt for nondisclosure preimplantation genetic testing with only nonaffected embryos chosen for implantation. Genetic information has the ability to affect more than just the individual whose genetic information is revealed.

In Iceland, the entire nation entered into an agreement with a private company, deCODE Genetics, Inc., in 1998 to set up an Icelandic Health Sector Database that was designed to provide information about the genetic causes of illness and help develop targeted drugs. The program was the subject of intense ethical debate, especially concerning the manner of consent and protection of privacy rights (Merz, McGee, and Sankar 2004). A key issue with the database was familial control over genetic information and that the medical records of deceased Icelanders were to be entered into the database without a provision for family members to object. In 2000, the daughter of a recently deceased man requested her father's information not be transferred to the database. The request was denied at the district court level, and the case was appealed to the Icelandic Supreme Court. Legally, a person's right of privacy dies when he or she dies. The question before the court was whether the information in the father's medical and genetic records could reveal information about the daughter that she had a right to keep private. Because of the nature of genetic and medical information, the court noted that medical records contain "medical treatment, lifestyles, social circumstances, employment and family.... Information of this kind can relate to some of the most intimately private affairs of the person concerned, irrespective of whether the information is seen as derogatory for the person or not" (*Guomundsdottir v. Iceland*, Icelandic Supreme Court, No. 151/2003, 2003). The database was unable to continue as originally devised, and the company was sold to Amgen in 2012. The case highlights the family nature of genetic information, and the tension between individual privacy rights and societal benefit. It is an issue that is sure to continue to be debated into the future.

## GENETICS AND IDENTITY

The identification of specific genetic mutations linked to disease susceptibility has led to enthusiasm for personalized medicine, but it has not been equaled by therapeutic discoveries. This has led to conflict about population-based genetic testing, as the identification of disease-linked genes may not eventually develop into manifest disease. The implication, however, that genes are linked to one's identity is a part of the complex interpretation that individuals must make in response to knowledge about their genetic risk factors. The lessons of history and the eugenics movement teach that the scientific association of identity to genetic factors may have troubling consequences.

Genetic science has provided us with an understanding of how certain disorders, such as Tay-Sachs, may be found most commonly among those of Ashkenazi ancestry, or sickle-cell trait may be associated with the black "race." Sickle cell was the first racialized disease, and because it was a disease of African Americans, it was invisible in the politics of the white-dominated South. In the 1960s, sickle cell became a symbol for the long-ignored suffering of African Americans. As Keith Wailoo wrote in *Dying in the City of the Blues: Sickle Cell Anemia and the Politics of Race and Health* (2001), the story of sickle cell demonstrates how clinical discovery, science, and politics work together to form identity.

It took decades before we realized that genetic traits are not a marker of race but rather a surrogate marker for environmental factors, including ancestral geographic origins, socioeconomic status, education, and access to health care (Collins 2004). Although race as a category has been scientifically undermined by knowledge of human genetics, it retains connotations of identity resulting from US political history. The critical examination of how the concept of race has political ramifications that most often work to the detriment of certain populations is an important line of inquiry for understanding how genetics shape our social identity more than our biologic identity.

# USE OF GENETIC TESTING IN LAW ENFORCEMENT

Historically, the genetics of behavior has been one of the most contentious aspects of human genetics. Research into schizophrenia and mental illness, intelligence, sexual orientation, addictive behaviors, and violence is linked to both genetic and political understandings of human beings. The nature versus nurture debate has been made more complicated by studies of the heritability of various human traits. For example, in the Ira Levin (1928–2007) novel *The Boys from Brazil* (1976), clones are made from Adolf Hitler's DNA and raised in different locations. That is the nature. The nurture is when the experimenters kill the boys' fathers because Hitler was thirteen when his father died. The fear is that governmental agents, who have great ability to control the environment, will manipulate genetics and environment in ways that prevent individuals from having truly free will to make their own choices.

The field of behavioral genetics is fraught with such methodological difficulties. Much of the work on heritability has been done with twin studies that reveal remarkable similarities, but also many differences, in twins reared in different environments. Public attention has shifted from a focus on environmental factors to a renewed emphasis on genetics as the genie in the bottle of human behavior. Legal authorities can use genetic information to identify individuals, or predict behaviors and place identified persons "at risk" for bad behavior into environments designed to lead to a desired outcome, but in doing so they may infringe on the individual's privacy to make one's own decisions in ways that invade individual freedom from external control.

## CRIMINAL CULPABILITY

The belief in free will is at the heart of the law's ability to punish individuals for wrongful acts. A utilitarian rationale suggests society would be better served to provide medical help for those not able to conform their acts to the demands of a civilized society. Courts in a criminal case are charged to "investigate the defendant's history in sufficient depth to dispel the illusion that he was free not to commit the crimes for which he is being condemned" (*Stewart v. Gramley*, 1997). Genetics can have effects on human behavior that may undermine notions of free will. For example, Tourette's syndrome, recently identified as having a strong genetic component, can cause sufferers to utter socially objectionable words. The utterances are out of their control. Two hundred years ago, these individuals would have been arrested. Five hundred years ago, they likely would have been burned at the stake. But we now know it is a disease that needs to be treated, and we no longer arrest, burn, or condemn Tourette's patients for their behavior. Similarly, claims in sentencing hearings may rely on genetic test results to provide evidence of the inability of a defendant to conform his or her behavior because of genetic traits. For example, in the 1956 film *The Bad Seed*, a young girl commits murder because of the evil genes she inherited from her serial-killer grandmother. A claim that "my genes made me do it," however, also promotes misunderstanding of the role of genetics in behavior and the performance of criminal or antisocial acts.

In the twenty-first century, genetic tests are routinely used in the investigation of crimes in which traces of genetic material are left by the criminal at the scene. In the 2010 film *Conviction*—based on a true story—a woman uses DNA evidence to prove her brother was imprisoned for a crime he did not commit. Inspiration for the movie may have come from the Innocence Project, which was started as an effort to utilize DNA to exonerate wrongly convicted inmates. It has grown into a national public policy organization. In 2004, Brandon Moon was released from prison in Texas after serving sixteen years of a seventy-five-year sentence for aggravated assault. Moon was exonerated using genetic evidence gathered at the scene of the crime. A number of legal and ethical questions are raised by the use of genetic technologies to exculpate convicted criminals. How many more prisoners have been wrongly convicted? What is the proper role of DNA in the criminal justice system? Should we require the use of genetics to exculpate innocent persons who were wrongly convicted? Finally, what is the role of genetic databases? These questions involve some of the most fundamental questions about what it means to be human, what it means to have free will, and how we should ascribe responsibility for actions that are influenced by genetic limitations or poorly understood illnesses.

## FORENSIC COLLECTION OF DNA

The US Supreme Court in *Maryland v. King* (2013) stated that "DNA technology is one of the most significant scientific advancements of our era." A woman in Maryland was raped in 2003 when a man broke into her home and covered his face. The woman reported the rape immediately and years later Alonzo King was arrested in 2009 for an unrelated assault. Maryland law authorized the collection of DNA from arrestees and his DNA was identified as a match to the DNA from the 2003 rape investigation. The case eventually ended up in the Supreme Court, where the issue presented was whether a warrantless collection of DNA from an arrestee is an unreasonable search under the Fourth Amendment. Although all fifty states allow collection of DNA from felony convicts, the collection from an arrestee would occur without conviction and prior even to a finding of probable cause, which would occur at arraignment. The court addressed this issue by saying the "expectations of privacy of an individual taken into police custody 'necessarily [are] of a diminished scope'" (*Maryland v. King*, at 24). The court weighed the need for the criminal justice system to identify perpetrators and make pretrial detention decisions before holding "that DNA identification of arrestees is a reasonable search that can be considered part of a routine booking procedure" (*Maryland v. King*, at 28). The 5–4 decision includes a dissent by Justice Antonin Scalia (1936–2016) that

> the Fourth Amendment forbids searching a person for evidence of a crime when there is no basis for believing the person is guilty of the crime or is in possession of incriminating evidence. That prohibition is categorical and without exception.... It is obvious that no such noninvestigative motive exists in this case. The Court's assertion that DNA is being taken, not to solve crimes, but to *identify* those in the State's custody, taxes the credulity of the credulous. (*Maryland v. King*, Dissent, at 1)

In a highly contested decision, this case may be one of the most important criminal procedure cases in decades because it allows law enforcement to collect genetic test results from anyone who is arrested, even if the arrest later turns out to be wrongful. Once in the law enforcement database, it can be used without consent or knowledge of the individual.

## EPIGENETICS

An individual's genetic inheritance is modified by environmental impacts that result in the insertion of methyl groups (one carbon and two hydrogen atoms) at positions in the DNA. These changes to the epigenome (literally, something that sits "upon the genome") result in varied transcription of the underlying gene, with some genes turned "off" or "on" because of the protein folding that results from the methylation changes. These epigenetic changes can be passed along from one generation to the next and provide a link to the challenges or advantages of prior generations. Like genetic testing, epigenetic testing raises important ethical issues.

Epigenetic trait analysis allows easy identification of behaviors such as tobacco use, alcohol consumption, and exposure to cannabis. When these epigenetic signals are present, it can be shown that the individual has had exposure to these substances, either through voluntary consumption or environmental exposure. Like genetic test results, these biochemical markers need to be interpreted carefully. As Cheryl Erwin notes in "Ethical Implications of Epigenetic Markers in Addiction and Recovery" (2015), because these markers are linked to behavior and other social conditions, it is important not to rely exclusively on a simple test result to make a medical determination of addiction or disease. The clinical use of epigenetics is only beginning to be explored in the ethics literature, and legal issues have been briefly identified.

Epigenetic profiles may be used to identify individuals, but it is not clear that epigenetic information is protected by the Genetic Information Nondiscrimination Act (GINA), which was signed into law in 2008. Additional consideration needs to be given to this issue to assure these technologies can be utilized to assist patients in recovery from harmful exposures, including recovery from alcohol and substance abuse. Because epigenetic changes to an individual's DNA can be transmitted from parent to child, new issues of intergenerational justice are raised concerning the obligation of parents to protect against genetic harms. Finally, a measurable knowledge of how environmental toxins alter the epigenome raises questions of environmental justice and the fair opportunity for all citizens to live in an environment free of harmful toxin. These issues are sure to generate ethical and legal questions as epigenetic technologies become more fully integrated into health care and forensic medicine.

# PRIVACY, CONFIDENTIALITY, AND DISCRIMINATION ISSUES RAISED BY GENETIC TESTING

As Warren and Brandeis wrote in "The Right to Privacy" (1890), all individuals have a right, recognized in law, to keep their thoughts and feelings away from the public and to reveal them only to those they choose. Respect for individual privacy can be traced back to the eighteenth-century common law (*Millar v. Taylor*, 1769). Privacy invokes the right of an individual to keep information from intrusion of others, whereas confidentiality involves a relationship of trust between two people who agree not to divulge information shared within that exclusive relationship. Genetic privacy and confidentiality are important legal constructs because genetic information can reveal the most intimate knowledge of an individual, and this information may be used in a discriminatory manner. As discussed previously, genetic tests may be conducted by police with no warrant.

Genetic information can be used for a broad range of reasons, some good, but others detrimental to the welfare of the individual about whom the information is shared. Genetic discrimination occurs when individuals are adversely treated in an unjust manner based solely on their genetic information from genetic test results or family history in the absence of manifests disease. Like in *Gattaca*, genetic discrimination may be experienced by individuals, families, or identifiable groups because of the perception of difference or the fear of illness. Studies of genetic discrimination were incorporated early into the Human Genome Project and indicated an area of concern for individuals wishing to undergo predictive genetic testing. Two areas of particular concern involved the potential for genetic discrimination in employment and health insurance (Rothstein 1998)

## PERCEPTIONS OF DISCRIMINATION

The medical and research literature on patient experiences after genetic testing developed more slowly than the identification of problematic gaps in legal protections for the new technologies of genetic testing. Early case law indicated such discrimination was occurring, including the genetic testing of employees without their consent or knowledge (*Norman-Bloodsaw v. Lawrence Berkeley Laboratory*, 1998). Because employers did not wish to divulge their illegal genetic surveillance activities, it became necessary to rely on self-reports of the perception that discrimination had occurred.

In 1996, an influential consumer survey by E. Virginia Lapham, Chahira Kozma, and Joan W. Weiss reported that 22 percent of individuals queried reported genetic discrimination in the context of health insurance and 13 percent in the context of employment. Most early studies of genetic discrimination focused solely on insurance and employment. Later studies, such as that by S. D. Taylor and others in 2008, included social stigma and intrafamily bias as a result of genetic discrimination. These studies raised the question of the broader implications of genetic discrimination, including how and whether laws affected perceptions of discrimination.

In 2010, the first large international study of genetic discrimination in HD, "Perception, Experience, and Response to Genetic Discrimination in Huntington Disease: The International RESPOND-HD Study" by Erwin and colleagues, looked at a broad range of experiences for individuals who had a family history of HD or had undergone genetic testing for HD but remained symptom free. Those who underwent genetic testing reported a higher perception of genetic discrimination than those who were at risk for the disease because of family history, but who had not chosen to undergo predictive testing. The study also reported higher perception of genetic discrimination in Australia and Canada as compared with the United States. Participants reported the greatest discriminatory effect in their personal relationships rather than in the spheres of employment or insurance. More than 32 percent of individuals reported changes in their relationships, with common perceptions that others changed the way they talked with them, made negative comments including discouraging them from having children, or discouraged them from pursuing their education. In the 2010 study "Personal Factors Associated with Reported Benefits of Huntington Disease Family History or Genetic Testing" by Janet Williams and her colleagues, however, 22 percent of respondents reported they had benefited from knowing their genetic status, primarily in the areas of understanding, life planning, and social support. These seemingly contradictory findings indicate there is not a one-size-fits-all approach to the risks of genetic discrimination, as some individuals are able to make better life plans and receive much needed support. There is widespread agreement, however, that all genetic test results need to be kept confidential within the limits of the law.

## LEGAL PROTECTIONS AGAINST GENETIC DISCRIMINATION

The Genetic Information Nondiscrimination Act (GINA) makes it illegal to discriminate against individuals in the areas of employment and health insurance. GINA provides that employers with more than fifteen employees cannot fail or refuse to hire, discharge, or otherwise discriminate against any employee with respect to compensation, terms, conditions, or privileges. The law also prohibits group or individual insurance plans from establishing rules for eligibility or premiums based on genetic information. GINA, however, was not designed to provide complete protection from genetic discrimination (Erwin 2008) The most important limitation is in the area of life and disability insurance, on which the law is silent. Individuals may still face barriers to obtaining these types of insurance.

The limited litigation following the passage of GINA provides a glimpse into the difficulty of bringing a successful challenge to employers or health insurers who discriminate. The US Equal Employment Opportunity Commission (EEOC) publishes a statistical report that lists the number of complaints under GINA since enforcement began. Comparing the number of GINA complaints with the total settlement amounts under all the statutes the EEOC enforces, it is clear that the settlements for genetic discrimination are modest. The lack of enforcement may be due in part to the burden of proving a case under the provisions of Title VII of the Civil Rights Act, which provides that the individual claiming discrimination must establish a *prima facie* case of discrimination before the burden shifts to the employer to provide a nondiscriminatory reason for their action.

Other laws provide limited protection against genetic discrimination. The 1996 Health Insurance Portability and Accountability Act (HIPAA) provides some limited legal protection for individuals who may face genetic discrimination. HIPAA prohibits group health plans from establishing rules for enrollment eligibility (including continued eligibility) based on certain health status–related factors, including genetic information. The Americans with Disabilities Act of 1990 protects individuals who have a disability or are regarded as disabled from discrimination in employment and public accommodations, and Section 504 of the Rehabilitation Act of 1973 protects individuals with symptomatic genetic conditions. The most important law protecting genetic information is the Patient Protection and Affordable Care Act of 2010, which requires guaranteed issue and renewability of health insurance and broadly prohibits preexisting condition exclusions, which include genetic conditions or predispositions.

# Summary

This chapter has highlighted the many issues raised by genetics. Although it is impossible for one chapter to fully explore all of the issues in depth, the key concepts are presented. Genetic technologies have challenged us to see ourselves in new ways. Genetics has changed the way we define a family, as well as how we create families. It has made us examine what it means to be human, and who we are. Genetics has not only led to revolutionary advances in personalized medicine. It has also changed the way we interact with the doctors who deliver that medicine. Genetic research allows us to create embryos with predetermined genetic traits and to make clones of entire organisms. Many of these applications of genetic technologies are deeply troubling and raise profound ethical and social issues that need to be debated and discussed.

The ability to predict future disease states allows us to make our own life plans and cherish the connections we have to family and friends who support us on that journey. This ability to see into our genetic inheritance also opens the door for genetic discrimination and loss of control over how others see us. There are possible government uses of genetic information for criminal or other reasons, and questions remain about how much information, and under what circumstances, the government may right use that information. Who we are and who we want to be are questions that strike at the core of our shared humanity. Although it is impossible to know what future issues may be raised by genetics, it is important to continue the conversation and become knowledgeable of both the power and limitations of information gained through genetic testing.

# Bibliography

American Academy of Pediatrics. "Ethical and Policy Issues in Genetic Testing and Screening of Children." *Pediatrics* 131, no. 3 (2013): 620–622.

American College of Medical Genetics and Genomics. "Technical Report: Ethical and Policy Issues in Genetic Testing and Screening of Children." *Genetics in Medicine* 15, no. 3 (2013): 234–245.

American College of Medical Genetics and Genomics, H. Hampel, R. L. Bennett, et al. "A Practice Guideline from the American College of Medical Genetics and Genomics and the National Society of Genetic Counselors: Referral Indications for Cancer Predisposition Assessment." *Genetics in Medicine* 17, no. 1 (2015): 70–87.

American Society of Reproductive Medicine. "Sex Selection and Preimplantation Genetic Diagnosis." *Fertility and Sterility* 82, Suppl. 1 (2004): S245–248.

Beecher, Henry. "Ethics and Clinical Research." *New England Journal of Medicine* 274, no. 24 (1966): 1354–1360.

Begos, Kevin. "Special Report: Against Their Will." *Winston-Salem Journal*, December 9, 2002.

Bernard, Claude. *An Introduction to the Study of Experimental Medicine*. Translated by H. C. Greene. New York: Dover, 1957. First published 1865.

Bliss, Michael. *William Osler: A Life in Medicine*. New York: Oxford University Press, 1999.

Collins, Francis S. "What We Do and Don't Know about 'Race,' 'Ethnicity,' Genetics, and Health at the Dawn of the Genome Era." *Nature Genetics* 36, no. 11 (2004): S13–S15.

Curzer, H. "The Ethics of Embryonic Stem Cell Research." *Journal of Medicine and Philosophy* 29, no. 5 (2004): 533–562.

Darwin, Charles. *On the Origin of Species*. London: J. Murray, 1859.

Edelstein, Ludwig. *The Hippocratic Oath: Text, Translation, and Interpretation*. Baltimore: Johns Hopkins University Press, 1943.

Erwin, C. "Ethical Implications of Epigenetic Markers in Addiction and Recovery." *Behavioral Sciences and the Law* (Summer 2015).

Erwin, C. "Legal Update: Living with the Genetic Information Nondiscrimination Act." *Genetic Medicine* 10, no. 12 (2008): 869–873.

Erwin, C., J. K. Williams, A. R. Juhl, et al. "Perception, Experience, and Response to Genetic Discrimination in Huntington Disease: The International RESPOND-HD Study." *American Journal of Medicine, Genetics B: Neuropsychiatric Genetics* 153B, no. 5 (2010): 1081–1093.

Friedlander, Henry. *The Origins of Nazi Genocide*. Chapel Hill: University of North Carolina Press, 1995.

Greely, Henry T. "Genotype Discrimination: The Complex Case for Some Legislative Protection." *University of Pennsylvania Law Review* 149, no. 5 (2001): 1483–1505.

Greely, Henry. T. "The Uneasy Ethical and Legal Underpinnings of Large-Scale Genomic Biobanks." *Annual Review of Genomics and Human Genetics* 8, no. 1 (2007): 343–364.

Innocence Project. "About Us." http://www.innocenceproject.org/about-innocence-project.

Ioannidis, John P. A. "Why Most Published Research Findings Are False." *PLoS Med* 2, no. 8 (2005): e124.

Katz, Jay. *The Silent World of Doctor and Patient*. New York: Johns Hopkins University Press, 1984.

Lapham, V. L., C. Kozma, and J. O. Weiss. "Genetic Discrimination: Perspectives of Consumers." *Science* 274, no. 5287 (1996): 621–624.

Lewis, C. S. *The Abolition of Man, Or, Reflections on Education with Special Reference to the Teaching of English in the Upper Forms of Schools*. Oxford: Oxford University Press, 1943. http://archive.org/stream/TheAbolitionOfMan_229/C.s.Lewis-TheAbolitionOfMan_djvu.txt.

Ludmerer, Kenneth M. *Genetics and the American Society: A Historical Appraisal*. Baltimore: Johns Hopkins University Press, 1972.

Mello, Michelle M., and Leslie E. Wolf. "The Havasupai Indian Tribe Case—Lessons for Research Involving Stored Biologic Samples." *New England Journal of Medicine* 363, no. 3 (2010): 204–207.

Merz, J. F., G. E. McGee, and P. Sankar. "Iceland Inc.? On the Ethics of Commercial Population Genomics." *Social Science and Medicine* 58, no. 6 (2004): 1201–1209.

Munos, Bernard. "23andMe: A Fumbling Gene in Its Corporate DNA?" Forbes.com. November 29, 2013. http://www.forbes.com/sites/bernardmunos/2013/11/29/23andme-a-fumbling-gene-in-its-corporate-dna/#30d5454e2656.

National Bioethics Advisory Commission. "Research Involving Human Biological Materials: Ethical Issues and Policy Guidance: Report and Recommendations of the National Bioethics Advisory Commission." Rockville, MD: National Bioethics Advisory Commission, 1999.

National Human Genome Research Institute. *Genetic Information Nondiscrimination Act* (GINA). 2008. http://www.genome.gov/24519851.

National Institutes of Health. *Stem Cell Basics*. 2015. http://stemcells.nih.gov/info/basics/Pages/Default.aspx.

Nelkin, Dorothy. "A Brief History of the Political Work of Genetics." *Jurimetrics Journal* 42, no. 2 (2002): 121–132.

Peabody, Francis. "The Care of the Patient." *Journal of the American Medical Association* 88, no. 12 (1927): 877–882.

Peikoff, Kira. "I Had My DNA Picture Taken, with Varying Results." *New York Times*, December 30, 2013. http://www.nytimes.com/2013/12/31/science/i-had-my-dna-picture-taken-with-varying-results.html?_r=0.

Philibert, R. A. "A Review of Epigenetic Markers of Addiction and Recovery." *Behavioral Sciences and the Law* (Summer 2015).

Philibert, R. A., N. P. Terry, C. Erwin, et al. "Methylation Array Data Can Simultaneously Identify Individuals and Convey Protected Health Information: An Unrecognized Ethical Concern." *Clinical Epigenetics* 6, no. 1 (2014): 28–33.

Reardon, Jenny. "Should Patients Understand That They Are Research Subjects?" *San Francisco Chronicle*, March 3, 2013. http://www.sfgate.com/opinion/article/Should-patients-understand-that-they-are-research-4321242.php.

Rothstein, M. A. "Genetic Privacy and Confidentiality: Why Are They So Hard to Protect?" *Journal of Law, Medicine, and Ethics* 26, no. 3 (1998): 198–203.

Rothstein, M. A., Y. Cai, and G. E. Marchant. "The Ghost in Our Genes: Legal and Ethical Implications of Epigenetics." *Health Matrix* 19, no. 1 (2009): 1–62.

Rowe, Laura B. "You Don't Own Me: Recommendations to Protect Human Contributors of Biological Material after *Washington University v. Catalona*." *Chicago-Kent Law Review* 84, no. 1 (2009): 227–269.

Scott, H. "Find Your Inner Neanderthal." *23andMe Blog*. 2011. http://blog.23andme.com/ancestry/find-your-inner-neanderthal/.

Skloot, Rebecca. *The Immortal Life of Henrietta Lacks*. New York: Crown, 2010.

Skloot, Rebecca. "Taking the Least of You." *New York Times Magazine*, April 16, 2006, 38–45.

Suter, S. M. "Whose Genes Are These Anyway? Familial Conflicts over Access to Genetic Information." *Michigan Law Review* 91, no. 7 (1993): 1854–1908.

Takahashi, K., K. Tanabe, M. Ohnuki, et al. "Induction of Pluripotent Stem Cells from Adult Human Fibroblasts by Defined Factors." *Cell* 5, no. 131 (2007): 861–872.

Taylor, S. D., S. Treloar, K. K. Barlow-Stewart, et al. "Investigating Genetic Discrimination in Australia: A Large-Scale Survey of Clinical Genetics Clients." *Clinical Genetics* 74, no. 1 (2008): 20–30.

Wailoo, Keith. *Dying in the City of the Blues: Sickle Cell Anemia and the Politics of Race and Health*. Chapel Hill: University of North Carolina Press, 2001.

Warren, Samuel D., and Louis D. Brandeis. "The Right to Privacy." *Harvard Law Review* 4, no. 5 (1890): 193–220.

Williams, Janet K., Cheryl Erwin, Andrew Juhl, et al. "Personal Factors Associated with Reported Benefits of Huntington Disease Family History or Genetic Testing." *Genetic Testing and Molecular Biomarkers* 14, no. 5 (2010): 629–636.

Wolf, S. M., F. P. Lawrenz, C. A. Nelson, et al. "Managing Incidental Findings in Human Subjects Research: Analysis and Recommendations." *Journal of Law, Medicine, and Ethics* 36, no. 2 (2008): 219–248.

## LEGAL CASES

*Association for Molecular Pathology v. Myriad Genetics*, 133 S.Ct. 2107 (2013).

*Bearder et al. v. State of Minnesota, et al.* 806 NW 2d 766 (2009).

*Beleno v. Lakey.* No SA-09-CA-188-FB (W.D. Tex. Sept. 17, 2009).

*Buck v. Bell.* 274 US 200 (1927).

*Conn v. U.S.* F880 F. Supp. 2d. 741 (S.D. Miss., 2012).

*Diamond v. Chakrabarty.* 447 US 303 (1980).

*Doe v. Marselle.* 675 A. 2d 835 (Conn. Sup. Ct. 1996).

*Grimes v. Kennedy Krieger Institute, Inc.* 782 A. 2d 807 (Maryland Ct. App. 2001).

*Guomundsdottir v. Iceland.* No. 151/2003 (Iceland Supreme Ct., Nov. 27, 2003).

*Harnicher v. University of Utah Medical Center.* 962 P. 2d 67 (Utah 1998).

*Havasupai Tribe of Havasupai Reservation v. Arizona Board of Regents.* 1 CA-CV 07-0454, 1 CA-CV 07-0801 (Ct. App. Ariz. 2008).

*In re Marriage of Buzzanca.* 72 Cal. Rptr. 2d 280, Ct. App. 1998.

*Johnson v. Calvert.* 851 P. 2d 776 (Cal. 1993).

*Maryland v. King.* 133 SCt 1958 (2013).

*Matter of Baby M.* 537 A. 2d 1227 (NJ 1988).

*McDonnell Douglas Corp. v. Green.* 411 US 792 (1973).

*Millar v. Taylor.* 4 Burr 2303 (English Court 1796).

*Molloy v. Meier.* Minn. 679 NW 2d 711 (Minn 2004).

*Moore v. Regents of the University of California.* 793 P. 2d 479 (Cal (en banc)1990).

*Norman-Bloodsaw v. Lawrence Berkeley Laboratory.* 135 F. 3d 1260 (9th Cir. 1998).

*Pate v. Threlkel.* 661 So. 2d 278 (Fla. 1995).

*Safer v. Estate of Pack.* 715 A. 2d 363 (NJ App. 1998).

*Sherley v. Sebelius.* 644 F. 3d 388: Ct. App. (DC Cir. 2011).

*Stewart v. Gramley.* 7th F. 3d 132 (7th Cir. 1996).

*Washington University v. Catalona.* 490 F. 3d 667 (8th Cir. 2007).

## LEGISLATION

Americans with Disabilities Act of 1990. 42 U.S.C. 12101 et seq.

Civil Rights Act of 1964, as amended. P.L. 88-352, 42 U.S.C. 21 et seq.

Employee Retirement Income Security Act of 1974. No. 113–97, 29 U.S.C. 18.

Executive Order 13145: To Prohibit Discrimination in Federal Employment Based on Genetic Information. 2000. http://www.eeoc.gov/eeoc/history/35th/thelaw/13145.html.

Genetic Information Nondiscrimination Act of 2008. P.L. 110–233, 29 CFR 1635.

Health Insurance Portability and Accountability Act of 1996. Pub. L. No. 104–191.

Newborn Screening. Tex. Health and Safety Code 33.011–33.056 (2016), see also https://www.dshs.state.tx.us/lab/nbsbloodspots.shtm.

Patient Protection and Affordable Care Act. P.L. 111–148, 42 U.S.C. 18001 et seq.

Protection of Human Subjects. 45 CFR 46.101 et seq.

Public Health Service Act of 1944 as amended. 42 U.S.C. 6A. https://www.gpo.gov/fdsys/granule/USCODE-2010-title42 /USCODE-2010-title42-chap6A.

Rehabilitation Act of 1973. 29 U.S.C. 701 et seq. https://www.google.com/url?sa=t&rct=j&q=&esrc=s&source=web&cd=1&cad=rja&uact=8&ved=0ahUKEwj5_4Ho35PLAhWIPiYKHQKcBS8QFggcMAA&url=https%3A%2F%2Fwww.gpo.gov%2Ffdsys%2Fpkg%2FSTATUTE-87%2Fpdf%2FSTATUTE-87-Pg355.pdf&usg=AFQjCNHCg4D-bKIWa29hER_c8TaJAyq6Hg&sig2=qa7l-6xg4-RADbaQi9VDg&bvm=bv.115277099,d.eWE.

Social Security Act of 1935. 42 U.S.C. 7. https://www.google.com/url?sa=t&rct=j&q=&esrc=s&source=web&cd=2&ved=0ahUKEwj-q9_R4JPLAhWJJCYKHY_ACkgQFggjMAE&url=https%3A%2F%2Fwww.gpo.gov%2Ffdsys%2Fpkg%2FCPRT-111WPRT52529%2Fpdf%2FCPRT-111WPRT52529.pdf&usg=AFQjCNE_BkFD3as-QDrLqhQLjvDVwB2PYA&sig2=mJ5t3zNF3BnO9TxPyprIaw&bvm=bv.115277099,d.eWE&cad=rja.

US Equal Opportunity Commission. "All Statutes." 1997–2014. http://eeoc.gov/eeoc/statistics/enforcement/all.cfm.

US Equal Opportunity Commission. "Genetic Information Non-discrimination Act Charges." 2010–2014. http://www.eeoc.gov/eeoc/statistics/enforcement/genetic.cfm.

US Patent Act, amend, 35 U.S.C. 101.

## FILM AND LITERATURE

Genetic testing has captured the imagination of writers for many decades. Where appropriate, these cultural reflections of our genetic anxieties have been mentioned in the text. The following list provides more information about these popular culture resources.

*The Bad Seed.* Dir. Mervyn LeRoy. 1956. Based on the play by Maxwell Anderson (New York: Dodd, Mead, 1955).

A young girl commits murder because of the evil genes she inherited from her serial-killer grandmother.

*The Boys from Brazil*. Dir. Franklin J. Schaffner. 1978. Based on the novel by Ira Levin (New York: Random House, 1976). Clones are made from Adolf Hitler's DNA and raised in different locations in the hope that one instance will re-create both the nature and nurture that gave rise to the dictator.

*College Holiday*. Dir. Frank Tuttle. 1936. College students are brought to a hotel to be used as guinea pigs in a eugenics experiment.

*Conviction*. Dir. Tony Goldwyn. 2010. A woman uses DNA evidence to prove her brother was imprisoned for a crime he did not commit.

*Do You Really Want to Know?* Dir. John Zaritsky. 2012. Documentary that follows three families dealing with the decision of whether to be tested for the Huntington's disease gene.

*Gattaca*. Dir. Andrew Niccol. 1997. An aspiring astronaut is kept out of the space program because his genes predict he will be a failure.

Genova, Lisa. *Inside the O'Briens*. New York: Gallery Books, 2015. A novel that depicts the lives of a family who discover they are carrying the gene for Huntington's disease. Author Genova's earlier novel concerning Alzheimer's disease, *Still Alice*, was made into an Academy Award–winning film in 2014.

*The Island*. Dir. Michael Bay. 2005. A utopian island is really the holding place for human clones who are designed to replace organs and body parts for others.

*Multiplicity*. Dir. Harold Ramis. 1996. A man who has too little time to get things done decides to clone himself.

*My Sister's Keeper*. Dir. Nick Cassavetes. 2009. Based on the novel by Jodi Picoult (New York: Atria, 2004). Parents of a child suffering from a leukemia disorder custom design a second fetus to become the older child's genetic match and tissue donor.

# CHAPTER 5

# Genetic Interventions: Therapy and Enhancement

**Keisha Ray**

*Postdoctoral Fellow, McGovern Center for Humanities and Ethics*
*University of Texas Health Science Center at Houston*

In the 2007 film *I Am Legend*, military scientist Robert Neville lives in New York City among zombie-like beings called dark-seekers. Dark-seekers were once normal human beings, but now they appear only at night to feed on human flesh. Dark-seekers are the result of scientists' attempt to genetically engineer the measles virus with the intention of using it to cure cancer. However, their attempts to manipulate the measles virus go tragically wrong. Instead of creating a much-needed cure for cancer, they create an airborne virus that turns most of the world's population into dark-seekers. Neville, however, is immune to the disease and spends his days in his New York City home trying to create a cure for the virus using his own blood and the dark-seekers that he has captured and sedated.

More recently, the 2011 film *Captain America: The First Avenger* (based on the popular comic book) tells the story of Steve Rogers, a sickly and physically unimpressive man with a strong sense of American pride. Rogers tries to enlist in the military during World War II, but he is denied admittance based on his lack of physical merit. Yet after a chance encounter with a military doctor who believes in Rogers's potential, he is allowed to enlist. After demonstrating superior moral character, he is chosen to be a part of the military doctor's super-soldier experiment. In the experiment, Rogers's DNA (deoxyribonucleic acid) is genetically altered in an attempt to make him a physically superior human being that can support America's war efforts. Immediately after undergoing the experiment, Rogers is much taller and has a much more muscular physique than he had before the experiment. Additionally, Rogers soon learns that he also has superhuman traits, including superhuman strength and speed.

The field of genetics drives the plot in both *I Am Legend* and *Captain America: The First Avenger*. Genetics is the study of who we are at the most fundamental level—our genes, which we inherit from our parents. The term *genes* is often used generically to refer to segments of DNA that code for certain traits, or characteristics. Specifically, a gene is a blueprint for a protein that builds these traits and characteristics. All of our genes together are referred to as our *genome*. The genome is encoded in DNA, which mainly resides in the nucleus of the cell. James D. Watson (1928–), Francis H. C. Crick (1916–2004), and Rosalind Franklin (1920–1958) discerned that the shape of DNA is a double helix. DNA is composed of chemical bases—adenine (A), thymine (T), guanine (G), cytosine (C)—and our genes are made up of the different arrangements of these bases that code for all of the

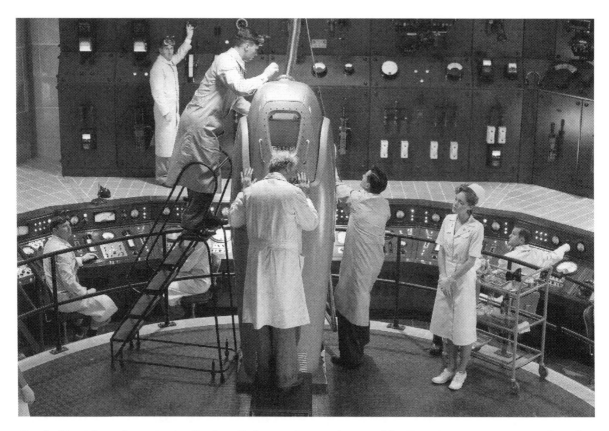

***Stanley Tucci (center) as scientist Abraham Erskine in* Captain America: The First Avenger, 2011.** *Set in the early 1940s, the film tells the story of Steve Rogers, a weak and sickly man whose DNA is altered in an attempt to make him physically superior in ways that can support America's war effort. Genetic enhancement—the process of modifying genes, not for therapeutic purposes but for imparting capabilities that surpass what is typical of humans—is a form of genetic intervention that tests the limits and ethical boundaries of medicine and science.* **AF ARCHIVE/ALAMY.**

proteins in the body. Think of the bases (A, T, G, C) as the letters of the genomic alphabet, and the genes as the sentences.

Each gene, or a combination of genes, is responsible for specific traits, such as hair color or eye color. How these genes are expressed (or transcribed into proteins) in a person will determine that person's hair color or eye color, as well as any of the many physical traits that genes control. Genes are also responsible for certain behaviors. Our likelihood of becoming addicted to alcohol, for example, is partially determined by our genes. Research also tells us that the likelihood that we will cheat on our spouses by engaging in extramarital relationships is partially determined by our genes. In sum, our genes tell us who we are, where we come from, and who we may be in the future.

Advances in our understanding of genetics, including genetic research like the Human Genome Project, paved the way for us to use what we have learned about genetics to make our lives better. One such way that advances in genetics have helped us is through the practice of genetic therapy. Discovering how genes work and how they make us who we are made it possible to cure some diseases and disorders by altering our genes. Then, as often happens, researchers and physicians began to question the limits of genetic therapy, particularly whether the limits of gene alteration could be expanded to include genetic enhancement. Genetic enhancement is the process of modifying genes, not for therapeutic purposes, but to give people capabilities that surpass what is typical of humans (i.e., superhuman powers). Collectively, genetic therapy and genetic enhancement are referred to as genetic interventions, and together they test the limits of medicine and science.

*I Am Legend* and *Captain America: The First Avenger* are fictional accounts of genetic interventions that employ fictional modes of gene alteration. Both films ask the kinds of questions that expanding the limits of our current and emerging technology in medicine and science force us to face: Is it ethical to use medical technology to change the most fundamental building blocks of our being? Is it ethical to use technology that will affect the traits of people in future generations of our family? Should we accept the risks associated with genetic interventions to find cures for incurable diseases? In their representation of the kinds of questions that genetic interventions raise, the stories of Steve Rogers in *Captain America: The First Avenger* and Robert Neville in *I Am Legend* also represent the benefits and the shortcomings of altering genes for therapy and enhancement purposes.

This chapter focuses on the benefits of genetic interventions and demonstrates how they represent a new form of human ingenuity. This chapter also discusses the shortcomings and criticisms of genetic interventions. Expectedly, a discussion of the benefits and shortcomings of genetic interventions also reveals broader but related issues, such as fairness in our health-care systems, what it means to be human, the value of disabilities, and our responsibility to our future children.

How we understand and discuss genetic interventions is constantly changing because we are continuously learning new things about the human mind, body, and genome. For example, just a few years ago, science held that the strands of unused DNA between useful genes were "junk." On the basis of the field known as *epigenetics,* we now believe that these strands' codes are deactivated genes that may be activated (or deactivated) to respond to stress or other changes. As knowledge and technology of genetic interventions advance, new concerns and new disagreements will emerge about how to use the interventions and who should have permission to use them.

## SOMATIC GENE THERAPY

Medical interventions that aim to restore, maintain, or improve health by preventing or curing a condition, impairment, illness, or disease are considered *therapy*. Providing therapy to people who are sick is a method of maintaining species-typical functioning. Species-typical functioning establishes a standard for what is normal human biological and physiological functioning. People who are unhealthy differ from this standard. Sick individuals generally have priority in health care based on the belief that when we are sick, or when we are functioning below what is normal, we cannot live good, happy lives.

According to popular bioethicist Norman Daniels (1942–), because of health care's special relationship with our opportunities, we are required to find a way to fairly distribute its limited resources to people. These resources include practices and techniques, goods (e.g., drugs and equipment), and the people like doctors and nurses who provide these goods and perform these techniques. One way to justify the obligations of medical facilities (i.e., hospitals and clinics) to provide therapy to people who are ill is to look at how health care can help us lead good lives. For example, Daniels argues that all people have a normal range of opportunities. A normal range of opportunities consists of the many opportunities, or life activities, that are available to people with ordinary talents. Because health is necessary for many of life's activities, people's normal range of opportunities is hindered if their species-typical functioning is not maintained.

Genetic therapy is a type of medical intervention that is meant to protect a normal range of opportunities by restoring people to normal functioning. The basic principle behind genetic therapy is that particular genes are associated with particular disorders. Genetic disorders, or disorders that we inherit from our parents' genes, are the result of improperly functioning genes, missing genes, or too many genes. Scientists estimate that there are at least two thousand genetic disorders. Therefore, genetic therapy consists in using genetic interventions to treat or prevent disease by replacing, adding, or deleting genes. This process is accomplished by inserting microscopic *vectors* into the cell where they carry out their work. Vectors are often viruses, such as *adenoviruses* (common cold), but they also may include proteins and fat particles called *liposomes*.

 Genetic therapy targets either somatic cells (cells that form organs such as the liver or lungs) or germ-line cells (cells that form sperm and eggs) for modification. Somatic gene therapy is the more common type. This type of therapy changes the genes of a single individual and those changes are not passed onto future generations. When performed on

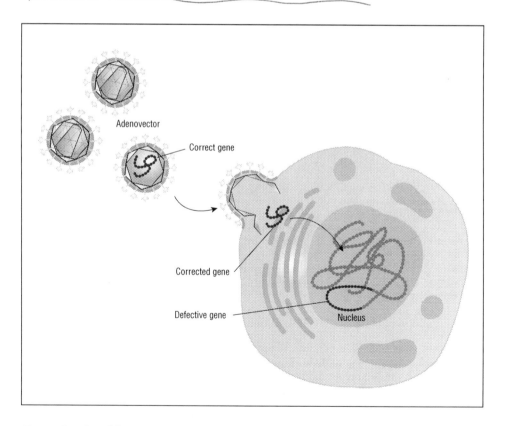

*Figure 5.1. Gene Therapy.* **COURTESY: NATIONAL HUMAN GENOME RESEARCH INSTITUTE.**

humans, somatic gene therapy is performed in one of two ways—*ex vivo* or *in vivo*. Ex vivo refers to the method in which genes are removed from patients' bodies, modified in a laboratory, and then inserted back into patient's body using a vector. In vivo refers to the method in which genes are not removed from patients' bodies but are modified while still in the body.

Somatic gene therapy inserts properly functioning genes into human bodies to either replace or repair improperly functioning cells that cause incurable diseases and disorders. Such therapies are being developed for incurable disorders, such as Parkinson's disease, a genetic disorder in which people lose control of their motor skills as the result of cells dying in parts of their brain, and cystic fibrosis, an incurable genetic disorder in which the body produces thick mucus that clogs the lungs, making breathing very difficult. Somatic gene therapy can also be used to treat diseases that are not genetic but are infectious. For instance, somatic gene therapy has been tested as a treatment for HIV and AIDS, in which antibodies are genetically altered to help people with HIV and AIDS fight off the disease.

Currently, somatic gene therapy is mostly considered to be experimental; however, it has had some real-life successes. Between 1999 and 2006, somatic gene therapy was used to treat some people with the genetic disorder severe combined immune deficiency (SCID). This disorder was depicted in the 2001 film *Bubble Boy*, in which the main character, played by Jake Gyllenhaal, lives in a plastic bubble to protect him from infections from which his body cannot protect him. People with SCID have a limited immune system, and their bodies cannot protect them from bacteria and viruses that most other people can fight. People with SCID have immune systems that cannot even protect them from typically nondeadly viruses that most people's immune system can protect them from, such as the virus that causes the common cold.

Between 1999 and 2006, children with SCID had some success with somatic gene therapy. To treat their SCID, viruses that were sterilized (i.e., the infectious component was removed) were used as carriers for good genes. The viruses were then introduced into SCID patients' bodies so the good genes could replace genes that were not working properly in the cells of their immune systems. After undergoing therapy, many of the children had their immune function restored. Five of the children with SCID, however, were diagnosed with leukemia caused by the somatic gene therapy. Four of those children had their leukemia successfully treated with chemotherapy and survived, but the fifth child died. Because of this failure, researchers have made changes to somatic gene therapy to render it safer, including changing the ways that genes are introduced into the body and conducting more tests.

Most of the successes from somatic gene therapy have only been shown during the testing phases of genetic research and experiments. For example, Parkinson's disease has shown to be somewhat successfully treated with somatic gene therapy, with some patients showing signs of improved muscle control after undergoing therapy. Currently, somatic gene therapy is available only to people enrolled in Parkinson's disease research trials.

Hemophilia has been treated somewhat successfully with somatic gene therapy. Hemophilia is a genetic disease in which people's blood has trouble clotting. These people lack the gene that codes for the protein that clots blood. If people with hemophilia experience an injury, even a minor injury, such as a small paper cut, they could lose a lot of blood, perhaps enough to cause death. During the testing phase of experiments, people with hemophilia are given the genes that they are missing. After therapy, many of the patients are able to form blood clots and have fewer occurrences of excessive bleeding. But more research is necessary to ensure that the procedure is safe for more people with hemophilia.

Other uses of somatic gene therapy also show promise of one day being used as widespread therapies for disorders. Using somatic gene therapy to treat blindness that is caused by inherited genes has shown to be successful in nonhuman animals like mice and dogs. Researchers hope that one day it will be successful at treating inherited blindness in humans. Somatic gene therapy is also on the horizon of being able to introduce a gene into the body that can produce a particular substance that the body cannot make on its own. This would be especially helpful to people who have diabetes and whose bodies do not produce enough insulin, or to people of short stature whose bodies do not produce enough growth hormone.

Somatic gene therapy offers the hope that it will be able to cure and treat many diseases that negatively affect these individuals' range of opportunities. Genetic therapy and genetic disorders are complicated: consider that some genetic disorders involve hundreds of genes. Understanding how a combination of genes is responsible for a disorder and the best way to treat that disorder can be quite complex.

## RISKS OF SOMATIC GENE THERAPY: THE CASE OF JESSE GELSINGER

Although generally not controversial, somatic gene therapy has raised several concerns. For instance, when a foreign substance, such as a new gene, is introduced into a body, the body's immune system will attack the foreign substance as a part of the body's natural inclination to protect itself. This is a risk when a person receives an organ transplant, because without treatment, the body would see the organ as foreign and attack it. It is similarly a risk when someone receives a DNA transplant. Although the immune system is doing its job, it is also voiding the somatic gene therapy, making it ineffective and potentially threatening the recipient's health.

Genetic therapy also has raised concerns about its link to cancer. In January 2015, the National Human Genome Research Institute, a branch of the US National Institutes of Health (NIH), released the statement "NIH Researchers Tackle Thorny Side of Gene Therapy," in which the NIH declares that a risk of cancer is associated with genetic therapy. Another study found an association between a type of genetic therapy and liver cancer. Currently, however, the NIH is seeing some success in tests of a new type of genetic therapy on mice that reduces the risks of cancer in the hopes of making genetic therapy safer for humans.

Another criticism of somatic gene therapy is the method of delivering added genes. When genetic therapy calls for adding genes to a person's body, as previously described, modified DNA is put into a virus and then that virus is inserted into a person's body. Once inside the body, the virus enters cells and the modified DNA attaches to those cells. The modified DNA then encourages the body to produce proteins that the body lacks. One concern with this method of genetic therapy is that the virus will infect the person with its disease. The well-known case of Jesse Gelsinger (1981–1999) is an example of this criticism. His story shone a spotlight on the delivery of added genes and on genetic therapy as a whole.

Gelsinger was an eighteen-year-old man with ornithine transcarbamylase deficiency (OTC), an often-deadly genetic disease in which the liver fails to remove ammonia from the body, causing the body to fill with deadly levels of ammonia. Screening of newborns can identify this disease, and the individual's life span can be extended with special diets in some circumstances. In 1999, Gelsinger participated in an OTC study at the University of

Pennsylvania, even though his OTC was adequately controlled with the help of nongenetic therapy and a proper diet. Researchers, as well as Gelsinger's father, confirmed that Gelsinger was told that the OTC study would not lead to a cure for him but could help find a cure for babies with OTC. As a part of the research, using somatic gene therapy, Gelsinger's liver was injected with an adenovirus that contained copies of the genes that people with OTC, like Gelsinger, are missing.

Although Gelsinger reportedly entered the study a healthy young man, he died four days after being injected with adenoviruses. A wrongful death lawsuit initiated by Gelsinger's family charged researchers with giving Gelsinger and his family misleading information about the study and its procedures. These charges were based on the belief that the adenovirus given to Gelsinger was more harmful than other vectors that were normally used to transmit genes. The charges also stemmed from the belief that researchers should have known this information because the adenovirus used in Gelsinger's therapy previously caused severe liver damage to another adult with OTC. Relatedly, the researchers kept increasing the concentration of the adenovirus that Gelsinger received despite rising levels of ammonia toxicity in his body. Last, the researchers were charged with not revealing that animals had died after being given the same adenovirus that Gelsinger was given.

As a result of Gelsinger's death and the many journalists and congressional hearings that investigated the incident, stricter rules were written about reporting the deaths of patients in genetic research. Gelsinger's case also spurred many genetic researchers to come together and reassess genetic therapy at a large-scale conference in 2000. At the meeting, the use of adenoviruses was reevaluated and it was determined that they should not be used on healthy patients. Another conference outcome was a moratorium on some research until genetic therapy could be made safer.

Although high-profile cases like Gelsinger's have revealed that there is much to learn about somatic gene therapy, the successful uses of somatic gene therapy show that it is likely not far from greater acceptance as a treatment.

## GERM-LINE GENE THERAPY

Germ-line gene therapy aims to eliminate the chance of developing diseases before a person is even born. Germ-line gene therapy modifies the heritable genes of male sperm or female eggs so that the resulting embryo has altered DNA. Sometimes germ-line gene therapy directly alters the cells of an already formed embryo. Whether sperm cells, egg cells, or embryos are modified, germ-line gene therapy aims to modify cells for therapeutic purposes—namely, to eliminate (or replace) genes responsible for disorders.

Overall, germ-line gene therapy and somatic gene therapy face the same criticism. Because germ-line gene therapy changes future humans, a baby born from altered genes is a different person than the embryo would have become if it had been allowed to develop without intervention. In addition, germ-line gene therapy changes the genetic makeup of all future generations—that is, the genetic makeup of any children, grandchildren, and great-grandchildren (and so forth) that come from that initially genetically altered person will also be changed.

Germ-line gene therapy can give us the ability to permanently eliminate genes that cause diseases so that future individuals do not inherit the disorders that are associated with the malfunctioning genes. But germ-line gene therapy comes with risks that are even more troublesome because those altered genes are passed on to future generations. Therefore, germ-line interventions currently are not performed on humans (only on plants and animals) in most countries. The US government prohibits federal money from being used to fund research on genetic interventions that alter germ-line cells, and genetic interventions that alter germ-line cells are banned in most of Europe.

Germ-line therapy requires an altruistic patient, because the people whose genes would be modified using germ-line gene therapy would not experience any of the benefits of therapy (unless an embryo is directly altered). Rather, the children of the people whose genes are being altered would experience the effects of germ-line gene therapy. This is where a lot of the controversy with germ-line gene therapy lies. Although germ-line gene therapy could be good for future generations because it could eliminate their experience of diseases, it could affect future generations in unexpected ways that we currently cannot predict. Germ-line gene therapy is also controversial because it treats future people without giving them a say in their own therapy; rather, someone else is making the decision for them.

Another risk associated with performing germ-line gene therapy on humans includes a higher chance for making mistakes based on the flawed method of administering genes—via viruses—and the great consequences of those mistakes. For example, consider a gene change that would not create problems in a patient until he or she was past fifty years of age. This problem would not appear until after the person has likely procreated, having already passed on the altered genes, and thus harming another generation.

These concerns about the ethical nature and the logistics of administering germ-line gene therapy are prevalent among doctors, researchers, and ethicists alike; however, some people support germ-line gene therapy. For example, in 2015 a group of Chinese researchers attempted to edit genomes in human embryos obtained from fertility clinics (the researchers used unviable embryos meaning they were incapable of being brought to full term) using an innovative tool called *clustered, regularly interspaced, short palindromic repeat* (CRISPR). CRISPR allows researchers to edit genomes much more efficiently than ever before. These Chinese researchers used CRISPR in their attempts to edit a gene in human embryos that causes a potentially fatal blood disorder. Their attempts resulted in mixed results, prompting them to acknowledge that more research is necessary before it is possible to successfully alter germ-line cells. As a result, an international body of gene therapy researchers elected to voluntarily ban human embryo gene editing, for now.

Somatic gene therapy and germ-line gene therapy are intended to be a more efficient way of ensuring that unhealthy people are healthy enough to pursue their life's activities. Genetic therapy, however, is controversial because of the accompanying risks to health. Genetic therapy, particularly germ-line gene therapy, is also controversial because of what therapy can turn into—enhancement, or using medical interventions for people without diseases to exceed species-typical functioning. Many of the medical therapies that we currently use to treat diseases have the potential to be used for enhancement, but the ways in which people are enhanced as a result of most of these medical therapies are minimal. The ways that genetic therapy can be used to enhance people's functioning, however, can be potentially species altering.

## THERAPY/ENHANCEMENT DISTINCTION

Although therapy is typically thought of as using medical interventions to maintain or restore species-typical functioning, enhancement employs medical interventions to improve health or human abilities beyond species-typical functioning. Enhancement occurs when people are already healthy and normal but either directly or indirectly use medical resources to develop abilities that surpass normal. Genetic enhancement is a type of enhancement in which people's genes are altered for the purposes of surpassing species-typical functioning that would likely occur naturally.

Distinguishing between medical interventions that are intended for therapy and medical interventions that are intended for enhancement is commonly referred to as the *therapy/enhancement distinction*. Based on the therapy/enhancement distinction, a fair distribution of resources means primarily allocating resources to people who want therapy and not to people who want enhancement. Similar to Daniels's concept of a normal range of opportunities, the therapy/enhancement distinction relies on the idea that we cannot have the best life possible if we have diseases. Therefore, health care has to provide us with resources to treat the diseases that stop us from doing the things that make us happy, such as pursuing our careers, participating in our hobbies, or spending time with our families and friends. Enhancement, however, is not typically seen as necessary to live the best life possible or pursue life's normal activities.

## SHOULD THE THERAPY/ENHANCEMENT DISTINCTION BE OUR MORAL GUIDE?

Enhancement is beyond health care's obligations to us, whereas therapy falls within health care's obligations to us. When using the therapy/enhancement distinction as a moral compass, guiding us when we have to make decisions about what is fair, we have to consider whether being able to draw a line between two different types of medical interventions necessarily means that health-care professionals are required to provide one type of intervention (e.g., treatment), but not another type of intervention (e.g., enhancement). For example, consider Bob, a young man training to be an Olympic swimmer who has trouble building muscle. His parents take him to a doctor who, after conducting tests, concludes that Bob has average muscle mass for his age. From the tests, the doctor also concludes that Bob does not have a medical condition that contributes to his inability to build the amount of muscle that Bob wants to build.

The doctor tells Bob and his parents that he will likely never be able to build the amount of muscle that he hopes to because muscle size is inherited. In fact both of Bob's parents are also unable to build a lot of muscle. Based on this information, Bob and his parents ask the doctor to genetically intervene so that Bob's body is encouraged to produce more muscle-building hormones. If Bob's body produces more of the muscle-building hormones that he is missing, he would be able to build more muscle.

Bob and his parents want genetic intervention for Bob because they claim that his lack of muscle, and its contribution to his lack of swimming power, makes him have low self-esteem and affects his sense of self-worth. His parents tell the doctor that he is frequently sad after his swimming competitions. They have tried to help him, but nothing has worked. They all believe that genetic intervention will help Bob feel better because it will help him achieve his life goal of becoming an Olympic swimmer. Bob's doctor understands their concerns and feels sorry for Bob, but because Bob is normal according to medical standards, the doctor denies their request for genetic intervention, which greatly saddens both Bob and his parents.

Todd is also a young man training to be an Olympic swimmer. Like Bob, he also lacks the ability to build more muscle despite his intense training. His parents take him to see a doctor who confirms that Todd's muscle mass is below average for his age. Todd and his parents tell the doctor that Todd's inability to put on muscle and athletically perform well affects his self-esteem and sense of self-worth. They have done some research and would like Todd to undergo genetic intervention. After a series of tests, Todd's doctor determines that his body is not properly producing muscle-building hormones, which is likely the cause of his inability to build muscle. The doctor also concludes that Todd's inability to build muscle is likely inherited from his parents. The doctor recommends that Todd undergo genetic intervention to correct the improper functioning of his body. After undergoing genetic intervention, Todd is able to build more muscle, which he attributes to helping him make the US Olympic swim team.

Based on the therapy/enhancement distinction, Bob is seeking enhancement. As such, the proper conclusion to draw is that Bob is not a priority in medicine and his doctor's decision to not genetically intervene is justified. Todd, in contrast, is seeking therapy for an improperly functioning body and is entitled to genetic intervention, based on the therapy/enhancement distinction. According to a clinical test, Todd has a disease, while Bob does not. The therapy/enhancement distinction does not consider that both young men have the same problem—inability to build muscle—or that Bob is mentally and emotionally suffering because of his lack of muscle mass just as Todd is suffering. When determining what is fair for Todd and Bob, Bob's decreased well-being matters less than the fact that his doctor has not found any medical reason for his lack of muscles. Todd's doctor, however, has found a medical reason for his lack of muscles, thus giving Todd a special claim on medicine's resources.

The example of Bob and Todd shows that sometimes the reasons that people want enhancement are similar to the reasons that people want therapy—namely, to be well, have access to life's opportunities, and generally live the best life that is available to them. The example of Bob and Todd also shows that in some cases the therapy/enhancement distinction does not always tell us how to fairly treat people because it does not account for overall well-being, which we may want to consider when deciding what is fair. But we have to find some way to distribute health care's resources. And if we want to use the therapy/enhancement distinction as our ethical guide for what are fair uses of medical resources, we have to (1) use it with the knowledge that it does not always match our obligations to people, and (2) be willing to consider all of the ways that people can be unhealthy that the therapy/enhancement distinction may overlook. The distinction also neglects likelihood of benefit. What if Bob (seeking enhancement) would benefit from intervention, but Todd (seeking treatment) would not? The therapy/enhancement distinction overlooks medical need and potential benefit.

The therapy/enhancement distinction, when applied to the example of Bob and Todd also raises the issue of fairness in sport. It particularly raises the issue of whether genetic interventions jeopardize at least one goal of sport—namely, that all athletes have an equal chance of winning. This was also an issue in the real-life case of Chinese athlete Ye Shiwen (1996–). In 2012, Ye, a sixteen-year-old top competitive swimmer, was accused of genetically enhancing her body, which she denied. Her superior swimming performance raised the suspicions of John Leonard, the American director of the World Swimming Coaches Association. Leonard believed that there was a strong chance that Ye genetically altered her body, and as a result, she was able to win swimming competitions. Leonard continues to believe that along with being tested for steroids and other banned substances in sports, athletes like Ye, who display unbelievable athletic performances, should also be tested for genetic manipulation.

*Gold medal winner Ye Shiwen of China on day two of the China National Swimming Championships, April 10, 2015, in Baoji, Shanxi Province, China.* In 2012 Ye Shiwen, then a sixteen-year-old top competitive swimmer, was accused of genetically enhancing her body, which she denied. Her superior swimming performance raised the suspicion of John Leonard, director of the World Swimming Coaches Association. Calling Ye's performance "unbelievable" and "disturbing," Leonard has advocated that athletes be tested for genetic manipulation in addition to the checks that are already in place for steroids and other banned substances. **GETTY IMAGES SPORT/GETTY IMAGES.**

Leonard's beliefs are based on the same ideas behind policies banning the use of enhancing substances in sport. Enhancing substances, such as steroids, are banned from sports based on the argument that professional sports are made unfair when some athletes receive an athletic advantage from drug use, whereas the athletes they compete against do not have this advantage. Athletes who take drugs have a better chance of winning competitions; they are able to modify their bodies in ways that athletes who do not take drugs will never be able to, giving athletes who take drugs superior abilities on the court or on the field. If genetic interventions can do the same things for athletes that drugs like steroids can do for them, then genetic interventions that enhance may also need to be banned in sports for the sake of fairness in competition.

Professional sports leagues ban performance-enhancing drugs, even though the leagues acknowledge that some banned drugs are also used by doctors to treat illnesses that athletes may experience. If athletes have illnesses that must be treated with drugs that are banned by their leagues, they can ask their leagues to make an exception for them by applying for a therapeutic use exemption (TUE). If approved, TUEs give some professional athletes permission to take banned drugs for therapy reasons, even if those drugs also enhance their bodies or minds.

Normally the therapy/enhancement distinction is used by sports leagues to justify bans on enhancing drugs. TUEs, however, stray from the normal uses of the therapy/ enhancement distinction. TUEs allow some instances of enhancement in the sport, because after all athletes who have permission to take some banned drugs could experience both the therapeutic and enhancing benefits of the drugs. Implementing TUEs is a sign that some sports leagues see a value in not strictly following the therapy/enhancement distinction.

Examples like Bob and Todd, Ye Shiwen, and TUEs show that sometimes therapy is not drastically different from enhancement. It may be more beneficial and compassionate to consider the lines between therapy and enhancement as malleable and, therefore, the conclusions drawn from the therapy/enhancement distinction as disposable as a means of including a wide range of people whom health-care professionals are obligated to help. Genetic engineering is another type of genetic intervention that is a necessary component of any discussion of the differences and similarities between therapy and enhancement. Fears of genetic engineering often spur people to draw distinct lines between therapy and enhancement. The legitimacy of these fears is the focus of the remainder of the chapter.

## GENETIC ENGINEERING

Some genetic interventions that are proposed for therapy purposes may one day be used for enhancement purposes. For example, muscular dystrophy is a debilitating disorder that is currently incurable. People who experience muscular dystrophy have very weak muscles and little to no muscle mass. They may lose the ability to walk, all because of improperly functioning genes. A proposed therapy for some types of muscular dystrophy is somatic gene therapy in which properly functioning genes are added to muscles to increase muscle strength. However, somatic gene therapy to increase muscle mass theoretically can also be used to increase the muscle mass of people without muscular dystrophy, turning what was once somatic gene therapy into genetic enhancement for normally functioning people.

Genetic enhancement is controversial for many reasons. One reason is that therapies, such as drugs, do not always work for healthy people in the same ways that they work for unhealthy people, their target population. When healthy people use drugs and medical practices that are intended to treat sick people, the therapies may do more harm to them than good. Second, genetic enhancement is controversial because of what it can evolve into—genetic engineering. Genetic engineering itself is controversial, largely because of fears that it can threaten the nature of what it means to be human.

### CHIMERAS

In a 2014 episode of the popular, long-running television show *The Simpsons*, the Simpson family's nemesis, Sideshow Bob, becomes the first person in their fictional town to undergo genetic engineering. He uses technology that is normally used to alter plants' genes to alter his own genes and give himself great strength and the traits of fish (e.g., gills), grasshoppers, and dolphins. To augment his newly created body, he kidnaps the most intelligent Simpson family member, Lisa, and plans to use her DNA and the DNA of other geniuses to make himself smarter. As in every episode in which Sideshow Bob attempts to hurt a member of

| Types of Genetic Interventions | Which cells are targeted? | Currently practiced in the United States or Europe? | Are future generations affected? | Is it considered human genetic engineering? |
|---|---|---|---|---|
| Somatic Gene Interventions | Somatic cells | Yes, in limited forms | No | No |
| Germ-Line Gene Interventions | Germ-line cells | No, but it is being researched | Yes | Yes |

**Table 5.1.** *Types of Genetic Interventions.* © GALE, CENGAGE LEARNING.

the Simpson family, his plan is thwarted with the help of the rest of the Simpson family and Sideshow's Bob own incompetence. This episode is a spoof of H. G. Wells's 1896 novel *The Island of Dr. Moreau*, in which a scientist creates a population of human-animal hybrids.

As depicted in *The Simpsons*, genetic engineering is a type of genetic intervention; more specifically, it is a type of genetic enhancement known as *chimerism*—the process of altering humans' genomes by adding genes to give healthy humans new traits. Because genes determine traits, if we add genes to people's bodies, we transfer the traits associated with those genes. As displayed by Sideshow Bob, genetic engineering can one day even give people traits that are not found in the human species, such as night vision or extraordinary strength, which would essentially create new kinds of humans. This is what makes genetic engineering so different from enhancement. Genetic engineering can give people new traits, whereas enhancement augments traits people either already have or are capable of developing.

As of the mid-2010s, human engineering is still in the research phase, so it amounts to mostly wishful thinking. Currently, human somatic cells are modified only for therapy purposes, not enhancement purposes. Human germ-line cells are not modified for either therapy or enhancement purposes in humans (see Table 5.1). Research is being conducted in the United States, the United Kingdom, and China (mostly for therapeutic reasons). So, in the near future, altering germ-line cells, as a part of the human engineering process, may become an actuality and no longer just wishful thinking.

### INTERNATIONAL POLICY

The Universal Declaration on the Human Genome and Human Rights serves as a good example of an argument against modifying germ-line cells and reflects the controversy surrounding genetic engineering. The declaration, adopted in 1997 by the United Nations Educational, Scientific, and Cultural Organization (UNESCO) and endorsed by the United Nations (UN) General Assembly the following year, affirms the rights of an individual whose genome is being used for research. National and regional lawmakers have relied on the declaration in legislation relating to medicinal and genetic research. The declaration is based on the belief that studying the genome can offer great benefits to individual research participants and to all of humankind, but the benefits must be balanced with a respect for human dignity and human rights. In support of this idea, the declaration asserts that "the human genome underlies the fundamental unity of all members of the human family, as well as the recognition of their inherent dignity and diversity" (Art. 1). Subsequently, the declaration asserts that altering germ-line cells is contrary to human dignity because it changes the natural course of human development. On the basis of this belief, many researchers and ethicists do not support altering germ-line cells for any reason.

Some observers take the opposite stance of the declaration. They assert that genetic engineering supports human dignity by giving us more control over our futures and the futures of our offspring. One such viewpoint is *transhumanism*, a school of thought that advocates using technology to redesign the human being to exceed species-typical functioning. And that includes manipulating the genome. Another perspective is based on the idea of *designing children*, or using available resources to create the best children possible. As with many other viewpoints on the merits of genetic interventions, these approaches are controversial. Some welcome the prospect of designing our genes as a sign of control over our future, whereas others view genetically engineering children as a threat to our humanity.

### ARE WE MORALLY OBLIGATED TO DESIGN THE BEST CHILDREN?

Genetic engineering could one day give us greater control over the kinds of people (i.e., children) that we bring into existence. After all, if we can give our children an advantage by giving them height, intelligence, kindness, or strength, then aren't we obligated to give them the best opportunity for success? We already have some control over this: When we choose partners with whom to have children, we are choosing the other half of our children's genetic makeup.

Julian Savulescu (1963–), a well-known Oxford University ethicist, defends the principle of *procreative beneficence* in the article "The Moral Obligation to Create Children with the Best Chance of the Best Life" (2009). In the article, he describes procreative beneficence as a moral duty to use whatever genetic interventions are available to bring into existence children who could have the best life possible. Savulescu argues that disease genes, genes that have the potential to be expressed as diseases or disorders, and nondisease genes, genes that determine characteristics like eye color and hair color, can both affect our likelihood of living a good life. Therefore, information about future children's disease genes and nondisease genes that are revealed in genetic testing should be used when determining which embryos ought to be brought to term.

The principle of procreative beneficence can also be extended to genetic interventions. If genetic interventions that allow us to genetically treat or prevent disease or to genetically engineer people become more widely available, based on the principle of procreative beneficence, it would be immoral not to use them. We would have to use genetic engineering to ensure that people had the characteristics that would give them the most well-being. For example, if a specific group of genes were found to determine intelligence, and genetic engineering allowed us to modify germ-line cells to ensure that embryos developed into intelligent people, then according to procreative beneficence, we must use genetic engineering to ensure that our offspring are intelligent.

The principle of procreative beneficence focuses on an objective sense of good and attempts to help people live a good life. Although this is generally a good thing, some people still may be critical of procreative beneficence and its assertion that as a matter of morality we must use genetic interventions, such as genetic engineering. Some criticisms of procreative beneficence stem from a belief in *procreative autonomy*, the principle that people have the freedom to autonomously choose what kind of persons they bring into existence. According to procreative autonomy, as long as the choice is made autonomously, any reproductive choice is moral. Procreative autonomy does not assert that we must use genetic interventions; rather, it allows us to define our own idea of well-being and pursue it for ourselves and for our future children, even if that means using or not using genetic interventions.

The idea of procreative autonomy is not without critics. Because procreative autonomy allows individuals to define well-being for themselves, we can essentially bring any kind of person, with any kind of traits, into existence. This means that people with traits that are normally not thought of as good traits, such as dishonesty (if a gene for dishonesty were found), or people with incurable diseases can be intentionally created. Also, the autonomy is held by a parent who will not be the person whom engineering affects—this is a proxy autonomy because the ultimate recipient of the genetic engineering has no choice in the matter.

Procreative autonomy and procreative beneficence have a shared aim—control over our lives and the lives of our children. Although procreative autonomy seems to embrace control by embracing the unknowns in life, the appeal of procreative beneficence seems to be controlling our lives by eliminating the unknowns in life. Life is filled with variables that can make us nervous about the future. Genetic interventions give us the chance to quiet some of the fears that we have about these variables. It also has been argued that genetic interventions give us a way to be prepared for what the future is sure to hold.

## BENEFITS OF GENETIC INTERVENTIONS: COMBATING CLIMATE CHANGE

Another potential benefit of genetic interventions is helping humans lessen their negative impact on the environment. S. Matthew Liao, Anders Sandberg, and Rebecca Roache make this argument in "Human Engineering and Climate Change" (2012), which asserts that climate change poses a difficult challenge for humans. Earth's temperatures are increasing, causing hotter and longer summers, colder and longer winters, and larger, more devastating natural disasters. These changes in the environment cause a lot of human suffering in the form of droughts, property damage, and the loss of human lives. The most unsettling part of climate change is that scientists tell us that it is only going to get worse, particularly because humans are not changing behaviors that contribute to the speed at which the climate is changing.

Public initiatives have encouraged people to help slow down climate change, such as grocery stores encouraging people to use reusable grocery bags in the place of plastic bags (or making patrons pay for the use of plastic and paper grocery bags and giving patrons discounts for using reusable grocery bags, which is the case in some counties in the city of Austin, Texas), and universities and businesses starting large-scale recycling programs to reduce garbage in landfills. Other solutions have been proposed and encouraged, including using automobiles less to reduce the harmful amounts of carbon monoxide in the atmosphere, which speeds up climate change. Governments also offer large companies financial incentives to reduce the amount of carbon monoxide they release into the environment. Liao and colleagues have questioned whether these modest solutions are enough to actually stop or significantly slow down climate change. They consider whether the best approach to climate change is to pair changes to human behaviors and incentives for large companies with practices that genetically modify humans.

Meat consumption is a good example of a human behavior that potentially could be targeted by genetic interventions for the sake of climate change. To produce an abundant supply of meat to accommodate human demand, many animals have to be farmed. Greenhouse emissions, particularly the methane gas released by cows, are a by-product of farming livestock. To keep humans supplied with an abundance of hamburgers, ribs, and other meat products, we have to farm a lot of animals that emit gas that is harmful to our environment and negatively changes our climate. If, however, we reduced the amount of meat we consumed, we would reduce the number of animals that exist solely for meat consumption by humans, thus significantly reducing the amount of harmful gases in the atmosphere.

Reducing the amount of meat that humans eat seems like a good idea, but there are a lot of meat eaters in the world. Getting people to give up their burgers and bacon would be a difficult project. To encourage individuals to give up meat, Liao and colleagues suggest creating intolerance for meat. Meat intolerance could be created by using genetic interventions to make our immune systems react negatively to proteins commonly found in meats, rendering them unpleasant to eat. This would be similar to lactose intolerance, in which people's bodies react negatively to lactose, which is found in milk and milk products.

Meat consumption is only one way that humans affect climate change that potentially could be limited with genetic interventions. Our physical size also affects climate changes. Liao and colleagues suggest the possibility of using genetic interventions to make us physically smaller in height and width. Essentially, the bigger we are, the more of Earth's resources we use to sustain ourselves in obvious ways, such as needing more food. But there are less obvious ways that bigger people require more resources that can contribute to climate change. For example, bigger people need more fabric to clothe themselves; to provide more fabric businesses must use more machines to create it and more automobiles to transport it, which uses more of Earth's resources and puts more harmful gases into the atmosphere. The overuse of Earth's resources and the creation of harmful gases in the atmosphere is also caused by our insatiable shopping habits, in which we buy things that we do not need and sometimes cannot afford. If our waistlines were smaller, or we were inches shorter, then our impact on the environment would be reduced. To limit these demands, Liao and colleagues suggest controlling human size using genetic interventions. We could only bring to term embryos of a certain height or use genetic interventions to control people's levels of growth hormone, which is the hormone responsible for our height.

One criticism of arguments for using genetic interventions to affect climate change is that the proposed uses of genetic interventions are not realistic from a policy-making point of view. However, it may be more feasible and desirable to provide better access to good education through good policy making and affect the number of people in the world this way. For genetic interventions to provide better options for reducing the human impact on the climate, the interventions must prove to be a more economically sound and effective policy than social options, such as access to better education.

The arguments presented by Liao and colleagues represent a conundrum that genetic interventions pose—should we use genetic interventions to fix problems, or would our time and efforts be best directed at changing those behaviors that create or worsen the problems? When we are not making simple modifications to our lifestyles that could make our environment more hospitable for ourselves and for future generations, perhaps the answer is to use human ingenuity, in the form of genetic interventions to transform ourselves. If we take the suggestion of genetically altering ourselves seriously, we also have to question what this says about humans. We have to consider whether genetic interventions change not only individuals but also the nature of what it means to be human for everyone in a changing world.

## WHAT'S WRONG WITH GENETIC INTERVENTIONS AND SHOULD WE CARE?

Leon Kass (1939–) is a well-known physician, ethicist, and public figure who frequently has argued against humans' use of genetic interventions that enhance people's abilities. In 2003,

Kass gave a popular lecture that summarizes the fears that genetic enhancement, including genetic engineering, seem to inspire:

> Let me begin by offering a toast to biomedical science and biotechnology: May they live and be well. And may our children and grandchildren continue to reap their ever tastier fruit—but without succumbing to their seductive promises of a perfect, better-than-human future, in which we shall be as gods, ageless and blissful. (Kass 2003, 9)

In the lecture, Kass argues that humans' desire to use genetic enhancement to change themselves (and their future children) represents a desire for perfection. And in fact, when people say that using genetic enhancement is like "playing God," what they really mean is that genetic interventions are used to attain a level of perfection that is impossible for humans to achieve and only possible for a god to reach.

Other than a desire to reach perfection, Kass gives three additional reasons that we should object to the use of genetic interventions that enhance people's bodies and minds. The first reason is safety. As mentioned previously, when healthy people use a drug intended to treat a disease, they may experience unintended side effects. In addition, current genetic engineering practices are still not safe enough to be performed on humans.

Second, Kass argues that we should object to genetic enhancement because it equates to cheating, a particular concern in sports, as seen in the case of Ye Shiwen, discussed earlier in this chapter. The concern is that genetic interventions give users an advantage over people who do not use genetic interventions, creating an issue of unfairness.

Third, Kass argues that we should object to genetic enhancement because it encourages control and a lack of freedom. To support this argument, Kass asserts that genetic enhancement gives parents an inappropriate amount of control over their children. Genetic enhancement, in the form of genetic engineering could also give people in one generation the ability to control the lives of future generations of their families. Genetic enhancement could also exert control over people's lives in the form of peer pressure. If many parents decide to genetically alter their children to give them traits that will help them succeed in school, other parents may feel pressure to genetically alter their children so they can keep up with the genetically altered children and also do well in school. Kass argues that genetic enhancement has the impossible goal of perfection, and in our pursuit of perfection, we miss out on the value of unbridled nature.

Michael Sandel (1953–), another well-known ethicist, wrote the popular article "The Case against Perfection" (2004), in which he makes an argument similar to Kass's. Sandel's argument is rooted in the idea that the value of life is embracing the unknowns and the mysteries of nature. As he sees it, enhancement tries to eliminate the unknowns in life by controlling nature, or by seeking perfection, as Kass argues. Sandel claims that his argument is not theological, but there are hints of theology in it, particularly the idea that nature was given to us (perhaps by God or some other godlike entity) and that we are to accept nature as it is, the good and the bad.

Sandel argues that the ways in which we normally discuss the bad aspects of genetic enhancement fail to really capture what we should find troubling about genetically altering humans. What we should find troubling about genetic enhancement has little to do with being able to direct our own lives, our rights, or what is fair. Consider the example of parents using genetic engineering to design their future children. An argument based on being able to direct our own lives would suggest that designing children is wrong because when we genetically engineer children, we deny them an open future. Rather than letting children turn into the individuals that they will naturally turn into, we use genetic engineering to preplan their future, thus preplanning the kind of person they will become.

According to Sandel, this argument gets genetic enhancement all wrong, in that it suggests that if parents did not design their children using genetic engineering, children would have the ability to naturally design themselves, which is impossible. No one chooses their genetic makeup because no one chooses their biological parents. The moral problem with genetic enhancement, as Sandel sees it, is that genetic enhancement represents our desire to master nature, specifically to control human nature. And a desire to master nature misguidedly supports the idea that everything in the world can be used at our disposal. Letting go of our desire for control and recognizing that everything in the world is not for our use requires a certain humility that is necessary to appreciate the mystery of life, which genetic enhancement does not encourage.

In *The Fabricated Man: The Ethics of Genetic Control* (1970), Protestant ethicist Paul Ramsey (1913–1988) argues against genetic engineering because it disengages humanity from nature and, ultimately, from the divine. On a practical level, he fears that if people are engineered to be more alike, then we may lose the genetic diversity that has been an important part of human evolution. On a humanistic side, he questions whether this technology ultimately means we become something other than human, a species that engineers its own obsolescence as it rapidly transforms into something else. Spiritually, Ramsey questions whether humans ought to practice technologies that can reshape an entire species, essentially acting like God but lacking omniscient wisdom.

Our evaluation of the arguments of Sandel, Kass, and Ramsey must take into account the many ways that we already alter our children and ourselves that we find acceptable. For example, Sandel accepts that parents shape their children's lives in many ways without using genetic engineering. Parents put their children in gymnastics classes, make them take piano lessons, or make them see a math tutor. Parents also regulate what music their children listen to and what movies they can watch, all with the aim of influencing what kind of adults they will become. In fact, we tend to applaud parents who do their best to positively shape their children's lives. For Sandel, parenting in this manner honors what it means to be a good parent, whereas genetic engineering does not. Being a good parent means accepting children as they are and not choosing for them who they must become, which as he sees it, is the purpose of genetic enhancement. But what Sandel's response does not acknowledge is that the ways that parents control their children's lives without genetic engineering can be just as limiting to their character as using genetic engineering to predetermine who they become.

We also exert control over nature in other ways. In the realm of cosmetics, we use makeup to give us the appearance that we wish genetics would have given us. We also use hair dye, hair extensions, and wigs to give us the hair that genetics did not give us. When we need to stay awake, we drink coffee or energy drinks, which are both enhancing substances. When considering the merits of genetic interventions, such as genetic enhancement and genetic engineering, we have to consider whether there are relevant differences between the nongenetic interventions (i.e., makeup, caffeine) that we use to make ourselves better, prettier, and happier and genetic interventions that we use to better ourselves. If we desire permanency, genetic enhancement is certainly more preferable to nongenetic enhancement. But if we take Sandel's and Kass's arguments seriously, relevant differences exist between nongenetic enhancement and genetic enhancement. At least one difference, according to their argument, is that genetic enhancement threatens our appreciation for life and the specialness that comes from not knowing what life is going to throw at us in a way that makeup or piano lessons do not.

Sandel's and Kass's concerns about genetic interventions mostly focus on individual uses of them. Their arguments warn us about what using genetic interventions reveals about the people who use them—namely, that they demonstrate a lack of humility and seek a level of perfection that is unattainable. Their arguments, however, do give some hints at how genetic interventions affect society as a whole. Kass's arguments concerning cheating and coercion, in particular, focus on how individuals' use of genetic interventions can have repercussions for many members of society. These kinds of arguments are important because it would be irresponsible to discuss genetic interventions without giving consideration to who is using them and how they will be used. Therefore, the great capabilities of genetic interventions have to be examined within the context of our society. The next section of this chapter examines how individual uses of genetic interventions affect other members of society, as well as the ideals that shape our society.

## INEQUALITY AND GENETIC INTERVENTIONS

Genetic interventions have been criticized for contributing to our misguided social preferences. For instance, individuals and societies as a whole tend to show preferences for certain human characteristics. And although preferences depend on the part of the world you find yourself in, generally we value good looks (and all that it entails) over bad looks. We also value certain talents and skills more than we value others. For instance, many people tend to value math, science, and business skills more than art and music skills. Considering these preferences, if we could determine the genes that correlate with traits that are necessary to succeed in business and in science, parents may use genetic interventions to ensure that their children have business traits and not traits for music and art in an attempt to secure their children's financial future.

Wanting to secure our children's financial future is a noble goal, one supported by the principle of beneficence. In US culture, however, we tend to place a lot of importance on money and its ability to make us happy. Rather than focus on happiness, we may be tempted to use genetic interventions to ensure that our children have the traits that we think will make them money, not the traits that will make them happy. Although we may have the best intentions, using genetic interventions in this way could backfire.

Genetic interventions also have been criticized for contributing to inequality by eliminating diversity in the world. Genetic diversity among humans occurs when different genes are present in the total population, creating diversity in race, gender, abilities, eye color, hair color, and other traits that make us unique. To preserve genetic diversity, people have to produce offspring with a wide variety of mates (or through other reproductive means) to maintain a variety of genes in the human population.

Genetic interventions pose a concern for genetic diversity, because the technology can be used to choose the traits that we want in people and to discard the traits that we no longer wish people to have. If we could use genetic interventions to change children's hair color to brown, for instance, when they would have been born with red hair if they were not genetically altered, eventually the number of people in the world with red hair will either be drastically lessened or completely eliminated. This scenario, and many other similar scenarios that involve eliminating diversity in our population, would be unfortunate because diversity is good for everyone. Living in a world in which everyone looks alike and acts alike would not be interesting or any fun. Diversity is also how we grow. People who are different from us help challenge our worldview and force us to think about the world from a different perspective, all which can make us better people. Diversity is also an evolutionary advantage. Having mutations and different genes allows a species to change and adapt to stressors. Losing this diversity can threaten a species' ability to survive over the long term. For these reasons, practices that could jeopardize diversity must be examined with a critical eye.

Genetic interventions can also contribute to class inequalities. The genetic interventions that are currently available are expensive, and the ones that will be available in the future will likely also be expensive. As such, they will be available only to people who have the financial means to pay for them—the rich. Subsequently, only the rich will have the means to genetically alter their children and give them traits that could make them even wealthier. The rich will have the means to eliminate diseases and disorders that prevent them from participating in life's activities. The poor, on the other hand, will not have access to genetic interventions or their benefits (assuming the only way to access genetic interventions is to pay for them ourselves). So, as critics assert, genetic interventions have the capacity to increase the existing gap between the wealthy and the poor, and because there is some connection between wealth and health (the wealthier you are the more likely you are to be healthy), these interventions may also increase the gap between healthy and unhealthy people.

## THE VALUE OF DISABILITIES

Genetic interventions, specifically genetic engineering, also challenge our views of disabilities and individuals with disabilities. Disabilities are commonly seen as things to be fixed or gotten rid of using the resources that are available to us. Some perspectives view people with disabilities as abnormal, as undesirable, or as having less well-being than people without disabilities. On the basis of these kinds of beliefs, we may be tempted to think that no one would want to intentionally bring a person into the world with a disability or even that it is wrong to knowingly bring people into the world with disabilities. Some scholars have argued that these kinds of beliefs fail to recognize an innate value for people with disabilities. These kinds of beliefs are mistakenly based on the idea that our world would be better without people with disabilities and that it would be better for people with disabilities if they did not exist. Beliefs like these fuel arguments that conclude we should use genetic interventions to eliminate disabilities such as Down syndrome.

These beliefs also lead to discrimination, stigmatization, and ostracism. For instance, if a physical condition can be eliminated before birth, then does having a disability become more stigmatized? If fewer people have a given trait, then those who have it become more ostracized. As a society, services are offered to help the differently abled navigate the world. Such services include braille signs, beeping walk signs, cut street corners, and elevators for wheelchairs. Many disability scholars argue that genetic engineering changes the person to fit society rather than adapting the lived environment for the real people who live within it. Because many communities of differently abled people have developed their cultures, is eliminating such traits from the gene pool a deliberate killing of a culture and way of life? And once most predictable differences can be eliminated, will it become child abuse for parents not to correct a foreseeable physical difference, such as deafness?

People typically have twenty-three pairs of chromosomes (a total of forty-six chromosomes), with each parent contributing half. According to the National Down

Syndrome Society, Down syndrome is the result of individuals having either a full or partial extra copy of the twenty-first chromosome. Genetic tests can determine whether embryos will have Down syndrome once they are brought to term and birthed.

If Down syndrome is seen as an unwanted disability, genetic therapy or genetic engineering could one day be used to eliminate Down syndrome by modifying embryos who show a likelihood of developing the disorder. Considering that Down syndrome is a good example of a disorder that some people stigmatize, it is quite possible that if more people could ensure that their children would not have Down syndrome, they would take that opportunity. This would leave few or possibly even no people with Down syndrome in the human population. Eliminating people with Down syndrome would limit diversity in the human population, thus limiting the kinds of people with whom we interact and narrowing the range of people we see on television and in magazines. Without people with Down syndrome, the world would be robbed of the richness that these individuals bring to the human population.

The lives of individuals with disabilities are intrinsically valuable, even if their lives do not benefit able-bodied people (i.e., people without disabilities) in any way. But we cannot ignore how individuals with disabilities do positively influence the lives of able-bodied people. In "The Case for Conserving Disability" (2012), Rosemarie Garland-Thomson upholds the value of disability and makes a case for preserving disabilities. One of her arguments is that, among other notable attributes, people with disabilities have rich narratives, or ways in which they experience the world. The lives of individuals with disabilities and their ability to challenge commonly held cultural standards of normalcy (which are often maintained and encouraged without reason) are to be valued rather than abolished.

Additionally, Garland-Thomson argues that people with disabilities challenge us to accept the unknowns and the unexpected events in life. Accepting people with disabilities as they are also shows all individuals, disabled or able-bodied, that we all have shortcomings. Whether we are poor runners, bad at math, or not the best at cooking a meal, we all have ways in which we fall short, but we all have a story worth telling. Overall, Garland-Thomson argues that although seemingly counterintuitive, disability is worth preserving because it forces us to face an "open future," an idea of our future selves that is not confined to expectations or concepts of normalcy, but one that is open to multiple possibilities.

## EUGENICS

Garland-Thomson's argument can be thought of as a counterargument to eugenics or as raising concerns about the reemergence of eugenics. Eugenics is the principle that certain desirable traits ought to be promoted in a population of humans, while certain other traits are undesirable and ought to be eliminated. Typically, supporters of eugenics propose that people who have the capacity to pass down certain genes that will result in undesirable traits, such as disabilities, should be discouraged or prevented from reproducing through medical intervention, such as sterilization.

In the first half of the twentieth century, eugenics was a driving force behind the Nazis' program to remove Jewish people from their homes, hold them in concentration camps, and eventually exterminate them. In the United States, eugenics stood behind efforts to force or encourage sterilization of Native Americans, African Americans, and people of all races who lived at institutions for the mentally disabled during much of the twentieth century.

Other than the classist and racist beliefs that formed the basic ideals of eugenics, one of the many problems with eugenics is that it is sometimes guided by incorrect ideas about genetics. Misguided beliefs about what kinds of traits can be passed on genetically to future generations ignore the importance of social environments to people's development. For example, past practices of eugenics were supported by misguided beliefs that laziness (which could lead to being poor), the devaluing of formal education (which could also lead to being poor), or uncontrollable sexual appetites (which could lead to individuals having the propensity to rape or to have more children than they could financially support) could all be passed genetically to future generations. The idea was that certain groups of people, such as African Americans, Latinos, or Jewish people, are more likely than other groups to have certain undesirable traits and, therefore, should not reproduce so that these traits can be eliminated from the collective human gene pool. Similar discriminatory beliefs about individuals with disabilities encouraged eugenics as well. The thought that individuals with disabilities ought to be eliminated from the population because their lives are "abnormal" and are not worth living encouraged eugenic actions against them.

Now genetic interventions face the charge that preventing or eliminating people with certain traits, including disabilities, is similar to practicing eugenics in the twenty-first century. How we use genetic interventions, now and in the future, reveals our social and cultural beliefs about what kinds of traits are not worth preserving, and ultimately, what kinds of individuals have moral worth. In essence, how we use genetic interventions reveals our biases. So when discussing the benefits and downsides of genetic interventions, we also have to consider the basis of our beliefs about certain kinds of traits and about people who are different from us, so that we do not repeat past misguided actions and perpetuate misguided ideologies, such as eugenics.

## Summary

Genetic interventions have the promise to significantly change the way that we view humans, including the limits of our cognitive and physical functioning. They also promise to change the way that we suffer from disease and from our natural shortcomings. But those promises must be balanced against the potential negative effects of genetic interventions. The promise of genetic interventions has to be weighed against social concerns, such as concerns for individuals with disabilities, concerns for our current and future children and our obligations to ensure their well-being, and concerns for growing disparities in economic wealth among social classes.

The promise of genetic interventions must also be weighed against safety concerns. Some genetic interventions are generally safe; however, some currently are not safe for humans and require more research into their safety and effectiveness. Because of safety concerns, as well as ethical and social concerns, many genetic interventions amount to wishful thinking. But in a sense, this is what science is all about; science as a field of study and as a practice concerns itself with using human ingenuity to turn ideas into reality. Science has made our lives easier, safer, and more enjoyable. The merits of genetic interventions have to be assessed for how they, too, can make life easier, safer, and more enjoyable. We can harbor a healthy dose of apprehension about genetic interventions without allowing fear to stifle human progress.

# Bibliography

Allen, Arthur. "Bioethics Comes of Age." *Salon.* 2000. http://www.salon.com/2000/09/28/caplan/.

Austin, Simon. "Lance Armstrong Is Said to Meet with USADA Chief in Bid to Cut Ban." *New York Times,* March 17, 2015. http://www.nytimes.com/2015/03/18/sports/cycling/lance-armstrong-is-said-to-meet-with-usada-chief-in-bid-to-cut-ban.html?_r=0.

Bognar, Greg. "When Philosophers Shoot Themselves in the Leg." *Ethics, Policy, and Environment* 15, no. 2 (2012): 222–224.

Buchanan, Allen, Dan W. Brock, Norman Daniels, et al. *From Chance to Choice: Genetics and Justice.* Cambridge: Cambridge University Press, 2000.

Bull, Andy. "Ye Shiwen's World Record Olympic Swim 'Disturbing,' Says Top US Coach." *Guardian* (London), July 30, 2012. http://www.theguardian.com/sport/2012/jul/30/ye-shiwen-world-record-olympics-2012.

Carroll, Rory. "Lance Armstrong Admits Doping in Oprah Winfrey Interview." *Guardian* (London), January 19, 2013. http://www.theguardian.com/sport/2013/jan/18/lance-armstrong-admits-doping-oprah-winfrey.

Colleton, Laura. "The Elusive Line between Enhancement and Therapy and Its Effects on Health Care." *U.S. Journal of Evolution and Technology* 18, no. 1 (2008): 70–78. http://jetpress.org/v18/colleton.htm.

Coune, Philippe G., Bernard L. Schneider, and Patrick Aebischer. "Parkinson's Disease: Gene Therapies." US National Library of Medicine, National Institutes of Health. 2012. http://www.ncbi.nlm.nih.gov/pmc/articles/PMC3312404/.

Cyranoski, David, and Sara Reardon. "Chinese Scientists Genetically Modify Human Embryos." *Nature,* April 22, 2015. http://www.nature.com/news/chinese-scientists-genetically-modify-human-embryos-1.17378?WT.mc_id=TWT_NatureNews.

Daniels, Norman. *Just Health Care.* New York: Cambridge University Press, 1985.

Daniels, Norman. "Normal Functioning and the Treatment-Enhancement Distinction." *Cambridge Quarterly of Healthcare Ethics* 9, no. 3 (2000): 309–322.

Elliott, Carl. *Better Than Well: American Medicine Meets the American Dream.* New York: Norton, 2005.

Friedman, Richard A. "Infidelity Lurks in Your Genes." *New York Times,* May 24, 2015. http://www.nytimes.com/2015/05/24/opinion/sunday/infidelity-lurks-in-your-genes.html?_r=0.

Galimidi, Rachel P., Joshua S. Klein, Maria S. Politzer, et al. "Intra-Spike Crosslinking Overcomes Antibody Evasion by HIV-1." *Cell* 160, no. 3 (2015): 433–446.

Gannett, Lisa. "The Human Genome Project." In *Stanford Encyclopedia of Philosophy,* edited by Edward N. Zalta. Winter 2008. http://plato.stanford.edu/archives/win2008/entries/human-genome/.

Garland-Thomson, Rosemarie. "The Case for Conserving Disability." *Bioethical Inquiry* 9, no. 3 (2012): 339–355.

Genetic Science Learning Center. "Challenges in Gene Therapy?" University of Utah. 2015. http://learn.genetics.utah.edu/content/genetherapy/gtchallenges/.

Genetic Science Learning Center. "Gene Therapy Success." University of Utah. 2015. http://learn.genetics.utah.edu/content/genetherapy/gtsuccess/.

Goering, Sara. "Eugenics." In *Stanford Encyclopedia of Philosophy,* edited by Edward N. Zalta. Fall 2014. http://plato.stanford.edu/archives/fall2014/entries/eugenics/.

Hancock, David. "Jose Canseco: 'Juiced.'" CBS News. August 5, 2008. http://www.cbsnews.com/news/jose-canseco-juiced/.

Hoch, Bryan. "Rodriguez Reveals he Cheated, Lied." MLB.com. February 10, 2009. http://m.mlb.com/news/article/3811116/.

Kass, Leon. "Ageless Bodies, Happy Souls." *New Atlantis: A Journal of Technology and Society* 2 (2003): 9–28. http://www.thenewatlantis.com/publications/ageless-bodies-happy-souls.

Lanphier, Edward, Fyodor Urnov, Sarah Ehlen Haecker, et al. "Don't Edit the Human Germ Line." *Nature* 519, no. 7544 (2015): 410–4111. http://www.nature.com/news/don-t-edit-the-human-germ-line-1.17111#/b4.

Liao, S. Matthew, Anders Sandberg, and Rebecca Roache. "Human Engineering and Climate Change." *Ethics, Policy and Environment* 15, no. 2 (2012): 206–221.

"Muscular Dystrophy." Mayo Clinic. 2014. http://www.mayoclinic.org/diseases-conditions/muscular-dystrophy/basics/definition/con-20021240.

Naish, John. "Genetically Modified Athletes: Forget Drugs. There Are Even Suggestions Some Chinese Athletes' Genes Are Altered to Make Them Stronger." *Daily Mail* (London), July 31, 2012. http://www.dailymail.co.uk/news/article-2181873/Genetically-modified-athletes-Forget-drugs-There-suggestions-Chinese-athletes-genes-altered-make-stronger.html.

National Human Genome Research Institute. "Germ Line Gene Transfer". 2006. http://www.genome.gov/10004764.

National Institutes of Health. "NIH Researchers Tackle Thorny Side of Gene Therapy." 2015. http://www.nih.gov/news/health/jan2015/nhgri-20.htm.

Plenke, Max. "A Team of Biohackers Has Figured Out How to Inject Your Eyeballs with Night Vision." Science.Mic. March 25, 2015. http://mic.com/articles/113740/a-team -of-biohackers-has-figured-out-how-to-inject-your-eye balls-with-night-vision.

Poston, Dudley L., Jr., Eugenia Conde, and Bethany DeSalvo. "China's Unbalanced Sex Ratio at Birth, Millions of Excess Bachelors and Societal Implications." *Vulnerable Children and Youth Studies* 6, no. 4 (2011): 314–320.

President's Council on Bioethics. "Human Genetic Enhancement." December 2002. https://bioethicsarchive.george town.edu/pcbe/background/humangenetic.html.

Ramsey, Paul. *The Fabricated Man: The Ethics of Genetic Control.* New Haven, CT: Yale University Press, 1970.

Regalado, Antonio. "Engineering the Perfect Baby." *MIT Technology Review,* March 5, 2015. http://www.techno logyreview.com/featuredstory/535661/engineering-the-per fect-baby/.

Sandel, Michael. "The Case against Perfection." *Atlantic Monthly* 293, no. 3 (2004): 51–62. http://www.theatlan tic.com/magazine/archive/2004/04/the-case-against-per fection/302927/.

Sander, Jeffrey D., and Keith Joung. "CRISPR-Cas Systems for Editing, Regulating and Targeting Genomes." *Nature Biotechnology* 32, no. 4 (2014): 347–355.

Savulescu, Julian. "Harm Ethics Committees and the Gene Therapy Death." *Journal of Medical Ethics* 27, no. 3 (2001): 148–150. http://jme.bmj.com/content/27/3/148.full.

Savulescu, Julian. "Procreative Beneficence: Why We Should Select the Best Children." *Bioethics* 15, nos. 5/6 (2001): 413–426.

Savulescu, Julian, and Guy Kahane. "The Moral Obligation to Create Children with the Best Chance of the Best Life." *Bioethics* 23, no. 5 (2009): 274–290.

Schrotenboer, Brent. "Lance Armstrong to Oprah: Story Was 'One Big Lie.'" *USA Today,* January 18, 2013. http://www .usatoday.com/story/sports/cycling/2013/01/17/lance-arm strong-oprah-winfrey-confession/1843641/.

Singleton, Marilyn M. "The 'Science' of Eugenics: America's Moral Detour." *Journal of American Physicians and Surgeons* 19, no. 4 (2014). Video presentation. https:// www.youtube.com/watch?v=VE0BtSSusIM.

"Types of Gene Therapy." Gene Therapy Net.com. 2015. http://www.genetherapynet.com/types-of-gene-therapy .html.

Universal Declaration on the Human Genome and Human Rights. 1997. http://portal.unesco.org/en/ev.php-URL_ID=1 3177&URL_DO=DO_TOPIC&URL_SECTION=201.html.

University of Missouri. "Gene Therapy and Genetic Engineering." School of Medicine. 2011. http://ethics.mis souri.edu/gene-therapy.aspx.

Walters, LeRoy. "Genetics and Bioethics: How Our Thinking Has Changed since 1969." *Theoretical Medicine and Bioethics* 33, no. 1 (2012): 83–95.

Wolpe, Paul Root. "Treatment, Enhancement, and the Ethics of Neurotherapies." *Brain and Cognition* 50, no. 3 (2002): 387–395.

Zhang, Sarah. "Everything You Need to Know about CRISPR, The New Tool That Edits DNA." Gizmodo.com. 2015. http://gizmodo.com/everything-you-need-to-know-about -crispr-the-new-tool-1702114381.

## FILM/TELEVISION/LITERATURE

*Alien: Resurrection.* Dir. Jean-Pierre Jeunet. 1997. Story of a half human/half alien woman.

*Bubble Boy.* Dir. Blair-Hayes. 2011. A boy, born without an immune system, must live his life in a bubble that protects him from infection.

*Captain America: The First Avenger.* Dir. Joe Johnston. 2011. An average man becomes a super-soldier in World War II after being engineered by scientists.

*Gattaca.* Dir. Andrew Niccol. 1997. The dangers of eugenics and genetic selection are highlighted through its main character, who was not conceived using genetic selection.

*Godsend.* Dir. Nick Hamm. 2004. A couple allows a scientist to clone their dead son, and the cloned son exhibits troubling behavior.

*I Am Legend.* Dir. Francis Lawrence. 2007. Based on the 1954 novel by Richard Matheson. A military scientist in New York tries to find a cure for the disease that has turned humans into night creatures.

*The Island of Dr. Moreau.* Dir. Don Taylor. 1977. A scientist on a remote island creates individuals who are a cross between humans and animals.

*The Lazarus Effect.* Dir. David Gelb. 2015. Researchers create a serum that can bring people back from the dead.

*The Simpsons.* "The Man Who Grew Too Much." Season 25, episode 13, 2014. Dir. Matthew Schofield.

Wells, H. G. *The Island of Dr. Moreau.* New York: Bantam Classics, 1994. First published 1896.

CHAPTER 6

# *Neuroethics*

**Karen S. Rommelfanger**
*Director, Center for Ethics Neuroethics Program; Assistant Professor,
Department of Neurology (School of Medicine) and Department of
Psychiatry and Behavioral Sciences
Emory University, Atlanta, GA*

**Julia Marshall**
*Graduate Student, Department of Psychology
Yale University, New Haven, CT*

**Paul Root Wolpe**
*Director, Center for Ethics; Professor, Departments of Medicine and
Pediatrics (School of Medicine) and Department of Sociology
Emory University, Atlanta, GA*

In the movie *Limitless*, an average man finds himself in possession of a pill, NZT, that gives him access to 100 percent of the computing capacity of his brain. For twelve hours, he is the smartest person in the universe. Unfortunately, the side effects are severe and deadly. The movie and the follow-up television show explore the lives of characters who take this pill. NZT does not exist, but some people in the real world take modafinil to seek a similar effect. A far distant second, modafinil is a narcolepsy drug used to promote alertness and wakefulness, which has gained a reputation for enhancing cognition, although it is not approved for such use. Still we see that what we once thought was purely science fiction has become less so with the rapid advances in neuroscience.

## HISTORY AND BACKGROUND OF NEUROETHICS

Research on the brain has been one of the fastest-growing areas in science since the mid-1990s. New technologies and more sophisticated analyses of "big data" have contributed to unprecedented insight into the structures and functions of the human brain. With the brain being the seat of self and identity, perhaps it is not surprising that many of these studies have challenged people's most cherished notions of themselves—notions such as the existence of free will, the nature of self and identity, how people make ethical decisions, and questions of agency and responsibility for action. As introduced above, neuroscience has also suggested some new mechanisms for manipulating cognitive and affective functioning, providing potentially powerful tools for human enhancement. In response to these and other questions generated by the increasing power of neuroscience and neurotechnology, the field of neuroethics was established and has been growing rapidly. In a relatively short time, it has become a significant contributor to the dialogue on thorny questions that arise as neuroscientific findings and neurotechnologies have begun to migrate out of laboratories and into society.

## DEFINITION OF NEUROETHICS

The term *neuroethics* was first used in clinical settings and was coined by Harvard Medical School physician Anneliese A. Pontius (1922–) in the paper "Neuro-ethics of 'Walking' in the Newborn" (Pontius 1973; Racine 2010). Pontius described concerns with "performance enhancement" interventions to accelerate walking abilities in newborns and emphasized the need to attend to neuroethical discourse: "In the present context, this concept [neuroethics] stresses the importance of being aware of neurological facts and implications while experimenting with the newborns' motility" (1973, 244).

The American neurologist Ronald Cranford (1941–2006) used the term in 1989 in relation to the role of the neurologist in clinical ethical discourse. Cranford called for a "neuroethicist" or "neuroethics consultant," by which he meant a neurologist who had an affinity for bioethical issues, becomes an active member of ethics committees at the institutional level, or acts as a consultant.

At the beginning of the twenty-first century, a group of bioethicists and neuroscientists recognized that the ethical and social questions neuroscience was generating were not limited to clinical medicine, and they established the field of neuroethics to explore those questions. The term *neuroethics* was popularized by the journalist William Safire (1929–2009), who wrote about neuroethics in his regular *New York Times* column. Safire was chairman of the Dana Foundation, an organization dedicated to promoting neuroscience for scientists and the public. In 2002, a seminal year in establishing the field, meetings of neuroscientists and ethicists were held by the University of Pennsylvania, the Royal Society of London, and Stanford University in partnership with the Dana Foundation.

The Stanford/Dana conference Neuroethics: Mapping the Field (2002) played a key role in the development of neuroethics. At this meeting, an interdisciplinary network of scholars and practitioners from neuroscience, law, and ethics met to discuss the accumulating impacts of neuroscience on society. It was here that Safire (2002) defined neuroethics "as a distinct portion of bioethics, which is the consideration of good and bad consequence in medical practice and biological research. But the specific ethics of brain science hits home as research on no other organ does."

Shortly after this meeting, philosopher Adina Roskies (1966–) described neuroethics as consisting of two distinct areas of inquiry (2002): (1) the "neuroscience of ethics," in which neuroscience uses its tools and theories to understand how humans engage in ethical reasoning and, eventually, behaviors; and (2) the "ethics of neuroscience," in which the ethical implications of emerging neurotechnologies and neuroscientific inquiry on society are discussed. Since then, other definitions of neuroethics have been proffered, such as "the examination of how we want to deal with the social issues of disease, normality, mortality, lifestyle, and the philosophy of living informed by our understanding of underlying brain mechanisms" (Gazzaniga 2004, xv). The exact boundaries of this new field of inquiry are still being debated, but its focus on the social and ethical implications of scientific and medical research on the brain, as well as on new technologies to understand and manipulate brain function, is well accepted.

Neuroethics is an interdisciplinary field that draws contributions from philosophers, sociologists, ethicists, neurologists, psychiatrists, neuroscientists, legal scholars, and policy makers, among others. It discusses topics ranging from brain imaging and the nature of self to the challenges of deep brain stimulation for depression, the use of pharmaceuticals for lifestyle enhancement, and debates over the neurological basis of criminality. With such a wide-ranging set of questions being explored by such a diversity of scholars, it is not surprising that there is still discussion over the exact definition of the field. Professional journals, professional societies, and even governmental bodies have accepted neuroethics as an important voice in determining the impact of the ever-growing understanding of the nature of the human brain.

## THE IMPORTANCE OF NEUROETHICS AS A FIELD

Early in the establishment of the field of neuroethics, some argued that research into the ethics of neuroscience was simply a subdiscipline of bioethics in general and not worthy of a new name and field (Rees and Rose 2004). But it quickly became clear that emerging neurotechnologies and new findings about brain function not only raised new ethical issues but also framed older bioethical questions in a new light. Defenders, such as the cognitive neuroscientist Martha Farah (1955–) and the sociologist Paul Root Wolpe (1957–), argued that "the brain is the organ of the mind and consciousness, the locus of our sense of selfhood.... Our moral and legal conceptions of responsibility are likewise susceptible to change as our understanding of the physical mechanisms of behavior evolves" (Farah and Wolpe 2004, 36).

For example, neuroscience studies on the nature of free will and brain development are challenging the current system of sentencing and punishment, especially of adolescents, and the courts have begun to take these findings into consideration. Other studies have questioned how persistent vegetative states and even brain death are defined. Clearly, studies of the brain have different implications than studies of any other part of the body.

Despite progress, understanding of the complexity of the brain has barely begun. As the neuroscience enterprise continues to grow, and as recognition of the brain's unfolding complexities increases, an ongoing ethical discourse on the practical problems and conceptual questions that arise becomes ever more crucial.

One of the purposes of bioethical inquiry is to anticipate future problems in science and medicine so that one can preempt problems or have solutions in hand when they arise. At times, therefore, neuroethicists may ask questions that appear far-fetched or years in the future given the current state of neurotechnology. However, it is important to acknowledge the speed at which neuroscience is advancing and assume that some of these ethical questions will become important in the future. One does not want to be caught short trying to avoid ethical problems after the technology is already in widespread use.

**American and European Initiatives.** For example, in 2013 President Barack Obama launched the BRAIN (Brain Research through Advancing Innovative Neurotechnologies) Initiative. The BRAIN Initiative's budget of more than US$300 million marked a turning point in the government's neuroscientific interest. The initiative, which aims to develop new technologies that will help people better understand brain circuitry and connectivity, will speed the "development of exciting new tools and technologies to understand how [brain] circuits work," according to National Institutes of Health (NIH) director Francis Collins (Regalado 2014). As he unveiled the project, President Obama commented, "There is an enormous mystery waiting to be unlocked, and the BRAIN Initiative will change that by giving scientists the tools they need to get a dynamic picture of the brain in action and

***US president Barack Obama shakes hands with National Institutes of Health director Francis S. Collins during a White House event announcing the administration's Brain Research through Advancing Innovative Neurotechnologies (BRAIN) Initiative, April 2, 2013.*** *The BRAIN initiative aims to develop new technologies that will promote better understanding of brain circuitry and connectivity. Neuroethics as a field is positioned to be the forum and the repository of social and ethical conversation and scholarship as exploration of the brain moves forward.* **MOLLY RILEY/AP IMAGES.**

better understand how we think, learn, and remember. That knowledge will be transformative" (Mooney 2013).

At the same time, President Obama tasked his Presidential Commission for the Study of Bioethical Issues (PCSBI) to explore the bioethical implications of the development of these advanced neurotechnologies. The work of the PCSBI culminated in two reports titled *Gray Matters* that discuss how the government should integrate neuroethical critique and considerations throughout the life of any neuroscience research endeavor. In the first report, the commission outlined four broad areas of interest: (1) neuroimaging and brain privacy; (2) dementia, personality, and changed preferences; (3) cognitive enhancement and justice; and (4) deep brain stimulation and the ethically difficult history of psychosurgery (topics discussed in more detail later in the text). The decision to task the PCSBI to set some ethical guidelines at the announcement of the emerging BRAIN Initiative and the more recent creation of a neuroethics advisory body, the NIH BRAIN Neuroethics Workgroup, emphasizes the importance of integrating neuroethics into the neuroscience enterprise.

The European Union has also prioritized funding brain-related research in the European Commission's Human Brain Project (HBP), which was established in 2013.

This €1.2 billion project is organized into thirteen subprojects, including theoretical neuroscience, neuroinformatics, brain stimulation, and high-performance computing, with an overarching goal to re-create a virtual human brain. The HBP has dedicated approximately 3 percent of its funding to addressing ethical issues. Controversy has swirled around the HBP, as scientists express frustration with the project's emphasis on simulations and building massive infrastructure (Frégnac and Laurent 2014).

What is clear from both the BRAIN and HBP enterprises, however, is that scientists have recognized the importance of addressing ethical issues in the brain sciences at the beginning of these massive undertakings. Neuroethics as a field is positioned to be the forum and the repository of social and ethical conversation and scholarship as the exploration of the brain moves forward.

**Public Interest.** Not only has neuroscience captured the minds of scientists, lawyers, ethicists, and the government, but it has also captivated the popular imagination, for better or for worse. As neuroscience news coverage has steadily increased in recent years, the public's interest in matters related to the brain has grown (O'Connor, Rees, and Joffe 2012). However, as brain science is featured in the media, some typical mistakes and misunderstandings have emerged when journalists and researchers try to convey neuroscience findings to the public (Racine 2010).

One prominent error has been called *neurorealism.* This fallacy occurs when one indicates that a psychological phenomenon such as pain, love, or anger truly exists because it appears on a brain scan. Such a biological approach may not provide any scientific insights or validation of psychological states better than asking someone if he or she is in love to ascertain if that person is in fact in love, yet the general public often believes that brain data are especially true or important simply because of their sophistication and complexity. Media representations of brain research often leave the public with an inaccurate understanding of the limitations of neuroscience research and result in misinterpretations about the nature of the mind, providing yet another example of why neuroethics remains a specialized field positioned to tackle specific questions about the intersection of brain sciences and ethics.

# OVERVIEW OF PRIMARY AREAS OF DISCUSSION IN NEUROETHICS

The field of neuroethics aims to tackle a wide array of issues, from distinguishing between medical treatment and enhancement to exploring the origin and nature of free will. This section discusses two primary neuroethical domains. The first, research and clinical neuroethics, largely deals with how researchers conduct neuroscientific research, including how subjects are protected and data are handled after a study's completion. Clinical considerations include the application of neurotechnologies to patients. The second, theoretical neuroethics, explores neuroscience's role in informing philosophical debates, including concepts such as free will and how ethical decisions are made.

## RESEARCH AND CLINICAL NEUROETHICS

Because of the unique nature of the brain, many sensitive neuroethical issues arise in neuroscience research. How should researchers in both clinical and nonclinical settings conduct neuroscientific research, and how should they protect and use the vast amounts of data they collect? Although these kinds of issues also arise in other kinds of human subject experimentation, neuroscience has some unique challenges. This section looks at three: informed consent, data management, and incidental findings.

**Informed Consent.** All humans engaged in research must be given full informed consent, meaning that all known risks involved in the research are clearly described to them, and they have full ability to decline participation without any kind of penalty. Of course, that also means that subjects must have the full capacity to understand the information, that they are not, for example, mentally impaired. Informed consent is uniquely challenging in neuroscience research because an individual's neurological or psychiatric condition might interfere with clear understanding of the consent form or explanation, or a patient is in a state that does not allow for verbal or written consent (Beauchamp and Childress 2001). Neurological disorders and psychiatric disorders might interfere to varying degrees with decision-making capacity.

In addition, some medical interventions in the brain might have effects on a patient's personality and autonomy. For example, one patient receiving experimental deep brain stimulation (DBS) for Parkinson's disease did have his symptoms alleviated when the DBS stimulation was turned on, but he also developed impulsive behavior that required psychiatric institutionalization. With the DBS electrode off, on the other hand, the patient was bedridden, frozen, and unable to move. The physicians were then faced with the question of whether to make the decision themselves or whether to ask the patient what he wanted to do, and when asking the patient, whether to ask when he had the stimulator turned on or off. Ultimately, the patient chose to be institutionalized with the stimulator on (Leentjens 2004). This is just one example of the need for neuroethical discourse in discussing future developments in neurological and psychiatric research and treatment.

**Privacy and Data Management.** Researchers, ethicists, and policy makers must also collaborate to determine how to manage and access the large amounts of data collected in neuroscientific research. Because brain-imaging studies are difficult to interpret, studies of sensitive areas can be misused and misunderstood by the public or by policy makers. In addition, brain scans of subjects contain information of a personal nature, sometimes even more personal than the subjects or researchers realize at the time, which can have legal, employment, or health-care insurance impacts. For these reasons, protecting the data generated in these studies can be important.

For example, brain-imaging studies have examined psychological traits such as unconscious racial attitudes (Hart et al. 2000; Phelps et al. 2000), sexual attraction and attempts to suppress attraction (Beauregard, Levesque, and Bourgouin 2001), and correlates of personality such as extraversion, neuroticism, risk aversion, pessimism, and empathy (Canli et al. 2002; Canli et al. 2001; Fischer et al. 2001; Johnson et al. 1999; Singer et al. 2004; Sugiura et al. 2000). Studies have even examined the neurocognitive correlates of kindergarteners' socioeconomic status (Noble, Norman, and Farah 2005).

To the researcher, these kinds of studies are often preliminary, results are inferred, and the number of subjects is small. But brain images are often interpreted by the public as more objective and accurate than they actually are (Dumit 2004). As the technology becomes more sophisticated, results of these studies could easily confuse employers, mislead juries, and be misused by law enforcement (Farah and Wolpe 2004). As impressive as some of these studies look, the technology generally cannot make predictions about future behaviors or even assess past behaviors, so these data could prove damaging taken out of the research context. Concerns about these issues, as well as data ownership, have spawned an area of interest called *neuroprivacy* and will necessitate conversation on how to protect privacy in both the short and long term (Ward 2011).

**Incidental Findings.** Finally, brain-imaging research can generate "incidental findings," that is, brain abnormalities unrelated to the goal of the experiment that are discovered during the course of the research project. Incidental findings have been identified in 2 to 8 percent of volunteers assumed to be healthy (Katzman, Dagher, and Patronas 1999; Kim et al. 2002; Weber and Knopf 2006), and so researchers have been developing ethical safeguards for such incidental findings. For example, a brain scan on a research volunteer in a cognitive study might uncover what appears to be an abnormality suggesting a brain tumor. The question arises whether the researchers, who are often not physicians, have a responsibility to report the abnormality to the volunteer or to the volunteer's primary care physician. Importantly, what if the volunteer does not wish to know, or what if a visit to a hospital does not reveal the tumor? As studies using neurotechnologies to identify characteristics of the brain increase, neuroethicists will need to continue to examine the unique contexts under which incidental findings may impact research volunteers.

## THEORETICAL NEUROETHICS

Questions of the nature of the mind are primarily the domain of the philosophy of mind. Modern neuroscience, however, is beginning to make inroads to these formerly purely philosophical questions, and though such questions are not fully within the field of neuroethics, their implications can influence how people think about morality and ethical behavior.

**The Mind-Body Problem.** In *The Matrix* films, the perceived world of humans is merely a simulation. Humans are cyborg slaves to a computer-generated universe. Moving one's "hand" moves a computer-generated hand, not the real thing. This image relates to some of the most puzzling and powerful of human questions: questions about the nature of the self—of consciousness, of identity, and of the relation of the concept of the self and will (mind) to its rootedness in the body. Philosophers have long contemplated the question of how the seemingly immaterial mind can effect changes in the material body. When I think, "I'll move my hand," how does the "mind" cause the brain to activate the motor cortex and my hand to move?

The mind-body problem has implications for the kinds of neurological interventions one might find ethical. Psychologist Henry Rutgers Marshall (1852–1927) argued (1904) that there is no inherent sense of self, that self is mutable and changing and is made up of various brain functions from which individuals construct the self in order to have a sense of coherence. With that perspective, brain enhancement does not generally threaten the sense of self because, even if it changes aspects of how individuals experience the self, those aspects can be assimilated into a new sense of self, which is in any case always changing.

Other concerns of the philosophy of mind—the nature of consciousness, the commonality of subjective experience (e.g., whether one's experience of the color red is the same as another person's, called *qualia*), and so on—are discussed and debated below, alongside discussions of neuroethics, and each to some degree informs the other.

**The Moral Brain.** Moral questions often elicit fervent debate and come in a variety of flavors. Is it morally wrong to not donate to charity? Is it morally right to kill one to save many? What if the person you have to kill is a close family member? Less abstractly and perhaps more timely, is the government morally obligated to provide health care to its citizens? At first, it may seem difficult to see how neuroscience can help to resolve these questions, and, in fact, it is difficult to argue that neuroscience has answered any of these questions. Nonetheless, neuroscientific methods, alongside behavioral research, have helped to elucidate why these questions may emerge in the first place.

Philosophy has been in the business of explaining and justifying moral distinctions for decades. For instance, philosophers (Kamm 1991) have proposed that allowing harm to happen is just as bad as inflicting harm, yet intuition sometimes suggests otherwise. Is throwing a drowning person a life preserver as morally wrong as pushing someone into the sea? Another distinction that has occupied philosophers is that intention and motivation matter; more specifically, similar actions with analogous consequences are not equally punishable if one action occurred accidentally. People's intuitions happen to coincide with this distinction; they find a person who premeditatively poisons and kills her husband more punishable than a person who gives a peanut-butter sandwich to a person who (unbeknownst to the sandwich-giver) is deathly allergic to nuts. Why do moral intuitions sometimes misalign with moral philosophy? Such a problem has motivated the growth of both moral psychology and the neuroscience of morality, as both disciplines are primarily interested in mapping the human moral terrain: when do moral intuitions match moral philosophical tenets, and when do they not?

*Trolleyology.* One of the most popular examples of substantiating a philosophical distinction in psychological and neurological terms is now commonly referred to as *trolleyology.* This body of work has its origin in a famous dilemma: A runaway trolley car is on a track where five individuals stand, and, unless a switch is activated changing the course of the trolley, they will be killed. However, pulling the switch redirects the trolley onto a track where one individual will be killed. Most respondents indicate that it is ethical to flip the switch, saving five even if causing a single death.

In a variant of this situation called the Footbridge Dilemma, respondents are asked to consider the same scenario of the runaway trolley, but here they are on a footbridge and can push one heavyset individual off the bridge onto the tracks to halt the trolley from killing the five individuals. Most respondents say that pushing the individual off a footbridge to save the five is unethical. Yet both scenarios result in one death to save five; why do people believe it is ethical to pull the switch but not to push the man off the bridge?

Joshua Greene and colleagues (2001) posited that these dilemmas tap into some human cognition distinction: the Footbridge Dilemma requires physically precipitating an action, whereas the Trolley Dilemma does not necessitate personally injuring another human being. The former type of moral scenario has hence been called a "personal" dilemma and the latter an "impersonal" dilemma.

In both scenarios, personal and impersonal, a choice to intervene (pull the switch or push the fat man off the bridge) has been described as a utilitarian decision. Utilitarianism in its simple form refers to the normative ethical stance that it is most right to save the greatest amount of lives or do the most amount of good. Thus, a choice to push the man or flip the switch is a utilitarian decision because doing either action saves the most amount of lives. A decision to not push the man or not flip the switch has been described as a deontological

***Illustration of the ethical dilemma known as the trolley problem: a runaway trolley car will claim the lives of five individuals, unless it is redirected to a track where only one person will be killed.*** *In a variant of this situation, respondents are asked to consider the same scenario of the runaway trolley, with a twist: they are on a footbridge and can push one person off the bridge onto the tracks to halt the trolley from killing the five individuals. Although both scenarios result in one death to save five, most respondents viewed the ethics of these actions quite differently, giving credence to the distinction between personal and impersonal dilemmas.* **CENGAGE LEARNING.**

decision, which is determined by rules or principles of what is morally right or wrong. One might see pushing the fat man off the bridge as actively killing someone, which violates the rule not to kill, even if it means saving other lives.

***Implications of Trolleyology.*** What is most fascinating about trolleyology is that in both versions of the scenario one life is pitted against five, yet intuitions, or gut feelings, about how to act in either case diverge. For this reason, psychologists have posited that there must be some sort of cognitively meaningful distinction between the two cases. The behavioral distinction between the two cases is relatively easy to illustrate; one can simply ask people whether it is morally permissible to flip the switch or push the person.

Perhaps more surprisingly, in a groundbreaking study, Greene and colleagues (2001) found that the distinction between impersonal and personal dilemmas emerged in neural responses as well. They found that the variations in responses to these scenarios with identical outcomes were related to differential activation in regions of the brain related to emotional processing. Responses to personal dilemmas elicited activation from areas of the brain associated with emotional processing, whereas responses to impersonal ones did not. In fact, the researchers found that the brain activation of participants responding to impersonal moral dilemmas was more similar to control dilemmas that included no moral content—such as choosing a pen over a pencil. To put it another way, these data lead to the following hypothesis: when people decide whether to pull the switch, they draw primarily on their rational, calculating circuitry of the brain, whereas when they consider pushing a person off a bridge, their emotional brain responses become primary.

In sum, trolleyology used a long-debated philosophical distinction between either personally or impersonally inflicting harm in addition to utilitarianism and deontology as a foundation to systematically map people's varying moral intuitions. Neuroscience research found that people demonstrated a strong preference for utilitarian decisions in impersonal scenarios and an opposite preference for deontological choices in personal scenarios. Neural data also supported an argument for the separation between utilitarian and deontological decision making. The neuroscience research helped illuminate and clarify a distinction that philosophers had debated for centuries by infusing the debate with information about the neural processes underlying utilitarian and deontological decision making.

Trolleyology, however, has not been immune to criticism. One criticism of such work is called the normative fallacy, a mistake in which someone infers that something ought to be a certain way because it has been found to be a certain way. For example, a researcher could find that the majority of people do not give to charity; however, that descriptive finding does not mean that people should not give to charity. In the context of trolleyology, one might wrongly conclude that it is immoral to push the man off the footbridge simply because most people make such a determination in most circumstances. Descriptive sciences like neuroscience can only give information about how people make ethical decisions; they cannot recommend or verify what is ethically right or wrong. What is ethical or not is a normative activity, that is, based on social and ideological values of the right and the good, which is not the realm of science in most cases. Scientific inquiry into moral cognition is therefore unlikely to put moral philosophers out of business.

Inquiry into moral cognition is not limited to the trolley problem; researchers continue to craft innovative ways to map people's moral intuitions and beliefs. For instance, they are now exploring how early in life people learn what is right and wrong or whether they are born already equipped to judge certain actions as morally right or wrong. Researchers have discovered that even infants prefer actors who help versus neutral characters (Hamlin, Wynn, and Bloom 2007). Neuroscientific inquiry into morality still has lessons to teach as it partners with other fields to try to understand exactly how human beings make moral decisions.

**Free Will.** For millennia human beings have grappled with the question of whether they have free will. Religion, especially Christianity, has grappled with the question as well. If God is omniscient, then God knows what decisions humans will make. But if God knows what decisions humans will make, then those decisions are already decided in some sense: people cannot make a decision other than the one God knows they will make. What then does it mean to say people have free will?

The question has also been prominent in philosophy, even from Presocratic times. Early determinists such as Democritus (c. 460–c. 370 BCE) wanted to wrest control of human fate from the gods, but in so doing he suggested that all things were determined materially and through "logical necessity" (the idea that everything that happens has a reason and must be the way it is). The idea was refuted by Aristotle (384–322 BCE), who brought the idea of chance or accident into human events as a fundamental explanation for actions. Aristotle's position suggested that there could be origins of things that were fundamentally uncaused by other things. (Though he did not grapple with free will per se, Epicurus [341–270 BCE], following Aristotle, taught that human beings could make autonomous decisions.) That dispute began a millennia-long conversation in philosophy over the nature of free will, whether human beings have it and to what degree.

Modern philosophy also engaged those questions, most famously through the dualism theory of the philosopher René Descartes (1596–1650), who gave the first systematic account of the relationship of the mind and body. Cartesian dualism (that is, dualism based on Descartes) holds that the immaterial mind and the material body are made of two different types of substances, though the two can interact. But it raises the question of exactly how a material brain influences an immaterial mind, or how a thought (I want to pick up my hand) translates into neural impulses in one's motor cortex such that one's hand goes up. Cartesian dualism has been credited (or blamed) for strongly influencing Western philosophy, and in many ways philosophers and neuroscientists still grapple with the questions of the nature of the physical brain and what seems to be a separate, nonmaterial mind.

In more recent years, neuroscience has reframed the question: How can a brain, subject to material and mechanical forces, generate free will? If all thought processes are determined by brain function, how can a person have an element of deciding separate from the deterministic functions of neurons firing in particular ways and patterns? Benjamin Libet (1916–2007), a pioneer in studies of consciousness and free will (Libet 1993), asked participants to report when they first became conscious of their desire to commit a volitional act, such as flexing a finger. At the same time, electrical recordings from the scalp using an electroencephalogram (EEG) traced cortical brain activity. A well-established electrical signal, the *Bereitschaftspotential* or readiness potential (Polich 2007; Verleger, Jaskowski, and Wascher 2005), has been shown to precede volitional movement. Libet found that participants reported becoming conscious of their desire to move their finger after the readiness potential had been recorded, suggesting that the participant became "aware" of wanting to move after the brain had already "decided" to move. In other words, "conscious" decisions may be no more than the brain informing one's awareness of what it has already decided.

Data such as these could suggest that human experience, free will, identity, and personhood could be simply interpreted as activity in the brain (Farah and Heberlein 2007; Gazzaniga 2011; Levy 2007). These data provoked an ongoing conversation about "free will" in neuroscience and neurophilosophy and generated much debate over how to interpret work such as Libet's. Some have refuted Libet's interpretation and suggested that there is still room for free will in neurological functioning (Nahmias 2014). The implications of these debates are real; how responsible people are for their acts has implications, for example, in law and jurisprudence, where criminal responsibility and personal agency are determined (the legal implications of neuroscience findings are discussed later).

**Neurotheology.** Almost all academic disciplines have puzzled over human religious behavior and have wondered why human beings have such a powerful impulse to organize around beliefs in higher powers and ritual. The ubiquity of religious behavior has led many to suggest that it might be hardwired in the brain (Wolpe 2006). Studies have begun to examine neural correlates to religiosity (Harris et al. 2009). Researcher Andrew Newberg and colleagues (2002) imaged the brains of Buddhist monks and nuns when they reached transcendent peaks or felt the presence of God. The researchers found that the portions of the brain that orient people in space and give a sense of being separate from one's surrounding environment were inhibited in meditators' brains when they reached a feeling of transcendence. Such studies have ushered in the new field of neurotheology, which looks at the correlates of human religious experience in the brain.

In Daryl Gregory's 2014 novel *Afterparty*, a designer drug recipe can be downloaded and printed out. A new drug called "numinous" is wreaking havoc because users find the "God center" of the brain permanently stimulated, giving them not only spiritual experiences but also their own personal imagined deity. Similarly, studies of religious experiences have popularized the notion of "God in the brain" (Biello 2007) and contributed to the idea that spirituality resides entirely in the brain (Beauregard and Paquette 2006). Epilepsy researchers such as Michael Persinger (1984) have noted that some patients felt they experienced God during their epileptic attacks. Using transcranial magnetic stimulation (TMS), a way of stimulating discrete areas of the brain by sending in electromagnetic impulses, Persinger and colleagues even managed to re-create religious or spiritual experiences in the brains of normal volunteers (Persinger et al. 2010). Neuromaterialists have therefore suggested that religious experience, and religion itself, are no more than humans' interpretations of brain impulses (Pinker 2003; Seybold 2005). As Steven Pinker puts it,

> Neuroscience is showing that all aspects of mental life—every emotion, every thought pattern, every memory—can be tied to the physiological activity or structure of the brain. Cognitive science has shown that feats that were formerly thought to be doable by mental stuff alone can be duplicated by machines, that motives and goals can be understood in terms of feedback and cybernetic mechanisms, and that thinking can be understood as a kind of computation. (in Gillespie and Bailey 2002)

Others refute that idea, offering various other interpretations of the religious experience outside a purely materialist one. They suggest, for example, that God designed people's brains to be able to perceive the Divine (Cunningham 2011; Newberg et al. 2002). Ultimately, the ability to experience religiosity has raised two primary questions, best summed up by the article titled "Is Our Brain Hardwired to Produce God, or Is Our Brain Hardwired to Perceive God?" (Fingelkurts and Fingelkurts 2009).

## SOCIETAL CONTEXTS FOR NEUROETHICS

Neuroscience continues to make its way into daily life. Seemingly no domain of society—from the clinical and legal contexts to commercial and national defense applications—is untouched by new neuroscience findings and emerging neurotechnologies.

### MIND READING

The idea of another creature being able to read one's innermost thoughts has always both intrigued and scared human beings. In Japanese mythology, monsters called Satori lurk in forests and confront people by relating back to them their thoughts as fast as the victim can think of them. Vampires, some mermaids, harpies, and elves have all been given the ability to read minds in some legends. Mr. Spock in *Star Trek* could "mind meld" to read others' thoughts, as can a variety of characters in horror movies (Freddy Krueger in *A Nightmare on Elm Street*), comic books (Charles Xavier in *X-Men*), and television (a variety of creatures in *Buffy the Vampire Slayer*), as well as video games and anime.

In more modern times, the fear that the government has the ability to read citizens' minds has been a common part of conspiracy theories and is believed by some people with mental illnesses. Although brain imaging has made some inroads into the ability to apprehend the subjective thoughts, perceptions, and states of people's brains, the research is still fairly crude and almost always involves people cooperating with the researcher while lying still in brain-imaging machines. Still, such developments raise pressing ethical questions about who should have access to such technologies should they become more sophisticated (Wolpe 2010).

**fMRI.** Technologies such as functional magnetic resonance imaging (fMRI) provide a noninvasive way for researchers to image an entire brain as a subject engages in certain tasks. Functional MRI is perhaps the most important internal imaging technology since the X-ray. Studies utilizing fMRI and other technologies can peer into the brain's activity and reveal others' experiences in a way never seen before. For example, brain-imaging studies have made some progress determining what kinds of visual stimulus or pictures a subject is seeing (Kamitani and Tong 2005; Haxby et al. 2001). In one study, scientists could tell through fMRI which of 1,750 images of natural scenes a subject had been looking at (Kay et al. 2008).

Other studies have tried to determine what people are thinking or feeling by examining brain patterns. In one famous study, researchers found a relationship between subjects' level of racist thinking and activation of a part of the brain known as the amygdala, the critical part of the brain mediating anxiety and fear, when those subjects looked at pictures of men of another race (Phelps et al. 2000). Another fascinating line of inquiry has attempted to link brain function to personality traits, finding, for example, that personality traits such as neuroticism or extraversion correlate with individual differences in brain activation (Canli et al. 2001). Studies like these suggest that humans might know something about how people feel or might react to things based entirely on brain-imaging studies.

Researchers have also attempted to predict participants' intentions using fMRI data. John-Dylan Haynes and his coauthors (2007) had people look at two numbers while in a scanner, decide whether they wanted to add or subtract the numbers, and then push a button to denote their decision. After studying images of people's brains after they made the decision, researchers were able to predict whether a participant had chosen to add or subtract before he or she pushed the button. In another groundbreaking experiment, a group from Carnegie Mellon University learned to predict with great accuracy the pattern of brain activation when subjects were thinking of particular nouns (Mitchell et al. 2008). Although researchers are not able to "read minds" in any meaningful sense, these and other experiments have brought them closer to being able to get glimpses into people's subjective minds while they are in fMRI machines.

Studies such as the ones described must be understood within the confines of their significant methodological and technological limitations. In most cases, participants engage in a specific protocol that is relatively simplistic and controlled. The number of subjects is small, and participants must remain perfectly still and cooperate fully while being brain-imaged. The information obtained is relatively simple. It is also still too early to understand how laboratory studies translate into real-world settings.

For example, the business world has developed a field called *neuromarketing*, in which researchers try to use imaging to shed light on people's preferences for certain commercial products (discussed below). However, the kinds of preferences willing subjects express while lying in brain scanners in carefully designed experiments may end up being very different from what a consumer actually buys in the marketplace. Researchers are still far from being able to use such technologies to "read people's minds" in any real way.

The notion that technology could one day truly read the mind of another would likely incite a major shift in how lawyers, employers, or the military operate. And such a prospect rightfully raises serious ethical concerns among the public about how such technologies ought to be used by an ever-growing list of stakeholders. Who should have access to brain imaging, and under what circumstances? For example, should courts be able to order a defendant to undergo brain imaging? Moreover, who will supervise the civil uses of brain imaging? How to interpret such data is still controversial.

**Lie Detection.** The ways in which brain information could be used in societal contexts continue to evolve. However, one of the most controversial applications is the use of brain imaging for lie detection (Wolpe, Foster, and Langleben 2005). Several studies have indicated that brain-imaging technologies might be used to determine whether a subject is attempting to deceive an investigator. Although the application and reliability of the findings remain unclear, two companies were quickly established to offer brain-imaging lie detection services, though neither was offering such services as of 2015.

The potential growth of a brain-imaging lie detection market has rightfully raised concerns among ethicists and researchers. Many have questioned the ability of the technology to accurately discern whether someone is telling the truth about a particular event (Kanwisher 2009). Because brain-imaging lie detection attempts are not highly reliable in real-world situations, some have called for regulation of lie detection information derived from fMRI, with particular attention to how the legal realm uses such information (Greely and Illes 2007).

The ethical and practical challenge of brain imaging involves the use of these technologies by the military, security, and intelligence agencies; by courtrooms and criminal law; and potentially by employers and the public at large. The technology has been tested primarily on small numbers of college students. It has not been researched on people with psychopathologies or other mental disorders, and little systematic research has been done on potential countermeasures. Because people can learn behaviors or even think thoughts that can undermine or alter the outcome of brain-imaging tests, including lie detection, the validity of these tests is questionable.

Even so, imaging has the potential to be coercive, or to invade privacy, potentially stripping a person of the right to refuse to divulge information and the right to say no (Wolpe, Foster, and Langleben 2005). The use of brain imaging in the legal domain raises a host of legal and constitutional questions. For example, defendants have a constitutional right not to testify against themselves. If a defendant were brain-imaged under court order and the image revealed evidence suggesting he or she was guilty, would that violate a constitutional right not to incriminate oneself (Stoller and Wolpe 2007)? Such questions may soon come in front of judges as these technologies are increasingly introduced into the courtroom.

## HEALTH AND ENHANCEMENT

Neurotechnology has also been used in various ways to mitigate or rehabilitate a diseased or injured brain and, beyond that, to simply improve the function of the brain. This section discusses some of these issues.

**Disorders of Consciousness.** It has long been assumed that patients who have been diagnosed as being in a persistent vegetative state have no cognitive abilities. However, recent studies indicate that some of them actually do. These patients are considered instead to be in a minimally conscious state (MCS) and have inconsistent but reproducible signs of awareness, such as being able to follow some simple commands and visually following objects (Giacino et al. 2002; Naci et al. 2012). Patients in a vegetative state (VS), on the other hand, show some signs of wakefulness, such as eye opening, and of physical arousal when stimulated, but show no signs of conscious awareness. Before brain imaging began to objectively detect signs of cognitive awareness, these measures of consciousness relied primarily on a physician's assessments of a patient's behavior, which are often unreliable.

A variety of neurotechnologies have been used to detect signs of consciousness by measuring signs of awareness (Phillips et al. 2011; Rosanova et al. 2012; Vanhaudenhuyse et al. 2010). For example, three studies have demonstrated that neuroimaging and EEG can detect patient awareness that was not apparent to their caretakers (Cruse et al. 2011; Monti et al. 2010; Owen et al. 2006). In one notable fMRI study (Monti et al. 2010), fifty-four MCS and VS patients were asked to engage in motor imagery tasks (imagine standing in a tennis court and swinging to hit a tennis ball) and spatial imagery tasks (imagine walking from room to room in a familiar space such as their home). Patients were then asked to respond yes or no by imagining a specific type of imagery (motor or spatial imagery).

Of these fifty-four patients, five were able to reliably modulate fMRI activity in response to experimenter commands. In other words, these patients' brains activated in the appropriate areas (such as their motor cortex when they were asked to imagine hitting a tennis ball), even though doctors had thought them to be completely lacking conscious awareness. One of these five patients was even able to respond to five of the six questions accurately by using visual or motor imagery.

Developing new diagnostic methods to determine which patients are in MCS is important because studies have revealed that an alarmingly high number of patients (40% or more) may be misdiagnosed as VS when they are actually MCS (Andrews et al. 1996; Monti 2012; Schnakers et al. 2009). As neuroimaging technologies and studies become more sophisticated, assessing the mental capacities of individuals in such states may become more accurate (Jox et al. 2012).

Once identified, however, it is not clear how patients in MCS should be treated. Some may benefit from therapy. Nicholas Schiff and colleagues (2007) describe a case study of an MCS patient who benefited from deep brain stimulation and was able to have meaningful interaction with his family, eat by mouth, and have increased mobility. In addition, this patient could respond vocally about certain preferences, such as whether he wanted to continue physical therapy, which restored at least a modicum of personal agency and autonomy. However, the question remains whether bringing these patients out of MCS into very impaired lives and greater awareness of their conditions truly aligns with the patients' notions of a good quality of life (Fins 2000, 2005).

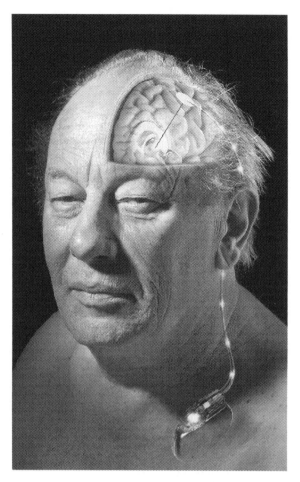

***Cutaway computer artwork illustrating the treatment known as deep brain stimulation (DBS).*** *DBS involves the surgical implantation of thin electrodes that send electrical impulses into deep structures of the brain. Popularized through its application for the neurodegenerative movement disorder Parkinson's disease, DBS is now being explored as potential treatment for a variety of psychiatric disorders and conditions.* TIM VERNON, LTH NHS TRUST/PHOTO RESEARCHERS, INC.

Another difficult ethical challenge is obtaining sufficient informed consent from patients who have disorders of consciousness. First, one must determine their mental capacity or competence, which is often difficult to do accurately, and then one must obtain their consent, often by asking yes or no questions and examining their brains through imaging or EEG. It will be necessary to establish careful criteria for competency and methodologies for determining it in these highly compromised populations. Then one must discuss whether patients who possess some level of "significant" mental capacity should be considered for pharmacotherapy, deep brain stimulation, or other therapies (Schiff et al. 2007). It is also difficult to know what such patients wish for their end-of-life care and what procedures to follow if an advance directive and their response through imaging or EEG conflict (Wilkinson et al. 2009).

**Deep Brain Stimulation.** Deep brain stimulation (DBS) involves the surgical implantation of thin electrodes that send electrical impulses into deep structures of the brain. DBS was popularized through its application for the neurodegenerative movement disorder Parkinson's disease (PD) (Kalia, Sankar, and Lozano 2013). Although it is effective for alleviating symptoms in some patients, DBS for PD has not been free from ethical concerns (Clausen 2010) because of rare but concerning side effects, such as personality and cognitive changes.

DBS is now being explored for psychiatric conditions, such as profound depression (Mayberg et al. 2005). However, using surgery on the brain for mental illness raises red flags among many because of the ethically fraught history of using psychosurgeries, such as frontal lobotomy, which was performed on thousands of Americans in the early twentieth century for reasons now considered misguided or even frivolous (Clausen 2010).

DBS is not necessarily lifesaving or curative; it primarily relieves symptoms. As with many treatments for mental illness, patients may not be able to truly comprehend and evaluate the risks and benefits of the surgery and may generally lack the capacity to consent (Bell, Mathieu, and Racine 2009). Recently, concerned groups have tried to issue some consensus guidelines for the ethical use of DBS for psychiatric disorders (Nuttin et al. 2014). The recommendations call for involvement of ethics committees, careful preoperative selection criteria of patients, the establishment of capacity to consent, clear informed consent procedures to facilitate realistic expectations of patients, close follow-up, and ongoing care with a multidisciplinary team.

Guidelines are important because studies are expanding applications for DBS into areas such as obesity (Kumar et al. 2015), Tourette's syndrome (Schrock et al. 2015), and anxiety disorders (Kuhn et al. 2009). There is also increasing discussion of the use of DBS for human enhancement (Suthana and Fried 2014; Synofzik and Schlaepfer 2008), which is covered in the following section.

**Cosmetic Neurology and Enhancement.** The increasing sophistication of neuroscience has led to hopes that new technologies might help enhance brain function beyond the therapeutic applications. After all, who doesn't want a better, more efficient brain? Both researchers and the public are anxious to explore if neuroscience might develop techniques for enhancing memory and learning, overcoming fatigue-related impairments in attention and focus, and improving mood, trust, and even moral decision making. Existing technologies range from pharmacological interventions to brain stimulation technologies; however, almost all of these brain enhancement techniques were initially developed for strictly therapeutic purposes. When should a medical technique be used for lifestyle purposes, what control should physicians retain over these technologies, and who should have access to them under these conditions? The field of neuroethics has been engaging such questions.

Before delving into methods of brain enhancement, a definition of the term *enhancement* is necessary. Human beings have been enhancing brain function for their entire recorded history. Almost every culture has ingested foods to change people's mood or function. In the Americas, native cultures used chocolate, maté, and guaraná to get their doses of caffeine, coca leaves to enhance attention and endurance for traveling or hunting, and tobacco for the stimulating effects of nicotine. People still have their coffee in the morning, chocolate when they feel down, and calming teas when agitated. In one sense, brain enhancement is as old as humanity.

However, modern neurological enhancement raises some novel issues. Modern enhancement is the use of sophisticated medical technologies to increase or improve one's functioning quickly, even beyond abilities that are considered normal or average for human beings. The word *enhancement* contrasts with *therapy*, which treats a disease or other pathology considered to reduce or impair normal function in order to bring the person back to baseline or normal functioning. Defining the terms *normal* and *undesirable*, however, is not simple. First, they are often subject to the cultural standards of a given time period. Second, is there a difference between improving one's own ability but still keeping it within a normal range (such as by taking an attention enhancement pill to improve concentration) and enhancing oneself beyond the capabilities of an average human being (if that were possible)? Finally, who determines what is normal or acceptable functioning, and what is enhancement?

**Enhancement Drugs.** In 2004, neurologist Anjan Chatterjee (1958–) popularized the term *cosmetic neurology* in a paper outlining the increasing tendency of patients to request drugs from their doctors for nonmedical uses to enhance their cognitive or affective abilities and states. For example, reports suggest that sales of "natural" supplements to middle-aged populations in the United States for memory improvement have reached billions annually (Hall 2003), despite scientific consensus that the treatments don't work (Birks and Grimley Evans 2009; Canter and Ernst 2007). Chatterjee has argued that, like cosmetic surgeons, neurologists will soon be asked by patients to regularly provide services that have no therapeutic necessity but are for pharmacological self-improvement.

On the other hand, the line between therapy and enhancement remains difficult to define. For example, memory decline is known to occur in the third decade of life onward and is often reported to be noticeably bothersome and troubling as early as the fourth decade of life (Craik and Salthouse 1992), even in "normal" and "healthy" individuals. Should the neurologist intervene in this circumstance?

*Stimulants.* Some of the most discussed cases and debates around enhancement concern the uses of stimulants in children diagnosed with attention deficit disorder (ADD). Ritalin and other stimulants are given to American students at a higher rate than anywhere else in the world and are given throughout college, where 5 to 25 percent of college students use prescription stimulants for cognitive enhancement. Many children receive these drugs who do not fit a diagnosis of ADD, often because parents push the drugs as a way to improve student performance. Even some professionals, including college professors and scientists, use these drugs to enhance performance (Sahakian and Morein-Zamir 2007; Maher 2008).

Should widespread use of cognitive enhancement drugs for those without a diagnosis of ADD be encouraged or allowed? Aside from the unknown effects of long-term use (Farah 2015), other ethical questions arise. Is it sending the right message to children when one offers a drug to encourage them to get better grades instead of asking them to do hard work? Will society use pills to enhance attention, calm one's mood, improve memory, and so on, until people lose the ability to develop these skills without drugs?

In addition, sometimes unexpected results come from the attempt to enhance oneself. A number of pharmaceutical companies are working on developing a pill to improve memory. However, studies of mice that were genetically improved to have enhanced memory found that they were bad at forgetting information they no longer needed and were also more sensitive to pain, presumably because the memory of the pain was more vivid (Wei et al. 2001).

How would cognitive enhancers such as these be fairly distributed? Could anyone who can afford these interventions have access to them? And what about the pressure to take enhancers to have a fair playing field in school or in the workplace? If my officemate is taking an attention enhancer and outperforming me, does that mean that I, and everyone else on my office, now have to take drugs to compete in the workplace? And does taking an enhancer for a test or to study actually constitute cheating? As of 2016, two universities (Wesleyan and Duke) had explicitly stated that using prescription drugs for enhancement was considered cheating.

In contrast, imagine that an enhancement drug made airline pilots more attentive and competent flyers. Chatterjee asked in his 2004 paper whether we might be willing to actually pay more for commercial flights with "enhanced" pilots. Others have suggested that some forms of enhancement should be compulsory, such as moral enhancement if a technology is ever developed that can do that (Rakić 2015). On the other hand, scholars such as Leon Kass have stated that the use of cognitive enhancers in general is a violation of authenticity (Kass 2003).

*Propranolol and SSRIs.* Other drugs being tested raise new interesting questions. In the 2004 film *The Eternal Sunshine of the Spotless Mind*, a couple break up and have their memories of each other erased from their brains to avoid their sadness. In the end of the film, even without their memories, they end up together. While we are far from such a science-fiction scenario, the story raises a contemporary concern about how tampering with memory in any sense might change our personal narratives. Propranolol, commonly used to treat high blood pressure, has been identified as a drug that could disrupt associative learning (such as when experience as a soldier makes someone associate a loud bang with a bomb) and so might be a treatment or preventive measure for post-traumatic stress disorder (PTSD).

Because propranolol may help diminish heightened physiological responses to painful memories (Argolo et al. 2015), the media reported that it can "erase" people's memories. Propranolol does not erase memories; it helps to reduce the emotional component of memories, which is what leads to PTSD. However, because other drugs and techniques seem to be able to actually reduce or eliminate memories in mice, there are worries that people without PTSD may use propranolol or other drugs to try to suppress memories they don't want (Evers 2007; Hurley 2007).

Other drugs have the potential to be used to encourage different kinds of behaviors, raising questions over the degree to which pharmaceutical agents should be used to encourage desired behaviors. For example, selective serotonin reuptake inhibitors (SSRIs), commonly used to reduce anxiety and depression, have been shown to modify some morally relevant behavior. In a game in which participants were asked to distribute money, participants given SSRIs were more likely to divide sums of money evenly (Tse and Bond 2002). In the Trolley Dilemma described earlier, participants taking SSRIs have a greater aversion to pushing a person over a footbridge (Crockett et al. 2010). Neil Levy and his coauthors (2014) speculate that SSRIs may have the potential to increase aversion to harming others and increase cooperation and fairness as a form of moral enhancement.

*Oxytocin.* Another example is oxytocin. Originally used in maternity wards to accelerate childbirth and stimulate milk ejection during lactation (Lee et al. 2009), it was then seen to influence maternal bonding behavior and social attachment and so was labeled the "love drug" by the media (Shen 2015). However, oxytocin is also involved in a larger reward system in the brain that may modify trust and cooperation within groups (Kosfeld et al. 2005).

Whereas oxytocin research has focused on clinical applications, there has been interest and popular speculation in using, marketing, and purchasing oxytocin to enhance trust among colleagues or increase or decrease fidelity in romantic partners (Levy et al. 2014; Wudarczyk et al. 2013). It may not be that simple; Carsten de Dreu and colleagues (2010, 2011) demonstrated that oxytocin administration also resulted in stronger bias and increased bias against those of a different race.

In these two examples, research has determined that naturally occurring brain chemicals that serve a function for the body can also be artificially introduced to encourage those behaviors. Should SSRIs be given to feuding parties to help facilitate compromise, or oxytocin to autistic children to encourage social bonding? Might oxytocin be given to paranoid schizophrenics to make them more trusting of their doctor, or to a couple undergoing marital counseling to increase their connection to each other?

**Brain-Machine Interfaces.** For a more mechanical example, there is William Gibson's 1984 novel *Neuromancer*. In this futuristic thriller, computer hacker Henry Dorsett Case is able to connect to the "matrix" (one of the first literary mentions of what is now called the Internet) through a wire plugged into his brain. With a direct brain-machine interface, he is able to manipulate computers at the speed of his thoughts.

In the real world, recent work on brain-machine interfaces, by which a brain interacts with a computer to facilitate human behavior or decision making, has garnered attention as a means of cognitive enhancement that does not involve taking a drug. Brain-machine interfaces are gaining in sophistication (Lebedev et al. 2011). In 2013, neuroscientist Miguel Nicolelis (1961–) succeeded in connecting the electrical activity of one brain to a second brain, allowing the transfer of neural information between the two (Pais-Vieira et al. 2013). The researchers taught a rat to learn which of two levers would deliver food and implanted wires into a second rat's brain from the first. Astonishingly, the second rat correctly chose the lever that would deliver food with no other input. More recently, two human brains were connected through EEG and TMS (transcranial magnetic stimulation, which involves no wires), which allowed the participants to play a video game in which activity from one brain prompted the finger in the second subject to successfully press a button to move a cursor (Rao et al. 2014).

The connecting of multiple brains in these ways raises several novel ethical issues (Trimper, Wolpe, and Rommelfanger 2014). Could transfers of information be hacked and changed (as has already been done with heart pacemakers)? Could false memories be implanted or introduced into one brain by another? Similarly, connecting brains may challenge notions of agency and identity. And if one person engages in an action during a brain-to-brain interface, how would one determine who was ultimately responsible?

## LAW AND POLICY

As should be evident by now, many neuroscience findings make problematic such notions as free will, agency, responsibility, and capacity. The implications of those findings are particularly important in law, where concepts of fairness, guilt, and other basic legal principles are based on the idea that individuals make free choices and are responsible for them. This section briefly reviews some of the ways neuroscience is influencing jurisprudence.

**A Historical Example.** In 1983, Brian Dugan kidnapped and killed ten-year-old Jeanine Nicarico in Naperville, Illinois. During the murder trial, his lawyers argued that Dugan suffered from psychopathy, a psychological condition associated with highly impulsive behavior and emotional deficits, and so should not be held fully responsible for his actions (Hughes 2010). In an attempt to mitigate Dugan's punishment for his horrific acts, his defense lawyers argued that Dugan was unable to understand the moral depravity of murdering a young girl and, as a consequence, should not be sentenced to death. To substantiate this claim, the legal defense team had a psychologist discuss Dugan's abnormal brain scan in court, marking the first criminal trial in which jurors weighed data collected via fMRI methods (Hughes 2010). Despite the inclusion of such information in the trial proceedings, Dugan was sentenced to death. Instances such as these are increasingly common in the legal realm (Davis 2012). Whether relying on an X-ray, fMRI scan, or another neuroscientific method, lawyers are now turning toward the brain sciences to make legal arguments.

Researchers have begun examining three distinct areas that draw from work in both neuroscience and law: diagnosis, intent, and truth and lie detection. Although researchers have made significant progress and claims about each, there also exists healthy skepticism about the relevance of such neural data to resolving legal questions. For instance, psychopathy is diagnosed through behavioral tests, and there is no agreed-upon diagnosis of psychopathology from brain images, so what is the role of an image of the brain in determining if someone is truly psychopathic? Do brain-imaging data provide jurors with information above and beyond psychological diagnostic tools, such as psychiatric interviews done by trained professionals? Can neuroscience information predict another person's future behavior with a high degree of accuracy? These questions are explored in the next three sections.

**Diagnosis in the Courtroom.** A problem that has plagued the legal world for centuries is determining whether, or the degree to which, defendants are or are not competent to stand trial or take responsibility for their actions. Attorneys regularly call upon psychologists and psychiatrists to speak about defendants' mental state at the time of a crime to craft a case that the defendants are not responsible for their actions, or to reduce sentencing.

Some argue (Schauer 2010; Batts 2009) that neuroscience may significantly aid in determining whether one is mentally competent. If a brain scan could help determine that Dugan was a psychopath, devoid of impulse control, should the legal realm take this information seriously? Dugan's defense lawyers believed that presenting brain data would provide converging evidence that Dugan was indeed morally compromised and impulsive. There are many other realms where brain data may seem useful. Many lawyers use standard IQ tests to ascertain whether one is competent to stand trial. When, how, and to what degree should scans be used to help determine competency? How should this information be weighed against other kinds of testimony in a courtroom setting? Should such tests take the place of careful questioning of patients, expert psychological testimony, and so forth?

Many prominent scholars have challenged the notion that neuroscience should alter the way the courts decide to punish criminals. One criticism challenges the assumption that neuroscience offers a superior diagnostic tool above and beyond already established and validated psychiatric tools. It is actually rare that a brain scan renders a different diagnosis than a psychological one, and, in such cases, there is substantial debate about which diagnosis to prefer. Second, although many resources are being devoted to better determining how brain data collected in a laboratory setting can predict the future behavior of someone outside the lab, there are still no robust methods for predicting the future behavior of a single individual.

At base there is a philosophical question and disagreement. How does a brain scan add to the understanding of competence? It is often unclear that a particular brain state influenced behavior in a particular way. Some people with perfectly normal-appearing brains engage in heinous crimes, whereas others who seem to have significantly misshapen brains seem to behave normally. A tumor on the brain may alter behavior, or it may not; having a tumor and engaging in a crime does not mean that the tumor caused the crime, and there is no way to know that it did. Even if it increased a person's compulsion to commit a crime, the person's responsibility is to find a way to resist giving in to that compulsion. How does a brain image illuminate these questions?

These open questions pose a serious challenge to the idea that brain data should be included in legal decisions. Nonetheless, if neuroscientists were at some point able to more definitively answer these questions, then perhaps the discussion surrounding the use of brain data in the courtroom would shift. However, given the diagnostic imprecision of neuroimaging techniques and the variability of such methods in predicting future behavior, the consensus seems to be that brain data may not be as transformative for courts as originally posited.

**Unpacking Intent.** People generally experience a feeling of control over their actions. If one were on a diet and saw a gooey, freshly made chocolate chip cookie, one would probably have a strong desire to eat the cookie. At the same time, one might also experience a desire to not eat the cookie because one wanted to adhere to a diet. In other words, one might feel as if one had self-control and that one should be responsible for the decision to eat or not eat the cookie. Now, if a neuroscientist could image one's brain right before one decides whether to eat the cookie, the researcher might find abnormal patterns of activity in the areas of the brain related to self-control. Would one be as responsible for eating the cookie as someone who does not exhibit these abnormal patterns? As another example, what if a neuroscientist could target certain areas of the brain to alter one's desire to eat the cookie via some neurostimulation device or a pharmaceutical drug? Would one still be responsible for eating the cookie? These are the types of questions philosophers, lawyers, and neuroscientists have discussed at length in recent years.

Such questions are not merely philosophical thought experiments. Situations analogous to the cookie situation crop up often in the legal realm. It has long been understood that damage to the brain can significantly impact personality and behavior. In fact, recent neuroscientific evidence has suggested that numerous and subtle brain modifications can elicit significant behavioral changes. For example, alcohol and stimulant drug use (Bechara et al. 2001) and severe neglect (Teicher et al. 2003) have been linked to substantial brain and behavior alterations throughout development. It is also known that there are individual differences in self-control and the proclivity to engage in violent behavior (Raine 2002). As neuroscience begins to build on the psychological research concerning the correlates of violent and criminal behavior, questions have been raised about the extent to which criminals are truly responsible for their actions.

The legal principle most closely related to this question is *mens rea*, the notion that people are accountable for their actions if they have the intent to break a specific law. This principle protects people from being legally responsible for involuntary actions and accidents. If Joey holds a gun to John's head and tells him to shoot Brad or he will die, a lawyer would likely argue that John was coerced, and so did not voluntarily kill Brad and thus should not be charged with murder. Similar arguments have been applied to actions while drawing on neuroscientific evidence; in such cases, certain behaviors, such as eating the cookie while exhibiting an abnormal neural activation in areas of the brain correlated with self-control, would be less punishable than another person eating the cookie without such a pattern. It is easy to then think that, although many of the details are different, the cookie situation and the John murder scenario follow a similar logical trajectory: it just so happens that in the cookie case it is not Brad holding a gun to John's head, but a hungry person equipped with faulty self-control mental machinery faced with an incredibly enticing cookie.

Situations such as these lead many to ask: if someone has less self-control than another person (and the difference can be corroborated via imaging), should the person with less self-control be punished similarly to the person with normal self-control patterns? Although this question seems like a legally relevant one, most legal scholars strongly urge that such debates be kept out of the courtroom. The primary argument against using neuroscience to determine *mens rea* revolves around the notion that providing a cause of a behavior (i.e., attenuated capacity for self-control) does not bear on a criminal's responsibility (Morse 2007).

Put another way, every crime has a prior cause—people do things for reasons—and a neuroscientific cause should not be privileged above other causes. Second, providing a neuroscientific cause does not bear on the notion that an individual did in fact commit a crime of some sort. Drawing on the cookie example, neuroscience data that suggest one has an abnormal self-control system do not negate that one did eat the cookie. If eating cookies were punishable by some bizarre rule, then one would still be responsible for eating a cookie even if one's lawyer could provide a sound scientific reason for why one engaged in the action in the first place.

## COMMERCIAL USES

Neuroscientific findings and technologies are often not held to the same scientific standards in commercial settings, leading to fears that commercialization of neurotechnologies may compromise scientific rigor and scientific transparency and even undermine scientific progress (O'Connell 2011).

**Neuromarketing.** In the 2002 film *Minority Report*, Chief John Anderton finds himself on the run in a mall. Holographic ads yell out his name as eye scanners find his identity and create custom ads to invite him to buy. For a marketer, this might be a dream—ads customized to every customer—but for a fugitive on the run, it's a nightmare. Similarly, as neuroscience developed, businesses began to wonder if brain scans might give them useful information about their customers. The resulting field of neuromarketing tries to track human brain responses to marketing stimuli (Murphy, Illes, and Reiner 2008; Renvoisé and Morin 2007). For example, researchers use brain imaging to examine how subjects respond to advertising campaigns or to help businesses decide which products to develop by looking at people's reactions to them (Ariely and Berns 2010).

Neuromarketing is based on studies that find correlations between activation of areas of the brain associated with reward and associated pleasant experiences or "liking." For instance, food odor, taste, and texture have been correlated with distinct brain regions, such as the orbital frontal cortex and the insula (de Araujo and Rolls 2004; Rolls 2006; Small and Prescott 2005). In one study, subjects who were unaware of the brand they were tasting, Pepsi or Coke, demonstrated brain activation related to not only the taste of a drink, but also the brand (McClure et al. 2004). Neuromarketing is used by many global corporations, but it has not yet proven that it can add value to the understanding of consumer behavior.

Principles of neuromarketing are also used to study voters. Studies have shown that subjects have complex brain responses to statements made by political candidates; specific areas of the brain are associated with subjects maintaining their political candidate preferences in response to advertisements, whereas other areas are associated with subjects changing their preferences in political candidates (Kato et al. 2009; Westen et al. 2006).

The challenge to neuromarketing is to show that the information it gives actually translates into consumer behavior. A brain activating in a certain way when a person is shown one brand of cookie does not necessarily mean that person will choose that cookie when shopping in the supermarket. In neuromarketing, brain-imaging technologies and EEG technologies replace or supplement people's subjective reports of their own preferences. In addition to skepticism about the value of neuromarketing, many critics worry that the data are not collected with adequate standards for legal protection and concern for privacy (Matthews 2015).

**Education and DIY Enhancement.** Neuroscience has also provided greater insight into how humans learn and can potentially help improve the learning process itself. Neuroscience has been employed to help design brain-based learning regimens (Gura

2005) and has even been suggested as a replacement for forms of standardized testing (Hoeft et al. 2011). The market has not been slow to pick up on this potential, and consumer products promising to use neuroscientific research to improve cognitive performance and learning are already big business.

*Brain-Training Games.* For example, brain-training games (BTGs) developed solely for the purpose of improving brain function have made great inroads into popular culture. BTG purveyors promise to their customers that as they improve performance on their games they will also improve in other cognitive tasks for which they have not trained, the so-called transfer effect. But although working memory tasks and improvements in working memory through training have been associated with neurophysiological changes (Jonides et al. 2008), and even with scholastic aptitude (Alloway and Alloway 2010), the overall efficacy of BTGs remains controversial (Rabipour and Raz 2012).

One concern is that many websites that sponsor BTGs collect data on their users, such as correlations of current cognitive capacity and behavioral predispositions, and this practice has implications for consumer participants' privacy (Purcell and Rommelfanger 2015). Unlike fMRI and EEG data, which raises concerns over the possibility of one day having the capability to garner detailed insights into a person's identity, personality, and behavioral predispositions, data collected from BTG companies are being interpreted right now as current demonstrations of existing behaviors and predispositions. Companies such as Lumosity have recently published data on the "smartest universities in the US," claiming to have used the largest human data set to date and concluding their paper with invitations for researchers to partner with them for future studies (Willett 2013).

If these data were indeed related to educational performance, they would typically be protected as education records. Yet there are no safeguards on these data, and in the event of the business's failure they are considered assets that can be sold. Lumosity has typically claimed to offer cognitive training to enhance performance, but the Federal Trade Commission fined Lumosity in January 2016 for false advertising, particularly for claims of delaying age-related cognitive decline (Federal Trade Commission 2016). Such a case outlines the regulatory entanglements of ambiguous neurotechnologies. If Lumosity is a recreational device, it should be regulated by the Federal Trade Commission. However, if Lumosity claims to have health-related benefits, such as delaying cognitive decline, then it may need to move under the purview of agencies such as the FDA.

*Transcranial Direct Current Stimulation.* Perhaps of greater concern is the explosion of interest in transcranial direct current stimulation (tDCS), a noninvasive brain stimulation device that is claimed to enhance attention, memory, and focus among its users (Dubljević, Saigle, and Racine 2014). Whereas some studies claim that tDCS may reduce symptoms of depression (Nitsche et al. 2009) and schizophrenia (Brunelin et al. 2012) and enhance performance on a variety of cognitive tasks (Kadosh et al. 2010), other studies have found no such effects (Horvath, Forte, and Carter 2015).

The controversy has not stopped both commercial and homemade tDCS devices from being widely used. Construction of a tDCS is relatively simple; one needs only a nine-volt battery, a couple of electrodes (even sponges dipped in saline will work), and some wires to build a circuit. This simple design has led to a burgeoning do-it-yourself (DIY) tDCS community alongside a commercial industry interested in selling such devices. The Internet is also full of blog entries and discussions with instructions on how to create a tDCS device with a few parts. It is unclear what benefits these devices provide when administered with such limited expertise and even less clear what the full extent of harms might be for people who decide to use tDCS devices on their own.

Given the increasing prominence of homemade and purchased neurostimulation devices, greater attention should be focused on understanding the potential safety risks associated with such gadgets. Currently, tDCS devices are not regulated. Some have proposed that tDCS should be considered a medical device to ensure that the development and use of these devices is subject to greater safety standards (Maslen et al. 2014). Perhaps of greatest concern, however, is the potential use of tDCS by enthusiastic parents on children, as very little is known about how brain stimulation technologies may affect typically and atypically developing brains.

## Summary

The explosion of interest in neuroscience has resulted in new discoveries, new technologies, and new interest in the workings of the human brain. Scientists are postulating new ways of looking at human traits such as free will and agency; questioning the nature of subjective phenomena such as religious experience; using technologies to try to read minds or determine who is lying; enhancing human abilities through pharmaceutical and other technologies; and creating new ways of understanding and manipulating people's brains.

Neuroscience offers many potential benefits, both in understanding the human condition and in potentially curing some terrible maladies. However, along with these great potential benefits come considerable ethical challenges.

First is the issue of safety. Both unintentional and intentional misuses of these technologies must be considered and guarded against fiercely. State actors may increasingly be tempted to use these technologies to coerce, drug, probe, control, or apprehend subjective information from citizens. Courts have serious decisions to make as to whether and how to use these technologies. Terrorists and authoritarian rulers may find new tools to use on their own citizens or external victims. It is important to put federal and international policies in place to guard against the misuse of these powerful technologies.

Unlike many other biotechnologies (such as much of genetic science, for example), many neurotechnologies are easily accessible to the public. Psychopharmaceuticals, TMS and tDCS, EEG, and other brain technologies can be used today by lay experimenters on themselves or others. Many are easily purchased on the Web.

Neuroscience therefore poses different challenges than other technologies. Brains are unlike other organs in that within them, as one understands human physiology, lie memories, a sense of self and identity, personalities, agency, and self-control. The science is moving much faster than society's ability to carefully consider its implications. For those reasons and others, a careful consideration of neuroethics, as well as the development of new ways to implement neuroethical standards and principles, is imperative as neuroscience advances into the future.[1]

## Endnote

1. The authors would like to thank Ross Gordon for his excellent research assistance for this chapter.

# Bibliography

Alloway, Tracy, and Ross Alloway. "Investigating the Predictive Roles of Working Memory and IQ in Academic Attainment." *Journal of Experimental Child Psychology* 106, no. 1 (2010): 20–29.

Andrews, Keith, Lesley Murphy, Ros Munday, et al. "Misdiagnosis of the Vegetative State: Retrospective Study in a Rehabilitation Unit." *BMJ* 313, no. 7048 (1996): 13–16.

Argolo, Felipe, Patricia Cavalcanti-Ribeiro, Liana Netto, et al. "Prevention of Posttraumatic Stress Disorder with Propranolol: A Meta-Analytic Review." *Journal of Psychosomatic Research* 79, no. 2 (2015): 89–93.

Ariely, Dan, and Gregory Berns. "Neuromarketing: The Hope and Hype of Neuroimaging in Business." *Nature Reviews Neuroscience* 11, no. 4 (2010): 284–292.

Batts, Shelley. "Brain Lesions and Their Implications in Criminal Responsibility." *Behavioral Sciences and the Law* 27, no. 2 (2009): 261–272.

Beauchamp, Tom, and James F. Childress. *Principles of Biomedical Ethics.* 5th ed. New York: Oxford University Press, 2001.

Beauregard, Mario, Johanne Levesque, and Pierre Bourgouin. "Neural Correlates of Conscious Self-Regulation of Emotion." *Journal of Neuroscience* 21, no. 18 (2001): RC165.

Beauregard, Mario, and Vincent Paquette. "Neural Correlates of a Mystical Experience in Carmelite Nuns." *Neuroscience Letters* 405, no. 3 (2006): 186–190.

Bechara, Antoine, Sara Dolan, Natalie Denburg, et al. "Decision-Making Deficits, Linked to a Dysfunctional Ventromedial Prefrontal Cortex, Revealed in Alcohol and Stimulant Abusers." *Neuropsychologia* 39, no. 4 (2001): 376–389.

Bell, Emily, Ghislaine Mathieu, and Eric Racine. "Preparing the Ethical Future of Deep Brain Stimulation." *Surgical Neurology* 72, no. 6 (2009): 577–586.

Biello, David. "Searching for God in the Brain." *Scientific American Mind* 18, no. 5 (2007): 38–45.

Birks, Jacqueline, and John Grimley Evans. "Ginkgo Biloba for Cognitive Impairment and Dementia." *Cochrane Library*, no. 1 (2009): CD003120.

Brunelin, Jerome, Marine Mondino, Leila Gassab, et al. "Examining Transcranial Direct-Current Stimulation (tDCS) as a Treatment for Hallucinations in Schizophrenia." *American Journal of Psychiatry* 169, no. 7 (2012): 719–724.

Canli, Turhan, Heidi Sivers, Susan Whitfield, et al. "Amygdala Response to Happy Faces as a Function of Extraversion." *Science* 296, no. 5576 (2002): 2191.

Canli, Turhan, Zuo Zhao, John Desmond, et al. "An fMRI Study of Personality Influences on Brain Reactivity to Emotional Stimuli." *Behavioral Neuroscience* 115, no. 1 (2001): 33–42.

Canter, Peter, and Edward Ernst. "Ginkgo Biloba Is Not a Smart Drug: An Updated Systematic Review of Randomised Clinical Trials Testing the Nootropic Effects of G. Biloba Extracts in Healthy People." *Human Psychopharmacology: Clinical and Experimental* 22, no. 5 (2007): 265–278.

Chatterjee, Anjan. "Cosmetic Neurology: The Controversy over Enhancing Movement, Mentation, and Mood." *Neurology* 63, no. 6 (2004): 968–974.

Clausen, Jens. "Ethical Brain Stimulation: Neuroethics of Deep Brain Stimulation in Research and Clinical Practice." *European Journal of Neuroscience* 32, no. 7 (2010): 1152–1162.

Craik, Fergus, and Timothy Salthouse. *The Handbook of Aging and Cognition.* Hillsdale, NJ: Lawrence Erlbaum, 1992.

Cranford, R. E. "The Neurologist as Ethics Consultant and as a Member of the Institutional Ethics Committee: The Neuroethicist." *Neurologic Clinics* 7, no. 4 (1989): 697–713.

Crockett, Molly, Luke Clark, Marc Hauser, et al. "Serotonin Selectively Influences Moral Judgment and Behavior through Effects on Harm Aversion." *Proceedings of the National Academy of Sciences* 107, no. 40 (2010): 17433–17438.

Cruse, Damian, Srivas Chennu, Camille Chatelle, et al. "Bedside Detection of Awareness in the Vegetative State: A Cohort Study." *Lancet* 378, no. 9809 (2011): 2088–2094.

Cunningham, Paul F. "Are Religious Experiences Really Localized within the Brain? The Promise, Challenges, and Prospects of Neurotheology." *Journal of Mind and Behavior* 32, no. 3 (2011): 223.

Davis, Kevin. "Brain Trials: Neuroscience Is Taking a Stand in the Courtroom." *ABA Journal*, November 1, 2012. http://www.abajournal.com/magazine/article/brain_trials_neuroscience_is_taking_a_stand_in_the_courtroom/.

de Araujo, Ivan, and Edmund Rolls. "Representation in the Human Brain of Food Texture and Oral Fat." *Journal of Neuroscience* 24, no. 12 (2004): 3086–3093.

de Dreu, Carsten, Lindred Greer, Michel Handgraaf, et al. "The Neuropeptide Oxytocin Regulates Parochial

Altruism in Intergroup Conflict among Humans." *Science* 328, no. 5984 (2010): 1408–1411.

de Dreu, Carsten, Lindred Greer, Gerben Van Kleef, et al. "Oxytocin Promotes Human Ethnocentrism." *Proceedings of the National Academy of Sciences* 108, no. 4 (2011): 1262–1266.

Dubljević, Veljko, Victoria Saigle, and Eric Racine. "The Rising Tide of tDCS in the Media and Academic Literature." *Neuron* 82, no. 4 (2014): 731–736.

Dumit, Joseph. *Picturing Personhood: Brain Scans and Biomedical Identity*. Princeton, NJ: Princeton University Press, 2004.

Evers, Kathinka. "Perspectives on Memory Manipulation: Using Beta-Blockers to Cure Post-Traumatic Stress Disorder." *Cambridge Quarterly of Healthcare Ethics* 16, no. 2 (2007): 138–146.

Farah, Martha. "The Unknowns of Cognitive Enhancement." *Science* 350, no. 6259 (2015): 379–380.

Farah, Martha, and Andrea Heberlein. "Personhood and Neuroscience: Naturalizing or Nihilating?" *American Journal of Bioethics* 7, no. 1 (2007): 37–48.

Farah, Martha, and Paul Root Wolpe. "Monitoring and Manipulating Brain Function: New Neuroscience Technologies and Their Ethical Implications." *The Hastings Center Report* 34, no. 3 (2004): 35–45.

Federal Trade Commission. "Lumosity to Pay $2 Million to Settle FTC Deceptive Advertising Charges for Its 'Brain Training' Program." January 5, 2016. https://www.ftc.gov/news-events/press-releases/2016/01/lumosity-pay-2-million-settle-ftc-deceptive-advertising-charges.

Fingelkurts, Alexander, and Andrew Fingelkurts. "Is Our Brain Hardwired to Produce God, or Is Our Brain Hardwired to Perceive God? A Systematic Review on the Role of the Brain in Mediating Religious Experience." *Cognitive Processing* 10, no. 4 (2009): 293–326.

Fins, Joseph. "Clinical Pragmatism and the Care of Brain Damaged Patients: Toward a Palliative Neuroethics for Disorders of Consciousness." *Progress in Brain Research* 150 (2005): 565–582.

Fins, Joseph. "A Proposed Ethical Framework for Interventional Cognitive Neuroscience: A Consideration of Deep Brain Stimulation in Impaired Consciousness." *Neurological Research* 22, no. 3 (2000): 273–278.

Fischer, Hakan, Maria Tillfors, Tomas Furmark, et al. "Dispositional Pessimism and Amygdala Activity: A Pet Study in Healthy Volunteers." *Neuroreport* 12, no. 8 (2001): 1635–1638.

Frégnac, Yves, and Gilles Laurent. "Neuroscience: Where Is the Brain in the Human Brain Project?" *Nature* 513, no. 7516 (2014): 27–29.

Gazzaniga, Michael. *The Ethical Brain*. New York: Dana Press, 2004.

Gazzaniga, Michael. *Who's in Charge? Free Will and the Science of the Brain*. New York: HarperCollins, 2011.

Giacino, Joseph, Stephen Ashwal, Nancy Childs, et al. "The Minimally Conscious State: Definition and Diagnostic Criteria." *Neurology* 58, no. 3 (2002): 349–353.

Gillespie, Nick, and Ronald Bailey. "Biology vs. the Blank Slate: Evolutionary Psychologist Steven Pinker Deconstructs the Great Myths about How the Mind Works." reason.com. 2002. https://reason.com/archives/2002/10/01/biology-vs-the-blank-slate/1.

Greely, Henry, and Judy Illes. "Neuroscience-Based Lie Detection: The Urgent Need for Regulation." *American Journal of Medicine* 33, nos. 2–3 (2007): 377.

Greene, Joshua, R. Brian Sommerville, Leigh E. Nystrom, et al. "An fMRI Investigation of Emotional Engagement in Moral Judgment." *Science* 293, no. 5537 (2001): 2105–2108.

Gura, Trisha. "Educational Research: Big Plans for Little Brains." *Nature* 435, no. 7046 (2005): 1156–1158.

Hall, Stephen. "The Quest for a Smart Pill." *Scientific American* 289, no. 3 (2003): 54–57, 60–65.

Hamlin, J. Kiley, Karen Wynn, and Paul Bloom. "Social Evaluation by Preverbal Infants." *Nature* 450, no. 7169 (2007): 557–559.

Harris, Sam, Jonas Kaplan, Ashley Curiel, et al. "The Neural Correlates of Religious and Nonreligious Belief." *PLoS One* 4, no. 10 (2009): e0007272.

Hart, Allen, Paul Whalen, Lisa Shin, et al. "Differential Response in the Human Amygdala to Racial Outgroup vs Ingroup Face Stimuli." *Neuroreport* 11, no. 11 (2000): 2351–2355.

Haxby, James, M. Ida Gobbini, Maura Furey, et al. "Distributed and Overlapping Representations of Faces and Objects in Ventral Temporal Cortex." *Science* 293, no. 5539 (2001): 2425–2430.

Haynes, John-Dylan, Katsuyuki Sakai, Geraint Rees, et al. "Reading Hidden Intentions in the Human Brain." *Current Biology* 17, no. 4 (2007): 323–328.

Hoeft, Fumiko, Bruce McCandliss, Jessica Black, et al. "Neural Systems Predicting Long-Term Outcome in Dyslexia." *Proceedings of the National Academy of Sciences* 108, no. 1 (2011): 361–366.

Horvath, Jared Cooney, Jason Forte, and Olivia Carter. "Quantitative Review Finds No Evidence of Cognitive Effects in Healthy Populations from Single-Session Transcranial Direct Current Stimulation (tDCS)." *Brain Stimulation* 8, no. 3 (2015): 535–550.

Hughes, Virginia. "Science in Court: Head Case." *Nature* 464, no. 7287 (2010): 340–342.

Hurley, Elisa. "The Moral Costs of Prophylactic Propranolol." *American Journal of Bioethics* 7, no. 9 (2007): 35–36.

Johnson, Debra, John Wiebe, Sherri Gold, et al. "Cerebral Blood Flow and Personality: A Positron Emission Tomography Study." *American Journal of Psychiatry* 156, no. 2 (1999): 252–257.

Jonides, John, Richard Lewis, Derek Nee, et al. "The Mind and Brain of Short-Term Memory." *Annual Review of Psychology* 59, no. 1 (2008): 193–224.

Jox, Ralf, James Bernat, Steven Laureys, et al. "Disorders of Consciousness: Responding to Requests for Novel Diagnostic and Therapeutic Interventions." *Lancet Neurology* 11, no. 8 (2012): 732–738.

Kadosh, Roi Cohen, Sonja Soskic, Teresa Iuculano, et al. "Modulating Neuronal Activity Produces Specific and Long-Lasting Changes in Numerical Competence." *Current Biology* 20, no. 22 (2010): 2016–2020.

Kalia, Suneil, Tejas Sankar, and Andres Lozano. "Deep Brain Stimulation for Parkinson's Disease and Other Movement Disorders." *Current Opinion in Neurology* 26, no. 4 (2013): 374–380.

Kamitani, Yukiyasu, and Frank Tong. "Decoding the Visual and Subjective Contents of the Human Brain." *Nature Reviews Neuroscience* 8, no. 5 (2005): 679–685.

Kamm, Frances. "The Doctrine of Double Effect: Reflections on Theoretical and Practical Issues." *Journal of Medicine and Philosophy* 16, no. 5 (1991): 571–585.

Kanwisher, Nancy. "The Use of fMRI in Lie Detection: What Has Been Shown and What Has Not." In *Using Imaging to Identify Deceit: Scientific and Ethical Questions*, 7–13. Cambridge, MA: American Academy of Arts and Sciences, 2009.

Kass, Leon R. *Beyond Therapy: Biotechnology and the Pursuit of Happiness.* New York: HarperCollins, 2003.

Kato, Junko, Hiroko Ide, Ikuo Kabashima, et al. "Neural Correlates of Attitude Change Following Positive and Negative Advertisements." *Frontiers in Behavioral Neuroscience* 3 (2009): 6.

Katzman, Gregory, Azar Dagher, and Nicholas Patronas. "Incidental Findings on Brain Magnetic Resonance Imaging from 1000 Asymptomatic Volunteers." *Journal of the American Medical Association* 282, no. 1 (1999): 36–39.

Kay, Kendrick, Thomas Naselaris, Ryan Prenger, et al. "Identifying Natural Images from Human Brain Activity." *Nature* 452, no. 7185 (2008): 352–355.

Kim, Brian, Judy Illes, Richard Kaplan, et al. "Incidental Findings on Pediatric MR Images of the Brain." *American Journal of Neuroradiology* 23, no. 10 (2002): 1674–1677.

Kosfeld, Michael, Markus Heinrichs, Paul Zak, et al. "Oxytocin Increases Trust in Humans." *Nature* 435, no. 7042 (2005): 673–676.

Kuhn, Jens, Wolfgang Gaebel, Joachim Klosterkoetter, et al. "Deep Brain Stimulation as a New Therapeutic Approach in Therapy-Resistant Mental Disorders: Ethical Aspects of Investigational Treatment." *European Archives of Psychiatry and Clinical Neuroscience* 259, Suppl. 2 (2009): S135–S1341.

Kumar, Rahul, Constance Simpson, Clifford Froelich, et al. "Obesity and Deep Brain Stimulation: An Overview." *Annals of Neurosciences* 22, no. 3 (2015): 181–188.

Lebedev, Mikhail, Andrew Tate, Timothy Hanson, et al. "Future Developments in Brain-Machine Interface Research." *Clinics (Sao Paulo)* 66, Suppl. 1 (2011): 25–32.

Lee, Heon-Jin, Abbe Macbeth, Jerome Pagani, et al. "Oxytocin: The Great Facilitator of Life." *Progress in Neurobiology* 88, no. 2 (2009): 127–151.

Leentjens, Albert. "Depression in Parkinson's Disease: Conceptual Issues and Clinical Challenges." *Journal of Geriatric Psychiatry and Neurology* 17, no. 3 (2004): 120–126.

Levy, Neil. *Neuroethics.* Cambridge: Cambridge University Press, 2007.

Levy, Neil, Thomas Douglas, Guy Kahane, et al. "Are You Morally Modified? The Moral Effects of Widely Used Pharmaceuticals." *Philosophy, Psychiatry, and Psychology* 21, no. 2 (2014): 111–125.

Libet, Benjamin. "The Neural Time Factor in Conscious and Unconscious Events." In *Experimental and Theoretical Studies of Consciousness* (CIBA Foundation Symposia Series, 174), edited by Gregory R. Bock and Joan Marsh, 123–146. Hoboken, NJ: Wiley, 1993.

Maher, Brendan. "Poll Results: Look Who's Doping." *Nature* 452, no. 7188 (2008): 674–675.

Marshall, Henry Rutgers. "The Mutability of the Self: Responsibility and Freedom." *Journal of Philosophy, Psychology, and Scientific Methods* 1, no. 21 (1904): 570–578.

Maslen, Hannah, Thomas Douglas, Roi Cohen Kadosh, et al. "The Regulation of Cognitive Enhancement Devices: Extending the Medical Model." *Journal of Law and the Biosciences* 1, no. 1 (2014): 68–93.

Matthews, Steve. "Neuromarketing: What Is It and Is It a Threat to Privacy?" In *Handbook of Neuroethics*, edited by Jens Clausen and Neil Levy, 1627–1645. Dordrecht, Netherlands: Springer, 2015.

Mayberg, Helen, Andrew Lozano, Valerie Voon, et al. "Deep Brain Stimulation for Treatment-Resistant Depression." *Neuron* 45, no. 5 (2005): 651–660.

McClure, Samuel, Jian Li, Damon Tomlin, et al. "Neural Correlates of Behavioral Preference for Culturally Familiar Drinks." *Neuron* 44, no. 2 (2004): 379–387.

Mitchell, Tom, Svetlana Shinkareva, Andrew Carlson, et al. "Predicting Human Brain Activity Associated with the Meanings of Nouns." *Science* 320, no. 5880 (2008): 1191–1195.

Monti, Martin. "Cognition in the Vegetative State." *Annual Review of Clinical Psychology* 8 (2012): 431–454.

Monti, Martin, Audrey Vanhaudenhuyse, Martin Coleman, et al. "Willful Modulation of Brain Activity in Disorders of Consciousness." *New England Journal of Medicine* 362, no. 7 (2010): 579–589.

Mooney, Alex. "Obama Seeks $100M to Unlock Mysteries of the Brain." CNN. April 2, 2013. http://www.cnn.com /2013/04/02/health/obama-brain-research/.

Morse, Stephen. "The Non-problem of Free Will in Forensic Psychiatry and Psychology." *Behavioral Sciences and the Law* 25, no. 2 (2007): 203–220.

Murphy, Emily, Judy Illes, and Peter Reiner. "Neuroethics of Neuromarketing." *Journal of Consumer Behavior* 7, nos. 4–5 (2008): 293–302.

Naci, Lorina, Martin Monti, Damian Cruse, et al. "Brain-Computer Interfaces for Communication with Nonresponsive Patients." *Annals of Neurology* 72, no. 3 (2012): 312–323.

Nahmias, Eddy. "Is Free Will an Illusion? Confronting Challenges from the Modern Mind Sciences." In *Moral Psychology*, Vol. 4: *Freedom and Responsibility*, edited by Walter Sinnott-Armstrong, 1–25. Cambridge, MA: MIT Press, 2014.

*Neuroethics: Mapping the Field.* Proceedings of the Dana Foundation Conference. Chicago: University of Chicago Press. 2002.

Newberg, Andrew, Eugene D'Aquili, and Vince Rause. *Why God Won't Go Away: Brain Science and the Biology of Belief.* New York: Ballantine Books, 2002.

Nitsche, Michael, Paulo Boggio, Felipe Fregni, et al. "Treatment of Depression with Transcranial Direct Current Stimulation (tDCS): A Review." *Experimental Neurology* 219, no. 1 (2009): 14–19.

Noble, Kimberly, M. Frank Norman, and Martha Farah. "Neurocognitive Correlates of Socioeconomic Status in Kindergarten Children." *Developmental Science* 8, no. 1 (2005): 74–87.

Nuttin, Bart, Hemmings Wu, Helen Mayberg, et al. "Consensus on Guidelines for Stereotactic Neurosurgery for Psychiatric Disorders." *Journal of Neurology, Neurosurgery, and Psychiatry* 85, no. 9 (2014): 1003–1008.

O'Connell, Garret. "Tracking the Impact of Neuroethics." *Cortex* 47, no. 10 (2011): 1259–1260.

O'Connor, Cliodhna, Geraint Rees, and Helene Joffe. "Neuroscience in the Public Sphere." *Neuron* 74, no. 2 (2012): 220–226.

Owen, Adrian, Martin Coleman, Melanie Boly, et al. "Detecting Awareness in the Vegetative State." *Science* 313, no. 5792 (2006): 1402.

Pais-Vieira, Miguel, Mikhail Lebedev, Carolina Kunicki, et al. "A Brain-to-Brain Interface for Real-Time Sharing of Sensorimotor Information." *Scientific Reports* 3 (2013): 1319.

Persinger, Michael. "Striking EEG Profiles from Single Episodes of Glossolalia and Transcendental Meditation." *Perceptual and Motor Skills* 58, no. 1 (1984): 127–133.

Persinger, Michael, Kevin Saroka, Stanley Koren, et al. "The Electromagnetic Induction of Mystical and Altered States within the Laboratory." *Journal of Consciousness Exploration and Research* 1, no. 7 (2010): 808–830.

Phelps, Elizabeth, Kevin J. O'Connor, William Cunningham, et al. "Performance on Indirect Measures of Race Evaluation Predicts Amygdala Activation." *Journal of Cognitive Neuroscience* 12, no. 5 (2000): 729–738.

Phillips, Christophe, Marie-Aurelie Bruno, Pierre Maquet, et al. "'Relevance Vector Machine' Consciousness Classifier Applied to Cerebral Metabolism of Vegetative and Locked-in Patients." *Neuroimage* 56, no. 2 (2011): 797–808.

Pinker, Steven. *The Blank Slate: The Modern Denial of Human Nature.* New York: Penguin, 2003.

Polich, John. "Updating P300: An Integrative Theory of P3a and P3b." *Clinical Neurophysiology* 118, no. 10 (2007): 2128–2148.

Pontius, Anneliese. "Neuro-ethics of 'Walking' in the Newborn." *Perceptual and Motor Skills* 37, no. 1 (1973): 235–245.

Purcell, Ryan, and Karen Rommelfanger. "Internet-Based Brain Training Games, Citizen Scientists, and Big Data: Ethical Issues in Unprecedented Virtual Territories." *Neuron* 86, no. 2 (2015): 356–359.

Rabipour, Sheida, and Amir Raz. "Training the Brain: Fact and Fad in Cognitive and Behavioral Remediation." *Brain and Cognition* 79, no. 2 (2012): 159–179.

Racine, Eric. *Pragmatic Neuroethics: Improving Treatment and Understanding of the Mind-Brain.* Cambridge, MA: MIT Press, 2010.

Raine, Adrian. "The Biological Basis of Crime." In *Crime: Public Policies for Crime Control*, edited by J. Q. Wilson and J. Petersilia, 43–74. Oakland, CA: ICS Press, 2002.

Rakić, Vojin. "We Must Create Beings with Moral Standing Superior to Our Own." *Cambridge Quarterly of Healthcare Ethics* 24, no. 1 (2015): 58–65.

Rao, Rajesh, Andrea Stocco, Matthew Bryan, et al. "A Direct Brain-to-Brain Interface in Humans." *PLoS One* 9, no. 11 (2014): e111332.

Rees, David A., and Steven P. R. Rose. *The New Brain Sciences: Perils and Prospects.* New York: Cambridge University Press, 2004.

Regalado, Antonio. "Obama's Brain Project Backs Neurotechnology." *MIT Technology Review*, September 30, 2014. http://www.technologyreview.com/news/531291 /obamas-brain-project-backs-neurotechnology/.

Renvoisé, Patrick, and Christophe Morin. *Neuromarketing: Understanding the "Buy Button" in Your Customer's Brain.* Rev. and upd. ed. Nashville, TN: Thomas Nelson, 2007.

Rolls, Edmund. "Brain Mechanisms Underlying Flavour and Appetite." *Philosophical Transactions of Royal Society B: Biological Sciences* 361, no. 1471 (2006): 1123–1136.

Rosanova, Mario, Olivia Gosseries, Silvia Casarotto, et al. "Recovery of Cortical Effective Connectivity and Recovery of Consciousness in Vegetative Patients." *Brain* 135, no. 4 (2012): 1308–1320.

Roskies, Adina. "Neuroethics for the New Millennium." *Neuron* 35, no. 1 (2002): 21–23.

Safire, William. "Neuroethics: Mapping the Field." July 1, 2002. http://dana.org/Cerebrum/2002/Neuroethics__Map ping_the_Field/.

Sahakian, Barbara, and Sharon Morein-Zamir. "Professor's Little Helper." *Nature* 450, no. 7173 (2007): 1157–1159.

Schauer, Frederick. "Neuroscience, Lie-Detection, and the Law: Contrary to the Prevailing View, the Suitability of Brain-Based Lie-Detection for Courtroom or Forensic Use Should Be Determined According to Legal and Not Scientific Standards." *Trends in Cognitive Sciences* 14, no. 3 (2010): 101–103.

Schiff, Nicholas, J. T. Giacino, K. Kalmar, et al. "Behavioural Improvements with Thalamic Stimulation after Severe Traumatic Brain Injury." *Nature* 448, no. 7153 (2007): 600–603.

Schnakers, Caroline, Audrey Vanhaudenhuyse, Joseph Giacino, et al. "Diagnostic Accuracy of the Vegetative and Minimally Conscious State: Clinical Consensus versus Standardized Neurobehavioral Assessment." *BioMedCentral Neurology* 9 (2009): 35.

Schrock, Lauren, Jonathan Mink, Douglas Woods, et al. "Tourette Syndrome Deep Brain Stimulation: A Review and Updated Recommendations." *Movement Disorders* 30, no. 4 (2015): 448–471.

Seybold, Kevin S. "God and the Brain: Neuroscience Looks at Religion." *Journal of Psychology and Christianity* 24, no. 2 (2005): 122–129.

Shen, Helen. "Neuroscience: The Hard Science of Oxytocin." *Nature* 522, no. 7557 (2015): 410–412.

Singer, Tania, Ben Seymour, John O'Doherty, et al. "Empathy for Pain Involves the Affective but Not Sensory Components of Pain." *Science* 303, no. 5661 (2004): 1157–1162.

Small, Dana, and John Prescott. "Odor/Taste Integration and the Perception of Flavor." *Experimental Brain Research* 166, nos. 3–4 (2005): 345–357.

Stoller, Sarah, and Paul Root Wolpe. "Emerging Neurotechnologies for Lie Detection and the Fifth Amendment." *American Journal of Medicine* 33, nos. 2–3 (2007): 359–375.

Sugiura, Motoaki, Ryuta Kawashima, Manabu Nakagawa, et al. "Correlation between Human Personality and Neural Activity in Cerebral Cortex." *Neuroimage* 11, no. 5 (2000): 541–546.

Suthana, Nanthia, and Itzhak Fried. "Deep Brain Stimulation for Enhancement of Learning and Memory." *Neuroimage* 85, no. 3 (2014): 996–1002.

Synofzik, Matthis, and Thomas Schlaepfer. "Stimulating Personality: Ethical Criteria for Deep Brain Stimulation in Psychiatric Patients and for Enhancement Purposes." *Biotechnology Journal* 3, no. 12 (2008): 1511–1520.

Teicher, Martin, Susan Andersen, Ann Polcari, et al. "The Neurobiological Consequences of Early Stress and Childhood Maltreatment." *Neuroscience and Biobehavioral Reviews* 27, nos. 1–2 (2003): 33–44.

Trimper, John, Paul Root Wolpe, and Karen Rommelfanger. "When 'I' Becomes 'We': Ethical Implications of Emerging Brain-to-Brain Interfacing Technologies." *Frontiers in Neuroengineering* 7, no. 4 (2014).

Tse, Wai, and Alyson Bond. "Serotonergic Intervention Affects Both Social Dominance and Affiliative Behaviour." *Psychopharmacology* 161, no. 3 (2002): 324–330.

Vanhaudenhuyse, Audrey, Quentin Noirhomme, Luaba Tshibanda, et al. "Default Network Connectivity Reflects the Level of Consciousness in Non-Communicative Brain-Damaged Patients." *Brain* 133, no. 1 (2010): 161–171.

Verleger, Rolf, Piotr Jaskowski, and Edmund Wascher. "Evidence for an Integrative Role of P3b in Linking Reaction to Perception." *Journal of Psychophysiology* 19, no. 3 (2005): 165–181.

Ward, Hester. "Privacy and Governance Implications of Wider Societal Uses of Brain Imaging Data." *Cortex* 47, no. 10 (2011): 1263–1265.

Weber, Frank, and Heinz Knopf. "Incidental Findings in Magnetic Resonance Imaging of the Brains of Healthy Young Men." *Journal of Neurological Sciences* 240, no. 1–2 (2006): 81–84.

Wei, Feng, Guo-Du Wang, Geoffrey A. Kerchner, et al. "Genetic Enhancement of Inflammatory Pain by Forebrain NR2B Overexpression." *Nature Neuroscience* 4, no. 2 (2001): 164–169.

Westen, Drew, Pavel Blagov, Keith Harenski, et al. "Neural Bases of Motivated Reasoning: An fMRI Study of Emotional Constraints on Partisan Political Judgment in the 2004 U.S. Presidential Election." *Journal of Cognitive Neuroscience* 18, no. 11 (2006): 1947–1958.

Wilkinson, Dominic, Guy Kahane, Malcolm Horne, et al. "Functional Neuroimaging and Withdrawal of Life-Sustaining Treatment from Vegetative Patients." *Journal of Medical Ethics* 35, no. 8 (2009): 508–511.

Willett, Megan. "America's Smartest Colleges." *Business Insider*, November 14, 2013. http://www.businessinsider.com/lumosity-smartest-colleges-2013-11.

Wolpe, Paul Root. "Is My Mind Mine? Neuroethics and Brain Imaging." In *The Penn Center Guide to Bioethics*, edited by Vardit Ravitsky, Autumn Fiester, and Arthur Caplan, 85–94. New York: Springer, 2010.

Wolpe, Paul Root. "Religious Responses to Neuroscientific Questions." In *Neuroethics: Defining the Issues in Theory, Practice, and Policy*, edited by Judy Illes, 298–296. Oxford: Oxford University Press, 2006.

Wolpe, Paul Root, Kenneth Foster, and Daniel Langleben. "Emerging Neurotechnologies for Lie-Detection: Promises and Perils." *American Journal of Bioethics* 5, no. 2 (2005): 39–49.

Wudarczyk, Olga, Brian Earp, Adam Guastella, et al. "Could Intranasal Oxytocin Be Used to Enhance Relationships? Research Imperatives, Clinical Policy, and Ethical Considerations." *Current Opinion in Psychiatry* 26, no. 5 (2013): 474–484.

## FILM/TELEVISION/LITERATURE

*Buffy the Vampire Slayer*. Created by Joss Whedon. 1997–2003. 20th Century Fox Television.

*Eternal Sunshine of the Spotless Mind*. Dir. Michel Gondry. 2004. Focus Features.

Gibson, William. *Neuromancer*. New York: Ace Books, 1984.

Gregory, Daryl. *Afterparty*. New York: Tor Books, 2014.

*Limitless*. Dir. Neil Burger. 2011. Relativity Media. Based on the novel *The Dark Fields* by Alan Glynn (New York: Bloomsbury, 2001).

*Limitless*. Created by Craig Sweeney. 2015–. Relativity Television.

*The Matrix*. Dir. The Wachowskis. 1999. Warner Brothers.

*Minority Report*. Dir. Steven Spielberg. 2002. Twentieth Century Fox. Based on the short story by Philip K. Dick.

*A Nightmare on Elm Street*. Dir. Wes Craven. 1984. New Line.

*Star Trek*. Created by Gene Roddenberry. 1966–1969. Paramount.

*X-Men*. Dir. Bryan Singer. 2000. Twentieth Century Fox.

CHAPTER 7

# Preparing for the End of Life

**Nicole M. Tolwin**
*Graduate Nursing Student*
*University of Illinois, Chicago*

**Craig M. Klugman**
*Professor of Bioethics and Health Sciences*
*DePaul University, Chicago, IL*

> Thou know'st 'tis common; that all lives must die,
> Passing through nature to eternity.
> —William Shakespeare, *Hamlet*, Act 1, Scene 2

William Shakespeare (1564–1616) wrote these lines in *Hamlet* for Queen Gertrude as she tries to comfort her son about his father's death. Death has been a companion to humanity as long as there have been humans. We experience many types of deaths as we die: social death, medical death, and biological death. How we interpret death and dying, what meaning we make of it, and what cultural practices we develop around it inform our perspective on the ethical issues the end of life raises. Our perceptions of death and dying have long been topics of film, literature, and art because the experience touches on a central human emotion and reality: we all die.

Artists often personify death in varied forms, from Gustave Doré's (1832–1883) engraving of *Death on a Pale Horse* (1865) as the terrifying grim reaper, to the gallant Brad Pitt (1963–) in *Meet Joe Black* (1998), in which Death seeks to understand the meaning of the end of life and the human experience of love.

In the play *Wit* (1999), Margaret Edson (1961–) tells the story of an English professor, Vivian Bearing, who finds herself facing stage-four ovarian cancer. As the character tells us, "There is no stage five." She becomes part of an experiment that puts her through a great deal of suffering, diminishes her autonomy, and isolates her from the rest of the world. She dies in a hospital, alone and in pain.

In the 2015 film *Selfless*, a businessman named Damian discovers he is dying of cancer. To avoid death, he undergoes a process of "shedding"— his consciousness is transferred into the body of a healthy, young man. This way, he can avoid his own death and continue living, but only at the cost of displacing the previous owner of the new body.

These stories examine potential outcomes when modern, and even futuristic, medical technologies are employed to prevent death. We live in an age in which death is seen as the

**Death on a Pale Horse,** *by Gustave Doré, 1865. Doré's grim reaper illustrates one of the ways that death is personified in the Bible book of Revelation (chapter 6).* **NIDAY PICTURE LIBRARY/ALAMY.**

enemy to life and death is viewed as a medical failure: there is always something more to be tried. This chapter will explore medical ethics at the end of life. We will first look at what death and dying are; explore the history of human dying, including how we die in the twenty-first century; and then review the right to refuse care/autonomy, foundational legal cases, advance-care planning, and provider issues in end-of-life care.

## DEFINITIONS OF DEATH

Advances in medical technology and research have increased our knowledge of the human body's diverse and often subtle processes that accompany death. Philosophically, these practices raise questions similar to discussions in Chapter 3 of this volume on abortion about when life begins. Death asks parallel fundamental questions about when human life ends. If one has lost the capacity for consciousness because of partial brain death, but the body still functions, is that death? Is a person who is unresponsive and not breathing dead? In a coma? In a persistent vegetative state? In a minimally conscious state? It would be convenient to offer a clear-cut, biological answer to what death is—for example, when the heart stops beating—but a deeper scientific understanding of the brain, and the human tendency to explore our existence, has deemed this too simplistic.

Because the definition of death is imprecise and declaring a specific moment of death is arbitrary, the notion of death is open to human interpretation. We use the terms *death* and *dying* interchangeably, and although both are part of the spectrum of the closing of a human life, they refer to different parts of it. *Dying* is the social, psychological, physiological, and cellular process that leads to death. *Passive dying* is when events happen to a person—retirement, being diagnosed with a disease, being treated for a disease, suffering from conditions of aging—that are part of the progression toward death, which may be years or decades in the future. *Active dying* is when a person has a life-limiting disease or condition with irreversible decline and is in the final days and hours of life.

### BIOLOGICAL DEATH

Commonly, we think of death as being an event, a demarcation between being alive and not alive. *Death* is the irreversible loss of the physiological integrity of the organism. The brain no longer controls the body and the body no longer works as a coherent unit. After this moment, the person cannot be put back together again. In this context, one is referring to the particular time and place at which life ended. There may be stray electrical discharges in the nervous system for a brief time and individual cells may be metabolizing, but they are not life.

*Biological death*, then, is the point at which the organism can no longer function as an integrated entity, and this loss cannot be reversed or augmented. Much like a puzzle, the pieces of the human body must be integrated to form the whole. The loss of the cohesiveness of the organism is what qualifies as biological death. On the micro level, *cellular death* occurs in the hours and days following organismal death, when bacteria and insects begin feasting on the corpse, leading to decay.

Even the notion of biological death can be controversial. Consider the case of Jahi McMath (2000–), which illuminates the difficulties that can arise surrounding such a seemingly clear-cut issue as stating when death has occurred.

In December 2013, thirteen-year-old McMath was admitted to Oakland Children's Hospital in California where she underwent surgery to relieve her sleep apnea. As a result of unforeseen blood loss, McMath had a heart attack. The loss of blood circulation caused whole brain death, and McMath was declared dead ten days after her surgery. A death certificate was issued by the coroner's office. McMath's mother, however, refused to accept the declaration of death by neurological criteria (i.e., brain death), and argued in court to have the death declaration overruled. The judge granted the mother's request for continuation of medical treatments to sustain breathing and blood circulation for a short period of time. Medical professionals at the hospital and across the country maintained that

***Attorney Christopher Dolan points to an MRI of Jahi McMath during a news conference at his San Francisco law office, October 3, 2014.*** *Thirteen-year-old McMath was declared dead ten days after surgery in December 2013, when complications arising from blood loss and a heart attack caused whole-brain death. However, her mother refused to accept the declaration of death by neurological criteria (i.e., brain death), arguing in court to have the declaration overruled. McMath was ultimately transferred to a care facility in New Jersey, where the law allowed for philosophical objection to a declaration of death on the basis of neurological criteria.* **ERIC RISBERG/AP IMAGES.**

McMath was dead and that continuation of support would be futile. During the time they were given by the courts, the family arranged to have McMath transferred to a care facility in New Jersey, where the law allowed for religious objection to a declaration of death on the basis of neurological criteria—meaning that she could be considered alive in New Jersey. As of 2015, McMath remains in New Jersey on body-sustaining treatment, where the supportive devices have maintained her cardiac flow and respiration.

## LEGAL DEATH

The need for a legal definition of death comes about from the necessity of knowing when it is acceptable to dispose of a body, to initiate probate (the legal process of distributing a person's goods), and to donate organs. For most of human history, death was known by signs of decay or the cessation of breathing and heartbeat. With the advent of organ transplant technologies, organs must be removed for transplant before decay occurs or bodily function must be maintained using ventilators, dialysis, and a variety of drugs that regulate processes. These technologies further muddy the water over when a person is *dead*. As a result, lawyers and physicians created the notion of *brain death* (or death by neurological criteria)—a period when the brain has ceased to function, the integrity of the organism is irreversibly lost, but the process of cellular death has not begun.

The Uniform Determination of Death Act of 1981 clarified the legal definition of death in the United States. This model law has been adopted, at least in part, by all states. Section one of the act states: "An individual who has sustained either (1) irreversible cessation of circulatory and respiratory functions, or (2) irreversible cessation of all functions of the entire brain, including the brain stem, is dead. A determination of death must be made in accordance with accepted medical standards" (National Conference of Commissioners on Uniform State Laws 1980).

Although the Uniform Determination of Death Act gave a concrete definition as to the legal definition of death among the US states, two states have adopted different interpretations of the act. In New Jersey, one can reject the whole brain death definition based on philosophical beliefs. In New York and New Jersey, if one is a member of a religion that does not accept the whole brain death definition, then the cardiopulmonary definition alone may be used. Because of this amendment in New Jersey, McMath's family transported her there from California so that she could be considered legally alive.

Once a person has been determined to have a complete cessation of all cardiopulmonary function or brain function by a licensed provider, a death certificate is issued. Death certificates are the government's official recognition that a person has died and allow for the collection of data on causes of death, death rates, and other related information.

## MEDICAL DEATH

Medical death can be understood as the physical assessment of physiological functions that allow us to determine that a patient has died. As technology advances, providers are able to use more accurate and descriptive methods to determine whether a patient has died. In the twenty-first century, rather than simply feeling for a patient's pulse or looking for bodily decay, providers use stethoscopes and heart monitors to observe cardiac and pulmonary functions. Pulse oximeters measure the percentage of oxygenation of the tissues, giving providers an idea of the body's ability to keep organs functioning, which is an indicator of how long the patient may have to live. These, and a variety of other tools, including blood pressure monitors and electrocardiogram heart monitor readings give providers the physical assessment information to determine the cardiopulmonary state of an individual and whether they have died as a result of loss of respiratory and heart function.

Determining the physical presence of brain death is a more involved task. In 1968, an ad hoc committee of the Harvard Medical School detailed a comprehensive list of physical assessment findings that determined brain death (see Table 7.1). Brain imaging and scanning now provide assessments of an individual's brain activity. Magnetic resonance imaging (MRI) allows us to observe the structure of the brain and look for anatomical issues that may indicate brain death. Positron emission tomography (PET) scanning allows for the assessment of blood flow to different areas of the brain, indicating brain activity (or a lack thereof). These advanced technologies allow providers to more closely observe a patient as he or she enters the last hours of life: certain vital signs such as heart rate, breathing pattern, and organ oxygenation change in consistent ways as individuals pass, and these technologies allow providers to be aware of this occurrence so that they can prepare patients and their families.

Both Harvard and the 1981 Uniform Determination provide criteria for *whole brain death*, not part. This means that the cerebrum, cerebellum, and medulla (brain stem) must cease to function for a person to meet *whole brain death* criteria. The cerebellum (or higher brain) is the location of our higher-order functioning, all of the traits and processes that make us human. The brain stem (or medulla) regulates the body's unconscious activities, such as breathing, digesting, and sleep-wake cycles. Whole brain death is final—the integrated organism cannot function when even basic brain function is lost. This perspective views the brain functions in terms of its ability to coordinate and integrate all functions of the body. Brain death requires an assumption that the brain is primarily what makes us human and alive.

Alternatively, one might argue for a *partial brain death* or *higher brain death* criteria. This standard suggests that death ought to be defined as "the irreversible cessation of the capacity for consciousness" (DeGrazia 2011). Thus death is when the upper brain is no longer capable of supporting consciousness, even though the brain stem may be supporting basic biological functioning. The philosophical notion is that it is higher brain function that makes us uniquely human and is the core of our existence in the world. If we lose the capacity for consciousness and for our individual identity, then there is no human life and that is sufficient for us to be viewed as dead. By this definition, a person in a persistent vegetative state would be considered dead. In the tradition of René Descartes's (1596–1650) logical-metaphysical dualism, this perspective assumes that a living human and a living biological organism are two separate things. For human life, response to stimuli, a sleep-wake cycle, and the processing of food (i.e., brain-stem function) are necessary but not sufficient to be alive as a human. Partial brain death also assumes that only being alive *as a human* is what makes life worth living. In this view, mere biological functioning without human consciousness is not alive.

**Harvard Ad Hoc Committee Determination of Brain Death**

The following clinical signs and symptoms are used to determine the mental state of an unconscious person and are to be repeated twice, twenty-four hours apart:

- Unreceptivity and unresponsiveness
- No movement or breathing
- No reflexes
- Flat electroencephalogram (confirmatory)

In addition, the following must be present:

- Body temperature ≥89.6°F (32°C)
- Absence of central nervous system depressants

SOURCE: Ad Hoc Committee of the Harvard Medical School to Examine the Definition of Brain Death 1968.

***Table 7.1.*** *Harvard Ad Hoc Committee Determination of Brain Death* © **GALE/CENGAGE LEARNING.**

One reason that the higher brain death position has not gained further traction in bioethics or legal communities is that it means a willingness to put someone like McMath or Terri Schiavo (1963–2005) into her burial plot, even though the body may still be breathing. The aesthetics of this offend some people and violate many people's religious beliefs.

## SOCIAL DEATH

Hunter S. Thompson (1937–2005) quips that "We are all alone, born alone, die alone" (1965, 225). Social death is part of the dying process—when a person loses parts of his or her engaged life. It is the loss of connections with people and places outside oneself. As a person dies from chronic disease or old age, his or her world becomes narrower—withdrawing from work, the public, and finally to a sickbed. Along the way, fewer people are part of the person's life. He or she loses regular contact with coworkers and clients, then acquaintances and friends, until the social network is a handful of people and medical professionals. This narrowing occurs for many different reasons, both physical and social, and leads to the eventual isolation of the individual from society, friends, and even family.

Social death also occurs when an individual can no longer contribute to the world in a way he or she finds meaningful. For example, the loss of hearing often begins this process of social death. When a sixty-five-year-old man cannot hear his friends' conversations at dinner, he begins to stay home more often, rather than socializing. The loss of vision also can have this effect, whether it stops a person from being able to drive, or simply disorients him or her to the point where he or she feels uncomfortable in public. These physical changes lead to the progressive decrease in social life.

Those with Alzheimer's disease experience an obvious form of social death as the disease progresses. The individual's ability to communicate normally with the world decreases to the point at which he or she is isolated from friends and family because his or her understanding of the world is limited. Those with Parkinson's disease often experience a social death because of decreased mobility and ability to continue physical activities that once provided him or her with social interactions like golf or walking. As a person's ability to complete activities of daily living, such as driving, gardening, cooking, or cleaning, decreases, his or her world diminishes. This narrowing can lead to feelings of inadequacy, hopelessness, and uselessness.

## PHILOSOPHICAL FRAMEWORK

The introduction to this volume included a discussion on the major ethical theories used in biomedical ethics. Among these was *principlism*, detailed by Tom Beauchamp (1939–) and James Childress (1940–) in their 1979 work *The Principles of Biomedical Ethics*. They describe four major principles of moral deliberation: autonomy, nonmaleficence, beneficence, and justice. *Autonomy* is an individual's right to self-governance in matters of medical care. *Nonmaleficence* is the requirement that a health-care provider should do no harm to a patient. *Beneficence* is a positive obligation to provide benefit to a patient and to take action to prevent harm. *Justice* asks what a person is due. According to Beauchamp and Childress, justice is the perspective that similar cases should be treated the same and that resources (such as hospital beds, medications, and physician time) should be distributed fairly. These principles are useful to understanding the importance of issues in death and dying, including attempts to increase patient autonomy, concerns about whether keeping the bodies of brain-dead patients functioning with mechanical technology is harming or helping, and even the decision of when care is futile. The distinctive definitions in death demonstrate the complexity of death and the challenges of defining it from a medical, legal, and social perspective. Personal understanding helps individuals exercise autonomy to make decisions and have conversations about the end of life. Professional understanding is important for physicians determining death, for policy makers creating laws and regulations, and for clinical ethicists helping families make tough decisions about their dying loved ones.

## HISTORY OF DEATH AND DYING

In previous eras of human history, defining the moment of death and acknowledging different types of death were not as important as they are in the twenty-first century. Our medicalization and institutionalization of death is a recent trend. Death has always held mystery, but as sociologist Allan Kellehear (1955–) writes in *A Social History of Dying* (2007), in previous eras it was viewed more as a part of life rather than as a sickness to be cured or controlled.

### MYTHOLOGY

Since the dawn of time, humans have sought explanations for why we die. In the myths of many cultures, humans are immortal or are long lived until some event brings death into the world.

According to the book of Genesis, death was a curse that God placed on humans after Adam and Eve violated his prohibition against eating from the Tree of Knowledge. As punishment for disregarding him, or gaining knowledge, God punished humans with pain, toil, and death.

One Native American myth holds that the first people lived forever, which led to overcrowding. The spirits met to take care of the problem and came up with the idea of temporary death—at any given time a certain part of the population would be dead and they would come back when their turn was over. Coyote—the trickster—did not like this idea, and so when it was time for the dead to return to life, he blocked the door back to life, making death permanent.

In ancient Greece, death enters when the gods Zeus and Prometheus have a disagreement. The resolution is Zeus creating a woman, Pandora, who later opens a forbidden box and releases death into the world.

### SOCIOLOGY

According to Kellehear (2007), there have been four ages of dying: the Stone Age, the Pastoral Age, the Age of the City, and the Cosmopolitan Age. In the Stone Age, death was sudden and occurred at all ages. Life was snuffed out by accident, animal attack, and less often by disease. This was an era where the moment of "death" was what the family said it was, since there was no greater expert. Dying as the social process of ending a life mostly occurred after biological death. The community would follow rites and rituals that would lead the soul to its reward in the beyond.

The Pastoral Age finds humans living in settlements as part of agrarian societies that adopted more sedentary lifestyles. Death was caused mostly by diseases, as well as war and human sacrifice. Dying could be better predicted, and dying would begin before death. One of the stresses of this age was having an awareness that one was dying, which permitted time to make plans for interment of the body and the distribution of wealth and property, and to seek absolution from a deity. This process was known as "the good death." A person was determined to be "dead" when his or her body rotted. In Europe, bodies were placed in charnel houses—a vault in which corpses and bones are stored—until the flesh decayed off the body and then the bones were buried. Part of the (social) dying process took place after death, during which time prayers would be said for the preservation of the deceased and for their ease in the afterlife.

In the Age of the City, a significant part of the population lived in cities. The period's characteristic feature of death was that the experience was managed. In the managed death, a team of specialists come and go from the bedside to ensure that the tasks of dying are accomplished. There are specialists to treat illness, to handle the body, to attend to mourners, to ensure inheritance, and to attend to spiritual needs. Here death needs to be controlled and kept at bay. The threshold between living and dying is a doctor's proclamation, not the self-awareness that existed in earlier ages. More of life is spent preparing for dying.

The Cosmopolitan Age is the modern era in which most people live a complex life. It is an era that worships energy, movement, strength, progress, and youth. Dying is not about a failing of the biological organism, but rather a moral statement that indicates one's economic and political value. Those who are no longer productive members of society are often moved to care facilities for the "aged." There, they can prepare for death and grow old out of sight of anyone else. This is the era of the "shameful death." From its origins as a community event, dying becomes private. In this era, Kellehear explains, we all die alone.

**Top Ten Causes of Death in the United States**

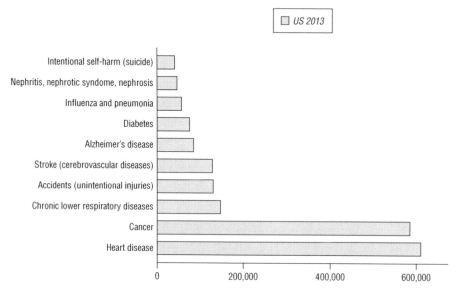

SOURCE: Centers for Disease Control and Prevention 2013.

***Figure 7.1.*** *Top Ten Causes of Death in the United States.* © **GALE/CENGAGE LEARNING.**

## DEATH AND DYING IN THE TWENTY-FIRST CENTURY

That we die has been a constant of human history, but what kills us has changed dramatically over time. For example, Figure 7.1 shows the top ten causes of death in the United States in 2013. At the top is heart disease followed by cancer. With the exception of influenza and pneumonia, the list does not include infectious diseases. One hundred years ago, this list would have shown several infectious diseases, such as tuberculosis, bronchitis, typhoid, diphtheria, and croup.

In the United States, violence is the highest cause of death (accident, suicide, homicide) for individuals younger than forty-five years of age. For individuals older than forty-five years of age, cancer is the leading cause of death and heart disease is second. After sixty-five years of age, these two causes switch spots on the list.

The rest of the world, however, looks quite different. Although heart disease is still the leading cause of death, respiratory infections, HIV/AIDS, and diarrhea are included in the top ten list for 2014 (see Figure 7.2). The differences between Figures 7.1 and 7.2 show how location and socioeconomic status has a strong effect on the risks of daily living that can cause death.

Like Vivian Bearing in *Wit*, almost 70 percent of people die in a hospital or long-term care settings. One trend shows that the number of days spent in the hospital, especially in the intensive care unit (ICU), before death are increasing. The unfortunate result of these numbers is deaths similar to Vivian's, where people die isolated from family and friends with more intense treatment than may be wanted.

**Top Ten Causes of Death Worldwide**

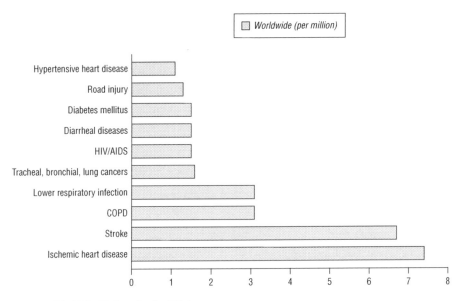

SOURCE: World Health Organization 2014.

***Figure 7.2.*** *Top Ten Causes of Death Worldwide.* © **GALE/CENGAGE LEARNING.**

### DEATH ANXIETY

The result of inheriting the age of the managed and shameful death is that those who are dying are isolated from the living. When death and dying occur offstage, those in the audience are left only with their imagination. According to Kellehear, death becomes a taboo topic that is not discussed and that is polluting to the living. For example, in Leo Tolstoy's (1828–1910) story *The Death of Ivan Ilyich* (1886), an officer of the court is dying after a fall. His disease is never diagnosed, but he finds himself in increasing physical and existential discomfort. His family is unsympathetic and is not interested in caring for him or even in simply visiting him. He finds caregiving in Gerasim, his young butler. With this modicum of compassion, Ivan spends his final three days alone contemplating the notion of suffering and the good life. He confronts his fears and anxiety of death—leaving a legacy, forgiveness, salvation, and finding a meaning to life. In the end, he finds in himself a capacity for forgiveness, and his fear of death vanishes.

Tolstoy's fear and existential angst is described by the term *death anxiety*: "Death anxiety is a multidimensional construct related to fear of and anxiety related to the anticipation and awareness of the reality of dying and death that includes emotional, cognitive, and motivational components that vary by developmental stage and sociocultural life occurrences" (Lehto and Stein 2009, 31–32). In other words, death anxiety is our unease and fearfulness when confronted with the notion of our own death. We are forced to face the fact that someday each of us will cease to exist. Because this anxiety is unpleasant, as a modern society, we have created a culture that denies death. As literary scholar Liran Razinsky discusses in *Freud, Psychoanalysis, and Death* (2013), we try not to think about it so that we can pretend it will never happen to us. Like Damian in *Selfless*, we yearn for a way to extend life, no matter the cost to ourselves or to others. Death becomes an enemy to be conquered.

Sometimes we are forced to confront mortality, our own or others, such as when facing a diagnosis of a life-threatening illness, facing a life-threatening event (e.g., a plane or car crash), seeing others die, or even facing situations that are beyond our control (such as flying on a plane in choppy weather). In these cases, death anxiety may become evident. If the feelings are strong enough, it may be clinically diagnosed as found in nurse Lynda Juall Carpenito's *Handbook of Nursing Diagnosis* (2013).

Death anxiety is so prevalent in modern society that it spawned the successful *Final Destination* series of films. In each of the many films, a group of teenagers is involved in an accident or event that should have led to their deaths. With some precognition, they are able to avoid the fatal stroke—for a time. The films then follow each character as he or she attempts to evade Death, who spins elaborate schemes to ensure the death occurs. The characters literally run away from death.

## WAYS OF DYING

### THE HOSPITAL AND ICU

*Steel Magnolias* (1989) is a film about Shelby Eatenton Latcherie, a young woman who, after getting married, becoming pregnant, and giving birth, experiences kidney failure as a complication of her type 1 diabetes and pregnancy. Despite a transplant donation from her mother, Shelby is unable to recover from the kidney disease and slips into a coma. Shelby is kept in the ICU at the hospital while her family makes the difficult decision to remove her body-sustaining treatment.

Body-sustaining treatment is sometimes called *life-sustaining treatment* or *life support.*
According to the American Medical Association (AMA), "Life-sustaining treatment is any
treatment that serves to prolong life without reversing the underlying medical condition"
(1994)—that is, a medical intervention that is intended to prolong life by maintaining or
replacing a vital function of the body but that does not cure the disease or condition. Such
measures include cardiopulmonary resuscitation (CPR, attempting to restart a patient's
heart when it stops), assisted ventilation (delivering air to the lungs), tube feeding (delivering
nutrition to the body), heart/lung bypass (pumping blood and oxygenating it), dialysis
(filtering the body's waste products), defibrillation (electrically shocking the heart to change
its rhythm), and pressors (drugs that artificially maintain blood pressure). These medical
interventions prolong organ function long after brain function diminishes past the point of
conscious life.

The ICU offers all of these interventions, providing every opportunity to keep patients'
hearts beating, blood filtered, and oxygen flowing through their bodies for an extended
period. For some patients, intensive care medicine provides extraordinary care to those
patients whose conditions can be cured. For those who are unable to recover, many
intensive treatments may simply cause more suffering. ICU care can cost $10,000 per day.
Despite the use of these interventions, the high nurse-to-patient ratio, and the use of
modern medical technologies, 18 to 20 percent of Americans die in the ICU. Often, these
patients are not conscious at the end of their life and are unable to communicate with their
loved ones as a result of the medical interventions they undergo in the ICU.

In *Steel Magnolias*, Shelby's husband and family decide together that she would have
wanted to end the body-sustaining support. The decisions and uncertainty in what Shelby
wanted cause much familial suffering (and entertainment for the audience). The film ends at
her funeral.

## HOSPICE

Vivian Bearing in *Wit* experiences unbearable pain and suffering at the end of her life. The
aggressive cancer treatments cause her to feel ill, cloud her mind, and keep her from doing
the things she wants to do with her last days. She is impaired to the point that she cannot
interact with doctors, nurses, or even the visitors who come to spend her last days with her.
As physician Benjamin F. Stump and bioethicists Craig M. Klugman and Barbara Thornton
write in *Last Hours of Life* (2008), this is not the way that most of us hope to die.

Despite our hopes for a quick death in familiar surroundings, most Americans will die
as a result of a chronic, progressive illness. Terminal illness is known to be the point at
which nothing more can be done to *cure* someone, but nurse Lorraine Fields notes in "DNR
Does Not Mean No Care" (2007) that it is often misinterpreted as the point at which
nothing more can be done to *help* someone. This idea gives the impression that no measures
should be taken to help these patients. Such a limited view of terminal illness puts no focus
on *comfort care*—pain management, symptom control, spiritual support, and emotional
factors that arise at the end of life. As was seen with Vivian, this view of terminal illness can
lead to isolation and ultimately increased suffering for patients and their families. Hospice
care exists so that we can experience a better end of life.

The term *hospice* is derived from the word *hospitality* and was used as early as 500 CE
when it meant a place of shelter for weary and ill travelers on a religious pilgrimage. *Hospice*
was first used in a medical context by Dame Cicely Saunders (1918–2005), a physician who

started her work with the terminally ill in 1948. In 1968, Saunders created the first modern-style hospice, St. Christopher's Hospice, in the United Kingdom. Hospice now refers to a journey toward death. Hospice is based in a philosophy of holistic—mind-body-spirit-social—multidisciplinary care focused on giving patients a "better" end-of-life experience. This philosophy stems from the idea that dying is a normal part of the process of living. As bioethicist Bruce Jennings and his coauthors note in "Access to Hospice Care" (2003), hospice provides comfort by focusing on quality of life rather than a cure. In hospice, end-of-life care typically takes place in the patient's home or a residential hospice center.

## DYING IN HOSPICE

To receive hospice care, two physicians must state that death can be expected within six months if the terminal disease follows its normal course. This does not mean that the patient must die within six months. Jennifer Temel and colleagues write in "Early Palliative Care for Patients with Metastatic Non-small-Cell Lung Cancer" (2010) that many hospice patients actually end up living longer than their counterparts who do not receive hospice care. Patients are reevaluated periodically to assess the state of their condition, and as long as the provider continues to agree that if the disease takes its normal course, the patient will die within six months, they can remain in hospice care.

To enter hospice, a patient will need to agree to stop medical treatments of curative intent. This is a momentous and often difficult decision for patients and their families because our current social view of death can cause this process to feel like "giving up." Patients in hospice care receive no aggressive medical interventions other than those that will relieve symptoms or provide comfort. Examples of these interventions include morphine for pain, eye drops for improved vision, and even physical therapy. Usually, these patients are not significantly impaired by the medications given to them in hospice. It is sometimes necessary, however, to give doses of medications, usually for pain, that alter the mental status of the patient. The goal of treatment in this type of care, though, always remains pain relief, symptom management, and emotional support (American Hospice Foundation 2014).

Each patient in hospice is assigned a social worker who will help with the social and emotional issues pertaining to end-of-life care. A social worker will work with the whole family to deal with issues of death anxiety, mending of familial relationships, grief, and guilt. Patients in hospice often have issues they would like to resolve before they die, whether it is a broken relationship with a child, or guilt about a poor life decision. According to Dona J. Reese in *Hospice Social Work* (2013), the social worker can help with these issues.

When a hospice patient is in the last stages of dying, the hospice will usually call a *vigil*, meaning that volunteers, nurses, family, and friends sit with the patient around the clock, reading, singing, playing music, or providing any activity that the patient has requested for his or her final hours. This personalization of care and the focus on patient's wants are indicative of the hospice philosophy of care and its focus on quality of life for its patients.

## PALLIATIVE CARE

In "What Is Palliative Care?" (1998), physician J. Andrew Billings explains that palliative care is a subspecialty of internal medicine that focuses on symptom management and pain relief. Although it shares many of the same clinical outcomes and goals as hospice care, palliative medicine is not restricted to those individuals at the end of life. Patients receiving palliative care are not required to stop receiving other forms of treatment, so in many cases cancer patients who are receiving aggressive chemotherapy treatments also work with palliative care to manage the symptoms of their treatments as well as their disease. Palliative care includes some of the social and spiritual services that are seen in hospice care and is often administered in the hospital or through out-patient medical clinics.

### AN EPIDEMIC OF PAIN

*Cake* (2015) is a film about Claire Bennett, a woman who is left in severe emotional distress and physical pain when a car accident injures her and kills her son. Although she is somewhat able to treat her physical pain with medication, Claire's husband and friends desert her because her physical pain, combined with her emotional suffering, causes Claire to become a distant, unpleasant, and emotionally unstable person.

Often the ideas of pain and suffering are lumped together, but it is important to differentiate between these two concepts. Pain is an unpleasant sensory and emotional experience associated with actual or potential tissue damage. The fever and chills, the strain in muscles, the stabbing in the stomach, and the shooting sharpness down a leg are all examples of pain. For Claire Bennett, physical pain was the pressure pushing on her spine and the tissue damage that occurred as a result of her accident. These observable injuries caused physiologically detectable pain in her breathing pattern, heart rate, and facial cues.

According to the Institute of Medicine, the United States is faced with an epidemic of pain. Pain is undertreated in the dying and in people with illness out of fears of addiction and the war on drugs. The American Hospice Foundation notes, however, that when dealing with a person who is dying, addiction should be of lesser concern than providing comfort. Patients approaching the end of life often experience large amounts of both pain and suffering. Physical pain, usually due to the progression of the patient's illness, can often be treated with medications. Alleviation of physical pain does a great deal of good for patients, allowing them to focus on family, friends, or any other matters they need to attend to with their remaining time.

Suffering, on the other hand, is the sadness, anger, frustration, and hopelessness that may or may not be related to physical pain. Claire Bennett shows her suffering in her depressed mood, her detachment from those around her, and her consistent dwelling on the negative aspects of her life. With patients at the end of life, suffering encompasses feelings of existential distress—questions like "Why me?" and "Why now?" This existential distress and death anxiety can cause fear and confusion. Existential pain can be approached directly through conversations with loved ones and spiritual advisers, and by providing time for reflection. These effects may even lessen the existential suffering of the individual.

## AUTONOMY AND THE RIGHT TO REFUSE

As mentioned earlier, autonomy means that a patient has a right to make his or her own health-care choices. The word *autonomy* derives from the Greek *autos* (self) and *nomos* (rule, governance, or law), or *self-rule*. The Greek notion gave autonomy to cities and states, but in more recent times, it is a right of individuals. The German philosopher Immanuel Kant (1724–1804) argued that every rational human being has free will and thus autonomy—the freedom to make choices free from outside influence. Kant's idea of autonomy relied on the idea of the human ability to reason and use logic to exercise free will.

In bioethics, autonomy is self-rule: a rational, competent person can make his or her own decisions, free of coercion. For patients to make truly autonomous decisions, the provider must give information about the potential treatments (or not treating), including risks, benefits, side effects, and alternatives. To act autonomously, a person must understand the options and must voluntarily make a choice. Legal autonomy requires that the individual be both competent and capable of communicating his or her own wishes to others. *Competency* is a legal status that an individual has the maturity, intelligence, and understanding to make his or her own decisions. *Capability* refers to the physical ability of a patient to make their wishes known. Most patients are able to vocalize their wishes, but some may have to write them, or be given direct questions to which they can respond by blinking or squeezing a hand. One is assumed to have competency upon reaching the age of majority, getting married, or in some states, giving birth. Incompetency—lacking legal competency—is declared by a judge after a hearing that provides evidence that a person is incapable of making rational and reasonable choices. This may occur because of intellectual deficits, psychological illness, or the individual's inability to communicate their wishes. Patients under the age of eighteen are considered incompetent: incapable of making decisions regarding their own health. A parent or guardian makes children's decisions.

*Capacity* is a person's ability to make a specific decision at a particular point in time. A five-year-old or a seventy-five-year-old with dementia may be able to choose between Jell-O or pudding but not whether to have major surgery. A patient's capacity is determined by the health-care provider. A person lacking capacity now may have it in a few hours or tomorrow. Capacity is fluid, whereas competency is more rigid.

The concept of autonomy in bioethics came about from the field's founding in the civil rights movement. Patients wanted to make their own decisions. Before patient autonomy was espoused, providers relied on their own ideas of morality and ethics to determine what was best for their patients. This left treatment outcomes in ethically ambiguous cases particularly difficult; legal cases often were needed to determine the precedent for future patients.

## EARLY COURT CASES

*Union Pacific Railway v. Botsford* was an 1891 US Supreme Court case involving a railroad passenger who suffered injuries to her brain and spine as a result of negligent construction of a car. The Union Pacific Railway Company claimed that it was entitled, without the patient's consent, to an opportunity to surgically examine her spine and brain to determine her diagnosis. The court disagreed, stating that "every individual [has] the right to the possession and control of his own person" (*Union Pacific Railway Co. v. Botsford* 1891). This case set the legal precedent for patient autonomy, giving individuals the right to refuse medical attention.

*Schloendorff v. Society of New York Hospital* was a 1914 case involving a woman who gave consent for surgical examination of her tumor. When the physician operated, however, he found the tumor to be cancerous and removed it. The court found that the operation to which the patient did not consent was considered medical battery, and thus illegal. This case set a precedent requiring expressed, documented, informed consent of the autonomous decisions of patients, thus reinforcing the right to refuse treatment.

## KAREN ANN QUINLAN

In 1975, twenty-one-year-old Karen Ann Quinlan (1954–1985) arrived home from a party where she experimented with multiple drugs and alcohol. Quinlan collapsed and stopped breathing. When she arrived at the hospital, Quinlan lapsed into unconsciousness, later determined to be a persistent vegetative state (PVS). Persistent vegetative state is defined by neurosurgeon Bryan Jennett and neurologist Fred Plum in "Persistent Vegetative State after Brain Damage" (1972) as a state of altered consciousness for more than four weeks. She suffered brain damage resulting from a lack of oxygen when she stopped breathing. She was put on a ventilator to breathe for her and doctors inserted a feeding tube.

After months of no change and with no likelihood of improvement, the Quinlan family requested that Karen's ventilator be removed, an act that doctors and the family alike felt would end her life. The hospital refused the family's request, acting on threats from the county prosecutor that homicide charges could be pressed if the ventilator was removed. In the subsequent court case, Quinlan's family argued that they simply wanted to end "extraordinary means" of continuing her life and that they wanted her returned to her natural state.

*Extraordinary means* is a term used in the Catholic tradition. The Catholic Church says that individuals are required to use *ordinary means*—medical interventions with a reasonable hope of benefit and not unduly burdensome—to preserve life and health. However, extraordinary means—medical interventions that merely prolong dying, have no reasonable hope of benefit, and may be excessively burdensome—may be withdrawn. The only exception is nutrition and hydration, which the Catholic Church says is ordinary care and thus must always be provided. It is worth noting that when a body is shutting down, introducing nutrition and hydration can cause pain and discomfort. Food in the stomach when the digestive system no longer works is uncomfortable and can be dangerous. Adding fluid in a body where the kidneys have ceased to function or methods of fluid removal have stopped can lead to painful swelling and stretching of the tissues that try to absorb the fluid. This distinction was an important clarification for the devout Quinlan family, as their religious beliefs would forbid ending Karen's life but would allow for an individual or his or her family to choose not to use extraordinary means to prolong life.

The New Jersey Supreme Court ruled in favor of the Quinlan family, setting a precedent that an individual or his or her medical power of attorney can make the decision to refuse medical treatment even if that intervention is sustaining the body. Quinlan's ventilator was removed. She surprised family and providers by sustaining her respiratory function, and she remained in a persistent vegetative state for more than nine years before dying of pneumonia.

This case is significant in three ways: (1) it confirmed a right to refuse life-sustaining treatment; (2) it established that a family could have a ventilator removed when there was no likelihood of recovery; and (3) it said that such decisions should be made by families in consultation with physicians and hospital ethics committees.

## NANCY CRUZAN

In January 1983, twenty-five-year-old Nancy Cruzan (1958–1990) lost control of her car and was thrown from the vehicle. She landed face down in a water-filled ditch and was later found by paramedics who resuscitated her. After being unconscious for three weeks, doctors determined that Cruzan was in a persistent vegetative state. Like the Quinlans, Cruzan's family wanted her removed from medical treatment prolonging her bodily functions so that she could die. The difference, however, was that Cruzan did not need respiratory assistance from a ventilator, only artificial nutrition and hydration through a feeding tube. Her family believed that this would be Cruzan's wish, had she the ability to advocate for herself. Her roommate stated that they had multiple conversations about the fact that she would not want to remain in a comatose state. Missouri law, however, stated that "clear and convincing" evidence of Cruzan's wishes was needed before removal of the feeding tube could be considered.

The Cruzans took their case to the Missouri courts, which ruled that the family did not have the evidence they needed to prove Cruzan's wishes. The family was not permitted to cease her medical treatments. Later, the family obtained corroborating testimony that satisfied the court, and a court order was written to remove artificial nutrition and hydration.

This case is significant in two ways: (1) it established the need to document one's wishes regarding end-of-life care to fulfill the "clear and convincing" standard; and (2) it set the precedent for removing artificial nutrition and hydration.

## TERRI SCHIAVO

In 1990, Terri Schiavo was a twenty-seven-year-old Florida woman taking fertility drugs while suffering from bulimia. In the middle of one night, the combination of drugs and the eating disorder stopped her heart long enough that her brain was starved for oxygen for an unknown period of time. She suffered severe brain damage as a result. After multiple months in a coma, Schiavo was diagnosed as being in a persistent vegetative state. She required a feeding tube for nutrition and hydration but was not on a ventilator. For two years, medical professionals attempted physical, speech, and even experimental therapies to improve Schiavo's condition, but she did not improve. In 1998, Schiavo's husband, Michael Schiavo, petitioned to have her feeding tube removed, saying that he and his siblings had talked to Terri Schiavo on multiple occasions and that she would not have wished to have her life dependent on such treatment. Schiavo's parents, however, opposed this decision, stating that they believed she would have wanted this treatment. Without an advance directive documenting her wishes, it was impossible to tell what Schiavo wanted. After extensive media coverage and multiple prolonged court hearings, the courts ruled that the feeding tube could be removed.

Schiavo's feeding tube was removed on April 24, 2001, but was reinserted several days later due to a court injunction that Schiavo's parents had filed. The court proceedings for this case took another two years, but it was determined again that Schiavo's parents would not have the right to keep the feeding tube in place. On October 15, 2003, the feeding tube was removed again.

As these proceedings occurred, media coverage of the case brought many different groups to advocate for both Terri Schiavo's parents and her husband. Perhaps the most vocal groups were those representing the pro-life and disability rights movements, who supported Schiavo's parents, arguing that Schiavo was living with a disability and that the removal of her feeding tube was discriminatory and amounted to murder.

Partially because of the extensive media coverage and the activism this case attracted, a law known as Terri's Law was passed quickly through the Florida legislature. This law gave the governor, Jeb Bush (1953–), the authority to intervene in Schiavo's case; he immediately ordered the feeding tube to be reinserted. After further court battles, Terri's Law was deemed unconstitutional, and the law was overturned. Finally, on May 18, 2005, Schiavo's feeding tube was removed for the third and final time. She died in hospice care on May 31, 2005.

This case is interesting in the field of bioethics because, unlike the cases of Quinlan and Cruzan, there were no new medical or ethical issues to debate. Schiavo chose her husband to be her agent in her medical power of attorney, so he had the right to remove her feeding tube. According to Craig Klugman in "Reframing Terri Schiavo" (2006), the case is significant in: (1) the interference of elected officials in a personal, family decision that should have been made between doctors and family; and (2) the influence of lobbying money and media portrayals on the case.

## PROLONGING DYING OR SUPPORTING A PERSON WITH A DISABILITY?

The Schiavo case raised the issue of how much brain function a person needs to have to be considered alive as a human. The notion of brain death presumes that humanness resides solely in the brain. A person in a persistent vegetative state not only lacks these capacities but also lacks the potential to ever have them again. Thus, when the brain dies, humanness dies. The technology supporting biological function can be removed because the person is already dead, the biological machine will just wind down.

On the other hand, if only part of the brain (e.g., the higher brain) is damaged or dead, then another perspective would hold that Schiavo was living with a disability. From this point of view, removing Schiavo's or Cruzan's feeding tube was morally wrong and illegal because that action would have constituted murder and discrimination against a person with a disability.

An MRI scan and postmortem autopsy showed that Schiavo had only 50 percent of the brain mass of a person her age and sex. The body had reabsorbed most of the higher brain (cerebellum). From this perspective, Schiavo's higher brain function was not compromised, it did not exist. Equating humanness with higher brain function, removing nutrition and hydration was acceptable because the person who was Schiavo was already dead. Certainly, her husband made this clear on her tombstone, which lists dates for "birth," "departed this earth," and "at peace."

## ADVANCE CARE PLANNING

In the graphic novel *Can't We Talk about Something More Pleasant* (2014), cartoonist Roz Chast (1954–) shares a memoir of her aging parents. Using words, drawings, and photographs, she illustrates her parents' descent into frailty, their final days, and their attempts to talk about the end of life. The book opens with an image of the artist as a child with her parents. The reader then sees nine comic panels. The author as character begins, "So … do you guys ever think about things?" In subsequent panels, her parents pretend to not know about what she was asking until the final panel in which they all appear to be relieved that they avoided such a conversation. The next 220 pages, however, show how important that conversation is.

Advance care planning may seem like an unusual section to have in a book about medical ethics or philosophy because it is practical and does not present controversial concepts or ideas. That is partly because there is no controversy about having a conversation about end-of-life choices—most religions and professional organizations endorse this. And partly it is because this is the practice of autonomy. These conversations are about ensuring others know your autonomous choices. Medicare even reimburses physicians for talking to patients about end-of-life care wishes. Physician Erik Fromme and his coauthors show in "Association between POLST Scope of Treatment Orders and In-Hospital Death in Oregon" (2014) that when your choices are known, you are more likely to have them followed.

The town of La Crosse, Wisconsin, is remarkable because 97 percent of adults have completed advance directives. This high number is attributed to the sole hospital in town having instituted a program of end-of-life conversations. The Respecting Choices program through Gundersen Health System has trained facilitators to have discussions with people about their future care goals. Their emphasis is not on completing documents, but rather on having conversations and assisting people in talking with their family and friends.

Another program is Death over Dinner, during which people sit around enjoying a multicourse dinner. With each course, the guests are presented with a new prompt for discussion. By the end of the evening, people who may or may not know each other have shared many ideas about end-of-life care and wishes. The idea is to associate the conversation with something fun.

Another variation is the Conversation Project, a website that provides guidelines and workbooks for helping people to have the conversation. Their free kit includes suggestions for opening lines and question prompts. Even the popular Five Wishes advance directive form has sections on comfort of the dying person, how the person wishes to be treated, and messages that one wants to leave for loved ones.

## ADVANCE DIRECTIVES

One response to death anxiety is to try to control it. The advance care planning movement evolved as a way to permit people to make decisions about end-of-life medical and social care at a time when they may have lost the capacity to exercise autonomy. These forms ideally document a conversation about one's wishes regarding treatment and values at the end of life.

In the 2011 film *The Descendants*, George Clooney (1961–) plays Matt King, a husband whose wife, Elizabeth, is in a persistent vegetative state. Faced with deciding medical care for her, King begs his wife to awaken. The physicians eventually tell King that she will never improve. Elizabeth has completed an advance directive. In multiple scenes, the viewer sees King discussing this document with other characters and sharing that Elizabeth did not want to be kept alive on life support. As a family, knowing what Elizabeth wanted makes the actual decision making easier. Accepting that choice is not so easy. As King tells Elizabeth's father, "They told me she isn't going to wake up. It's for sure now.... She has a will, see, saying we have to do it like this. We both do. That's why I got you. We're letting her go."

Advance directives are a set of documents that provide guidance for future health-care decisions. In other words, a person creates one today to help guide physicians and families to make future choices when the patient can no longer make or express decisions. In 1977, California became the first state to pass an advance directive act. The California Natural Death Act permitted people to construct such a legal document. Other states soon adopted similar laws, and in 1990 the US Congress enacted the Patient Self-Determination Act. This law stated that an individual has a right to create a document that states his or her future health-care wishes and to appoint a surrogate decision maker to choose among available options when the patient can no longer make decisions. In addition, the law requires that hospitals must ask whether patients have an advance care directive when being admitted to a hospital.

All fifty states and the federal government have advance directive statutes. Each one varies in terms of language, what choices can be made, who can make decisions, and how the documents are certified (whether a notary or witness signatures or both). In some states, the directive must follow state law and language exactly (such as in Nevada and Texas). In other states, there may be a suggested form but almost any document form can be used. All states have friendly state statutes—meaning that forms from other states will be respected as far as their law allows. This means that a person who lives in California and has a directive there does not need to have a new directive for every state he or she drives through when traveling to New York. One should have a directive in the state of residence (where your driver's license is and, if applicable, where you pay state taxes). Ideally, these should be updated every five years. When traveling overseas, such documents may not exist in other countries or be honored.

In most cases, the advance directive can consist of up to four documents: a directive to physician and family, a power of attorney for health care, an advance directive for mental health, and physician orders for life-sustaining treatment (POLST)/out-of-hospital do-not-resuscitate order. Each of these will be discussed in turn.

## LIVING WILL

The living will or *directive to physician and family* is the legal document in which a person states what health-care choices he or she would want in future care. Patients and future patients can state what procedures they do or do not want, what their values are, and what should be considered in making choices. Most documents come into effect only when a person (1) is no longer capable of making decisions or can no longer communicate decisions (i.e., is incapacitated or incompetent), and (2) has a terminal illness or irreversible condition. For example, a person who is in a persistent vegetative state lacks the capacity to make decisions, has an inability to share them, and is in an irreversible condition. The exact trigger that activates the document varies by state.

Documents often allow a person to state how much body-sustaining treatment he or she desires. Body-sustaining treatment includes any medical intervention that replaces a function of the body. For example, a ventilator can take over breathing. A feeding tube can take over eating and drinking. In the event that a person's heart stops beating, cardiopulmonary resuscitation (CPR) and other resuscitative techniques (shocking, pressors, and compression) can be used to attempt to restart the heart. You can choose to have some of these efforts, all of these, or none of these.

Other directives allow a person to state preferences for specific procedures, such as resuscitation, antibiotics, blood and blood products, respiratory support, palliative surgeries (intended to decrease pain, not to cure), artificial nutrition and hydration, and dialysis. A patient's choices in these procedures is limited as to whether they are medically necessary and beneficial. For example, a person could request respiratory support, but if he or she is breathing fine on his or her own, then such support is not medically necessary.

In some directives, a person can add other requests such as being free from pain and having a period of trying medical interventions before removing them. Directives may even state value preferences, such as holding a preference for quantity of life (simply existing) over quality of life or vice versa. In some other cases, a person can state his or her organ donation choices, whom he or she wishes to be by the bedside, funeral arrangements, and more.

Advance directives are widely available online and in hospitals, doctors' offices, or attorneys' offices. Lawyers often help people complete them when writing a last will and testament. An attorney is not required to complete these documents; they are available for free online.

People with directives are more likely to have their wishes honored than people who do not have them. Such individuals are also more likely to choose hospice or palliative care over aggressive care. Their families are likely to have an easier mourning because they know they made the decision that the patient wanted.

These documents also have their problems. Consider the philosophical issue raised by health law scholar Rebecca Dresser and neurologist Peter Whitehouse, who believe that the person who needs the directive is a different person from the one who created it. They express concern that the wishes of a self from a former time should rule over a self in a later time. The latter self may have different values, believes, and opinions about quality of life and what makes a good life. On the other side of this debate is philosopher Ronald Dworkin, who believes that what counts is the integrity (values) of a life. Thus, the decisions of a former self in time should govern a current self who may lack capacity and competency.

Pragmatically, directives often cannot be located when most needed. They can be confusing and difficult to complete, thus leading to questions concerning whether they represent what a person truly wants. People may not understand the medical procedures they are being asked about or may not have an understanding of what life is like in a coma or a persistent vegetative state. A directive is often completed long before it is needed: a person may have changed his or her mind. Also consider that it is not possible to anticipate every possible decision that will need to be made or even what the patient's situation will be. Depending on the state, the document may not be applicable if one is pregnant.

About 25 percent of all US adults have completed advance directives. Completion is positively correlated with higher education, being Caucasian, having a disease, having a higher income, and being older. According to bioethicist Craig M. Klugman and nursing student Nicole Tolwin in "Examining Autonomous Selections in an Advance Directive" (2015), people over fifty are more likely to choose to refuse medical interventions, whereas those under fifty are more likely to want them.

## DURABLE POWER OF ATTORNEY FOR HEALTH CARE

A second document in the advance directive allows for a person to appoint a surrogate decision maker. This is a proxy who makes decisions for the patient when the patient is no longer able to do so because of a lack of capacity or ability to communicate. Different states have different names for this appointment, which may be durable power of attorney for health care (DPAHC), power of attorney for health care, medical power of attorney, and surrogate decision maker.

While just about anyone over the age of eighteen can be selected as a surrogate, a few categories of individuals cannot. To avoid conflicts of interest, your health-care provider or anyone who is an employee of your health-care provider or hospital in which you are a patient cannot serve as a surrogate. One should also not choose someone who will inherit one's estate or who is one's attorney.

The surrogate is not supposed to make a decision that he or she wants, nor the one that the physician claims is in the best interest of the patient. A *best interest* standard is where an authority decides what is best for the patient. The surrogate instead is charged with making the decision that the patient would have made, a *substituted judgment*. Thus, it is best if the surrogate and the patient have talked extensively. A surrogate, however, in many states has limits on his or her abilities. The surrogate may not be permitted to consent to terminating a pregnancy or to voluntary mental-health commitment, psychosurgery, electroshock therapy, or refusal of comfort care.

As a surrogate for the patient, this individual has access to the patient's entire medical record and speaks with the legal authority of the patient. A medical power of attorney becomes effective when a patient is unable to communicate decisions. Unlike the living will, the diagnosis of a terminal illness or irreversible condition usually is not required. For example, if a person faints from heat stroke and is otherwise healthy, the DPAHC comes into effect until the patient regains consciousness, whereas the living will would not be active in this scenario.

Complications occur when the family is unaware of who is the surrogate or when the surrogate is unaware of his or her role. For example, in an episode of the television show *Malcolm in the Middle*, the father, Hal, learns that he is the surrogate for a neighbor when an attorney knocks on the door. Hal has little knowledge of the neighbor, and they never had a conversation about end-of-life wishes. The result is that Hal cannot make a decision.

Often people will say, "My family knows what I want" or "My loved ones will make the right choice" and so do not choose a surrogate. What happens if a person does not select a surrogate? In some states, the statute includes a hierarchical list of decision makers. These individuals often include a spouse or partner, adult children, parents, siblings, close relatives, close friends, or clergy members. If there is no named DPAHC, then by these laws the spouse makes the decision; if there is no spouse, then the adult children; and so on. In other states, no list is made, but the physician must gather all of the significant people in a patient's life and ask them to choose who will make the decisions.

Several states grant more rights and powers to a DPAHC than to a surrogate from the default list. For example, in Illinois, an appointed surrogate can choose to withdraw treatment, but a person who makes decisions by virtue of being on the default list cannot.

## DIRECTIVE FOR MENTAL ILLNESS

In some states, a person can complete a directive for treatment of mental illness. This form is usually only completed by people who know they have a mental illness that can take away their capacity to make decisions. In such cases, they can indicate decisions for mental health treatment, such as preferences for voluntary hospitalization, electroshock therapy, medications, and use of restraints. Most of these are controversial therapies, as well as ones that can change a personality. Thus, it is desirable to have a person's input before such procedures might be necessary. Most people, however, will not complete this directive.

## POLST/OUT-OF-HOSPITAL DNR

In one scene in *Wit*, Vivian Bearing has a late-night conversation with Susie, her nurse. They discuss the idea of code status. If her heart should stop beating, does Vivian want to have resuscitative measures to try to restart her heart, or should the hospital staff just let her die, a practice known as *do not resuscitate* (DNR). Vivian chooses DNR. Unfortunately, this choice is ignored when her heart does stop and an overeager physician calls for her to be resuscitated.

The DNR order is a hospital-based, physician-written order stating that if a patient's heart stops or the patient ceases to breathe, no efforts will be made to resuscitate the patient. That means no CPR, no pressors, no intubation, and no electroshocking. In some places, the DNR order is known as the "do not attempt resuscitation" (DNAR) order, reflecting that one can attempt to resuscitate a patient but success is not guaranteed. In fact, chances of success range from 1 to 50 percent depending on the circumstances, such as observed versus unobserved code and presence of a comorbidity. Also in use is the phrase *allow natural death* (AND), advocating a perception that the cause of death is the underlying disease and not the lack of resuscitation. Those who believe that the act of not resuscitating is the cause of death, call not performing medical interventions *passive euthanasia*, reflecting a moral judgment that such actions must always be made to avoid being the cause of a patient's death (for more on this causality distinction, see the section "Withdrawing versus Withholding"). This latter position is not widely held or supported in mainstream bioethics.

What happens if the patient is outside of the hospital—at home, at work, or even in the ambulance? Because a DNR is a hospital-based order, it has no bearing outside of the hospital, including with emergency medical services (EMS). If one calls 911, EMS must perform resuscitation, even if there is an advance directive and even if there was a DNR order from a hospital. One answer to this situation is the out-of-hospital DNR. In some states, this is a physician-written order that applies to situations outside of the hospital, mainly when EMS is called. If EMS arrives on scene, and they see such a document, they can cease (or not begin) resuscitative efforts.

An alternative to the out-of-hospital order is the *physician/provider orders for life-sustaining treatment* (POLST) paradigm. In some states, this may be known as the practitioner orders for life-sustaining treatment, medical orders for life-sustaining treatment, clinician orders for life-sustaining treatment, medical orders for scope of treatment, or physician orders for scope of treatment. This document is for patients with a serious illness or frailty—a patient whom the doctor believes has less than one year of life remaining. Unlike other medical orders that stay with the care provider or hospital, a POLST stays with the patient and thus travels from site to site. Usually, it is a brightly colored form, which makes it easy to find. The goal is to ensure that patient's wishes for end-of-life treatment are known at all times.

## ORGAN/BODY DONATION

A final aspect of the advance directive documentation is to consider being an organ or body donor. Most states have online registries on which individuals can indicate a desire to donate and choose what organs or tissues they are willing to offer. A donation wallet card is often mailed that can be used to inform others of your donor status. In some states, this designation can be made when getting a driver's license and a demarcation is added to the license. This topic is discussed in greater detail in Chapter 14 of this volume.

One can also choose to donate one's body to science. Medical schools or sometimes statewide organizations coordinate people who wish to donate. Such bodies are used in medical education and research.

Having donor documents together with the other parts of the advance directive can be helpful in creating a record of your values and end-of-life treatment choices. It is important that these documents be available when needed. Even though most people store them in a safe, in a safe-deposit box, or with their last will and testament, by the time anyone accesses those locations, it is too late. Advance directives should be distributed widely to the physician, surrogate decision maker, spouse, closest friends, local hospital, and attorney. Many online repositories also exist for storing these documents and making them accessible through a website or a scannable card; individuals can even keep a copy on their Facebook profile. These documents should not just be put in a drawer and forgotten; they should be made readily available and should be updated on a regular basis (approximately every five years or during major life events).

Although the documents are important, having the conversation is critical. The documents supplement and record the conversation, but do not replace it.

## PROVIDER ISSUES IN END-OF-LIFE CARE

### WITHDRAWING VERSUS WITHHOLDING

The question in *Malcolm in the Middle*, *Steel Magnolias*, and *The Descendants* is whether and when body-sustaining treatment should be withdrawn. Once it is stopped, then the most likely outcome is that the patient will die soon thereafter (although as Quinlan shows, that is not always the case).

In *withdrawing*, a medical intervention that sustains the body has been started and is then discontinued. This is a different action than *withholding*, when a medical intervention is not begun in the first place. For example, if a patient has a DNR order or a POLST, then sustaining treatment may never be initiated. In the television series *The Big C*, Cathy Jamison is dying from melanoma. The character spends three seasons dealing with dying, from hearing the bad news, to coming to terms, to making plans. In the fourth season, Jamison is in hospice care after deciding to forgo further cancer treatment that has little chance of benefit but would impose a large burden. She also chooses to be DNR and to avoid any body-sustaining treatment. *Withholding* treatment is the decision to not provide treatment before it is started.

In "Biases in How Physicians Choose to Withdraw Life Support" (1993), physician-sociologist Nicholas Christakis and physician-ethicist David A. Asch explain that some health-care providers have a moral concern when asked to withdraw treatments like feeding tubes or ventilators because they feel that their actions (e.g., removing the feeding tube) are directly causing the death of a patient. Conversely, withholding treatment is rarely seen as a dilemma because providers see these deaths as caused by the condition of the patient, rather than the provider's lack of action. Philosophically, withdrawing and withholding are the same thing. According to physician-ethicist Bernard Lo's *Resolving Ethical Dilemmas* (2013), the causative agent of death in both cases is the underlying disease, not the actions of the provider. The difference and difficulty comes from the aesthetics and the actions (or lack of action) involved.

### FUTILITY

When a patient has a terminal illness, he or she may reach a point at which medical interventions will no longer provide any physiological or psychological benefit. To continue such treatments at this point would violate the bioethical principles of beneficence and nonmaleficence. Beneficence is the obligation to actively do good for a patient, by providing cure, treatment, or comfort. When further treatment is nonbeneficial, only comfort care remains. Nonmaleficence is the notion of "do no harm." In this scenario, any intervention over comfort care is a burden to the patient, causing pain and discomfort. Thus, to act violates the notion of nonmaleficence.

Like the doctors in *The Descendants*, the health-care providers will inform the patient and family that nothing more can be done to prolong life or to improve the patient's condition. Further treatment would be *futile* and *nonbeneficial*. Despite the fact that the treatment will provide no physiological or psychological benefit, sometimes the patient or the family will request to have treatment continued because they are unwilling to accept the fact that nothing more can be done.

Avoidance of futile treatment has been a goal of the medical profession since the fifth century BCE, when among the ethics of the Hippocratic physicians was "to refuse to treat those who are overmastered by their diseases" (Jecker 1991, 5). The challenge is to determine when treatment is futile. One might argue that interventions may bolster hope and thus no treatment is truly futile. As physician Thanh Huynh and colleagues write in "The Frequency and Cost of Treatment Perceived to be Futile in Critical Care" (2013), treatment can be perceived as futile when the burdens of treatment grossly outweigh the benefits, when treatment could never reach a patient's goals, when death is imminent, or when the patient would never be able to survive outside of an intensive care setting.

Futility also can be defined in both qualitative and quantitative terms. Quantifying futility focuses on the statistical likelihood that a patient improves with a specific treatment. Qualitative analysis of futility focuses on analyzing the importance of improvement provided by a treatment. Clearly, futility in medical care is a difficult topic to characterize. This makes legal precedents for futility difficult to determine.

The Texas Advance Directive Act of 1999, known euphemistically as the Texas Futility Law, is one of the few laws in the United States to address futility. This law does not define futility itself, but rather leaves the decision to determine whether care is futile to the providers. When at least two physicians feel that care is no longer beneficial and the family or patient disagrees, the law creates a process for resolution. The hospital must inform the family or patient in writing of the process: (1) determination by two physicians that further aggressive care will not provide benefit with burdens that outweigh the risks; and (2) a meeting with the ethics committee to which the family is invited. The committee will review the case and determine whether it supports the physicians. If the committee does, then the family has ten days to find a facility that is willing to accept the patient as a transfer. After ten days (unless there is a court order staying the removal of sustaining treatment), the hospital may withdraw body support (but not comfort care), even if the family protests.

In addition to beneficence and nonmaleficence, when discussing futile care, the principle of justice suggests that one should consider the availability and allocation of medical resources. Justice forces us to ask: should we continue to use limited hospital resources on patients who will not recover or benefit from the treatment rather than using these resources to help patients who have the potential to recover? For example, consider a pandemic flu in which thousands of people may need ventilators to help them breathe and vaccines to protect the uninfected. There are probably only enough ventilators to help a small number of patients. The sickest individuals, those who require the greatest use of resources (physician time, ventilators, antivirals) and are still likely to die, may not receive aggressive care. Justice in triage ethics says that resources should go to those most likely to benefit, not to those who are the sickest (which is the justice standard used in conventional situations).

In an extreme case, during the 2014–2015 Ebola outbreak, some hospitals in the United States established *unilateral DNR orders* for those infected with Ebola. In brief, this meant that no Ebola patients would receive CPR or other resuscitation. These orders were given based on the fact that once patients suffering from Ebola had reached the point at which they required resuscitation, the patient's condition was terminal. Also, resuscitation of these patients put health-care providers at high risk for contracting the disease. Resuscitations are messy with sharp instruments being used quickly and exposure to the patient's bodily fluids. In addition, providers would be wearing biohazard suits, giving them limited dexterity and movement. The chances of a mishap are high. The decision to impose a unilateral DNR is based on two reasons: continuation of futile treatment would (1) not benefit the patient and (2) poses a high risk for the care providers.

## Summary

Throughout history, death has fascinated humankind with a sense of mystery. This curiosity is apparent in the variety of books, films, plays, music, and art that deal with the topics of death and dying. An analysis of these art forms, as well as an understanding of the mythology and sociology of the history of death, indicates that death was not always viewed as it is in the twenty-first century—a sickness to be cured or controlled. Rather, death was seen as a natural part of the living process. Our definition and understanding of death now is much more complex, expanding from ideas of simple biological death to defining medical, legal, and social death.

The philosophical question of when human life ends generates controversy over whether humanness resides in the brain, the higher brain, or the whole organism. This debate influences conversations about futility (physiological nonbeneficence), withdrawing versus withholding, and technological efforts to avoid death. Such medical advancements have blurred the lines of life and death by giving medical professionals the ability to sustain organ function past the point of conscious life. Court cases, such as *Union Pacific Railway Co. v. Botsford* and *Schloendorff v. Society of New York Hospital*, and ethical cases, such as those involving Quinlan, Cruzan, and McMath, are representative of the ethical and legal issues that arise with the use of body-sustaining treatments to avoid death.

The Uniform Determination of Death Act provides a legal definition of death as the cessation of all cardiopulmonary function or the loss of whole brain function. Some states allow philosophical and religious exemptions, and some groups desire a higher brain function standard.

Invasive medical interventions at the end of life most often take place in the hospital, ICU, or long-term care setting, where more than 70 percent of deaths occur despite the fact that most Americans would prefer to die at home, free of painful or aggressive medical interventions. The hospice philosophy is an alternative to aggressive treatments that focuses on providing the patient's view of a "good death" by ceasing all forms of curative treatment and focusing on pain and symptom management, as well as the emotional and social processes that accompany the patient and their family as death approaches.

Talking about one's values, approach, and beliefs about death and dying are an attempt to alleviate death anxiety and to make one's preferences clear. Discussions should include matters of necessity, such as property allocation, as well as desired medical interventions and emotional needs (e.g., wanting family near). These conversations should be supplemented, but not replaced, by the use of advance directive documents, including the living will, power of attorney for health care, and the provider's order for life-sustaining treatment.

# Bibliography

Ad Hoc Committee of the Harvard Medical School to Examine the Definition of Brain Death. "A Definition of Irreversible Coma." *Journal of the American Medical Association* 205, no. 6 (1968): 85–88.

Aging with Dignity. "Five Wishes: Changing the Way We Talk about and Plan for Care at the End of Life." July 5, 2015. http://www.agingwithdignity.org/five-wishes.php.

American Medical Association. "Opinion 2.20: Withholding or Withdrawing Life-Sustaining Medical Treatment." *American Medical Association Code of Medical Ethics.* June 1994. http://www.ama-assn.org/ama/pub/physician-resources/medical-ethics/code-medical-ethics/opinion220.page?.

Arenella, Cheryl. "Use of Opiates to Manage Pain in the Seriously and Terminally Ill Patient." American Hospice Foundation. 2014. http://americanhospice.org/caregiving/use-of-opiates-to-manage-pain-in-the-seriously-and-terminally-ill-patient/.

Beauchamp, Tom L., and James F. Childress. *Principles of Biomedical Ethics.* 7th ed. New York: Oxford University Press, 2013.

Billings, J. Andrew. "What Is Palliative Care?" *Journal of Palliative Medicine* 1, no. 1 (1998): 73–81. doi: 10.1089/jpm.1998.1.73.

Bureau of the Census. "Mortality Statistics: 1910." Bulletin 109. Department of Commerce and Labor. 1912. http://www.cdc.gov/nchs/data/vsushistorical/mortstatbl_1910.pdf.

Byock, Ira. *The Four Things That Matter Most.* New York: Atria, 2014.

Carpenito, Lynda Juall. *Handbook of Nursing Diagnosis.* 14th ed. Philadelphia: Lippincott Williams & Wilkins, 2013.

Centers for Disease Control and Prevention. "Detailed Tables for the National Vital Statistics Report (NVSR) Deaths: Final Data for 2013." http://www.cdc.gov/nchs/data_access/Vitalstatsonline.htm.

Christakis, Nicholas A., and David A. Asch. "Biases in How Physicians Choose to Withdraw Life Support." *Lancet* 342, no. 8872 (1993): 642–646.

Death over Dinner. "Let's Have Dinner and Talk about Death." 2015. http://deathoverdinner.org/.

DeGrazia, David. "The Definition of Death." In *The Stanford Encyclopedia of Philosophy,* edited by Edward N. Zalta. 2011. http://plato.stanford.edu/entries/death-definition/.

Dresser, Rebecca, and Peter Whitehouse. "The Incompetent Patient on the Slippery Slope." *The Hastings Center Report* 24, no. 4 (1994): 6–12.

Dworkin, Ronald. *Life's Dominion.* New York: Vintage, 1993.

Fields, Lorraine. "DNR Does Not Mean No Care." *Journal of Neuroscience Nursing* 39, no. 5 (2007): 294–296. http://www.medscape.com/viewarticle/567654.

Fromme, Erik K., Dana Zive, Terri Schmidt, et al. "Association between POLST Scope of Treatment Orders and In-Hospital Death in Oregon." *Journal of the American Geriatrics Society* 62, no. 7 (2014): 1246–1251.

Goodman, Ellen. The Conversation Project. 2015. http://theconversationproject.org.

Hui, D., Z. Nooruddin, N. Didwaniya, et al. "Concepts and Definitions for 'Actively Dying,' 'End of Life,' 'Terminally Ill,' 'Terminal Care,' and 'Transition of Care': A Systematic Review." *Journal of Pain and Symptom Management* 47, no. 1 (2014): 77–89. doi: 10.1016/j.jpainsymman.2013.02.021.

Huynh, Thanh N., Eric C. Kleerup, Joshua F. Wiley, et al. "The Frequency and Cost of Treatment Perceived to Be Futile in Critical Care." *AMA Internal Medicine* 173, no. 20 (2013): 1887–1894.

Institute of Medicine. *Relieving Pain in America: A Blueprint for Transforming Prevention, Care, Education, and Research.* Washington, DC: National Academies Press, 2011.

Jecker, Nancy S. "Knowing When to Stop: The Limits of Medicine." *The Hastings Center Report* 21, no. 3 (1991): 5–8.

Jennett, Bryan, and Fred Plum. "Persistent Vegetative State after Brain Damage. A Syndrome in Search of a Name." *Lancet* 1, no. 7753 (1972): 734–737.

Jennings, Bruce, True Ryndes, Carol D'Onofrio, and Mary Ann Baily. "Access to Hospice Care: Expanding Boundaries, Overcoming Barriers." *The Hastings Center Report* Supp. (2003): S3–S7, S9–S13, S15–S21 passim.

Kellehear, Allan. *A Social History of Dying*. New York: Cambridge University Press, 2007.

Klugman, Craig M. "Reframing Terri Schiavo: One Family's Story of Morality, Ethics and Politics." *Internet Journal of Law, Healthcare, and Ethics* 4, no. 1 (2006). http://www.ispub.com/ostia/index.php?xmlFilePath=journals/ijlhe/vol4n1/schiavo.xml.

Klugman, Craig M., and Nicole Tolwin. "Examining Autonomous Selections in an Advance Directive." *Journal of Clinical Ethics* 26, no. 3 (2015): 212–218.

Landau, Elizabeth. "When 'Life Support' Is Really 'Death Support.'" CNN. December 29, 2013. http://www.cnn.com/2013/12/28/health/life-support-ethics/.

Lehto, Rebecca Helen, and Karen Farchause Stein. "Death Anxiety: An Analysis of an Evolving Concept." *Research and Theory in Nursing Practice* 23, no. 1 (2009): 23–31. http://deepblue.lib.umich.edu/bitstream/handle/2027.42/66464/Death+Anxiety+An+Analysis+of+an+Evolving+Concept.pdf?sequence=1 doi: 10.1891/1.541-6577.23.1.23.

Lo, Bernard. *Resolving Ethical Dilemmas: A Guide for Clinicians*. 5th ed. Philadelphia: Lippincott Williams & Wilkins, 2013.

National Conference of Commissioners on Uniform State Laws. Uniform Determination of Death Act. Chicago: National Conference of Commissioners on Uniform State Laws, 1980.

Physician Orders for Life-Sustaining Treatment Paradigm. 2015. http://www.polst.org.

Razinsky, Liran. *Freud, Psychoanalysis, and Death*. New York: Cambridge University Press, 2013.

Reese, Dona J. *Hospice Social Work*. New York: Columbia University Press, 2013.

*Schloendorff v. Society of New York Hospital*. 211 N.Y. 125, 105 N.E. 92 (1914).

Schneiderman, Lawrence J., Nancy S. Jecker, and Albert R. Jonsen. "Medical Futility: Response to Critiques." *Annals of Internal Medicine* 125, no. 8 (1996): 669–674.

Stump, Benjamin F., Craig M. Klugman, and Barbara Thornton. "Last Hours of Life: Encouraging End-of-Life Conversations." *Journal of Clinical Ethics* 19, no. 2 (2008): 150–159.

Temel, Jennifer S., Joseph A. Greer, Alona Muzikansky, et al. "Early Palliative Care for Patients with Metastatic Non-small-Cell Lung Cancer." *New England Journal of Medicine* 363, no. 8 (2010): 733–742. doi: 10.1056/NEJMoa1000678.

Teno, Joan M., Pedro L. Gozalo, Julie P. W. Bynum, et al. "Change in End-of-Life Care for Medicare Beneficiaries: Site of Death, Place of Care, and Health Care Transitions in 2000, 2005, and 2009." *Journal of the American Medical Association* 309, no. 5 (2013): 470–477. doi: 10.1001/jama.2012.207624.

*Union Pacific Railway Co. v. Botsford*, 141 US 250 (1891).

World Health Organization. "The Top 10 Causes of Death." May 2014. http://www.who.int/mediacentre/factsheets/fs310/en/.

## LITERATURE AND DRAMA

Chast, Roz. *Can't We Talk about Something More Pleasant?* New York: Bloomsbury, 2014.

Edson, Margaret. *Wit: A Play*. New York: Faber and Faber, 1999.

Shakespeare, William. *Hamlet*. Act 1, Scene 2. 1603.

Thompson, Hunter S. *The Proud Highway: Saga of a Desperate Southern Gentleman, 1955–1967*. New York: Ballantine, 1965.

Tolstoy, Leo. *The Death of Ivan Ilyich*. New York: Bantam Dell, 1981. First published 1886.

## FILM AND TELEVISION

*The Big C*. Created by Darlene Hunt. 2010–2013. Sony Pictures Television.

*Cake*. Dir. Daniel Barnz. 2015. Freestyle/Cinelou Releasing.

*The Descendants*. Dir. Alexander Payne. 2011. Fox Searchlight.

*Final Destination*. Dir. James Wong. 2000. New Line Cinema.

*Malcolm in the Middle*. "Living Will." Season 6, episode 12, 2005. Dir. Steve Love.

*Meet Joe Black*. Dir. Martin Brest. 1998. Universal Pictures.

*Self/less*. Dir. Tarsem Singh. 2015. Focus Features.

*Steel Magnolias*. Dir. Herbert Ross. 1989. TriStar Pictures.

# CHAPTER 8

# Physician-Assisted Suicide and Euthanasia: Death as Treatment?

**Lois Snyder Sulmasy**
*Director, American College of Physicians Center*
*for Ethics and Professionalism*[1]
*Philadelphia, PA*

In July 2015, a judge in California dismissed a lawsuit challenging state law that makes it a crime to aid another person's suicide. The plaintiffs bringing the case claimed a right to prescriptions for lethal doses of medicine and suicide advice from physicians. They argued that such assistance is just an extension of the right to refuse life-sustaining treatments, such as ventilators, artificial nutrition, and hydration. After the judge's ruling, one of the plaintiffs in the case with advanced lung cancer, Christy O'Donnell, stated, "I don't have much time left to live. These options are urgent for me" (Dembosky 2015). Ironically, she was saying:

> I need to kill myself because I don't have much time left.

Think about O'Donnell's words. Why would one want a right to physician-assisted suicide if natural death is imminent and the right to refuse treatment is well established? Is physician-assisted suicide merely an extension of the right to refuse life-sustaining treatments, or is it something different? In the early days of the physician-assisted suicide (PAS) movement, advocates said PAS was a right needed for terminally ill patients in excruciating pain and with other severe suffering. Over time, it has become clearer that, as for the plaintiffs in this case, it is actually more about controlling the timing and manner of death. And this, among other things, highlights ethical and philosophical questions about how society views and cares for those near death, as well as the idea of seeking death. It also raises questions about whether physicians should be involved in such practices as PAS and whether the medicalization of suicide is a good idea and should be a goal of society.

PAS and euthanasia pose the question of whether death is the ultimate treatment. Proponents say PAS and euthanasia are humane and dignified ways to die. But when physicians participate in such practices, the nature and role of medicine in society is changed, with significant implications for the patient-physician relationship. Physicians—and society—validate the patient's request as a medical one. They also validate the patient's conclusion that he or she is better off dead. Does this signal to individuals, and especially certain vulnerable populations, that there is little or no value to their lives? That there is a duty to die? Could the frail elderly, the disabled, and those on the margins of society come to believe they are a burden and that they should end their lives—especially in an atmosphere of concerns about the costs and availability of health care? What does this sort of approval of a choice to die do for trust in the patient-physician relationship? Or in the profession of medicine? What about the loved ones who are left behind after suicide through physician assistance or euthanasia?

Debate continues about the ethical implications of physician-assisted suicide and euthanasia and their consequences for both individuals and society at large. In part, misunderstandings about end-of-life care—and the fact that care of the dying is still inadequate in the United States—fuel public interest as patients and families fear the prospect of what they think will be a prolonged, undignified, and painful death. But perhaps a solution is to address patient and family fears and concerns. Also, although progress has been made in palliative and hospice care, access to it continues to be uneven and barriers to care, such as counterproductive reimbursement policies, persist.

There also remains a great deal of confusion about what is meant by the terms *physician-assisted suicide* and *euthanasia*, along with the practical and theoretical parameters of these acts and others at the end of life. Often, people use unclear terms or talk about different practices using the same terms, which makes debate difficult. Definitions will be provided in the next section of this chapter.

In the 1990s, Dr. Jack Kevorkian (1928–2011) was a leading spokesperson for what he called "death with dignity." In 1999, a Michigan jury rejected his attempt to blur legal lines with his "Thanatron" death machine. He said dying was not a crime. But the jury found that killing was and convicted him of murder. In 2014, Brittany Maynard (1984–2014) became a leading advocate for PAS after being diagnosed with the brain cancer glioblastoma and moving to Oregon from California to take her life under Oregon's PAS law. She was twenty-nine and presented a very different face of well-organized efforts to legalize physician-assisted suicide.

Medical ethics and the law recognize a right to refuse medical treatment, including life-sustaining treatment. Patients exercise this right every day. But is there a right to die? Are physician-assisted suicide and euthanasia just an extension of refusal of treatment? Or are these acts distinguishable? What do PAS and euthanasia look like in jurisdictions that allow them? Do safeguards that are put in place for their implementation actually work? Should PAS and euthanasia be seen as treatments that the profession of medicine provides? What is their relationship to end-of-life care? Should they be viewed as merely additional end-of-life care options? Some argue that individuals who voluntarily stop eating and drinking with physician assistance when they can otherwise eat and drink are merely forgoing life-sustaining medical treatment. They say this is an alternative to PAS. Others argue that it is PAS.

These issues, including the ethical arguments for and against physician-assisted suicide and euthanasia, are considered in this chapter. Hopefully this exploration will shed light on whether society should encourage individuals to view physician-assisted suicide or euthanasia as end-of-life care options and permit the practices—or whether supportive palliative and hospice care, trusting relationships, compassion, and social support should be the focus of medicine and the highest priority for those who fear suffering or an undignified death.

Some of these questions and issues have been dramatized on film. For example, in the 2014 Israeli farce *The Farewell Party*, residents of a senior independent-living home design a suicide machine for use by their friend with terminal cancer. Max wants to die but assisted suicide is illegal in Israel. Ethical dilemmas escalate as more people (a woman with lung cancer who is outside the group of friends, as well as the inventor's wife, who has dementia) learn about the device. This fictional film is based on real-life ethical dilemmas in medicine and law. The 2010 HBO film *You Don't Know Jack* is a sympathetic portrayal of the life of Jack Kevorkian. The 2004 Spanish film *The Sea Inside* is a dramatized account of the true story of Ramón Sampedro (1943–1998), a quadriplegic who fought in the Spanish courts for what he called the right to die.

## LANGUAGE MATTERS: DEFINITIONS AND CONTEXT

Language is important and can subtly, or not so subtly, influence debate. The debate in the United States about these issues has, to date, centered on physician-assisted suicide. Advocates for PAS have cast the movement as one for recognition of physician aid in dying or physician-assisted death and what they say are expanded end-of-life options. They see PAS as "death with dignity," an often used phrase. Opponents do not see dignity in this act; they believe it is the intrinsic humanity of human beings and the way people deal with death that defines dignity. They also see many dangers in societal approval of helping people kill themselves, even—or especially—if a physician is to provide the assistance.

Regardless of whether one's views are pro or con, terms such as *physician aid in dying* that lump categories together can cloud the issue and the ethics of what is at stake and should be avoided. So, to begin at the beginning, some definitions are needed.

Dictionaries define *suicide* as intentionally ending one's own life. The *Oxford English Dictionary* says *suicide* is "the act of taking one's own life, self-murder." The word comes from the Latin *suicidium*, or "self-killing," and appears in the Romance languages: *suicidio* in Italian, Portuguese, and Spanish; *suicide* in French. The *Oxford Dictionary of Law* defines *suicide* as "the act of killing oneself intentionally."

That suicide is defined as a killing is important and will be discussed in more depth later in this chapter. It will also be compared to and contrasted with the concept of allowing someone to die. The term *suicide* is not a commentary on those who either contemplate or actually take their own lives. It is merely an objective description based on common definitions that state it is an intentional killing of self.

Suicide and attempted suicide are no longer illegal in the United States. Assisting a suicide, however, has been and continues to be a specific statutory offense in most states. Assisted suicide is helping another individual end that individual's life. Physician-assisted suicide is the participation of a physician in advising or providing, but not directly administering, the means and/or information to help an individual intentionally end his or her life. The means is usually a lethal dosage of medication prescribed by a physician for that purpose.

PAS does not mean the withholding or withdrawal of life-sustaining medical care based on patient refusal of treatment (which will be discussed below). PAS is also distinguishable from euthanasia. Euthanasia is the act of taking a life to relieve pain and suffering. In euthanasia, it is the physician who performs the act specifically intended to end another's

**KEY TERMS**

**Suicide:** the act of killing oneself intentionally.

**Physician-assisted suicide:** participation of a physician in advising or providing, but not directly administering, the means and/or information to help an individual intentionally take that person's own life (usually through ingesting a lethal dosage of medication prescribed for that purpose).

**Euthanasia:** the act of taking a life to relieve pain and suffering; lethal injection performed by a physician is the most common example of euthanasia.

**Voluntary euthanasia:** when a person with decision-making capacity consents to euthanasia; voluntariness is usually required by euthanasia laws.

**Involuntary euthanasia:** when a person with decision-making capacity has not consented to euthanasia.

**Nonvoluntary euthanasia:** when a person lacks decision-making capacity and cannot consent to euthanasia.

*Table 8.1. Key Terms.*

life. Lethal injection is the most common example of euthanasia. Euthanasia can be voluntary, involuntary, or nonvoluntary (see Table 8.1).

As an ethical—and clinical—matter, it is important to clarify the differences between these practices. Suicide and, particularly, assisted suicide are social acts with effects on family, community, and society. Physician-assisted suicide, when legalized, becomes a new social service (Byock 1997).

Against all logic, the Oregon Death with Dignity Act, enacted in 1997, specifically says that actions taken in accordance with it "shall not for any purpose constitute suicide, assisted suicide, mercy killing or homicide, under the law." But declaring that so does not make it so. The Dutch began their social experiment with the very inclusive and benign-sounding phrase "medical decisions at the end of life." This phrase was used to put physician-assisted suicide, euthanasia, and refusal of treatment all within the purview of the medical encounter (Thomasma 1996), casting them as morally equivalent ways of dying. But they are not. More recently, the Dutch have spoken of euthanasia more honestly in recognizing, for example, that "if a death is due to euthanasia, it cannot be certified as 'natural'" (Verhagen and Sauer 2005).

## WHERE PHYSICIAN-ASSISTED SUICIDE AND EUTHANASIA ARE LEGAL

To date, the focus of legalization efforts in the United States has been on physician-assisted suicide. As of 2015, PAS had been legalized through voter-approved ballot initiatives in Oregon and Washington and through legislation in Vermont and California. A court decision in Montana allows a patient's request to be used as a defense for a physician who participates. A court authorized PAS in New Mexico, but that ruling was struck down in 2015. Legalization efforts increased in 2015, when the District of Columbia and twenty-five states considered PAS legislation, all of which failed except for in California. In addition, Canada's Supreme Court legalized physician-assisted suicide for terminally ill Canadians in early 2015, with the ruling to take effect in a year. PAS and euthanasia were tolerated in the Netherlands starting in the 1980s and legalized in 2002. Both are also legal in Luxembourg. Euthanasia is legal in Belgium and Colombia. Switzerland also decriminalized assisted suicide—that is, no one will be prosecuted for it, and anyone may assist with a suicide; consequently, assisted suicide in Switzerland includes but is not limited to PAS.

Belgium permits euthanasia of infants, children, and adults. In the Netherlands, euthanasia is permitted for anyone age twelve and older; it has not been formally legalized for children under the age of twelve, but for infants, it is not prosecuted if the Groningen Protocol (guidelines and requirements for newborn euthanasia developed at University Medical Center Groningen) is adhered to (Verhagen and Sauer 2005).

## THE RIGHT TO REFUSE TREATMENT

Patients have the right to refuse treatment, including life-sustaining treatment. This is based on a weighing of patient autonomy and self-determination interests against societal interests. It is not, however, a "right to die." What has been established (and the ethical principles that undergird it) is the protection of one's interests in bodily integrity and in being left alone. A patient has the right to refuse medical treatment—including life-sustaining treatment, such as a ventilator or feeding tube—even if doing so will accelerate the dying process.

The withholding or withdrawing of life-sustaining treatment based on patient wishes has been ethically and clinically distinguished from physician-assisted suicide and euthanasia. It has been legally distinguished by state appellate court decisions and all of the decisions regarding treatment refusal and PAS by the US Supreme Court. And it is distinguished by common sense as well. Advocates for PAS argue that there is no distinction because this serves their cause. Will the line that has been drawn between refusal of treatment and PAS/euthanasia stand?

## KILLING VERSUS ALLOWING TO DIE

Some people argue that if a physician can legally and ethically give morphine to a dying patient knowing that this might speed up death and that the patient desires death, this is no different from killing the patient (more on this under the section on "Double Effect"). Similarly, it is argued that stopping a ventilator based on patient wishes and taking a lethal dose of medicine prescribed for that purpose are equivalent because both actions end in the patient's death. But these are, in fact, distinguishable acts, and understanding the distinctions is critically important (Sulmasy 1998).

If, for example, a patient named Jones is terminally ill with a few weeks to live and is in the hospital on a ventilator and feeding tube, he may elect to have those medical treatments withdrawn. This will hasten his death. Having consented to those treatments, he can now refuse them. Were it not for those interventions he originally agreed to, he would have died from his underlying disease. Discontinuing them now, with his consent, would allow him to die a natural death from that underlying disease. If Jones is receiving life-sustaining treatments but Smith stops them without Jones's consent, Smith has killed Jones. In both instances, Jones dies after the discontinuation of medical treatments—but in very different ways as a matter of ethics and law (and medicine).

The right to refuse life-sustaining treatment arose in response to growing use of medical technologies to prolong life. Such technologies can be lifesaving. But when they merely prolong the dying process, many people decide to discontinue them. Also, without the right to refuse treatment, patients would be very reluctant to try a treatment, fearing that they would be stuck with it if they later decided it was unwanted. Or, they might avoid medical care altogether.

So why are the examples above different? Think about the definitions of *homicide*, *murder*, and *manslaughter* and the importance of intent and causation in those definitions. Dictionaries define *homicide* as a killing. Not all killings, however, are a crime (for example, self-defense). *Murder* is an intentional killing, with different degrees depending on premeditation, whereas *manslaughter* is killing without "malice aforethought." If Jones runs over Smith with his car, there may be no crime (although there may be civil liability if his behavior was negligent). Jones may have committed involuntary manslaughter (if he was reckless), or he may be guilty of some degree of murder (because of extreme disregard for human life if, for example, Jones was driving drunk without a license or if he previously planned and set out to run over Smith). What if Smith had been in the street about to shoot himself with a gun when Jones ran him over? Or, what if Smith had pancreatic cancer when Jones ran him over? Does Jones avoid culpability? The answer is clearly "no."

Medicine and the law have long maintained that killing a person and allowing a person to die are different acts. It may be helpful to analyze three cases to consider the distinctions between physician-assisted suicide and allowing natural death to see where to draw lines. In all of the following cases, the patients have the capacity to make their own decisions:

(1) An older man requests barbiturates that he will use to end his life when he deems his suffering from leukemia to be unbearable. His doctor understands his intent and provides a prescription for a lethal dose of the medication.

(2) A middle-aged woman has end-stage cancer of the esophagus (food pipe), which has also damaged her windpipe. She now has pneumonia and is on a ventilator. She says she is finished with fighting; she wants the ventilator removed and refuses treatment with antibiotics.

(3) An elderly couple decide together that each person will stop eating and drinking. Neither is dying nor terminally ill. They say they are "tired of living." They ask their physician to admit them to the hospital so that they can receive sedation and comfort care while they refuse food and fluids.

The first case is clearly an example of physician-assisted suicide. How similar to or different from the first one are the second and third cases? What causes death? Is it an underlying disease, the withdrawal of care, or another act? Commissions (acts) versus omissions (failures to act) are not alone determinative—the physician in the second case would actively be stopping the ventilator (a commission). So what else is at work? What is the significance of the act? What is the intent of the participants?

In all three cases, the patients desire death. In the first and third cases, however, the proximate (direct) cause of death is something new: the use of a lethal dose of drugs (case one) and starvation/dehydration (case three). In the third case, the patients are not severely ill and do not have a natural loss of appetite or an inability to eat and drink because of underlying illness or pathophysiology. In the first and third cases, it is the patients' intent to die—and it is the physicians' intent to assist them. They help the patients hasten their deaths through new pathophysiology: the lethal dose of medicine or starvation/dehydration. The patients would not otherwise have died of an overdose or starvation/dehydration; the acts causing the deaths are not related to the underlying condition.

In contrast, the act and the intent of the patient and physician in the second case is to withdraw treatment that the patient determines is burdensome and to refrain from providing care that she has determined is no longer in keeping with her goals of care. This allows her to die a natural death from her underlying illness.

The second case is an example of refusing of life-sustaining treatment and allowing natural death. Here, nature would be taking its course. Though there is the commission of an act—withdrawal of the ventilator—the act merely removes an intervention that was preventing a preexisting condition from running its course. It is not an affirmative act to kill

(Sulmasy 1998). The patient also declines antibiotics. To continue the ventilator or insist on antibiotics would be to force treatments. This would be unethical and in violation of patient rights.

In the famous Karen Ann Quinlan case (*In Re Quinlan*, 1976), the patient's parents argued for a right to refuse a ventilator that they said she would not have consented to, arguing it was unwanted care (a feeding tube was also in use but that was not refused). Based on a right to self-determination and on the principle of autonomy, they argued that under the doctrine of informed consent, if you must consent to treatment, then you have the right not to consent as well.

The court employed a balancing test in its reasoning, finding that state interests (in the preservation of life, in the protection of innocent third parties, and in maintaining the ethical integrity of the medical profession) should be weighed against the individual's right. The court said that the state's interest weakens and the rights of the individual grow as the degree of bodily invasion of the treatment increases and the prognosis dims.

Under the facts of the Quinlan case, the court found that the individual right outweighed state interests. The ventilator was discontinued. Quinlan lived on in a persistent vegetative state with a feeding tube in place for nine years until her death from pneumonia. But her parents had exercised her rights to refuse an unwanted burdensome treatment, as they thought she would have.

Case law in the United States, including the decision by the US Supreme Court in *Cruzan v. Director, Missouri Dept. of Health* (1990), has determined that artificial nutrition and hydration are medical treatments that can be refused in the same way as other life-sustaining treatments under appropriate conditions. Refusing a feeding tube is not suicide. Later in this chapter, refusal of artificial nutrition and hydration will be compared and contrasted to the voluntarily stopping of eating and drinking (VSED) with the assistance of a physician, which is the scenario in case three. VSED with physician assistance has been proposed as an alternative to PAS, but it can be strongly argued that VSED is actually a form of PAS.

A fundamental point illustrated by these three cases (as in the Quinlan case) is that patient self-determination is much more at stake in the refusal of treatment: to impose unwanted care is a bodily invasion, a violation of bodily integrity that does not respect patient wishes and rights. Not assisting the patients in cases one and three is not a bodily invasion. This was one of the lines of argument that the US Supreme Court explicitly used in ruling that there is no constitutional right to assisted suicide in the *Quill v. Vacco* and *Washington v. Glucksberg* PAS cases (see below).

## US SUPREME COURT DECISIONS ON PAS

The US Supreme Court decided two cases in 1997 on PAS. It held that there is no constitutional right to PAS, that PAS is not equivalent to the withholding or withdrawal of life-sustaining treatment based on a patient's refusal of treatment, and that state bans of assisted suicide are constitutional.

Different arguments were made in each of the two cases. One focused on due process (the protection of certain fundamental rights from government interference). The other focused on equal protection (treating individuals or classes of individuals the same if they are similarly situated).

In *Compassion in Dying v. Washington* (1996), the Ninth US Circuit Court of Appeals became the first federal appellate court to decide a case on physician-assisted suicide. There, it was held that individuals have a right to choose how and when they die. As applied to a terminally ill adult with decision-making capacity who wanted a physician's prescription for a lethal dose of medication, the Washington State criminal statute banning physician-assisted suicide was found to be unconstitutional as a violation of the due process clause of the Fourteenth Amendment. The due process clause says a state may not "deprive any person of life, liberty, or property without due process of law."

Another federal appellate court, the Second Circuit, in another case at the same time, said it would decline to "identify a new fundamental right in the absence of a clear direction from the Court whose precedents we are bound to follow," recognizing other decisions by the US Supreme Court. Instead, in *Quill v. Vacco* (1996), a New York law was found to be unconstitutional by the Second Circuit on much narrower grounds. It found a violation of the equal protection clause of the Fourteenth Amendment that says that no state shall "deny to any person within its jurisdiction the equal protection of the laws." The Second Circuit ruled that the New York law violated that clause because dying patients with decision-making capacity were being treated differently: some patients could refuse life-sustaining treatment and thereby hasten death, but others were prohibited from seeking prescriptions from physicians to hasten death.

The US Supreme Court did not find either of the lower court decisions persuasive. Instead, in *Vacco v. Quill* (1997) and *Washington v. Glucksberg* (1997), the withdrawal or withholding of life-sustaining treatment based on refusal of treatment by a patient was found to be very different from physician-assisted suicide. The court said refusal of treatment is about being free of the bodily invasion of unwanted medical treatment, not a right to something. This negative right—many American rights and freedoms take this form—is entirely different from a positive right to secure assistance to kill oneself and control the manner and timing of death. Although the US Supreme Court ruled that there is no constitutional right to assisted suicide and that states may prohibit it, the court also left open the possibility that individual states could legalize it.

Very significantly, in her concurring opinion in *Washington v. Glucksberg*, Justice Sandra Day O'Connor lent support to the rule of double effect as it is applied in medicine (see below). She explained that although there was no right to commit suicide or receive assistance in doing so, patients could receive pain control to alleviate symptoms, even at levels that might hasten death. She said:

> Death will be different for each of us. For many, the last days will be spent in physical pain and perhaps the despair that accompanies physical deterioration and a loss of control of basic bodily and mental functions. Some will seek medication to alleviate that pain and other symptoms.

> The Court frames the issue in this case as whether the Due Process Clause of the Constitution protects a "right to commit suicide which itself includes a right to assistance in doing so," *ante*, at 18, and concludes that our Nation's history, legal traditions, and practices do not support the existence of such a right. I join the Court's opinions because I agree that there is no generalized right to "commit suicide." But respondents urge us to address the narrower question whether a mentally competent person who is experiencing great suffering has a constitutionally

cognizable interest in controlling the circumstances of his or her imminent death. I see no need to reach that question in the context of the facial challenges to the New York and Washington laws at issue here.... The parties and *amici* agree that in these States a patient who is suffering from a terminal illness and who is experiencing great pain has no legal barriers to obtaining medication, from qualified physicians, to alleviate that suffering, even to the point of causing unconsciousness and hastening death. (Justice O'Connor, concurring opinion, *Washington v. Glucksberg*, 1997)

## BENEFICENCE, NONMALEFICENCE, RESPECT FOR AUTONOMY, AND SOCIAL JUSTICE

The law defines what can be thought of as a moral minimum in society. Medical ethics demands more of the medical profession, requiring that positive duties be fulfilled. The principles that are the foundation for these duties are beneficence, nonmaleficence, respect for autonomy, and social justice.

Beneficence is the obligation to promote the good of the patient and act in the patient's best interests. This means putting the patient first and serving as the patient's advocate. Nonmaleficence is the requirement to avoid doing harm. These duties, dating back to the dawn of medicine as a profession, form the core of the individual physician's and the profession's responsibility to patients. They are weighty responsibilities. Given the nature of the relationship and the power differential between the patient (who seeks help) and the physician (who offers and can often provide such help), physicians are expected to abide by these principles to be trustworthy and to serve the patient's interests. According to the 2012 sixth edition of the *American College of Physicians Ethics Manual*:

> The patient-physician relationship entails special obligations for the physician to serve the patient's interest because of the specialized knowledge that physicians possess, the confidential nature of the relationship, and the imbalance of power between patient and physician.... The physician's primary commitment must always be to the patient's welfare and best interests, whether in preventing or treating illness or helping patients to cope with illness, disability, and death. The physician must respect the dignity of all persons and respect their uniqueness. The interests of the patient should always be promoted regardless of financial arrangements; the health care setting; or patient characteristics, such as decision-making capacity, behavior, or social status. (Snyder for the American College of Physicians Ethics, Professionalism, and Human Rights Committee 2012, 75)

Contemporary medical ethics recognizes two additional principles: (1) the duty to respect patient autonomy to facilitate and protect patients' right to make treatment choices, and (2) consideration of issues of social justice to help ensure the equitable distribution of health care and the promotion of health throughout society.

Major US medical associations oppose the legalization of PAS and euthanasia as breaches of the physician's ethical duties of beneficence and nonmaleficence and specific prohibitions against them since medicine's beginnings. They find these acts to be inconsistent with the physician's role as healer and comforter, as well as a threat to the patient-physician relationship and to trust in the relationship and the profession. While respecting patient autonomy, they also recognize that autonomy is not absolute and does not trump all other principles and values. They also raise social justice issues related to dangers for vulnerable populations, questions about safeguards, and slippery-slope concerns.

The *American College of Physicians Ethics Manual* and the college's 2001 position paper on physician-assisted suicide make these arguments. The position paper recognizes that "medicine should not arrogate to itself the task of relieving all human suffering, even near the end of life. Our culture's goal of eliminating death is a false goal, the pursuit of which has led to bad medical care. Likewise, the medical profession must humbly realize that the elimination of all human suffering is also a false goal that, if pursued, will ultimately lead to bad medical care" (Snyder and Sulmasy for the American College of Physicians-American Society of Internal Medicine Ethics and Human Rights Committee 2001).

There are some things medicine simply cannot do, including ending all suffering. Physicians must be compassionate, but compassion also must be based on reason (Pellegrino 1993). The college further explains:

> Physicians ought to use their skills to eliminate or ameliorate the medical conditions that occasion human suffering at the end of life. This includes the palliation of both somatic symptoms such as pain and nausea, and of psychological syndromes such as depression or anxiety. But the feeling of helplessness shared by both patient and physician when the patient continues to suffer despite the power of contemporary medical palliative technology is not sufficient to justify assistance with suicide. Etymologically, to be compassionate means to "suffer with" another person. The physician who remains with the dying patient but has not participated in assisted suicide upon the patient's request has not acted without compassion, nor has she or he abandoned the patient. When patients continue to suffer from physical symptoms or psychiatric syndromes despite the best efforts at palliation, physicians ought vigorously to pursue the amelioration of these symptoms even at the risk of unintentionally hastening death. But when the occasion of the patient's suffering is interpersonal, existential, or spiritual, the tasks of the physician are to remain present to the patient, to "suffer with" the patient in compassion, to affirm his or her value as a person, and to enlist the support of clergy, social workers, family, and friends in healing those aspects of suffering that are beyond the legitimate scope of medical care. (Snyder and Sulmasy for the American College of Physicians-American Society of Internal Medicine Ethics and Human Rights Committee 2001, 212)

The specific prohibition against euthanasia and assisted suicide—against physicians taking active steps to intentionally accelerate death—dates back to the Hippocratic Oath. The most fundamental principles of the oath are acting in the best interests of the patient and, recognizing the immense power physicians hold, setting ethical limits like this one to prevent abuses of that power. Stopping treatment when patients are "overmastered by disease," however, is ethical and appropriate—another Hippocratic precept.

The major US medical organizations find that PAS and euthanasia also compromise the patient-physician relationship and the trust necessary to sustain it. They argue that these practices undermine the integrity of the profession and shift much-needed focus away from how to improve the care of the dying and the experiences of dying patients and their families. The powers of prescribing assisted suicide or performing euthanasia are tremendous. They also harbor huge potential for misuse.

The American Medical Association's policy is set forth in "Opinion 2.211—Physician-Assisted Suicide" (1996):

> Physician-assisted suicide occurs when a physician facilitates a patient's death by providing the necessary means and/or information to enable the patient to perform

the life-ending act (e.g., the physician provides sleeping pills and information about the lethal dose, while aware that the patient may commit suicide).

It is understandable, though tragic, that some patients in extreme duress—such as those suffering from a terminal, painful, debilitating illness—may come to decide that death is preferable to life. However, allowing physicians to participate in assisted suicide would cause more harm than good. Physician-assisted suicide is fundamentally incompatible with the physician's role as healer, would be difficult or impossible to control, and would pose serious societal risks.

Instead of participating in assisted suicide, physicians must aggressively respond to the needs of patients at the end of life. Patients should not be abandoned once it is determined that cure is impossible. Multidisciplinary interventions should be sought including specialty consultation, hospice care, pastoral support, family counseling, and other modalities. Patients near the end of life must continue to receive emotional support, comfort care, adequate pain control, respect for patient autonomy, and good communication. (American Medical Association 1996)

Medical societies are consistent in their opposition to killing by physicians: they also strongly oppose physician participation in capital punishment.

## BALANCING PRINCIPLES: AUTONOMY IS NOT ABSOLUTE

Respect for patient autonomy is an important principle and value, but not the only one. Ethical medical practice is also guided by the principles of beneficence, nonmaleficence, and social justice. Society restricts individual autonomy frequently, including with requirements as simple as red lights and seat-belt and helmet laws. Society limits the choice of individuals who would seek the right to sell themselves into slavery, in that way limiting their freedom to give up freedom and rights. Nor does autonomous choice compel the assistance of others in one's choice. Even if a condemned prisoner wanted to die and requested execution by lethal injection, it would not make participation in the execution by a physician ethical.

There are many examples of legitimate limits to patient autonomy in everyday health-care encounters. Patients do not have a right to treatment or tests that are not medically indicated, to prescriptions for drugs that are illegal, or to care that can potentially harm others. Physicians may decline requests for care that in their medical judgment is too risky. A physician cannot be forced to perform an unnecessary operation, need not provide an MRI for early-onset back pain, or prescribe antibiotics for a viral upper-respiratory infection. Patient autonomy has limits.

Does justifying PAS as maximizing patient autonomy and choice de-medicalize death, or does it medicalize suicide? Tania Salem (1999) makes the argument that it is the latter. She finds that PAS "is widely but incorrectly represented as a further step in the demedicalization of death begun by the patients' rights and right to die movements." Proponents see PAS and euthanasia as putting the patient in control (and halting the frequent tubes and technology that can be an unwanted part of the dying process, thereby de-medicalizing death). But she asserts that PAS "implies not a resistance to but an extension of medical power over life and death" (1999). It is an extension of power most physicians do not want and have explicitly resisted since the time of Hippocrates. It is a daunting power for one human being to have over another, and for a profession to hold.

# BALANCING ON SLIPPERY SLOPES

Slippery-slope arguments maintain that one action will lead to other undesired actions and unintended consequences. The *Merriam-Webster Unabridged Dictionary* defines slippery-slope arguments as "a process or series of events that is hard to stop or control once it has begun and that usually leads to worse or more difficult things." Here, the slippery slope points to questions about how to limit euthanasia or physician-assisted suicide. Proponents say it is possible to restrict these practices to a small group of individuals, such as terminally ill patients who have full decision-making capacity and can consent to these acts. They say safeguards can work.

Opponents worry that physician-assisted suicide leads to euthanasia; that euthanasia for the terminally ill leads to euthanasia for the chronically ill or those who are not ill at all; that voluntary euthanasia leads to involuntary euthanasia or nonvoluntary euthanasia; that euthanasia by doctors leads to euthanasia by nurses; and that euthanasia for adults leads to euthanasia for infants and children.

Experiences in Belgium and the Netherlands seem to confirm these kinds of concerns over time. Recent articles report findings about practices that go beyond the law and guidelines in those countries. In addition, the definition of what constitutes unbearable suffering has expanded with time. In the Netherlands, the End-of-Life Clinic was set up in 2012 as a mobile clinic for second opinions when physicians in the community declined requests for PAS or euthanasia. But this contradicts the ideas that it is physicians in the community who know patients best, which was supposed to be an important safeguard. The following are some trends over the course of a recent year at the End-of-Life Clinic: those age eighty and older constituted 54 percent of those approved for PAS or euthanasia; almost 50 percent of requests were approved for individuals who said part of their suffering was loneliness; almost 7 percent were approved because they said they were "tired of living" (Lerner and Caplan 2015).

In the Netherlands, one in thirty deaths were by euthanasia in 2012, triple the percentage in 2002. In Flanders, Belgium, euthanasia accounted for one in twenty-two deaths in 2013, an increase from about 2 percent of all deaths (in 2007) to 4.6 percent. Concerns similar to those in the Netherlands are seen in Belgium, despite safeguards that are supposed to be in place (Lerner and Caplan 2015). In both countries, underreporting is suspected. According to Barron Lerner and Arthur Caplan (2015):

> The increasing rates of euthanasia may alternatively represent a type of reflexive, carte blanche acquiescence among physicians to the concept of patient self-determination. Or worse, is it simply easier for physicians to accede to these sad and ailing patients' wishes than to reembark on new efforts to relieve or cope with their suffering? As one Dutch ethics professor has said, "The risk now is that people no longer search for a way to endure their suffering." In other words, are the Netherlands and Belgium turning to physicians to solve with euthanasia what are essentially psychosocial issues? And one additional question: Did physicians in the End-of-Life Clinic diagnose unbearable suffering in patients previously not given that diagnosis because they are better diagnosticians or because the clinic was set up by Right to Die NL, a proeuthanasia organization? (Lerner and Caplan 2015)

Also troubling is a lack of attention to advance care planning, an important mechanism for implementing patient rights. In a study of nursing homes in Flanders, Belgium (De Gendt et al. 2013), researchers found a very low prevalence of advance care planning among deceased residents, many of whom had dementia and were dependent on others for their care. For only 50 percent of residents was there evidence of advance care planning (defined as advance directives or physician's orders) and, of those, only 5 percent had advance directives (directly spelling out the residents' health-care goals and wishes should they lose decision-making capacity). Less than 3 percent had documentation of refusal of artificial nutrition and hydration. A legal representative to speak on behalf of a nursing-home resident was documented for less than one in ten residents. In one-third of cases, no palliative care was provided. In addition, two residents (0.2%) documented their potential wish for terminal sedation and eight (0.7%) for euthanasia. This does not seem to be in accord with the frequency of euthanasia and terminal sedation (to death) being reported.

Are these societies addressing the underlying problems and suffering of their people, especially the elderly, the disabled, the depressed, the lonely, and the weary? Are they providing opportunities for patients to express their preferences and exercise their rights through advance care planning? Or are euthanasia and PAS turned to as simpler solutions?

The ride down the slippery slope can accelerate when an activity becomes routine. Rachel Aviv's June 2015 article in the *New Yorker* gave voice to some of those concerns with an interview of the anguished son of a depressed woman who "was chatting and laughing" in the car on the way to her euthanasia appointment. The article reported that other Belgians had been euthanized for autism, anorexia, chronic fatigue syndrome, and adult-onset deafness. Another category, as noted above, includes those who are "tired of living." Yet another is "an inability find a meaningful purpose or goal in life." The article chronicled the activities of one of Belgium's leading euthanasia advocates and practitioners, who seems desensitized to the act of killing he views as a "treatment."

Proponents of PAS in Oregon say the law there works well, and they point to what they say is a low number of individuals (about nine hundred) dying under the law in the first eighteen years of implementation (Oregon Public Health Division 2015). But others say that there is underreporting and that implementation of the law is problematic, with a change in attitudes about medical care and strained patient-physician relationships because patients fear they are being pointed toward PAS. The law requires psychological exams if a physician suspects depression or mental illness in a patient requesting PAS, but this rarely happens—in 2014, only three of 105 individuals who died under the law were referred for a psychological exam. This seems low for referrals given that, for example, among cancer patients receiving palliative care, 18 percent express transient wishes and 12 percent have persistent wishes for death. Of the latter group, 52 percent have a diagnosable mental condition, mostly depression (Wilson et al. 2014). Linda Ganzini and colleagues noted in 2008 that "although most terminally ill Oregonians who receive aid in dying do not have depressive disorders, the current practice of the Death with Dignity Act may fail to protect some patients whose choices are influenced by depression from receiving a prescription for a lethal drug."

In a 2012 article, José Pereira documented instances that go beyond what the law allows in various jurisdictions: involuntary euthanasia (when a person with decision-making capacity has not consented); nonvoluntary euthanasia (when a person lacks decision-making capacity and cannot consent); large numbers of unreported cases despite mandatory reporting requirements; euthanasia performed by nurses where the act is required to be performed by a physician; lack of second opinions and consultations; and other disregard of safeguards mandated by law.

Furthermore, restricting PAS and euthanasia to the terminally ill or to adults with full decision-making capacity, or denying euthanasia to someone who cannot physically commit PAS, raises concerns about arbitrary discrimination against those individuals. In fact, the broadening of these practices to include nonconsenting and nonterminally ill persons has already happened outside the United States.

## IS PAIN CONTROL THAT HASTENS DEATH EUTHANASIA? THE RULE OF DOUBLE EFFECT

Patients' fears about the end of life often include fear of the prospect of unrelieved pain or other symptoms, such as breathlessness. Some patients with terminal illness are under-medicated. Physicians have their own fears and sometimes undertreat pain because they mistakenly fear that terminally ill patients will become tolerant or addicted to the medication. But physicians should be competent in treating pain and other symptoms, administering medications with skill and knowledge and also addressing the patient or family's concerns, which can also interfere with good care. Some physicians are reluctant to use effective doses of opioids because they fear that high doses may hasten death through respiratory suppression. In most cases, adequate pain relief does not hasten death. But there is that possibility and, in those instances, the rule of double effect applies.

The rule of double effect says that an action undertaken with the intention of achieving some good is morally permissible, even if it has a bad side effect—provided that the side effect is not intended, the side effect is not the cause of the good outcome, and the good outweighs the bad.

Consequently, vigorous management of pain for those who experience it at the end of life is ethically acceptable, even when the risk of hastening death is foreseeable—if the intent is to relieve pain. The good effect is pain relief. The potential bad effect is respiratory suppression, which may or may not happen, but which is not intended. If the intent of the act were to cause death, or to cause death to relieve pain, it would not be permissible under the rule of double effect. It would also not be in keeping with the rule of double effect to use aggressive pain relief to treat loneliness, depression, a sense of being tired of living, or psychological or existential suffering.

In euthanasia, death is intended, it is not a side effect. Furthermore, in euthanasia, death is the cause of the relief of suffering. These characteristics violate the rule of double effect.

## SEDATION TO DEATH (TERMINAL SEDATION) VERSUS DOUBLE-EFFECT SEDATION (AND MORE ON WHY LANGUAGE MATTERS)

The use of sedation in certain patients near the end of life is controversial. The terminology varies, as do the circumstances under which it is used, so it is not entirely clear that commentators are speaking of the same practice. Some of the terms that have been used include *terminal sedation, palliative sedation, continuous deep sedation, sedation of the imminently dying,* and *sedation for intractable distress in the dying.* It is an option of last resort to control intractable symptoms. But it must be clear what the intent is of the patient and the clinician in this practice in order to determine whether it is ethically permissible. Is the aim to treat a symptom, understanding that it may require doses that make the patient unconscious, or is the aim to make the patient unconscious as the way to treat the symptoms? This matters. A more accurate description of an appropriate and ethical practice is *double-effect sedation*. In double-effect sedation, the intent is symptom relief, and it is permissible to treat severe symptoms, even if doing so renders the patient unconscious.

By contrast, if the aim is sedation to the point of unconsciousness as way of uncoupling the patient from the experiences of suffering, with a plan to withhold feeding and keep the patient unconscious until death, the practice is more accurately called sedation to death. The Dutch seem to use terminal sedation this way, as a variant of euthanasia—sometimes with consent, sometimes not—making the patient unconscious as a way to treat symptoms. But they see it as separate from euthanasia. They define it as "bringing the patient into deep sedation while forgoing artificial nutrition and hydration" (Rietjens et al. 2006), and this practice accounted for 4 to 10 percent of all documented deaths in the Netherlands in 2001. Both are routine clinical practices, as reflected in the title of the article, "Terminal Sedation and Euthanasia: A Comparison of Clinical Practices" (Rietjens et al. 2006). The authors state that "terminal sedation is typically used to address severe physical and psychological symptoms in dying patients to avoid further suffering, while the patient or the patient's representatives may accept loss of control of the dying process. For patients requesting euthanasia, perceived loss of dignity during the last phase of life is a major problem" (Rietjens et al. 2006, 753). Patients receiving terminal sedation in this study were older, had cardiovascular disease more often than cancer, and 41 percent of the time were not involved in the decision-making process. Here, terminal sedation seems more like a slower version of euthanasia of the elderly, often without the individual's consent.

## KILLING VERSUS ALLOWING TO DIE REVISITED: VSED AND PAS

Another controversial proposed practice is *voluntarily stopping eating and drinking* (VSED) with physician assistance. It has been proposed as an alternative for patients who deem their suffering to be intolerable and who seek death in places where PAS has not been legalized. (Schwarz 2007). Some commentators have maintain that VSED is the forgoing of life-sustaining medical treatment. It has been argued that physicians should assist patients who elect to stop eating and drinking (Quill 2012). VSED, however, is not the forgoing of life-sustaining medical treatment. VSED with the assistance of a physician is ethically equivalent to PAS. A direct comparison between *naturally stopping eating and drinking* (NSED) and VSED helps demonstrate why.

NSED occurs when patients cannot eat or drink (or can do so only with great difficulty) because of an underlying fatal medical condition. Forgoing artificial nutrition and hydration in a patient experiencing NSED is a well-recognized right; it is an instance of allowing the patient to die. In contrast, true VSED is best characterized as a form of suicide because the patient can eat but chooses not to. Consequently, a physician who assists with VSED is engaged in a form of physician-assisted suicide. More succinctly, in NSED, a patient who cannot eat because of underlying illness refuses the medical treatment of artificial feeding. In VSED, a patient who can eat chooses not to eat, asks not to be artificially fed, and seeks assistance with this process (see the case of the elderly couple above). These are different cases.

A few proponents have acknowledged that VSED with the assistance of a physician is assisted suicide. But they think it is morally justified. They are more forthright and call the practice *voluntary palliated starvation* (White, Willmott, and Savulescu 2014; Savulescu 2014). This more honest language allows for a more honest debate about the ethics of—and what constitutes—care at the end of life and physician-assisted suicide.

## END-OF-LIFE CARE, PALLIATIVE CARE, AND HOSPICE CARE

Americans are fighters. But the societal and cultural emphasis on cures and medicine's emphasis on intervention—as well as the wishes of many patients and their families that physicians do everything possible for dying patients—have sometimes been at the expense of good end-of-life care. Adoption of the attitudes, practices, and principles of hospice and palliative care, especially pain-control techniques, has been slow. Reimbursement disincentives for comfort care continue, and concerns about cost pressures regarding health care—especially care at the end of life—are very real. Some patients get unwanted aggressive care as they near the end of life; some do not get needed care. Paradoxically, some get both—a lot of unwanted inappropriate care plus little of the palliative, pain, pastoral, or other supportive comfort care that would ease the dying process. They do not get the right care at the end of life.

What patients should get is good palliative and hospice care. Palliative care improves the quality of life for patients with serious illness—and their families—through treatment of physical and psychological symptoms, spiritual support, and coordination of care. An emphasis on good communications helps ensure that care plans are made and implemented as determined by the patient's goals of care. Hospice care is the provision of palliative care to dying patients in the last months of life (Kelley and Morrison 2015). However, many people die of chronic diseases that they live with for quite some time.

In the age of high-tech medicine, there has been conclusive data since the 1990s that many Americans do not die well. The $28-million study SUPPORT (Study to Understand Prognoses and Preferences for Outcomes and Risks of Treatment) provided much evidence for the need for greater attention to pain control, physician communication with patients (and families), and clinical decision making associated with end-of-life care. The cultural norm of medicine and of hospital life is to fight hard to preserve life, which in most cases is the right thing to do. However, inappropriate aggressive care at the end of life can be both emotionally and physically harmful to patients and their families. SUPPORT found that patients and/or their families were often not being asked about their treatment wishes, and advance directives were not being used or were not being used effectively to implement care preferences (Phillips et al. 2000; The SUPPORT Principal Investigators 1995).

In 1997, an Institute of Medicine (IOM) report titled *Approaching Death: Improving Care at the End of Life* also demonstrated that end-of-life care in the United States was lacking in many ways, which confirmed the SUPPORT findings. In 2014, the IOM revisited these issues and found continued problems in care, but there had been improvements. How to make better care possible is known; it is just very hard to implement. The 2014 IOM report, *Dying in America: Improving Quality and Honoring Individual Preferences Near the End of Life*, stated that though palliative care had become more established, challenges remained in delivering quality end-of-life care to a growing elderly population, with increased cultural diversity and access barriers, as well as communications, time-pressure, and care-coordination issues. This does not sound like an environment in which PAS and euthanasia, even with safeguards, are cures to what ails individuals.

Providing good end-of-life care is an ethical duty of the medical profession. Physician-patient communication must be a high priority, and patient refusals of treatment according to now well-established ethical, clinical, and legal standards for the withholding or withdrawal of medical interventions must be followed. Good pain control is an ethical imperative and should be a high priority. Doing all that can be done through effective hospice care and supportive services and validating patients as persons by supporting and promoting the quality of their lives, even while dying, is the opposite of abandonment.

In the United States, Medicare policy has been a barrier to widespread use of hospice care. Traditionally, patients have only been able to qualify for hospice care if they are predicted to survive with their disease or illness for only six months or less (the definition of terminal illness). In addition, Medicare would not pay for such hospice services as pain management, counseling, and nursing care unless patients discontinued curative care, such as chemotherapy. This has forced patients to make a choice between comfort care or trying to keep their options open. Many patients do not use the hospice benefit, and those who do often do so very late, with only a few days or weeks left to live. In 2015, Medicare announced a new initiative to test concurrent coverage of hospice and curative care that will run through 2020. This will allow patients and families to be cared for longer in hospice, as well as to build relationships and trust with the hospice team that enhance care during the dying process. Studies show patients near the end of life who receive earlier palliative care have lived longer and better, even though they receive less aggressive care. Medicare will also allow payment for expanded advance care–planning discussions between patients and physicians starting in 2016. Lack of reimbursement for these time-intensive conversations was another barrier to good end-of-life care.

In a review of the state of palliative and hospice care in the United States in 2015, Drs. Amy Kelley and R. Sean Morrison noted that a survey of adults found that 90 percent of them did not know or had little understanding of what palliative care was. When read a definition of it, more than 90 percent said they would want it for themselves or family members. If patients and families felt confident they could depend on palliative and hospice care to ease their suffering and that their wishes would be respected at the end of life, there would likely be less demand for physician-assisted suicide.

The culture of fear around dying in America and the gaps and barriers to the delivery of end-of-life care, however, need to change to make that happen. Necessary changes include increasing access to and length of time in hospice care; improving physician training in the principles, science, and practice of palliative and hospice care; providing palliative care earlier in the course of illness, along with curative treatments if desired by the patient; doing a better job of addressing pain and other symptoms; addressing spiritual needs as desired by patients; improving the capabilities of hospitals and nursing homes to provide high-quality care; removing financial and reimbursement impediments to good care and to advance care planning; encouraging more advance care planning (written directives for care and appointment of a proxy decision maker); and creating an atmosphere of openness in discussing care at the end of life and death in a culture that often avoids such issues (Kelley and Morrison 2015). Such changes could potentially reduce patient concerns, anxiety, and fear about death and go a long way toward improving the experience of patients and families during the last phase of life. But it would not eliminate all requests for PAS.

Please see Chapter 7, "Preparing for the End of Life," for further discussion of these issues.

## THE ETHICS OF PAS AND EUTHANASIA: PRO AND CON

Ethics is not merely a matter of consensus. Majority support for an issue does not make it ethical (for example, slavery in the South in the nineteenth century). But polling data can be of interest. It is especially important to look at the actual questions being asked. A 2015 Gallup poll found that almost seven of ten Americans support physician-assisted suicide (PAS), and that support has been increasing. But the survey questions were confused and confusing, sometimes equating suicide with euthanasia, and containing a leading question about PAS. A leading question, of course, is one that prompts the person responding to answer in a certain way. The PAS question was as follows: "When a person has a disease that cannot be cured and is living in severe pain, do you think doctors should or should not be allowed by law to assist the patient to commit suicide if the patient requests it?" This question assumes severe pain and poses a very scary scenario. But pain, including severe pain, can be effectively treated (Dugan 2015).

Another 2015 poll, conducted by the Marist College Institute for Public Opinion, posed the following question: "In some states, legislation is being considered which would allow doctors to prescribe a fatal drug dose to adults who have been told they have less than six months to live so they can take their own life if they want to. Do you strongly support, support, neither support nor oppose, oppose, or strongly oppose such legislation?" Here, 43 percent of respondents said they supported such legislation.

Why do people support PAS? In general, they seem to fear painful and prolonged suffering and the unknowns associated with the process of dying. Some who desire suicide are depressed and, especially among terminally ill patients, this wish is often not stable over time. Others who support the right fear severe pain or a protracted death involving unwanted ventilators, feeding tubes, and other technology. Some regret having watched loved ones die without effective pain and symptom control, and they are also concerned they will not receive good care when they need it. Many are concerned about becoming a burden to their families. They fear loss of dignity or self-image, as well as the idea of winding up in a long-term care facility or other setting. Cognitive decline is another big concern.

Data from Oregon and elsewhere show that most of the individuals who have actually committed suicide with physician assistance, however, do so because they want to control the manner and timing of death, and they fear not being able to enjoy the activities of daily life. But why do they not choose suicide or assisted suicide by other means? Why physician-assisted suicide?

Committing suicide can be accomplished in other ways, but those methods are often seen as disturbing, violent, or not always effective. Some people might seek physician validation that their desire for suicide is medically indicated and doctor approved. Arguments for PAS start from an absolute view of patient autonomy—patients should have the right to control how and when they die based on how they view suffering. It is about maximizing individual freedom and liberty.

Proponents say that as a society, American pets are treated better than humans, because pets can be euthanized when they are sick or old and when their suffering is judged too great. Opponents question how anyone could propose treating humans the way animals are treated.

Proponents see intentionally accelerating death as a good thing. Opponents question this. The last phase of life can be a valuable experience and time for patients and for their loved ones. Unlike PAS, good palliative and hospice care can be emotionally and physically supportive of dying patients and the loved ones they leave behind. Some point to the irony of the difficulties in Oregon of getting coverage for palliative services and pain drugs under the state's Medicaid program although there is no problem having PAS paid for as a covered service. One commentator asks, "Supporters claim physician-assisted suicide gives patients choice, but what sort of choice is it when life is expensive but death is free?" (Toffler 2015).

The ethical arguments in support of physician-assisted suicide and euthanasia focus on the duty of physicians to relieve patient suffering based on an understanding of the duty to respect patient autonomy as an exclusive value, elevating it above all other interests and values. This extends a trend in bioethics emphasizing patient autonomy. Proponents argue that when physician-assisted suicide is not an option, physicians are abandoning patients. They see physician-assisted suicide or euthanasia as acts of compassion respecting patient choice that demedicalize death because they put a stop to what they perceive as an indiscriminate use of high technology at the end of life.

Shouldn't more careful use of high technology in accord with patient wishes be a goal in itself in the care of patients at the end of life? Does physician-assisted suicide demedicalize death—or does it medicalize suicide? End-of-life care, palliative medicine, and hospice care are still evolving fields. Medicine—and society—can and should do better at meeting patient and family needs, alleviating fears, and openly discussing the dying process and what can be expected. Family and loved ones, clergy members, social workers, and other health professionals can contribute greatly to a person's final phase of life, as desired by the individual. Shouldn't we strive to make dying less medical, not more?

Opponents question whether intentionally hastening death should be the role of the physician. They argue physicians should heal when possible and comfort always—not be agents of death. Assistance with suicide or euthanasia can compromise the patient-physician relationship and the trust in the profession and in individual doctors necessary to sustain it. It also undermines the integrity and social role of the medical profession, and alters the meaning of beneficence and the duty to do good and promote the best interests of the patient. When a cure is not possible, care and compassion are still required. Giving up on the care of the patient and validating a desire for suicide is seen as abandonment.

Society in general—and the medical profession in particular—have obligations to safeguard the value of human life and to protect the most vulnerable members of the community: the elderly, the disabled, the sick, the poor, minorities, and other potentially vulnerable individuals and groups. Euthanasia and PAS raise social justice concerns. Might some individuals come to believe they are a burden to family members or society and therefore have a duty to die?

Although autonomy is an important value, does respect for individual autonomy trump all other values? Does one have the right (of self-determination) to give up all self-determination? Are there some limits on individual autonomy? Does a broad right to suicide undermine the very meaning of autonomy? Autonomy and respect for persons is about far more than just control. What are the purposes and consequences of such self-determination for the individual and for society? Should this form of self-determination require, ironically, the assistance of others? Should those others be members of a healing profession?

On a practical level there are many concerns and questions about slippery slopes. Ultimately, can access to physician-assisted suicide be successfully restricted to terminally ill adults with decision-making capacity? The scope of who is eligible for PAS and euthanasia has widened fairly quickly in Europe. And would there be claims of discrimination by others who suffer who are not terminally ill if these services are restricted? What about the individual with Alzheimer disease who fears for the future and wants euthanasia when the time comes but who will not possess decision-making capacity at that time? Is it discriminatory to restrict the practice to certain categories of individuals? To physician-assisted suicide (versus euthanasia)? Also, on a practical level, are there many potential opportunities for abuse, especially in a health-care environment where costs of care are a growing concern and where patients may not have a long-standing relationship with a physician who knows them well?

In an interactive feature in 2013, the *New England Journal of Medicine* published a vignette titled "Physician-Assisted Suicide" about a seventy-two-year-old man in Oregon with metastatic pancreatic cancer who was considering PAS. Included were commentaries by experts, both pro and con, and the opportunity for readers (physicians and nonphysicians) to vote. The commentators opposing PAS recognized the patient's concerns and the need for the request for PAS to be addressed—but not carried out. They recognized the patient's right to refuse treatment and the physician's responsibility to relieve pain and suffering and provide palliative care, but drew a line stating that PAS was incompatible with the physician's role as healer. From their perspective, "healers commit to accompanying patients throughout the illness trajectory" ("Physician-Assisted Suicide" 2013, 1451). The commentary found that advocates were intentionally confusing physician-assisted suicide with palliative care and, in doing so, were trying to get the public to see PAS as a clinically and ethically accepted end-of-life care "treatment." They reviewed slippery slope arguments. But most fundamentally, the commentary discussed principles underlying the debate and pointed to flaws in placing individual autonomy above all other values and interests.

The pro-PAS commentary asserted that death can be a relief and that, for some patients, taking action is better than waiting for death to occur. Though it said that responding to a carefully considered request for PAS can be compatible with the goals and ethos of medicine, the commentary offered no argument as to how and only asserted that physicians should use their skills to alleviate all patient suffering. This commentary said safeguards in other countries were working, noting that not all the individuals who asked about PAS actually killed themselves, allowing individuals to have more options even if they did not exercise them.

Evidently there were some problems with the interactive features and voting process, but all told, about 65 percent of voters said that PAS should not be allowed in the case (Colbert, Schulte, and Adler 2013). This was the case:

> John Wallace is a 72-year-old man with metastatic pancreatic cancer. At time of diagnosis, the cancer was metastatic to his regional lymph nodes and liver. He was treated with palliative chemotherapy, but the disease continued to progress. Recently he has become jaundiced, and he has very little appetite. He has been seeing a palliative care physician and a social worker on an ongoing basis. His abdominal pain is now well controlled with high-dose narcotics, but the narcotics have caused constipation. In addition to seeing the social worker, he has also been seeing a psychologist to help him to cope with his illness.

Mr. Wallace has been married to his wife, Joyce, for 51 years, and they have three children and six grandchildren. He and his wife have lived in Salem, Oregon, for the past 23 years, and most of his family lives nearby. He understands the prognosis of the disease, and he does not wish to spend his last days suffering or in an unresponsive state. He discusses his desire for euthanasia with his wife and family members, and they offer him their support. The next day, he calls his physician and asks for information about physician-assisted suicide. ("Physician-Assisted Suicide" 2013)

Although the case mentions euthanasia, it ends with a phone call by the patient to his physician to ask for information about PAS. The feature posed the following question: "Do you believe that Mr. Wallace should be able to receive life-terminating drugs from his physician?"

Looking at the case, however, Mr. Wallace actually appears to be doing fairly well. His symptoms, including pain, are well controlled, although the high-dose narcotics he is taking are causing constipation. He has a loving family and social and psychological support. Readers are informed that he understands his disease. But evidently, medication for his opioid-induced constipation has not been offered and he has not been told that in his current state, and with natural loss of appetite, death is likely not far off. He assumes he will be suffering and no one has otherwise addressed these concerns with him and his family. This seems more like a failure of his treating physicians—he even has a palliative care physician—and not a compelling case for PAS.

## NO GENERAL RIGHT TO HEALTH CARE IN THE UNITED STATES

Is it ironic to have a right to PAS in the United States, a country that has no general right to health care? Holland and Belgium both have universal health care. They also have more homogeneous populations. Culturally sensitive delivery of care is another issue in the United States, where some groups actively distrust the health-care system and infrequently access palliative care for fear of being denied care.

## Summary

The legalization of physician-assisted suicide (and/or euthanasia) remains a difficult issue that divides both the public and the medical profession. Although PAS is legal in a few jurisdictions in the United States, and PAS and/or euthanasia are legal or tolerated in other parts of the world, assisting a suicide is a specific statutory offense in most states, and euthanasia is illegal in all states.

There will always be compelling and tragic cases of suffering at the end of life, and many of the arguments of the supporters of the legalization of physician-assisted suicide are significant. But do those arguments for legalization outweigh the other interests and values at stake and longstanding core ethical arguments of the medical profession?

Proponents and opponents view data about the experiences with legalization differently. Proponents say that the laws work, that the numbers of individuals using PAS and euthanasia are relatively small, and that the floodgates have not opened. Opponents see expansion of the practices over time in addition to underreporting. Overall, the evidence does seem to indicate slippage on the slippery slope, especially outside of the United States.

In view of the ethical arguments and the data, and on practical and theoretical grounds, much more consideration needs to be given to the implications of the legalization of PAS and euthanasia for the patient-physician relationship and the trust necessary to sustain the relationship. Legalization should be evaluated in light of the goals of medicine and the medical profession's role in society, as well as the value society places on the lives of vulnerable patients, especially the disabled, the incapacitated, infants, children, the elderly, and those experiencing health disparities. The implications of approving killing by physicians, including the ramifications for physician participation in capital punishment, must be considered.

Physician-assisted suicide and euthanasia are issues in medicine and bioethics that will define who Americans are and who they want to be both as individuals and as members of society. In the United States, there is no general right to health care. Should death be routinely available as a treatment?

There is, however, a well-developed right to refuse treatment in the United States. Is physician-assisted suicide (or euthanasia) just an extension of that right? Do ethical and legal arguments back up such a right? The withdrawal of treatment based on patient wishes respects a patient's right to bodily integrity, to be free of unwanted medical treatment. Are physician-assisted suicide and euthanasia fundamentally different?

Individuals facing the end of life who really want to end their lives cannot be prevented from committing suicide. Opponents of PAS and euthanasia argue that society should discourage them and care for them, providing the necessary social support, health care (including mental health care, hospice and palliative care, spiritual care), and compassion. Perhaps this should be the focus of medicine so that no one should have to fear an undignified or pain-filled life or death. Individuals either do not know or do not know much about what palliative care is, but when told its definition, they overwhelmingly respond that they would want it for themselves or their family members if they were severely ill.

In some ways, the continuing inadequacies of palliative and hospice care and the ability to provide comfort and compassion at the end of life fuel the desire for access to PAS. Health professionals, families, and communities can do a better job of caring for, meeting the needs of, and demonstrating support for those who would perceive suicide as their best option. Improvements in end-of-life care have really just begun.

Who lives, who dies, and how? Is it the role of medicine to give to individuals the control over the manner and timing of death that some seek? Throughout life, and as death is approached, the medical profession must strive to give patients the care, compassion, and comfort they need and deserve. The way we die and the role of physicians in life and death are, and will likely continue to be, matters for intense debate.

## Endnote

1. The views expressed herein do not necessarily reflect the policies of the American College of Physicians.

## Bibliography

American Medical Association (AMA). "Opinion 2.211— Physician-Assisted Suicide." Issued June 1994; updated June 1996. http://www.ama-assn.org/ama/pub/physician-resources/medical-ethics/code-medical-ethics/opinion2211.page/.

Aviv, Rachel. "The Death Treatment." *New Yorker*, June 22, 2015. http://www.newyorker.com/magazine/2015/06/22/the-death-treatment.

Byock, Ira. "Physician-Assisted Suicide Is Not an Acceptable Practice." In *Physician-Assisted Suicide*, edited by Robert F. Weir, 107–135. Bloomington: University of Indiana Press, 1997.

Callahan, Daniel. "When Self-Determination Runs Amok." *The Hastings Center Report* 22, no. 2 (1992): 52–55.

Colbert, James A., Joann Schulte, and Jonathan N. Adler. "Physician-Assisted Suicide—Polling Results." *New England Journal of Medicine* 369, no. 11 (2013): e15.

Coleman, Carl H., and Alan R. Fleischman. "Guidelines for Physician-Assisted Suicide: Can the Challenge Be Met?" *Journal of Law Medicine and Ethics* 24, no. 3 (1996): 217–224.

De Gendt, Cindy, Johan Bilsen, Robert Vander Stichele, and Luc Deliens. "Advance Care Planning and Dying in Nursing Homes in Flanders, Belgium: A Nationwide Survey." *Journal of Pain and Symptom Management* 45, no. 2 (2013): 223–234.

Dembosky, April. "California Judge Throws Out Lawsuit on Medically Assisted Suicide." NPR and KQED. Updated July 24, 2015. http://www.npr.org/sections/health-shots/2015/07/24/425753398/california-judge-to-throw-out-lawsuit-on-medically-assisted-suicide.

Dugan, Andrew. "In US, Support Up for Doctor-Assisted Suicide." Gallup poll. May 27, 2015. http://www.gallup.com/poll/183425/support-doctor-assisted-icide.aspx?utm_source=physician assisted suicide&utm_medium=search&utm_campaign=tiles.

Emanuel, Ezekiel J., Diane Fairclough, Brian C. Clarridge, et al. "Attitudes and Practices of US Oncologists regarding Euthanasia and Physician-Assisted Suicide." *Annals of Internal Medicine* 133, no. 7 (2000): 527–532.

Field, Marilyn J., and Christine K. Cassel. *Approaching Death: Improving Care at the End of Life*. Institute of Medicine (IOM). Washington, DC: National Academy Press, 1997.

Ganzini, Linda, Elizabeth R. Goy, and Steven K. Dobscha. "Prevalence of Depression and Anxiety in Patients Requesting Physicians' Aid in Dying: Cross-Sectional Survey." *BMJ* 337 (2008): a1682.

Gaylin, Willard, Leon R. Kass, Edmund D. Pellegrino, and Mark Siegler. "Doctors Must Not Kill." *Journal of the American Medical Association* 259, no. 14 (1988): 2139–2140.

Hardwig, John. "Is There a Duty to Die?" *The Hastings Center Report* 27, no. 2 (1997): 34–42. Originally published online (2012). doi: 10.2307/3527626.

Hippocrates. "The Oath." In *Hippocrates I*, edited by W. H. S. Jones, 289–301. Cambridge, MA: Harvard University Press, 1923.

Institute of Medicine (IOM). *Dying in America: Improving Quality and Honoring Individual Preferences near the End of Life*. Washington, DC: National Academies Press, 2014.

Kelley, Amy S., and R. Sean Morrison. "Palliative Care for the Seriously Ill." *New England Journal of Medicine* 373, no. 8 (2015): 747–755.

Lerner, Baron H., and Arthur L. Caplan. "Euthanasia in Belgium and the Netherlands: On a Slippery Slope?" *JAMA Internal Medicine* 175, no. 10 (2015): 1640–1641. doi: 10.1001/jamainternmed.2015.4086.

Loggers, Elizabeth Trice, Helene Starks, Moreen Shannon-Dudley, et al. "Implementing a Death with Dignity Program at a Comprehensive Cancer Center." *New England Journal of Medicine* 368, no. 15 (2013): 1417–1424.

Marist College Institute for Public Opinion. "The End of Life Debate: A Survey of Americans." March 2015. http://www.kofc.org/un/en/resources/communications/end-of-life-debate04152015.pdf.

Miller, Franklin G., Timothy E. Quill, Howard Brody, et al. "Regulating Physician-Assisted Death." *New England Journal of Medicine* 331, no. 2 (1994): 119–122.

Momeyer, Richard. "Does Physician-Assisted Suicide Violate the Integrity of Medicine?" *Journal of Medicine and Philosophy* 20, no. 1 (2000): 13–24.

New York State Task Force on Life and the Law. *When Death Is Sought: Assisted Suicide and Euthanasia in the Medical Context*. Albany: Author, 1994.

Oregon Public Health Division. Oregon's Death with Dignity Annual Reports: "Oregon's Death with Dignity Act—2014." 2015. http://public.health.oregon.gov/ProviderPartnerResources/EvaluationResearch/DeathwithDignityAct/Pages/ar-index.aspx.

Pellegrino, Edmund D. "Compassion Needs Reason Too." *Journal of the American Medical Association* 270, no. 7 (1993): 874–875.

Pellegrino, Edmund D. "Nonabandonment: An Old Obligation Revisited." *Annals of Internal Medicine* 122, no. 5 (1995): 377–378.

Pereira, José. "Legalizing Euthanasia or Assisted Suicide: The Illusion of Safeguards and Controls." *Current Oncology* 18, no. 2 (2011): e38–e45.

Phillips, Russell S., Mary Beth Hamel, Kenneth E. Covinsky, et al. "Findings from SUPPORT and HELP: An Introduction." *Journal of the American Geriatrics Society* 48, no. 5 (2000): S1–S5.

"Physician-Assisted Suicide." *New England Journal of Medicine* 368, no. 15 (2013): 1450–1452.

Quill, Timothy E. "Physicians Should 'Assist in Suicide' When It Is Appropriate." *Journal of Law, Medicine and Ethics* 40, no. 1 (2012): 57–65. doi: 10.1111/j.1748-720X.2012.00646.x.

Rietjens, Judith A. C., Johannes J. M. van Delden, Agnes van der Heide, et al. "Terminal Sedation and Euthanasia: A Comparison of Clinical Practices." *Archives of Internal Medicine* 166, no. 7 (2006): 749–753.

Salem, Tania. "Physician-Assisted Suicide: Promoting Autonomy—or Medicalizing Suicide?" *The Hastings Center Report* 29, no. 3 (1999): 30–36.

Savulescu, Julian. "A Simple Solution to the Puzzles of End of Life? Voluntary Palliated Starvation." *Journal of Medical Ethics* 40, no. 2 (2014): 110–113.

Schwarz, Judith. "Exploring the Option of Voluntarily Stopping Eating and Drinking within the Context of a Suffering Patient's Request for a Hastened Death." *Journal of Palliative Medicine* 10, no. 6 (2007): 1288–1297.

Snyder, Lois, for the American College of Physicians Ethics, Professionalism, and Human Rights Committee. *American College of Physicians Ethics Manual.* 6th ed. *Annals of Internal Medicine* 156, no. 1, part 2 (2012): 73–104.

Snyder, Lois, and Daniel P. Sulmasy, for the Ethics and Human Rights Committee of the American College of Physicians-American Society of Internal Medicine. "Physician-Assisted Suicide." *Annals of Internal Medicine* 135, no. 3 (2001): 209–216.

Sulmasy, Daniel P. "Killing and Allowing to Die: Another Look." *Journal of Law, Medicine and Ethics* 26, no. 1 (1998): 55–64.

Sulmasy, Daniel P., and Edmund D. Pellegrino. "The Rule of Double Effect: Clearing Up the Double Talk." *Archives of Internal Medicine* 159, no. 6 (1999): 545–550.

The SUPPORT Principal Investigators. "A Controlled Trial to Improve Care for Seriously Ill Hospitalized Patients." *Journal of the American Medical Association* 274, no. 20 (1995): 1591–1598.

Thomasma, David C. "When Physicians Choose to Participate in the Death of Their Patient: Ethics and Physician-Assisted Suicide." *Journal of Law, Medicine, and Ethics* 24, no. 3 (1996): 183–197.

Toffler, William L. "A Doctor-Assisted Disaster for Medicine." *Wall Street Journal*, August 17, 2015. http://www.wsj.com/articles/a-doctor-assisted-disaster-for-medicine-1439853118.

Verhagen, Eduard, and Pieter J. J. Sauer. "The Groningen Protocol—Euthanasia in Severely Ill Newborns." *New England Journal of Medicine* 352, no. 10 (2005): 959–962.

White, Ben, Lindy Willmott, and Julian Savulescu. "Voluntary Palliated Starvation: A Lawful and Ethical Way to Die?" *Journal of Law and Medicine* 22, no. 2 (2014): 376–386.

Wilson, Keith G., Tracy L. Dalgleish, Marvey Max Chochinov, et al. "Mental Disorders and the Desire for Death in Patients Receiving Palliative Care for Cancer." *BMJ Supportive and Palliative Care* (March 5, 2014). doi: 10.1136/bmjspcare-2013-000604.

## COURT CASES

*Compassion in Dying v. Washington*, 79 F.3d 790 (9th Cir. 1996).

*Cruzan v. Director, Missouri Dept. of Health*, 110 S.Ct 2841 (1990).

*Quill v. Vacco*, 80 F.3d 716 (2d Cir. 1996).

*In Re Quinlan*, 355 A.2d 647 (NJ 1976).

*Vacco v. Quill*, 117 S.Ct. 2293 (1997).

*Washington v. Glucksberg*, 117 S.Ct. 2258 (1997).

## FILM AND TELEVISION

*The Barbarian Invasions.* Dir. Denys Arcand. 2003. Miramax.

*The Farewell Party.* Dir. Tal Granit and Sharon Maymon. 2014. Samuel Goldwyn Films.

*In the Matter of Karen Ann Quinlan: Murder or Mercy.* Dir. Glenn Jordan. 1977. NBC.

*The Sea Inside.* Dir. Alejandro Amenábar. 2004. New Line Cinema.

*You Don't Know Jack.* Dir. Barry Levinson. 2010. HBO Films.

# Part Two:
# Professionalism—Fiduciary Relationship

Historically, medicine, law, and the clergy were the three professions. One characteristic of these professions is that the individual is called to the work, and another is that the focus is on the client or patient, not on personal wealth, fame, or satisfaction. Today, professions are defined by their attributes, which often include self-regulation of training and education (and who gets access to that training), a long process of education as an adult, a legally recognized licensure practice that is controlled by members of the profession, high social status and income, a strong personal identification with the profession, and freedom from lay control. Professions also usually have a code of ethics that spells out how a member of the profession is expected to behave. Part Two of this volume looks at several of these expected behaviors.

Health-care professionals are expected to tell the truth (Chapter 9), preserve confidentiality (Chapter 10), secure patient consent (Chapter 11), and avoid conflicts of interest (Chapter 12). These behaviors are virtuous in a health-care provider because they help preserve trust in a fiduciary relationship. A fiduciary relationship is a special legal connection formed when a vulnerable person comes to an expert for help. The vulnerable person must share secrets, and the expert is supposed to provide benefit. For the vulnerable person to feel confident enough to expose confidential information, there must be trust that the expert will not abuse any information shared and will not harm the person in need. In a fiduciary medical relationship, the patient is dependent on the physician or other health-care provider. Thus, the virtuous behaviors are required to ensure that health-care providers are trustworthy in their practice.

CHAPTER 9

# Truth and Deception in Health Care

**Julija Kelecevic**
*Regional Ethicist*
*Hamilton Health Sciences, ON, Canada*

**Andrea Frolic**
*Director, Office of Clinical and Organizational Ethics*
*Hamilton Health Sciences, ON, Canada*

"It's a basic truth of the human condition that everybody lies. The only variable is about what."

—*House M.D.*, Season 1

One of the most touching literary descriptions of the experience of being lied to about a terminal diagnosis was depicted in *The Death of Ivan Ilych* (1886) by Leo Tolstoy (1828–1910):

> What tormented Ivan Ilych most was the deception, the lie, which for some reason they all accepted, that he was not dying but was simply ill, and that he only need keep quiet and undergo a treatment and then something very good would result. He however knew that do what they would nothing would come of it, only still more agonizing suffering and death. This deception tortured him—their not wishing to admit what they all knew and what he knew, but wanting to lie to him concerning his terrible condition, and wishing and forcing him to participate in that lie. Those lies—lies enacted over him on the eve of his death and destined to degrade this awful, solemn act to the level of their visitings, their curtains, their sturgeon for dinner— were a terrible agony for Ivan Ilych. And strangely enough, many times when they were going through their antics over him he had been within a hairbreadth of calling out to them: "Stop lying! You know and I know that I am dying. Then at least stop lying about it!" But he had never had the spirit to do it. The awful, terrible act of his dying was, he could see, reduced by those about him to the level of a casual, unpleasant, and almost indecorous incident (as if someone entered a drawing room defusing an unpleasant odour) and this was done by that very decorum which he had served all his life long. (Tolstoy [1886] 2015, 41–42)

We see a doctor's perspective on deception in the short story "The Doctor's Word" (1943) by R. K. Narayan (1906–2001). It features Dr. Raman, an astute diagnostician, who is facing an ethical dilemma when treating his good friend Gopal. Dr. Raman is known for "certain curt truthfulness; for that very reason his opinion was valued; he was not a mere doctor expressing an opinion but a judge pronouncing a verdict" (Narayan [1943] 2006, 21). But when facing Gopal's health crisis, Dr. Raman deviates from his practice after his dear friend asks him about truthful prognosis. Although Dr. Raman is certain that Gopal is dying, he felt that it would "virtually mean a death sentence and destroy the thousandth part of a chance that the patient had of survival" (25) if he is truthful with his friend.

These literary examples illustrate the ethical tensions commonly experienced between the core principles of bioethics in situations involving disclosure. Although questions about truth-telling to patients can be traced back to the works of Hippocrates (late fourth century BCE) and Maimonides (1135–1204), in modern health care the theoretical underpinnings of truth-telling arise from Western, mainly Anglo-American, philosophy and laws (e.g., the laws about informed consent). The core principles of bioethics emphasize individual rights related to health and health care, specifically the rights to self-determination and autonomous decision making, as well as rights to confidentiality and privacy of personal health information. Bioethics also emphasizes professional health-care providers' fiduciary duties to reduce harm and provide positive benefit to their patients, their colleagues, their profession, and the society in general.

According to James Childress in *Who Should Decide?* (1982), ethical tensions between the professional's desire to shield the patient from bad news and the patient's right to information have become more common in the wake of the civil rights movement as the notion of paternalism (physician's behavior that limits patient's self-determination) has been reassessed. In the past, as noted by Ezekiel J. Emanuel and Linda L. Emanuel in their 1992 article "Four Models of the Physician-Patient Relationship," health-care providers either directly made a decision for the patient or selected the type of information to present to the patient to create a pretense of a choice, when, in fact, the details were clearly skewed toward the choice favored by the health-care professional. Historical examples of intentional deception, writes Albert R. Jonsen in *The Birth of Bioethics* (1998), forced health-care providers, scientists, and policy makers to examine what would be the best way to ensure that people—especially those considered vulnerable—are in a position to make an informed choice. The ethical principles and guidelines that ensure shared decision making and respect for a person's autonomous choice have been outlined in the *Belmont Report* (1979). Tom Beauchamp and James Childress explain in *Principles of Biomedical Ethics* (2009) that although the report focused on research involving human participants, the concepts have been adopted for the general field of bioethics.

## TRUTH-TELLING IN HEALTH CARE: A TWENTIETH-CENTURY INNOVATION

In the twenty-first century, honesty, openness, truth-telling, veracity, and disclosure are considered the norms of contemporary relationships between patients and health-care providers in the United States, Canada, and, increasingly, other parts of the world. Childress (1982) explains that these concepts are understood as central postulates of therapeutic relationships, guiding actions in clinical decision making, for example, through the process of informed consent. Although there are subtle differences in the meanings of these terms, this chapter will use them interchangeably.

Popular television shows, however, don't necessarily reflect such idealized behaviors. Dr. House from *House M.D.*, is guided by the credo "everyone lies." Throughout the run of the show, House is often proved correct, as many of his patients lie about their illnesses. They either outright lie about possible reasons for their medical issues (especially when they are involved in sexual infidelities) or they fail to disclose pertinent information they find embarrassing or unimportant. House believes that patients lie for a good reason. In his interactions with patients, he often uses deception and even manipulation to get results. For example, in the 2005 episode "TB or not TB" (season 2, episode 4), although House knows that the patient has tuberculosis, he deceives him about his condition. The patient, who is a doctor working in Africa, would refuse lifesaving treatment based on the fact that his patients would not have access to the same medications, so House lies to him to administer the treatment.

Why do people lie? Psychological research has provided us with a better understanding about the motivations and the mechanisms of lying and deception. John Seiter, Jon Bruschke, and Chunsheng Bai compiled a comprehensive overview of the literature on the topic in their article "The Accept-ability of Deception as a Function of Perceivers' Culture, Deceiver's Intention, and Deceiver-Deceived Relationship" (2002), describing different typologies of lying. The classifications were based on the motivation, the interpersonal relationship between the deceiver and the deceived, the consequences of lying, and the cultural acceptability of lying. For example, in "Predicting the Acceptability and Likelihood of Lying: The Interaction of Personality with Type of Lie" (2008), Beverly McLeod and Randy Genereux identified four types of intentions and reasons why people lie: (1) altruism, (2) avoidance, (3) social acceptance, and (4) self-gain. Richard Maier and Paul Lavrakas's 1976 study "Lying Behavior and Evaluation of Lies" revealed that research participants found lies that shortchanged people of resources to be more unacceptable.

In reality, no clear distinction exists between truth-telling and lying, and not all kinds of deception have the same consequences. People interact with each other based on preexisting relationships, individual motivations, preferred consequences, and social circumstances. When discussing the concepts of truth-telling and deception, perhaps it is more useful not to think about these terms as simply black and white, but rather to examine them along the *deception spectrum*, depicted in Figure 9.1.

It would be impractical to plot each speech act on this three-dimensional graph; however, conceptually, this can ground our understanding of how lying and deception occur in health care and the nature of their consequences. For example, historically, physicians acted paternalistically by not disclosing *bad news* to patients to protect them from emotional upset, particularly those whom they considered vulnerable. According to Figure 9.1, physicians' motivation in such cases could be considered altruistic (to protect others) because the type of deception was almost always passive (omission of pertinent information rather than outright lying). This type of deception has significant consequences for patients who are denied key information that may affect not only their health decisions but also other aspects of their lives.

The power shift in health care from a model of expert clinician to a collaborative and shared decision-making model in which patients are experts in their own experiences of illness, challenges the practice of paternalism, including withholding truthful information or deceiving patients. The research data support this shift. Evidence shows that physicians and

**The Deception Spectrum**

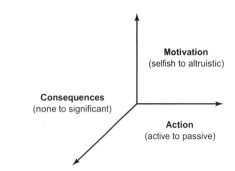

**Figure 9.1.** *The Deception Spectrum.*

other health-care professionals significantly modified their behaviors regarding the disclosure of diagnosis and associated prognosis in the second part of the twentieth century. For example, in the case of cancer diagnosis, in a span of less than two decades, physicians' attitudes changed from almost never disclosing an oncology diagnosis (Oken 1961) to the situation in which 98 percent of physicians would do so (Novack et al. 1979). Special circumstances, such as a patient's cognitive inability to understand the diagnosis, emotional stability, age, and the family's wishes to not disclose "bad news," became exceptions to the rule of full disclosure (Novack et al. 1979). Such a drastic change seems to result from the shift in societal expectations of how physicians ought to behave in clinical encounters when disclosing bad news and physicians' respect for truth-telling as a cornerstone of patient-physician relationships.

In the twenty-first century, truth-telling has become so ingrained in clinical practice that it is now a public expectation and professional doctrine. But what is really meant by truth-telling? Where do ethical issues related to truth-telling arise in contemporary health care? What are some strategies for practicing the art of truth-telling in a multicultural society? This chapter explores truth-telling in contemporary health-care practice, describing current norms, innovative practices, and areas of continued controversy and ambiguity. We will try to unpack these concepts not only from a strictly philosophical perspective, but also use information from social sciences (anthropology, sociology, and psychology) to better understand truth-telling and deception. In addition, we will expand the discussion from strictly patient-provider relationships and begin to understand these concepts from a systems perspective. We hope to deliver some practical recommendations to future health-care providers for navigating ethical challenges in truth-telling.

## TRUTH-TELLING AND INFORMED CONSENT

The concept of truth-telling may be oversimplified if understood as a unidirectional process in which a physician or other health-care professional presents the biomedical facts about the patient's disease to inform decision making. When reflecting on such an approach, physician-ethicist Antonella Surbone (2006) suggests two seemingly opposite problems. First, this approach to informed consent positions the physicians and other health-care professionals as experts, ensuring the passive role of their patients. Thinking about this approach another way, by presenting *objective facts* about the disease in a neutral way, physicians and other health-care professionals delegate decision making completely to their patients, leaving no space for shared decision making. Surbone advocates for "an open-ended dynamic process of ascertainment and constant reassessment of a truth shared" (2006, 944). In her view, the physician-patient relationship is ideally a reciprocal exchange of pertinent and hopefully truthful information to reach the best possible outcome for patients in a collaborative manner.

In a 2014 editorial, Steven Edwards pointed out that health-care students almost uniformly agree that all adult and competent patients have a right to know what is going on with their health. This is congruent with the students' worldview, in which almost all of them would like to be told what is going on with their health. The students also observed that some of the clauses in the guiding documents for health-care professionals, like codes of ethics, are confusing, appearing to justify withholding the truth from the patients in some circumstances, such as when it would cause the patient extreme distress. The students were additionally puzzled when witnessing their clinical preceptors' behavior, citing examples when experienced practitioners have not been completely truthful to their patients. It became clear that conceptually there should be no ambiguity about whether truth-telling should be a mandatory part of physicians' and other health-care professionals' practices, but in reality, clinical encounters demonstrate a lack of uniformity about how truth (or some version of it) is communicated to the patients. Students and novice health-care practitioners may be educated in the theoretical doctrine of truth-telling, but more often than not, they have not been provided with the skills to be successful in the art of disclosure. The process of disclosure is not a simple one; it is a nuanced interaction resulting from a complex social reality in which both patient and health-care provider exist. The section "Culture and Truth-Telling" will deal with the art of truth-telling in a multicultural society.

## LYING AND DECEPTION IN HEALTH CARE: PROVIDERS' ROLE

According to Meredith Grey, the lead character in the television show *Grey's Anatomy*, doctors lie:

> Doctors give patients a number of things. We give them medicine, we give them advice, and most of the time, we give them our undivided attention. But, by far, the hardest thing you can give a patient is the truth. The truth is hard. The truth is awkward, and very often, the truth hurts. I mean, people think they want the truth, but do they really? … The truth is painful. Deep down nobody wants to hear it, especially when it hits close to home. Sometimes we tell the truth because the truth is all we have to give. Sometimes we tell the truth because we need to say it out loud to really hear it for ourselves. And sometimes we tell the truth because we just can't help ourselves. And sometimes, we tell them, because we owe them at least that much. (*Grey's Anatomy*, "Let the Truth Sting," 2007)

In her theoretical work, Jennifer Jackson (1991) argued that physicians and nurses have a *prima facie* duty to be truthful, and that both lying and deception are wrong from a utilitarian standpoint. She also observed that such a theoretical approach does not provide justification of why either one of the actions is inherently wrong. She claimed that there is a moral difference between lying and deception: physicians are obligated not to lie, but they are not obliged to avoid deception because deception may not lead to erosion of trust in patient-physician relationships. This conclusion has been challenged by Piers Benn (2001) who explored whether there is qualitatively a moral difference between outright lying to a patient and deceiving the patient without lying, whether the deception is verbal or nonverbal. He concluded that these actions may have detrimental consequence on a therapeutic relationship.

A 1989 study by physician Dennis Novack and colleagues provides an interesting analysis of physicians' justification for engaging in deception, especially when such action does not harm the patient and leads to the physicians' personal gain. Here, physicians commented that they would misrepresent a screening test as a diagnostic test to ensure payment from the insurance companies, raising the possibility that "offering 'creative diagnoses' to third-party payers may be a widespread practice" (Novack et al. 1989, 2984). Because physicians' earnings are closely tied to the volumes of the delivered services, and referrals to other specialties are less lucrative, it would be interesting to explore whether physicians tend to omit treatment options that are outside of their specialty—for example, whether a surgeon would offer only surgical procedures and would not present nonsurgical options to a patient. In extreme situations, physicians actively lie to patients for obvious personal gain, like the case of a Michigan oncologist who falsely diagnosed people with nonexistent cancers and administered unnecessary chemotherapy (Steensma 2016). He also prescribed chemotherapy to end-of-life patients who may not have benefited from it and who suffered significantly from the side effects of the medication. The total scope of his scam is unknown, but it has been estimated that he defrauded approximately US$35 million. The detrimental impact of his deception on affected patients and families is immeasurable.

In contrast, like the example of Dr. Raman, lying for the benefit of patients appears to be endemic in certain clinical contexts. A special set of circumstances in which physicians intentionally lie has been identified when physicians communicate false information to third parties to secure payment approval for what they consider to be necessary procedures. In "Lying for Patients: Physician Deception of Third-Party Payers" (1999), physician Victor Freeman and colleagues assessed physicians' willingness to lie to secure payment approval through six clinical vignettes. Each of the vignettes represents a common case related to referrals for specialized medical services. The cases escalate from medically appropriate and urgent care (coronary bypass surgery for a patient with serious cardiac illness) to cosmetic rhinoplasty (for an elective procedure for a patient who has body image issues and may benefit more from counseling than surgery). The findings revealed that physicians were more likely to lie in cases in which a patient requires a more serious procedure (e.g., more than half of them would create false statements to ensure that patients are covered for bypass surgery, whereas only 2.5 percent would do so to ensure patient access to rhinoplasty). Physicians who practice more in managed-care settings and those who spend less time in direct patient care also were more likely to engage in deception.

Another clinical context in which deception could be perceived as morally acceptable is in the use of deception in administrating psychiatric medications. Nonadherence to the proposed treatment remains one of the great challenges in caring for mentally ill patients. Many of these patients, if they don't take prescribed medications, inevitably will deteriorate to the point of harming themselves or others, and potentially they could be forced to take the medications, just at a later date. K. S. Latha (2010) wonders whether it would ever be ethically justifiable to secretly administer psychiatric medications to competent patients, acknowledging that there may be a qualitative difference in using deception to administer medications in situations in which the patient lacks capacity to consent to the treatment and their substitute decision maker agrees to the treatment. Similarly, in patients with Alzheimer's disease, covert, deceptive treatment should be considered only after the interprofessional team has reached consensus with the family that this is the best option (Blythe 2000). Gary Mitchell used a case study to illustrate what he described as therapeutic lying to ensure medication adherence among patients with Alzheimer's disease. He stated that nurses caring for patients with this type of dementia "are at war with the legal, ethical, and clinical issues that surround therapeutic lying practices" (2014, 845).

Pediatrics is another setting in which paternalistic deception is almost a norm. As in the case of adult patients who have lost the capacity to make health-care decisions, the justification for not including children in the conversation about their health or not exercising full disclosure is similar: if a substitute decision maker acts appropriately in her role and is informed and agreeable to the plan, deception is justifiable. Philosopher Sissela Bok argued that children, "more than all other, need care, support, protection. To shield them, not only from brutal speech and frightening news, but from apprehension and pain—to soften and embellish and disguise—is as natural as to shelter them from harsh weather. Because they are more vulnerable and more impressionable than adults, they cannot always cope with what they hear" (1978, 10).

Bok did not advocate for blatant deception of children. Rather, she argued that lying to children carries risks of tainting relationships when the child discovers the lie. She has highlighted the need to develop communication skills with children to present "what is at stake ... so that they will be able to respond 'appropriately'—neither too casually, nor too intensely if it is a present danger, and without excess worry if it is a future danger" (1978, 11).

These examples of special clinical circumstances, in which physicians and other health-care providers justify lying, deception, or omission of all or part of relevant information as part of therapeutic intervention, seem to be qualitatively distinct from those situations in which health-care professionals engage in deception for personal gain. In such exceptional circumstances, patients either never had the capacity or have lost the capacity to make personal decisions, making them vulnerable individuals. Therefore, health-care professionals may feel that they have special duties to protect the vulnerable, which would justify use of any of the actions along the deception spectrum.

## LYING AND DECEPTION IN HEALTH CARE: PATIENTS' ROLE

Health-care professionals are not the only ones who may act less honestly than desired. If truth-telling is seen as a bidirectional and dynamic process, it should be expected that patients also have a duty to be truthful. Without doubt, as the television character House teaches, patients may lie, intentionally deceive, omit facts, or distort the information shared with their physicians or other health-care providers. In contrast to physicians and other health-care providers who engage in deception because of either personal gain or a misguided sense that they are protecting a patient, most patients lie because of prior negative experiences within the health-care system or society as a whole. For example, in the television series *The Big C*, Cathy Jamison initially hides her cancer diagnosis from her family because she wants time to figure out her new life with cancer on her own. She does not wish to burden her family, and wants to help them maintain a "normal" life for as long as possible.

Patients may lie or omit relevant facts during health-care encounters due to feelings of shame. Psychiatrist Aaron Lazare reports in "Shame and Humiliation in the Medical Encounter" (1987) that people experience humiliation or shame because they have a negative relationship with their own self-identity. For the shamed person, like the fictional Ivan Ilych, this may have a moral meaning, as people see themselves as not good enough or somehow flawed. Lazare examined the issues of shame in clinical encounters and proposed that the following three factors contribute to incomplete or inaccurate transfer of information during clinical encounters: "(1) the shame-inducing event; (2) the vulnerability of the subject; and (3) the social context, which includes the roles of the people involved" (1987, 1654). A lie or omission can then be expected as one of the responses to deal with difficult situations in a health-care setting. Patients tend to lie about socially stigmatizing topics: sexuality, mental health, addiction, and participating in risky behaviors, just to name a few.

Many marginalized groups have reported not fully disclosing information to their health-care providers. For example, in "Being Lesbian—Does the Doctor Need to Know?"

A Qualitative Study about the Significance of Disclosure in General Practice" (2007), Mari Bjorkman and Kirsti Malterud explored how lesbian women decide to disclose their sexual orientation to primary care providers. The researchers discovered that although lesbian women prefer to offer up-front disclosure of their sexual orientation to their primary care providers, their prior negative experiences create barriers to doing so. Similar findings have been reported in the Trans PULSE project, conducted among transgendered and transsexual people in Ontario:

> For trans people who have the option of passing as cissexual [having a gender identity that matches one's birth sex], the choice often exists as to where and when and to whom to disclose. Yet choice is often an illusion in which all options carry risks. For example, a trans person in need of emergency health care has the "choice" to self-disclose his or her medical history and hormone use. Disclosure involves the risk of denial of care or mistreatment; lack of disclosure involves the risk of inappropriate health care and possible unintentional disclosure through medical examinations or testing. (Bauer et al. 2009, 357)

Another group that often omits relevant information during clinical encounters are pregnant women. The fear of being judged as *bad mothers* is real, as the general population cannot fathom that any pregnant woman would intentionally do anything to harm an unborn child. This could include use of alcohol, tobacco, or illicit drugs. Pregnant women traditionally underreport participation in any kind of risky behavior. For example, in "Prenatal Tobacco Exposure and Cotinine in Newborn Dried Blood Spots" (2014), Logan Spector and colleagues examined how well pregnant women's self-reporting of smoking corresponded with the level of cotinine, an alkaloid found in tobacco, in their babies' dried blood spots. Twenty-nine percent of newborns whose mothers reported that they were tobacco-free actually had detectable levels of cotinine. Even taking into account corrective factors, such as that the newborns were exposed to tobacco through their pregnant mothers' exposure to secondhand smoke, such underreporting is undoubtedly due to other factors, such as shaming pregnant women for any behavior that could cause harm to their fetuses.

Beside the small group of patients who may engage in pathological lying to their physicians and other health-care providers, patients frequently are dishonest when they perceive that they may be judged for who they are or what they do. As the literature suggests, patients who belong to vulnerable populations seem to be less open to disclose facts that may be perceived as morally wrong, which could lead to receiving inappropriate or dangerous care. The onus is on physicians and other health-care providers to create a safe environment in which disclosure can occur.

## CULTURE AND TRUTH-TELLING

Shifting the gaze from individual to community, culture substantively modifies the phenomena of truth-telling and disclosure in clinical encounters throughout the continuum of health care. Where a patient and her family come from largely influences their attitudes and beliefs about health care, including their expectations surrounding communication about their health status or disease. Therefore, patients hold a tacit expectation that health-care professionals understand their cultural context and that they are able to disclose relevant information in a culturally safe manner. For example, as nurses Megan-Jane Johnstone and Olga Kanitsaki write in "Ethics and Advance Care Planning in a Culturally Diverse Society"

(2009), physicians or other health-care providers should know how, when, where, by whom, and to whom health information should be shared, and be able to perform the ritual of disclosure in a way that is not offensive to the patient's cultural reality. A number of cultural safety initiatives have been put in place—in, for example, New Zealand (see Papps and Irihapeti 1996), Australia (see Taylor and Guerin 2010), and Canada (see Walker et al. 2009)—with the goal of achieving flexible service delivery to accommodate the preferences and needs of diverse cultural groups. Numerous resources, including Patricia Marshall's "Anthropology and Bioethics" (1992) and Rosemarie Tong and Michael Boylan's *New Perspectives in Health Care Ethics* (2007), note that there is a difference between how trained health-care professionals and patients and their families approach truth and truth-telling in a health-care setting. The gap is even wider if the patients and their family members come from a minority culture. The assumption that trust is built through truth-telling may not be true for all patients.

In all cultures, strict taboos exist about what is considered appropriate to talk about in any given context. Such observations extend to taboos about people's health conditions, their bodies, and the physiological and pathological changes people experience. Medical anthropologists have collected and shared enormous amounts of information about these topics. What often is described in tight-knit communities about truth-telling and disclosure is that some groups perceive disclosure as harmful to a person's sense of well-being, to a degree that is much more severe than the harm that a disease can cause her physically (see, e.g., Blackhall et al. 1995; Mitchell 1998). By insisting on disclosing all aspects of a severe or life-limiting illness, physicians and other health-care providers are in clear violation of the principle of nonmaleficence.

For example, physician Joseph Carrese and anthropologist Lorna Rhodes (2000) described how communication about bad news about health is perceived among Navajo people in the United States. The researchers observed that the participants felt discomfort thinking and talking about these bad things, including diagnoses about serious or life-limiting diseases. According to Gary Witherspoon's *Language and Art in the Navajo Universe*, to remediate the distress of learning unwanted, bad news, Navajo people should turn to "thinking and speaking the Beauty Way" (1977, 34), a manifestation of living according to a traditional Navajo notion of *hózhó*.

Similar observations were described by Russell Searight and Jennifer Gafford in "It's Like Playing with Your Destiny," when examining views about advance directives and end-of-life decision making among Bosnian immigrants to the United States: "I think it's cruel to tell somebody you have cancer and you will die" or "I would be worried about my children if everyday I was sad, upset and depressed. … If I was going to die, it's better if I knew for a short time … it's better than being upset for years … better for my family" (2005, 199).

In "A Report from East Asia: Self-Determination vs. Family Determination: Two Incommensurable Principles of Autonomy" (1997), physician-philosopher Ruiping Fan (1997) correspondingly highlighted the different ethos of East Asian cultures when examining attitudes toward cancer diagnoses among people from China, Hong Kong, South Korea, and Japan. He reported that a much larger emphasis has been laid on family-determination rather than self-determination in the context of health care in these cultures.

Social work scholar Pamela McGrath and her coauthors discovered in "The 'Right Story' to the 'Right Person'" (2005) that truth-telling and disclosure are not limited only to the accuracy of the shared information; rather, the *rightness* of the process is crucial. The "right story" must be shared in the "right way" to the "right person" to avoid anxiety among Aboriginal people from the Northern Territory of Australia who are suffering from grave illnesses. The importance of communicating culturally safe information is vividly illustrated by the following examples:

> She was there with all the doctors, [she thought] the doctors told her—You have to go back to your family, you got to see your family and you have got to pass away in 12 weeks time. ... We had an incident recently. It was explained that this gentleman was going to die so the family took him home and painted him up and put him under a tree for 3 days because they thought he was going to die right there and then. So that whole communication thing. (McGrath et al. 2005, 310)

In both cases, the intent was to truthfully communicate the need to redefine and revisit the goals of care in collaboration with the patient and her family. However, the health-care professionals' message was received as statements about imminent death.

Johnstone and Kanitsaki recount that in other more communitarian groups, a central part of the family role is to act as "protector-advocate and gatekeeping" (2009, 411). The intention is to protect the patient from bad news and to ensure interactions with physicians and other health-care providers "that does not deny hope and/or plunge their loved ones into a state of soul destroying and hopeless despair" (411). As discussed earlier, this is evident among Chinese patients (Tse, Chong, and Fok 2003), but this attitude is also evident in reports about Asian Indian Hindus, such as Ardith Doorenbos and Mary Nies's "The Use of Advance Directives in Population of Asian Indian Hindus" (2003); Native Americans in the United States, such as Carrese and Rhodes's work "Bridging Cultural Differences in Medical Practice" (2000); Middle Eastern Lebanese, such as Jouhayna Gebara and Hera Tashjian's "End-of-Life Practices at a Lebanese Hospital" (2006); Australian Aboriginal people, such as McGrath et al.'s "The 'Right Story' to the 'Right Person'" (2005); British South Asians, such as Kelvin Karim's "Informing Cancer Patients: Truth-Telling and Culture" (2003); and Bosnian immigrants to the United States, such as Searight and Gafford's "It's Like Playing with Your Destiny" (2005).

Anthropologist Cecil Helman (1990) has contemplated what can benefit patients more: being told accurate information about their diagnosis and prognosis or living unaware of what is happening with their bodies. He considered whether straightforward truth-telling, veracity, and disclosure are problematic because they can cause a *nocebo* effect, that is, "the negative effect on health beliefs and expectations—and therefore the exact reverse of the 'placebo' effect" (Helman 1990, 257). Culturally inappropriate processes of disclosure of health information may be viewed as so harmful that the actions of physicians and other health-care providers may be perceived as "wishing death" on that person (Johnstone and Kanitsaki 2009). Acknowledging that patients are inherently vulnerable during clinical encounters by the very virtue of being ill, and adding to that the experience of *otherness* in a Western health-care system, it is not unexpected, as Lucy Candib (2002) notes, that patients report that truth-telling can be experienced as disrespectful, paternalistic, demeaning, authoritarian, and unhelpful, even when disclosure was compassionate and well-intended.

From physicians' and other health-care professionals' perspective, providing culturally safe care is not easy. One example is the story documented in the book *The Spirit Catches You and You Fall Down* (1997) by Anne Fadiman. In this true account, a young Hmong girl with epilepsy is in a tug of war between an unassimilated immigrant family and a medical system that prioritizes Western biomedical approaches to care. The misunderstanding leads to compromised medical care and a family in distress.

Some attempts have been made to overcome the disconnect between the health-care professionals' duties to disclose all relevant health information about their patients' conditions to get informed consent and the patients' preferences on how such communication should occur. Literature shows plenty of examples in which physicians and other health-care providers intentionally modify the process of disclosure of information to accommodate the cultural expectations of patients they are treating.

Philosopher Benjamin Freedman was truly insightful in "Offering Truth" when he wrote that "a patient's knowledge of diagnosis is not all-or-nothing. It exists along a continuum, anchored at one end by purely theoretical 'absolute ignorance' and at the other by the unattainable 'total enlightenment'" (1993, 574). Freedman compared his approach of "offering truth" to a dance, in which a patient and a physician or other health-care provider are engaged along the continuum of how much information the patient wants to have: "a patient will be offered an opportunity to learn the truth, at whatever level of details the patient desires" (574). The "truth offering" is supposed to balance the provider's fiduciary duties with the cultural expectations of the patient's experience in a health-care setting.

In research with Bosnian immigrants, not sharing negative information was seen as "humane and emotionally sensitive" (Searight and Gafford 2005, 199). Withholding accurate information about devastating diagnosis was understood as preferable to either disclosing truthfully the facts or outright lying. Searight and Gafford also described an alternative to disclosure in which the family initially is informed with the expectation that the family members will have a conversation with the patient, to ease him or her into bad news.

In "Breaking Bad News: A Chinese Perspective" (2003), C. Y. Tse, Alice Chong, and S. Y. Fok defined three types of family involvement among Chinese people in decision making about health, depending on how much information patients are told and how actively patients participate in the decision-making process about their own health. The first model highlights the relational aspect of the process, in which both the patient and the family are told the bad news, and they together decide on the next steps. This model most closely resembles the expected process of communicating bad news and participating in the shared decision making as expected by the Western-trained physicians and other health-care professionals. A slight difference may be that patients are not explicitly asked for consent to information sharing with family members; rather, the disclosure to everyone present occurs more spontaneously.

In the second model of disclosure, Tse, Chong, and Fok (2003) described how the patient delegated the decision-making power to the family and opted not to be burdened by hearing bad news. Although this expression of self-determination is rarely seen among patients identifying themselves with Western cultural context and those who have capacity to make their own decisions, this, in fact, is an example of exercising autonomous decision making. The patient does not expect to be deceived or lied to; instead, the patient relies on family members who can make decisions according to the known wishes and beliefs they share as a family unit.

The third model of disclosure is the case in which the patient wants to have information about the diagnosis, but the family attempts to block physicians' and other health-care providers' access to the patient. This is justified by the claim that the patient would be harmed much more by the news about severe illness than by the illness itself.

This can make therapeutic relationships almost impossible, as Johnstone and Kanitsaki argue: "in some cultures, talking about end stage illnesses and plans for managing care at the end stage of life can be interpreted as a portent of death and, hence, something to be avoided, which again can pose significant challenges for health care providers" (2009, 410).

## DISCLOSURE OF ERRORS IN HEALTH CARE

Although most communication about diagnosis, prognosis, and care planning still occurs in a clinical setting between the patient and the health-care team, some disclosures about patient care have become institutionalized. This is especially the case surrounding the disclosure of adverse events and errors. According to Philip Hébert, Alex V. Levin, and Gerald Robertson in "Bioethics for Clinicians" (2001), this is a relatively new movement in health care to ensure transparency and public trust. If disclosures about adverse events and errors do not occur, this represents an act of deception that can perpetuate harms to the patient beyond the initial erroneous event.

As David Hilfiker writes in "Facing Our Mistakes" (1984), communicating an error to a patient is perhaps one of the most difficult situations physicians and other health-care providers may face in their professional careers, especially if the consequences of the error are grave. Although professional guidelines and institutional policies emphasize the frankness of the process, as Marc Newman explains in "The Emotional Impact of Mistakes on Family Physicians" (1996), this is not an easy task and takes an emotional toll on the persons who participate in the disclosure.

The disclosure of adverse events and errors is considered a norm and should be done to avoid erosion of trust among all involved: the patient and the health-care provider; the patient and the health-care system; or the health-care provider and the health-care organization. Although physicians in principle agree that the full disclosure of errors should became standard practice, the results of the study conducted by Lisa Iezzoni and her colleagues (2012) reveal that physicians do not always act in the way as they say they should, primarily because of the fear of litigation. This stands in contrast with the theoretical underpinnings of a culture of safety in health care. The study results describe a climate of *shame and blame* in which truth-telling may have broader consequences than described in institutional policies and professional guidelines.

## SUPPORTING PATIENT-CENTERED TRUTH-TELLING

During their training, physicians and other health-care professionals are indoctrinated into truth-telling. They are taught the theoretical foundations of the concept and its importance for building and maintaining trusting relationships with their patients, and they are expected to be able to apply it during clinical encounters. The expectations increase as learners move on to become registered health-care professionals.

When examining the readiness of third-year medical students to address ethical conflicts in clinical settings in "Deception, Discrimination, and Fear of Reprisal" (2005), physician-ethicists Catherine Caldicott and Kathy Faber-Langendoen reported that deception and deliberate lying were the predominant issues described by students. Caldicott and Faber-Langendoen explained that although students understood the importance of being truthful, they had to balance between the commitment to the patient and other competing interests (e.g., advancement in their academic careers): "the student weighed her need to learn and to establish a positive relationship with her preceptor against her intention to respect the patient's wishes" (Caldicott and Faber-Langendoen 2005, 871). This demonstrates that although students are probably well-equipped to deal with strictly clinical skills, they "lack the necessary tools to navigate these dilemmas with moral sensitivity and commitment" (871).

Sometimes, political powers shape laws in ways that force physicians to lie to their patients. Examples include legal guidelines in Florida that interfere with evidence-informed practice in screening for domestic violence or in counseling patients about firearm safety to avoid risks to children as recommended by the American Academy of Pediatrics (2014). In another example, Arizona abortion law, as described by John C. Jennings in "Commentary: Arizona Law Forces Ob/Gyns to Lie to Patients" (2015), requires doctors to inform women seeking an abortion that (contrary to scientific evidence) medical abortion may be reversed after it is initiated. When politics enter the patient-physician relationship, there is a considerable chance that truth is sacrificed.

So, how can patient-centered truth-telling occur in light of these challenges? Some attempts have been made to overcome the disconnect between health-care professionals' duty to disclose all relevant health information about their patients' conditions and patients' preferences about how such communication should occur. In "Therapeutic Privilege: Between the Ethics of Lying and the Practice of Truth" (2010), physicians Claude Richard, Yvette Lajeunesse, and Marie-Thérèse Lussier proposed an algorithm for reflexive and dialogical decision-making processes in order to reconcile ethical and practical challenges of disclosure in a clinical setting.

Perhaps we do not have to develop a complex framework on truth-telling and the professional duty to disclose; rather, a simple strategy is what is needed. Protected time and opportunities to reflect with colleagues about the nuances of truth-telling would support patient-centered care. A simple statement to patients could be sufficient to mitigate the competing interests that hinder truth-telling, address cultural diversity among patients, and reflect the complexity of the health-care system. For example:

> Mr. X, I have more information about what you have complained about. Some of my patients want to know everything, including information from every single test; others want to know in general what is going on with their health. What kind of patient are you? Is there any information you wouldn't want me to tell you? Also, legally only you are entitled to have information about your health, but I understand that you may want to consult with the people in your life who can help you navigate the system and can assist you in making decisions about your health. Do I have permission to share your health information with anyone?

Starting conversations about truth-telling by normalizing the fact that there are a range of truths to be told in every situation, and a range of ethically acceptable approaches to disclosure, would be one simple way to address the plethora of challenges described in this chapter.

---

## Summary

Historically, telling the truth to patients was not part of medical practice, but with the rise of bioethics, truth-telling is a *prima facie* duty. Ethical tensions lie at the core of the bioethics concept of disclosing information to patients. This tension exists at the intersection of motivations, consequences, and action. On the one hand, physicians want to protect patients from bad news, stigma, and their own errors. On the other hand, patients need to know their health information to make informed choices regarding their medical options and life plans. Honesty, openness, and disclosure are the norms in health care in the United States and Canada, but they may not be in other parts of the world or in subcultures within North America.

Physician lies can negatively affect trust in a provider-patient relationship and compromise a patient's ability to give informed consent. At times, lying may benefit the physician or patient, such as when changing a diagnostic code to ensure insurance coverage for a procedure or to get a higher level of coverage. Sometimes this helps the patients and other times it harms them, such as when patients are given unneeded treatment. Deception to patients is more common toward patients with psychiatric conditions, who may resist taking medication that can address their acute symptoms. The cost of noncompliance or nonadherence can be mental deterioration to the point of becoming a harm to themselves and others. Deceiving children is not unusual because young people may lack the competency and capacity to comprehend their health conditions, although such deception runs the risk of injuring trust and thus should be minimized.

As Dr. House tells us, patients lie. Most often, patients lie when they are embarrassed or feeling stigmatized, or when they have had negative experiences disclosing in the past. Health-care providers need training on the ethical and legal bases of truth-telling. But more importantly, they need to learn how to speak to patients about these issues to maintain a patient-centered approach.

Truth-telling is viewed differently in different cultures. In some populations, it is the family rather than the individual who makes health-care choices and determines how much information the patient is told. In a Western setting, this can have several effects. For instance, patients may not want to know about health information that is being pushed on them. Or patients may want to have a diagnosis, but families actively work to prevent them from knowing this information. It is important to recognize that culture plays a strong role in how truth-telling will be received and desired. Equally, one should not presume that just because people belong to a cultural group, that their preferences regarding disclosure are the same as the norm in that culture.

## Bibliography

American Academy of Pediatrics. "American Academy of Pediatrics Condemns Ruling against Physicians' Right to Counsel on Firearm Safety." 2014. https://www.aap.org/en-us/about-the-aap/aap-press-room/pages/American-Academy-of-Pediatrics-Condemns-Ruling-Against-Physicians%E2%80%99-Right-to-Counsel-on-Firearm-Safety.aspx.

Bauer, Greta R., Rebecca Hammond, Robb Travers, et al. "'I Don't Think This Is Theoretical; This Is Our Lives': How Erasure Impacts Health Care for Transgender People." *Journal of the Association of Nurses in AIDS Care* 20, no. 5 (2009): 348–361.

Beauchamp, Tom L., and James F. Childress. *Principles of Biomedical Ethics.* 6th ed. New York: Oxford University Press, 2009.

*Belmont Report.* US Department of Health and Human Services. April 18, 1979. http://www.hhs.gov/ohrp/humansubjects/guidance/belmont.html.

Benn, Piers. "Medicine, Lies, and Deceptions." *Journal of Medical Ethics* 27, no. 2 (2001): 130–134.

Bissonette, R., R. M. O'Shea, M. Horwitz, and C. F. Route. "A Data-Generated Basis for Medical Ethics Education: Categorizing Issues Experienced by Students during

Clinical Training." *Academic Medicine* 70, no. 11 (1995): 1035–1037.

Bjorkman, Mari, and Kirsti Malterud. "Being Lesbian—Does the Doctor Need to Know? A Qualitative Study about the Significance of Disclosure in General Practice." *Scandinavian Journal of Primary Health Care* 25, no. 1 (2007): 58–62.

Blackhall, Leslie, Sheila Murphy, Geyla Frank, et al. "Ethnicity and Attitudes toward Patient Autonomy." *Journal of the American Medical Association* 274, no. 10 (1995): 820–825.

Blythe, Jenny. "Study Questions Ethics of Covert Medication." *BMJ* 321, no. 7258 (2000): 402.

Bok, Sissela. "Lying to Children." *The Hastings Center Report* 8, no. 3 (1978): 10–13.

Caldicott, Catherine V., and Kathy Faber-Langendoen. "Deception, Discrimination, and Fear of Reprisal: Lessons in Ethics from Third-Year Medical Students." *Academic Medicine* 80, no. 9 (2005): 866–873.

Candib, Lucy. "Truth Telling and Advance Care Planning at the End of Life: Problems with Autonomy in a Multicultural World." *Family Systems and Health* 20, no. 3 (2002): 213–228.

Carrese, Joseph A., and Lorna A. Rhodes. "Bridging Cultural Differences in Medical Practice." *Journal of General Internal Medicine* 15, no. 2 (2000): 92–96.

Childress, James F. *Who Should Decide? Paternalism in Health Care*. New York: Oxford University Press, 1982.

Doorenbos, Ardith Z., and Mary A. Nies. "The Use of Advance Directives in Population of Asian Indian Hindus." *Journal of Transcultural Nursing* 14, no. 1 (2003): 17–24.

Edwards, Steven. "Telling the Truth?" *Nursing Ethics* 21, no. 4 (2014): 383–384.

Emanuel, E. J., and Linda L. Emanuel. "Four Models of the Physician-Patient Relationship." *Journal of the American Medical Association* 267, no. 16 (1992): 2221–2226.

Fan, Ruiping. "A Report from East Asia: Self-Determination vs. Family Determination: Two Incommensurable Principles of Autonomy." *Bioethics* 11, nos. 3–4 (1997): 309–322.

Fox, R. C. "The Evolution of American Bioethics: A Sociological Perspective." In *Social Science Perspectives on Medical Ethics*, edited by George Weisz, 201–217. Philadelphia: University of Pennsylvania Press, 1990.

Freedman, Benjamin. "Offering Truth: One Ethical Approach to the Uninformed Cancer Patient." *Archives of Internal Medicine* 153, no. 5 (1993): 572–576.

Freeman, Victor G., Saif S. Rathore, Kevin P. Weinfurt, et al. "Lying for Patients: Physician Deception of Third-Party Payers." *Archives of Internal Medicine* 159, no. 19 (1999): 2263–2270.

Gebara, Jouhayna, and Hera Tashjian. "End-of-Life Practices at a Lebanese Hospital: Courage or Knowledge?" *Journal of Transcultural Nursing* 17, no. 4 (2006): 381–388.

Hébert, Philip C., Alex V. Levin, and Gerald Robertson. "Bioethics for Clinicians: 23. Disclosure of Medical Error." *Canadian Medical Association Journal* 164, no. 4 (2001): 509–513.

Helman, Cecil. *Culture, Health and Illness*. London: Wright, 1990.

Hilfiker, David. "Facing Our Mistakes." *New England Journal of Medicine* 310, no. 2 (1984): 118–122.

Huijer, M., E. van Leeuwen, A. Boenink, and G. Kimsma. "Medical Students' Cases as an Empirical Basis for Teaching Clinical Ethics." *Academic Medicine* 75, no. 8 (2000): 834–839.

Iezzoni, Lisa I., Sowmya R. Rao, Catherine M. DesRoches, et al. "Survey Shows That at Least Some Physicians Are Not Always Open or Honest with Patients." *Health Affairs* 31, no. 2 (2012): 383–391.

Jackson, Jennifer. "Telling the Truth." *Journal of Medical Ethics* 17, no. 1 (1991): 5–9.

Jennings, John C., on behalf of the American Congress of Obstetricians and Gynecologists. "Commentary: Arizona Law Forces Ob/Gyns to Lie to Patients." April 8, 2015. http://www.medscape.com/viewarticle/842792.

Johnstone, Megan-Jane, and Olga Kanitsaki. "Ethics and Advance Care Planning in a Culturally Diverse Society." *Journal of Transcultural Nursing* 20, no. 4 (2009): 405–416.

Jonsen, Albert R. *The Birth of Bioethics*. New York: Oxford University Press, 1998.

Karim, Kelvin. "Informing Cancer Patients: Truth-Telling and Culture." *Cancer Nursing Practice* 2, no. 3 (2003): 23–31.

Latha, K. S. "The Noncompliant Patient in Psychiatry: The Case For and Against Covert/Surreptitious Medication." *Mens Sana Monographs* 8, no. 1 (2010): 96–121.

Lazare, Aaron. "Shame and Humiliation in the Medical Encounter." *Archives of Internal Medicine* 147, no. 9 (1987): 1653–1658.

Maier, Richard A., and Paul J. Lavrakas. "Lying Behavior and Evaluation of Lies." *Perceptual and Motor Skills* 42, no. 2 (1976): 575–581.

Marshall, Patricia A. "Anthropology and Bioethics." *Medical Anthropology Quarterly* 6, no. 1 (1992): 49–73.

McGrath, Pamela, Katherine Ogilvie, Robert Raynar, Hamish Holewa, and Mary Anne Patton. "The 'Right Story' to the 'Right Person': Communication Issues in the End-of-Life Care for Indigenous People." *Australian Health Review* 29, no. 3 (2005): 306–316.

McLeod, Beverly A., and Randy Genereux. "Predicting the Acceptability and Likelihood of Lying: The Interaction of Personality with Type of Lie." *Personality and Individual Differences* 45, no. 7 (2008): 591–596.

Mitchell, Gary. "Therapeutic Lying to Assist People with Dementia in Maintaining Medication Adherence." *Nursing Ethics* 21, no. 7 (2014): 844–849.

Mitchell, Jill L. "Cross-Cultural Issues in the Disclosure of Cancer." *Cancer Practice* 6, no. 3 (1998): 153–160.

Newman, Marc C. "The Emotional Impact of Mistakes on Family Physicians." *Archives of Family Medicine* 5, no. 2 (1996): 71–75.

Novack, Dennis H., Barbara J. Detering, Robert Arnold, et al. "Physicians' Attitudes toward Using Deception to Resolve Difficult Ethical Problems." *Journal of the American Medical Association* 261, no. 20 (1989): 2980–2985.

Novack, Dennis H., Robin Plumer, Raymond L. Smith, et al. "Changes in Physicians' Attitudes toward Telling the Cancer Patient." *Journal of the American Medical Association* 241, no. 9 (1979): 897–900.

Oken, Donald. "What to Tell Cancer Patients: A Study of Medical Attitudes." *Journal of the American Medical Association* 175 (1961): 1120–1128.

Papps, Elaine, and Irihapeti Ramsden. "Cultural Safety in Nursing: The New Zealand Experience." *International Journal for Quality in Health Care* 8, no. 5 (1996): 491–497.

Richard, Claude, Yvette Lajeunesse, and Marie-Thérèse Lussier. "Therapeutic Privilege: Between the Ethics of Lying and the Practice of Truth." *Journal of Medical Ethics* 36, no. 6 (2010): 353–357.

Searight, Russell, and Jennifer Gafford. "'It's Like Playing with Your Destiny': Bosnian Immigrants' Views of Advance Directives and End-of-Life Decision-Making." *Journal of Immigrant Health* 7, no. 3 (2005): 195–203.

Seiter, John S., Jon Bruschke, and Chunsheng Bai. "The Acceptability of Deception as a Function of Perceivers' Culture, Deceiver's Intention, and Deceiver-Deceived Relationship." *Western Journal of Communication* 66, no. 2 (2002): 158–180.

Spector, Logan G., Sharon E. Murphy, Katherine M. Wickham, Bruce Lindgren, and Anne M. Joseph. "Prenatal Tobacco Exposure and Cotinine in Newborn Dried Blood Spots." *Pediatrics* 133, no. 6 (2014): e1632–e1638.

Steensma, David P. "The Farid Fata Medicare Fraud Case and Misplaced Incentives in Oncology Care." *Journal of Oncology Practice* 12, no. 1 (2016): 51–54.

Surbone, Antonella. "Telling the Truth to Patients with Cancer: What Is the Truth?" *Lancet Oncology* 7, no. 11 (2006): 944–950.

Taylor, Kerry, and Pauline Guerin. *Health Care and Indigenous Australians: Cultural Safety in Practice*. South Yarra, Australia: Palgrave Macmillan, 2010.

Tong, Rosemarie, and Michael Boylan. *New Perspectives in Healthcare Ethics: An Interdisciplinary and Crosscultural Approach*. New York: Prentice Hall, 2007.

Tse, C. Y., Alice Chong, and S. Y. Fok. "Breaking Bad News: A Chinese Perspective." *Palliative Medicine* 17, no. 4 (2003): 339–343.

Walker, Roger, Helen Cromarty, Len Kelly, and Natalie St Pierre-Hansen. "Achieving Cultural Safety in Aboriginal Health Services: Implementation of a Crosscultural Safety Model in a Hospital Setting." *Diversity in Health and Care* 6, no. 1 (2009): 11–22.

Witherspoon, Gary. *Language and Art in the Navajo Universe*. Ann Arbor: University of Michigan Press, 1977.

## LITERATURE

Fadiman, Anne. *The Spirit Catches You and You Fall Down: A Hmong Child, Her American Doctors, and the Collision of Two Cultures*. New York: Farrar, Straus and Giroux, 1997.

Narayan, R. K. "The Doctor's Word." In *Malgudi Days*. London: Penguin Classics, 2006. Originally published 1943.

Tolstoy, Leo. *The Death of Ivan Ilych*. Translated by Louise and Aylmer Maude. First published 1886. An Electronic Classics Series Publication. April 15, 2015. http://opie.wvnet.edu /~jelkins/lawyerslit/stories/death-of-ivan-ilych.pdf.

## TELEVISION

*The Big C.* Created by Darlene Hunt. 2010–2013. Showtime Networks.

*Grey's Anatomy.* Created by Shonda Rhimes. 2005–. ABC Television.

*Grey's Anatomy.* "Let the Truth Sting." Season 4, episode 3, 2007. Dir. Daniel Minahan.

*House M.D.* Created by David Shore. 2004–2012. Fox Network.

*House M.D.* "TB or not TB." Season 2, episode 4, 2005. Dir. Peter O'Fallon.

*House M.D.* "Three Stories." Season 1, episode 21, 2005. Dir. Paris Barclay.

# CHAPTER 10

# *Confidentiality*

**Robert S. Olick**
*Professor, Bioethics and Humanities*
*SUNY Upstate Medical University, Syracuse, NY*

In 2005, the television drama *Grey's Anatomy* premiered, introducing the world to a cast of residents and attending physicians in a Seattle hospital. One scene from the pilot episode showed three physicians talking about a patient by name in a crowded hospital elevator. While the physicians may have thought this was a routine, permissible conversation with a consulting provider, this is actually an egregious example of violating a patient's confidentiality—talking about a case in a public space and using a patient's identifying information when not necessary.

Most people know what it means to keep a secret. Most also know how it feels when their secrets are revealed without permission and when promises and trust are broken. Keeping someone else's personal information private is a general moral obligation. But it takes on special significance when this information derives from the nature of relationships, such as being a family member, friend, or coworker. For members of a profession, such as lawyers, clergy, accountants, physicians, and other health-care providers, the duty of confidentiality is a role-related obligation, a fundamental requirement of the professional relationship with a client or patient. In health care, the duty to maintain confidentiality of patient information obtained in the course of the health-care encounter is a core principle of medical ethics. It is articulated in oaths, codes, and statements of professional organizations across medicine and is firmly established in law.

This chapter examines the concepts of confidentiality and privacy in health care from both ethical and legal perspectives. Among the topics addressed are the nature and relationship between the concepts of privacy and confidentiality, the ethical basis for the professional duty of confidentiality, and an introduction to legal rules governing both, in particular the Privacy Rule of the 1996 Health Insurance Portability and Accountability Act (HIPAA). An important theme of the discussion is the interplay between ethics and law.

The principle of confidentiality is sacrosanct in the health professions, but it is not absolute. Rather, confidentiality is best understood as *prima facie* binding, as a principle that must sometimes yield to competing concerns for the welfare of others, such as family members or the public, and to the obligation to follow the law. This chapter discusses two sorts of leading exceptions and challenges to strict confidentiality, and both illustrate the *prima facie* nature of the principle. First, mandatory reporting laws require disclosure of patient information to government entities for the purpose of safeguarding the public health and welfare, most notably the reporting of infectious and contagious diseases to the department of health. Second, physicians must decide whether it is justified to breach confidentiality to protect or warn third parties in situations in which reporting laws may not fully address the issue, or the law's guidance is unclear or even in conflict with ethically sound judgment. Four such scenarios are presented here: the psychiatric patient who threatens to kill another person; the patient with HIV/AIDS who refuses to tell his partner about his HIV status; the driver whose impairment poses significant risk of a motor vehicle accident; and the patient who insists her genetic condition be kept secret from potentially affected family members. Each case poses a difficult ethical-legal dilemma, in which it may well be asked, "it's ethical, but is it legal?"

Later sections of the chapter offer brief discussions of three important and emerging issues: those posed by adolescent patients who desire to keep sensitive information private from parents; new rules and special challenges presented by the emergence of electronic health records, in particular for the privacy of mental health, drug and alcohol abuse, HIV, and genetic and other information; and the implications of social media in today's information age, when patient information is shared, intentionally or accidentally, on various platforms with the click of a mouse.

As with most treatments of confidentiality, the paradigmatic frame of the discussion is the physician-patient relationship. Confidentiality is no less foundational for nurses, social workers, physician assistants, respiratory therapists, imaging technicians, and other allied health professionals; for ethics consultants, health-care administrators, and institutions; and for government agencies that possess or have access to health information.

## CONFIDENTIALITY AND PRIVACY

Although the terms and concepts of confidentiality and privacy are often used interchangeably, they have both overlapping and distinct meanings. The idea that each person has a *zone of privacy*—that is, a set of ideas and behaviors that involve self-governance and creation of boundaries that keep others out, both with respect to our physical person and access to personal information—is quite familiar.

The broad idea of privacy can be more specifically defined under the rubric of four domains:

1. *physical privacy* concerns interests in the boundaries of one's personal space and intrusions on one's physical person, as well as visual privacy;

2. *informational privacy* concerns one's interests in controlling the access of others to what one considers to be personal information;

3. *decisional privacy* concerns one's interests in freedom to choose without restriction or interference from law, government, or other third-parties; and

4. *proprietary privacy* concerns one's interests in the use by others of one's property, likeness, or human personality, such as when a personal photo is appropriated without permission.

The first three of these domains are the most relevant to health care. With respect to both physical and decisional privacy, both ethics and law establish a right to be left alone, to be shielded from intrusion or interference of others, and to refuse unwanted medical interventions upon our bodies. The right of privacy in health care is perhaps best known as our constitutional right to be protected against government interference, such as the right to use contraception in the security of our own homes, prohibitions against laws that infringe on a woman's right to choose abortion, and laws that establish a dying patient's right to refuse unwanted life-sustaining treatments.

The subject of this chapter, confidentiality, falls under the domain of informational privacy. The concepts of confidentiality and informational privacy are both grounded in the idea that patients should have control over access to their personal health information, and that in most instances, patients must give consent for others to obtain or disclose their health information. Patients have rights of confidentiality and of privacy, and health-care professionals have corresponding duties to respect and protect these rights.

A key distinction emerges when informational privacy is divided into two main elements. The first, most closely aligned with privacy, concerns access to patient information. The second, most closely aligned with confidentiality, concerns use and disclosure of patient information by health-care professionals with legitimate access to that information. From the standpoint of the rights of patients and corresponding professional responsibilities, discussions of privacy often concern whether health-care providers have legitimate access to patient information, whereas analyses of confidentiality typically concern whether physicians or other providers may disclose information obtained in the course of patient care and treatment to others outside the physician-patient relationship. To illustrate, when a physician talks about a patient's colon cancer diagnosis in a crowded hospital elevator, this is an unauthorized disclosure, a breach of confidentiality and of patient privacy. When a nurse snoops in the medical record of a coworker, or when a resident snaps a cell-phone photo of a patient during surgery without permission, privacy and HIPAA have been violated, even if the information and the photo are not shared with anyone else.

Importantly, confidentiality and privacy are broken only when the patient is identifiable, that is, when others know or reasonably may know the name or identity of the patient. In various circumstances, information about patients is shared with others without the patient being identifiable to the recipient of the information. For example, a physician may seek advice from a colleague by describing the patient's condition without revealing who the patient is (a practice known as informal consultation). Another example is the use of health data in research when data are stripped of identifying information (de-identified), such as names, addresses, occupation, and other facts that might personally identify the patient.

Confidentiality applies to information obtained within the parameters of the physician-patient relationship. Conversations that occurred before the physician-patient relationship was formed or after it has ended, information acquired in one's role as friend or citizen, or information that is publicly available are not required to be kept confidential. Physicians, nonetheless, should exercise appropriate judgment and discretion, remaining aware that patients may feel that privacy and confidentiality have been violated regardless of whether the information was obtained in the professional relationship. Furthermore, duties of confidentiality and privacy continue after treatment has concluded, whether the patient has chosen a new physician or the physician-patient relationship has otherwise ended. One might expect that the principle of confidentiality comes to an end upon the patient's death. To the contrary, physicians, hospitals, and others must continue to keep medical records and information private and confidential. Under HIPAA, this rule applies for at least fifty years after the patient has died.

Finally, privacy and confidentiality should be distinguished from the physician-patient privilege. This is a narrow concept: a rule of law that gives patients the right to prevent their physicians from giving testimony or otherwise disclosing confidential information in a legal proceeding.

With these conceptual and practical foundations in mind, the next sections address the ethical argument for why confidentiality matters, its place in professional oaths and codes, and some of the most important legal rules governing confidentiality and privacy of patient information.

## THE ETHICAL BASIS OF THE PRINCIPLE OF CONFIDENTIALITY

The principle of confidentiality is a cornerstone of the physician-patient relationship. It is widely understood as an express or implied vow, duty, and promise of the physician. It is found in writing in the patient's bill of rights, in hospital admission packets, and in the notice of privacy practices given to patients under HIPAA. Every code of ethics for physicians and the other health-care professions contains a core commitment to confidentiality.

Why confidentiality matters can be explained in either of two ways. From the standpoint of consequentialism (utilitarianism), rules of confidentiality produce good consequences for the patient and promote broader societal interests in our collective health and welfare. Hence, confidentiality has instrumental value. From a rule-based (deontological) perspective, confidentiality respects patient autonomy and the dignity and unique moral worth of the patient. As such, confidentiality has intrinsic value. On the former view, confidentiality builds trust in the physician that is instrumental to good patient care; on the latter view, trust is a value in itself that is respectful of patients.

It is standard practice for physicians to take a health history and a social history from patients in the clinical encounter. Without assurance of confidentiality, patients may be less trusting of their physicians and unwilling to be fully honest and forthright in describing their health concerns and in answering questions posed by health-care providers. Patients may be unwilling to submit to necessary exams or tests. Confidentiality engenders trust, which in turn strengthens the physician-patient relationship for the benefit of the patient. Conversely, failure to keep information confined to the physician-patient relationship—in other words, breaches of confidentiality—can have potentially serious adverse consequences for patients, such as damage to relationships with family and friends, stigma, discrimination, or loss of employment. These same consequences can adversely affect patients' families. Accordingly, a strong and clearly understood commitment to confidentiality is essential to accurately, fully, and properly diagnose and treat patients, to do so in accordance with their wishes and best interests, and to prevent harmful outcomes that would likely result if patients could not expect and rely upon confidentiality in the health-care encounter.

From the standpoint of population health, these patient concerns are multiplied exponentially. Knowing that duties of confidentiality are firmly established is an inducement if not a reason to seek health care. But if confidentiality is in question, people may choose not to seek health care, even when they are sick. Serious consequences may follow, including possibly the spread of infectious and contagious diseases, such as tuberculosis and sexually transmitted diseases. This concern was manifest in the early years of the HIV/AIDS epidemic, as shown in the 1993 film *Philadelphia*. In an effort to encourage testing, counseling, and treatment for those who were or might be at risk of infection, and to control the spread of HIV, laws were passed to establish strong rules of confidentiality and privacy.

By contrast, a rule-based approach posits that patients have autonomy-based rights to make their own health-care decisions. The principle of respect for autonomy has emerged since the 1960s as another foundational principle of medical ethics. Autonomy includes the right to act as a moral agent to decide about our own health care, including access to personal health information, sharing and permitting access to some while excluding others. From this stance, confidentiality derives from respect for autonomy. The principle of respect for patient autonomy means that health-care professionals should solicit and honor patients' autonomous choices. Seeking consent and honoring the patient's decision recognizes the intrinsic moral agency, dignity, and worth of the patient.

Numerous studies confirm that patients value confidentiality and privacy for both intrinsic and instrumental reasons. They want control over their health information, are apprehensive about violations of privacy and loss of confidentiality, and would be less forthcoming with their physicians or might simply avoid medical care absent strong, reliable assurances of confidentiality. Long-standing fears of discrimination in health insurance and employment persist, notwithstanding strong legal protections, and patients fear they will be treated differently in their social community and elsewhere based on their disability and health status.

As we will see in the following section, strong ethical and legal protections coexist alongside many exceptions for legitimate, justified disclosures of confidential information. Decisions about whether to disclose confidential information without the patient's permission often start with the strong presumption to maintain the patient's confidence and respect the patient's choice, and go on to look to the consequentialist framework to determine whether overriding autonomy is justified. As a general matter, when keeping confidentiality is at issue, neither the deontological nor utilitarian rationale uniformly trumps the other.

## OATHS AND CODES

The origin of the principle of confidentiality in modern medicine can be traced to the Hippocratic Oath, attributed to the ancient Greek physician Hippocrates (late fourth century BCE). Among its provisions, the oath calls on physicians to hold sacred and secret, and not speak to others about, information learned in the course of caring for patients. The Hippocratic Oath is the foundation for the many medical codes and oaths developed by physician and other health professional groups and organizations over the centuries. Countless medical students have sworn some version of the Hippocratic Oath over the years. In the Hippocratic tradition, keeping the patient's secrets was justified on the ground that, in the physician's judgment, this benefited the patient. On some interpretations, this suggests physicians could also decide when it was appropriate to disclose patient information without asking the patient. The modern shift to an additional autonomy-based rationale that recognizes patients' rights to control access to information can be found in contemporary versions of the oath that link protecting patient confidentiality and respecting patient choice in the text and recitation of the oath.

One of the hallmarks of a profession is the adoption of a code of ethics or conduct for the members of the profession. The leading code of ethics in health care is the American

Medical Association's (AMA) *Code of Medical Ethics*, first adopted in 1847 and since revised in response to changes in the science and practice of medicine. The AMA Code contains a number of provisions devoted to confidentiality, grounding the physician's obligation in both respect for patient autonomy and the good consequences for patients and society that confidentiality produces. Similar statements can be found in the codes and policy statements of the American Nurses Association, the American Public Health Association, the American Pharmacists Association, and the World Medical Association's Declaration of Geneva.

Professional codes, far more than oaths, are important sources of guidance for the practice of medicine. They help physicians and others to internalize the ethical principle of confidentiality and can be a resource for difficult cases. But in the daily practice of medicine, when issues and uncertainty arise about the nature, scope, and exceptions to confidentiality, health-care providers frequently turn to both ethical principles and the law. One reason to look to the law is that violations of law typically carry more serious consequences than unethical conduct or failure to abide by an oath or professional code. Another is that with respect to confidentiality, as with many issues in bioethics, law and ethics are closely intertwined. Legal rules often embody widely shared ethical principles for the practice of medicine. This is very much the case with confidentiality, although as explained in the following section, there are important areas in which laws may differ from state to state and cases in which the law may fail to squarely support sound ethical judgment.

## INFORMATIONAL PRIVACY, CONFIDENTIALITY, AND THE LAW

The legal landscape governing privacy and confidentiality in the United States is composed of both state and federal law. All states impose strong requirements on health-care providers to maintain the privacy and confidentiality of patient information. Federal law, most importantly HIPAA, strengthens privacy protections and establishes uniform standards for the privacy, confidentiality, and security of patient information and medical records. At the same time, HIPAA generally defers to numerous state laws across the fifty states that establish special protections for especially sensitive information, such as alcohol and drug abuse, HIV/AIDS, psychiatric conditions, and genetically associated conditions; that govern the rights of children and the parent-child-physician relationship; and that carve out exceptions to confidentiality. Because state laws take different approaches to some issues, there are no universal rules across all fifty states for the various circumstances in which disclosure of confidential information is prohibited, permitted, or required. But there are areas of strong consensus, such as mandatory reporting of infectious and contagious diseases. In other areas, the law may vary considerably from state to state, in such cases as whether and when the physician has a duty to warn or protect third parties. Both of these areas and the ethical-legal dilemmas they present are discussed in the following sections. First, it is important to understand the basic rules and protections of HIPAA.

### HIPAA

Enacted in 1996, HIPAA is best known for its privacy protections, but it also includes important protections against discrimination in health insurance. HIPAA's Privacy Rule is set forth in regulations from the Department of Health and Human Services, as amended in 2013. The Privacy Rule applies to hospitals, outpatient clinics, private practice offices, and other health-care providers who transmit health information in electronic form. Privacy protections apply to all individually identifiable health information, called *protected health information*, but they do not apply to de-identified information that cannot be recognized as belonging to a particular individual. The underlying purposes of HIPAA are both to define the scope of privacy protections and to delineate those circumstances in which health information may be used and disclosed by hospitals, physicians, and other providers. HIPAA creates a minimum set of privacy protections. States may establish more rigorous standards if they choose to do so.

At the heart of HIPAA is the rule that use and disclosure of health information require the patient's consent (the HIPAA term is *authorization*). But the right to control access to information does not mean that patients must give express consent whenever a health-care provider looks at their medical record or enters their hospital room or whenever a physician talks to a nurse or submits a claim for payment to an insurance company. HIPAA permits disclosure in a range of circumstances without specific patient consent. It is common practice for general consent that authorizes routine, daily access to numerous health-care providers with responsibility for the patient's care to be obtained at the time of hospital admission or annually at the physician's office. This same approach asks patients for permission to transmit information to insurance companies, Medicaid, Medicare, or other financial sources before receiving services (but because refusing to do so means the patient must pay out of pocket, this is hardly a free and voluntary choice for most patients).

In most respects, disclosure and transfer of patient information for treatment, payment, and health-care operations codifies standard pre-HIPAA practices in the delivery of health care. HIPAA directs that uses and disclosures are to be limited to the *minimum necessary* to serve the purposes for disclosure. Hence, transfer of information may be limited to a portion of the medical record, and payors and health-care providers should not request and should not be sent the patient's entire historical record without good reason.

Under HIPAA, patients receive a written Notice of Privacy Practices (NOPP), typically upon hospital admission or annually at the physician's office. The NOPP states the provider's duty to protect privacy, describes the provider's practices regarding how protected health information will be used and disclosed, and explains the patient's privacy rights, including the right to receive a copy of one's own record, amend the record, seek an accounting of disclosures made by the provider, and complain about perceived violations of privacy.

The number of people who potentially see the patient's personal health information may be surprising. When one reflects on the number of physicians, residents, nurses, social workers, respiratory therapists, imaging technicians, medical students, and others who may be involved in the patient's care over a lengthy hospital stay in an academic medical center, this number can be considerable. Often, the patient gives no express consent to the involvement of many of these providers and their access to the patient's medical record. Rather, consent (permission) is implied, commonly through the hospital admission process. Whether the traditional practice of relying on implied consent remains the most ethically sound approach has engendered an important debate. A growing consensus argues that at least for some providers, most notably medical students and residents, there should be more express consent to their role, with the patient having the opportunity to refuse participation in their care, and hence access to their health information.

HIPAA carves out special protections for psychotherapy notes. Informed consent from the patient is required before psychotherapy notes may be used or disclosed outside the therapeutic relationship. With respect to psychiatric treatment, HIPAA essentially codifies and makes uniform established ethical and legal principles recognizing that a long history of stigma and discrimination against those with mental health problems makes diagnosis and treatment an especially personal matter, in need of strong privacy and confidentiality protections. HIPAA, however, does not establish added safeguards for other possibly sensitive information as many states have done. This shortcoming raises important issues for the electronic health record, discussed below.

The US Office for Civil Rights is charged with enforcing HIPAA. Violations are punishable by civil fines, with the possibility of imprisonment in extreme cases. In one case, a major pharmacy chain was fined for improperly disposing of labeled prescription pill bottles. In another case, a health system was cited for a HIPAA violation and was required to change its policies after a nurse left too much information about the patient's medical condition on the voice mail of the patient's daughter. Hospitals have implemented sophisticated procedures for monitoring HIPAA compliance. Confirmed violations may result in restriction of privileges, suspension, or termination of employment. Health-care providers have been fired from their jobs for snooping in the health records of celebrities. In one case reported in the media, hospital employees were fired for passing information about motor vehicle injuries to an attorney referral service.

Finally, HIPAA expressly permits (but does not necessarily require) disclosure of protected health information without patient permission for twelve specified "national priority purposes," including disclosure to address an imminent threat to health and safety, to protect victims of domestic abuse and violence, to comply with court or other legal proceedings, to cooperate with law enforcement, and to facilitate organ donation and transplantation. With respect to these areas, HIPAA mostly defers to the rules established by the states, and health-care providers should look to the law of their state for guidance. Mandatory reporting laws hold a prominent place in the legal landscape.

## MANDATORY REPORTING LAWS

In the exercise of their police powers to provide for the public health, safety, and welfare, all states require reporting of a wide range of health information, including vital statistics (births and deaths); morbidity and mortality for specific diseases; population-based research (such as incidence of diabetes); a long list of infectious and contagious diseases (pertussis, measles, tuberculosis, HIV, and many others); smallpox, anthrax, and other bioterrorism agents; sexually transmitted diseases; gun and knife wounds; and child abuse, domestic abuse, and elder abuse. States vary regarding which diseases and conditions are reportable, when and under what circumstances a report must be made, and which state agency has responsibility for specific types of health information. The US Centers for Disease Control and Prevention (CDC) maintains its own list and database of nationally notifiable (reportable) diseases for the purpose of preventing and controlling disease, based largely on information collected and transmitted by state-level agencies. The CDC and the states update their lists periodically. For communicable diseases, a positive test or diagnosis triggers the report (often by the testing lab). The reporting obligation is typically also imposed on physicians, nurses, health-care facilities, infection control practitioners, public health authorities, and others, and it may be assigned to designated hospital personnel. Notification to a government agency should be appropriately tailored to disclose the minimum necessary to achieve the law's purpose, not the entire medical record. Coordination among health agencies and the central role of the CDC is depicted in the fictional film *Contagion*, in which the CDC works closely with the Minnesota Department of Health, the World Health Organization, and many others to investigate and track an unknown deadly virus that is quickly spreading across the globe.

In the balance between the interests of society and those of individual patients, reporting laws favor disclosure and reporting to safeguard public health and welfare and to provide for the greater good. At the same time, because they contain patient information, government-maintained registries and databases are subject to their own privacy and confidentiality rules. Statistical data are publicly available in a variety of forms, but identifiable information is confidential and not available to the public. Changes to the list of reportable conditions can be controversial, as they necessitate compromises and decisions about the relative importance of individual privacy when weighed against the public good.

Mandatory reporting laws address many, but by no means all, of the situations in which it can be justified for health-care providers to breach confidentiality. The next section presents several case vignettes that pose challenging ethical-legal dilemmas for physicians and other health-care professionals, dilemmas that are either not fully resolved by reporting to government authorities or are not addressed by the law.

## PROBLEMS IN CONFIDENTIALITY: IT'S ETHICAL BUT IS IT LEGAL?

A mental health patient tells his psychiatrist he plans to kill his ex-girlfriend. An AIDS patient refuses to tell his partner he is HIV-positive. A patient suffers from dementia and impaired motor function and could have a motor vehicle accident at any time. Another patient has a serious genetic disorder but does not want her family to know. Each of these cases presents a tension in the physician-patient relationship between maintaining confidentiality and a duty to protect or warn third parties at risk. These dilemmas are especially challenging because ethics and law are not always in agreement. Physicians sometimes must ask, "it's ethical, but is it legal?"

Recall that confidentiality is a *prima facie*, not absolute, principle that may be trumped for good reasons. A widely accepted analytical approach is to assess the consequences of maintaining confidentiality compared with the consequences of disclosure, for the patient, third parties at risk, the physician, or other significantly affected parties. Specifically, a sound analytical framework should take careful account of the (1) imminence and likelihood of the risk for the third party; (2) likelihood and magnitude of potential harm; (3) likelihood disclosure will be effective to prevent or mitigate the harm and any other possible benefits for the third party; (4) potential harm to the patient that may result from disclosure, such as loss of employment and damage to relationships; (5) possibility that loss of trust in the physician will lead the patient to go elsewhere or discontinue treatment altogether; and (6) possible benefit to the patient from disclosure, such as avoidance of self-harm. Consequences for the physician—in particular, legal jeopardy associated with choosing either confidentiality or disclosure—also must be considered. Physicians may find themselves on the horns of an ethical-legal dilemma: if ethical analysis favors disclosure, the aggrieved patient may bring a lawsuit for breach of confidentiality; if it supports keeping confidentiality, the injured third party may sue for failure to warn.

In the following cases, it is sometimes a duty-to-protect principle and sometimes a duty-to-warn principle that best describes the physician's duties to shield others from harm. The two concepts are sometimes used interchangeably, but it is important to understand how they differ. Among the core distinguishing features are that a duty to warn entails direct communication with an identified at-risk third party, whereas a duty to protect sometimes applies to the public at large and often may be met by reporting to public health agencies (as in *Contagion*) or to other responsible authorities. Both the distinction and the confusion between the two concepts are illustrated by the well-known *Tarasoff* case.

### PSYCHIATRY: WHEN THE PATIENT THREATENS TO HURT SOMEONE

Our contemporary approach to the tension between confidentiality and the duty to protect or warn derives in many respects from issues in psychiatry and the seminal case of *Tarasoff v. Regents of the University of California* (1974, 1976). The pertinent facts of the case are straightforward. In the late 1960s, a University of California, Berkeley, graduate student, Prosenjit Poddar, dated another student, Tatiana Tarasoff. After a brief time, Tarasoff rebuffed him. Poddar did not take the end of the relationship well and suffered an emotional crisis. During therapy with a university hospital psychologist, he confided his intention to

*Twenty-year-old University of California (UC) student Tatiana Tarasoff and her estranged boyfriend, UC graduate student Prosenjit Poddar.* Tarasoff was brutally stabbed to death by Poddar on the doorstep of her Berkeley, California, home in 1969. During therapy sessions with a university hospital psychologist two months earlier, Poddar confided his intention to kill Tarasoff. The therapist notified campus police, but Poddar was released after questioning. Tarasoff's parents later brought a civil suit in which they claimed that the doctor and his colleagues had a duty to warn either them or Tatiana. The rulings that resulted have strongly influenced both legal and ethical understandings of the tension between confidentiality and duties to third parties. **AP IMAGES.**

kill Tarasoff. The therapist notified the campus police that Poddar suffered from paranoid schizophrenia and recommended that he be civilly committed as a danger to himself and others, namely Tarasoff. The police detained Poddar, but he was released after questioning; the police found him to be rational and he promised to stay away from Tarasoff. About two months later, Poddar killed Tarasoff. He then called the police, turned himself in, and was arrested and charged with murder. His conviction of second-degree murder was later set aside for failure to consider his diminished capacity. A second trial was not held on condition that he leave the country and return to his native India.

Tarasoff's parents brought a civil suit in which they claimed that the psychologist and his psychotherapist colleagues had a duty to warn either them or Tatiana and that she had died because of their failure to do so. In two controversial rulings (1974 and 1976), the California Supreme Court first held that mental health professionals have a duty to warn known persons at risk and that there was here an obligation owed directly to either Tarasoff or her parents to tell them of Poddar's threat. The later ruling described the therapist's obligation more broadly as a duty to exercise reasonable judgment to protect a known third party from harm. How this obligation is met depends on what is reasonable and appropriate under the circumstances. Here, directly warning the intended or foreseeable victim, notifying authorities (the police), or seeking civil commitment for the patient on grounds he posed a danger to others were all reasonable options. The decision establishing the mental health professional's duty allowed Tarasoff's parents to continue to pursue their claim that the psychologist and colleagues had failed to exercise reasonable care to protect their daughter.

Developments in the law post-*Tarasoff* have been varied. Some states impose a duty to protect or warn against serious threats, while others permit but do not require that mental health professionals take action, and still others have not enacted laws to address *Tarasoff*-type cases. State laws also vary with respect to applicable standards for breaking confidentiality, such as how explicit, imminent, or serious the patient's threat to harm others must be. Obligations of mental health professionals have been tested and subjected to scrutiny in several tragic campus attacks carried out by students in recent years.

The *Tarasoff* rulings have strongly influenced both legal and ethical understandings of the tension between confidentiality and duties to third parties well beyond psychiatry. Across medicine, it is now well established that an ethical, and perhaps legal, obligation may arise to breach confidentiality for the benefit of others. A duty to warn or protect may exist even though no relationship exists between the physician and the third party; physicians have a duty to people who are not their patients. And that obligation is not limited to patient threats to do physical harm to others. The duty to warn or protect applies to known or foreseeable persons at risk of harm from the patient; disagreement exists as to the scope of foreseeability and whether the duty applies to the public at large. Post-*Tarasoff*, physicians are expected to exercise reasonable judgment to evaluate the likelihood and seriousness of harm to others, and the likelihood disclosure will produce a positive outcome, as well as the other criteria set forth previously. Physicians may claim such predictions are inherently uncertain (as they did in *Tarasoff*), but they will be held to a standard of reasonable, ethically sound judgment and conduct.

The following cases illustrate how the duty to warn or protect applies to other patient care situations.

## THE HIV-POSITIVE PATIENT: TELLING THE PATIENT'S PARTNER

Consider Joe, a thirty-five-year-old patient just diagnosed with HIV. As part of posttest counseling, the physician urges Joe to share this information with his wife. She should get tested and seek treatment, and they should take appropriate precautions. But Joe is scared for his own health and afraid this news will destroy his marriage. He refuses to tell his wife and insists the physician must keep his secret too. Should the physician break confidentiality and warn Joe's wife that she may have been exposed to HIV?

The Academy Award–winning film *Philadelphia* presents a poignant look at how the issue would likely have been addressed in the early 1990s and offers a useful reference point for the evolution of ethics and law. Set in the early years of the epidemic, the film tells the story of a young man with HIV/AIDS who struggles with the personal, social, legal, and ethical dimensions of privacy, confidentiality, stigma, discrimination, and loss of employment while confronting the dying process with the support and comfort of his same-sex partner. The lead character tells his partner he has the virus. Had he not done so, it is unlikely the physician would have. In roughly the first decade of the HIV/AIDS epidemic, both ethics and law sided with a policy of strict confidentiality. As noted earlier, one rationale was that strict confidentiality would serve the greater good by encouraging more people to seek testing and treatment. Another was to shield those affected by HIV/AIDS from discrimination. Law also established mandatory reporting to the department of health (typically a direct report from the testing lab) with partner notification and contact tracing to be carried out by the department based on names or other identifying information shared by the patient and reported by the physician. Anonymous testing is offered as an option to ensure privacy and encourage testing.

The reporting and partner notification features of the legal framework remain in force in the twenty-first century, but the approach to protecting known partners at risk has changed. With advances in medicine, HIV/AIDS has become much more a chronic, manageable condition with proper care and treatment, and laws against discrimination have taken hold. Most states have moved away from a strict duty of confidentiality in favor of a physician's permission to warn potentially affected partners. This means that if patients name their sexual or needle-sharing partners, the physician may, but is not required to, notify and warn them directly of their risk. If the steps prescribed by law are followed in good faith, including telling patients that their partners will be contacted, and a good ethical argument is made for doing so, then physicians are given legal immunity against patients' later claims that confidentiality was wrongfully breached. If sound judgment is to keep confidentiality, immunity applies to a later claim by exposed partners for failure to warn.

After reporting to the department of health, Joe's physician might decide that his obligations are met and choose to do no more. But it could take days to weeks for the partner notification program to become involved in Joe's case. Should the physician rely on the government agency, or is there an ethical obligation to contact and warn Joe's wife? Considering the potential benefits to Joe's wife of avoiding HIV infection or seeking early intervention, there is a strong argument for breaking confidentiality. But this is not an easy decision, as the marriage likely faces negative consequences and Joe may no longer trust his physician enough to continue care and treatment. It is not uncommon for physicians to side with keeping the patient's confidence and to rely on the partner notification program.

## IMPAIRED DRIVERS: CAN YOU TAKE AWAY THE KEYS?

Mary, a seventy-five-year-old woman showing signs of dementia, reports to her primary care physician that on the way to the doctor's office she forgot where to turn and her legs were slow to hit the brakes when she nearly hit a pedestrian. The physician counsels Mary to take self-corrective action: perhaps to voluntarily stop driving, seek a thorough evaluation and treatment of her impairment, and take responsibility by telling others about her condition, in particular her husband and adult children. But Mary protests that she is fine and that her husband does not drive and relies on her for all their transportation needs. She implores the physician to keep this their secret.

Nearly all states have laws for reporting impaired drivers to the department of motor vehicles (DMV). The DMV is charged with the general duty to protect the public against impaired drivers. Most states leave reporting to the discretion and judgment of the physician; some mandate reporting. Once reported, driver evaluation could result in suspension or revocation of an impaired driver's license. But if keeping the patient's secret risks a motor vehicle accident that could (seriously) harm the patient, her family, or others, is it ethically justified not to report the patient to the DMV, or to rely on the DMV process that could take four to six weeks?

In cases like Mary's, the prospect that an accident may occur at any time, including while administrative action is pending, leaves many uncomfortable. A strong argument can be made not only to notify the DMV but also to reach out to the family to monitor and modify Mary's driving privileges or even take away the keys. Under family pressure, Mary might agree to seek needed help. On the other hand, disclosure threatens loss of freedom and independence, may impose particular burdens on the family, and may instead move Mary deeper into denial. The AMA counsels that reliance on the DMV meets the physician's obligation but that reporting is justified based on clear evidence of substantial driving impairment, if this poses a strong threat to the patient and others. On this standard, arguably more protective of confidentiality than the approach delineated earlier, it may be premature to notify the DMV, let alone contact the family.

The problem of impaired drivers is a growing concern with an aging population. But it is hardly limited to the elderly. Alcohol and drug abuse, seizures, disability, sleep disorders, depression, and a range of other medical conditions can all impair driving competence. That commercial truckers and airlines have their own standards and procedures for identifying and responding to employee impairment evidences the significance of the issue (and presents its own set of confidentiality concerns). Whether reporting to the DMV is legally required or merely permitted, it may be an imperfect response to the risk, calling on physicians to decide whether it is ethical to break confidentiality to prevent potentially serious harm to others.

## IT'S IN OUR GENES: DUTIES TO FAMILY MEMBERS

Donna Safer, thirty-six years old and recently married, has a cancerous blockage of the colon and multiple polyposis. After surgery to remove part of her large intestine, additional metastatic cancer was detected, leading to removal of her left ovary, followed by more chemotherapy. During the course of treatment, Donna underwent genetic testing and counseling. She learned that she had a genetic mutation for her disease and that hers was an inheritable condition. Curious to know more about her father's death years earlier, she requested his medical records. The surprising and disturbing discovery was that her father had died from the very same condition. Had she known—had her father's physician informed her of her genetic risk for familial adenomatous polyposis (FAP)—regular screenings, removal of polyps, and other measures might well have allowed her to control her disease without the need for major surgery. Did the physician have an ethical obligation to warn Donna?

The facts here are based on a New Jersey court case, one of the very few to address the question of a physician's duty to disclose genetic information to family members. In the legal case, Donna asserted that her father's physician had breached his duty to warn her and that she had suffered serious harm as a result. The court agreed. The case stands for the proposition that in some circumstances a physician has a duty to warn potentially affected family members of their genetic risk. By contrast, some genetic privacy laws (including the current New Jersey law) suggest a rule of strict confidentiality. But this is a new and slowly developing area for which there are few cases or statutes on the specific question of disclosure to family members without patient consent and thus little legal guidance for physicians. Acting on sound ethical judgment to tell potentially affected family members (again, when patients refuse to take on this responsibility themselves) when the law is silent makes the physician's dilemma more difficult—even more so if state law directs the keeping of genetic secrets without the grant of permission to disclose, as found in most HIV/AIDS laws.

A key factor in the ethical analysis is what medicine has to offer. For Donna and patients like her, there is significant benefit from knowledge, early detection, and intervention. By contrast, for those with a family history of Huntington's disease (HD), a late onset, progressive neurological disorder for which there currently is little medicine can do beyond palliation of some symptoms, other factors also shape decisions to disclose genetic risk. Studies have shown that for those with a family history of HD, knowing their genetic risk may be of critical importance to decisions to marry, have children, and plan a family; this is true for various other genetic conditions as well. Taking a good social and genetic history may reveal that a patient's genetic risk raises questions about disclosure to potentially affected siblings both for the patient and the physician. Psychosocial dynamics within the family, portrayed in the 2014 film *Still Alice* when the mother is diagnosed with early-onset Alzheimer's disease, play an important role in the disclosure decision and often are a reason that patients insist on their genetic secrets. In this film, two of three children undergo genetic testing for Alzheimer's with the result that one is destined to have the disease and one is not. The question not raised in the film is whether a patient has an obligation to tell his or her children that there may be a risk to their future health. So, too, patients and families may be concerned about the risks of social stigma and of discrimination in health insurance or employment should genetic information become known. Physicians and genetic counselors bear a special responsibility in this regard to know that extant law provides strong protections against genetic discrimination in both of these areas and to explain this to patients and families.

With inexorable advances in genetic and medical science, disclosure of genetic information is a question of rising interest not only with respect to diagnosis and disease management, but also with adoption, in vitro fertilization, preimplantation genetic diagnosis, and other assisted reproductive practices. Those with a particular interest in the ethical and social implications of genetics will likely enjoy (and be troubled by) the 1997 film *Gattaca*, set in a futuristic society of genetic determinism in which parents choose the genetic makeup and the future of their children, while those with "inferior" genes belong to a genetic underclass labeled "degene-erates."

***Scene from the film* Gattaca, *1997.*** Gattaca *centers on issues that stem from eugenics and the development of a genetic underclass, but also touches on confidentiality of medical information. In this futuristic society, automated DNA testing replaces less effective means of identification, and is also a commonplace consumer service (for example, to screen a potential romantic partner). The main character's identity and key medical details are displayed for his employer via an automated DNA test.* MOVIESTORE COLLECTION LTD/ALAMY.

## OTHER ISSUES IN CONFIDENTIALITY

The responsibility to protect patient privacy and confidentiality, and challenges to doing so, apply throughout medicine. The next sections present three areas of important and emerging interest. The move to electronic health records, required by federal law, not only holds great promise for patient care but also brings new challenges to patient privacy. So, too, social media in the information age requires careful consideration of privacy and confidentiality in digital platforms. First, we turn to the unique issues raised when the patient is an adolescent with strong interests in keeping sensitive information strictly between himself or herself and the physician.

### CONFIDENTIALITY AND THE ADOLESCENT PATIENT

Confidentiality is critical to the care of adolescent patients. Absent strong assurance of confidentiality, adolescents may be unwilling to reveal information critical to care and treatment. Issues of confidentiality can be especially delicate, particularly when adolescents want their diagnosis, treatment, or decisions kept secret from their parents.

Generally, parents have the legal right and authority to make health-care decisions for their children until they reach age eighteen, the age of majority. But as children enter adolescence and grow to adulthood, both ethics and law support giving them more control over their own medical decisions before eighteen years of age. Laws across the country have long recognized the rights of adolescents to make their own decisions about contraception, pregnancy, sexually transmitted diseases, HIV testing, mental health counseling, and other matters. In other situations, adolescent patients may be treated as mature or emancipated minors who are able to consent to diagnosis and treatment. Applying the rule that confidentiality follows consent, adolescents who make their own health-care decisions also have the right to decide who has access to their health information, including whether to exclude their parents. It is routine practice for young patients (perhaps age thirteen and older) to see their pediatricians without their parents present, to discuss confidentiality, and to be asked whether all, none, or only some information should be shared with parents. Adolescent requests for confidentiality are typically honored. Oftentimes, even though parents are making decisions, it is appropriate and necessary to have the assent and cooperation of adolescent patients. Pediatricians commonly try to respect adolescent requests for confidentiality, even when formal consent from parents is required. Conversely, it is sometimes parents who ask that information be withheld from their child, perhaps wanting to shield the child from bad news. How information will be submitted to insurance when statements are sent to a parent as the policyholder also must be determined.

Requests to keep secrets from parents, or from the child, are familiar terrain for experienced pediatricians, but they can be difficult to navigate. At times, keeping confidentiality conflicts with another fundamental ethical principle—truth-telling—especially when physicians are asked a direct question by the patient or parents. As a general matter, whether it is the patient or parents who want to withhold information from the other, perceived obligations to the family unit counsel facilitating agreement about open communication. When these efforts are not successful and disagreement persists, exceptions to confidentiality can involve balancing the dual patient-centered obligations to respect autonomy and to promote the patient's best interests. If parental involvement is critical to the patient's health and welfare—for example, when parental support is important to ongoing treatment for diabetes—honoring confidentiality may yield to the patient's best interests. Conversely, on rare occasions, adolescent patients' mature and autonomous refusals of life-sustaining treatment have been respected, even over their parents' objection. How an adolescent's decision to say when enough is enough may be honored and how it may implicate patient confidentiality is depicted in the film *My Sister's Keeper* (2009), in which a teenage girl, conceived through preimplantation diagnosis to be a bone marrow donor for her older sister who has leukemia, seeks medical emancipation from her parents so she can refuse to continue donating (but does not want her parents to know that she and her sister have agreed because the sister wants to be allowed to die).

Child and domestic abuse reporting can be among the most difficult ethical issues faced by pediatricians. The decision to report child abuse commonly rests on the reliability of the child's verbal account, sometimes substantiated by signs of physical injury sufficient to form the reasonable belief that agency investigation is needed. Awareness of the consequences of involving government authorities with the power to take custody away from parents or remove someone from the home, and of the fear, anger, and risk of further physical abuse within the family, also plays an important role. Pediatricians sometimes err on the side of maintaining confidentiality, at least until stronger evidence of abuse becomes known. Risks of suicide or harm to others, HIV status, and reproductive choices are also among the challenging ethical-legal dilemmas in which confidentiality, reporting, disclosure, and obligations to adolescent patients and others are all in tension.

## ELECTRONIC HEALTH RECORDS

Both HIPAA and the Patient Protection and Affordable Care Act of 2010 direct hospitals and other health-care providers to transition to the use of electronic health records (EHRs) and to phase out use of paper records. Computerized records are intended to create a unified historic patient record to replace the traditional and fragmented system of a multiplicity of paper records held in different locations with each of the patient's primary care physicians and specialists, and that are created anew when one becomes a patient at the hospital, outpatient clinic, or nursing home. The move to EHRs is designed to benefit both patients and health-care providers by giving physicians and the health-care team easy access to the patient's longitudinal and complete history. This also helps to reduce medical errors and improve safety, as hospitals are now better able to learn about a patient's prescription history, allergies, risks of drug interactions, and what the patient was treated for on a prior admission to another hospital. The EHR creates the pathways for remote access on laptops, tablets, and smartphones. It is also touted as a means to improve efficiency and reduce administrative costs.

At the same time, EHRs introduce unique concerns about privacy and confidentiality. Many areas of the United States have established regional health information sharing networks that link a patient's medical history and records, including visits with different providers and admission to different facilities over the years. As a result, with admission to the hospital or other medical encounters, the treating physician and many others have the means to access the full patient record, some of which has no relevance to the patient's current problem. Reports of early implementation of EHR systems suggest they do a poor job of shielding sensitive information other than psychotherapy notes from general access in the record. At present, the EHR may not be designed to elicit and accommodate patients' privacy concerns with regard to HIV status, domestic abuse, genetic diagnosis, dementia, family history, or other matters. Rules for restricted access to that portion of the record would offer greater privacy protection. For all their promise, EHRs do not remove long-standing apprehensions about privacy and confidentiality that sometimes incline patients to hide information from their physician.

## SOCIAL MEDIA

Physicians and patients increasingly seek, post, and exchange information over Web 2.0 interactive platforms, including e-mail, blogs, Facebook, Twitter, text-messaging, and online education resources. Today's information age holds the promise of enhanced knowledge and communication, but it also poses special challenges and pitfalls. Personal and cultural conceptions of privacy and social media can blur the boundary with professional obligations. Illustrating the tension, physicians and residents are divided on whether it is appropriate to friend patients on Facebook.

The physician's time-honored commitment to patient privacy and confidentiality applies with equal force whether information is acquired or disclosed face-to-face, online, or via cell phone. Physicians, nurses, and medical students have faced disciplinary action and dismissal for tweets, Facebook posts, and blogs about patients. It may be believed that sharing anonymized information with identifiers masked or removed (no names, locations, or other unique descriptors) sufficiently protects confidentiality, but this can be mistaken.

Few guidelines are available to help physicians and others navigate the practice of medicine in the digital age. The American College of Physicians and the Federation of State Medical Boards urge physicians to maintain appropriate boundaries between the professional and the personal in the use of social media. These organizations recommend that physicians not use social networking sites to interact with past or current patients and that they pay careful attention to security protocols when information is stored, transmitted, and disclosed in any electronic form.

## Summary

The time-honored principle of confidentiality is a cornerstone of medical ethics, firmly established in professional oaths and codes, in statements of professional organizations, in the law, and in the culture of medicine. Confidentiality and privacy share core commitments to patients' rights to control their personal health information. Privacy is generally concerned with access to patient information. Confidentiality is commonly concerned with the use and disclosure of information. The physician's duties to keep patient information confidential and to respect patient privacy are role-related obligations grounded in the physician-patient relationship. The importance of confidentiality and privacy rests on both consequentialist (utilitarian) and rule-based (deontological) grounds. On the former, adherence to the principle of confidentiality promotes truthfulness and sharing by patients, trust in physicians, and consent to tests, diagnosis, and treatment, all of which lead to better patient care and outcomes. On the latter, keeping confidentiality is grounded in respect for autonomy and patient rights, itself a core principle of medical ethics, and it honors the patient's unique moral agency, dignity, and worth.

State and federal laws protect privacy and require confidentiality in the medical encounter. The Privacy Rule of HIPAA, the most significant federal law, provides essential uniform guidance for the privacy, security, and confidentiality of health information. Laws across the fifty states also address privacy and confidentiality. Because state laws vary on some important issues, there are no universal rules for when disclosure of confidential information is prohibited, required, or permitted. One important exception to confidentiality in force across the fifty states is required reporting to government agencies to promote the public health and welfare, most notably reporting of infectious and contagious diseases.

Because confidentiality is a *prima facie*, not absolute, principle, keeping the patient's secrets must sometimes be balanced with and yield to concerns for the welfare of others, such as family members or the public, and to the obligation to follow the law. There are a number of cases in which physicians must decide whether it is justified to breach confidentiality to protect or warn third parties, situations in which the law of the state may not support or be consistent with sound ethical judgment. Four such scenarios were presented: the psychiatric patient who threatens to kill another person; the patient with HIV/AIDS who refuses to tell his partner about his HIV status; the driver whose impairment poses significant risk of a motor vehicle accident; and the patient who insists that her genetic condition be kept secret from potentially affected family members. In each case, the physician must balance confidentiality against the duty to warn or protect, taking into account the consequences of maintaining confidentiality and of notifying third parties at risk, respectively. In cases like these, the tension between ethics and law sometimes raises the question, "it's ethical, but is it legal?"

Unique issues about the strength and scope of confidentiality arise with adolescent patients. Although parents make many health-care decisions for their children under age eighteen, adolescents may make their own decisions on a range of matters, and sometimes want sensitive information (sexual activity, pregnancy, HIV, or sexually transmitted disease status) kept private from their parents. In this regard, the question is whether to maintain or break confidentiality for the benefit of the patient and the family.

The emergence of the EHR brings new rules and also special challenges, in particular for the privacy of mental health, drug and alcohol abuse, HIV, genetic, and other information. So, too, in today's information age, when we freely access social media with the click of a mouse, patient information has been shared, intentionally or accidentally, on various platforms in contravention of patients' rights of privacy and confidentiality.

In sum, confidentiality is foundational in the practice of medicine, but it is also riddled with exceptions. Health-care professionals should look to both principles of medical ethics and to the law for guidance regarding the rules and justified exceptions for the privacy and confidentiality of patient information.

## Bibliography

Allen, Anita L. "Genetic Privacy: Emerging Concepts and Values." In *Genetic Secrets: Protecting Privacy and Confidentiality in the Genetic Era*, edited by Mark A. Rothstein, 31–59. New Haven, CT: Yale University Press, 1997.

American Academy of Pediatrics. "Standards for Health Information Technology to Ensure Adolescent Privacy." *Pediatrics* 130, no. 5 (2012): 987–990.

American Medical Association and National Highway Traffic Safety Administration. *Physician's Guide to Assessing and Counseling Older Drivers*. 2nd ed. Chicago: Author, 2003.

American Medical Association Council on Ethical and Judicial Affairs. *Code of Medical Ethics of the American Medical Association, 2014–2015*. Chicago: Author, 2015.

Annas, George J. "HIPAA Regulations—A New Era of Medical-Record Privacy?" *New England Journal of Medicine* 348, no. 15 (2003): 1486–1490.

Bayer, Ronald. "Public Health Policy and the AIDS Epidemic: An End to HIV Exceptionalism?" *New England Journal of Medicine* 324, no. 21 (1991): 1500–1504.

Bayer, Ronald, John Santelli, and Robert Klitzman. "New Challenges for Electronic Health Records: Confidentiality and Access to Sensitive Health Information about Parents and Adolescents." *Journal of the American Medical Association* 313, no. 1 (2015): 29–30.

Beauchamp, Tom L., and James F. Childress. *Principles of Biomedical Ethics*. 7th ed. New York: Oxford University Press, 2013.

Berg, Jessica. "Grave Secrets: Legal and Ethical Analysis of Postmortem Confidentiality." *Connecticut Law Review* 34, no. 1 (2001): 81–122.

Berger, Jeffrey T., Fred Rosner, Pieter Kark, and Allen J. Bennett. "Reporting by Physicians of Impaired Drivers and Potentially Impaired Drivers." *Journal of General Internal Medicine* 15, no. 9 (2000): 667–672.

Chretien, Katherine C., Jeanne M. Farnan, Ryan Greysen, and Terry Kind. "To Friend or Not to Friend? Social Networking and Faculty Perceptions of Online Professionalism." *Academic Medicine* 86, no. 12 (2011): 1545–1550.

Farnan, Jeanne M., Lois Snyder Sulmasy, Brooke K. Worster, et al. "Online Medical Professionalism: Patient and Public Relationships: Policy Statement from the American College of Physicians and the Federation of State Medical Boards." *Annals of Internal Medicine* 158, no. 8 (2013): 620–627.

Ford, Carol A., Susan G. Millstein, Bonnie L. Halpern-Felsher, and Charles E. Irwin. "Influence of Physician Confidentiality Assurances on Adolescents' Willingness to Disclose Information and Seek Future Health Care."

*Journal of the American Medical Association* 278, no. 12 (1997): 1029–1034.

Gallup Organization, Institute for Health Freedom. "Public Attitudes toward Medical Privacy." 2000. http://www.forhealthfreedom.org/Gallupsurvey.

Gostin, Lawrence O. *Public Health Law: Power, Duty, Restraint*. Berkeley: University of California Press, 2000.

Herbert, Paul B., and Kathryn A. Young. "*Tarasoff* at Twenty-Five." *Journal of the American Academy of Psychiatry and the Law* 30, no. 2 (2002): 275–281.

HIPAA Privacy Rule, as amended 2013. www.hhs.gov/ocr/privacy/hipaa/administrative/privacyrule/.

Moskop, John, Catherine A. Marco, Gregory Luke Larkin, et al. "From Hippocrates to HIPAA: Privacy and Confidentiality in Emergency Medicine—Part I: Conceptual, Moral, and Legal Foundations." *Annals of Emergency Medicine* 45, no. 1 (2005): 53–59.

Office for Civil Rights, Department of Health and Human Services. "Summary of the HIPAA Privacy Rule." May 2003. http://www.hhs.gov/ocr/privacy/hipaa/understanding/summary/.

Offit, Kenneth, Elizabeth Groeger, Sam Turner, et al. "The 'Duty to Warn' a Patient's Family Members about Hereditary Disease Risks." *Journal of the American Medical Association* 292, no. 12 (2004): 1469–1473.

Perkins, Henry S., and Albert R. Jonsen. "Conflicting Duties to Patients: The Case of a Sexually Active Hepatitis B Carrier." *Annals of Internal Medicine* 94, no. 4, pt. I (1981): 523–530.

Rothstein, Mark A. "*Tarasoff* Duties after Newtown." *Journal of Law, Medicine, and Ethics* 42, no. 1 (2014): 104–109.

Sankar, Pamela, Susan Moran, Jon F. Merz, and Nora L. Jones. "Patient Perspectives on Medical Confidentiality: A Review of the Literature." *Journal of General Internal Medicine* 18, no. 8 (2003): 659–669.

*Tarasoff v. Regents of University of California*, 551 P.2d 334 (Cal. 1976).

Ubel, Peter, Margaret M. Zell, David J. Miller, et al. "Elevator Talk: Observational Study of Inappropriate Comments in a Public Space." *American Journal of Medicine* 99, no. 2 (1995): 190–194.

US Centers for Disease Control and Prevention. "Summary of Notifiable Diseases." Updated September 19, 2014. Accessed May 28, 2015. http://www.cdc.gov/mmwr/PDF/wk/mm6153.pdf.

Veatch, Robert M. *Hippocratic, Religious, and Secular Medical Ethics*. Washington, DC: Georgetown University Press, 2012.

Woodward, Beverly. "The Computer-Based Patient Record and Confidentiality." *New England Journal of Medicine* 333, no. 21 (1995): 1419–1422.

### FILM

*Contagion*. Dir. Steven Soderbergh. 2011. The US Centers for Disease Control and Prevention leads a worldwide race to identify and combat a lethal airborne virus that threatens humanity.

*Gattaca*. Dir. Andrew Niccol. 1997. A genetically inferior man secretly assumes the identity of a superior one to pursue his lifelong dream of space travel in a futuristic society committed to genetic determinism and discrimination.

*My Sister's Keeper*. Dir. Nick Cassavetes. 2009. Based on the 2004 novel by Jodi Picoult. A teenage girl seeks medical emancipation from her parents who relied on her to be an organ donor for her older sister who is dying from leukemia.

*Philadelphia*. Dir. Jonathan Demme. 1993. When a man with AIDS is fired from his law firm, he hires a homophobic small-time lawyer as the only willing advocate for a wrongful dismissal suit.

*Still Alice*. Dirs. Richard Glatzer and Wash Westmoreland. 2014. Based on the 2007 novel by Lisa Genova. A linguistics professor and her family confront her diagnosis of early-onset Alzheimer's disease.

# CHAPTER 11

# *Consent*

**Stephen S. Hanson**
*Associate Professor, Department of Philosophy*
*University of Louisville, KY*

Mary Schloendorff went to the hospital in December 1907 for treatment for indigestion. Before her release after getting her indigestion under control, her physician discovered a lump that could not be further diagnosed without an examination under ether. Ether was the surgical anesthesia of choice at the time, but here it was being recommended to allow a nonsurgical examination with her muscles completely relaxed. Mrs. Schloendorff had been aware of the lump for approximately five years and was not overly disturbed by it; still, she allowed an examination under ether to get a more accurate diagnosis. She explicitly refused, multiple times, to allow any operation. Her physician agreed to performing the examination without any operation being done.

The lump turned out to be a uterine fibroid tumor, which is a nonmalignant type of tumor that forms in the muscle tissue of the uterus. While fibroid tumors are not cancerous and pose little risk themselves if they are not causing burdensome side effects, surgical removal was often recommended by some, although not all, doctors at the time. While Mrs. Schloendorff was under anesthesia, the surgeon at the hospital performed a hysterectomy to remove the tumor.

Mrs. Schloendorff sued. She actually lost the case; the court did not hold the hospital liable for the injuries that came about from her unwanted surgery. However, the decision, written by Justice Benjamin Cardozo early in his career, carries strong language against the behavior of her physicians:

> Every human being of adult years and sound mind has a right to determine what shall be done with his own body; and a surgeon who performs an operation without his patient's consent, commits an assault. (*Schloendorff v. Society of New York Hospital* 1914, 130)

In ruling this way, Justice Cardozo argued that the decision whether to undergo medical treatment, and what treatment may be performed, must be made by the patient. Justice Cardozo was not the first to argue this, and that he made this statement in a decision that nonetheless denied Mrs. Schloendorff any relief is disheartening. Still, this powerful statement has had a significant effect on the development of consent in the medical field.

Modern readers may be surprised at the necessity of making such a statement; however, the history of medicine before the twentieth century is not congenial to patient participation in decision making. The Hippocratic Oath says nothing about patient consent; the Tuskegee Syphilis Study was not unique in its recruitment of subjects without informing them that they were to be subjects in a research study. The term *informed consent*, which now plays such an important role in medical encounters, was not even coined until the case of *Salgo v. Leland Stanford Jr. University Board of Trustees* in the 1950s. The modern focus on informed consent is modern: it has only been recently developed.

However, the recent nature of the development of consent as a vital part of medical practice means that we can see with clarity how this development has come about. One of the best and clearest statements of what informed consent ought to be, and why, comes from another court case, *Canterbury v. Spence* (1972). In 1963, Jerry Canterbury sued his physician, Dr. William Spence, for insufficiently informing him of the potential risks of a procedure performed on him. Mr. Canterbury was a young man suffering from back pain, and his physician, Dr. Spence, recommended a surgical procedure called a laminectomy, which is the removal of the back part of the vertebra that covers the spinal canal. This is an aggressive form of treatment for radiating back pain that carries significant risks, about many of which Dr. Spence informed Mr. Canterbury and his mother. The operation was also known to have a small chance of causing paralysis, but Dr. Spence did not inform Mr. Canterbury of this possibility. After Dr. Spence performed the operation, Mr. Canterbury did suffer from significant paralysis after a fall from his hospital bed during his recovery period.

Mr. Canterbury had agreed to the surgery, but the court held that mere agreement was not sufficient for true consent. For consent to be legitimate, the patient must be informed well enough to evaluate the risks and benefits of the alternatives available. There are alternatives to any medical treatment, even if the alternative option is only nontreatment. Patients might prefer an alternative to the procedure the physician thinks is best. Physicians cannot refuse to provide information that a reasonable person would need to have in deciding what course of action to take.

The most important part of the *Canterbury* decision is the justification for why physicians need to inform their patients, which is that "it is the prerogative of the patient, not the physician, to determine for himself the direction in which his interests seem to lie" (781). Patients, not physicians, decide what treatment to undergo because patients, not physicians, know which of their interests are to be promoted by engaging in medical treatment. This fairly simple understanding can actually help clarify many possible difficulties in examining the idea of consent.

## INTRODUCTION AND CHAPTER OVERVIEW

Consent in medicine is a vital part of the interaction between physicians and patients. Clinical treatment and clinical research involve risks and benefits, and the individual patients and subjects that undergo these therapies are the ones who will experience these results, both good and bad. They must be voluntary participants.

The ideal means of consent is *informed consent*, a term coined in the mid-twentieth century but with a rich philosophical history. Informed consent is the considered decision and action of an autonomous person after careful reflection over the available options. Informed consent requires being informed and consenting, and both parts of the concept must be present for the informed consent to be valid. *Consent* requires that the person consenting be capable of making the decision being discussed, and that the consent is voluntary and competently given. Being *informed* requires not only having information available, but actually understanding that information and being able to use it in a careful analysis of the risks and benefits of differing options. A true informed consent must be given without being manipulated by coercion, deception, or misleading language about risks and benefits.

**Informed consent must be**
- Well informed
- Information must be understood
- Without coercion or manipulation
- Made by a person capable of consenting
- After consideration of reasonable alternatives

*Table 11.1. Informed Consent.*

Barriers to good consent can include lack of capacity to make good decisions, time constraints in providing and obtaining informed consent, challenges in receiving information and being able to use it well, and difficulties in accommodating differing value sets into the Western medical practice of consent. A good understanding of the moral underpinnings of the practice of informed consent will help resolve many of these difficulties and give insight into how to address others.

## THE MORAL IMPORTANCE OF INFORMED CONSENT

Consent is morally important, as well as legally required, and for much the same reasons. The principle of respect for a person's ability to make and act on his or her own autonomous decisions has a long history of moral importance, although respect for patients' rights to make their own decisions has been slower to be recognized. Consent to treatment was initially put forth (e.g., in *Schloendorff*) as morally justified because of this right that individuals have to make their own decisions, and the right to control what happens to their bodies. This is correct, but it is incomplete.

### AUTONOMY

If one only looks at respect for individual autonomy as the moral basis of consent, a particular sort of error becomes easy to make. One can mistakenly perceive consent (or, more frequently, refusal to grant consent for a physician's preferred form of treatment) as a way for patients to interfere with physicians doing what is best for them. The patients would be exercising their autonomy, but they would be harming themselves by doing so. Physicians know what can be medically done, and they wish to do the most appropriate treatment for the best interests of their patients. This error suggests that when patients refuse that treatment, or prefer a different treatment, they prevent a physician from doing what is best for them.

If this were the case, then it might still be appropriate to allow persons to refuse unwanted treatments. After all, the importance of allowing persons to make and act upon their own decisions, even risky or bad decisions, is well established as a moral value. John Stuart Mill's rejection of paternalism in Chapter 5 of *On Liberty* is but one example:

> When there is not a certainty, but only a danger of mischief, no one but the person himself can judge of the sufficiency of the motive which may prompt him to incur the risk: in this case, therefore, (unless he is a child, or delirious, or in some state of excitement or absorption incompatible with the full use of the reflecting faculty) he ought, I conceive, to be only warned of the danger; not forcibly prevented from exposing himself to it. (1859, 182)

It would probably be sufficient reason to justify consent to and refusal of treatment to appeal to individual autonomy. However, there is further justification for informed consent.

### PATIENT BENEFIT

Consent is not exclusively about the autonomy of a person. It is also about choosing from among the options available that option which best allows a person to seek his or her best interests. Recall the statement from the court in the *Canterbury* case: "it is the prerogative of the patient ... to determine for himself the direction in which his interests seem to lie." Therefore, consent and autonomy are not in conflict with the best interests of the chooser; rather, they are necessary to know what the best interests are. Consent is morally justified not only by respect for the autonomy of individuals but also by the obligation to do what is (truly) in another's best interests.

The reason for this is that decisions in modern medicine often are choices between various options, each with significant positive and negative features. For example, medical decisions often require choosing aggressive attempts to cure a disease that have a small but real chance to be successful, but also have serious and damaging side effects, or palliating the symptoms as best as possible without attempting to cure the underlying illness. There is no single answer as to whether it is better to choose the small chance at eliminating the problem while suffering serious side effects, and possibly dying unpleasantly through the attempt to cure the illness, or to choose to relieve the symptoms and die as peacefully as possible.

Which of these options is the choice that is truly best for a patient depends entirely on the values and preferences of the patient. Different patients will have different valuations of the importance of avoiding the side effects of a treatment; they will also differently value the importance of a relatively comfortable and peaceful death. The same patient may also value these differently at different times of life. A significant chance of survival may be important for someone anticipating the birth of a grandchild, hoping to graduate college, or anticipating some other important life milestone. Later in life, that same person may be far less concerned with the possibility of survival and far more concerned with a peaceful death. Consequently, the only way to know what is in a patient's best interests is to have a clear, informed consent.

## COMPETENCE AND CAPACITY

There are two terms that are used, sometimes interchangeably, to discuss the ability to give consent: competence and capacity. A distinction has historically been drawn between these two, in which competence has been a legally defined term whereas capacity is a clinical assessment. Although the two terms are not always carefully distinguished, the two ideas do need to be.

### COMPETENCE

In the clinical setting, legal competence is a fairly simple determination based on the age of a patient, possibly modified by a court decision. Anyone over the age of eighteen is presumed to have the competence to make their own decisions unless there is a legal judgment otherwise. Conversely, anyone below the age of eighteen is legally assumed not to have decision-making ability unless there is a legal judgment of competence (such as being declared an emancipated minor). Although there may be times when a clinician thinks it might be prudent to seek a change in a patient's legal status, this is rarely the issue at hand regarding patient consent. If a court has established the incompetence of an individual, then she or he may still be able to assent to treatment (see the section on "Assent" further in this chapter).

Note: Eighteen is the age of majority in most countries, as well as in US states and territories. Clinicians should consult their local laws for any variations. Furthermore, there are various mature minor laws that may apply in some cases in many jurisdictions.

## CAPACITY

Capacity to give consent is a clinical assessment. Capacity means that a person has the ability to make decisions, can adequately consider the benefits and burdens of the options available, and can evaluate the effects of the various options on their life. Because medical prognosis is statistical in nature, nearly always giving the likelihood of particular results rather than certainty, capacity is a complex ability. It is a combination of the ability to reflect on the importance of various results, including an ability to weigh and choose between different values and interests that are particular to the person deciding, and being able to make evaluations based on the likelihood of the various results.

Therefore, capacity is not something that a person either has or does not have. It develops over time and can differ from decision to decision. Whether a patient should be thought to have decisional capacity can depend upon the complexity of the decision and the options being evaluated. A seven-year-old can have the capacity to decide whether she prefers ice cream or cupcakes for dessert while still being incapable of making decisions about chemotherapy.

Similar to any opportunity for case-by-case analysis, this makes the clinical assessment of capacity an area open for abuse. However, this is a worthwhile risk because this also enables clinicians to make proper decisions when the blunt legal assessment of competence is too simplistic. Consider the following case.

**Spondyloptotic Spinal Column Fracture.** A fifteen-year-old Jehovah's Witness (a Christian faith that generally refuses blood transfusions on biblical grounds), who was four months pregnant and had a serious cervical spine fracture, was suffering from paralysis from this injury. She was transferred to a different hospital three weeks after being injured in an automobile accident in the hopes that her quadriplegia could be alleviated or removed by an operation on her injured spine. In addition, she was severely anemic and refused transfusion of blood products because of the tenets of her religious faith; blood transfusion would normally be required for this type of surgery. It was hoped that the specialists at this hospital could devise a variation of the surgery that would not require blood products. Her parents, who were also Jehovah's Witnesses, agreed with this plan.

If the patient were to be incompetent to make her own decisions, then the decision would revert to her parents. Although the parents would have refused to consent to a blood transfusion for their child, physicians often seek a court order to transfuse minor children of Jehovah's Witnesses. The rationale is that one can autonomously choose to risk one's own life for a religious belief, but not someone else's. If she were not considered capable of making her own medical decisions, then she would likely have received the standard therapy (with blood products) to obtain the greatest likelihood of a medically successful operation.

As a fifteen-year-old unemancipated minor, the patient's lack of legal competence was clear. Interestingly, even knowing how this is so shows the limitations of legal competence for cases similar to this: in some states, she would have been presumed competent to make her own medical decisions because she was pregnant, but that was not the law in the locality where this occurred. However, the simple legal answer oversimplifies the case.

Almost any fifteen-year-old will have developed some ability to evaluate risks and benefits and to compare medical options on the basis of those risks and benefits. Therefore, the physicians took plenty of time to discuss the options with her. They wanted to know if she understood the risks of each operation, including a greater chance of dying from the nonstandard operation. They worried that her faith-based requests might be overly influenced by her parents, and they questioned whether she was capable of appropriately weighting the risks and benefits. After multiple conversations with her, the physicians concluded that she was capable of making her own decisions, and they performed the bloodless procedure.

Thus, the legal declaration of competence or incompetence is not definitive of patient capacity. A clinical assessment of capacity or incapacity should be made at the time of the discussions surrounding a decision to determine the current clinical ability of a patient to make good decisions.

# ASSENT

For persons not capable of making their own medical decisions, especially those who are incapable because of young age, there is the option of assent to treatment. Because the important part of consent is that persons are able to guide their medical treatment in a way that best fits their values and interests in life, even persons who are too young to consent to treatment can provide input into their treatment decisions. Likewise, even if a person is not old enough to make his or her own decisions yet, he or she ought to be well informed about what is being contemplated and should be able to participate in discussions about that treatment. This becomes more and more true as persons become more and more able to make decisions. Assent is the tool that has been developed for this.

Assent is a similar to consent in that it is a decision to participate made after an adequate attempt is made to inform patients of their options, risks, and benefits. However, there are two important differences. The level of information provided in an assent is frequently much less than that required for a fully informed consent, and the assent alone is not sufficient to allow a treatment to be performed. Assent is always done in conjunction with an actual informed consent provided by an appropriate surrogate decision maker because without the consent it does not serve a clear purpose.

In medical research, many researchers require an assent from a juvenile subject (sometimes even from subjects as young as seven years of age) before enrolling a subject in a research protocol. Therefore, in that case, assent can serve as a true opportunity for potential underage subjects to partially control their participation in research: they can refuse to participate, although they could not choose to participate in the research via assent without a valid consent from an authorized surrogate. Assent can serve as a means for noncompetent decision makers to exercise their autonomy to refuse to become research subjects.

However, medical treatment is different from medical research in this respect. Although researchers can generally choose to allow any potential subject to refuse to be a subject for their research, especially for ethical reasons, clinicians may feel more obligated to provide medical treatment that is the standard of care. Not only do patients need appropriate treatments in a timely manner, but physicians are professionally obligated to provide timely and appropriate treatment to their patients. If a young patient refuses to assent to a treatment (e.g., as would have been the case with the young Jehovah's Witness), then a physician does not always have the ability to accept that refusal. Therefore, there are numerous cases of treatment being imposed even on older adolescents who refuse treatment but do not have the legal ability to do so.

These facts lead to an interesting question: what is the ethical value of an assent or a refusal to assent? One can understand the importance of informed consent as enabling competent patients to select from among treatment options to receive the treatment that best matches their values and life goals, but an assent does not do this. An assent also does not allow one to choose or refuse treatment, nor does it necessarily allow older minor patients to allow their goals and values to guide treatment (although a thoughtful clinician can make that a part of the assent process, it is not required). Therefore, the moral value of an assent is unclear.

Perhaps the best interpretation of the moral value of assent is that it enables the participation of noncompetent patients in the discussion about their treatment as much as possible in an environment where consent is required. They are not competent decision makers at the time of the decision, and to treat them as if they were competent decision makers by fully respecting their decisions would be inappropriate. At the same time, to completely exclude them would fail to respect their limited (and, in the case of minors, developing) abilities to be decision makers. Engaging in the process of assent is valuable as a practice for the assenter, even if the assent itself is not yet as important as consent.

## INFORMATION VERSUS UNDERSTANDING

As can be seen from the *Canterbury* case, consent to treatment is only worthwhile if the persons consenting know what they are agreeing to. Not only do they need to know about the treatment a physician prefers, but they also need to know other possible alternatives, including no treatment at all. They need to be well informed about the risks and possible benefits of these treatments so that they can determine which seems most in line with where their interests lie. Without this information, a decision may be a consent to or refusal of a treatment, but it is not a morally interesting consent.

Understanding is critical to the moral validity of any consent; but here the legal underpinnings of informed consent fail us. *Canterbury* (and similar cases) involved physicians who did not mention a particular risk of a treatment. Although legal judgments hold that one must be well informed to make a good informed consent, they also focus on the failure of a physician to reveal salient pieces of information as the reason why a given consent was faulty. Although it is true that a decision cannot be well informed if the decision maker does not have access to the relevant information, having the information is not sufficient. A decision maker must also be able to use the information to evaluate different decisions. This means that the decision maker must understand the information.

There are many ways that information can be disclosed to a patient in a way that cannot be adequately understood. Disclosing too much information, especially too quickly, is one recipe for failed understanding. Use of jargon, inability of patients to cope with receiving information on top of an unexpected or serious diagnosis, difficulty with literacy, difficulty with numeracy, and many other things can also convert what might be an adequate disclosure of information into a situation in which a patient does not understand well enough to make an informed consent. In addition, many people are not willing to admit that they do not understand, especially to physicians in medical settings.

Therefore, it is crucial to ensure not just disclosure of relevant information but also that patients understand and can use that information. How best to do this is an active field of study, but there are some helpful guidelines.

### ELIMINATE JARGON

This guideline is widely recognized, and many clinicians and researchers recognize the importance of avoiding complicated or technical language in speaking with their patients. There are still many ways that persons can have trouble understanding even simplified language; therefore, this step is not enough, but it is the first step toward making difficult information understandable. There is no simple algorithm for how to simplify difficult language, but aiming for a fifth-grade reading level is recommended.

Eliminating jargon is not a one-size-fits-all method. There are a wide variety of factors that can affect a person's ability to interpret and understand the various options available. Low educational levels and poor literacy are two of the more obvious barriers to comprehension, but there are others. Persons who speak English as a second language can have additional problems, and even those who are native speakers may know little about the language of clinical concepts. It is wise to aim at simple language at first and adjust to more complex language if appropriate as one moves forward.

Jargon can mean more than just big words. For example, it is also medical jargon to say something as simple as "take one pill twice daily." Most readers of this work will probably recognize that this means to take two pills each day, one at a time, separated by (at least roughly) twelve hours. However, there is nothing in the phrase itself that actually says that, and a patient might conclude, as one patient in the American Medical Association (AMA) video *Health Literacy and Patient Safety: Help Patients Understand* does, that it is acceptable to take two in the morning to make sure that both pills are taken each day. In fact, the language of medical terminology is filled with concepts that skilled users do not even recognize as jargon, which is why it is difficult to completely eliminate it. Other tools are vital for producing good understanding.

### TEACH-BACK

The teach-back method is a tool for evaluating whether someone has absorbed a specific piece of information. It is similar to the concept of testing students after information is provided by a teacher. If recipients are able to teach the material back to the person who provided it, in their own words, then they have understood the material. This can be used as a part of the process of providing information. Patients should be regularly asked to repeat, in their own words, what they have been discussing, what they understand about their condition, what they understand about the treatment options, and so on. These questions should be asked in a manageable fashion (not, "Can you summarize the last thirty minutes of conversation?" but "Can you tell me about the treatment we just discussed?") and should be open-ended. "Do you understand?" is not an opportunity for teaching back, but "Tell me how you will take your medications" is.

### REPEATED DISCUSSIONS OVER TIME

Informed consent is not an event that occurs when a decision is made or a form is signed. It is a process that occurs over time. Recognizing this allows persons who are making difficult decisions time to think about their decisions, recognize what they do and do not understand, and ask questions. Because the process of consent involves both the person deciding and the clinicians who will be providing therapy, multiple conversations over the course of time between patients and clinicians can be an opportunity to re-inform, test understanding, and generally make a consent much more accurately informed.

## INFORMED CONSENT IN RESEARCH

Much of what has been said about the practice of consent in clinical matters also applies to research. However, there are several differences that require examination.

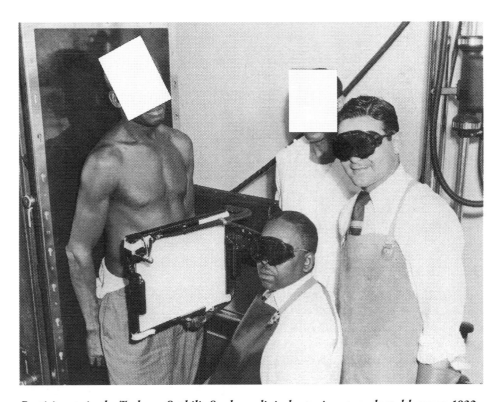

***Participants in the Tuskegee Syphilis Study, a clinical experiment conducted between 1932 and 1972 that examined the progression of untreated syphilis on African American men in Alabama.*** *The study, which promised participants free health care from the US government, recruited and retained subjects without fully informing them of their role in a research study.* CENTERS FOR DISEASE CONTROL AND PREVENTION.

Medical research has an uglier recent history than clinical treatment (see also Chapter 15, "Modern Research Ethics: A Historical Perspective"). Not only are the atrocities of the Nazis still in living memory, but the rest of Western medical research also does not fare well. According to the revelations in Henry Beecher's "Ethics and Clinical Research" (1966), the Willowbrook study, the Tuskegee Syphilis Study, and many others tarnish even the most compelling accounts of the success of medical research. Partly in response to some of these studies, the US Public Health Service established policies (which in 1974 were made into federal regulations) that authorized the creation of what are now called *institutional review boards* (IRBs) to examine research involving human subjects to ensure the protection of those subjects. One goal of this is ensuring that subjects are well informed about the research they are to participate in and that they consent to participate.

Subjects in research are informed about the procedures they will undergo somewhat differently from how patients are informed about clinical treatments. The process is superficially similar because in each case the procedures and alternatives are described and individuals choose whether or not to participate. However, there are important differences that make the consent process different. First, research is done according to carefully constructed protocols so that each subject is treated in the same way. This helps to ensure that the results derived from the research will be scientifically valid. This means that the entire process of providing the procedure, medication, or surgical intervention being researched is designed before any subject receives any procedures.

At the same time, research by definition involves procedures in which the effects of the procedure are not well known. The risks of a new procedure or a newly developed medication are discovered through testing, and even when a drug with a known set of side effects is being studied for use to treat a new condition, the complete risks and benefits of the treatments being studied are not known. A subject cannot be fully informed of the risks and benefits because no one knows what they are.

Finally, nearly all medical research involves comparing the treatment to be studied against either the standard treatment or a placebo, most of the time without the subject knowing which of the two is being received. To fully understand and consent to the study, a subject must understand the risks and benefits of not only the study procedure but also the placebo/standard treatment procedure. Subjects must also properly understand the concepts of randomization and blinding, which is keeping both subjects and clinicians from knowing whether the subject is receiving the treatments under study or the placebo.

Putting these three together, combined with the obligation to make the informed consent clear and explicit, has led to informed consent documents and procedures for research that are long, in depth, and often confusing. Not only must the consent process involve a discussion of the entire set of procedures to be performed over the entirety of the research, but it must also present a listing of all of the common and/or serious side effects, with an idea of how dangerous and how likely these side effects are. This must be done for the treatment being studied and for the standard treatment (or placebo treatment), and it may also need to clarify that the researchers do not know what all of the side effects are of the study procedure. Difficulties with numeracy may affect subjects' abilities to understand the concept of randomization, and this must be carefully considered. This makes the documents and discussions unwieldy. It also interferes with potential research subjects understanding what is proposed, not because the information is not available, but because

| Informed Consent | Implied Consent | Emergency Consent | Presumed Consent |
|---|---|---|---|
| Is the standard, and should be used in most cases | Applies only in well-understood, common, and generally noninvasive procedures | Used when patients cannot give consent | Used when patients are unable to give consent, including organ donation after death |
| Requires time | Is easily revoked | Can be revoked by prior request of patient | Requires significant justification |
| Requires active patient participation | Used for conscious, competent patients, but does not involve active patient participation | Used when patients are in immediate need of life-saving treatment or other serious medical need | |
| Can justify any appropriate treatment, whether normal or unusual, invasive or not, experimental, and so forth | Should not be used if there is any doubt about the case | | Should be appealed to rarely (if at all) |

**Table 11.2.** *Types of Consent.*

there is so much of it that even competent decision makers can go into information overload.

Nevertheless, these concerns can be addressed, although researchers must be careful. Subjects cannot be fully informed about what the likelihood of the success of their therapy will be, but they can be informed about what is known, and what the expected risks and benefits of the research procedure and the standard procedure (or placebo) are. They cannot know which they are receiving, but they can understand that they could receive either. The process of the consent is more complicated, and what needs to be discussed differs, but the concept of it is not radically different.

## IMPLIED AND PRESUMED CONSENT

Informed consent is the gold standard for consent because it is a voluntary agreement made as a rational act by someone well-enough informed of the alternatives to be able to choose an alternative if that were in fact preferable. However, there are other kinds of consent that occur in medical practice that need consideration to differentiate between them and to ensure that they are properly used.

### IMPLIED CONSENT

Implied consent in medical care is the granting of permission for some form of health care without a formal agreement between the patient and the health-care provider. A commonly used example (e.g., see *Mosby's Medical Dictionary*, 8th ed.) is the implied consent given to a medical provider to diagnose a patient when that patient makes an appointment with the physician with a specific complaint. Implied consent is appropriate for commonly understood features of health care that are recognized by both patient and provider as agreed upon without need for a specific agreement. As such, it covers many routine procedures but ought not be used to assume consent in any questionable cases.

The moral justification for implied consent comes from the fact that the activity and the role that each person plays in this activity is clearly understood by patients and providers either because it is a commonly understood feature of medical practice or because these particular persons have regularly participated in these actions. In other words, implied consent is valid because all participants understand what they are proposing to do and agree to it, which are the exact same reasons that informed consent is justified. If this is not true, then implied consent does not exist.

This can be seen by the fact that a case of purported implied consent can be revoked by a patient. Consider the following case.

**Revoked Implied Consent.** John J. has a family history of Huntington's disease, a genetic illness that strikes its victims in midlife and begins a years-long and eventually fatal process of mental and physical deterioration. (Although there now is a genetic test that can detect the disease in a carrier while still asymptomatic, there is still no cure nor any treatment. Because of this, many persons do not choose to have the genetic test.) Mr. J. visits his doctor because of increased difficulty in organizing and prioritizing tasks. Because his father, who died from the disease when Mr. J. was ten years old, was first affected by physical impairments, and perhaps because he has been effectively in denial, it has not occurred to Mr. J. that this could be an early symptom of Huntington's. However, as his doctor's questions begin to focus on his family history and other possible symptoms that Mr. J. recognizes, he stops the doctor mid-question and prepares to leave. He does not want any further progress toward his diagnosis to occur until he has had time to think it over, at home, for a few days.

Even if Mr. J.'s physician has a clear idea of what the diagnosis might be, and even if (for example) the physician already has a blood sample that could be tested for the gene, there is no consent to provide that diagnosis or to do tests on the blood to confirm it. The consent that was implied was based on a misunderstanding on Mr. J.'s part about what diagnosis could mean in this case. Once the actual information about what the diagnosis could be becomes clear, it also becomes clear that there is no consent for it any longer. Had the physician provided the diagnosis before Mr. J. had realized and stopped the process, then the physician would not have been blameworthy because there was every reason to expect that there was implied consent; however, once Mr. J. made it clear that he had not actually been appropriately informed, then there is no consent, implied or otherwise.

**Where Consent Cannot Be Implied.** This allows for the correction of a common sort of error about implied consent. For example, some might argue that patients give implied consent to being seen by medical students and by student doctors when they come to be treated in a teaching hospital. It is part of the procedure of treatment at teaching hospitals that medical students and residents participate in the care of patients; by opting for care at this hospital, rather than another, patients have given implied consent to this kind of care.

However, closer analysis suggests that this implied consent is hard to justify. After all, the argument must hold that patients know that this is a teaching hospital and have chosen to be treated in this hospital knowing what that means. Neither of these claims is likely to be true for most patients arriving in a teaching hospital. For this to follow, these patients would have to understand the way medical education proceeds—medical students, interns, residents, and attending physicians and the various ways they interact with patients. There is no reason to think the general public actually does understand this. They would also have to have chosen this hospital for that reason, rather than all of the myriad of other reasons persons choose hospitals (e.g., their personal physician has admitting privileges at this hospital, it was the closest when an emergency occurred, or it is the one that takes their insurance). Implied consent may be present for the medical school dean who eagerly anticipates seeing the educational experience from the side of the patient; however, that does not mean it can be assumed for the uninsured patient who has come there for treatment because no other hospital would provide it.

## EMERGENCY CONSENT

Although this is often considered to be a form of implied consent, it is worth breaking emergency consent out for its own consideration. Emergency consent occurs when a patient is unable to give consent and is in imminent danger of death or severe harm. In general, it is used with regard to lifesaving procedures necessary in such a case, but it could also be applied to procedures that would prevent or reverse serious harm in the same circumstances (e.g., if a patient were not conscious, no surrogates could be found, and a limb needed to be reattached as soon as possible to prevent permanent loss of the limb, then emergency consent could be appealed to). Emergency consent allows emergency medical technicians (EMTs) and emergency room staff to perform lifesaving measures in the appropriate time frame—immediately—when there is no way to discuss with the patient what treatments the patient would value.

Emergency consent is morally justified by an assumption that the patient would agree to the treatments if capable; therefore, it is only applicable in extraordinary circumstances. For example, life-sustaining, limb-retaining, or brain-protecting treatments are treatments that would normally be agreed to by most persons, and which in many cases must be done immediately on patients who are incapable of communicating. When there is no way to confirm this, and waiting to get confirmation is effectively choosing not to act, assuming that a patient would agree to these procedures is morally justified by appeal to what is reasonably assumed to be the patient's best interests and autonomy.

However, this means that emergency consent can be assumed where, in fact, it does not exist. Patients who would choose not to be treated, or not to be treated in particular ways, can be treated by emergency consent because health-care providers do not know the patient's preferences. In some cases, the emergency consent can be reversed later on; for example, if a patient has a strong preference not to be on a ventilator, but is intubated in an emergency room while unconscious, then that ventilator can be removed later after the patient has recovered the ability to make a preference known. However, sometimes the reversal is not possible. If a Jehovah's Witness is transfused while unconscious, then the blood cannot be removed later on. Therefore, care should be taken when invoking emergency consent. In addition, persons who know they have preferences outside of the norm for emergency treatment can and often do document their preferences (e.g., on wallet cards), and an effort should be made to locate such documents when possible before using emergency consent.

## PRESUMED CONSENT

Presumed consent is similar to implied consent in that it is consent that is assumed to exist unless explicitly rejected. It could apply in multiple circumstances; for example, emergency consent could be considered a form of presumed consent. But presumed consent has been used most commonly as a policy regarding organ donation after death. Many European countries have a policy of presumed consent for organ donation after death, where it is assumed that a person is willing to donate organs after death unless that person has explicitly indicated, while alive, a preference not to donate.

Presumed consent assumes consent where there is no evidence of either consent or refusal, whereas under normal circumstances we presume refusal unless explicit consent is given. The reason for the standard of presuming refusal is clear from the legal history presented earlier. *Schloendorff* clearly roots the justification for the need for consent in the right to be free from unwanted touching. The kind of physical contact necessary for a physician to diagnose or treat a patient is often personal or even invasive. It would be illegal in most cases for someone to make this sort of contact with another person without that person's express permission. With informed consent, a surgical operation is good medical care; without it, it is cutting someone open with a knife. As an example, see the film *Extreme Measures* (1996), in which Gene Hackman plays a researcher who experiments on homeless men without their permission. Although he is seeking a cure for paralysis from spinal cord damage, and he may be achieving some success, he is not a hero but a villain.

Thus, for presumed consent to be justified, there must be strong reasons to reverse this normal orientation. The argument for presumed consent for organ donation, despite the normal presumption of refusal, is threefold. First, individual rights to bodily integrity are not absolute and can be overridden for good enough reasons. Second, there is a great need for donated organs, and it is hoped that this policy would lead to an increased number of organs donated. This is based in part on the thought that most people would wish to be donors but do not take the time to indicate their preference officially or to loved ones before their deaths. Third, although there is the risk of a violation of a person's autonomy by

*Gene Hackman stars as neurosurgeon Dr. Lawrence Myrick in the 1996 crime thriller* Extreme Measures. *In an attempt to find a cure for paralysis, Myrick secretly performs spinal experiments on homeless people without their consent.* **AF ARCHIVE/ALAMY.**

presuming consent when it would not have been given, the harm of this violation is thought to be diminished because the donor is already dead.

From this, it can be seen that the justification of presumed consent is difficult; therefore, it is rare that any case of truly justified presumed consent will actually occur. In fact, even this case may not be justified because the evidence is unclear that presumed consent would actually lead to increased organ availability, and it is possible to achieve high donation rates without it. Presumed consent should only be used carefully, if at all.

# CULTURAL CHALLENGES

The policy of informed consent discussed herein is grounded in a Western and perhaps specifically American concept of individual autonomy and negative rights. This can lead to challenges when obtaining consent from persons with a cultural heritage that considers other values more strongly than the individualistic norms on which this is based. Because these values can be held by a wide variety of persons with varying cultural mores, it makes the most sense to organize these by category of challenge. Although some guidance can be given for these cases, they can be true challenges to the concept of consent without a simple solution to the problems raised.

## FAMILY DECISION MAKING

The form of consent discussed previously is one in which an individual makes a decision about the treatment that that individual person will receive. It is focused almost entirely on the preferences, the deliberation, and the decision of one individual. The patient, who is the person who will be receiving treatments, is also the person who is informed, must understand, and makes the decision (unless unable to).

However, some families function in a different fashion in which important decisions are made either by the family as a whole or by some subsection of the family (frequently family elders). A competent patient choosing treatments based on the recommendation of family members is not morally problematic, but the challenge in this sort of case comes when a family may request that information not be given to the patient but rather to the family, who will then dole out information to the patient (or not) as they choose. The patient will not be informed about treatment options and will not be able to choose among them because this job will be performed by the family.

There are two ways in which this sort of challenge can occur, only one of which is a serious difficulty. The first version is where the patient joins the family's request and chooses not to participate in the decision-making process. This can still count as a form of consent because in such a case a decision is still being made by the patient (in this case, the decision is to defer the decision making to the family). As long as the patient is aware that this decision can be recanted at any time, and can choose to be the primary decision maker again, a (revocable) waiver of the right to make one's own decisions is consistent with the moral principles of consent described here.

Take as an example of this *Grey's Anatomy*, season 2, episode 5. Here, a Hmong woman has a tumor on her spinal cord that will render her paralyzed if not surgically removed. Although she is an adult, she says that her father must make the decision for her. Because of Hmong cultural beliefs in opposition to some Western medicine, he (initially) refuses. (For further discussion of Hmong culture, see, e.g., Anne Fadiman, *The Spirit Catches You and You Fall Down* [2012].) After having a Hmong healing ceremony performed in the hospital, the patient's father consents to the surgery.

The second version of this challenge is where a family requests that a competent patient be removed from the decision-making process without that patient being a part of the request. Information is to be provided to the family, and the family will choose the treatments to be provided with input from or information to the patient only as the family chooses. This version is a serious challenge because the patient is rendered unable to consent by this.

One possible solution to this second sort of challenge is to turn it into the first sort. A clinician may discuss the family's preferences with the patient, and if the patient agrees to let the family decide, then the situation becomes one of a revocable waiver discussed above. Alternatively, if the patient prefers to be informed and make decisions, then the clinician must accept that, but the clinician can appeal to the patient's specific request as justification. If the family refuses even to allow this conversation with the patient, then clinicians may be caught between obligations of differing cultures, but they should not be trapped by this. The law requires that competent patients give informed consent; thus, a clinician is bound by the law to deal with the patient even if the family prefers otherwise.

## DIFFICULTY DISCUSSING BAD NEWS

Some persons have difficulty planning for future medical decisions because of a fear, or a cultural barrier, of discussing possible bad futures or disclosing bad news. Opposition to this discussion can range from beliefs that it is impolite to reveal bad news to a belief that speaking of bad results makes them more likely to come true. True consent involves an informed analysis of the options available. If a patient prevents a clinician from discussing the risks of proposed medical treatments, then that patient cannot really make an informed decision.

Patients do not have to be in charge of consenting for their own treatment. If a patient or patient's family feels that discussing bad news with the patient is inappropriate, then a physician can discuss this with the patient. For example, if the patient chooses not to be informed about test results, then that can be allowed. The physician should ensure that the patient knows that the physician will discuss these matters with the patient at any time if desired. The only challenge remaining here is that someone must be able to consent for the patient. Any person or set of persons the patient chooses can consent for the patient (who this is should be clearly documented in the patient's chart), although it should not be the physician or another health-care provider because the potential for conflict of interest is too great.

## LANGUAGE BARRIERS

If it is difficult to obtain understanding about health-care matters when two persons are communicating in a language that they are both fluent in, translation difficulties can make this even harder. The solution to even moderate translation difficulties should be to obtain a translator, ideally a professional or trained translator. Translators should provide a word-for-word translation and should ask the physician to rephrase or explain any terms that they do not themselves fully understand. Whenever possible, one should avoid using family members as translators because the matters discussed in a physician/patient conversation are confidential and can involve matters that one does not wish to discuss with one's grandmother.

## Summary

Consent is a vital part of modern medical practice. It is vital for preserving the autonomy of patients and research subjects, and it enables health-care providers to act in the best interests of their patients. To achieve these goals, consent must be performed by a person who is currently capable of making decisions and is currently competent to make medical decisions. That decision maker should not only have been well informed about the risks and benefits of the procedure to be performed, and alternative procedures that could also be performed, but he or she should also have correctly understood that information. This allows the patient or research subject to choose in accordance with his or her own values and preferences.

## Bibliography

Abadie, Alberto, and Sebastien Gay. "The Impact of Presumed Consent Legislation on Cadaveric Organ Donation: A Cross-Country Study." *Journal of Health Economics* 25, no. 4 (2006): 599–620.

Beauchamp, Tom L., and James F. Childress. *Principles of Biomedical Ethics.* 7th ed. New York: Oxford University Press, 2013.

Beecher, Henry. "Ethics and Clinical Research." *New England Journal of Medicine* 274, no. 24 (1966): 1354–1360.

*Canterbury v. Spence*, 409 U.S. 1064 93 S. Ct. 560 34 L. Ed. 2d 518 (1972) U.S.

Coleman, Doriane Lambelet, and Philip M. Rosoff. "The Legal Authority of Mature Minors to Consent to General Medical Treatment." *Pediatrics* 131, no. 4 (2013): 786–793.

Donate Life California. "Presumed Consent: An Attractive Concept with Unattractive Results." http://donatelifecalifornia.org/education/faqs/presumed-consent/.

Faden, Ruth R., and Tom L. Beauchamp. *A History and Theory of Informed Consent.* New York: Oxford University Press, 1986.

Fadiman, Anne. *The Spirit Catches You and You Fall Down: A Hmong Child, Her American Doctors, and the Collision of Two Cultures.* New York: Farrar, Straus and Giroux, 2012. First published 1997.

Feigenbaum, Frank, Daniel P. Sulmasy, Edmund D. Pellegrino, and Fraser C. Henderson. "Spondyloptotic Fracture of the Cervical Spine in a Pregnant, Anemic Jehovah's Witness: Technical and Ethical Considerations." *Journal of Neurosurgery* 87, no. 3 (1997): 458–463.

Hern, Eugene, Barbara Koenig, Lisa Jean Moore, and Patty Marshall. "The Difference That Culture Can Make in End-of-Life Decision-Making." *Cambridge Quarterly of Healthcare Ethics* 7, no. 1 (1998): 27–40.

Holland, Jimmie C., Natalie Geary, Anthony Marchini, and Susan Tross. "An International Survey of Physician Attitudes and Practice in Regard to Revealing the Diagnosis of Cancer." *Cancer Investigation* 5, no. 2 (1987): 151–154.

*Institutional Review Board Guidebook.* Updated 1993. http://www.hhs.gov/ohrp/archive/irb/irb_guidebook.htm.

Kagawa-Singer, Marjorie, and Leslie J. Blackhall. "Negotiating Cross-Cultural Issues at the End of Life: 'You Got to Go Where He Lives.'" *Journal of the American Medical Association* 286, no. 23 (2001): 2993–3001.

Katz, Jay. *The Silent World of Doctor and Patient.* Baltimore: Johns Hopkins University Press, 2002. First published by the Free Press in 1984.

Kripalani, Sunil, Rachel Bengtzen, Laura E. Henderson, and Terry A. Jacobson. "Clinical Research in Low-Literacy Populations: Using Teach-Back to Assess Comprehension of Informed Consent and Privacy Information." *IRB: Ethics and Human Research* 30, no. 2 (2008): 13–19.

Lombardo, Paul A. "Phantom Tumors and Hysterical Women: Revising Our View of the *Schloendorff* Case." *Journal of Law, Medicine, and Ethics* 33, no. 4 (2005): 791–801.

Mill, John Stuart. *On Liberty.* 1859. https://www.gutenberg.org/files/34901/34901-h/34901-h.htm.

*Mohr v. Williams* (104 N.W. 12) Minn. (1905).

*Pratt v. Davis*, 118 Ill. App. 161, 79 N.E. 562 (1905).

*Salgo v. Leland Stanford Jr. Univ. Bd. Trustees*, (1957) 154 Cal. App. 2d 560, 317 P.2d 170.

*Schloendorff v. the Society of the New York Hospital*, Court of Appeals of New York. 211 N.Y. 125; 105 N.E. 92 (129–130) (1914).

Searight, H. Russell, and Jennifer Gafford. "Cultural Diversity at the End of Life: Issues and Guidelines for Family Physicians." *American Family Physician* 71, no. 3 (2005): 515–522. http://www.aafp.org/afp/2005/0201/p515.html.

Stewart, William H. "Surgeon General's Directives on Human Experimentation." 1966. http://history.nih.gov/research/downloads/Surgeongeneraldirective1966.pdf.

Washington, Harriet A. *Medical Apartheid: The Dark History of Medical Experimentation on Black Americans from Colonial Times to the Present.* New York: Doubleday, 2008.

Yeo, Gwen, and Nancy Hikuyeda. "Cultural Issues in End-of-Life Decision Making among Asians and Pacific Islanders in the United States." In *Cultural Issues in End-of-Life Decision Making*, edited by Kathryn L. Braun, James H. Pietsch, and Patricia L. Blanchette, 101–125. Thousand Oaks, CA: Sage, 2000.

## FILM AND TELEVISION

American Medical Association. *Health Literacy and Patient Safety: Help Patients Understand.* https://www.youtube.com/watch?v=cGtTZ_vxjyA.

*Extreme Measures.* Dir. Michael Apted. 1996. A British doctor working at a hospital in New York makes unwanted inquiries when the body of a man who died in his emergency room disappears. He is led to an eminent surgeon, but he finds himself in danger from people who wish to keep the hospital's secret undiscovered.

*Grey's Anatomy.* "Bring the Pain." Season 2, episode 5, 2005. Dir. Shonda Rhimes et al. ABC.

# CHAPTER 12

# *Conflicts of Interest*

**Howard Brody**
*Independent Scholar*
*Galveston, TX*

In 1983, philosopher Albert Jonsen described the core of medical ethics as a paradox between altruism and self-interest (Jonsen 1983). On the one hand, physicians generally adopted the stance of placing the care of the patient foremost. On the other hand, physicians did not fare badly as a result—they normally managed a rewarding lifestyle.

Although Jonsen described the relation between altruism and self-interest as a paradox, physicians tend to conceal the paradox. They tend to disclose the altruistic portions of their behavior and motives and to soft-pedal all aspects of self-interest, which becomes easier to do because of the fiduciary nature of much of a physician's activity. In general, patients must accept on trust the fact that the physician is seeking the outcome that will genuinely aid the patient rather than the outcome that will provide the physician with the greatest personal benefit.

Cases in which two sets of interests may collide (such as the patient's and the physician's) are generally described as *conflicts of interest*. We will see that conflicts of interest describe a wide field, in only a portion of which would we say that the physician (or other professional) was engaged in wrongdoing. However, even cases in which no personal wrongdoing can be ascribed may be illustrative of ethically important factors.

This chapter will proceed by laying out two case studies—the first fictional and the second real. *Conflict of interest* will then be defined and analyzed using the example of the pharmaceutical industry. After that discussion, two other examples of conflicts of interest will be studied: (1) boundary crossings and boundary violations; and (2) physician self-referrals. Possible ways to resolve conflicts of interest will then be explored.

## FICTIONAL CASE STUDY: *THE CONSTANT GARDENER*

*The Constant Gardener* was published as a novel by John le Carré in 2001 and produced as a motion picture in 2005. Justin Quayle, a low-level British diplomat in Kenya, learns that his wife Tessa, a member of an activist group, has been murdered. Tessa had been in the company of a physician, Arnold Bluhm, and Quayle initially suspects a sexual intrigue. However, Bluhm is later discovered to have been murdered at the same time and is revealed to have been gay.

The story follows Quayle's investigation into Tessa's death. He eventually learns that an international pharmaceutical company, "KVH," has been performing experiments of a new drug for tuberculosis, "Dypraxa." KVH had been hoping to capitalize on the need for new medicines for multidrug-resistant tuberculosis and was hiding evidence of serious adverse reactions to Dypraxa. Quayle eventually learns that some of his own colleagues in the British foreign service had been complicit in the concealment. The colleagues are eventually revealed, but not before Quayle himself is killed by company hit men.

Novelist le Carré based his plot loosely on Pfizer's experience with the drug trovafloxacin (Trovan), an antibiotic eventually withdrawn because of its tendency for serious liver damage. In Kano, Nigeria, in 1996, Trovan was tested for pediatric meningitis, with the control group being given an inadequate dose of another antibiotic, ceftriaxone, in a trial that was conducted without proper government authorization and without adequate informed consent of subjects' parents.

The film included a statement from le Carré's novel: "Nobody in this story, and no outfit or corporation, thank God, is based upon an actual person or outfit in the real world, but I can tell you this, as my journey through the pharmaceutical jungle progressed, I came to realize that, by comparison with the reality, my story was as tame as a holiday postcard" (le Carré 2001, 568).

The novel and film deviate from reality in one significant way. No people have been assassinated by hit men hired by drug companies in any case that has yet been reported. One reason for this difference between reality and the plot of the novel is that the drug industry has not yet found any real need for a crude tactic such as assassination. The total amount of money spent per year by the drug industry for marketing in the United States has been estimated at US\$57 million, equivalent to US\$61,000 per practicing physician (Gagnon and Lexchin 2008). This is much greater than the total cost of all physician education. Thus far, the pharmaceutical industry has found the medical profession sufficiently responsive to money to eliminate the need for less respectable alternatives.

KVH had an ethical duty to ensure that any drug it sold, including Dypraxa, was effective and safe. Patients trust products urged upon them by physicians and lack the ability and the resources to check out each case. To abandon ethical duty in order to make a profit by selling an unsafe drug represented a serious conflict of interest.

## REAL CASE STUDY: MEDTRONIC AND INFUSE

The June 2011 issue of the *Spine Journal* contained an unusual set of articles accompanied by an editorial (Carragee et al. 2011). The writers surveyed published research on the chemical recombinant human bone morphogenic protein-2 (rhBMP-2; InFuse), manufactured by Medtronic, used in spinal fusion surgery. This surgery treats chronic back pain by firmly attaching adjacent bones (vertebrae) to each other.

The fusion technique previously involved inserting a bit of bone taken from the hip, which required an extra incision with corresponding pain. With rhBMP-2, this extra procedure was eliminated. The chemical was contained within a small wire cage and placed in contact with the vertebrae. The chemical would then stimulate new bone growth to fuse the adjacent vertebrae.

The rhBMP-2 also had the potential to cause several adverse reactions, including inflammation, persistent pain, inability to urinate, and inappropriate bone growth from leakage of the chemical outside of the wire cage. In some cases, the inappropriate growth caused nerve compression and increased pain, precisely what the spinal fusion surgery was meant to correct.

The editorial compared articles published by authors associated with Medtronic with articles from other sources. In seven published reports by Medtronic-affiliated authors, not a single adverse reaction was noted. By contrast, the estimates of risks of complications in the articles by nonaffiliated authors ranged from ten to fifty times that suggested by the Medtronic authors.

The editorial also noted that the affiliated authors had received large sums from Medtronic, adding that one single trial had apparently netted its investigators a total of US$26 million in payments. A popular press account had earlier reported that five surgeons who performed many spinal fusions had received a total of US$7 million in royalty and consulting payments during the first nine months of 2010 alone (Carreyrou and McGinty 2010). (A single patient's surgery can call for the use of US$20,000 worth of Medtronic devices.)

These payments raised another question. The surgeons were heavy users of rhBMP-2 and received large payments. However, Medtronic reported they were paid not for rhBMP-2 but for other company-manufactured devices. According to Medtronic, this factor eliminated the risk that the surgeons would have a serious conflict of interest. However, the company never supplied a description of the other products and what special knowledge these surgeons had about them. It seemed instead that Medtronic was simply trying to hide the significance of the payments.

The editorial in the *Spine Journal* concluded flatly, "The core of our professional faith … is to first do no harm. It harms patients to have biased and corrupted research published" (Carragee et al. 2011, 466). The following year, the US Senate Committee on Finance (2012) issued a report of its own investigation. The Senate committee concluded that Medtronic exerted an undue influence over its studies and the way they were reported in journals.

Medical firms are near the top of the list of companies revealed to be engaged in illegal activities; therefore, it would be no surprise if Medtronic simply went about its business after these events. However, for whatever reason, the company performed an abrupt about-face. Medtronic approached Yale University and a physician faculty member, Dr. Harlan Krumholz, to perform an independent assessment of rhBMP-2. Dr. Krumholz, known to be a strong critic of pharmaceutical companies and their conflicts of interest in medical research, later detailed the agreed-upon study plan (Krumholz and Ross 2011). Medtronic would turn over all of the relevant raw data. Yale would then oversee the creation of two separate committees, made up of public representatives and academic experts, each of which would separately review the data and issue a report on its findings.

The Medtronic-InFuse case thus began as a classic illustration of conflict of interest in medical research, with the company apparently using its influence over investigators to suppress reports of adverse effects from its chemical and with physicians apparently willing to accept the huge sums of money and do the company's bidding. However, in the end, the case illustrates what appears at this time to be perhaps the most successful turnaround, with a promising method to expose and to police the company's behavior. We do not yet know the outcome of the review process, and it seems unlikely that this process can be applied on a wide scale. However, at least thus far, it appears to signal the greatest willingness of any drug or device company to come clean under public scrutiny.

# DEFINING CONFLICT OF INTEREST

*Conflict of interest* has proven to be a controversial phrase to define. To get oriented, Edmund Erde (1996) suggested associating conflicts of interest with the general concept of *trust in a social role*. Professional roles are often seen as generating *fiduciary relationships*, defined as relationships in which one holds something in trust for another. To do the work, the professional requires considerable discretion and power over the life and health of the patient. The average patient lacks the knowledge to judge critically what the professional is doing. Therefore, the patient has no choice but to trust the professional. For this reason, we generally hold fiduciaries to a high standard of behavior (Rodwin and Okamoto 2000). Other people generally have to trust those occupying the roles to efficiently and responsibly perform those duties. Conflicts of interest address one way that those duties might be threatened.

From Erde's analysis, one can develop a definition of conflict of interest as follows. A conflict of interest exists in medicine when all of the following are true:

- The physician has a duty to advocate for the interests of the patient (or public).
- The physician is also subject to other interests—either his or her own or those of a third party.
- The physician becomes a party to certain social arrangements.
- Those arrangements, as viewed by a reasonable onlooker, would tempt a person of normal human psychology to neglect the patient's or the public's interests in favor of the physician's (or third party's) interests. (Brody 2011)

Let us illustrate this definition by thinking of the physicians who wrote the Medtronic-sponsored articles about the absence of adverse reactions to rhBMP-2:

- The physicians (reporting on medical research, relied upon by others to be true) had a duty to generally advocate for the interests of patients.
- The physicians also became involved in other interests arising from their association with Medtronic (including the money to be made and their assumptions regarding the superior performance of rhBMP-2).
- The physicians became party to certain social arrangements (royalties and consulting fees paid by Medtronic, apparently hidden by not being explicitly tied to rhBMP-2).
- These arrangements appear to have led the physicians to underreport the actual adverse reactions caused by rhBMP-2 in the studies, thereby creating a misleading impression of the safety of the chemical.

The phrase "appear to have led" highlights the unknowns in this account. It may have been purely by chance, or through some other legitimate factor, that the results of the Medtronic physicians' experiments were unlike those of other investigators, and those physicians honestly reported their findings. This example further illustrates one of Erde's concerns about conflicts of interest—that its bad outcomes are suspected much more often than actually documented. In the Medtronic case, the difference between studies performed by paid versus disinterested scientists was between ten and fifty times the risk of complications. Systematic reviews of differences between studies funded by drug companies and by neutral parties routinely show a four to five times greater likelihood among the former of the company's drug being shown to be superior (Lexchin et al. 2003;

Perlis et al. 2005). In one recent study of systematic reviews of studies of sugar-sweetened beverages and obesity, 83 percent of the findings contained in papers showing no conflicts of interest concluded that the use of such beverages is associated with obesity, whereas 83 percent of the findings in papers by conflicted authors stated inability to discover any association (Bes-Rastrollo et al. 2013). However, one cannot exclude the possibility that the results of any given study are based solely on purely honest experimental and interpretive measures.

## DESCRIPTIVE AND PERFORMATIVE ASPECTS

Erde then suggested some further distinctions, as shown in Table 12.1. Erde argued that most uses of the term *conflict of interest* had both a descriptive and a performative intent. The speaker attempts to inform listeners how the world is arranged so that they will take appropriate action based on their moral assessment of that arrangement. He recognized that the term was used almost exclusively in situations leading to moral unease if not actual moral disapproval.

The two descriptive possibilities Erde foresaw are:

1. The individual appears motivated to act in a way that might compromise a professional duty because of the existence of a competing interest.

2. Social arrangements exist that might tempt the individual to act contrary to professional duties, although the individual is highly motivated to remain true to those duties.

The social arrangements in possibility 2 might include general relations with pharmaceutical sales representatives, monies paid for consulting arrangements with industry, and the like. A common response from industry defenders is how silly it would be to suggest that a physician can be bought for a sandwich or a doughnut. If one were to interpret that charge under the heading of "motives," then it would seem reasonable to ask how valuable a gift one would have to receive to tilt one's motives away from scientific integrity and in the direction of commercialism. However, under the general heading of "social arrangements," the question is different. Physicians become used to social arrangements in which they routinely receive gifts from industry. Each gift is perhaps of little value. What ultimately sways their allegiance, if it is swayed, is not any individual gift or the sum of these gifts. Rather, it is the general sense that one is entitled to these gifts and that one then owes a sense of loyalty and gratitude to the gift giver. Many misplaced objections to industry

SOURCE: Adapted from Erde 1996.

***Table 12.1.*** *Aspects of Conflict of Interest Decisions.* **ADAPTED FROM ERDE 1996.** © **GALE, CENGAGE LEARNING.**

conflicts of interests assume that one's personal motives are being questioned, when instead a more subtle network of social arrangements is being pointed out.

The performative possibilities are:

- No breach of professional duty has yet occurred. The personal motives or social arrangements seem to tempt the individual in the direction of such a breach. Therefore, a warning is appropriate.
- A breach of professional duty has already occurred; the responsible individual must now be held accountable.

Again, the seriousness of the charge of conflict of interest depends on which of these two can be shown. In most instances related to pharmaceutical marketing, it is much easier to demonstrate a temptation to breach one's duty rather than an actual breach.

## FURTHER DIFFICULTIES

These observations raise questions about when conflicts of interest in medicine should be labeled and avoided. Consider the fact that physicians are paid for their services. No one has yet devised a system that will pay physicians when, and only when, they provide beneficial care for patients. Fee-for-service schemes risk paying physicians when they do procedures that are not beneficial, salaries and capitated payments risk rewarding physicians even when they refuse to do needed procedures, and pay-for-performance schemes have numerous problems of their own. At the same time, no one has discovered a way to get physicians to provide needed services for the population without paying them. Therefore, even when all known payment methods include some conflicts of interest, it seems necessary to pay physicians in one way or another.

Conflicts of interest arising from payments from drug and device manufacturers seem on further analysis to present a different situation. Examples of these behaviors are seen in the 2010 film *Love & Other Drugs*. In this romantic comedy, Jamie Randall is a successful pharmaceutical representative who is wooing a patient that he sees at a physician's office. The film is based on the 2005 book *Hard Sell*, a real-life memoir by Jamie Reidy about selling Viagra. Both demonstrate salespeople trying to become friendly with physicians, giving away free samples, and offering free meals, all in an attempt to encourage a physician to prescribe their drug more than the competitor's. In fiction and in real life, practicing physicians and medical investigators may receive any of the following from manufacturers:

- Free meals accompanied by brief discussions of drugs by sales representatives
- Other gifts, such as textbooks and office materials
- Trips to medical conferences
- Advertisements in medical journals and on television
- Continuing medical education financed by the drug industry
- Industry support for professional societies and organizations
- Research grants
- Consulting fees related to research
- Editorial assistance in preparing articles for publication (the extreme version is ghostwriting, in which the article is written by drug company staff but appears under the physician's name)

*Jake Gyllenhaal (left) and Oliver Platt in* Love & Other Drugs, *a 2010 romantic comedy about philandering pharmaceutical sales rep Jamie Randall (played by Gyllenhaal).* The film, based on the book Hard Sell, *a real-life memoir about selling Viagra, features salespeople trying to influence physicians—giving away free samples, offering free meals—in an attempt to encourage a doctor to prescribe their company's drug more frequently than the competitor's.* **PHOTOS 12/ALAMY.**

Moreover, these influences may occur at several levels. Individual physicians may be approached for meals and gifts. Research support may be granted to an academic department or school. Funds may be given to a professional society. Medical journals may receive money from companies that is difficult to ignore. The medical profession as a whole may be presented with a compelling account of a disease that favors treatment with brand-name drugs, whereas equally plausible accounts that favor nondrug therapy may receive much less coverage.

It is not necessary for physicians to accept free meals and other gifts, consulting fees, and other rewards from these companies to perform their medical responsibilities. The social arrangement provided by those gifts and fees are long-standing and have become commonplace, but they are nonessential for medical practice.

The social arrangements that now characterize typical payments from drug and device companies generally appear to have two characteristics:

1. The arrangements carry a serious risk of undermining the public trust in medicine and its social role.
2. The arrangements are avoidable—physicians can fulfill their social roles without them. (Brody 2011)

## OPPOSING VIEWS

Although concerns about conflicts of interest appear to be the majority view, some believe that closer relations with industry are wiser than an arm's-length posture. One typical statement is:

> Industry provides the backbone to healthcare; it is responsible for the design and development of hospitals, operating theatres, imaging equipment, and sophisticated surgical instruments and many other key elements of health-care provision, including medicines. It is imperative that scientists and clinicians collaborate with industry on these developments if we are to continue to have a health service that is innovative and meets the need of new health challenges. (Forsyth 2014, g7197)

Of course, such a view is compatible with criticisms of specific industry actions. A few critics have taken more striking positions of support for industry. Thomas Stossel has argued that "conflicts of interest" is empirically meaningless and driven instead by ideology (Stossel 2007a, 2007b). Michael Weber has attacked the term as "pejorative and misleading" (Weber 2009, 533). Philosopher Lance Stell has claimed, "The frame 'conflict of interest' carries bias, and begs the moral questions: what are the costs and benefits associated with the relationships?" (Stell 2010, 28).

To a large extent, these critics view the world differently from the more common view represented by most who use the term *conflicts of interest* (Abramson 2004; Angell 2004; Avorn 2004; Brody 2007; Kassirer 2005). The former group sees the pharmaceutical and device industries as continually advancing medical science and improving the quality of care. The episodes stressed by the common view, in which major harms have occurred because of the overpromotion of flawed medicines, are seen by the critics as merely a few bad apples in the barrel. For example, the risk of increased cardiovascular events among patients taking the analgesic rofecoxib (Vioxx) was shown at least as early as 2000, although the drug company made efforts to conceal it until Vioxx was taken off the market in 2004 (Curfman, Morrissey, and Drazen 2005). It was later calculated that between 88,000 and 140,000 additional cases of serious coronary artery disease were caused by the continued use of rofecoxib in the United States during those four years (Graham et al. 2005). The majority view was that this discovery was probably just the tip of the iceberg and that many similar adverse drug events had gone unreported, considering the unusual amount of extra attention paid to the cyclooxygenase-2 (COX-2) analgesics (Wright 2002). The critics would presumably reply either that rofecoxib was an unusually unsafe drug, or that its dangers had been vastly miscalculated, or both.

## PROPOSED SOLUTIONS

We have seen that conflicts of interest with regard to the pharmaceutical and device industries do, under certain circumstances, pose considerable ethical dangers. What, then, ought to be done to mitigate the problem? The complexity of the issue is indicated by the lack of convincing, practical solutions.

A group from the University of Oklahoma, led by Jensen T. Mecca, sought advice to resolve conflicts of interest from a multidisciplinary group of faculty investigators (Mecca et al. 2015). They identified five approaches to conflicts of interest:

1. Disclosure,

2. Self-removal,

3. Accommodation,

4. Denial,

5. Recognition of complexity.

Most professional and academic journals require authors to disclose all financial conflicts of interest when they submit the article for consideration in publication. These disclosures are usually printed alongside the article.

Disclosure of a conflict of interest is a necessary first step, but ultimately it is an inadequate response. For instance, to report that an author has ties with Company X usually does not inform journal readers what interests Company X has in the outcome of the study. The research might be about a drug manufactured by Company X, and the question is whether the study overstates evidence in favor of the drug. The research might be about a drug that is a major competitor to a product made by Company X, and the question is whether the research unfairly makes the competitor's drug appear worse than it is. What the alert reader needs to know to accurately judge the conflicts of interest pertaining to any one article is generally more than is stated in usual disclosures, but it would become unduly burdensome if routinely required.

If the disclosure solution is usually only partial, then self-removal—requiring that any investigator who has any appearance of conflict of interest not do the research—seems extreme and is ill-suited when conflict of interest generally suggests a suspicion of a possible breach of ethics ("warnings") rather than an actual violation. If disclosure is often an inadequate solution, then self-removal would appear to be overly harsh and would mean that some studies could not be conducted by the most appropriate investigators.

Approaches 3 and 4, accommodation and denial, are described by Mecca and colleagues as largely an avoidance strategy, in which conflict of interest is either denied or minimized. The fifth option, recognition of complexity, is at least honest and forthright, but it generally leads to no clear, practical solution. Thus, Mecca and colleagues describe the following typical outcomes in cases of conflicts of interest:

- Deny or minimize the problem.

- Disclose the conflict of interest—a necessary but hardly sufficient response.

- Remove oneself from the research completely—an extreme and often unnecessary response.

- Admit the complexity of the situation, without any ability to recommend a practical solution.

None of these options provides an optimal ethical framework.

## LEVELS OF THE PROBLEM

Sarah Wadmann, a health services researcher at the University of Copenhagen, offers an in-depth study of Danish hypertension research, 78 percent of which is funded by industry (Wadmann 2014). The investigators accept per-capita contract payments from the drug industry and generally find that these payments provide additional funds so that they can do needed research on the side. Wadmann reports that these scientists see themselves as running a research "business." They see industry ties not as binding and restrictive, but as generating independence and autonomy. The funds allow investigators to pay residents and PhD students and to support preparations for future grant submissions. According to Wadmann, industry collaboration becomes a moral obligation for the medical research collective.

This relationship between investigator and industry is not without tensions. The specific research required by the companies, and paid for under contract, is often seen by the investigators as routine and even boring. The side projects that they can do with the leftover funds become, for them, the "real" research. The companies then struggle to police these arrangements where investigators are suspected of placing their maximum efforts into studies that are not the ones that the industry needs or is paying for. In addition, investigators are sensitive to charges of conflicts of interest; therefore, they are anxious to claim that they personally make no money off of these arrangements.

Wadmann concludes that the end result is a "blame game" when conflicts of interest are described solely in financial terms. It is assumed that motives of financial gain are the major factor, and political priorities in the public-private collaboration are often overlooked. Here, Wadmann shows the advantages of Erde's (1996) framework, in which "social arrangements" can substitute for "motives" and generally provide a more accurate description of the situation.

Wadmann restricts her perspective to relationships between the individual investigator and industry. The problem is that neither side has any motive to say what the difficulty really is—the questionable scientific worth of much industry-sponsored research. If one were to expand one's purview beyond that of individual investigators, one might decide that the real question is why politicians in Denmark and most other advanced countries insist on allowing industry to foot the bill for the huge majority of research and why they will not vote for more research funding from public sources.

The ethics of the relationship between health care and the pharmaceutical and device industries ultimately require close attention to relations at many different levels, from the individual to social and governmental (Brody 2007). For example, several US authors have called for the creation of a new division of the National Institutes of Health (NIH) (Angell 2004; Avorn 2004; Brody 2007; Krimsky 2003). The goal of this division is to reverse the present tendency to have drug companies directly pay for so much pharmaceutical research. Firms currently pay investigators to do the required research, which gives the company effective control over the conduct of the research trial and the way that it is eventually reported in a medical journal. It also creates a system in which physician-investigators who do research the way that the company wishes, even if the full truth is sacrificed, are first in line for later research grants. Under the various proposals for a reformed system, the drug firms would specify the sort of research needed, and pay the funds to the NIH section, which would independently contract with investigators to conduct the research. The likelihood of getting further research funds in the future would presumably then depend on the quality of the study and not on whether the investigators found results that favored the marketing of the drug.

Attorney Marc Rodwin has noted that it is often easier to ensure the avoidance of conflicts of interest than to monitor the behavior of fiduciaries in the face of conflicts of interest (Rodwin and Okamoto 2000). Allowing drug companies to continue to directly fund research, while hoping to monitor the research to prevent unduly favoring the companies' drugs, is an example of the latter approach. The problem is that the monitoring of the research has to occur at such a fine grain of detail that the plan becomes unrealistic. It is relatively easier to adopt a major change in the relationship between the party paying for the research (the drug company) and the party actually overseeing the research (the new NIH division).

However, Rodwin also noted that in changing the incentives to increase services and the incentives to reduce services, one often ends up creating new conflicts of interest. In the end, he favors a power-sharing arrangement among the various sectors—physicians, hospitals, patients, insurers, and drug and device manufacturers—that he believes will provide an overall balance of interests.

## BOUNDARY CROSSINGS AND BOUNDARY VIOLATIONS

Financial conflicts of interest represent one example of physicians being tempted to prioritize personal interests over professional values. Boundary issues present a similar set of circumstances. The patient-caregiver relationship is notably unequal, with the patient in a more vulnerable and the caregiver in the more powerful position. Boundaries generally assist a patient in maintaining clarity about the nature and limitations of the relationship with the caregiver. As part of this relationship, the patient ought to be provided with a connection that will serve the ends of healing and protection from harm (Sawyer and Prescott 2011).

It is common to distinguish boundary *crossings* from boundary *violations* (Martinez 2000; Nasrallah, Maytal, and Skarf 2009; Sawyer and Prescott 2011). Boundary crossings are generally nonpejorative labels given to practices that may or may not be justified and beneficial to patients. Boundary violations suggest that the patient has been coerced or exploited and that harm to the patient far exceeds benefit.

At one extreme, physicians engaging in sex with patients would clearly represent a serious boundary violation. At the other extreme, a physician might briefly describe a bit of

| Type | Risk of harm to patient and relationship | Coercive and exploitative elements | Potential of benefit to patient and relationship | Professional intentions and motives | Recommendations | Examples |
|---|---|---|---|---|---|---|
| I | High | Present | None or low | Professional self-interests over patient interests | Discouraged and prohibited | Sexual contacts with patients |
| II | High | Ambiguous | Low | Professional self-interests blur patient interests | Rarely justified; highly discouraged | Professional offers patient work at low pay in professional's home |
| III | Low–middle | Absent | Middle–high | Patient interests predominate over professional self-interests | Justified; encouraged as benefit increases | Going to lunch with patient |
| IV | None–low | Absent | Middle–high | Patient interests over professional self-interest | Strongly encouraged and justified as benefit increases | Home visits; sharing some personal information |

SOURCE: Adapted from Martinez 2000.

*Table 12.2. Graded-Risk Model of Boundary Crossings.* **ADAPTED FROM MARTINEZ 2000.** © GALE, CENGAGE LEARNING.

his or her own background or experiences, such as an episode of illness or a reaction to a drug, in the process of discussing a similar situation with a patient. This disclosure would be a minor boundary crossing, and assuming proper caution and discretion could easily be the favored course of action.

A psychiatrist, Richard Martinez, has noted that much of the literature on boundary issues has taken a "slippery-slope" approach (Martinez 2000). On this view, any boundary crossing is potentially dangerous because a nonharmful action of a milder nature is at risk for leading to further actions that are coercive or exploitive. Martinez thinks the slippery-slope perspective fails to take into account the fact that some boundary crossings may be appropriate and justified. These defensible boundary crossings might focus more on the humanistic aspects of medical care and lead to more innovative ways of helping patients.

Martinez favors a graded-risk model over the more usual slippery-slope approach. By this model, he divides boundary crossings into four types, as presented in Table 12.2.

An illustration of a boundary crossing that Martinez would classify as type III or IV is discussed in a detailed case study by Elizabeth Vig and Mary Beth Foglia (2014). A terminally ill patient, long known to a physician and nurse before the illness, repeatedly invited the two of them out to a steak dinner. The patient greatly enjoyed good food, hated to cook, and disliked going to restaurants alone. The physician and nurse consulted their local ethics program and reviewed several considerations. In the end, the physician bought the steak, and she and the nurse prepared dinner at the nurse's home, to which the patient was invited. The dinner in the end was a success from everyone's standpoint.

As the physician and nurse went down through the ethicists' list of concerns, the possible negative effect of the dinner, under various alternative scenarios, was discussed at length. However, the damage potentially done to the patient and to the relationship by refusing to have the dinner was not thoroughly considered. The patient could easily have become offended and disturbed by the failure of the physician and nurse to respond to a well-meant, innocent request. This factor seems a good argument against a slippery-slope reasoning approach and in favor of Martinez's graded-risk approach.

Much of the work on boundary crossings has been done by mental health professionals. These professionals are more likely than other health workers to have patients whose reactions may be difficult to predict and who may interpret events in unusual ways. These factors appear to justify different approaches to boundary crossings. For example, consider a patient receiving counseling, who becomes especially animated and engaged in the conversation just as the scheduled time is about up. A primary care physician counseling the patient might appropriately feel it a justified, minor boundary crossing to allow the visit to run overtime on this occasion and only to intervene if the patient seems intent on repeating the extension at future visits. A mental health professional might feel it necessary to end the visit at the agreed-upon time and to feel that allowing the visit to run over creates an unfortunate precedent. This difference in viewpoint appears justified based on the different populations served.

## SELF-REFERRAL

In addition to pharmaceuticals and boundary crossings, a third area for conflicts of interest is physicians' referrals of patients to facilities that the physicians own. Jean Mitchell provided a general review of studies of self-referrals to laboratories and imaging facilities. For example, in Florida, 45 percent more magnetic resonance imaging (MRI) scans were performed for Medicare beneficiaries in the late 1980s, with almost all of the extra scans being performed in physician-owned facilities; the total charges for MRI scans performed in these physician-owned imaging centers exceeded the national average by 118 percent. In general, physicians owning these facilities referred patients two to four times more frequently for tests (Mitchell 1996).

A particular source of concern is physician-owned specialty hospitals. Specialty hospitals, such as children's hospitals, cancer hospitals, and psychiatric hospitals, are generally not owned by physicians. In 2010, there were only 265 physician-owned hospitals among approximately 7,000 US hospitals, but the attention paid to this group has been disproportionately large (Cole 2013).

The creation of this sort of hospital is related to the Stark law of the early 1990s, which sought to prohibit self-referral and kickbacks but also created safe harbors. One safe harbor was the "whole hospital exception." Physicians were prohibited from referring their patients to a section of a hospital that they partly owned, but they were allowed referrals if their ownership was in the entire hospital.

To a critic, physician-owned specialty hospitals appear to be a use of the Stark law exception to negate the actual intended purpose of the law. The new hospitals—providing services such as orthopedics or cardiology—resemble much more those sections of hospitals to which the Stark law intended to prohibit self-referrals. Physician-owned specialty hospitals often lack sections and services, especially emergency departments, that one would expect to find in a "whole hospital" (Cole 2013).

Physician-owned specialty hospitals are disproportionately located in a small number of states that lack certificate-of-need laws. They are overwhelmingly for-profit and tend to admit less severely ill patients with good insurance and to avoid Medicaid admissions. The typical physician who owns a part of a specialty hospital typically also has privileges in a general hospital and will selectively refer the more-profitable patients to the first site. A general hospital routinely offers services that are both well and poorly reimbursed and aims to keep a balance between them. Physicians who own specialty hospitals upset this balance by referring the more lucrative patients to the specialty hospital and restricting their referrals to the general hospital to the poorest-paying patients (Babu, Rosenow, and Nahed 2011).

Physicians stand to make significant money from these arrangements. Partial ownership of a specialty hospital ideally represents an opportunity to "triple-dip"—the physician is paid for doing a surgical procedure, is paid a share of the profits made by the hospital, and finally earns additionally as the total value of the investments increase. One specialty hospital in Austin, Texas, was reported to have advertised to physicians that from an initial US$4 million investment, they could make a profit of US$55 million over six years (Kahn 2006).

Proponents of physician-owned hospitals claim several advantages. They claim that these hospitals can operate more efficiently, enhancing patient care, increasing patient choice, and operating as a positive competitive option in the marketplace (Cole 2013). They also stress that physician owners can have more direct influence on policies than is now the case in the more usual general hospital, especially one that has been subjected to multiple mergers (Iglehart 2005). Critics cite the basic problem of conflicts of interest, arguing that when so much money can be made, the money might easily take priority over the quality of patient care (Kahn 2006). Because of the effects of competition, the deleterious consequences of conflicts of interest are not restricted to specialty hospitals, but spill over into nearby general hospitals (Cole 2013).

The critical perspective so far has been dominant. The Patient Protection and Affordable Care Act (2010) restricted the formation of new physician-owned hospitals in the United States, requiring them to have additional features, such as more twenty-four-hour coverage and emergency departments. Although one major court suit opposing these new restrictions was rejected, the situation appears far from legally settled (Cole 2013).

# CONCLUSION

Erde summarizes:

> [One could] say … that the physician acted from a [conflict of interest] even though he lacked any sense of conflict. This strengthens the argument that [conflicts of interest] constitute a family resemblance both to cases of motives and to causes (social structures) that undermine trust in clinicians. And, as a further point about the meaning of the phrase, we can say that a [conflict of interest] can properly be mentioned even if the physician does not do wrong, that is, even if the [conflict of interest] does not mature into a breach of obligation. For he may both resist temptation and, without having had any temptation, be immersed in social structures that are compromising. Both of these are part of what we bring into focus by means of the concept of [conflict of interest]. (Erde 1996, 27, italics omitted)

In addition:

> Thus far, we have found that to have a [conflict of interest] is neither to be in a state of temptation nor in a dilemma, for although these might pertain, it is also true that neither must. Rather, to have a [conflict of interest] is to be in a situation in which one might plausibly be thought to do something immoral due to a motivation that might tempt most role holders (or this individual). The implication is that many persons of typical moral fiber would be likely to neglect the duties of their roles for the sake of their own values of any sort (not just economic, safety, friendship, etc.). (Erde 1996, 30)

Let us return to some of the examples in this chapter. Boundary violations of the sort that Martinez has labeled types I and II, such as having sex with patients, seem a clear-cut example of serious breaches of moral duty. The evidence also suggests that self-referral to a hospital or facility of which one owns a partial share is so likely to lead to the overuse of medical resources, and/or higher costs to patients, that it should also be morally prohibited.

The numerous social structures within which physicians operate to take advantage of conflicts of interest with pharmaceutical and device manufacturers present a much broader target. We have seen that the most common attempts to police these activities tend to yield more confusion than insight, with physicians being told either to avoid all conflicts of interest or else that merely proclaiming the conflict is sufficient (Mecca et al. 2015).

Erde (1996) has one suggestion that seems to move matters closer to resolution. He recommends, as a thought experiment, turning an argument about a possible conflict of interest into a public complaint about its being betrayed. For example, in the InFuse case, the question is: Would a spine surgeon complain publicly about not being paid a consulting fee amounting to as much as millions of dollars in exchange for performing a study in which it is likely that the risks attached to the use of the procedure would be underreported? Stating the issue in this way is tantamount to deciding it, because it seems obvious that no spine surgeon would be willing to seek publicity in this fashion.

Consider another case. A surgeon has invented a new device. It has passed all necessary prior research and is now ready for its first trial in humans. The inventor of the device is the most skilled at using it, and to ask other surgeons to do the trial would be to ask the research subjects to consent to suboptimal conditions. The device inventor has a financial stake in the device's success. He has also organized a review system that will subject all of his decisions, in the course of the research, to extra scrutiny with regard to patient safety. It would appear that a good case could be made for allowing the inventing surgeon to play a key role in the research, despite the conflict of interest. In addition, the surgeon would presumably not hesitate to publicly make the case.

While Erde's suggestion for testing conflicts of interest seems to hold promise, it is worrisome that it seems capable of revealing only conflicts that occur at the individual level. One of the problems in the relationship between medicine and the pharmaceutical industry (for example) is that the relationship is multilayered, and the individual physician represents only one component of a complex system (Brody 2007). In addition, both sides of the relationship, the physicians and the drug companies, have strong incentives to hide the true nature and extent of their interests. (Recall in the InFuse case study how Medtronic aided spine surgeons in pretending that their consulting fees were being paid for unrelated reasons.) A good deal more work will need to be done regarding conflicts of interest in medicine before substantial progress can be made.

## Summary

Conflicts of interest arise frequently in medicine, where one is supposed to prioritize patient care but is understandably concerned with self-interest. These conflicts of interest represent a wide variety of possible cases. In some, moral rules have clearly been violated. In others, there are grounds for initial suspicion, and warnings may be due about proceeding farther. In at least a few instances, the action may on final analysis be praiseworthy.

Altruism regarding patients is highly regarded, whereas self-interest is often frowned upon although it is secretly encouraged. This means that much of the discussion about conflicts of interest is not completely honest—physicians tend to claim altruism as their sole motive and to deny self-interested intentions. In the end, honest and persistent self-inquiry may be the best ethical tool to minimize problems caused by conflicts of interest at the individual level. At social and organizational levels, new regulations and laws will be required.

## Bibliography

Abramson, John. *Overdo$ed America: The Broken Promise of American Medicine*. New York: HarperCollins, 2004.

Angell, Marcia. *The Truth about the Drug Companies: How They Deceive Us and What to Do about It*. New York: Random House, 2004.

Avorn, Jerry. *Powerful Medicines: The Benefits, Risks, and Costs of Prescription Drugs*. New York: Knopf, 2004.

Babu, Maya A., Joshua M. Rosenow, and Brian V. Nahed. "Physician-Owned Hospitals, Neurosurgeons, and Disclosure: Lessons from Law and the Literature." *Neurosurgery* 68, no. 6 (2011): 1724–1732.

Bes-Rastrollo, Maira, Matthias B. Schulze, Miguel Ruiz-Canela, and Miguel A. Martinez-Gonzalez. "Financial Conflicts of Interest and Reporting Bias regarding the Association between Sugar-Sweetened Beverages and Weight Gain: A Systematic Review of Systematic Reviews." *PLoS Medicine* 10, no. 12 (2013): e1001578.

Brody, Howard. "Clarifying Conflict of Interest." *American Journal of Bioethics* 11, no. 1 (2011): 23–28.

Brody, Howard. *Hooked: Ethics, the Medical Profession, and the Pharmaceutical Industry.* Lanham, MD: Rowman and Littlefield, 2007.

Carragee, Eugene J., Alexander J. Ghanayem, Bradley K. Weiner, et al. "A Challenge to Integrity in Spine Publications: Years of Living Dangerously with the Promotion of Bone Growth Factors." *Spine Journal* 11, no. 6 (2011): 463–468.

Carreyrou, John, and Tom McGinty. "Top Spine Surgeons Reap Royalty, Medicare Bounty." *Wall Street Journal,* December 20, 2010. http://www.wsj.com/articles/SB1000 14240527487033952045760240233361023138.

Cole, Cristie M. "Physician-Owned Hospitals and Self-Referral." *Virtual Mentor* 15, no. 2 (2013): 150–155.

Curfman, Gregory D., Stephen Morrissey, and Jeffrey M. Drazen. "Expression of Concern: Bombardier et al., 'Comparison of Upper Gastrointestinal Toxicity of Rofecoxib and Naproxen in Patients with Rheumatoid Arthritis.'" *New England Journal of Medicine* 353, no. 26 (2005): 2813–2814.

Erde, Edmund L. "Conflicts of Interest in Medicine: A Philosophical and Ethical Morphology." In *Conflicts of Interest in Clinical Practice and Research,* edited by Roy G. Spece, David S. Shimm, and Allen E. Buchanan, 12–41. New York: Oxford University Press, 1996.

Forsyth, Stewart. "Re: Medical Journals and Industry Ties." Rapid Response letter. *The BMJ* 349 (2014): g7197.

Gagnon, Marc-Andre, and Joel Lexchin. "The Cost of Pushing Pills: A New Estimate of Pharmaceutical Promotion Expenditures in the United States." *PLoS Medicine* 5, no. 1 (2008): e1.

Graham, David J., D. Campen, R. Hui, et al. "Risk of Acute Myocardial Infarction and Sudden Cardiac Death in Patients Treated with Cyclo-Oxygenase 2 Selective and Non-selective Non-steroidal Anti-inflammatory Drugs: Nested Case-Control Study." *Lancet* 365, no. 9458 (2005): 475–481.

Iglehart, John K. "The Emergence of Physician-Owned Specialty Hospitals." *New England Journal of Medicine* 352, no. 1 (2005): 78–84.

Jonsen, Albert R. "Watching the Doctor." *New England Journal of Medicine* 308, no. 25 (1983): 1531–1535.

Kahn, Charles N. "Intolerable Risk, Irreparable Harm: The Legacy of Physician-Owned Specialty Hospitals." *Health Affairs* 25, no. 1 (2006): 130–133.

Kassirer, Jerome P. *On the Take: How Medicine's Complicity with Big Business Can Endanger Your Health.* New York: Oxford University Press, 2005.

Krimsky, Sheldon. *Science in the Private Interest: Has the Lure of Profits Corrupted Biomedical Research?* Lanham, MD: Rowman and Littlefield, 2003.

Krumholz, Harlan M., and Joseph S. Ross. "A Model for Dissemination and Independent Analysis of Industry Data." *Journal of the American Medical Association* 306, no. 14 (2011): 1593–1594.

le Carré, John. *The Constant Gardener.* New York: Penguin, 2001.

Lexchin, Joel, Lisa A. Bero, Benjamin Djulbegovic, and Otavio Clark. "Pharmaceutical Industry Sponsorship and Research Outcome and Quality: Systematic Review." *BMJ* 326, no. 7400 (2003): 1167–1170.

Martinez, Richard. "A Model for Boundary Dilemmas: Ethical Decision-Making in the Patient-Professional Relationship." *Ethical Human Sciences and Services* 2, no. 1 (2000): 43–61.

Mecca, Jensen T., Carter Gibson, Vincent Giorgini, et al. "Researcher Perspectives on Conflicts of Interest: A Qualitative Analysis of Views from Academia." *Science and Engineering Ethics* 21, no. 4 (2015): 843–855. doi: 10.1007/s11948-014-9580-6.

Mitchell, Jean M. "Physician Joint Ventures and Self-Referral: An Empirical Perspective." In *Conflicts of Interest in Clinical Practice and Research,* edited by Roy G. Spece, David S. Shimm, and Allen S. Buchanan, 299–317. New York: Oxford University Press, 1996.

Nasrallah, Sandra M., Guy Maytal, and Lara M. Skarf. "Patient-Physician Boundaries in Palliative Care Training: A Case Study and Discussion." *Journal of Palliative Medicine* 12, no. 12 (2009): 1159–1162.

Perlis, Roy H., Clifford S. Perlis, Yelena Wu, et al. "Industry Sponsorship and Financial Conflicts of Interest in the Reporting of Clinical Trials in Psychiatry." *American Journal of Psychiatry* 162, no. 10 (2005): 1957–1960.

Rodwin, Marc A., and Etsuji Okamoto. "Physicians' Conflicts of Interest in Japan and the United States: Lessons for the United States." *Journal of Health Politics, Policy, and Law* 25, no. 2 (2000): 343–375.

Sawyer, Steven, and David Prescott. "Boundaries and Dual Relationships." *Sexual Abuse* 23, no. 3 (2011): 365–380.

Stell, Lance K. "Avoiding Over-Deterrence in Managing Physicians' Relationships with Industry." *American Journal of Bioethics* 10, no. 1 (2010): 27–29.

Stossel, Thomas P. "Divergent Views on Managing Clinical Conflicts of Interest." *Mayo Clinic Proceedings* 82, no. 8 (2007a): 1013–1014.

Stossel, Thomas P. "Regulation of Financial Conflicts of Interest in Medical Practice and Medical Research: A Damaging Solution in Search of a Problem." *Perspectives in Biology and Medicine* 50, no. 1 (2007b): 54–71.

US Senate Committee on Finance. *Staff Report on Medtronic's Influence on Infuse Clinical Studies*. October 2012. http://www.finance.senate.gov/imo/media/doc/Medtronic_Report1.pdf.

Vig, Elizabeth K., and Mary Beth Foglia. "The Steak Dinner—A Professional Boundary Crossing." *Journal of Pain and Symptom Management* 48, no. 3 (2014): 483–487.

Wadmann, Sarah. "Physician-Industry Collaboration: Conflicts of Interest and the Imputation of Motive." *Social Studies of Science* 44, no. 4 (2014): 531–554.

Weber, Michael A. "Academic Physicians Confront a Hostile World: The Creation of ACRE." *Journal of Clinical Hypertension* 11, no. 10 (2009): 533–536.

Wright, James M. "The Double-Edged Sword of COX-2 Selective NSAIDs." *Canadian Medical Association Journal* 167, no. 10 (2002): 1131–1137.

## FILM

*The Constant Gardener*. Dir. Fernando Meirelles. 2005. Based on the novel by John le Carré (New York: Penguin, 2001). Suspense-thriller based on efforts of a fictional drug company to conceal side effects of drugs for tuberculosis in Africa.

*Love & Other Drugs*. Dir. Edward Zwick. 2010. Comedy loosely based on the nonfiction book by Jamie Reidy, *Hard Sell: The Evolution of a Viagra Salesman* (Riverside, NJ: Andrews McMeel, 2005).

*Side Effects*. Dir. Kathleen Slattery-Moschkau. 2006. Comedy about drug detail salespersons based on the personal experiences of the director.

CHAPTER 13

# Clinical Ethics Consultation

**D. Micah Hester**
*Chief and Professor of Medical Humanities*
*University of Arkansas for Medical Sciences, Little Rock*

In season five of *Designing for the Sexes*, a television series on HGTV hosted by interior designer Michael Payne, a young couple, Jan and Dave, have recently purchased their first home together, but neither feels equipped to make design decisions about the living or dining room. The current furniture consists of matched, off-white couches against an off-white floor and walls. Although they both agree the room needs a facelift, their stated visions for the room differ wildly. Jan wants "a rich, stylish, eye-catching atmosphere." She likes "comfortable" and "casual." Dave, on the other hand, "envisions a simple blend of old and new, comfortable furnishings." He wants "rugged" and "a little bit country." Seemingly at an impasse, they are stuck in decorating paralysis, and the room remains bland and unloved by both parties.

Rather than continue to live with the space as is and realizing their own limitations, Jan and Dave call Payne to consult about it. His goal is to help create a space that both can enjoy and to resolve the design tensions that have Jan and Dave frustrated and ill at ease in their own home.

While their design struggles persist, imagine that Jan's mother, Betty, has recently had a stroke that has left her unable to speak for herself. Betty requires complex, intensive medical interventions, and should she survive her stay in the hospital, she would have to go to a nursing home that can deal with such complex care—a nursing home that most likely will be many hours from the family's hometown. Jan, as one of two daughters to Betty, is wrestling with what Betty would want and, thus, what is best for her. Jan believes that Betty is a fighter and would want every chance to continue living and get better. Betty's other daughter, Pam, believes that her mother has only a very small chance of "meaningful" recovery, and she believes it might be best to stop the intensive treatments and only provide comfort for Betty's pain and suffering until she dies. At an impasse, Jan, Pam, and Betty's physicians are unsure how best to proceed, and thus, they remain at status quo, with Betty lying in the intensive care unit for weeks. Jan wonders out loud whether there is a health-care equivalent to Michael—someone who can help work through these health-care decision differences to find a reasonable resolution for her mother's care.

Turns out there is.

## THE RESPONSIBILITIES OF HEALTH-CARE PROFESSIONALS

Medicine is neither easy to learn nor to practice. Health-care professionals are tasked with helping individuals (even society) live healthy lives. But to do this, several things must

279

happen. First, communities and governments must help develop the conditions for healthy living. Among other things, streams of water must be free of contaminants; sewage must be taken away from where people live; air must have oxygen in it and pollution out of it. Second, people must visit health-care professionals, both to help prevent illness and to treat disease or injury. Avoiding the physician or lacking access to medical care undermines the ability of health care to help. Finally, health-care providers must get to know not only the biophysiology of their patients, but also patient interests and values that shape the meaning of what "healthy living" means to each patient.

Given these three important requirements at the intersection of health care and healthy living, both states and their citizens, laypeople and patients, providers and other health-care professionals all have responsibilities, and these responsibilities rest on value determinations. Is it more important to provide clean water or to allow businesses small levels of contamination so that they can stay in business? Should access to health care be universal for all citizens of the state, thus raising tax levels, or should market forces be the primary factor in determining health-care access? Or, to make this all more specific and personal, what care options are best for Betty, and who is best positioned to make those decisions?

This latter set of questions that arises in hospitals and clinical settings is the catalyst for what is known as *clinical ethics consultations*. Since the mid-1970s, clinical ethics consultations, whether by individual ethicists, teams of consultants, or committees of health-care and lay professionals, have become increasingly common in large hospitals across the United States and internationally. But although this fairly young health-care practice is quite common, the decades to come will continue to see the practice of ethics consultation both adjust to the changes in medicine and grow with the needs of medical providers and patients alike.

This chapter will look at the purposes, premises, and practices of clinical ethics consultation. It will explore why they are requested, how consults are done, and how they might help. The chapter focuses on how the moral character of medicine results in the need for careful ethical reflection, on how ethicists can help in those reflections, and what occurs in a consultation that systematically moves reflection forward to help in patient care.

## THE ETHICAL WORLD OF MEDICINE

In the following scene from the television series *The West Wing*, at a preprimary presidential campaign talk in Vermont, Governor Jed Bartlet is speaking before a small audience in a VFW hall.

FARMER: Governor Bartlet, when you were a member of Congress, you voted against the New England Dairy Farm Compact. That vote hurt me, sir. I am a businessman, and that vote hurt me to the tune of, maybe, ten cents a gallon. … And I'm here, sir, and I'd like to ask you for an explanation.

[*Grumbling in audience; pause before responding*]

JED BARTLET: Yeah—I screwed you on that one—

FARMER: I'm sorry?—

JED BARTLET: I screwed you; you got hosed—

FARMER: Sir, I—

JED BARTLET: And not just you, a lot of my constituents. I put the hammer to farms in Concord, Salem. ... You guys got Rogered, but good.

Today, for the first time in history the largest group of Americans living in poverty are children. One in five children live in the most abject ... poverty any of us could imagine.... If fidelity to freedom and democracy is the code of our civic religion, then, surely, the code of our humanity is faithful service to that unwritten commandment that says, "We shall give our children better than we ourselves receive."

Let me put it this way: I voted against the bill because I did not want to make it hard for people to buy milk. I stopped money from flowing into your pocket. If that angers you, if you resent me, I completely respect that. But if you expect anything different from the President of the United States, you should vote for someone else.

Thanks very much, everybody. Hope you enjoyed the chicken.

(*The West Wing*, 2000)

*Ethics* is a term that lends itself to multiple meanings. Colloquially, the term *ethics* concerns how each individual deals with right and wrong, good and bad. As with Governor Bartlet's claim that what you see is what you would get as president, personal integrity and habits of action are at stake. We think of ethics, in this light, as speaking to who we are, the beliefs and interests that we take to be fundamental or integral to us, and the reputations we have and cultivate. Taken in this way, ethics is about *values* and *character*.

In addition, however, all individuals have their place in society. We all are members of a family, of communities, of professions—that is, role-based considerations come into play. From these roles arise commitments and obligations. Governor Bartlet owes his constituents an accounting for why he voted as he did. Married spouses should not cheat on each other or abandon the family. Community members should help one another in times of crisis and follow the laws of the society. Professionals should abide by the codes of conduct set forth by the profession itself. Again, the roles we play place on us responsibilities and obligations, and others hold us accountable for fulfilling these responsibilities. This use of ethics often is associated with judgments of what actions or behaviors are *right* and *wrong*.

Finally, carrying values is not unique to any one individual but is ubiquitous across humankind. Often, between personal interests, cultural values, professional and relational obligations, it is not uncommon that conflict will arise between people and even with(in) institutions. But such conflicting concerns can lead to questions about ends to be pursued and what means are appropriate in those pursuits. Children live in poverty; milk prices are high; farmers want to get fair pay. Whose values trump the other? Should state interests trump individual citizens? And whichever values trump, what ways are there to fulfill the values we believe should be championed? This way of seeing ethics can be characterized as weighing *good* and *bad, better* and *worse*.

The history of Western moral philosophy shows that many thinkers have attempted to determine which sense of ethics is the proper conception to hold. It seems clear, however, that each of the given meanings of ethics captures something important about moral life, and thus, no one of these three senses of ethics should be ignored, nor is any one of them always dominant. It is worth noting that each of us is a "values carrier," whether as a product of biology, nurturing, education, or some other means. Furthermore, we do, in fact, find ourselves in relation to others—familial, professional, and so forth—and those relationships commit us to others and to expectations for which we are held accountable. At the same time, in a finite universe of limited abilities and resources, with a plurality of individual and communal interests, we often are confronted by concerns for what we should do, and why.

Ethics, then, concerns each of these aspects of moral living—values (character), duties (roles), and goods (ends). We might say, then, the field of ethics—that is, the territory of values and interests covered by moral considerations—includes those *evaluations* of human (and some other animal) values-based conduct, both arising from and affecting character, which result in appraisals of good and bad, right and wrong.

If ethics, then, concerns human conduct, medical practice, as a form of human conduct, falls within the realm of ethics. Of course, that does not make medicine unique, but that is, in part, the point. Medical practice, like all human practice, implicates character, roles, and outcomes for patients and professionals alike. Although medicine does involve specialized knowledge and skill, that knowledge and skill are implemented in the service of human beings, affected by the values and interests of those it is in service to. As such, it is rife with ethical issues. Medicine's aim is to promote healthy living for patients through physiological and psychological interventions, and this is no insignificant matter to human beings. Medical decisions and actions, as well as the character of practitioners and patients, are readily on display, and the implications can be of intimate and vital human importance. As philosopher John Dewey (1859–1952) notes,

> Healthy living is not something to be attained by itself apart from other ways of living. A man needs to be healthy in his life, not apart from it, and what does life mean except the aggregate of his pursuits and activities? … [W]hat a man needs is to live healthily, and this result so affects all the activities of his life that it cannot be set up as a separate and independent good. (1920, 175)

Healthy living is personal and cultural, not just cellular and functional. As such, the challenge of providing good medicine is a moral, not simply a biophysiological, challenge. Health-care decisions are made in light not only of lab values and imaging studies but also of individual interests and communal values.

# WHY HEALTH-CARE ETHICS COMMITTEES AND CLINICAL ETHICS CONSULTATION?

> Patrick was born with Hirschsprung's disease, a disorder of the digestive tract, and after years of surgery to snip out parts of his intestine, he was left unable to digest food.… Patrick was … on a ventilator suffering from pneumonia, with a tube down his throat to help him breathe. He was conscious, and he was miserable. His feeding line was working in fits and starts, clogged by infection. He was being simultaneously kept alive and tortured by a nightmare of an antifungal drug called amphotericin B.
> …
>
> "He'll need a new line soon … ," [noted the physician]. "We know he'll need another one after that and another one after that. Do we keep opening his chest over and over? Without a new line, he'll starve. Which is worse?" …
>
> [Questions like these] seem dramatic and rare until you spend any time at all in a hospital. Then you realize that questions this complicated are asked every single day. (Belkin 1993, 4–7)

Given that medicine is a moral endeavor, medical practice requires moral sensitivity, even insight. As physician and bioethicist Edmund Pellegrino (1920–2013) has said, "In making the 'right' decision for an individual patient … , personal, social, economic, and psychological characteristics of the patient must be factored in" (1979, 181). As Albert Jonsen writes in *The Birth of Bioethics* (1998), to help develop that sensitivity and insight, over the past forty-plus years, health-care schools and colleges have provided ethics instruction, courses, and curricula. Although the content of that instruction varies widely among professional disciplines and colleges, the purpose of such education intends to make health-care professions better able to deal with the daily ethical issues and concerns that arise in their practices.

During the same forty-plus years, clinical ethics consultation has arisen as a professional practice in medical centers. Philosophers, religious ethicists, lawyers, clinicians, and others have stepped into the role of "ethics consultant," listening to complex cases, helping clarify ethical concerns, and even making recommendations about decision making and ethically appropriate care options. With several generations of health-care providers being taught ethics during their training, it is reasonable to ask why the practice of clinical ethics consultations exists and whether it is needed at all. Bioethicist Mark Aulisio raised this very concern when he notes, "Some have suggested that there is no need for ethics consultation, since doctors, nurses, and other health professionals can and should handle ethical issues as they arise" (Aulisio, Arnold, and Youngner 2003, 4). Furthermore, he adds, "some would argue that medical practice was done quite well without such outside intrusions as ethics committees and consultation services" (5). Let us follow this logic a bit.

It is hard to disagree with the claim that physicians and other health-care providers, themselves, have a responsibility to deal with ethical concerns as they arise. Particularly, if we argue that medicine is constitutively a moral practice, one simply cannot do medicine without accepting the moral implications of the practice. Take this analogy as an example of what this means: the heart and its functions are central to healthy living, and thus, to medical practice. In fact, every physician has training in cardiovascular physiology and pharmacology, to diagnose and treat heart-related illness. And yet, the medical profession has developed a subspecialty in cardiology, and we encourage the practice of consulting such subspecialists when patients have significant issues with their heart.

The reasons for such specializing in medicine is that the human body and healthy living are complex, not simple. Having the knowledge, skills, insights, and training necessary to deal with the intricacies of medicine requires special attention. Of course, every health-care provider requires some level of knowledge of all organ systems, among other things, but we would place patients in greater peril if we did not produce professionals capable of being able to hyperfocus on more delimited areas of medicine. Is ethics the kind of discipline and knowledge area that requires this kind of hyperfocus? On one view, maybe it is not. For all the discussion about duties and consequences and character, you might simply say that each of us is raised with values, and we are all confronted with questions of right or wrong and good or bad throughout our lives. Why is this not enough to be well-equipped in these matters?

We must be careful, however, not to confuse the field of ethics and confronting ethical concerns with the careful reflection and practice of ethics. The former is most assuredly a part of the human condition, but the latter requires training. Just think for a moment about Patrick's situation and the concerns and questions of his physician. In the everyday business of growing up in a family, with friends, becoming educated in school, maybe having religious values, what in all that would necessarily make any individual prepared to deal with the complexities and consequences of the decisions to be considered for Patrick? Motivating values must be identified; significant obligations must be met; potential consequences must be weighed. But which values matter, what obligations win, and how are consequences weighted? These are not easy questions for anyone to answer, but there are learned reflections that exist on these questions that most everyday people do not have the time to understand. The history of moral philosophy has given us many ethical theories and methods—Aristotle's (384–322 BCE) virtue ethics, Immanuel Kant's (1724–1804) deontology, John Stuart Mill's (1806–1873) utilitarianism, and Carol Gilligan's (1936–) ethics of care, casuistry, narrative ethics, pragmatism, and so forth—and the much briefer history of bioethics has a variety of reflective methodologies. However, short of a full-blown course in (bio)ethical theory and method, no one can be expected to have a firm handle on all of these theories. Short of such a robust education, reflections on ethical issues may be compromised.

Each of our actions is not performed in isolation, nor are policies written in a vacuum. *Reasons and justifications are necessary* components of ethical determinations, whether concerning particular situations or institutional policies. Furthermore, consistency of considerations is not unimportant either. Consistent reasoning stems from justified principled positions, and those positions arise from long processes of inquiry into the moral life itself. It is not good enough simply to care about the consequences of our actions for some issues and about our dutiful obligations toward others depending on our mood. We must be able to account for the legitimacy of the methods and theories that underlie the deliberations we perform and decisions we make.

Closer to home, we might also say that there is a "kind of progress possible through reflection in ethics" (Buermeyer 1923, 323), which may be noted in four types: First, ethical reflection can bring our own values to light, "values which we might otherwise overlook" (323). Second, reflection aids in clarifying our aims and desires. Third, ethical reflection allows us to separate wheat from chaff, helping "us see what problems really are most vital, and thus bring[ing] us nearer to actual solutions" (324). And fourth, reflection leads us to own our actions, making "our conduct more fully our own, more voluntary and less of a blind obedience to custom" (324).

These are laudable, even necessary, goals to strive for, and so, again, simply put, there is no reason to expect health-care professionals to be fully equipped to do this kind reflection without the aid of persons trained in ethics. Again, as Aulisio points out, "today's complex medical decision making goes on in a broader societal context of value heterogeneity and a growing recognition of the implications of individual rights for that decision making, which combine with the current clinical reality to create the need for ethics consultation" (Aulisio, Arnold, and Youngner 2003, 6).

## WHAT IS A HEALTH-CARE ETHICS COMMITTEE AND CONSULTATION SERVICE?

Julian Byrd ... had read of a few hospitals that had ethics committees, and he decided to form one at [his institution].... For several months, the small group discussed ethics only in the theoretical sense. They developed a list of committee bylaws and a statement of purpose, but they didn't hear a case. Then one morning in

October … Randy Gleason, the hospital's lawyer, arrived at a meeting with the tale of a seventy-three-year-old woman who had peripheral vascular disease. The circulation to one leg was so poor that the leg would have to be cut off. She refused the operation, and her doctor asked Randy for his opinion. The Ethics Committee was in business. (Belkin 1993, 69–70)

Beginning in the 1960s with decisions about who should get kidney dialysis, suggested by courts in the 1970s, required by the Baby Doe regulations in the 1980s, and proliferated in response to the Joint Commission on Accreditation of Healthcare Organizations' (known as the Joint Commission as of 2007) accreditation requirements in the 1990s, health-care ethics committees (HECs) are now mainstays of hospitals in the United States. According to Ellen Fox and her coauthors (2007), exact numbers are not available, but a conservative estimate would be that thirty thousand people (and probably double that) in the United States currently serve in some manner on an HEC.

*What is an ethics committee?* Most HECs were developed to be the mechanisms that handle ethically challenging issues in a hospital or other health-care institution. The membership of an ethics committee typically is composed of institutional staff members—physicians, nurses, social workers, even chaplains, administrators, and sometimes legal counsel (these last three groups are not always included because of conflict-of-interest concerns). Many employ community or unaffiliated people as well to serve as a check on institutional bias and to provide greater insight. When available, someone educated in philosophical or religious ethics is often included as well.

*What functions does an ethics committee serve?* The traditional threefold mission of an HEC has not changed substantially since the President's Commission for the Study of Ethical Problems in Medicine and Biomedical and Behavioral Research formulated it in 1983. The most visible and controversial role is to consult on difficult clinical decisions. Equally important, although sometimes forgotten, are the other two functions of an HEC: (1) formulating institutional policies (consistent with the organization's function and mission) to guide the professional staff in making ethical decisions, and (2) educating hospital personnel about these policies and about health-care ethics in general.

Not all committees perform all three functions, as some institutions have a separate ethics consult service and some ethics committees may do little to no policy review or other "organizational" ethics activities—instead, these may be done by other committees or by a compliance or ethics officer in the institution. The Joint Commission's mandate that ethical issues be handled in some way, however, does put emphasis on the function of case consultation, and consults may occur in three general ways:

- Singular consultant—an individual (one hopes well trained) is tasked (either by the institution or the committee) with consulting. That person would take the call and respond as needed. This process allows for maximum expediency and flexibility, but a minimum of perspective.

- Small team consult—some institutions use a small team (typically three to five people from the larger ethics committee) to consult. This process provides a bit less flexibility and expediency than the single-consultant model, but in turn, it provides more perspectives.

- Full committee consult—at least a quorum of the entire committee meets to discuss an ongoing case. Needless to say, this is the least expedient and flexible approach, but it maximizes the perspectives brought to bear.

The details of how a consult occurs will be specific to each institution. In fact, some institutions may use a combination of the consulting models just listed, depending on the type and source of the consult request. Furthermore, in most institutions, a consultation can be requested by a wide variety of people—not simply by attending physicians or unit directors, but by almost anyone in the institution, including patients and family members. Once a request comes in, the consultation process begins, and it is the purpose and process of consultation, whether by individuals, teams, or committees, that are the focus of the rest of this chapter.

## THE PURPOSE OF CONSULTATION

CARLA ASTON: When designing for couples, has there ever been one person in a relationship who tried to dominate all the creative decisions that needed to be made in a project? If so, how did you help the other half find and exert their voice?

MICHAEL PAYNE: Yes. This happened several times on *Designing for the Sexes*. One instance that sticks out in my mind was the time where the woman of the household actually said this on camera …

"*You don't need to speak with … Joe, because I actually do this sort of thing for a living.… So you don't need to speak with him at all.*"

Obviously, she was being completely dismissive of her husband. So, after learning long ago that you can say just about anything with a smile on your face, I replied …

"*Well that may be the case in the past, but this is now, and this is a show, and I really want to know what Joe feels about all this. I want to know his tastes, too.*"

After I made my point, I launched into asking her about her taste, her preferences, her style, and her likes and dislikes. Then I questioned her on what she didn't like about [the] room we were to design, why she wanted to change it, and what her expectations were.

After listening to her responses, I then—almost literally—turned my back on her and said …

"*Okay, Joe. Let's talk about this. What do you have in mind? What are you seeing that's going to be in this new space?*"

And whenever she would try to sort of jump in, I'd say, "*No. I really want to know what Joe feels like about this.*"

Honestly, the feedback I received was oftentimes better when I was spotlighting Joe, because he was speaking from the bottom of his heart.

Finally, after collecting his input and her input, I sat down and designed their space, making sure he got a lot of what he wanted, and she got a lot of what she wanted.

(Payne and Aston 2012)

Not unlike the competing differences that stimulated the design intervention at the opening of the chapter or the concerns expressed by Payne in this interview with Carla Aston, the practice of clinical ethics consultation arises in light of the complexity of health-care decision making and the diversity of values, interests, and beliefs that patients, families, and professionals carry with them into challenging medical contexts. Surely, health-care professionals are expected to develop an awareness and sensitivity to ethical issues in their practice, and patients and families have the responsibility to grapple with the ethical considerations that health status and decision making present, but being able to analyze, synthesize, and act on the ethical challenges may be too great a burden to place on people not otherwise trained in, or at least decidedly determined to provide, ethical analysis, especially when they have specific investments in the situation that might blind or bias them to outcomes that otherwise do not hold up to ethical scrutiny of the given situation.

> Mary is an infant with hypoplastic left heart syndrome (the left side of her heart is small and nonfunctioning) and other congenital anomalies that resulted in her living her entire nine months of life in the cardiac intensive care unit of a children's hospital. Her mother lives over an hour away and has two other young children. She visits Mary about every three to four weeks.

> Whenever Mary's mother is asked by the attending physician if she would like to continue intensive care and keep Mary as a "full code" (providing CPR [cardio-pulmonary resuscitation] if her heart stops), her mother says, "yes." The nurses at the bedside are distressed because they believe that Mary is suffering and that the care that is being provided is, in their words, "futile." They are also upset that the mother does not visit, and they believe that she is not truly an engaged parent. However, they feel compelled to continue their intensive treatments because of the stated wishes of Mary's mother.

While designers like Payne are called in to navigate design challenges between couples, clinical ethics consultations are employed in cases like Mary's to take on ethically difficult situations in health care, addressing moral matters head-on by filling the gaps in knowledge, skills, or even perspective. How this gap is (or should be) filled is a matter of some debate.

In its report, *Core Competencies for Healthcare Ethics Consultation*, the American Society for Bioethics and Humanities (ASBH) states, "Healthcare ethics consultation … is a set of services provided by an individual or group in response to questions from patients, families, surrogates, healthcare professionals, or other involved parties who seek to resolve uncertainty or conflict regarding value-laden concerns that emerge in health care" (ASBH 2011, 2). Again, medical practice is not merely about the conditions, function, and effects of human biophysiology. Health care is value laden. Clinical ethics consults, per ASBH, are directed toward "resolving" value-laden concerns that are "uncertain" or "in conflict." Accordingly, constitutive of clinical ethics consultation is an aim toward resolution. But not everyone agrees.

> In discussion with different stakeholders, it is discovered that the surgeons believe that further surgery for the heart could keep the child alive for many months, maybe a couple of years, if other co-morbidities do not make living impossible. Thus, they offer to keep Mary on intensive care if the mother desires. Also, Mary's mother has no transportation, and must rely on others to get her to the hospital.

Some argue that the aim of consultation is primarily both situational and "values" clarification. Admittedly, such clarification is not merely an end-in-itself, but it may provide a means to the end of resolving ethical dilemmas. However instrumental, situation and values clarification is taken by some to be a worthy "end in view" that, if achieved, marks the limits of clinical ethics consultations—ceding the responsibility to achieve "resolution" to the affected parties. Although such clarification is a useful, even necessary, part of a consultation, it ends precisely where many of the parties involved need the most help—namely, adjudicating and weighing the values at play to move forward in the case. Physicians feel obligated to offer surgery, even though the long-term prognosis is dismal. Nurses feel compelled to act on parental decisions, even though they believe those decisions are causing bad outcomes for Mary. Mary's mother chooses to continue to keep her child alive, but she is hampered by circumstances to share much in her daughter's life. For each of the affected parties, ethical challenges arise. And, again, recognizing and working through ethical issues takes training, not just life experience.

Given the pressures of health-care decision making and the kinds of conflicts (as in Mary's case) that create ethics consults, there is little dispute that the driving purpose of clinical ethics consultation is resolution, although debates about the form of and the parties affected by that resolution do remain.

## MODELS OF CONSULTATION

The following scene from the "Twelve Angry Men," a 1954 episode of *Studio One in Hollywood*, occurs in a jury room after a six-day trial of a nineteen-year-old male who is accused of killing his father.

[JUROR NUMBER] THREE: Do you really believe he's not guilty?

EIGHT: I don't know.

SEVEN: After six days, he doesn't know.

TWELVE: In six days I could learn calculus. This is A, B, C.

EIGHT: I don't believe that it is as simple as A, B, C.

THREE: I never saw a guiltier man in my life.

EIGHT: What does a guilty man look like? He is not guilty until we say he is guilty. Are we to vote on his face?

THREE: You sat right in court and heard the same things I did. The man's a dangerous killer. You could see it.

EIGHT: Where do you look to see if a man is a killer?

Some situations in life, like the preceding deliberation in "Twelve Angry Men," appear uncompromising. The parties are set off against each other. The decisions are resolute, although they also may be unspoken. This happens in legal matters, in relationships, in business, and certainly in health care. But ethics consultations, as we have said, aim at resolution, and if this is true, then consultation models should be structured to achieve that aim. In this light, some have suggested what ASBH has termed the *pure facilitation* (1998) or *pure consensus* (2011) model. This model is predicated on the idea that resolution is met through the development of consensus among the affected parties. Some individual values and practices are morally questionable, however, and the "pure" consensus model could lead to "resolutions" that "fall outside the boundaries of widely accepted ethical and legal norms and standards" (ASBH 2011, 7). Also, some ethical conflicts are morally intractable, and seeking consensus as the primary aim of a consult in those cases would necessarily leave the consult without resolution.

Two models, then, have been proposed that are intended to achieve resolution of an ongoing case, where possible, but not rely solely on group agreement to get there. These two models are *ethics facilitation* (ASBH 1998, 2011) and *bioethics mediation* (Dubler and Liebman 2004, 2011).

## ETHICS FACILITATION

Ethics facilitation is considered by ASBH to be "most appropriate" (ASBH 2011, 7) for clinical ethics consultation and is probably the most common method of consultation in the United States. It consists of helping to "elucidate issues, aid effective communication, and integrate perspectives of the relevant stakeholder" (7). Ethics facilitation relies on skills of active listening and the clarification of values. While it does not necessarily aim for recommendations, it "does not preclude making recommendations.... On the contrary, specific recommendations are often helpful and appropriate" (8).

## BIOETHICS MEDIATION

Even with the broad practice of ethics facilitation in US hospitals, bioethics mediation has become increasingly popular as a model for performing an ethics consultation. Although the facilitation approach often can be fairly unstructured and makes the consultant the locus for ethically evaluating the situation, bioethics mediation involves the consultant taking on the role as mediator to negotiate an ethically "principled resolution ... that is comfortable for all parties" (Dubler and Liebman 2011, 13). The mediator, rather than carrying the burden of fashioning an ethical outcome, works with the conflicting parties to ensure that each party is able to exercise his or her autonomy, that the decisions made are well informed, and that relevant aspects of the mediation remain confidential. The process begins with an ethically informed mediator and invites parties to the table to work through a dispute. Bioethics mediation must come to resolution, even if that resolution is "a series of default rules for determining who makes decisions" (Dubler and Liebman 2011, 24).

As noted, both facilitation and mediation as models of case consultation are implemented in the midst of ongoing patient situations. However, moral concerns often linger, regardless of outcomes for the patient, family, and health-care providers, and some have argued that it is in retrospect or, at least, in some distance from the actual experience, that ethical reflection can best occur. In this light, some have suggested that consultants do a form of "debriefing" with professionals. Dutch professionals (see, e.g., Molewijk et al. 2008) have implemented a process called *moral case deliberations* instead of providing bedside consultations.

## MORAL CASE DELIBERATIONS

The purpose of moral case deliberation is to provide a determined time and place in which professionals can reflect on moral aspects of their practice by reviewing cases. Although this can occur while a case is still ongoing, often this process happens after a case has been completed. Like ethics facilitation, moral case deliberation involves multiple people but is not necessarily aimed at a specific resolution or recommendation. Like bioethics mediation, the ethics consultant is not tasked with developing the moral evaluation but rather is trained to facilitate a structured discussion among the individuals who attend. Unlike both facilitation and mediation, moral case deliberation is restricted to professional participants, not families and patients.

Arguments have been made for each model of consultation described previously (as well as some others), but clinical ethics consultants are probably best served by having facility with each of the models and using one or the other depending on specifics of the situation at hand. But models are large frameworks that must be operationalized, and we will call that operationalizing a consultation *method*. Many methods of consultation have been suggested and are in use around the country. The Veterans Administration, for example, uses what they call the CASES method, in which a consult is broken into five steps: clarifying the consultation request, assembling the relevant information, synthesizing the information, explaining the synthesis, and supporting the consultation process. In "Ethics Consultation Process" (2012), Jeffrey Spike has suggested *GiNo's DicE*, an acronym to remind a consult of the necessary activities for a comprehensive consult: get information, negotiate options, document the consult, and evaluate the outcomes and processes. Similarly, Wayne Shelton and Dyrleif Bjarnadottir (2008, 58) describe a method of structuring a consult around what should be reported clinically: demographic information, reason for consult request, informants, a systematic description of the case (utilizing a framework adapted from Jonsen, Siegler, and Winslade 2002), assessment, discussion and analysis, and recommendation.

Further examples of consultation methods can be enumerated, but I offer up a discussion of my own particular method that is applicable in many ways to any of the consult models mentioned thus far. Unlike some other models, it is not intended to be comprehensive regarding all steps of the consultation, but instead it is intended to focus specifically on those moments during a consultation that are focused on ethical evaluation of a case. As such, it is decidedly aligned with the facilitation (recommendation) model, because facilitation is the most common model currently used for clinical ethics consultations.

## A METHOD OF CONSULTATION

Consider the following situation adapted from an ethics consultation chart note:

*Situation*: The patient, Mr. Q (26 years old) was brought to an outside medical facility with severe head pain. He was told to go to the academic medical center (AMC) 45 miles away after CT scan at the outside facility indicated a large brain mass. At the AMC, the patient arrived at the Emergency Department and was immediately admitted for surgery on a brain tumor.

Unfortunately, during his stay, his brain hemorrhaged, rendering him completely unresponsive and requiring a ventilator, tracheotomy, and feeding tube. Patient remained in ICU for 3 weeks, and was able to be moved to step-down on week 4. The patient is unable to respond meaningfully to questions, and part of his skull has been removed until his head stops swelling.

With the patient's condition now stable after surgery, the neurosurgeon indicates that the patient can be moved out of the hospital, though it will be many months before another surgery will be performed to replace the missing part of his skull. Case management has discussed future discharge options with family. The case manager discussed nursing home options, and noted that his state-based insurance was going to stop paying for his care in the hospital within a couple of weeks. To all this, the family expressed concern that the patient was being moved out prematurely.

That patient lives with his grandmother, and his father lives nearby. There are conflicting reports from both family and health-care providers about whether Mr. Q suffered from some mild form of developmental delay prior to this hospitalization.

Ethics was contacted by risk management after learning that the family contacted the newspaper to complain about the patient being discharged because they could not pay. The ethical concern was that the hospital's resources were being unduly taxed by caring for a patient who could be served in a rehab or long-term care facility.

The clinical ethics consultant talked with bedside nursing, a resident, and the attending physician to better understand the medical situation. He also discussed the patient's situation with the family every day for one week. These discussions led to three health-care team conferences.

That family felt obligated to protect the patient from undue harm that they believed would more easily occur if not in the hospital. They were not interested in moving to a nursing home, believing that nursing homes would not be able to provide adequate care. They were confused by why their loved one was being sent somewhere else when his head was still not fully recovered, and they were not clear on how long it would be until that recovery might occur.

While the health-care providers recognized the family's distress, they also did not believe that keeping the patient in the hospital was, in fact, protecting him from undue harm. Hospital-acquired infections and other problems can arise in acute-care facilities. They also believed that as an acute-care facility, they should not be obligated to take on chronic-care patients whenever the family was uncomfortable with long-term care options.

The risk manager was concerned that the hospital's reputation had taken a hit that it did not deserve, that it was obligated to find an appropriate long-term care facility, and once one was found that could take the patient, funding would run out.

Most clinical ethics consultations, then, have at their core the aim of stimulating moral reflection on different aspects of the medical situations that call forth consultations. Moral reflection is an important and complex process. It aims at better understanding of morally challenging situations and, possibly, providing insight and direction for morally acceptable responses to those challenges. On its face, moral reflection, then, seems a skill worthy of cultivation, but it can be difficult to motivate such development.

On the one hand, as Dewey has noted (1922), morality simply is social. We grow up acting in a world of others, and others do hold us accountable for those actions. From the earliest age, parents tell us what is and is not acceptable, and they correct us when we miss the target of acceptability. But moral direction is not simply supplied by adults to children, peer-to-peer evaluations also occur when our friends and playmates challenge and condemn us for what we do and say. Given this, we can readily say we are beings ever immersed in morality, and as such, suggesting there is a need to cultivate our moral processes is, at best, redundant and, at worst, patronizing.

On the other hand, however, experience alone is unsystematic, producing unreflective habits at best, and generally we believe that careful development of our habits in light of the purposes to which we would like to put them affords the opportunity to improve them. Surely, every person with working muscles in her arm and hand can throw a ball. But when that "natural" experiential ability is tasked with throwing a baseball sixty feet, six inches to cross a fifteen-inch surface at a height roughly between twelve and forty-eight inches off the ground, many are unsuccessful. As such, no one seems taken aback when it  is suggested that if not simply throwing but pitching a baseball is your desire, you should develop a systematic approach to develop the "arm mechanics" to get the ball consistently over the plate for a strike. Such an example (and many others) seem obvious. Driving a car, shaving our faces or legs, or shooting a basketball are all readily seen not simply as muscular movements but rather as habits that require some reflection and cultivation to make them work for us regularly and successfully. We must be careful that we do not let the physical nature of these activities fool us into thinking that careful habit formation is merely for physical processes. Mental and cognitive aspects of our lives are prone to be habituated as well, and like their muscular counterparts, they can be developed over time, not simply set loose. That is, we can think, emote, and respond differently to the world around us than we do by "nature." Yes, our brains will produce thoughts and ideas without any purposeful reflection, intentionally brought to bear. But we would, then, never be able to read or write, discern classical from pop music, or enjoy the complexities of wines and craft beers.

So, again, having desires about what you want and see as good is our natural starting point for morality, but it is not the end. The world is full of moral challenges that involve others' interests and desires, values and beliefs. Navigating all this complexity implicates the full scope of moral considerations. To leave our moral sensibilities to their own devices without some careful attempt at mature development and habituation seems foolish, at best—and unethical at worst. Put differently, why should our cognitive and moral "habits" be any different than our physical ones, especially given that some moral challenges we face are significantly complex?

As we have discussed, medicine is rife with moral issues, complexities, and considerations. Clinical ethics consultations, thus, attempt to flex reflective, considered habits of moral reflection, habits that must be cultivated. To build those habits and have them operate in the professional sphere, in conference with others, at the bedside of patients, the process of consultation must be carefully developed and enacted. That process can be broken down into different, but intimately related, parts: moral evaluation, moral considerations, moral instrumentation, and moral argumentation.

## MORAL EVALUATION

Clinical ethics consults are forms of moral evaluation in which ethical problems are identified and solutions explored. Some of these consultations result in ethically grounded recommendations, and others simply provide the opportunity to think through the ethical issues and values at play. But either way, a moral evaluation occurs, and careful evaluation is multifaceted.

Clinical ethics consultations begin as a hallway conversation, a phone call, or an e-mail. A nurse or resident physician, an attending physician or social worker, even a patient or family member, is troubled by some aspect of a situation in the hospital. People wonder whether what is going on is "right" or "good," and this leads them to reach out. The clinical ethics consultant, then, is confronted by a request for help and that request typically is predicated on there being a problem to avoid or solve. In fact, a frequent question the ethicist will ask early on is, "What do you think the ethical problem is?"

Problems are puzzles to be solved, irritations to be eliminated, or concerns to be met. They are the stimulants for reflective thought, and they set the agenda for that reflection. Every identified problem only admits to a finite set of solutions, and thus, a well-developed problem is half solved. Thus, carefully understanding and investigating the problem itself is an important first step in consultation.

Once a problem (or set of problems) has been identified, consultants begin to explore the range of possible, reasonable solutions. Any ethically challenging situation is precisely a challenge because goods compete or obligations conflict. In such situations, obviously acceptable solutions are not readily identified because multiple, competing solutions have their supporters and detractors. For a physician to tell a woman that she is at risk of a sexually transmitted disease from a patient who is her philandering husband would meet the good of protecting her. At the same time, it would violate the obligation of confidentiality. Both meeting her good and fulfilling the obligation to him have good reasons that would support going in one direction or the other. Is it clear on its face which should win? If not, then we must investigate both further before making a final, morally based decision. If so, what do you tell the party whose good you denied or obligation you violated were the reasons for doing so?

This last question, then, leads to another aspect of moral evaluation—justification. To say something is wrong or bad versus right or good simply stimulates the next question: what makes it wrong or bad versus right or good? "It just is" is the weakest answer possible, for the claim is one of moral ontology and intuition—that is, the claim is that some things just *are* good or *are* bad. But again, in the face of competing possible solutions to the moral problem, such a response rings hollow. What is required are reasons and justification. In the development of reasonable solutions, an investigation ensues. Strengths and weaknesses are explored. Values and principles are brought to bear. And this provides the support for any of the reasonable solutions being investigated, and justifications are required precisely because competing values and solutions are at play.

Through the investigation, it is hoped that the moral situation and morally acceptable solutions come clear. If so, the clinical ethicist should put forth a recommendation in light of the results of the investigation, which completes the moral evaluation.

## MORAL CONSIDERATIONS

You will note that in discussing moral evaluation, nothing was said about what should be investigated and what kinds of data and concepts make for moral justification. So, although the evaluation is a process, what, then, is the content? To look at content comprehensively, I suggest the use of the following acronym: GRACE.

**G—Get the Whole Story.** As mentioned earlier, clinical ethicists will often ask what the requestor believes is the moral problem, but why take his or her word for it? Furthermore, problems lead to solutions, but what solutions are reasonably available in any given situation? To answer these questions, the clinical ethicist must find out what is going on. Individual lives and communal or cultural experience can be seen as different life stories or narratives. Clinical situations are no different. What is the medical condition of the patient? What is the prognosis, and on what evidence is it based? Who are the stakeholders, decision makers, and affected parties? What are their personal stories? How do their values and beliefs affect the actions and choices in the case? What are the policies and laws that are implicated by the situation?

For example, in the consultation about Mr. Q, the medical facts are that his neurological condition requires long-term nursing care. Furthermore, his grandmother is ill-equipped to provide that care at home. Neither his grandmother nor his father want him to go to a nursing home, in part because they believe that high-end hospital care is safer than the care he would get at a nursing home. All this, and much more, is part of the story that shapes the decisions to be made.

Clinical ethics addresses real-life issues that happen in real time. To understand the ethical issues at play, the concerns to be addressed, and the problems to be solved, the clinical ethicist must investigate the ongoing narratives in the situation, because those narratives give rise to the moral issues, and it is those narratives that will be affected by the process and product of clinical ethics evaluation.

To put it differently, a common claim made by clinical ethicists is this: good ethics begin with good facts.

**R—Recognize Obligations.** One set of facts (debatable as they may be) is the collection of obligations that each of us carry with us. As mentioned earlier in the chapter, each of us takes on roles and commitments that obligate us. If we have a spouse, we are obligated through marriage to meet certain expectations of that spouse. If we practice a religion, religious maxims and tenets exist that we should fulfill. And if we are professionals, the professions we serve require that we act and practice in particular ways to remain within the bounds of the profession.

All of these, and many more, are obligations that come out in ethics consultations. You can see in Mr. Q's case that his grandmother, as caregiver, is deeply concerned about making decisions that might put her grandchild in harm's way. She feels obligated to fight to provide him the best care available. Physicians, nurses, and other health-care providers all experience the constraint of obligations—whether that be keeping patient conversations confidential or demanding blood transfusions for pediatric patients whose parents refuse but allowing such refusals by adult patients.

The clinical ethicist, then, must attempt to map out the many obligations at play in the situation. To fulfill or violate an obligation takes an understanding of its value in relation to other obligations and ethical considerations. Although they may not be determinative by themselves, these obligations have moral weight in any ethical evaluation.

**A—Accept Responsibilities and Avoid Overreaching.** One of the challenging things about obligations is that sometimes they compete. A physician, for example, may need to be home after school gets out to pick up his or her children and feed them dinner. That same physician may also get a page at 4:00 PM that requests his or her expertise on a patient matter right away. Determining which to fulfill will be based on a number of factors: Is the physician the only one available to take the call? Can the children remain at school in an after-care program? Is there a spouse? Is he or she available? However it gets worked out, there are responsibilities to be fulfilled, and the physician *must* fulfill them. If the physician decides to pick up the children, she or he must find another physician to cover the call. If the physician decides to stay at work, the children or spouse need to be alerted to the change in familial planning. Accepting these responsibilities, not just merely acknowledging them, is of vital importance.

Furthermore, in determining obligations to be fulfilled, professionals often are confronted by their own personal values—that is, values they have come to hold because of their lives outside their profession, whether from families, religions, or education. As professionals, however, the ethical situations that call forth consultations must be navigated carefully so that the professional does not "overreach." In practice, there is a concept known as "scope of practice," in which professionals are expected to do only what is in their training to do. Physicians, qua physicians, are not spiritual guides. Nurses, qua nurses, are not psychotherapists. Social workers, qua social workers, are not police officers. This, too, holds for ethical considerations. Physicians, qua religious believers, cannot let their belief in the healing power of a deity interfere with providing evidence-based medical care. Nurses, qua spouses, cannot let their concern for a wife's unknown risk of a sexually transmitted disease undermine their obligation to confidentiality of their patient. Social workers, qua citizens, cannot have hospital security hold an adult patient against his or her will simply because the patient has a mental illness.

In a clinical ethics consultation, is it necessary not only to map out the obligations at play but to look at what responsibilities will need to be fulfilled. Who owes what to whom? How will that reckoning take place? And what happens when some responsibilities go unfulfilled?

**C—Consider Consequences.** Whichever obligations are fulfilled or responsibilities accepted, all choices promote actions that lead to consequences. Even the best of intentions to fulfill necessary obligations can go astray—as the saying goes, the road to hell is paved with good intentions. Consequences matter. In fact, whatever our motivations, they lead us to an attempt to achieve some end, and those ends should be evaluated, not simply accepted.

Admittedly, in ethical deliberation, although some consequences have more evidence and some much less, all consequences under consideration are speculative. Thus, consequential considerations are challenging. Will Mr. Q get an infection in the hospital? Will the nursing home meet its obligations to care for him properly? We must act on probability and pragmatics—that is, what we think will happen and what we believe is most worth our efforts in trying to achieve it given our lack of certainty that it will, in fact, come to pass. The former turns on evidence, the latter on character.

**E—Evaluate Character.** A final consideration, then, concerns who we are and who we want to be—personally, professionally, and institutionally. As with Mr. Q's situation, risk managers, while primarily managing risk, are often concerned about "how will it look?" This can smack of being unduly self-serving, but all our actions say something about us—as people, as professionals, and institutions. The obligations we fulfill or violate say something about us and about our roles. The consequences that follow our actions affect our future pursuits—validating or undermining our values, beliefs, decisions, and processes. To make choices is to express our values through the choices we make. And the result of actions are ours to own.

Each clinical ethics consultation has the potential to say something about the many parties at play. But even further, the decisions and outcomes say something about the institution in which they occur. The consultant needs to keep this in mind to fashion an outcome that can be owned by the institution (or, more importantly, must be owned by the institution). For this reason, some ethics consultations lead to policy review and development.

## MORAL INSTRUMENTATION

Moral considerations are but one aspect of evaluation. With obligations seemingly coming from every direction and consequences of all stripes following from actions, how do we take all these considerations and begin to reason through them? Moral considerations function in a moral evaluation like wood, wallboard, cement, and paint do in building a house. They are the raw material. The material becomes a structure (or becomes structured) using instruments or tools. In home building, those tools are hammers, power drills, mixers, and brushes. The tools of moral evaluation are principles, maxims, rules, and more.

Elsewhere in this text you will have read about basic biomedical principles, such as respect for autonomy, beneficence, and justice. We might also enumerate principles of utility and fidelity, among others. But even more broadly, we might use principles to guide action, such as "only act so as to promote good and minimize harm to all those affected by the propose action," or "cultivate habits that moderate among extreme outcomes." We also follow maxims, such as "treat others as you would want to be treated" or "act in a way that you would be willing for anyone else to act under similar circumstances." Furthermore, we abide by moral rules, such as "do not harm innocent others," "tell the truth," and "be kind."

Each of these concepts are moral instruments (i.e., ethical norms) that can be applied in situations given the moral considerations under scrutiny. Which ones to bring to bear, however, is probably the most challenging question of all. Clinical ethicists, like their theoretical counterparts, come in all ethical stripes. Every ethicist should do as comprehensive a job as possible rooting through and out the moral considerations in a case, but which tools to use to put those considerations into an evaluation is highly individualized. Some ethicists are primarily worried about meeting certain moral demands or duties; others are moved mostly by consequences; still others find that focusing on moral virtues best moves thought forward. Whichever approach is taken, ultimately, decisions must be made and justification given.

## MORAL ARGUMENTATION

Moral evaluation as a process of identifying moral problems and attempting solutions results in taking a moral position. To do so requires comprehensive work on moral considerations honed by moral instrumentation both crafted by and resulting in moral argumentation. An argument is not simply a dispute between people. In fact, some arguments are done so well that at the end of it, there is no dispute at all. What is meant, then, by argument is a logical structure that puts data and evidence (sometimes called *premises*) together to support a claim (or *conclusion*).

Data and evidence can be physical facts or moral beliefs, cultural norms or statistical outcomes, emotional responses, or scientific discoveries. They are fit together with principles of support—whether of the kinds of moral instruments just mentioned or logical tools such as creating valid deductive arguments or identifying argument fallacies. Without the fit, data are bare and meaningless. Principles give data meaning. For example, an argument could be made as follows:

Kareem Abdul-Jabbar scored more points than any other NBA player (38,387). (This is a premise.)

He won six NBA and three NCAA championships. (This is another premise.)

Therefore, he is the greatest basketball player ever. (This is conclusion.)

This is an argument because it contains both data and evidence for support and a conclusion from that data. Now, you might disagree. Some, in fact, argue that Michael Jordan (1963–) is the greatest basketball player ever. But how can that be? The data given about Kareem Abdul-Jabar (1947–) are true; they are facts that cannot be contested. So, how can we contest the conclusion? Simple, really. We can contest the *meaning* of the given data. Why should we accept that both (or either) 38,000-plus points and total championships won mean that you are the greatest basketball player? Well, hidden in the argument are a number of unstated premises that are doing a lot of the logical work. This premise is what is making the data meaningful for the purpose of the argument. It might go something like this:

> Winning games, championship games, is the whole point of playing competitive sports. (This is an unstated premise.)
>
> Basketball games are only won if points are scored. (This is an unstated premise.)
>
> A player scoring more points puts you in the position to win. (This is an unstated premise.)

Other options for unstated premises would still give useful meaning to the data in relation to the conclusion, but the point is that whatever the unstated premises are, they are doing the work of what has been called a *warrant*—that is, what makes bare data meaningful in an argument.

In an ethics consultation, the data and evidence are gathered through the process of getting the whole story (talking with professionals, families, friends, and the patients—where possible), recognizing the obligations at play, accepting responsibilities that flow from those obligations, considering possible consequences that would follow from proposed actions, and evaluating the character of those people and institutions affected by the decisions to be made. But then, clinical ethicists are challenged with connecting all the data elements up into an argument, and that connection occurs through the use of moral instruments that bring ethical meaning to the data.

It would be impossible to recount in full detail all the elements of a case consultation in anything less than a short book, but the chart note at the start of this section gives an idea of how some of these elements come together (both explicitly and implicitly) irrespective of the method (GRACE, CASES, etc.) used. To understand where cases sometimes end up, the follow-up notes are provided:

> *Recommendation*: The case highlights ethical tensions among doing what is best for the patient, what his decision makers are requesting, and the appropriate stewardship of medical resource. The hospital is obligated to provide the best care possible, but tertiary, acute care hospitals are not the best environment for long-term care patients. The family's concern about nursing homes was motivated, in part, by having very little knowledge of what kinds of nursing homes were available in their area. It is recommended that the family be given the opportunity to visit nursing homes in their area in order to identify a suitable long-term care facility. Furthermore, the family would like better head protection of the patient before leaving the hospital, and it is recommended that an occupational therapy (OT) helmet be ordered and fitted. Finally, the family appreciates the work of the neurosurgeon, and so it is recommended that the neurosurgeon take the time to explain carefully, slowly, and comprehensively the current situation, short-term processes, and long-term prognosis.

> *Resolution*: After three care conferences with the family and different members of the health-care team, the family indicated that they understood that the patient's care was going to take months, maybe even years, and that the hospital was not the best place for the care to occur. They were assured that he would be given more surgery for his head and skull, but only after his brain had recovered enough. The patient was eventually moved to a nursing home within 10 miles of his family.

# A BRIEF CODA: SCOPE OF PRACTICE

The preceding consult note shows not only ethical concerns about beneficence, harm, and familial duties, but also about how or whether health-care providers do a good job of conversing with family, hearing their needs or concerns, and speaking their language. In practice, it is certainly not the case that all ethics consultations rely on merely moral evaluations. Clinical ethicists often are called on to triage challenging issues that ultimately are referred to other experts in the institution—risk management, social work, psychiatry, and more. Furthermore, as a practical matter, many consults are the result of poor or erratic communication among important parties in the situation. Health-care providers disagree about what is best for the patient, and this can be an ethical issue. But the conflicts are exacerbated by the team members not talking about these differences among themselves. Families may struggle with what is best for their loved one, and surely this raises some moral concern. But underlying family dynamics that undermine their ability to talk among themselves, rather than differences in values or fundamental moral beliefs, often lead to decision-making struggles.

Clinical ethicists, while not always the best trained or positioned to handle these kinds of communication problems, often are called on to work with the various parties because institutions do not always have other professionals who are available and trained to do so. The question then becomes: should the clinical ethicist take up the role of communication facilitator because otherwise no one will, or should the clinical ethicist take a pass on these kinds of requests so as not to practice outside his or her expertise? There is no single right answer to this question, and different ethicists will take on or push off these responsibilities, depending on their comfort level and the resources otherwise available. What must be weighed are not just professional but moral considerations—or more precisely, the ethics of professional considerations. To take on such consults is to put patient needs first, but it comes with its own risks—namely, practicing beyond one's (typical) training in ethics. Just like the need to avoid overreaching by physicians and nurses, ethicists, too, must identify the limits of their scope of practice. And yet, if no one helps work through conflicts of communication, problems persist and ethical issues arise.

## Summary

Gyges was a shepherd in the service of the king of Lydia; there was a great storm, and an earthquake made an opening in the earth at the place where he was feeding his flock. Amazed at the sight, he descended into the opening, where, among other marvels, he beheld a hollow brazen horse, having doors, at which he stooping and looking in saw a dead body of stature, as appeared to him, more than human, and having nothing on but a gold ring; this he took from the finger of the dead and re-ascended. Now the shepherds met together, according to custom, that they might send their monthly report about the flocks to the king; into their assembly he came having the ring on his finger, and as he was sitting among them he chanced to turn the collet of the ring inside his hand, when instantly he became invisible to the rest of the company, and they began to speak of him as if he were no longer present. He was astonished at this, and again touching the ring he turned the collet outwards and reappeared; he made several trials of the ring, and always with the same result—when he turned the collet inwards he became invisible, when outwards he reappeared. Whereupon he contrived to be chosen one of the messengers who were sent to the court; where as soon as he arrived he seduced the queen, and with her help conspired against the king and slew him, and took the kingdom. (Plato 1892, 359d–360b)

Medicine, like Gyges, begins humbly. People fall ill, as bodies are vulnerable to disease and injury. But medicine is also powerful stuff, and its ultimate power can be unknown even to the one who creates or discovers it. The power can further be corruptive, as particular goals create questionable outcomes. Medicine, as with the Ring of Gyges, may be all too consuming, too tempting to use its abilities in unjust ways. And yet, the Ring could be used for good as well. The cloak of invisibility is a power that can lead to good ends for others, for communities, not just the selfish interests of one. So, too, with medicine, and it is the moral core of medicine that must keep the corrupting power of the Ring at bay. In this world, clinical ethics consultations are an instrument employed to keep medicine just, focused on the service of patients and public health through careful consideration of the moral conditions at play in any given health-care situation brought forth. Consultants are tasked to help resolve the ethical tensions experienced by both health-care providers and patients and families, through the use of ethical consideration to evaluate ethically challenging cases.

## Bibliography

American Society for Bioethics and Humanities (ASBH). *Core Competencies for Healthcare Ethics Consultation.* Glenview, IL: Author, 1998.

American Society for Bioethics and Humanities (ASBH). *Core Competencies for Healthcare Ethics Consultation.* 2nd ed. Glenview, IL: Author, 2011.

Aulisio, Mark P., Robert M. Arnold, and Stuart J. Youngner. *Ethics Consultation: From Theory to Practice.* Baltimore, MD: Johns Hopkins University Press, 2003.

Belkin, Lisa. *First, Do No Harm.* New York: Fawcett, 1993.

Buermeyer, Laurence. *An Introduction to Reflective Thinking.* Boston: Houghton Mifflin, 1923.

Dewey, John. *The Later Works*, Vol. 5. In *The Collected Works of John Dewey, 1882–1953*, edited by J. A. Boydston. Carbondale: Southern Illinois University Press, 1991.

Dewey, John. *The Middle Works*, Vol. 12. In *The Collected Works of John Dewey, 1882–1953*, edited by J. A. Boydston. Carbondale: Southern Illinois University Press, 1991.

Dubler, Nancy N., and Carol B. Liebman. *Bioethics Mediation: A Guide to Shaping Shared Solutions.* New York: United Hospital Fund of New York, 2004.

Dubler, Nancy N., and Carol B. Liebman. *Bioethics Mediation: A Guide to Shaping Shared Solutions.* Rev. ed. Nashville, TN: Vanderbilt University Press, 2011.

Fox, Ellen, Sarah Myers, and Robert A. Pearlman. "Ethics Consultation in United States Hospitals: A National Survey." *American Journal of Bioethics* 7, no. 2 (2007): 13–25.

Jonsen, Albert. *The Birth of Bioethics.* New York: Oxford University Press, 1998.

Jonsen, Albert, Mark Seigler, and William Winslade. *Clinical Ethics: A Practical Approach to Ethical Decisions in Clinical Medicine.* 5th ed. New York: McGraw-Hill, 2002.

Molewijk, Bert, Ezra van Zadelhoff, Bert Lendemeijer, and Guy Widdershoven. "Implementing Moral Case Deliberation in Dutch Healthcare—Improving Moral Competency of Professionals and the Quality of Care." *Bioethica Forum* 1, no. 1 (2008): 57–65.

National Center for Ethics in Health Care. *Ethics Consultation: Responding to Ethics Questions in Health Care.* 2nd ed. Washington, DC: US Department of Veterans Affairs, 2015.

Payne, Michael (interviewee), with Carla Aston (interviewer). "Michael Payne Explains How Couples Can Share Creative Control in Design Projects." *Carla Aston Designed.* 2012. http://carlaaston.com/designed/michael-payne-explains-how-couples-share-creative-control-design-project.

Pellegrino, Edmund D. "The Anatomy of Clinical Judgments: Some Notes on Right Reason and Right Action." In *Clinical Judgment: A Critical Appraisal: Proceedings of the Fifth Trans-disciplinary Symposium on Philosophy and Medicine*, edited by H. T. Engelhardt Jr. and S. F. Spicker, 169–194. Dordrecht, Netherlands: D. Reidel, 1979.

Plato. *The Dialogues of Plato.* Translated by B. Jowett. New York: Random House, 1892.

Shelton, Wayne, and Dyrleif Bjarnadottir. "Ethics Consultation and the Committee." In *Ethics by Committee: A Textbook on Consultation, Organization and Education for Hospital Ethics Committees*, edited by D. Micah Hester, 49–78. Lanham, MD: Rowman and Littlefield, 2008.

Spike, Jeffrey. "Ethics Consultation Process." In *Guidance for Healthcare Ethics Committees*, edited by D. Micah Hester and Toby Schonfeld, 41–47. New York: Cambridge University Press, 2012.

**TELEVISION**

*Designing for the Sexes*. "Dining/Living Room Combination." Season 5, episode 2, 2003. HGTV.

*Studio One in Hollywood*. "Twelve Angry Men." Season 7, episode 1, 1954. Dir. Franklin J. Schaffner. CBS.

*The West Wing*. "In the Shadow of Two Gunman: Part I." Season 2, episode 1, 2000. Dir. Thomas Schlamme. NBC.

# Part Three:
# Social Justice

The final part of this volume looks at equity, or the fair sharing of benefits and burdens in a society. These are issues that affect more than one person (patient) or more than one relationship (patient-provider). These chapters examine common goods, services, and products that are shared by a population.

One question raised by social justice is how to fairly distribute goods and services in a society. Consider a limited resource, such as a newly developed vaccine. One could distribute in an egalitarian manner in which each person is treated as equal. The fair system here would be either first come/first served or a lottery. A need-based system looks solely at the medical need for a service. In other words, the sickest person gets the good. Another option would be a merit system, whereby a person receives what he or she has earned through good deeds to others, a remarkable achievement, or celebrity status. The contribution method looks at what a person can do to gain the good or service; the most common example would be which person can pay the most money for it. And the last method is desert (pronounced "dessert"), which asks who is deserving of the good or service and determines this by how much an individual's actions are responsible (or not) for the need. For example, should a liver transplant go to a person who is an alcoholic and has taken no steps to gain control over this problem?

Chapter 14 looks at the question of justice in terms of procuring and distributing organs. Protecting individuals who make the choice of participating in research is the subject of Chapter 15, which surveys the history of abuse of humans as subjects in research, and the development of ethics and law in this area. The justice question here is making sure that the benefits of research and the burdens of being research subjects are fairly shared. And finally, Chapter 16 proposes that an ethic based in common goods is necessary for community-level decisions. Public health ethics asks how a society protects the aggregate health of its population while being cognizant of individual rights.

# CHAPTER 14

# *Organ Transplants*

**Aviva M. Goldberg**
*Associate Professor, Department of Pediatrics and Child Health,*
*Faculty of Health Sciences*
*University of Manitoba, Winnipeg, Canada*

Since the first successful human organ transplant, a kidney transplant between identical twin brothers in 1954, both the medical community and society at large have struggled with the opportunities and ethical challenges of transplantation. As the demand for organs has outpaced the supply of donors, the transplant community has been challenged to ensure that the highest ethical standards continue to be paramount in both obtaining and distributing organs.

Per the Organ Procurement and Transplantation Network (OPTN, the source of all data in this chapter unless otherwise indicated), more than 29,000 organ transplants were performed in the United States in 2014. Despite this success, there are not enough organs to meet the increasing demand; as of June 2015, more than 123,000 people were waiting for a transplant. Although some types of organ failure can be managed temporarily with bridging strategies (like dialysis for kidney failure, and external ventricular assist devices for heart failure), transplantation is often the only way to save or extend a patient's life. If a suitable organ is not found in time, a person with end-stage organ failure may become one of more than six thousand people who die in the United States every year while waiting for a transplant that they will not receive.

Kidneys are the most commonly transplanted organ, followed by liver, heart, lung, small bowel, and pancreas transplantation. Some organs can come only from deceased donors, like hearts, whereas other can be obtained from either living or deceased sources. Composite transplants (including face, hands, and uterus) are still quite rare and available only at a few specialized centers, but these are increasing in frequency.

After an organ transplant, it is necessary for the transplant recipient to take medications, usually for the rest of his or her life. These medications suppress the patient's immune system so that the body does not recognize it as foreign material and reject it. These immunosuppressants require close adherence to a medication schedule and regular medical follow-up, often have side effects that may require other medications to manage, and increase the patient's risk for developing other conditions, like diabetes and cancer. Overall, organ transplantation can be lifesaving and life enhancing, but it requires a lifetime commitment to medical care.

Because of the issues of supply and demand, and the medical care required to keep a transplant functioning, organ transplantation creates some special ethical challenges. This chapter will outline some of the major ethical issues related to organ donation, recipient selection, and allocation. It will mainly deal with the ethics of solid organ transplantation (as opposed to bone marrow, stem cell, and blood donation) and will not address experimental types of donation (artificial organs and xenotransplantation) or composite transplants. Of course, transplant ethics is a vast subject, and all the issues and philosophical debates cannot be addressed in a single chapter. The bibliography directs the interested reader to a number of well-written books and journal articles that outline these issues in greater detail.

Aside from being an interesting area for medical personnel and bioethicists, organ transplantation has also been a popular theme in literature and visual art. Movies, television shows, and novels have explored both the promise and peril of organ transplant, as well as how the ethical issues raised by transplant technology can affect families, relationships, and society as a whole. Throughout the chapter, the reader will find references to the bibliography that highlight how a particular ethical issue in transplantation has been discussed in a popular medium.

## DECEASED DONORS

Deceased donation involves removing organs from people who have died and transplanting them into living people who suffer from organ failure. Modern organ transplantation in the United States would not exist without deceased donation, because even for organs with a potential living source, the majority of organs are received from deceased donors, including approximately 70 percent of kidney transplants and 96 percent of liver transplants. This section will deal with the ethical issues of defining death, donation after neurologic determination of death (NDD), donation after cardiocirculatory death (DCD), opt-in versus opt-out strategies for obtaining organs, and the use of organs from executed prisoners.

### DEFINING DEATH AND DONATION AFTER NEUROLOGIC DETERMINATION OF DEATH

The *dead donor rule* (DDR) is a long-established standard that dictates that a person should not be killed by the process of removing organs for transplant (i.e., the donor needs to be dead before the organs are removed). The intent of the rule is to maintain nonmaleficence—not wanting to harm a person by killing him or her for their organs. It may seem on the surface to be both sensible and self-evident, but the DDR is controversial both because it can be difficult to accurately define death and because maintaining or rejecting the rule will significantly affect who can be considered a candidate for deceased donation.

There was relatively little controversy in defining death until the advent of life-sustaining therapies (LSTs) like ventilators in the 1960s. Before that time, a dying person's heart, lungs, and brain would all stop working at approximately the same time, because the lack of oxygen from the cessation of heart or lung function would rapidly lead to the cessation of all body functions. Although it could sometimes be difficult to determine the exact moment at which these processes ceased (as in an ancient Hebrew tract, which considers how to determine death in a person buried in an earthquake, when neither the pulse nor respiration can be observed), the issues quickly became moot as there was no way to replace heart or lung function for any prolonged length of time. With the advent of ventilator therapy in the middle of the twentieth century, new situations arose in which a critically brain-injured patient's breathing could be taken over by machines, so the heart could go on beating long after the brain and lungs ceased independent function. First described as a *coma dépassé* by Pierre Mollaret and Maurice Goulon in 1959, these individuals would never regain consciousness or even minimal brain function, but it became difficult to know how and when to shut off the ventilators to which they were attached.

To better define a time at which resuscitative efforts and intensive care unit (ICU) therapies could be ethically discontinued, and so that the relatively new practice of deceased organ donation could continue without violating the DDR, a landmark 1968 paper from a team at Harvard Medical School outlined a condition they called *irreversible coma* as a new criterion for defining death. The authors defined a permanently unconscious brain as one in which there was:

1. Unreceptivity and unresponsivity

2. No movement or breathing

3. No reflexes

4. Flat electroencephalogram (EEG, a test that monitors brain activity)

The Harvard group recommended that all the tests to establish irreversible coma be repeated after twenty-four hours and stated that the decision to do a brain-death test and the responsibility for removing the patient from mechanical support should be made by a physician, since leaving the decision to the family would be "unsound and undesirable." Many jurisdictions now have specific rules for the conditions that must be met in order to declare a patient dead by NDD criteria, which build upon these earlier works.

A 1981 presidential commission further clarified the legal and medical status of brain death as a valid definition of death, and this was followed by the Uniform Determination of Death Act, which defined death as either "(1) irreversible cessation of circulatory and respiratory functions, or (2) irreversible cessation of all functions of the entire brain, including the brain stem … in accordance with accepted medical standards." As of 2016, all but two US states allow physicians to remove mechanical support after NDD; commonly referred to as *brain death*). In New York and New Jersey, the laws dictate that the moral and religious views of a family must be considered before removing ventilators and other machines. This has played out in several cases in which families of those declared dead by NDD criteria have fought to continue the ventilators for their loved ones (see, e.g., articles by Belluck 2005; Foht 2014; Gostin 2014).

Although brain death is accepted by many in both the medical community and the public at large, there is controversy over whether this definition, and the DDR, are the best way to decide from whom we are allowed to procure organs for transplantation. Ethicists Franklin Miller and Robert Truog are two of the most vocal proponents of this viewpoint, arguing in "Is It Time to Abandon Brain Death?" (Truog 1997) and *Death, Dying, and Organ Transplantation* (Miller and Truog 2012) that the current definition of death by neurological criteria is a legal fiction and a "medical charade" that makes the medical community and the public more comfortable with organ removal. They argue that people who meet criteria for NDD may maintain integrative body function for years (i.e., their other body functions can continue even after the brain is declared dead), and therefore they question whether NDD is truly death, as it has been classically understood. They further argue that abandoning the DDR would not mean abandoning deceased donation, because organs could be ethically removed from those who were near death and who had consented to the procedure. They suggest that rejecting the DDR and basing the decision to remove organs on the principles of autonomy (by respecting the would-be donor's wishes to donate) and nonmaleficence (because donors will not be harmed if they are dying anyway), actually may do more good for donors and donor families, because it would allow those who could not be donors in the current system (because they do not meet current death criteria) to have their wishes regarding donation respected.

Others, like Samuel Birch writing in "The Dead Donor Rule: A Defense" (2013), defend the DDR, stating that it is consistent with the general duty of physicians to not kill their patients and that the traditional distinction between killing (as would happen when organs are removed before death) is morally different than allowing someone to die and then removing their organs. Many people, as well as the President's Council on Bioethics (2008), assert that maintaining the DDR is necessary to prevent exploitation of the vulnerable, like patients in a persistent vegetative state who may been seen as viable donors if there is no requirement for death before donation. Current law and practice in the United States has maintained that the DDR is necessary for ethical organ procurement, and attempts to justify the retrieval of organs from patients who are severely brain injured but not yet dead generally have not achieved broad consensus.

## DONATION AFTER CARDIOCIRCULATORY DEATH

The DDR also becomes important when discussing DCD, which now accounts for up to 25 percent of deceased donor kidneys transplants in some regions. There are two types of DCD: controlled and uncontrolled. Controlled DCD occurs in hospitals, after an anticipated cardiac arrest, usually in critically injured patients for whom a decision has been made to withdraw LSTs. As Iván Ortega-Deballon, Laura Hornby, and Sam Shemie outline in "Protocols for Uncontrolled Donation after Circulatory Death" (2015), uncontrolled DCD is generally initiated outside of the hospital following an unanticipated cardiac arrest (e.g., at an accident scene). This section will focus on controlled DCD because it is the only type in common practice in the United States at this time.

The modern age of DCD began with the publication of the Pittsburgh Protocol in 1993, which outlined the ethical concerns and justification for proceeding with a policy that would allow the use of organs from those who were gravely ill, in whom a decision had been made to withdraw LST, but who did not meet criteria for NDD (see also DeVita and Snyder 1993). Protocols vary among centers, but the general process is as follows:

1. A decision is made to withdraw LST in a person who is so critically ill that he or she is not expected to recover, but who does not meet NDD criteria.

2. If the patient appears to be medically suitable (e.g., has no transmissible diseases), the family or substitute decision maker is asked for permission to proceed with DCD.

3. If permission is obtained, the patient is prepared for removal of LST and the organ procurement team awaits the patient's death.

4. After the LST is withdrawn, the medical team waits for a proscribed amount of time (usually two to five minutes) after the heart is stopped. After this time, the patient is declared dead and the organ procurement team removes the transplantable organs. If the heart does not stop within a certain amount of time, say, two hours, the donation does not proceed and the patient is returned to the ICU.

This intricately organized approach is necessary because organ quality rapidly deteriorates after the heart stops delivering oxygen, so organ retrieval must take place as quickly as possible after the donor's death. The original protocol met with significant criticism and was the subject of a special 1993 issue of the *Kennedy Institute of Ethics Journal* (to which the reader is directed for several excellent articles on this debate), including one in which prominent bioethicist Renee Fox deemed the practice an "ignoble form of medically rationalized cannibalism" and called for its prohibition (1993, 238).

As outlined by religion scholar Christopher Kaczor in his 2011 chapter "Organ Donation following Cardiac Death," the three main ethical concerns with DCD are as follows:

1. The potential conflicts of interest between providing the best care for the patient who is a potential DCD donor and obtaining organs for the intended recipients (e.g., because preparation for organ removal in DCD must occur before the declaration of death, there is concern that the ICU staff may have conflicting obligations to the potential donor and the intended recipient).

2. The potential need for antemortem interventions (those done to the donor patient before death) that help maintain organ quality but do no good for the intended donor (e.g., the administration of heparin and vasodilators to the patient to maintain the quality of the organs before LST is withdrawn).

3. The difficulties in determining death by cardiorespiratory criteria (e.g., what qualifies as irreversible cessation of cardiac function, how long a waiting time should be required between the heart stopping and the start of organ removal, whether there is a possibility of the heart restarting even after relatively prolonged periods without oxygen).

Despite these issues, many believe that these concerns can be addressed ethically as long as proper protocols and safeguards are in place. The ethical justification for the Pittsburgh Protocol was based primarily on respect for the autonomy of the patient and family to make medical decisions, including the opportunity to donate organs if they choose, after receiving sufficient information to do so. Shemie, an intensive care physician who has led the establishment of DCD in Canada and elsewhere, agrees that DCD is ethical if proper safeguards are in place. In the paper "Donation after Cardiocirculatory Death in Canada," which he authored with colleagues in 2006, Shemie suggests several core values that can guide the ethical implementations of DCD, including the following:

1. Respect for the life and dignity of all people, including the donor.

2. Optimal end-of-life care that respects the holistic well-being of the dying patient.

3. Respect for the autonomy of the dying patient, including his or her wish to donate or not donate.

4. Support for the grieving family, including giving them the opportunity to donate in situations that would not be possible without DCD.

5. Identification and management of real and perceived conflicts of interest and maintenance of public trust.

6. Respect for the professional integrity of those involved in end-of-life care, donation, and transplantation.

Although debate continues, DCD has become more and more common, and according to the standards of the Joint Commission on Accreditation of Healthcare Organizations (2006), hospitals are now required to address DCD in their policies, even if they choose not to perform such transplants in their centers. The ethical concerns have been evaluated and considered to be surmountable by many medical associations and organizations. For example, the Committee of Bioethics of the American Academy of Pediatrics identifies several points along the organ donation process where careful attention and avoidance of conflicts of interest could be managed, like decoupling the discussion of LST withdrawal from the organ donation discussion; provision of integrated palliative care, including sedation and analgesia to all potential DCD donors; and separation of the transplant team and ICU team to the greatest degree possible. They also assert that although hospitals should be required to provide access to DCD to families who request it, individual's health-care professionals should not be forced to participate.

## OPT-IN AND OPT-OUT MODELS OF CONSENT FOR DECEASED DONATION

Two methods are commonly used for determining whether people want to be organ donors after they die: opt-in strategies or opt-out strategies (sometimes called *presumed consent*). Opt-in requires potential donors to positively signify their intent to be a donor (e.g., by registering on an online donor registry or making a declaration at their local department of motor vehicles). As the strategy is currently practiced in the United States, the families of potential donors must still be approached for consent to donate, even if there is no record of the person having registered as a donor (i.e., failing to opt-in does not prevent donation). In an opt-out strategy, people are presumed to want to be organ donors unless they specifically state that they do not want to be. Opt-out strategies are used in several countries, including, most famously, Spain. With one of the highest deceased donor rates in the world, Spain has been suggested as a country on which lower-performing countries could model their organ retrieval practices. David Foster, a composer who runs a charitable foundation to help patients in need of organ transplants, advocates for adopting an opt-out approach in the United States and Canada by stating "Opt-out, really, it makes so much sense…. Hey, you're an organ donor unless you say you don't want to be one. That makes perfect sense" (Grant 2014).

An opt-out strategy has the potential benefit of increasing the overall deceased donor rate, because it would bypass the inertia that keeps people from registering to be donors. It can be ethically justified as respecting autonomy, because the autonomy of those who do not want to donate can be protected by allowing them to opt out. The same inertia, however, that keeps people from registering their positive intent to donate could prevent people from registering their dissent, so it is not clear that those who do not register their dissent truly wish to become donors. This theoretically could result in a case in which a person who does not want to donate dies without having made an opt-out designation and becomes an organ donor against his or her wishes.

Would presumed consent, even if it results in some errors in determining donor wishes, really result in any harm, because the organs are removed from a person who has died? In his notable 2011 book *Ethics and the Acquisition of Organs*, bioethicist Timothy Wilkinson defends a form of the opt-out system by arguing that, in the cases in which there is no good reason to suspect that a deceased person would have opposed organ donation, no rights are being violated. Thus, organ retrieval is not harmful to the donor or donor family, and its use could well be helpful to the potential recipient. Wilkinson stresses that a procedure for presumed consent would require the consequences of failing to make a choice (i.e., that your organs will be removed for transplantation) to be so well publicized so that all potential donors and nondonors are aware of what it means to make a "null choice" (i.e., choosing neither the donate or refuse to donate option), but he admits there is little evidence that current levels of public education can achieve that goal (Wilkinson 2014).

A major problem with presumed consent, as it is touted as a way to increase organ supply, is that it may not actually do so. Spain, the country often held up as the model for presumed consent, has employed many other innovations to increase its deceased donor rate, including early identification of potential donors, training for all medical staff involved even indirectly in organ donation, and extensive public engagement. Even the leaders of transplant in those countries do not credit presumed consent as the cause of their success: Rafael Matesanz, director of the Organización Nacional de Trasplantes in Spain, coauthored a paper with John Fabre and Paul Murphy in which they called presumed consent "a distraction in the quest for increasing rates of organ donation" (Fabre, Murphy, and Matesanz 2010, c4973). James Childress, a well-known bioethicist, has suggested in "Are Systems of Presumed Consent and Sales the Answer to the Need for More Organs for Transplantation?" (1992) that this presumed consent policy actually would engender mistrust in the public, prompting more people to register as nondonors and therefore reduce the number of organs donated. One can easily imagine a scenario in which a presumed consent case were to go awry (e.g., a person becomes a donor and is later revealed to have been against donation) and the inevitable ensuing media coverage, which could irreparably damage trust in the organ donation system.

Another difficulty with presumed consent is that it would likely require what has been called the "strong" model to be effective—that is, families would not be allowed to refuse donation unless the dead person had registered his or her dissent while alive. A "weak" model of presumed consent (where families are asked for consent to donate even if no antemortem dissent was registered) would have little advantage over the current opt-in model, because the ultimate decision would remain with the family. A family presented with clear evidence that their loved one wanted to donate (as would be the case with an opt-in model in which the patient took proactive steps to register his or her wishes) might be more likely to consent than would a family in which the patient's wishes could only be presumed. A strong model may increase donor rates in the short term, but it risks offending and alienating donor families, who would not be allowed to participate in the decision. Overriding family decision-making authority would remove one of the benefits of deceased donation, which is aiding the donor family during their grief. Thus, overriding family decision making would be difficult to gain traction with ICUs and organ procurement organizations, who are understandably focused on building trusting relationships with donor families. Finally, evidence from other countries has shown that it does not work; a hard model of presumed consent in Brazil was revoked after less than two years because of these types of concerns from both the public and medical professionals.

Given the concerns about public trust, the inadequate evidence that presumed consent actually can increase the number of organs available for transplant, and concerns that autonomy may be violated by such a policy, a 1993 United Network for Organ Sharing (UNOS) subcommittee on the issue recommended against adopting presumed consent in the United States. Instead, they advocated for registered choice, in which all individuals applying for driver's licenses would be required to make a choice to either donate, not donate, or leave the decision to their family. As Justin List notes in "To Donate or Not: Is That the Question?" (2005), both Texas and Virginia have experimented with this model, but the results have been discouraging, with many people deciding not to donate or simply refusing to make a decision. In the more than two decades since the UNOS report was published, there has been continued debate on the issue, but the opt-in model continues to be the US standard.

### PRISONERS AS DECEASED ORGAN DONORS

Because capital punishment is legal in many US states, it has been suggested that obtaining organs after execution may be one way to increase the donor pool, but in "The Use of Prisoners as Sources of Organs—An Ethically Dubious Practice" (2011), bioethicist Arthur Caplan argues against any use of organs from the condemned. In addition to the practical issues that he identifies (the small number of donors, the requirement to restrict methods of execution to those that would not damage the transplantable organs, and others), he raises many ethical concerns. Physicians would have to be involved in the execution, something that the American Medical Association already opposes because it is inconsistent with the physician's duty to heal. Caplan argues that accepting any type of altruism from the condemned may allow him or her some positive feedback or notoriety in the final days, which can negatively affect the families of the victims and decrease the retributive nature of the punishment. Furthermore, many Americans disagree with capital punishment entirely. Those individuals may fear that allowing organ donation from the condemned may make judges or juries more likely to sentence the convicted to death, because of the benefit of possible donation that could not be realized by lifetime imprisonment.

Despite these concerns, some argue that the practice should be supported. Physician Shu Lin, nurse Lauren Rich, and their coauthors (2012) assert that even if death row donation only results in a small number of donors, the effect on those receiving the organs would be lifesaving, and that the debate over the morality of capital punishment is not relevant to the consideration of organ donation after execution, because it is currently a legal option in many states. Bioethicist L. Syd Johnson (2011) rejects the argument that donation undercuts the morality of execution by allowing some degree of redemption, pointing out that other redemptive acts, like apologizing to the families of victims and seeking spiritual awakening are accepted and even encouraged in a prisoner's final days.

The world has clearly denounced the use of organs from executed prisoners in China (an area that will be explored further in the section on transplant tourism). Execution in the US justice system has been shown to be inequitably applied, especially punishing nonwhites, and the United States was one of the last countries in the world to stop executing juveniles and those with developmental disabilities. So, is it reasonable to assume that using condemned prisoners as organ donors in the United States will be done more ethically than in the Chinese system? It makes little sense for the transplant community to justify the use of organs from the condemned in one country while remaining passionately opposed to the practice in another. At present, the UNOS ethics committee opposes any changes to the law that would make procuring organs after execution possible, and there are no known cases in which a condemned prisoner's offer to donate has been accepted.

## LIVING DONATION

Kazuo Ishiguro's novel *Never Let Me Go* (2005, made into a 2010 film starring Keira Knightley and Carey Mulligan) follows three children, Ruth, Tommy, and Kathy, from their childhood at a strange English boarding school called Halisham through Tommy's death (euphemistically called "completion"). It is revealed through the novel that the children are clones who have been created to become organ donors and that they "complete" after their vital organs are removed for transplantation. The novel challenges the reader to consider whether the clones are breaking Immanuel Kant's (1724–1804) injunction to treat all rational beings as ends in themselves, not merely as means, and what degree of sacrifice we are willing to accept from living donors.

Living donation has been responsible for much of the growth in transplant rates over the past two decades. Living donors were once only blood relatives, but now spouses, friends, coworkers, and even Internet-based acquaintances can potentially become living donors. What are the ethical issues involved in accepting an organ donation from a living person? Do the obligations of the transplant team to accept or reject a donor candidate change with the organ, the recipient, or other factors? Is there an obligation to offer to be a living donor, whether to a family member, friend, or stranger?

To be a living donor, an individual usually needs to be blood-type compatible with the intended recipient and must be a reasonable immunological match (i.e., the recipient's body is not expected to reject the donor organ). The donation surgery involves the removal of one kidney, a part of the liver, or a lobe of the lung, depending on which organ the recipient requires. Although most healthy individuals can continue to function well after the removal of one or part of these organs, it is clear that a potential living donor is exposed to some risks. Transplant surgeon Francis Moore (1913–2001) commented in his 1964 article "New Problems for Surgery" that many in the field were uncomfortable with living donor transplantation because "for the first time in the history of medicine a procedure is being adopted in which a perfectly healthy person is injured permanently in order to improve the wellbeing, not of himself, but of another" (391). Kant's injunction to treat all rational beings as ends in themselves, not solely as means, would require us to reject living donation if all the benefits accrued to the recipient, and all the risks to the donor. Living donation, however, can be ethically justified if we consider the psychological benefits to the donor, like the satisfaction of having saved a life, or the emotional connection maintained when a loved one is saved by transplant. Living donors do report being highly motivated to save a loved one's life and those who do donate generally report satisfaction with their decision and generally good mental health (see, e.g., Fehrman-Ekholm et al. 2000; Gross et al. 2013; Tong et al. 2012).

To avoid risks as much as possible, each potential donor must undergo a thorough physical and psychological screening program. Those who pursue donation must display adequate capacity to provide informed consent, which requires them to understand the risks and benefits, make and express an informed choice, and be free from coercion as much as possible in making a decision (as with other medical interventions). Some centers enforce a "cooling off" period between donor assessment and the actual surgery, to give the potential donor a chance to renege, or employ an independent donor advocate to further evaluate the donor's capacity and motivation. The medical team caring for the recipient (e.g., the patient's nephrologist) must be excluded from any evaluation of potential donors to avoid undue influence and conflict of interest.

Is there a level of risk that is too high to accept, even from the highly motivated donor? In the "My Chopped Liver" episode of the television show *Scrubs*, a man donates a part of his liver to his brother, but nearly dies from complications of the surgery. This episode raises the ethical issue of how much risk is reasonable to accept from those willing to act as living donors and whether the relational ties of family make these risks more acceptable. The risk of death resulting from kidney donation is low (around three in ten thousand), but even well-screened patients face a higher lifetime risk of high blood pressure and other medical issues. Recent studies have shown a relatively high rate of later kidney failure in those who donate, about eleven times higher than the general population, even though end-stage kidney disease is still relatively rare in donors (about 0.5 percent after fifteen years of follow-up, according to Geir Mjøen et al. in their 2014 article "Long-Term Risks for Kidney Donors"). Katrina Bramstedt reports in "Living Liver Donor Mortality: Where Do We Stand?" (2006), that the risks are much higher for liver transplantation, with a risk of morbidity (serious complication) of 50 percent and mortality between 1 and 2 percent. A donor death in the United States in 2002 sparked controversy and a call from some to outlaw the use of living liver donors entirely. Although that did not happen, Denise Grady writes in "Donor's Death at Hospital Halts Some Liver Surgeries" (2002) that donation rates decreased and still account for only 4 percent of liver transplants in the United States.

Few guidelines clearly delineate an acceptable threshold for donor risk, because the risks and benefits to each particular donation scenario are dependent on the medical characteristics of the donor, as well as on the relationship between donor and recipient. For example, a transplant team might be more willing to accept higher medical risks for a father donating a kidney to his child than they would for a person who wants to donate to his workmate because the psychological benefits are perceived to be greater for the father than for the coworker. In addition, transplant nephrologist and epidemiologist Peter Reese has pointed out that "setting thresholds on the lifetime probability of complications such as end-stage renal disease might perpetuate or worsen disparities in access to kidney transplantation in minority groups" (Reese, Boudville, and Garg 2015, 2009) because in-family donors may be difficult to find in communities where hypertension, obesity, and other diseases are more common.

Transplant teams generally reserve the right to deny a donor application if the team feels that the risk is too high, even if the potential donor is willing to accept the risk. The justification for this is that the transplant team, who ultimately must protect the donor from harm, should not have to participate in a procedure they consider unethical. Interestingly, this is one of the last examples in which fairly paternalistic decision making is generally accepted—decisions that are made by the medical team that limit the patient's autonomy but that are justified as being for the patient's own good. Part of the reason for this is that donation, unlike treatment for a patient's own illness, is always optional, even for highly motivated donor candidates, and this generally is regarded as being supererogatory—that is, beyond what is required in normal human interaction, a "meritorious act, but one that is not legally or morally required" (Simmerling et al. 2004, 22).

## DONATION BETWEEN INTIMATES AND MEDICAL EXCUSES

The previous section pointed out that any potential living donor candidate must be capable of making an informed decision, which includes ensuring that the decision is being made voluntarily and without coercion. Although obviously unacceptable examples of coercion can be ferreted out in the donor assessment (e.g., a donor who states that he is coming forward only because he has been threatened by the recipient's family), some types of pressure and coercion may be unavoidable. Family relationships are unavoidably complex (and some are admittedly more complex than others). Donation to a family member certainly involves some degree of altruism, but it also may be somewhat self-serving and even expected, as pointed out by ethicists Walter Glannon and Lainie Ross, who note that "the family member who is a potential donor has a *prima facie* obligation to donate because of the nature of relationships within the family" (2002, 156). For example, if a woman who is the breadwinner in her family requires a kidney transplant, her husband may come forward to donate for any number of interrelated reasons. He may be donating to display altruism in general, to act on his love for his wife, to fulfill his vow to stay "in sickness and in health," to keep his children from becoming motherless, to protect the family's livelihood, or to avoid the stares and recriminations from family members if he does not volunteer. It would be unrealistic to accept only offers that came from pure altruism, as likely few could pass such stringency, nor would such a threshold fit with the usual conception of family that we accept in practically every other aspect of society.

Although donation between intimates, then, can be ethically acceptable even if it is not purely altruistic, what of the potential donor who is evaluated and approved, but who really does not want to donate? Some living donor assessment programs offer these reluctant candidates (sometimes called "black sheep donors") a medical excuse that they can back out of donating without admitting their reluctance to their intended recipient (e.g., stating that the donor is not blood-type compatible, even when this is untrue). A medical excuse potentially can reduce coercion and maintain family relationships or friendships that otherwise would be strained, but philosopher Mary Simmerling and colleagues argue that it is inherently deceptive and may damage trust toward the transplant team if the recipient discovers the excuse to be false. In "When Duties Collide: Beneficence and Veracity in the Evaluation of Living Organ Donors" (2007), Simmerling and her coauthors also point out that this is a difficult lie to maintain, especially in a situation in which a donor later changes his mind about donating or wants to donate to another family member, as commonly may be the case for genetic kidney diseases. Even if the evaluation team does not lie directly to the recipient and simply provides a convenient excuse for the potential donor to take back to her family (e.g., "I have too many arteries going into my kidney"), this could be seen a violation of the trust placed in health-care professionals and amounts to abuse of that powerful relationship. Instead of a medical excuse, they advocate a straightforward approach at the outset that would explain "up front to all parties that the program has the right to refuse a living donation without detailed explanation" (Simmerling et al. 2007, 191).

Ethicist Aaron Spital disagrees with this analysis, maintaining that deception can be justified because it protects the potential donor, to whom the donor evaluation team owes its fidelity. In his 2008 article "Providing a Medical Excuse to Organ Donor Candidates Who Feel Trapped: Concerns and Replies," he further asserts that assisting the donor to lie is not the same as lying directly to the recipient, so should not be considered unacceptable in the same way that other medical lies are (like lying to a patient about a terminal diagnosis). Physician ethicist Ross takes a nuanced approach in "What the Medical Excuse Teaches Us about the Potential Living Donor as Patient" (2010), distinguishing between the unacceptable "false medical excuse" (like fabricating an anatomical abnormality), from the ethically justifiable "blameless excuse," which would be a general statement that the potential donor is unsuitable and would be provided whether the donor's unsuitability stems from medical reasons, psychological issues, or simple reluctance. She also suggests that these discussions regarding what will and will not be disclosed should take place even before blood-type testing or human leukocyte antigen (HLA) testing (the initial blood tests to which a potential donor submits), because these simple tests done early in the process can be seen as the point of no return for some donors.

## DONATION FROM NONINTIMATES (NONDIRECTED DONATION)

*Seven Pounds* (2008) is a film starring Will Smith that examines the motivations of a man who wants to donate all his vital organs. Smith's character, Tim, is attempting to make amends for killing seven people in a motor vehicle collision that he caused. He subsequently

**Will Smith stars as a man on a journey to change the lives of seven strangers in the 2008 drama** Seven Pounds, **directed by Gabriele Muccino.** *In the movie, Smith's character is attempting to make amends for killing seven people in a motor vehicle collision that he caused. He subsequently donates his organs to seven "good" people, whose worthiness he determines by surreptitiously interviewing them. Here, Smith's character speaks to one of his intended recipients, played by Woody Harrelson.*
MOVIESTORE COLLECTION LTD/ALAMY.

donates his organs to seven "good" people, whose worthiness he determines by surreptitiously interviewing them. The two final recipients of his gifts get their transplants (heart and corneas) after he commits suicide, and all his recipients get posthumous letters from him explaining his motivation.

Donation between blood relatives was the only type of accepted living donation for many years, not only because the degree of matching between donor and recipient was likely to be better but also because the donor motivations for an in-family donor were more obvious. Over time, better transplant medications have reduced the need for close matching of HLA types, and those who were emotionally connected to their recipients (spouses, stepparents, close friends, and so on) but not blood related were accepted as living donors. For example, in the *Scrubs* episode "My Unicorn," a man who needs a kidney transplant seeks out his estranged son to be a donor. The reluctant son eventually agrees, but the workup reveals that he is not the man's biological son. The team struggles with whether or not to tell him about his true parentage. In the end, they reveal the truth, and the son donates his kidney anyway.

Another category of donors took a little longer to take hold in the transplant community: people who come forward to donate but have no relationship with any wait list candidate. The donors, commonly referred to as *living nondirected donors* (LNDs) or *nondirected altruistic donors* (NDADs), initially were viewed with suspicion, and their offer to donate was often seen as a sign of mental illness. These potential donors express many types of motivation, including fulfillment of religious directives, a general sense of wanting to help another human being, or an attempt to make amends for previous wrong doing (as in *Seven Pounds*).

With careful psychiatric evaluation, it became clear that, at least for a portion of these NDADs, their motivation was primarily altruistic and they had the capacity to provide an informed choice. Most programs now accept NDADs, either to donate to the top person on the deceased donor list or to start a domino chain (a topic beyond the scope of this chapter). As Ross and colleagues argue in "Should All Living Donors Be Treated Equally?" (2002), it may be acceptable for NDADs to take on the risks of donation, but the degree of risk should be less than we allow for intimates because the NDAD who is prevented from donating has not been prevented from discharging his duty (since he had none to begin with), whereas an intimate may have such a duty. One ongoing debate is whether these donors should be allowed to direct their organ to a person they have heard of but do not know (e.g., after a public solicitation attempt). Also concerning is whether potential donors and intended recipients who meet in less traditional forums (e.g., on the Internet) should be treated the same as traditional intimate donors—who we let direct their donation to the recipient of their choosing—or if we should insist that all nonintimate donors donate to the person that the transplant team has deemed to be the most in need. This discussion challenges us to discuss how relationships are formed in the new millennium—with so much of our time being spent online, are these new types of friendships so different from the old? Proponents would argue that friendships can be formed in many ways, and it is not the transplant team's place to judge the intimacy of a bond or hold it to outdated standards of sincerity. Detractors question what information the intended donor received before embarking on a friendship with the intended recipient, as well as the recipient's need, the risks of donation, and the other people on the waiting list.

Although it is unlikely that a real-life Tim (from *Seven Pounds*) would pass the psychological screening that is necessary to become a living donor, it is technically possible that his heart and cornea donations would be accepted, because directed donation to a named recipient is consistent with US law. The film was critically panned because of it sentimentality and unbelievability, but is an interesting twist on the issue of donor motivation, especially for LNDs. It also leads the viewer to question what makes a "worthy" organ recipient, because the current organ allocation generally sees evaluation of social worth to be an indefensible allocation criterion.

## MINORS AS ORGAN DONORS

Jodi Picoult's *My Sister's Keeper: A Novel* (2004, made into a 2009 movie starring Cameron Diaz and Abigail Breslin) tells the story of Anna, a thirteen-year-old girl who was conceived as a "savior sibling" for her sister Kate, who is suffering from cancer. Although the initial bone marrow donation works well, Kate eventually relapses and her kidneys fail, prompting her family to ask Anna to donate a kidney to Kate. Anna dissents and takes her parents to court, suing for emancipation. Both the novel and film, despite their medical inaccuracies, were highly successful, and the story raises the question about whether it is ever ethically acceptable for minors to act as living donors.

Living organ donation has been discussed earlier as an ethically valid procedure for adults who are motivated and healthy enough to donate, but should minors be allowed to donate under some circumstances? Young children's medical decision making is usually the responsibility of their parents or legal guardians, but adolescents often have some say in the decisions regarding their own medical care, and they may be allowed to make autonomous decisions in some situations (e.g., regarding contraception). To make their own decisions, adolescents are expected to show capacity, to demonstrate the ability to understand the proposed therapy and its alternatives, and to make an informed choice. The more serious or risky a decision, the more capacity is expected to be displayed: a thirteen-year-old may easily be trusted to make an informed decision regarding school electives but would not be expected to be solely responsible for decisions regarding cancer chemotherapy.

For living organ donation, the bar for capacity can justifiably be raised even further, because there is no physical benefit to the donor, and a small but real chance of physical harm. Because young donors need to live their entire adult lives with a single kidney, the risk of developing kidney disease themselves over a lifetime is higher. A study by David MacDonald and colleagues (2014) examining the long-term effects of donation on adolescent donors could not show that their risk is lower than that of adult donors; an accompanying editorial by Aviva Goldberg and Leroy Storsley (2014) argued that this does not mean that potential harms do not exist. Another potential harm is the increased coercion that a minor donor may experience from his or her family, especially if an adult parent is the decision maker for both the intended recipient and donor.

Because of the psychological benefits that donation may allow, young adults over the age of majority are allowed to serve as living donors. These benefits (helping a loved one, saving a life, improved self-esteem) theoretically could accrue to the minor donor, especially if the donor had a close emotional connection to the intended recipient (e.g., a teen parent donating to his or her own child). Francis Delmonico and the Council of the Transplantation Society, an international consensus panel, recommended in "A Report of the Amsterdam Forum on the Care of the Live Kidney Donor" (2005) that those under eighteen years old never be allowed to donate as living donors, because the outcomes for their recipients would not be better than that expected if they received adult donor kidneys. This approach seems to focus only on the risk-benefit ratio to the recipient and overlooks the situations in which there are significant benefits to the donor from donating. A more nuanced approach was put forward by two major expert panels in the United States, the American Academy of Pediatrics (AAP) Bioethics Committee in 2008, and the Live Organ Donor Consensus Group in 2000, which outlines four conditions under which a minor could donate. The AAP endorsed the findings of the earlier group and added a fifth condition recommending that minors be allowed to donate only when the following criteria are met:

1. Donor and recipient are both highly likely to benefit.
2. Surgical risk for the donor is extremely low.
3. All other deceased and living donor options have been exhausted.
4. The minor freely assents to donate without coercion (established by an independent advocacy team).
5. Emotional and psychological risks to the donor are minimized.

These criteria seem generally acceptable, although are not without controversy. N. J. Webb and P. M. Fortune (2006), for example, argue that the decisional capacity of an adolescent and an adult may be equivalent in some situations and that when it has been determined that an adolescent possesses sufficient capacity to donate, the requirement to exhaust any adult donor potential may put undue coercion on adult family members to donate.

Although this issue has primarily been discussed in regard to kidney transplantation, the increasing use of living liver donors has sparked the same conversation. According to Laura Capitaine and her coauthors in "Should Minors Be Considered as Potential Living Liver Donors?" (2013), it has not yet been recommended as an ethically viable option because the risk to living liver donors is much higher than that to kidney donors.

## TRANSPLANT TOURISM AND ORGAN TRAFFICKING

The film *Dirty Pretty Things* (2002) follows two undocumented immigrants (played by Audrey Tatou and Chiwetel Ejiofor) who participate in an illegal organ-vending scheme in the hotel in which they work. They struggle with the morality of their actions, which include performing transplant retrieval surgery in the hotel and selling a kidney to obtain a fake passport. Although the scheme stretches the limits of believability (they first discover what is going on by finding a human heart plugging one of the hotel's toilets), the film does an excellent job of dramatizing the desperate situations in which a person may consider vending his or her organs.

The US National Organ Transplant Act forbids the sale of organs for money or any "valuable consideration," and the same is true for most countries in the world. The sale of organs from the living is legal in Iran, and a flourishing black or gray market for organs exists in many other countries, including Bangladesh, the Philippines, and former Soviet bloc countries. Anthropologist Nancy Scheper-Hughes has documented these practices in several publications, including her 2003 paper "Keeping an Eye on the Global Traffic in Human Organs." In 2012, Monir Moniruzzaman, another anthropologist, published an in-depth investigation into the organ trafficking markets of Bangladesh, including interviews with those who had sold their organs. People who sell their organs in these markets are not donors, because they are getting paid for the exchange and more correctly are referred to as *vendors*.

Few argue that the black or gray market can be justified ethically. There is potential benefit to the recipient (who otherwise might have died while waiting on the deceased donor list), but there is ample evidence of harm to those who sell their organs. Vendors usually work through a broker or intermediary. The broker connects the vendor to a person in need of a transplant, or a medical center willing to do the organ removal surgery, and is paid for producing the vendor. Although some of the money that the broker receives is passed on to the vendor, these brokers profit much more from the transaction than do the vendors, and often they provide little information to the vendor about the risks of the surgery or the potential long-term effects. Vendors are given little chance to make a truly informed decision. Often, they have serious regrets about their decision to vend, and the money that they make generally is not enough to improve their lives in any permanent way. The anthropological work of Scheper-Hughes in "The Global Traffic in Human Organs" (2000) and elsewhere brought to light this global market, which clearly benefits those from wealthier countries over those with lower levels of socioeconomic development.

In response to the growing international market in organs, an international group of more than 150 professionals developed the 2008 Declaration of Istanbul on Organ Trafficking and Transplant Tourism, which condemned unregulated markets and outlined six principles that built on the United Nations' Universal Declaration of Human Rights (1948). The final principle condemns the practice of transplant tourism, stating that it "violate[s] the principles of equity, justice, and respect for human dignity and should be prohibited" (3).

In addition to the illegal and unethical practice of paying poor people to give up their organs while alive, evidence indicates that governments have also sold organs from executed prisoners for the purpose of transplantation. Canadians David Matas, a human rights lawyer, and David Kilgour, a former politician, investigated and published the evidence on the use of organs from executed prisoners in China in their report *Bloody Harvest* (2009). This practice has since been rejected by the transplant community as a violation of nonmaleficence, especially because evidence shows that some groups are targeted for arrest and execution specifically to supply organs for donation.

## FINANCIAL INCENTIVES IN A REGULATED LEGAL SYSTEM

Although an unregulated global market in organs cannot be justified, could there be a way to ethically incentivize donation? In "Living and Deceased Organ Donation Should Be Financially Neutral Acts" (2015), Delmonico and colleagues report that consensus is wide that current financial disincentives to donation (e.g., due to taking time off work to donate) should be addressed by adequate donor medical coverage, medical follow-up, and reasonable compensation for expenses. There is still disagreement, however, on whether the law prohibiting the sale of organs should be changed to allow for true incentives (those that leave the donor better off financially by the act of donation).

Lianne Barnieh and her coauthors report in "Attitudes toward Strategies to Increase Organ Donation" (2012) that public opinion polls are mixed, but some evidence suggests that a portion of the general public supports financial incentives. This could be a payment of a fixed amount of money (in "In Defense of a Regulated System of Compensation for Living Donation" [2008], transplant surgeon Arthur Matas, nephrologist Ben Hippen, and kidney transplant recipient and psychiatrist Sally Satel estimate that between $10,000 and $45,000 would be fair), lifetime health insurance, a tax credit, or, in the case of deceased donors, payment of funeral expenses. Matas, one of the most vocal proponents of a regulated market, claims in "A Regulated System of Incentives for Living Donation: A Challenge to Define and Understand the Objections" (2014), that it is both practical and ethically acceptable to design regulated systems that can offer financial incentives to those willing to sell their organs. He points out that people are paid for jobs that we consider to be altruistic (firefighters, police officers, etc.) and that we allow people to accept some risk of bodily injury in their jobs (miners, etc.), and therefore, it is equally acceptable to consider paying people for something we consider to be altruistic or risky. He argues that a regulated market (which would, among other things, offer incentives only from a state or state-recognized authority that is of similar value to all recipients, and limit vendors to citizens or legal residents of the country that will allocate the organs) avoids many of the ethical issues of unregulated markets.

The debate has garnered interest among the general public as well, outside of medicine. The repugnance argument contends that selling organs is an unacceptable commodification of the body—just as we reject slavery, indentured servitude, and prostitution, there are limits to what we will allow people to do with their bodies. On the other hand, a 2014 *Wall Street Journal* article by economists Gary Becker and Julio Elias rejects repugnance as a valid argument, because we have found ways to legally and ethically commodify the body in other ways, such as gestational surrogacy.

There is an equally impassioned debate concerning rejection of any type of market in organs, even if regulated. A 2015 editorial by Delmonico and other prominent transplant professionals calls for the continued prohibition. Their objections can be summarized as follows:

1. Financial incentives do not promote autonomy because they rely on the constrained choice of the economically disadvantaged to sell their organs.

2. Organ vendors would be motivated to be less honest in their evaluations than would altruistic donors, which could put both the vendor and recipient at risk for more complications.

3. The evidence from Iran, where organ sales are legal, is not encouraging. Organ vendors are unhappy with their choice to vend, report high rates of medical and psychological sequelae, and often are involved in side deals with recipients to negotiate additional payments.

4. More ethical methods to increase the donor pool have not yet been exhausted, and efforts should focus on these rather than a regulated market in organs.

Although there is no move, at the present time, to remove the prohibition on organ sales in the United States, the debate continues. It is clear that the discussion involves consideration of both the practical opportunities and drawbacks that a regulated system would create as well as a larger discussion of the human body, its ownership, and how its commodification would affect not only the transplant community but also the greater society.

## ALLOCATION AND RECIPIENT ISSUES

In Season 3 of *Scrubs*, "My Rule of Thumb" focused on a man denied a liver transplant because he drank a small amount of alcohol in violation of hospital transplant policy. A young woman, who was felt by the medical team to be more deserving and more likely to be adherent, receives the liver transplant instead.

The evaluation of a potential transplant recipient is usually done by a team of experts, and not all people with organ failure will be considered "good" transplant candidates or eligible for a transplant. Medical reasons could exclude someone from transplant: the patient's other conditions could make the transplant surgery too dangerous (e.g., a person with kidney disease whose heart is too weak to undergo major surgery) or may be worsened by the transplant (e.g., a person with malignant cancer, whose cancer would be worsened by the medications required after a transplant), or the patient's condition may not improve even with a successful transplant (e.g., heart-lung failure that has weakened the body past the point of potential repair).

The medical factors seem to be relatively easy to justify, but the transplant eligibility system also takes into account psychosocial factors, such as the following:

1. Alcohol and substance use.

2. Presence of psychiatric conditions that could limit ability to adhere to post-transplant regimen (e.g., depression, schizophrenia, etc.).

3. Ability to adhere to the medical plan post-transplant (taking medications, attending follow-up appointment, etc.).

4. Ability to afford ongoing medical care, including expensive transplant medications.

Although these psychosocial criteria, at first glance, also seem relatively intuitive, there is a potential for them to be misused or misapplied, especially because the evidence to support them often is weak. To be ethically acceptable, psychosocial criteria should be based, as much as possible, on empirical evidence that the restriction results in better outcomes for the recipient and in better use of the organs available for transplant (e.g., it maximizes utility). For example, most transplant programs require individuals waiting for a liver transplant because of alcoholic liver disease to demonstrate at least six months of sobriety before receiving a transplant. If it can clearly be demonstrated that lack of sobriety leads to liver graft loss, then it would be reasonable to restrict access based on these grounds. When the psychosocial criteria are based on more limited evidence or public opinion of social worth or deservedness, they become less ethically defensible and may violate justice. For example, in "Alcohol and Substance Use in Liver Transplant Patients" (2011), Andrea DiMartini, Catherine Crone, and Mary Amanda Dew support the idea of some period of abstinence from alcohol pretransplant, but they have pointed out that those with alcoholic liver disease are less likely to even be referred for transplant evaluation and are considered to be of lower priority by physicians and the public when compared with other cirrhosis patients, suggesting some biases that go beyond empirical medical criteria. The UNOS Ethics Committee, in its statement on "Ethical Principles to Be Considered in the Allocation of Human Organs" (2015), recognizes that the allocation of organs, since they are viewed as a public resource, may need to consider the views of the public even when there is no clear cause and effect, stating "past behavior that results in organ failure should not be considered a sole basis for excluding transplant candidates. However, additional discussion of this issue in a societal context may be warranted."

## LIMITING TRANSPLANT OPPORTUNITIES BASED ON SOCIAL FACTORS

In "Haunted by the 'God Committee': Reciprocity Does No Justice to Eliminating Social Disparities" (2004), Elisa J. Gordon discusses the famous work of the "God committees," which decided which patients would receive access to dialysis in Seattle in the 1960s. Gordon highlights how social worth criteria can be misused, even by seemingly well-meaning people, to perpetuate social disparity. These committees, composed mainly of community members (a labor leader, lawyer, clergy member, housewife, etc.), reviewed the files of patients with end-stage kidney disease and determined who would be given access to dialysis, which was an extremely limited option at the time. A landmark 1962 article in *Life* magazine by Shana Alexander (1925–2005) discussed how the God committees reached their determinations. All patients were considered to be of equal need, because all would die without the treatment. It was clear that social worth criteria (level of education, church attendance, and even ability of the patient's wife to remarry if he were to die) were considered to be valid factors in allocating the dialysis chairs, and those who did not fit the committee's interpretation of a worthy person were excluded. The UNOS allocation system is designed to avoid or reduce these types of social judgments, by relying as much as possible on objective medical criteria, stating that "all members of the public are morally entitled to fair access." Inequalities in accessing the list, however, still limit the opportunities of certain groups or types of patients.

Despite relatively objective allocation criteria, major disparities persist in access to transplantation based on race and geography. For example, according to Amit Mathur and colleagues in "Racial and Ethnic Disparities in Access to Liver Transplantation" (2014), analysis of the liver transplant waiting list shows a significant disparity in access, with African Americans getting less access than whites, not only to transplantation but also to other steps in their disease journey, such as therapy for hepatitis C and cirrhosis. In "Racial

Differences in Determinants of Live Donor Kidney Transplantation in the United States"
(2013), T. S. Purnell and colleagues note that on the kidney transplant waiting list,
predialysis care and insurance also limit the opportunities of nonwhite patients.
Additionally, even objective criteria can limit access; heavy emphasis on HLA typing, for
example, can disadvantage minorities because they are less likely to find a perfect match in
the donor pool. There is ongoing work to reduce and eliminate these disparities, but equal
access has not yet been achieved. There are also fewer living donors from minority
communities, which further disadvantages this group.

Social worth continues to play a role in access to the waiting list. Because little evidence
suggests that social worth is any indication of how well the organ will survive in the recipient
(i.e., utility), such an approach generally should be rejected because it violates the principle
of justice. As with other inequities in the health-care system as a whole, this is important not
only because it is the right way to treat human beings, but also because the public relies on
the transplant system to be fair and transparent. Policies that violate this fairness may reduce
trust in the entire system.

One debate has centered on undocumented immigrants. UNOS does not specifically
limit access to these individuals, but difficulties in health-care access, including payment for
the transplant surgery and subsequent medication costs, have significantly marginalized this
population. Some, like nephrologist Eli Friedman and transplant surgeon Amy Friedman,
argue that undocumented residents should not be entitled to federally funded transplants
because the US system cannot be expected to provide expensive health care for these
individuals when it is not providing basic health care for many US citizens. They also
question whether undocumented residents will be responsible recipients, because their "very
presence in the United States represents a determination to disregard regulations" (2007,
22). Goldberg, Simmerling, and Joel Frader, writing in "Why Undocumented Residents
Should Have Access to Kidney Transplantation" (2007), disagree, arguing that the cost to
the system is not a valid argument in that transplantation saves the federal system money
because it is cheaper over the long run than dialysis. Additionally, evidence suggests that
undocumented residents contribute both to the US financial system (through their labor)
and the organ system (because some become deceased donors if they die in the United
States). They argue that these individuals, especially if they arrived in the United States
before they knew of their illnesses, are therefore members of the larger US community and
should be considered similarly to other residents for access. Some hospitals, programs, and
states do now provide assistance for transplant to these individuals.

Developmentally disabled individuals have been excluded from transplant evaluation in
the past. The initial concern was that their other comorbidities might limit the success of
transplantation or that their intellectual disability would prevent them from being able to
adhere to the post-transplant regimen. The evidence in this regard, albeit limited, does not
seem to bear this out—the outcomes for graft and patient survival are similar to that of the
general population, and recipients and their caregivers report improvements in quality of life
after transplant, similar to other patients. This success is likely the result of the supports that
are already built in to the care of the individual with developmental disability: they often
need the long-term support of a caregiver and that person also can help with their transplant
medications and follow-up appointments, thus increasing the chances of success. Goldberg,
Sandra Amaral, and Asha Moudgil (2015) offered a framework for evaluating children with
comorbidities for transplant, arguing that it is only justifiable to restrict access if the burdens
of transplant clearly outweigh the benefits. They also stress that this needs to be a discussion

between the parents and the transplant team, because benefits and burdens may be valued differently by different parties.

## CONDITIONAL AND DIRECTED DONATION AND PUBLIC SOLICITATION FOR ORGANS

In the United States, the Final Rule allows deceased donor organs to be directed to a particular, named recipient (i.e., the organ can be directed to a particular person, thus bypassing the usual allocation system). In analyzing the ethics of directed donation in these high-profile cases, one must consider that the vast majority of living donation is already directed; that is, living donors usually donate to people they know. Generally, directed donation is accepted in the living donor case because it is recognized that familial bonds, or the emotional commitments between friends, are a motivation for donation, and that the act of donation can strengthen these bonds. There is also the concern that living donors will donate only if their autonomy in selecting a recipient is respected, so that utility will be harmed by reducing the number of willing living donors. This acceptance of partiality in the living donor scheme, in some ways, does violate justice, because those without a willing living donor are relegated to the deceased donor waiting list, where they will wait longer for an organ and may receive one of lower quality.

In contrast, the deceased donor waiting list is more strongly rooted in justice: once active on the waiting list, patients rise to the top based on strict, objective allocation criteria. This system places little importance on the autonomy of the deceased donor or family, at least after consent for organ donation is obtained. The system generally is immune to personal pleas (e.g., a nephrologist cannot make a challenge to move her patient higher up on the allocation list because she feels the patient is more "deserving" than others on the wait list).

Despite the heavy weighting for justice in the general allocation system for deceased donor organs, when a deceased donor organ is, in rare cases, directed to a particular recipient, media reports generally have been positive, like the transplants from a daughter to a father (see the 1994 *New York Times* article "Father Receives Heart Transplant from Daughter") and from a fourteen-year-old boy to his schoolmate (see Meyer's 2004 article "Teen Who Always Gave of Self Gives Gift of Life"). In "Directed and Conditional Deceased Donor Organ Donations" (2010), Antonia Cronin and James Douglas describe a case in the United Kingdom, where directed donation at the time was not allowed, in which a public uproar followed a decision to refuse to direct a kidney from a deceased woman to her mother who was on the transplant waiting list. Although media reception is not, of course, the sole standard by which ethical behavior should be judged, it is interesting that the public response in both cases seemed to support the decision to allow such donation between family members.

The recognition that two parallel systems place different weight on ethical principles (autonomy for the living donor system and justice for the deceased donor system) has led some to question whether the deceased donor system should be allowed to be more partial. For example, would it be acceptable for a donor family to insist that their loved one's organs go to a particular type of individual (someone of a certain race or religion) or even that their organs not be donated to a person of a certain race or religion? This type of conditional donation generally has been rejected by the transplant community because it violates the principle of justice, and it may reduce trust in the transplant system as a whole. As stated by a British panel that examined this issue after organs were accepted with the condition that they be transplanted only into white people, "to attach any condition to a donation is unacceptable, because it offends against the fundamental principle that organs are donated altruistically and should go to patients in the greatest need" (UK Department of Health 2000, 25).

Physicians Michael Volk and Peter Ubel agree in their 2008 article "A Gift of Life: Ethical and Practical Problems with Conditional and Directed Donation" that conditional donation remains ethically problematic, both on consequentialist grounds (because it may actually result in fewer transplants as a result of reduced trust in the system) and because it furthers discrimination against those with undesirable social habits or characteristics, thus violating justice. Medical-legal scholar David Price disagrees in his 2008 article "Conditional Organ Donation: A View of the Ethicist," arguing that a conditional donation may be acceptable when directed toward a class of people that does not exclude another class of people based on "illegitimate discriminatory criteria" (1540), as would be might the case, for example, with a directed donation to children. Bioethicist Wilkinson argues in "What's Not Wrong with Conditional Organ Donation?" (2003) that even directions to a particular race of people may be acceptable when the race is one that has been historically marginalized in organ access (like African Americans in the United States, or indigenous populations in Canada, Australia, and New Zealand). He further argues that although the request for conditional donation may be racist or otherwise distasteful, accepting it can still be ethically acceptable, because the increased number of organs benefits the entire waiting list, even those who were denied that particular organ. Even if conditional donation could be justified on these grounds, it would remain problematic. Would a transplant team with a conditional offer be required to sort through wait-list candidates like an old-fashioned matchmaker, discarding those who did not meet the donor's criteria and bringing acceptable matches forward for scrutiny? Besides being an obvious violation of patient confidentiality, such an obligation would be difficult to discharge, especially in the time-sensitive donation situation.

Under the current US rules, conditional donations are not allowable, but directed donations may be. This legislation allows some individual to launch public solicitation campaigns (e.g., on televisions, billboards, or online) to find a living or deceased donor. Solicitation of smaller audiences (e.g., family members, church communities, or coworkers) has been accepted and even encouraged, presumably because of the assumption that a preexisting emotional relationship exists and that the personal campaign may encourage donors who otherwise would not have donated. There is criticism, however, when this solicitation extends to the wider spheres of television audiences or Internet users, because there is little likelihood that a prior relationship does exist. Physician and writer Robert Steinbrook points out in "Public Solicitation of Organ Donors" (2005) that there are risks to recipients who launch these campaigns because they might be asked for payment or otherwise exploited by potential donors. In addition, it remains unclear whether donors who receive organs from these campaigns have received an organ that otherwise might not have been donated at all or potentially diverted an organ that would have been allocated according to the normal criteria. Others argue that the Internet does give special access to those that are willing or able to use this technology and that this seems to violate the principle of justice, at least when it involves deceased donor organs. In fact, as Goldberg explains in "Advertising for Organs" (2005), the highly regulated OPTN system was developed, in part, because of the public solicitations for organs that were occurring in the unregulated past, and the harms that were seen as a result of them.

Detractors of directed donation also worry that its widespread use will allow those with celebrity status or compelling personal stories to bypass the organ allocation criteria that puts the neediest patient (by objective medical criteria) at the top of the list, as has been suspected in some cases. One way to minimize this risk is to do what has been suggested by the Transplantation Society (in a 2008 statement authored by transplant researcher Annika Tibell) and limit the recipients to those with whom the donor or donor family has had a "personal or long standing emotional relationship" (1539). This, however, requires a judgment to be made at the time of donor offer, when there are only a few hours in which to obtain consent, have the donor surgery performed, and send the organs for allocation. This can put the medical team in a difficult situation: a close family member seems to obviously fit this category, but what about an acquaintance or coworker? What if the donor family wants to donate to a celebrity who they have never met, stating that the donor was "his biggest fan?" Ideally, there would be some confirmation from the donor family that the donor, while alive, made some indication that he or she would have wanted to donate to that particular individual (e.g., recollection of a conversation or a written addendum in a health-care directive). Until that time, directed donation will remain a rare but difficult situation for a transplant team to navigate, especially when the donor-recipient relationship is not obviously a close one.

## CHALLENGING THE ALLOCATION SYSTEM

As long as demand for organs exceeds supply, it will be necessary to rank potential recipients to allocate the organs available. Although this organ allocation system is developed and managed by experts, it is not immutable, and the system changes with increasing evidence, with changes in public opinion, and with further ethical debate on the correct balance of utility and equity. The OPTN's kidney transplant allocation system, for example, recently underwent a major change in an attempt to better match the expected survival of the donated kidney to the expected survival of the recipient (e.g., transplanting kidneys with the highest expected survival into recipients with expected best outcomes, instead of relying only on waiting times and degree of matching).

Although the need for experts to reexamine the allocation criteria is obvious, what should be done when the request for reevaluation comes not from the organ expert group but from a recipient candidate or family who feel that they should move higher up the rank list? This concept was tested for the lung allocation system in 2013 when the parents of a young girl with cystic fibrosis challenged the criteria that they felt were keeping their daughter from receiving a lung transplant, through a public relations campaign and a later legal challenge.

Many felt that the parents' actions were the understandable action of desperate family members who were trying to save their daughter's life (a similar argument to that used to justify transplant tourism and public solicitation for organs). Proponents also point out that lung allocation criteria at the time were based on limited evidence that gave children less priority than similarly sized adults, and therefore, it unfairly discriminated against children. These proponents argue that the patient did not receive undue favoritism because of her appeal, but was simply allocated organs more fairly than the previous system allowed. In fact, the lung allocation policy did change after this case to allow exceptions to the normal allocation policy for children under twelve years old who were felt to be morphologically similar to older candidates.

Critics of the legal intervention maintain that the action was unjust, because it allows those with better access to media or legal resources to advocate over those with less, and it gives preference to personal stories over more objective criteria. These critics argue for maintaining stewardship of the allocation program in the hands of medical experts (including bioethicists) who should consider public opinion in reaching their decisions but not be beholden to it.

Ultimately, the current allocation system is a good attempt to balance equity and justice, but it is far from perfect and needs regular reevaluation. Who should be allowed the privilege of challenging the system (wait-list candidates, organ experts, legislators, or the public?) remains unclear.

## Summary

Organ transplantation is an ethically charged area both because of its inherent supply-and-demand issue and because transplantation requires cooperation, not only of medical teams and recipients but also from the donors, their respective families, and the general public. Deceased donation requires a good understanding of the settled and controversial areas in death determination, both for neurologic death and cardiac death. The DDR continues to be the standard for deceased donation at this time, but philosophers, bioethicists, and medical professionals debate whether this is a rule that needs updating or outright rejection. Living donation involves a balance of the risks and benefits, not just to one person but to both the donor and recipient, and it must never use the donor simply as a means. Organ allocation highlights the difficulties inherent in an attempt to balance utility and justice and how important it is to maintain public trust in a system that receives both its organs and its financial support from that public.

Overall, although transplantation will directly affect only a small portion of the population, it is an interesting lens though which to examine these ethical issues that are common to other types of medicine. It is also a relatively young field; as technology continues to advance, we can expect some of the ethical issues in this chapter to be resolved or become irrelevant, while new ethical issues arise to challenge the transplant community.

## Bibliography

Abecassis, M., M. Adams, P. Adams, et al. "Consensus Statement on the Live Organ Donor." *Journal of the American Medical Association* 284, no. 22 (2000): 2919–2926. https://www.kidney.org/sites/default/files/docs/jama_article.pdf.

Alexander, Shana. "They Decide Who Live, Who Dies." *Life Magazine*, November 9, 1962, 102–125.

American Medical Association. "Opinion 2.06: Capital Punishment." Issued in 1980 and since updated. http://www.ama-assn.org/ama/pub/physician-resources/medical-ethics/code-medical-ethics/opinion206.page?.

Barnieh, L., S. Klarenbach, J. S. Gill, et al. "Attitudes toward Strategies to Increase Organ Donation: Views of the General Public and Health Professionals." *Clinical Journal of the American Society of Nephrology* 7, no. 12 (2012): 1956–1963.

Becker, Gary S., and Julio J. Elias. "Cash for Kidneys: The Case for a Market for Organs." *Wall Street Journal*, January 18, 2014. http://www.wsj.com/articles/SB100014 24052702304149404579322560004817176.

Belluck, Pam. "Even as Doctors Say Enough, Families Fight to Prolong Life." *New York Times*, March 27, 2005. http://www.nytimes.com/2005/03/27/us/even-as-doctors-say-enough-families-fight-to-prolong-life.html?_r=0.

Birch, Samuel C. "The Dead Donor Rule: A Defense." *Journal of Medicine and Philosophy* 38, no. 4 (2013): 426–440.

Boudville, Neil, and Amit X. Garg. "End-Stage Renal Disease in Living Kidney Donors." *Kidney International* 86, no. 1 (2014): 20–22.

Bramstedt, Katrina A. "Living Liver Donor Mortality: Where Do We Stand?" *American Journal of Gastroenterology* 101, no. 4 (2006): 755–759.

Capitaine, Laura, Kristof Thys, Kristof Van Assche, et al. "Should Minors Be Considered as Potential Living Liver Donors?" *Liver Transplantation* 19, no. 6 (2013): 649–655.

Caplan, Arthur. "The Use of Prisoners as Sources of Organs—An Ethically Dubious Practice." *American Journal of Bioethics* 11, no. 10 (2011): 1–5.

Childress, James F. "Are Systems of Presumed Consent and Sales the Answer to the Need for More Organs for Transplantation?" *UNOS Update*, November 8, 1992.

Committee on Bioethics. "Ethical Controversies in Organ Donation after Circulatory Death." *Pediatrics* 131, no. 5 (2013): 1021–1026.

Cronin, Antonia J., and James F. Douglas. "Directed and Conditional Deceased Donor Organ Donations: Laws and Misconceptions." *Medical Law Review* 18, no. 3 (2010): 275–301.

Csillag, C. "Brazil Abolishes 'Presumed Consent' in Organ Donation." *Lancet* 352, no. 9137 (1998): 1367.

Declaration of Istanbul on Organ Trafficking and Transplant Tourism. 2008. http://multivu.prnewswire.com/mnr/transplantationsociety/33914/docs/33914-Declaration_of_Istanbul-Lancet.pdf.

"A Definition of Irreversible Coma. Report of the Ad Hoc Committee of the Harvard Medical School to Examine the Definition of Brain Death." *Journal of the American Medical Association* 205, no. 6 (1968): 337–340.

Delmonico, Francis L., Council of the Transplantation Society. "A Report of the Amsterdam Forum on the Care of the Live Kidney Donor: Data and Medical Guidelines." *Transplantation* 79, Supp. 6 (2005): S53–S66.

Delmonico, Francis L., D. Martin, B. Dominguez-Gil, et al. "Living and Deceased Organ Donation Should Be Financially Neutral Acts." *American Journal of Transplantation* 15, no. 5 (2015): 1187–1191.

deSante, Jennifer, Arthur Caplan, Benjamin Hippen, et al. "Was Sarah Murnaghan Treated Justly?" *Pediatrics* 134, no. 1 (2014): 155–162.

DeVita, Michael A., and James V. Snyder. "Development of the University of Pittsburgh Medical Center Policy for the Care of Terminally Ill Patients Who May Become Organ Donors after Death following the Removal of Life Support." *Kennedy Institute of Ethics Journal* 3, no. 2 (1993): 131–143.

DiMartini, Andrea, Catherine Crone, and Mary Amanda Dew. "Alcohol and Substance Use in Liver Transplant Patients." *Clinics in Liver Disease* 15, no. 4 (2011): 727–751.

Fabre, John, Paul Murphy, and Rafael Matesanz. "Presumed Consent: A Distraction in the Quest for Increasing Rates of Organ Donation." *The BMJ* (Clinical Research ed.) 341 (2010): c4973.

"Father Receives Heart Transplant from Daughter." *New York Times*, August 26, 1994. http://www.nytimes.com/1994/08/26/us/father-receives-heart-transplant-from-daughter.html.

Fehrman-Ekholm, I., B. Brink, C. Ericsson, et al. "Kidney Donors Don't Regret: Follow-Up of 370 Donors in Stockholm since 1964." *Transplantation* 69, no. 10 (2000): 2067–2071.

Foht, Brendan P. "Is 13-Year-Old Jahi McMath Alive or Dead? Doctors Say There's No Hope: Her Mother, with Faith That God Will Decide, Has Gone to Court." *Wall Street Journal*, January 2, 2014. http://www.wsj.com/articles/SB10001424052702304325004579296290047481758.

Fox, Renee C. "'An Ignoble Form of Cannibalism': Reflections on the Pittsburgh Protocol for Procuring Organs from Non-heart-Beating Cadavers." *Kennedy Institute of Ethics Journal* 3, no. 2 (1993): 231–239.

Friedman, Amy L., and Eli. A. Friedman. "Illegal Aliens Are Not Entitled to Federally Funded Organ Transplants." *Transplantation* 83, no. 1 (2007): 21–23.

Gentry, S. E., D. L. Segev, Mary Simmerling, et al. "Expanding Kidney Paired Donation through Participation by Compatible Pairs." *American Journal of Transplantation* 7, no. 10 (2007): 2361–2370.

Glannon, Walter, and Lainie F. Ross. "Do Genetic Relationships Create Moral Obligations in Organ Transplantation?" *Cambridge Quarterly of Healthcare Ethics* 11, no. 2 (2002): 153–159.

Goldberg, Aviva. "Advertising for Organs." *Virtual Mentor* 7, no. 9 (2005). doi: 10.1001/virtualmentor.2005.7.9.msoc2-0509.

Goldberg, Aviva M., Sandra Amaral, Asha Moudgil. "Developing a Framework for Evaluating Kidney Transplantation Candidacy in Children with Multiple Comorbidities." *Pediatric Nephrology* 30, no. 1 (2015): 5–13.

Goldberg, Aviva M., Mary Simmerling, and Joel E. Frader. "Why Undocumented Residents Should Have Access to Kidney Transplantation: Arguments for Lifting the Federal Ban on Reimbursement." *Transplantation* 83, no. 1 (2007): 17–20.

Goldberg, Aviva, and Leroy Storsley. "Teen Donors, Adult Problems? Evaluating the Long-Term Risks of Living Kidney Donation from Adolescents." *Pediatric Transplantation* 18, no. 4 (2014): 319–320.

Gordon, Elisa. J. "Haunted by the 'God Committee': Reciprocity Does No Justice to Eliminating Social Disparities." *American Journal of Bioethics* 4, no. 4 (2004): 23–25; discussion W35–37.

Gostin, Lawrence O. "Legal and Ethical Responsibilities following Brain Death: The McMath and Munoz Cases." *Journal of the American Medical Association* 311, no. 9 (2014): 903–904.

Grady, Denise. "Donor's Death at Hospital Halts Some Liver Surgeries." *New York Times*, January 16, 2002. http://www.nytimes.com/2002/01/16/nyregion/donor-s-death-at-hospital-halts-some-liver-surgeries.html.

Grant, Kelly. "Automatic Organ Donation: A New Campaign for 'Presumed Consent' Gets a Push from Composer David Foster." *Globe and Mail*, September 21, 2014. http://www.theglobeandmail.com/life/health-and-fitness/health/composer-david-foster-pushes-presumed-consent-for-organ-donations/article20705846/#dashboard/follows/.

Gross, C. R., E. E. Messersmith, B. A. Hong, et al. "Health-Related Quality of Life in Kidney Donors from the Last Five Decades: Results from the RELIVE Study." *American Journal of Transplantation* 13, no. 11 (2013): 2924–2934.

Henderson, Antonio J., Monica A. Landolt, Michael F. McDonald, et al. "The Living Anonymous Kidney Donor: Lunatic or Saint?" *American Journal of Transplantation* 3, no. 2 (2003): 203–213.

Johnson, L Syd. "The Ethically Dubious Practice of Thwarting the Redemption of the Condemned." *American Journal of Bioethics* 11, no. 10 (2011): 9–10.

Joint Commission on Accreditation of Healthcare Organizations. "Revisions to Standard LD.3.110." *Joint Commission Perspectives* 26, no. 6 (2006): 7.

Kaczor, Christopher. "Organ Donation following Cardiac Death: Conflicts of Interest, Antemortem Interventions, and Determination of Death." In *The Ethics of Organ Transplantation*, 95. Washington, DC: Catholic University of America Press, 2011.

Kluge, Eike-Henner. "Designated Organ Donation: Private Choice in Social Context." *Hastings Center Report* 19, no. 5 (1989): 10–16.

Lin, Shu S., Lauren Rich, Jay D. Pal, and Robert M. Sade. "Prisoners on Death Row Should Be Accepted as Organ Donors." *Annals of Thoracic Surgery* 93, no. 6 (2012): 1773–1779.

List, Justin. "To Donate or Not: Is That the Question?" *Virtual Mentor* 7, no. 9 (2005). http://journalofethics.ama-assn.org/2005/09/msoc1-0509.html.

MacDonald, D., A. K. Kukla, S. Ake, et al. "Medical Outcomes of Adolescent Live Kidney Donors." *Pediatric Transplantation* 18, no. 4 (2014): 336–341.

Matas, Arthur J. "A Regulated System of Incentives for Living Donation: A Challenge to Define and Understand the Objections." In *Organ Transplantation: Ethical, Legal and Psychosocial Aspects*, 304–308. Lengerich, Germany: Pabst Science, 2014.

Matas, Arthur J., Benjamin Hippen, and Sally Satel. "In Defense of a Regulated System of Compensation for Living Donation." *Current Opinion in Organ Transplantation* 13, no. 4 (2008): 379–385.

Matas, David, and David Kilgour. *Bloody Harvest: Organ Harvesting of Falun Gong Practitioners in China*. Woodstock, Ontario: Seraphim, 2009.

Mathur, Amit K., Douglas E. Schaubel, Qi Gong, et al. "Racial and Ethnic Disparities in Access to Liver Transplantation." *Liver Transplantation* 16, no. 9 (2010): 1033–1040.

Meyer, H. G. "Teen Who Always Gave of Self Gives Gift of Life." *Chicago Tribune*, June 16, 2004.

Miller, Franklin, and Robert Truog. *Death, Dying, and Organ Transplantation*. New York: Oxford University Press, 2012.

Miller, Franklin G., Robert D. Truog, and D. W. Brock. "The Dead Donor Rule: Can It Withstand Critical Scrutiny?" *Journal of Medicine and Philosophy* 35, no. 3 (2010): 299–312.

Mjøen, Geir, Stein Hallan, Anders Hartmann, et al. "Long-Term Risks for Kidney Donors." *Kidney International* 86, no. 1 (2014): 162–167.

Mollaret, P., and Maurice Goulon. "The Depassed Coma (Preliminary Memoir)." *Revue neurologique* 101, no. 1 (1959): 3–15.

Moniruzzaman, Maurice. "'Living Cadavers' in Bangladesh: Bioviolence in the Human Organ Bazaar." *Medical Anthropology Quarterly* 26, no. 1 (2012): 69–91.

Moore, Francis D. "New Problems for Surgery: Drugs that Act on the Cell Nucleus Affect the Surgeon's Work on Cancer and on Transplantation." *Science* 144, no. 3617 (1964): 388–392.

OPTN/UNOS Ethics Committee. "Ethical Principles to Be Considered in the Allocation of Human Organs." 2015. http://optn.transplant.hrsa.gov/resources/ethics/ethical-principles-in-the-allocation-of-human-organs/.

OPTN/UNOS Ethics Committee. "Ethics of Organ Donation from Condemned Prisoners." http://optn.transplant.hrsa.gov/resources/ethics/the-ethics-of-organ-donation-from-condemned-prisoners/.

Ortega-Deballon, Iván, Laura Hornby, and Sam D. Shemie. "Protocols for Uncontrolled Donation after Circulatory Death: A Systematic Review of International Guidelines, Practices and Transplant Outcomes." *Critical Care* 19, no. 1 (2015): 268–283.

Participants in the International Summit on Transplant Tourism and Organ Trafficking Convened by the Transplantation Society and International Society of Nephrology in Istanbul, Turkey, April 30–May 2, 2008. "The Declaration of Istanbul on Organ Trafficking and Transplant Tourism." *Transplantation* 86, no. 8 (2008): 1013–1018.

President's Council on Bioethics. *Controversies in the Determination of Death: A White Paper by the President's Council on Bioethics.* Washington, DC: Author, 2008.

Price, David. "Conditional Organ Donation: A View of the Ethicist." *Transplantation* 85, no. 11 (2008): 1540–1541.

Purnell, T. S., P. Xu, N. Leca, and Y. N. Hall. "Racial Differences in Determinants of Live Donor Kidney Transplantation in the United States." *American Journal of Transplantation* 13, no. 6 (2013): 1557–1565.

Reese, Peter P., Neil Boudville, and Amit X. Garg. "Living Kidney Donation: Outcomes, Ethics, and Uncertainty." *Lancet* 385, no. 9981 (2015): 2003–2013.

Ross, Lainie F. "What the Medical Excuse Teaches Us about the Potential Living Donor as Patient." *American Journal of Transplantation* 10, no. 4 (2010): 731–736.

Ross, Lainie F., Walter Glannon, M. A. Josephson, et al. "Should All Living Donors Be Treated Equally?" *Transplantation* 74, no. 3 (2002): 418–421; discussion 421–422.

Ross, Lainie F., and J. R. Thistlethwaite Jr., Committee on Bioethics. "Minors as Living Solid-Organ Donors." *Pediatrics* 122, no. 2 (2008): 454–461.

Scheper-Hughes, Nancy. "The Global Traffic in Human Organs." *Current Anthropology* 41, no. 2 (2000): 191–224.

Scheper-Hughes, Nancy. "Keeping an Eye on the Global Traffic in Human Organs." *Lancet* 361, no. 9369 (2003): 1645–1648.

Shemie, Sam, Andrew J. Baker, Greg Knoll, et al. "Donation after Cardiocirculatory Death in Canada." *Canadian Medical Association Journal* 175, Supp. 8 (2006): S1–S24.

Simmerling, Mary, Peter Angelos, Aviva Goldberg, and Joel Frader. "Do Gifts Create Moral Obligations for Recipients?" *American Journal of Bioethics* 4, no. 4 (2004): 20–22; discussion W35–37.

Simmerling, Mary, Joel Frader, John Franklin, and Peter Angelos. "When Duties Collide: Beneficence and Veracity in the Evaluation of Living Organ Donors." *Current Opinions in Organ Transplantation* 12, no. 2 (2007): 188–192.

Spital, Aaron. "Providing a Medical Excuse to Organ Donor Candidates Who Feel Trapped: Concerns and Replies." *Cambridge Quarterly of Healthcare Ethics* 17, no. 1 (2008): 124–127; discussion 128–130.

Steinbrook, Robert. "Public Solicitation of Organ Donors." *New England Journal of Medicine* 353, no. 5 (2005): 441–444.

Tibell, Annika. "The Transplantation Society Statement on Directed and Conditional Donation." *Transplantation* 85, no. 11 (2008): 1538–1539.

Tong, Allison, Jeremy R. Chapman, Germaine Wong, et al. "The Motivations and Experiences of Living Kidney Donors." *American Journal of Kidney Diseases* 60, no. 1 (2012): 15–26.

Truog, Robert D. "Is It Time to Abandon Brain Death?" *Hastings Center Report* 27, no. 1 (1997): 29–37.

Truog, Robert D., and F. G. Miller. "The Dead Donor Rule and Organ Transplantation." *New England Journal of Medicine* 359, no. 7 (2008): 674–675.

Truog, Robert D., F. G. Miller, and S. D. Halpern. "The Dead-Donor Rule and the Future of Organ Donation." *New England Journal of Medicine* 369, no. 14 (2013): 1287–1289.

UK Department of Health. "An Investigation into Conditional Organ Donation." Report of the panel. London: Author, 2000.

Uniform Determination of Death Act. 1981. http://www.uniformlaws.org/shared/docs/determination%20of%20death/udda80.pdf.

"University of Pittsburgh Medical Center Policy and Procedure Manual. Management of Terminally Ill Patients Who May Become Organ Donors after Death." *Kennedy Institute of Ethics Journal* 3, no. 2 (1993): A1–A15.

US Department of Health and Human Services. "An Evaluation of the Ethics of Presumed Consent and a Proposal Based on Required Response: A Report of the Presumed Consent Subcommittee of the Ethics Committee." June 30, 1993. http://optn.transplant.hrsa.gov/resources/ethics/an-evaluation-of-the-ethics-of-presumed-consent/#5.

Volk, Michael L., Scott W. Biggins, Mary Ann Huang, et al. "Decision Making in Liver Transplant Selection Committees: A Multicenter Study." *Annals of Internal Medicine* 155, no. 8 (2011): 503–508.

Volk, Michael L., and Peter A. Ubel. "A Gift of Life: Ethical and Practical Problems with Conditional and Directed Donation." *Transplantation* 85, no. 11 (2008): 1542–1544.

Webb, N. J., and P. M. Fortune. "Should Children Ever Be Living Kidney Donors?" *Pediatric Transplantation* 10, no. 7 (2006): 851–855.

Wilkinson, Timothy M. *Ethics and the Acquisitions of Organs.* New York: Oxford University Press, 2011.

Wilkinson, Timothy M. "Taylor on Presumed Consent." *Journal of Medical Ethics* 40, no. 9 (2014): 638–639.

Wilkinson, Timothy M. "What's Not Wrong with Conditional Organ Donation?" *Journal of Medical Ethics* 29, no. 3 (2003): 163–164.

## NOVELS

Ishiguro, Kazuo. *Never Let Me Go.* New York: Knopf, 2005.

Picoult, Jodi. *My Sister's Keeper: A Novel.* New York: Atria, 2004.

## FILM

*Dirty Pretty Things.* Dir. Stephen Frears. 2002.

*Seven Pounds.* Dir. Gabriele Muccino. 2008.

## TELEVISION

The television series *Scrubs*, which ran for nine seasons from 2001 to 2010, dealt with transplant topics in several episodes. Although there are accuracy issues with how the organs are allocated (almost all end up in the same hospital as the donor, something that would likely not occur with current UNOS allocation rules), many of the episodes manage to deal with complex transplant issues in a concise, humorous, and thoughtful manner:

"My Rule of Thumb." Season 3, episode 10, 2003. Dir. Craig Zisk.

"My Unicorn." Season 4, episode 11, 2004. Dir. Matthew Perry.

"My Chopped Liver." Season 5, episode 17, 2005. Dir. Will Mackenzie.

"My Happy Place." Season 8, episode 4, 2009. Dir. Ken Whittingham.

CHAPTER 15

# Modern Research Ethics:
# A Historical Perspective

**Sean Philpott-Jones**
Chair, Department of Bioethics
Clarkson University, Capital Region Campus, Schenectady, NY

In *The Constant Gardener* (2005), an award-winning film based on the John le Carré novel of the same name, actor Ralph Fiennes portrays Justin Quayle, a low-level British diplomat stationed in Kenya. When his activist wife Tessa and her Kenyan driver are found brutally murdered on a deserted roadside, suspicion immediately falls on a physician colleague with whom Tessa was rumored to be having an affair. As Justin continues to investigate his wife's death, however, he discovers that she was investigating a suspicious trial of an antituberculosis drug called "Dypraxa." Despite knowing about the harmful side effects of Dypraxa, the pharmaceutical company continues to test the drug using unsuspecting and ill-informed Kenyan participants. Tessa was killed because she threatened to publicize this fact, which would shut down the clinical trials and cost the drug company hundreds of millions of dollars in lost sales and redevelopment costs.

Although fictional, the story was inspired by an actual clinical trial in Nigeria. In 1996, during an outbreak of meningococcal meningitis in the northern city of Kano, the pharmaceutical company Pfizer conducted a study in which one hundred children were randomized to receive a new antibiotic called Trovan, while another one hundred children received standard treatment with ceftriaxone. During the course of that trial, eleven children died. Subsequent investigation raised a number of questions about the ethical design and conduct of the study. These questions included whether the study was reviewed and approved by an independent ethics committee, whether investigators obtained voluntary and informed consent from the parents of the children enrolled, and whether researchers gave children in the control arm a substandard dose of ceftriaxone to skew the trial results and make Trovan look more effective. Survivors and the families of those enrolled in the study later sued Pfizer for damages, eventually resulting in a US$75 million out-of-court settlement.

This case, and the subsequent book and film it inspired, provide an example of the ethics (or lack thereof) of research involving human subjects. Research ethics looks at how the planning and conducting of research is designed to protect the well-being of study participants and to protect them from harm. Unfortunately, although we'd like to think that cases like these are rare, they are disturbingly common. In fact, the current ethical frameworks and regulatory mechanism that are used to design, review, conduct, and oversee research involving human subjects were developed in response to scandalous cases like this.

Starting in the latter half of the twentieth century, notorious cases of research subject abuse, including the Tuskegee Study of Untreated Syphilis in the Negro Male (1932–1972), the Jewish Chronic Disease Hospital Study (1963), and the Willowbrook Study of Infectious Hepatitis (1963–1966), were paraded in the peer-reviewed literature and the popular press. These cases, in turn, prompted proposals for government regulation, including the current US system for requiring independent ethics committee review of all research involving human subjects. For example, in response to public outrage about the Tuskegee study, the US Congress passed the National Research Act in 1974, establishing the modern institutional review board–based (IRB) system for the review and oversight of all federally funded human-subjects research, a system that has since been adopted worldwide. The National Research Act also established the US National Commission for the Protection of Human Subjects of Biomedical and Behavioral Research. This commission published the seminal *Belmont Report* in 1979, which established the now famous trinity of principles—respect for persons, beneficence, and justice—that govern modern research ethics. However, the first internationally recognized statement of research ethics, the Nuremberg Code, was written decades earlier in response to the horrors of Nazi experimentation among concentration camp inmates and Allied prisoners of war.

# THE NUREMBERG CODE

The Nuremberg Code, a list of ten requirements for the ethical conduct of research, was written in the aftermath of World War II. The US War Crimes Tribunal drafted the code in 1947 during the trials of war criminals before the Nuremberg Military Tribunals (also known as the Subsequent Nuremberg Trials or more commonly as the Nazi Doctors' Trial). In brief, the requirements for ethical research outlined in the Nuremberg Code are as follows:

1. The voluntary and informed consent of subjects with full legal capacity must be obtained.

2. The experiment should be designed to yield fruitful results for the good of society, results that cannot be procured in some other way.

3. The study should be scientifically justified on the basis of prior research, including animal experiments.

4. The research protocol should be designed to avoid unnecessary physical and mental suffering or injury.

5. No study should be conducted if there is a reason to believe that death or debilitating injury will occur, *except in cases in which the researchers also serve as subjects.*

6. The research risks should be commensurate with the social benefits and humanitarian importance of the problem to be solved.

7. Proper preparations must be taken and adequate facilities must be provided that protect the subjects against the risk.

8. Only properly trained and qualified researchers should conduct the study.

9. The subjects must be free to quit the study at any time if they are mentally or physically unable to go on.

10. The researchers must be prepared to stop the study at any time if they believe that continuation would result in a subject's injury, disability, or death.

Interestingly, although the Nuremberg Code was included in the verdict of the Nazi Doctors' Trial and presents the first internationally recognized set of research ethics principles, it has little binding legal force. For example, it was not incorporated into US, British, or German law. It has been incorporated, however, into the laws of several other countries and a handful of US states. Despite this lack of binding legal force, the Nuremberg Code laid the groundwork for later declarations of research ethics principles, including the 1948 World Medical Association (WMA) Declaration of Geneva, the 1948 United Nations (UN) Universal Declaration of Human Rights, the 1949 WMA International Code of Medical Ethics, and the 1964 WMA Declaration of Helsinki. The Nuremberg Code and subsequent ethical guidelines also influenced the US National Commission for the Protection of Human Subjects and helped provide the foundation for existing US regulations on human-subjects research, including the Common Rule (Code of Federal Regulations 2009).

To appreciate fully the effect that the Nuremberg Code has had on modern research practices, however, it is important to understand the historic context that led to the drafting of these principles.

## THE NUREMBERG WAR CRIMES TRIALS

The Nuremberg Code was delivered as part of the verdict in the Nuremberg war crimes trials, a series of military tribunals established after World War II to prosecute Nazi leaders for war crimes and other crimes against humanity. The second set of the war crimes trials focused on crimes committed by twenty-three prominent doctors and medical researchers, including Dr. Karl Brandt (1904–1948), who had initiated the Nazi eugenic-euthanasia program, and Dr. Josef Mengele (1911–1979), who conducted research on twins while serving as chief medical officer at Auschwitz-Birkenau. A total of 1,750 victims were identified in the indictment, although this represents only a small proportion of those who were killed or injured as a result of medical experimentation in the concentration camps. In *The Nazi Doctors and the Nuremberg Code* (1992), lawyer-bioethicist George Annas and physician-bioethicist Michael Grodin provide a detailed descriptive review and historical analysis of the Nuremberg trials.

What is surprising, however, is that before and even during World War II, Germany itself had the most sophisticated and progressive system of regulations designed to protect the rights of patients who were the subjects of medical and scientific research. As befits the theme of this chapter, these regulations had evolved in response to scandals, like the public outrage over an experimental vaccine that caused the deaths of seventy-two children in the German village of Lübeck in 1930. Responding to these scandals and to the critiques of reformers like the German-Jewish psychiatrist Albert Moll (1862–1939), Germany's progressive Weimar Republic adopted the world's most stringent set of research ethics regulations in 1931. As evident in the translation by historian Hans-Martin Sass, these regulations included a number of key ethical concepts that appear in later guidance documents and national laws:

> Medical science, if it is not to come to a standstill, cannot refrain from introducing in suitable cases New Therapy using as yet insufficiently tested agents and methods. Also, medical science cannot dispense completely with Human Experimentation.
>
> Medical ethics rejects any exploitation of social or economic need in conducting New Therapy.
>
> (a) Without consent, non-therapeutic research is under no circumstances permissible.

(b) Any human experimentation which could as well be carried out in animal experimentation is not permissible. Only after all basic information has been obtained should Human Experimentation begin. This information should first be obtained by means of scientific biological or laboratory research and animal experimentation for reasons of clarification and safety. Given these presuppositions, unfounded or random Human Experimentation is impermissible. (Grodin 1992, 128–132)

These regulations thus mandated scrutiny to ensure scientific validity, required experiments on animals as a prerequisite for experiments on humans, and stipulated that researchers must obtain the informed voluntary consent of patients before they could be subjected to medical research. Germany was, in fact, the only country at that time to have such a stringent set of regulations in place.

When the Nazis came to power in 1933, they not only inherited these research regulations, they tightened them further by prohibiting vivisection. Specifically, the Nazi regime banned any research involving invasive operations on living animals and thus effectively eliminated almost all medical research on animals—guinea pigs could no longer

*Karl Brandt, personal doctor of Adolf Hitler and initiator of the Nazi eugenic-euthanasia program, listens to his verdict during the Nazi Doctors' Trial at Nuremberg, Germany, August 20, 1947. Brandt was sentenced to death by hanging and was executed on June 2, 1948, at Landsberg prison in Bavaria. The Nazi Doctors' Trial considered the fate of twenty-three German physicians and medical researchers who either participated in the Nazi program of mass murder under the guise of euthanasia or who conducted experiments on concentration camp prisoners without their consent. Sixteen of those charged were found guilty, and seven were executed.* DPA PICTURE ALLIANCE/ ALAMY.

serve as "guinea pigs." For example, a National Socialist German Workers' Party (NSDAP/Nazi Party) press release from 1933 reads as follows:

> The Prussian minister-president Goering has ... stated that starting 16 August 1933 vivisection of animals ... is forbidden. Persons who ... participate or perform vivisections on animals ... will be deported to concentration camps.

> Among all civilized nations, Germany thus was the first to put an end to the cultural shame of vivisection. The New Germany not only frees man from the curse of materialism, sadism, and cultural Bolshevism, but gives the cruelly persecuted, tortured, and until now, wholly defenseless animals their rights.

> What Reichschancellor Adolph Hitler and Minister-president Goering have done and will do for the protection of animals should set the course for the leaders of all civilized nations! (Grodin 1992, 128–132)

At that time, despite the economic problems that Germany faced, it was considered to be the world leader in scientific research and pharmaceutical development. These new regulations prohibiting animal experimentation, however, put Germany's top scientists, research institutions, and pharmaceutical companies in a bind. When a pharmaceutical company like Behringwerke AG, which was working in collaboration with the Robert Koch Institute of Berlin to develop a new antityphus vaccine, needed to conduct the preclinical studies necessary to prove that the new vaccine was safe for first-in-human trials, they had to find a population of subjects that qualified neither as human patients or laboratory animals.

At that time, the Nazi Party's policy of "racial hygiene" included laws allowing the compulsory sterilization for conditions such as schizophrenia, epilepsy, alcoholism, and other forms of social deviance (e.g., the 1933 Law for the Prevention of Hereditarily Diseased Offspring). Additionally, its quasi-legal programs, such as Action T4, allowed for involuntary euthanasia of the disabled, invalids, and other *Ballastexistenzen* (or dead-weight existences). Gradually, Jews, Roma, homosexuals, and Allied prisoners-of-war were added to this list of *Ballastexistenzen*. Thus, when the German Air Force (*Luftwaffe*) wanted to design aircraft that could fly at higher altitudes and needed equipment that would protect pilots against sudden changes in atmospheric pressure, or when the German Navy (*Kriegsmarine*) needed gear to protect sailors against the frigid waters of the North Sea, or when the German Army (*Heer*) needed new vaccines to protect soldiers against tropical diseases in Africa, they tested them on these *Ballastexistenzen*, a population of subjects who were seen as neither human patients nor laboratory animals.

It was only after the defeat of Nazi Germany by Allied forces that the extent to which German physicians and research scientists engaged in research on this population of unwilling subjects became widely known. This research included experiments in which concentration camp inmates were put into hypobaric (i.e., lower atmospheric pressure) chambers to see how long they could survive with little oxygen, prisoners of war were forced to remain in baths of freezing water for several hours, patients were deliberately infected with typhus or malaria to test new vaccines or drugs, or captives were forced to inhale mustard gas or burned with phosphorus to develop new medical treatments.

## THE AMERICAN MEDICAL ASSOCIATION'S ROLE

Dr. Andrew Ivy (1893–1978), the official American Medical Association (AMA) observer at the Nazi Doctors' Trial, asserted that the German "experiments performed on human subjects without their consent, or by coercion, is contrary to the laws of humanity and the ethical practices of the medical profession which have been in practice for 22 centuries" (*Trials of War Criminals before the Nuernberg Military Tribunals under Control Council Law No. 10*, 1949). Aside from the laboratories that Ivy himself directed and those that abided by the 1931 German research regulations, no major professional society or research institution anywhere in the world—including the United States—subscribed to the rules of ethical conduct that he attributed to them. Ivy's assertions about research ethics was applicable to the practices in his own laboratory, but otherwise were utterly without historical foundation. In fact, the only real code of research ethics in the United States at the time of the Nuremberg trials was a direct result of Ivy's efforts. After meeting with the prosecutors at Nuremberg, Ivy returned to the United States and urged the AMA to adopt a set of research ethics principles to differentiate legitimate medical (i.e., American and British) research from unethical medical (i.e., Nazi) research.

In December 1946, the AMA's House of Delegates adopted a version of Ivy's proposed principles. These principles stipulated that ethical research on humans requires (1) the voluntary consent of the subject, (2) prior animal experimentation, and (3) proper medical supervision. The AMA principles, however, did not require that consent be informed or that experiments be for the good of society, that the research yield information unprocurable by other means, or that it precludes the likelihood of unnecessary suffering, disability, or death. Nonetheless, these were the first principles of research ethics embraced by any official body or professional organization in the United States. Ivy then used the AMA's endorsement of these principles to testify before the Nuremberg tribunal that Nazi researchers had violated the principles and standards followed by civilized researchers everywhere. This perjured testimony laid the foundation for a code of universally accepted basic rules of research ethics that the court would use to condemn the Nazi researchers and their research as uncivilized, unethical, and criminal.

This is not to say that the Nuremberg judges were wrong in condemning the Nazi doctors—even though their actions did not violate the letter of Nazi law or existing norms of research that existed at the time. Because the Nuremberg court had been convened under international law, this mythical conception of research-ethics principles was thus elevated onto the international stage. Before 1945, however, there were no internationally recognized standards of research ethics and few formal research regulations of any kind.

Horror at the Holocaust and the need to relegitimate medical research on human subjects led to the creation of this new standard of research ethics. Additional subsequent standards included the WMA Declaration of Geneva, the UN Universal Declaration of Human Rights, the various iterations of the WMA Declaration of Helsinki, and, more recently, the code of international research ethics, the Council of Europe's 1997 Convention for the Protection of Human Rights and Dignity of the Human Being with Regard to the Application of Biology and Medicine: Convention on Human Rights and Biomedicine.

## RESEARCH ON HUMAN SUBJECTS AFTER NUREMBERG

As mentioned, although the Nuremberg Code is the first internationally recognized statement of research ethics—and is still mentioned by ethics committees, researchers, and subject advocates alike, particularly when describing a research study as potentially unethical—the code itself has little legal force except in those few countries and localities in which it has been incorporated formally into existing legislation. Moreover, if adhered to as written, the code presented a number of challenges for researchers in the years that followed the judgments at Nuremberg. Ignoring for the purposes of this discussion some of the more ethically problematic parts of the Nuremberg Code, such as the provision allowing experiments that pose a high risk of injury or death so long as the investigators themselves volunteer to be subjects, consider its key ethical principle: "The voluntary consent of the human subject is absolutely essential." Elaborating on that point, however, the Nuremberg Code goes on to state that

> This means that *the person involved should have legal capacity to give consent* [emphasis added]; should be so situated as to be able to exercise free power of choice, without the intervention of any element of force, fraud, deceit, duress, over-reaching, or other ulterior form of constraint or coercion; and should have sufficient knowledge and comprehension of the elements of the subject matter involved, as to enable him to make an understanding and enlightened decision. (*Trials of War Criminals before the Nuernberg Military Tribunals under Control Council Law No. 10*, 1949, 2:181)

The requirement that all subjects of human research must have the legal capacity to give consent, however, excludes a large number of people from research because they lack the legal capacity to give consent, either because they are children under the age of majority or because they are incapacitated due to mental or physical disability or injury. The Nuremberg Code thus precludes any research on children, preventing investigators from studying childhood illnesses or developing and testing new drugs or treatments for pediatric populations. Similarly, the code would prohibit any research on the mentally ill or developmentally disabled, victims of trauma, or patients in the intensive care or critical care unit who lack the capacity to give consent. In the absence of a provision for research-subject surrogacy, a great deal of important clinical research would be prohibited as unethical, even in cases in which study participants would benefit from a direct therapeutic.

## THE WORLD MEDICAL ASSOCIATION'S PRINCIPLES

To address this issue of consent, in 1954 the WMA issued its Principles for Those in Research and Experimentation, which recapitulated the main themes of the Nuremberg Code but revised the principle of voluntary and informed consent. Specifically, the WMA's principles allowed for surrogate consent on behalf of legally incompetent or incapacitated patients. Some researchers—particularly US and British investigators—would rebel against these principles and later codes of research ethics, but the WMA's efforts in this case (and particularly its revision of the Nuremberg Code's key principle of voluntary informed consent to permit surrogate decision making) helped to transform "an obscure legal judgment pronounced at Nuremberg into the founding document for all codes governing human-subjects research and for international bioethics generally. The 1954 surrogacy revisions permitted the Nuremberg Code to enter into the real world of clinical research, thereby making research ethics a practical clinical possibility" (Baker 1998, 253).

Moreover, these revisions were quickly yet quietly adopted by a number of professional organization and government agencies in Europe, starting in 1955 when the Public Health Council of the Netherlands issued a policy that implemented the WMA's Principles for Those in Research and Experimentation in Dutch clinical contexts. As part of that policy, the Public Health Council called for the formation of an independent advisory committee to oversee the application of these ethical principles to research practice, one of the first examples of the use of a research ethics committee, or IRB, to review human-subjects protocols. Building on the WMA Principles, the WMA's Medical Ethics Committee drafted a new set of research ethics principles that would be adopted at the Eighteenth General Assembly in Helsinki, Finland, in 1964. It has since been amended nine times, most recently in 2013 by the Sixty-Fourth WMA General Assembly in Fortaleza, Brazil. Like the Nuremberg Code, it is not a legally binding instrument in international law, holding legal sway only in those countries where its principles have been codified in local legislation and regulations. It is largely ignored in countries like the United States.

In fact, the events in Nazi Germany, the resulting Nuremberg Code, and the subsequent WMA Principles for Those in Research and Experimentation and Declaration of Helsinki were not considered to be relevant by US or British researchers historically. Following World War II, the US government increased funding for medical research, and the demand for human subjects increased concomitantly. Researchers in the United States largely resisted regulation and oversight, however, and US researchers largely refused to acknowledge the Nuremberg Code or the WMA's Principles. Instead, they asserted their nobility of character and purpose and defended the value and necessity of research on humans while simultaneously disowning notorious examples of research impropriety by claiming that the investigators involved either lacked integrity or were "unbalanced." Until 1972, for example, codes of research ethics were regarded as a proper response to the madness of Nazi medicine. The prevailing attitude was that although the Nuremberg Code had been a good code to indict the Nazis, it was irrelevant to US research practices. Ethical constraints were necessary for Nazis, but not for civilized researchers who naturally would conduct themselves honorably. As historian David Rothman notes, "the violations had been the work of Nazis, not doctors … not scientists. Madness not medicine was implicated at Nuremberg. The prevailing view was that [the defendants] were Nazis first and last; by definition nothing they did, and no code drawn up in response to them, was relevant to the United States" (1991, 62–63).

## THE OFFICE OF THE SURGEON GENERAL'S REGULATIONS

When the US Army Office of the Surgeon General reissued the Nuremberg principles as a set of rules regulating all military and all military-funded research on human subjects in 1954, researchers on the faculty at Harvard Medical School protested. Rejecting the surgeon general's regulations as overly restrictive, the board of administrators of Harvard Medical School instead adopted a set of principles that included a requirement for informed consent and a provision for peer review, but that was applicable only to *nontherapeutic contexts*. Henry Beecher (1904–1976), who was then the Henry Isaiah Dorr Professor of Anesthesia Research at Harvard, drafted this set of principles. Beecher later would publish an article that drew public attention to examples of unethical clinical research that risked patients' lives, but at the time, he felt that requiring informed consent for therapeutic research was not only difficult but also unnecessary. Informed consent and peer review was only required for experiments that offered no clinical benefit to subjects. For therapeutic research, the rights and safety of subject-patients would be protected by the "character, wisdom, experience, honesty, imaginativeness and sense of responsibility of the investigator, who in all cases of doubt or where serious consequences might remotely occur, will call in his peers and get the benefit of his counsel" (Advisory Committee on Human Radiation Experiments 1996, 91). Not only was Harvard successful in obtaining an exemption from the surgeon general's rules, but also the Office of the Surgeon General later revised its regulations on human-subjects research to recognizing an exemption for so-called therapeutic research. As philosopher Robert Baker notes, "Since most biomedical research on human subjects is performed in clinical environments with the aim of developing new therapies, a therapeutic exclusion would exempt almost all biomedical research from the requirement of informed subject consent" (1998, 256).

Moreover, this opinion was not uniquely American. In fact, researchers around the globe resisted oversight and regulation by emphasizing Nazi exceptionalism. Shortly after the Office of the Surgeon General revised its rules, the British Medical Association and the British Medical Research Council (MRC) issued research guidelines exempting therapeutic research from the ethical requirement to obtain informed consent. Similarly, as Maurice Pappworth writes in "Human Guinea Pigs—A History" (1990), when the WMA issued its Principles for Those in Research and Experimentation (which would be revised a decade later to become what is now known as the Declaration of Helsinki), British physicians and scientists objected on the grounds that it would impede medical research. Later, the WMA would include a therapeutic exemption in its original 1964 Declaration of Helsinki, allowing physicians to try a new therapy on patients without consent if it "offers hope of saving life, re-establishing health or alleviating suffering." Obtaining informed consent for therapeutic research was, as articulated in this document, an aspirational goal but not a moral obligation.

## DECADES OF ABUSE

Unfortunately, much of the history of research involving human participants in the United States is shameful. For most of the twentieth century, the burdens of serving as research subjects fell largely on the poor, while the benefits of research (including new treatments and advances in medical care) went primarily to the wealthy. US and British researchers' honor proved to be insufficient to prevent abuses of human subjects, even after whistle-blowers like Beecher (see 1966a, 1966b) and Pappworth (1962, 1967) called professional and public attention to this scandalous state of affairs by publicizing cases of abusive research in major hospitals and institutions, conducted by leading researchers, funded by prestigious sources, and published in leading medical journals. Beecher's article "Ethics and Clinical Research" (1966b) in the *New England Journal of Medicine*, for example, described the unethical treatment of human subjects as reported in twenty-two papers written by top researchers (from institutions like Harvard, Sloan-Kettering, and the US National Institutes of Health [NIH]), funded by major public and private sponsors (including the NIH, US Office of the Surgeon General, US Public Health Service [PHS], and pharmaceutical company Merck), and published in leading US and British medical journals between 1948 and 1965. Similarly, Pappworth's 1962 article "Human Guinea Pigs—A Warning" described a series of fourteen unethical experiments conducted by some of Great Britain's top researchers, including one experiment in which insulin was deliberately withheld from forty-three patients with diabetes until they became comatose, at which point liver and renal biopsies were obtained. His subsequent book, *Human Guinea Pigs* (1967), expands on this list, describing 205 unethical experiments cited in British institutions and prisons, including seventy-eight studies conducted by researchers in National Health Service hospitals.

The cases described by Beecher and Pappworth included, but were not limited to, a few of the more egregious examples of research abuse in the twentieth century: the Tuskegee

Study of Untreated Syphilis in the Negro Male (1932–1972), the US Human Radiation Experiments (1944–1974), the US PHS Sexually Transmitted Diseases (STD) Inoculation Study in Guatemala (1946–1948), the Jewish Chronic Disease Hospital Study (1963), Milgram's Experiments on Obedience to Authority (1963)—presented in the 2015 film, *Experimenter*—and the Willowbrook Study of Infectious Hepatitis (1963–1966). These cases are but a few of the examples of unjust experimentation in the United States and Europe before and after the Nuremberg trials.

Consider the 2015 movie *The Stanford Prison Experiment,* based on a real-life experiment that is now held as an example of the failure of researchers to adequately protect study participants. This film opens with viewers watching potential human subjects being interviewed for a social psychology experiment. The college-age men who volunteered for the study would be randomly assigned as a "guard" or a "prisoner" in a mock prison set up in the basement of Stanford University's psychology department building. The goal was to see whether ordinary people could be made to act in abusive and inhuman ways simply by putting them in a specific authoritarian context. As unabashedly shown in the file, after only a few days the study's principal investigator, Phil Zimbardo (1933–) loses objective perspective, the guards became verbally and physical abusive, and the prisoners are subjected to abuse. Two subjects quit and the experiment was finally stopped six days later after a psychology graduate student persuaded Zimbardo to end it.

Similarly, as described in *Acres of Skin* (1999) by Allen Hornblum (1947–), numerous experiments were conducted on prisoners throughout the United States, including high-risk cancer treatments, the application of strong skin creams, new cosmetics, dioxin, and high doses of LSD. According to Nathaniel Comfort in "The Prisoner as Model Organism" (2009) and Franklin G. Miller in "The Stateville Penitentiary Malaria Experiments" (2013), during one such experiment—the Stateville Penitentiary Malaria Study—four hundred prisoners in Illinois were deliberately infected with malaria in the 1940s to study the effects of new experimental treatments. Although one prisoner died after suffering a heart attack following several bouts of fever, the researchers insisted that the death was unrelated to their research. As documented in Pulitzer Prize–winning series of articles by Eileen Welsome (and later summarized in her 2000 book *The Plutonium Files*), for decades the US Armed Services, the US Atomic Energy Commission, and collaborating institutions and hospitals conducted experiments using radioactive materials on thousands of vulnerable or ill-formed subjects, including experiments in which subjects were injected with plutonium, pregnant women were given drinks containing radioactive iron, and developmentally disabled children were fed food contaminated with uranium and polonium. For more on these cases, also see E. Samei and Kimberly J. Kearfott's "A Limited Bibliography of the Federal Government–Funded Human Radiation Experiments" (1995).

## RESPONSE TO ABUSE

In recent years, these revelations have led to government inquiries and eventually public apologies and recompense for the victims of unethical studies. For example, in 1994 President Bill Clinton (1946–) and his secretary of energy, Hazel O'Leary (1937–), appointed the Advisory Committee on Human Radiation Experiments in response to Welsome's articles. In 2010, Secretary of State Hillary Clinton (1947–) and Secretary of Health and Human Services Kathleen Sebelius (1948–) apologized for the Guatemala Syphilis experiments conducted in the late 1940s by the US PHS. Before the 1970s, however, the public and private response to most of these scandals was muted. As typified by the response to the Jewish Chronic Disease Hospital Study, for example, the medical and research profession largely reacted to revelations of whistle-blowers like Beecher and Pappworth as one does to any trauma: denial, anger, negotiation, and (eventually) reluctant acceptance. In this case, the public and professional treatment of Sloan-Kettering researcher Dr. Chester Southam (1919–2002) is indicative of the research community's general refusal to acknowledge any external ethical critique of its conduct.

To test existing theories on cancer immunosurveillance and immunoediting—the idea that most people are protected against cancer by their immune system, whereby lymphocytes and other cells of the immune system act as sentinels in recognizing and eliminating newly transformed cells—Southam conducted a series of experiments in which he injected live cancer cells into prisoners, including women who had just undergone hysterectomies, and dying Jewish patients (e.g., see the research described in Aizawa and Southam [1960], Itoh and Southam [1963], Levin et al. [1964]). In most cases, the subjects of Southam's research were not informed that they were being injected with cancerous materials, only that they were undergoing "tests of immunity." It was only after Southam began experimenting on elderly patients at Brooklyn Jewish Chronic Disease Hospital, most likely because of Jewish sensitivities to research contrary to the principles of the Nuremberg Code, that ethical concerns about these experiments were raised. In response, the New York State Board of Regents suspended Southam's license to practice medicine for one year. Despite the suspension, Southam was elected vice president and then president of the American Association for Cancer Research in 1966 and 1967, respectively, because the results of his experiments advanced scientific understanding of the nature of cancer.

This is not to say that there weren't a handful of research professionals, in addition to well-known whistle-blowers like Beecher and Pappworth, who raised questions or proposed policies to improve the ethical conduct of research in the United States and elsewhere at that time. In 1965, for example, the director of the US NIH proposed that all research funded by the NIH or by the PHS undergo independent peer review to ensure that the rights of research subjects were protected. Despite this proposal, as research professionals saw nothing wrong with honoring researchers like Southam, whose work had been condemned publicly as unethical, effective regulation of research would prove to be difficult, if not impossible. It wasn't until Associated Press writer Jean Heller broke the Tuskegee Syphilis Study scandal in 1972 that real movement on this issue started, and not because the medical profession or the researchers were shocked—they weren't. Change occurred only because the timing of this particular scandal resulted in an unprecedented civic and political outcry that threatened to undermine the public legitimacy of human-subjects research entirely.

## THE RISE OF REGULATORY OVERSIGHT IN AMERICAN RESEARCH ETHICS

Although US and British researchers were quick to condemn the exploitation of unwilling prisoners as research subjects in Nazi concentration camps as a particularly flagrant injustice, even after the horrors of Nazi German and (less so) Imperial Japanese experimentation were made widely known, they themselves continued to engage in exploitative and unethical research. Beginning in the 1930s, for example, the Tuskegee Syphilis Study used disadvantaged, rural black men to study the untreated course of a disease that is by no means confined to that population. This study continued for decades, with subjects deprived of demonstrably effective treatment to avoid interrupting the project, long after such treatment became generally available.

For a detailed description of the design and conduct of what is properly called the Tuskegee Study of Untreated Syphilis in the Negro Male, the reader is referred to such classic texts as James H. Jones's *Bad Blood* (1993) and Wellesley historian Susan Reverby's *Examining Tuskegee* (2009), as well as the play and 1997 film *Miss Evers' Boys*. For four decades (1932–1972), the US PHS studied the effects of untreated syphilis on African American men in Macon County, Alabama, near Tuskegee. Almost four hundred men with syphilis participated in the Tuskegee Syphilis Study, and an additional two hundred men without syphilis served as experimental controls. Most of these poor and undereducated men were recruited without informed consent, were not told that they had syphilis, and were regularly misinformed that some of the procedures done in the interest of the research (e.g., spinal taps) were actually "special treatment" (Jones 1993, 127). More egregiously, as Raymond Vonderlehr and Taliaferro Clark report in "Untreated Syphilis in the Male Negro" (1936), although arsenic-based treatments like arsenobenzol were available during the early 1900s and penicillin became widely available as an inexpensive cure for syphilis by the late 1940s, the study continued and the men were left uninformed and untreated even after it became apparent that more of the infected men than the controls had developed complications.

The study continued even though John R. Heller and P. T. Bruyere reported in "Untreated Syphilis in the Male Negro: II. Mortality during 12 Years of Observation" (1946) that the death rate among those with syphilis was about twice as high as among the controls. Similarly, treatment continued to be actively withheld despite a 1955 review by Jesse J. Peters and his colleagues of autopsy results that found almost a third of the subjects with untreated syphilis had died as a direct result of advanced syphilitic lesions in the cardiovascular or central nervous system. According to Allan M. Brandt in "Racism and Research: The Case of the Tuskegee Syphilis Study" (1978), the withholding of treatment was systematic and deliberate, with US PHS investigators providing local physicians, the Alabama Health Department, and even the US Army Draft Board with a list of participants who should remain untreated for syphilis.

All told, more than a dozen articles describing the devastating consequences of untreated syphilis were published in the peer-reviewed literature, yet there was no professional condemnation of the study. In fact, the US PHS and the US Centers for Disease Control and Prevention (CDC) evaluated the study on several occasions, including as late as 1969. Each time, the reviewers recommended that the study continue and the men still enrolled remain untreated. The Tuskegee study continued unabated until 1972 when, acting on information provided by former PHS employee and whistleblower Peter Buxtun, Heller published her article "Syphilis Victims in U.S. Study Went Untreated for 40 Years." The timing of Heller's article was impeccable, as it was published at the height of the US civil rights movement. Describing in detail forty years of unethical experimentation on poor black men by educated white elites in the rural South, that article caused public outrage.

## PASSAGE OF THE NATIONAL RESEARCH ACT

Following this outcry, in August 1972 the US Department of Health, Education, and Welfare (DHEW) established the Tuskegee Syphilis Study Ad Hoc Advisory Panel to review the project. Focusing on two key questions—had the participants given their informed consent, and should treatment with penicillin have been provided when it became widely available—this panel determined that the study was unjustified and ordered its termination. Despite the fact that a similar panel convened by the CDC just four years earlier had recommended that the study continue unabated, the members of the Tuskegee Syphilis Study Ad Hoc Advisory Panel concluded the following:

1. In retrospect, the Public Health Service Study of Untreated Syphilis in the Male Negro in Macon County, Alabama, was ethically unjustified in 1932. This judgement made in 1973 about the conduct of the study in 1932 is made with the advantage of hindsight acutely sharpened over some forty years, concerning an activity in a different age with different social standards. Nevertheless, one fundamental ethical rule is that a person should not be subjected to avoidable risk of death or physical harm unless he freely and intelligently consents. There is no evidence that such consent was obtained from the participants in this study.

2. Because of the paucity of information available today on the manner in which the study was conceived, designed and sustained, a scientific justification for a short term demonstration study cannot be ruled out. However, the conduct of the longitudinal study as initially reported in 1936 and through the years is judged to be scientifically unsound and its results are disproportionately meager compared with known risks to human subjects involved. (US Department of Health, Education, and Welfare, 1973)

In addition to the decision by DHEW to terminate the Tuskegee study, a series of congressional hearings was held by the Subcommittee on Health of the Committee of Labor and Public Welfare to investigate the study. Chaired by Senator Edward Kennedy (1932–2009), the hearings led Congress to pass the National Research Service Award Act of 1974 (Public Law 93-348, hereafter referred to as the National Research Act).

The approval of the National Research Act marks a watershed moment in US research ethics. First, the law established the current IRB-based system for ethical review of federally funded research in the United States, as well as the establishment of a federal office to oversee human-subjects research. IRBs are human-subjects review boards that examine proposed research to ensure that the protocols meet federal regulations and local policies and that they adequately protect human subjects. Shortly after the US government implemented these recommendations as policy, international organizations followed suit. In 1975, for example, the Tokyo amendment to the Declaration of Helsinki recommended peer review of all human-subjects protocols by independent research ethics committees or IRBs.

More importantly, the National Research Act also established the National Commission for the Protection of Human Subjects of Biomedical and Behavioral Research, the first body to shape research ethics policy in the United States. This multidisciplinary panel of eleven members, supported by staff members of the newly established Kennedy Institute of Bioethics at Georgetown University, was specifically ordered to:

(i) conduct a comprehensive investigation and study to identify the basic ethical principles which underlie the conduct of biomedical and behavioral research involving human subjects, (ii) develop guidelines which should be followed in such research to assure that it is conducted in accordance with such principles, and (iii) make recommendations to the Secretary (I) for such administrative action as may be appropriate to apply such guidelines to biomedical and behavioral research conducted or supported under programs administered by the Secretary, and (II) concerning any other matter pertaining to the protection of human subjects of biomedical and behavioral research. (National Commission for the Protection of Human Subjects of Biomedical and Behavioral Research 1979)

Thus empowered, the National Commission provided the DHEW secretary with a series of reports and practical recommendations for the regulation and oversight of US research, including research on children and fetuses, research on prisoners, research on the developmentally disabled, and the structure and function of IRBs designated to review and approve human-subjects research. In the latter report, the National Commission also recommended that, "all institutions receiving federal support for the conduct of research involving human subjects should be governed by uniform federal regulations applicable to the review of all such research." Although this approach was not fully implemented until 1991, all federally funded research is now guided by a set of uniform regulations known as the Common Rule, which establishes strict requirements for obtaining and documenting informed consent from research participants and for ensuring appropriate review by an independent review board.

### RELEASE OF THE *BELMONT REPORT*

The National Commission's most important contribution to research ethics came with the release of the 1979 *Belmont Report: Ethical Principles and Guidelines for the Protection of Human Subjects of Research* (published in the *Federal Register* in 1979). Named after the conference center where the National Commission met, the *Belmont Report* stated that research on human subjects needed to be justified in terms of three basic ethical principles. To this day, these principles provide the ethical foundation for the US federal government's existing human-subjects regulations. Instead of providing recommendations for new laws or policies, the *Belmont Report* articulated the ethical principles for regulatory proposals that already had been acted on, and thus became a seminal document for US research ethics and research ethics generally.

## THE *BELMONT* PRINCIPLES

As articulated in the *Belmont Report*, the three ethical principles for human-subjects research are as follows:

1. Respect for persons: Obtaining voluntary and informed consent from research participants and including special protections to protect the rights and safety of vulnerable persons.

2. Beneficence: Minimizing or avoiding risks and harms to research subjects while maximizing the benefits to subjects and/or society.

3. Justice: Ensuring reasonable, non-exploitative and well-considered procedures to ensure that potential subjects are recruited fairly and equitably, and that individuals and groups enrolled in research studies benefit from their participation. (National Commission for the Protection of Human Subjects of Biomedical and Behavioral Research 1979).

These three principles thus would require that: (1) participants enroll in a research trial only after being fully informed of the risks and benefits of participating, and without being coerced or improperly enticed through unreasonable promises of financial compensation or of a level of medical care that otherwise is not available in the community; (2) the risks to participants have been properly minimized and the benefits maximized; and (3) individuals and communities recruited to participate in the trial are chosen because they will benefit from the results of the research. These benefits may be derived perhaps through access to safe and effective products tested in the trial or through capacity-building efforts like community education and improvements to existing health-care systems. A frequently overlooked fact, but one that is critical to remember, is that the *Belmont Report* does not privilege any one of the three principles over the others.

## RESPECT FOR PERSONS

Consider, for example, the obligations to obtain informed consent placed on researchers by the principle of respect for persons. Except in rare circumstances in which a waiver of consent may be granted, this principle requires that researchers obtain informed consent from all study participants. Indeed, the requirement to obtain informed consent is a central component of US (and most international) research ethics policies. Respect for persons is thus, in some ways, the most tightly regulated but also easiest of the three ethical principles to achieve in practice. What is often overlooked, however, is the fact that informed consent has three important components: (1) full disclosure of information, (2) comprehension and understanding, and (3) confirmation that the decision to participate is free of coercion or undue influence. All of these components must be addressed to fully meet the ethical obligations of respect for persons.

Although informed consent is one way in which investigators demonstrate respect for the autonomy of potential study participants, in some circumstances individuals may have diminished capacity. Consider that subjects may be children under the age of majority, they may be mentally ill or developmentally disabled, or they may lack the capacity to give consent as a result of acute illness or trauma. These individuals are often described as *vulnerable*, and existing research ethics regulations often include provisions designed to protect subjects who fall into this protected class.

## BENEFICENCE

Similarly, the *Belmont* principle of beneficence requires that trial participants be treated ethically, "not only by respecting their decisions and protecting them from harm, but also by making efforts to ensuring their well-being. Two general rules have been formulated as complementary expressions of beneficent actions: 1) do no harm, and 2) maximize possible benefits and minimize potential harms" (National Commission for the Protection of Human Subjects of Biomedical and Behavioral Research 1979, sec. B2).

Often, this principle of beneficence is interpreted to mean that the trial must have a favorable risk-benefit ratio. That is, the benefits to individual participants or the trial community must outweigh the risks of study participation. Of course, it is more appropriate to say that the *anticipated* risks of study participation must be commensurate with the *potential* benefits to participants and the trial community. The first of the two rules of beneficence mentioned in the *Belmont Report*—do no harm—implies that researchers have an obligation to ensure that any new drug or intervention be rigorously tested for safety in laboratory and animal models before being used in clinical trials. Other study-related procedures also should be restricted only to those that are as safe possible and that are necessary for the study to be scientifically valid. It is the second of these two rules— maximizing the benefits and minimizing the harms of study participation—that can prove to be problematic in practice, particularly with respect to placebo-controlled trials. For example, this ethical principle would seem to imply that researchers must provide all trial participants with access to treatments and interventions that are known be safe and effective.

Conversely, researchers cannot deny participants access to safe and effective treatments that already exist within the trial community. Note that the obligation to maximize benefits is not limitless. Using the principle of beneficence, one can argue that investigators conducting research in resource-poor regions have an obligation to provide health care for endemic illnesses like malaria or tuberculosis, even if these diseases are not under study. After all, these interventions also would provide a direct benefit to trial participants, albeit one that is not directly relevant to the research question. Although some ethicists and researchers believe it is morally praiseworthy to provide such services, there is considerable disagreement about whether this should be considered obligatory; see, for example, Participants in 2006 Georgetown University Workshop on Ancillary-Care Obligations of Medical Researchers Working in Developing Countries (2008). In particular, other researchers and ethicists, such as the National Institute of Mental Health Collaborative HIV/STD Prevention Trial Group (2007), argue that such an expansive interpretation of the principle of beneficence would place an undue burden on clinical trials, depleting already limited resources and limiting the number and quality of trials that could be conducted.

## JUSTICE

The least understood, and most often debated of the three bioethical principles articulated in the *Belmont Report* is justice. Until recently, the notion of justice has focused primarily on the need to protect potential and actual research subjects from harm, abuse, and exploitation. As philosopher Tom Beauchamp (1939–) and religious studies scholar James Childress (1940–) point out in the 2008 edition of their *Principles of Biomedical Ethics*, in the past twenty years, justice as fair access—both participation in research and access to the benefits and results of research—became as important as protection from exploitation.

In Book 5 of his *Nicomachean Ethics*, Aristotle (384–322 BCE) describes three types of justice: distributive justice, rectificatory justice, and reciprocal justice. The first and the last of these are applicable to the ethical design and conduct of research studies. Distributive justice is the notion that all things must be distributed fairly. This includes the risks and benefits of participating in research. Similar to the earlier description of *The Constant Gardener*, offering trial participants in a developing country like Kenya experimental interventions and standardized treatments that are inferior in both scope and effectiveness to those offered to trial participants in an industrial country like the United States may be unjust. The risks to individual volunteers in the United States and Kenya would be the same in terms of study-related harms, but the benefits would differ substantially in terms of prevention services offered to participants in the developed and developing world, respectively.

Reciprocal justice is the second type of justice relevant to the ethical design and conduct of research studies. The underlying idea behind reciprocity is that individuals who voluntarily take the risks associated with research participation deserve proportionally more benefit than those who do not take on these risks. A South African woman who volunteers to take part in a trial of a new HIV vaccine, for example, might expect to receive a level of treatment and other types of medical care that otherwise would not be available to women in the community. Reciprocity demands that she have access to state-of-the-art HIV prevention tools, or some other equivalent benefit like improved medical care, to compensate her for the potential risks she faces as a trial participant.

In short, the principle of justice requires that the selection of research subjects be scrutinized to determine whether some classes (e.g., welfare patients, particular racial and ethnic minorities, or people confined to institutions) are being systematically selected simply because of their easy availability, their compromised position, or their manipulability, rather than for reasons directly related to the problem being studied. It also requires that the study participants and the community should benefit from the results of the research. Research should not unduly involve people from groups unlikely to be among the beneficiaries. Finally, whenever research supported by public funds leads to the development of therapeutic devices and procedures, justice demands that these developments not provide advantages only to those who can afford them.

As bioethicist Ruth Macklin explains in *Double Standards in Medical Research* (2004), however, the principle of justice does not require that investigators and donors provide the exact same level of care and services to all participants at all trial sites. Under this less expansive view of justice, researchers can provide a different level of care and services to trial participants at different sites, as long as specific sites are not chosen solely because local circumstances preclude or exclude their prevision. For example, consultant Kathy Shapiro and physician-ethicist Solomon Benatar argue in "HIV Prevention Research and Global Inequality: Towards Improved Standards of Care" (2005) that the types of services that researchers are ethically required to provide to trial participants depend not only on the specific nature of the research but also on the local context, needs, and preferences of the trial community. It may not feasible, for example, for researchers to provide study participants in rural Tanzania with the level of treatment and care that would be achievable in United States. Economic, logistical, and political barriers may prevent research clinicians from using the latest diagnostic tools or providing the most modern and effective drugs. That does not, however, reduce the obligations of these investigators to provide a standard of care that is equivalent to the best achievable in that socioeconomic context. Moreover, researchers may also be obligated to provide additional resources that are designed to provide sustainable improvements to the existing public health-care system. In addition to distributive justice between sites in industrial versus developing countries, they encourage researchers to take into account the potential impact of "introduc[ing] new inequalities or further exacerbat[ing] existing inequalities in health in the community where research is being conducted" (Shapiro and Benatar 2005, 45). Justice requires, at a minimum, that researchers not select a community solely because they do not or cannot provide a particular level of care to trial participants—to do so would be exploitative.

## OTHER RESEARCH ETHICS FRAMEWORKS

Since they were first promulgated, the *Belmont* principles have become the most commonly cited and used framework in the research ethics literature. In one form or another, these principles are the basis for many of the international guidance documents discussed earlier, including new research ethics guidelines from organizations like the Joint United Nations Program on HIV/AIDS (UNAIDS) and the World Health Organization's (WHO) *Ethical Considerations in Biomedical HIV Prevention Trials* (2007). Other (often related) bioethical frameworks also speak to the issues at hand. For example, a slightly different articulation of these fundamental ethical principles was put forward in 2002 by the Nuffield Council on Bioethics, an independent ethics body that specifically addresses the challenges of conducting research in developing countries. The Nuffield Council principles strongly mirror those articulated in the *Belmont Report*, but they address more explicitly issues of culture, justice, and exploitation and include (1) the duty to show respect for persons,

(2) the duty to alleviate suffering, (3) the duty to be sensitive to cultural differences, and (4) the duty not to exploit the vulnerable or less powerful.

Examples of other common research ethics frameworks include standards of care, therapeutic obligation and clinical equipoise, the duty of rescue, and casuistry and virtue ethics. The first three of these alternative frameworks are described in the following section.

## STANDARD OF CARE

The standard-of-care argument maintains that it is unethical to conduct a clinical trial in which some participants receive a level of care that falls below established treatment guidelines. The source of considerable debate and confusion, however, has been what is the appropriate point of reference for determining this standard? Is the standard of care defined by the best-proven intervention anywhere in the world or is the standard defined locally or nationally? As Hans-Jörg Ehni writes in "The Definition of Adequate Care in Externally Sponsored Clinical Trials" (2006), part of the reason for this ambiguity is the conflicting definitions of the word *standard*.

In the descriptive sense of the word, *standard* describes what is usually done as a matter of fact. Philosopher Alex John London defined this as the *de facto* standard of care in his articles "The Ambiguity and the Exigency" (2000) and "Equipoise and International Human-Subjects Research" (2001)—that is, *standard of care* refers to the actual set of medical practices in a community. Often the result of empirical observation on the part of local physicians and researchers, this sort of routine practice reflects local context, local experience, and expert judgment rather than careful and rigorous scientific evaluation of different and competing approaches to treatment or prevention.

By contrast, the normative sense of the word *standard* describes the level of care that should be provided in the community. This standard of care, according to London, the so-called *de jure* standard of care, would be the optimum type and level of care that should be provided in the community, as defined by national norms, medical and scientific experts, or other regulatory authorities. To draw an analogy from the field of cardiovascular research, the use of β-adrenergic blockers (beta-blockers) to prevent myocardial infarction would be an example of *de jure* versus *de facto* standards of medical care. In the 1980s, use of beta-blockers by patients recovering from heart attacks was found to reduce overall mortality in randomized trials. Almost thirty years later, however, these drugs still are prescribed to only a small minority of patients in the United States. In this case, the standard of care given to most heart attack patients is considerably less than has been confirmed scientifically to be best practice. Although the use of beta-blockers to prevent heart attacks prophylactically would be the *de jure* standard of care for cardiac patients, the *de facto* standard of care is no treatment at all.

**Local versus Global Standards.** Note that there are local and global or universal versions of both the *de jure* and the *de facto* standard. The global *de jure* standard is what experts think is the best proven therapy available anywhere. The local *de jure* standard is what national experts and public health norms have determined is best practice for that population in that setting. In many developing countries, the local *de jure* standard of care is defined by national guidelines or through expert consultation but, because of resource constraints, the *de facto* standard of care may be nothing at all. Most ethicists (and prevention trial investigators) agree that the local *de facto* practice is not an adequate moral guide to inform research conducted in situations of scarcity. As Macklin (2004) explains, in resource-poor regions where existing health inequities mean that many trial participants otherwise might have little access to existing treatments, allowing trials to define the level of treatment provided in terms of *de facto* standards of care could allow researchers to provide few, if any, treatments or benefits.

The current and more progressive view argues that a *de jure* standard should apply to all research, grounded in the researchers' obligation to ensure that subjects of clinical trials are not knowingly exposed to foreseeable and preventable harms. This leaves open the question of whether the *de jure* standard that should apply is the global standard (e.g., the best-known treatment or prevention recommended anywhere or endorsed by global experts, such as the WHO) or the national *de jure* standard. Central to this debate is the issue of whether it is ever ethically defensible for the standard of care to vary among settings, or whether one universal standard must always be applied.

Macklin also argues that knowingly having standards that differ by setting, particularly between industrial and developing countries, is always unacceptable. By contrast, other ethicists, including Benatar and Peter A. Singer in "A New Look at International Research Ethics" (2000) and Adnan Hyder and Liza Dawson in "Defining the Standard of Care in the Developing World" (2005), argue that local socioeconomic and cultural contexts should influence the types and level of services that researchers plan to provide.

From a historical perspective, consider the controversial ACTG 076 trials to prevent mother-to-child transmission of HIV. The first ACTG 076 trial, involving the administration of a combination of oral and intravenous zidovudine (AZT) to pregnant HIV-positive women in the United States in the early 1990s, demonstrated that this treatment—coupled with oral administration of AZT to the newborn and avoidance of breast-feeding—reduced the likelihood of perinatal HIV transmission of HIV threefold. Because of the cost of the drugs, the need for extensive prenatal treatment, and the necessity to avoid breast-feeding, however, this so-called long-course AZT regimen was not and could not be implemented in most developing countries at that time.

Because there was some evidence that a short-course regimen consisting of oral AZT during the last few weeks of pregnancy and the first few days postdelivery could also reduce rates of mother-to-child transmission of HIV, the NIH and CDC sponsored a series of trials in which HIV-positive pregnant women in countries like Thailand and Cameroon were randomized to receive short-course AZT or placebo. This shorter course of treatment also proved effective, albeit less so, at preventing mother-to-child transmission of HIV, but a series of articles published shortly thereafter in the *New England Journal of Medicine* and *Lancet* (e.g., see Angell 1997, 2000; Lurie and Wolfe 1997; Wolfe and Lurie 1999) questioned the ethics of randomizing women to receive a placebo when the original study had demonstrated that an alternate course of treatment with AZT had already been shown to reduce perinatal transmission of HIV in the United States. To deny women enrolled in the ACTG 076 trial access to long-course AZT, they felt, violated the principle of justice—NIH and CDC researchers were willing to take advantage of these women's poverty and vulnerability to test an obviously inferior course of treatment.

Others, including Edward Mbidde in "Bioethics and Local Circumstances" (1998), David Resnik in "The Ethics of HIV Research in Developing Nations" (1998), and Harold Varmus and David Satcher in "Ethical Complexities of Conducting Research in Developing Countries" (1997), believe trials like this can be ethical—even if they could not be done ethically in a country like the United States—so long as the goal is to improve the health of trial participants in the countries and communities where the research is done. Although the principle of justice would appear to require that the risks and benefits of research be distributed equally, the socioeconomic circumstances or special health needs of resource-poor communities can justify the use of a placebo control even when an effective treatment exists elsewhere or can justify offering different health packages to participants in different settings. In the case of the ACTG 076 trial, for example, philosopher Resnik argued that denying women in developing countries access to long-course AZT treatment did not violate the principle of justice for two reasons. First, the research addressed a health problem of concern to the trial communities. Second, the treatment under investigation, because it proved effective, was made available to the study population once the research was completed.

Moreover, according to physician-bioethicist Robert Levine's 2000 "Revision of the CIOMS [Council for International Organizations of Medical Science] International Ethical Guidelines" and Macklin (2004), one of the reasons that the women in the controversial ACTG 076 trials did not receive the longer course of AZT treatment, for example, was they also would have had to abstain from breast-feeding. At the time, WHO, UNAIDS, and the United Nations Children's Fund (UNICEF) had issued *HIV and Infant Feeding: A UNAIDS/ UNICEF/WHO Policy Statement* (1997), which recommended exclusive bottle-feeding (or other alternatives to breast-feeding) by HIV-positive women to reduce the likelihood of mother-to-child transmission of HIV, thus meeting the universal *de jure* standard of care. Avoidance of breast-feeding was, for a variety of cultural and economic reasons, neither the universal *de facto* standard nor the local *de jure* or *de facto* standard for HIV-infected women in most developing countries. To implement the universal *de jure* standard, researchers would have had to convince women both to resist centuries-old cultural expectations of proper child care and to risk communicating their HIV status—a difficult if not impossible task. Moreover, encouraging exclusive bottle-feeding without providing sustained access to formula and clean water potentially would have increased the chances that the babies of women enrolled in the trial could die from malnutrition or diarrhea.

In addition, implementing the full ACTG 076 regimen in Africa, with its requirement for exclusive bottle-feeding runs counter to the medical ethics notion that "ought implies can." Often but erroneously attributed to Immanuel Kant (1724–1804), the principle of "ought implies can" states that if someone is ethically obligated to do something—say, to avoid breast-feeding her child or to provide comprehensive HIV prevention to all trial participants—then that person or agent must have the power or ability to achieve this. Conversely, if a person cannot do something—because social expectations require her to breast-feed her child or women do not present for prenatal care early enough to implement the ACTG 076 regimen—this weakens the claim that the agent is ethically obligated to do it. In the context of a clinical research trial, ethical obligations are binding only if they can be implemented. In the case of the ACTG 076 trial, if requiring abstinence from breast-feeding would be socially unacceptable or, alternatively, would put more children at risk of injury or death from malnutrition than likely would be saved from HIV infection, this could obviate an ethical obligation for researchers to provide long-course AZT treatment.

## THERAPEUTIC OBLIGATION AND CLINICAL EQUIPOISE

Therapeutic obligation is the notion that physicians—and by extension physician-researchers—have an obligation to do what is best for their patients. This idea is one of the oldest traditions in medicine and derives from the Hippocratic Oath: "I will follow that system or regimen which, according to my ability and judgment, I consider for the benefit of my patient and abstain from whatever is deleterious and mischievous" (Pellegrino and Sulmasy 2003, 14).

This section of the Hippocratic Oath obligates the physician to do what is best for each patient, without consideration of other personal or social obligations (Veatch 2005; Buchanan and Miller 2006). Two separate but related concerns pertain to this oath: acts of *commission* (what the physician does to the patient) and acts of *omission* (what the physician fails to do or provide to the patient)

Building on the *Belmont Report*, particularly the principles of beneficence and justice, philosopher Don Marquis (1935–) argued that no trial participant should receive an intervention known to be inferior to other treatments in the trial or to existing standards of care (1983). Marquis first applied the phrase *therapeutic obligation* to randomized clinical trials, like those used to test novel HIV prevention tools.

Bioethicist Benjamin Freedman in "Equipoise and the Ethics of Clinical Research" (1988), Levine in *Ethics and Regulation of Clinical Research* (1988), and physician-philosopher Charles Weijer in "The Ethical Analysis of Risk" (2000), among others, have argued that randomized controlled clinical trials, by their very nature, violate a physician's therapeutic obligation unless the medical community is uncertain as to whether the treatment under investigation is better or worse than existing standards of care. Freedman called this state of uncertainty *clinical equipoise*, writing that randomized controlled trials are ethical only when there is "no consensus within the expert clinical community about the comparative merits of the alternatives to be tested" (1988, 144).

The interrelated notions of therapeutic obligation and clinical equipoise most often are applied to ongoing debates about the use of placebos in clinical trials. Freedman (1988), for example, argued that placebo-controlled trials violate the concept of clinical equipoise when proven effective therapy is available. According to Karin Michels and Kenneth Rothman's "Update on Unethical Use of Placebos in Randomised Trials" (2003), placebo-controlled trials compromise a participant's right to receive the best care possible and violate the *Belmont* principle of beneficence and the therapeutic obligation of physicians to offer optimal medical care. Freedman later argued in "Placebo-Controlled Trials and the Logic of Clinical Purpose" (1990) that placebo-controlled trials are appropriate only when (1) there is no standard therapy for the condition under study, (2) existing therapy is no better than placebo, (3) the standard treatment is placebo, (4) there is sincere doubt about the therapeutic advantage of the standard versus experimental therapy, or (5) the standard treatment is unavailable. Physicians David Solomon, Edward Gilbert, and Milton Packer have argued that placebo-controlled trials are acceptable under the twin arguments of therapeutic obligation and clinical equipoise in studies where participants "do not have a response to the conventional treatment or cannot tolerate its adverse effects" (Solomon 1995, 62) or in add-on studies in which participants in both the placebo and treatment groups "receive all medications that would normally be prescribed" (Gilbert and Packer 1995, 61).

Although long an article of faith of research ethics, some ethicists have come to question the appropriateness of grounding obligations to research participants in the physician's therapeutic obligation. The most expansive critique to date has been that of two ethicists at the NIH Clinical Center, philosopher Miller and physician-ethicist Howard Brody. Although their position is not widely accepted within the ethics community, Miller and Brody have argued that key differences exist between medical care and biomedical research—differences that call into question the applicability of concepts like therapeutic obligation and clinical equipoise to clinical trials. For example, in "Clinical Equipoise and the Incoherence of Research Ethics" (2007), Miller and Brody assert that researchers are not providing personalized medical care to the participants enrolled in a clinical trial. In routine medical care, physicians are obligated to offer personalized therapy to particular patients consistent with existing standards of care. The risks of diagnostic and treatment interventions are justified by the prospect of medical benefit to the patient. In contrast, research trials differ from routine medical care in their purpose, methods, benefits, and risks. The primary goal of a research trial is to develop knowledge that can lead to improving the care of future patients, not to promote the interests of individual participants enrolled in the trial.

According to Steven Joffe and Miller in "Bench to Bedside: Mapping the Moral Terrain of Clinical Research" (2008), the clinical services provided in randomized controlled clinical trials are quite different from the clinical care that an individual receives as part of the normal doctor-patient relationship. The researcher typically is not the primary physician of the study participants and thus is not subject to the same therapeutic obligation that governs medical care. In addition, by their very nature, clinical trials sometimes must limit the types of treatments made available to volunteers. They also subject participants to additional procedures necessary to achieve the scientific goals of the study that have some (albeit small) risk of harm or discomfort—such as additional blood draws—but that do not offer any direct medical benefit. Thus, clinical trials by necessity often involve medical procedures or therapeutic restrictions that would not be justifiable within the strict ethical framework of therapeutic obligation. The risks of these procedures and restrictions, however, are ethically justifiable by the value of the knowledge to be gained from the research.

Other ethicists do not take such as extreme position as Miller and Brody with respect to the therapeutic obligations of researchers versus physicians, but still question the applicability of Freedman's concept of equipoise to clinical research. For example, Robert Veatch (2006, 2007) has argued that evaluation of treatment alternatives is a subjective process: a continuum exists between the point at which an HIV prevention trial meets Freedman's strict definition of clinical equipoise and the point at which the research community concludes that a new intervention, such as a new HIV prevention tool, has been found to be safe and effective for all at-risk populations worldwide. Along similar lines, London (2001) has offered a more operationally precise definition of equipoise that takes into account differences in study design and trial populations. Just because a new treatment has proven safe and effective in one trial, its safety or effectiveness in a different setting still may be questionable—for example, even if an HIV vaccine is found to be safe and effective in the current phase III trial of injection drug users in Thailand, this doesn't mean that the vaccine will be equally safe and effective for heterosexually exposed women in Zambia. Only once a similar trial of the vaccine is conducted among heterosexually exposed women, or once there is broad consensus that the differences between the two populations are unlikely to significantly affect safety and effectiveness, would equipoise be disturbed and researchers be obligated to make this new vaccine available.

Once again, as with the debate over standards of care, we have to consider the notion that ought implies can. Researchers should strive to provide as high a level of care and prevention as possible, so long as doing so would not place an impossible burden on researchers or sponsors to provide a level of care that is not achievable or sustainable.

## GOOD SAMARITAN OBLIGATIONS AND THE DUTY OF RESCUE

The last of the ethical frameworks discussed in this section, Good Samaritan obligations and the duty of rescue, derives its name from a biblical parable in which only a single traveler (out of hundreds, the so-described Good Samaritan) on the road from Jerusalem to Jericho stopped to render aid to a man left half dead by bandits. From this story arises the notion that everyone has an obligation, often called the *duty of rescue,* to help those in need. Many philosophers and ethicists, however, would argue that this duty is limited. Although it is morally praiseworthy to come to the aid of a drowning boy, for example, there is no obligation to risk one's own life to save another. Under the duty of rescue, a passerby who could not swim would not be expected to leap into the water in an attempt to save the child's life. A competent swimmer, on the other hand, would have a duty to rescue the child.

Applying this parable to biomedical research, in the same way that the principle of beneficence requires researchers to maximize the benefits and minimize the risks of trial participation, the duty of rescue suggests that researchers have a moral obligation to provide at least some level of care beyond that which is required to conduct the study. As with the discussion of the *Belmont* principle of beneficence, the challenge lies in determining just how far this obligation extends.

The Good Samaritan obligation to provide appropriate care and treatment to those in need does have limits. Researchers conducting trials in many resource-poor regions of the world, for example, frequently work in places where existing public health clinics are overburdened, underfunded, or do not exist. Beyond providing prevention and care services necessary for the safe and ethical conduct of the trial, researchers working in these areas often are called on to provide ancillary care—that is, "care which is not required to make a study scientifically valid, to ensure a trial's safety, or to redress research injuries" (Belsky and Richardson 2004, 1494). As long as the cost of the additional medical supplies and the burden of providing ancillary care is not so large as to threaten the trial itself, some would argue, including Henry Richardson and Leah Belsky in "The Ancillary-Care Responsibilities of Medical Researchers" (2004) and Jennifer Hawkins in "Exploitation and the Enterprise of Medical Research" (2008), there is no compelling reason why the researchers do not have a moral obligation to provide as many additional medical and social services to study participants as possible.

## THE POST-*BELMONT* ERA

Despite the regulatory requirements imposed by the National Research Act and subsequent adoption of the Common Rule, in the absence of scandal, considerable resistance persists on the part of US investigators, study sponsors, and government regulators to new requirements or restrictions on the design and conduct of human-subjects research. The existing regulatory landscape in the United States also has remained largely unchanged since the promulgation of the Common Rule in 1991, despite scientific advances that have called into question many of the ethical and procedural requirements imposed by these federal regulations. The requirements and expectations to obtain voluntary and informed consent for all study participants, for example, have been challenged by a number of changes, including the growth of biobanks and specimen repositories (which call into question existing definitions of *human subjects* and the validity

***Henrietta Lacks.*** *During treatment for cervical cancer at Johns Hopkins Hospital in 1951, Lacks unwittingly provided sample tissue to researcher George Otto Gey, who used it to develop the first immortalized line of human cells for medical research. The eponymous HeLa cells are now commonly used in biomedical research.* **JESSICA WILSON/SCIENCE SOURCE.**

of blanket consent for future research) and the increasing use of the Internet for participant recruitment and data collection. This inertia may soon be overcome, however, thanks to yet another scandal: the federal government's apology for a previously unknown series of research studies conducted in Guatemala in the 1940s.

As described by Reverby in her 2011 article "'Normal Exposure' and Inoculation Syphilis: A PHS 'Tuskegee' Doctor in Guatemala, 1946–1948," from 1946 to 1948, US-based researchers, with the help of the Pan American Sanitary Bureau (the precursor to the Pan American Health Organization) and several Guatemalan health ministries and officials, conducted a series of experiments in which they deliberately exposed soldiers, prisoners, and mental patients to syphilis, gonorrhea, and other sexually transmitted infections to test whether or not antibiotics could be used prophylactically to prevent infection after exposure. As Reverby notes, the Guatemalan study has several parallels to the forty-year Tuskegee Syphilis Study, including the fact that the two studies shared at least one investigator—doctor John Charles Cutler (1915–2003)—but there are important differences. Although the Tuskegee experiment followed the natural progression of syphilis in those already infected, in Guatemala the researchers deliberately exposed healthy people to the disease. Unlike the studies in Macon County, Alabama, where the participants were already infected, an ample supply of uninfected study participants were available in Guatemala. Moreover, although subjects in Guatemala were allegedly given antibiotics when they contracted the disease (unlike having treatment withheld in Alabama), it is unclear from existing records whether all infected parties were cured. Although 1,300 subjects were deliberately infected, only seven hundred received some sort of treatment.

In response to these revelations, not only did the US government immediately apologize to the government of Guatemala and the survivors and descendants of the study participants, but the United States also asked the Institute of Medicine to conduct a review of these experiments. Similarly, the Obama administration's Presidential Commission for the Study of Bioethical Issues (PCSBI) convened a panel of international experts to review this study, concluding that "the Guatemala experiments involved unconscionable basic violations of ethics, even as judged against the researchers' own recognition of the requirements of the medical ethics of the day" (2011, 92). As part of this review, the PCSBI was also asked to conduct a thorough analysis of existing regulations and policies designed to protect the subjects of research to "ensure that all [US-sponsored] human medical research conducted around the globe today meets rigorous ethical standards" and that such incidents are not be repeated (PCSBI 2011, 2).

Concurrently, in 2011 the Office of the Secretary of Health and Human Services, in coordination with the Executive Office of the President's Office of Science and Technology Policy (OSTP) proposed nineteen changes to the Common Rule designed to streamline the ethics review process and update existing regulations in light of scientific advances (particularly the increase use of biobanked specimens [e.g., biological samples that are collected and stored for research]) while still protecting the rights and safety of research participants (76 *Federal Register* 44512–44531, 2011). In doing so, the Department of Health and Human Services was responding to the various scandals, controversies, and presidential orders that had called into question the adequacy of existing human-subjects regulations, including a lawsuit by the Havasupai Indians over the unauthorized use of biobanked DNA specimens by Arizona State University researchers (*Havasupai Tribe v. Arizona Board of Regents*, 2008) and the publication of Rebecca Skloot's best-selling book *The Immortal Life of Henrietta Lacks* (2010), which describes how cancerous tissue harvested from a socioeconomically disadvantaged African American woman was used to create the first immortalized cell line without her family's knowledge and without compensation. In announcing those proposed changes, the department posed seventy-four questions and invited public comment on seven aspects of human-subjects protections in the United States: (1) ensuring risk-based protections, (2) streamlining IRB review of cooperative studies, (3) improving informed consent, (4) strengthening data protections to minimize information risks, (5) collecting data to enhance system oversight, (6) extending federal regulations, and (7) clarifying and harmonizing regulatory requirements and agency guidance. Over a three-month public comment period, a total of 1,051 comments were received from researchers and research organizations, disease and patient advocacy groups, bioethicists and IRB members, and research subjects themselves.

These comments, along with the 2011 PCSBI report on the Guatemala study, were reviewed by the Department of Health and Human Services Office of Human Research Protections. In September 2015, the department released a new Notice of Proposed Rulemaking outlining its planned revisions to the Common Rule (80 *Federal Register* 53931–54061, 2015). These proposed changes were opened for public comment and debate, and by early 2016 it remained unclear what the final regulations would look like. Among the proposed changes, however, are new requirements regarding the length and complexity of informed consent documents (acknowledging that voluntary informed consent is a process, not a form), new rules requiring broad consent for storage and secondary research on biobanked specimens, and a new category of review that would make many minimal risk studies (particularly those in the social and behavioral sciences) largely exempt from IRB review. These proposals, not surprisingly, are hotly debated within the research and ethics community, and it remains to be seen whether or not they truly streamline the research process while still maintaining (or even improving) current human-subjects protections. Only time (and scandal) will tell.

## Summary

For investigators, ethicists, and study participants alike, to fully appreciate the current principles and policies that regulate human-subjects research, it is important to understand their historical origin and evolution. It is a story of abuse and harm, and most of our current regulations and ethical frameworks are a reaction to such public scandals as the Nazi experiments on concentration camp prisoners, the deliberate withholding of treatment from syphilis patients by US PHS investigators, and the deliberate infection of institutionalized patients or prisoners with diseases such as hepatitis, malaria, and gonorrhea. Key international guidance documents like the Nuremberg Code and the Declaration of Helsinki were a direct response to these scandals and, in some ways, represent a desperate attempt by investigators and other stakeholders to rebuild and ensure public trust in the biomedical research enterprise. More important, scandalous and unethical research like the Tuskegee Syphilis Study resulted in the promulgation of new regulations in the United States that not only formally established of the current IRB-based system of human-subjects protection and research review (a model widely replicated in most countries to some extent) but also resulted in the promulgation of the best-known ethical framework for human-subjects research, the *Belmont Report*, which established the holy trinity of research ethics principles (albeit derived from previous guidance and codes of ethics). Those three principles—respect for persons, beneficence, and justice—provide not only the moral justification for current US regulations regarding human subjects, they are also used globally in one form or another to define ethically appropriate research. Although our ethical and regulatory frameworks continue to evolve, either in response to scandal or as a result of scientific advances that open up new avenues of inquiry, the principles of respect for people, beneficence, and justice remain the key moral hallmarks of ethical research.

## Bibliography

Advisory Committee on Human Radiation Experiments. *The Human Radiation Experiments*. New York: Oxford University Press 1996.

Aizawa, Miki, and Chester M. Southam. "Serum Antibodies following Homotransplantation of Human Cancer Cells." *Annals of the New York Academy of Sciences* 87, no. 1 (1960): 293–307.

Angell, Marcia. "The Ethics of Clinical Research in the Third World." *New England Journal of Medicine* 337, no. 12 (1997): 847–849.

Angell, Marcia. "Investigators' Responsibilities for Human Subjects in Developing Countries." *New England Journal of Medicine* 342, no. 13 (2000): 967–969.

Annas, George, and Michael Grodin. *The Nazi Doctors and the Nuremberg Code*. New York: Oxford University Press, 1992.

Aristotle. *Nicomachean Ethics*. 2nd ed. Translated by Terence Irwin. Indianapolis, IN: Hackett, 1999.

Baker, Robert. "A Theory of International Bioethics: The Negotiable and the Non-negotiable." *Kennedy Institute of Ethics Journal* 8, no. 3 (1998): 233–273.

Barenblatt, Daniel. *A Plague upon Humanity: The Secret Genocide of Axis Japan's Germ Warfare Operation*. New York: HarperCollins, 2004.

Beauchamp, Tom L., and James L. Childress. *Principles of Biomedical Ethics*. 1st ed. New York: Oxford University Press, 1979.

Beauchamp, Tom L., and James L. Childress. *Principles of Biomedical Ethics*. 5th ed. New York: Oxford University Press, 2008.

Beecher, Henry K. "Consent in Clinical Experimentation: Myth and Reality." *Journal of the American Medical Association* 195 (1966a): 34–35.

Beecher, Henry K. "Ethics and Clinical Research." *New England Journal of Medicine* 274, no. 24 (1966b): 1354–1360.

Belsky, Leah, and Henry S. Richardson. "Medical Researchers' Ancillary Clinical Care Responsibilities." *BMJ* 328, no. 7454 (2004): 1494–1496.

Benatar, Solomon R., and Peter A. Singer. "A New Look at International Research Ethics." *BMJ* 321, no. 7264 (2000): 824–826.

Brandt, Allan M. "Racism and Research: The Case of the Tuskegee Syphilis Study." *The Hastings Center Report* 8, no. 6 (1978): 21–29.

Buchanan, David R., and Franklin G. Miller. "A Public Health Perspective on Research Ethics." *Journal of Medical Ethics* 32, no. 12 (2006): 729–733.

Code of Federal Regulations, Title 45, Part 46, Protection of Human Subjects. July 14, 2009.

Comfort, Nathaniel. "The Prisoner as Model Organism: Malaria Research at Stateville Penitentiary." *Studies in History and Philosophy of Science* 40, no. 3 (2009): 190–203.

Department of Health and Human Services, Office of the Secretary. Federal Policy for the Protection of Human Subjects. 80 *Federal Register* 53931–54061 (September 8, 2015).

Department of Health and Human Services, Office of the Secretary. Human Subjects Research Protections: Enhancing Protections for Research Subjects and Reducing Burden, Delay, and Ambiguity for Investigators. 76 *Federal Register* 44512–44531 (July 28, 2011).

Ehni, Hans-Jörg. "The Definition of Adequate Care in Externally Sponsored Clinical Trials: The Terminological Controversy about the Concept 'Standard of Care.'" *Science and Engineering Ethics* 12, no. 1 (2006): 123–130.

Freedman, Benjamin. "Equipoise and the Ethics of Clinical Research." *New England Journal of Medicine* 317, no. 3 (1988): 141–145.

Freedman, Benjamin. "Placebo-Controlled Trials and the Logic of Clinical Purpose." *IRB: Ethics and Human Research* 12, no. 6 (1990): 1–6.

Gilbert, Edward M., and Milton Packer. "The Use of Placebo Controls." *New England Journal of Medicine* 332, no. 1 (1995): 60–62.

Grodin, Michael. "Historical Origins of the Nuremberg Code." In *The Nazi Doctors and the Nuremberg Code*, edited by George Annas and Michael Grodin, 121–144. New York: Oxford University Press, 1992.

Harkness, Jon M. "Nuremberg and the Issue of Wartime Experiments on US Prisoners. The Green Committee." *Journal of the American Medical Association* 276, no. 20 (1996): 1672–1675.

*Havasupai Tribe v. Arizona Board of Regents*. 204 P.3d 1063, 1067 (Ariz. Ct. App. 2008).

Hawkins, Jennifer S. "Exploitation and the Enterprise of Medical Research." In *Exploitation and Developing Countries*, edited by Jennifer S. Hawkins and Ezekiel Emanuel, 246–285. Princeton, NJ: Princeton University Press, 2008.

Heller, Jean. "Syphilis Victims in U.S. Study Went Untreated for 40 Years." *New York Times*, July 26, 1972, A1.

Heller, John R., and P. T. Bruyere. "Untreated Syphilis in the Male Negro: II. Mortality during 12 Years of Observation." *Journal of Venereal Disease and Infection* 27 (1946): 34–38.

Hornblum, Allen R. *Acres of Skin: Human Experiments at Holmesburg Prison*. London: Routledge, 1999.

Hyder, Adnan A., and Liza Dawson. "Defining the Standard of Care in the Developing World: The Intersection of International Research Ethics and Health Systems Analysis." *Developing World Bioethics* 5, no. 2 (2005): 142–152.

Itoh, Tetsuo, and Chester M. Southam. "Isoantibodies to Human Cancer Cells in Healthy Recipients of Cancer Homotransplants." *Journal of Immunology* 91, no. 4 (1963): 469–483.

Joffe, Steven, and Franklin G. Miller. "Bench to Bedside: Mapping the Moral Terrain of Clinical Research." *The Hastings Center Report* 38, no. 2 (2008): 30–42.

Joint United Nations Programme on HIV/AIDS and the World Health Organization. *Ethical Considerations in Biomedical HIV Prevention Trials: UNAIDS/WHO Guidance Document*. Geneva, Switzerland: UNAIDS, 2007.

Jones, James H. *Bad Blood: The Tuskegee Syphilis Experiment*. New York: Free Press, 1993.

Kimmelman Jonathan, Charles Weijer, and Eric M. Meslin. "Helsinki Discords: FDA, Ethics and International Drug Trials." *Lancet* 373, no. 9657 (2009): 13–14.

Levin, Arthur G., D. B. Custodio, Emanuel E. Mandel, and Chester M. Southam. "Rejection of Cancer Homotransplants by Patients with Debilitating Non-neoplastic Diseases." *Annals of the New York Academy of Sciences* 120 (1964): 410–423.

Levine, Robert J. *Ethics and Regulation of Clinical Research*. New Haven, CT: Yale University Press, 1988.

Levine, Robert J. "Revision of the CIOMS International Ethical Guidelines: A Progress Report." In *Biomedical Research Ethics: Updating International Guidelines. A Consultation*, edited by R. J. Levine and S. Gorovitz. Geneva, Switzerland: Council for International Organizations of Medical Science (CIOMS), 2000.

London, Alex John. "The Ambiguity and the Exigency: Clarifying 'Standard of Care' Arguments in International Research." *Journal of Medicine and Philosophy* 25, no. 4 (2000): 379–397.

London, Alex John. "Equipoise and International Human-Subjects Research." *Bioethics* 15, no. 4 (2001): 313–332.

Lurie, Peter, and Sidney M. Wolfe. "Unethical Trials of Interventions to Reduce Perinatal Transmission of Human Immunodeficiency Virus in Developing Countries." *New England Journal of Medicine* 337, no. 12 (1997): 853–856.

Macklin, Ruth. *Double Standards in Medical Research*. Cambridge: Cambridge University Press, 2004.

Marquis, Don. "Leaving Therapy to Chance." *The Hastings Center Report* 13, no. 4 (1983): 40–47.

Mbidde, Edward. "Bioethics and Local Circumstances." *Science* 279, no. 5348 (1998): 155.

Michels, Karin, and Kenneth Rothman. "Update on Unethical Use of Placebos in Randomised Trials." *Bioethics* 17, no. 2 (2003): 925–926.

Miller, Franklin. "The Stateville Penitentiary Malaria Experiments: A Case Study in Retrospective Ethical Assessment." *Perspectives in Biology and Medicine* 56, no. 4 (2013): 548–567.

Miller, Franklin, and Howard Brody. "Clinical Equipoise and the Incoherence of Research Ethics." *Journal of Medicine and Philosophy* 32, no. 2 (2007): 151–165.

Miller, Franklin, and Howard Brody. "What Makes Placebo-Controlled Trials Unethical?" *American Journal of Bioethics* 2, no. 2 (2002): 3–9.

Monagle, John F., and David C. Thomasma. *Health Care Ethics: Critical Issues for the 21st Century*. 2nd ed. Sudbury, MA: Jones and Bartlett, 2004.

National Commission for the Protection of Human Subjects of Biomedical and Behavioral Research. *Belmont Report: Ethical Principles and Guidelines for the Protection of Human Subjects of Research*. Washington, DC: US Department of Health, Education, and Welfare, 1979. http://ohsr.od.nih.gov/guidelines/belmont.html.

National Institute of Mental Health Collaborative HIV/STD Prevention Trial Group. "Ethical Issues in the NIMH Collaborative HIV/STD Prevention Trial." *AIDS* 21, Suppl. 2 (2007): S69–S80.

Nuffield Council on Bioethics. "The Ethics of Research Related to Healthcare in Developing Countries." April 2002. http://nuffieldbioethics.org/project/research-developing-countries/.

Pappworth, Maurice H. "Human Guinea Pigs—A History." *BMJ* 301, no. 6766 (1990): 22–29.

Pappworth, Maurice H. "Human Guinea Pigs—A Warning." *Twentieth Century* (Autumn 1962): 66–75.

Pappworth, Maurice H. *Human Guinea Pigs: Experimentation on Man*. London: Routledge, 1967.

Participants in 2006 Georgetown University Workshop on Ancillary-Care Obligations of Medical Researchers Working in Developing Countries. "The Ancillary-Care Obligations of Medical Researchers Working in Developing Countries." *PLoS Medicine* 5, no. 5 (2008): e90.

Pellegrino, Edmund D., and Daniel Sulmasy. "Medical Ethics." In *Oxford Textbook of Medicine*. 4th ed. Vol. 1: Sections 1–10, edited by David A. Warrell, Timothy H. Cox, John D. Firth, and Edward J. Benz Jr., 14–16. New York: Oxford University Press, 2003.

Peters, Jesse J., James H. Peers, Sidney Olansky, John C. Cutler, and Geraldine Gleeson. "Untreated Syphilis in the Male Negro: Pathologic Findings in Syphilitic and Nonsyphilitic Patients." *Journal of Chronic Disease* 1, no. 2 (1955): 127–148.

Presidential Commission for the Study of Bioethical Issues (PCSBI). *"Ethically Impossible": STD Research in Guatemala from 1946 to 1948*. Washington, DC: Author, 2011.

Resnik, David. "The Ethics of HIV Research in Developing Nations." *Bioethics* 12, no. 4 (1998): 286–306.

Reverby, Susan M. *Examining Tuskegee: The Infamous Syphilis Study and Its Legacy*. Chapel Hill: University of North Carolina Press, 2009.

Reverby, Susan M. "'Normal Exposure' and Inoculation Syphilis: A PHS 'Tuskegee' Doctor in Guatemala, 1946–1948." *Journal of Policy History* 23, no. 1 (2011): 6–28.

Richardson, Henry S., and Leah Belsky. "The Ancillary-Care Responsibilities of Medical Researchers: An Ethical Framework for Thinking about the Clinical Care That Researchers Owe Their Subjects." *The Hastings Center Report* 34, no. 1 (2004): 25–33.

Rothman, David. *Strangers at the Bedside: A History of How Law and Bioethics Transformed Medical Decision Making*. New York: Basic Books, 1991.

Samei, E., and Kimberly J. Kearfott. "A Limited Bibliography of the Federal Government–Funded Human Radiation Experiments." *Health Physics Journal* 69, no. 6 (1995): 885–891.

Shapiro, Kathy, and Solomon R. Benatar. "HIV Prevention Research and Global Inequality: Towards Improved Standards of Care." *Journal of Medical Ethics* 31, no. 1 (2005): 39–47.

Skloot, Rebecca. *The Immortal Life of Henrietta Lacks*. New York: Crown, 2010.

Solomon, David A. "The Use of Placebo Controls." *New England Journal of Medicine* 332, no. 1 (1995): 60–62.

*Trials of War Criminals before the Nuernberg Military Tribunals under Control Council Law No. 10*. Vol. 2: *The Medical Case*. Washington, DC: US Government Printing Office, 1949.

US Department of Health, Education, and Welfare. *Final Report of the Tuskegee Syphilis Study Ad Hoc Advisory*

Panel. Washington, DC: US Government Printing Office, 1973.

US Food and Drug Administration. "Human Subject Protection: Foreign Clinical Studies Not Conducted under an Investigational New Drug Application." Final rule. 73 *Federal Register* 22800–22816 (October 27, 2008).

Varmus, Harold, and David Satcher. "Ethical Complexities of Conducting Research in Developing Countries." *New England Journal of Medicine* 337, no. 14 (1997): 1000–1005.

Veatch, Robert M. *Disrupted Dialogue: Medical Ethics and the Collapse of Physician-Humanist Communication.* New York: Oxford University Press, 2005.

Veatch, Robert M. "The Irrelevance of Equipoise." *Journal of Medicine and Philosophy* 32, no. 2 (2007): 167–183.

Veatch, Robert M. "Why Researchers Cannot Establish Equipoise." *American Journal of Bioethics* 6, no. 4 (2006): 55–57.

Vonderlehr, Raymond A., and Taliaferro Clark. "Untreated Syphilis in the Male Negro." *Journal of Venereal Disease and Infection* 17 (1936): 262.

Weijer, Charles. "The Ethical Analysis of Risk." *Journal of Law Medicine and Ethics* 28, no. 4 (2000): 344–361.

Weindling, Paul. "The Origins of Informed Consent: The International Scientific Commission on Medical War Crimes, and the Nuremberg Code." *Bulletin of the History of Medicine* 75, no. 1 (2001): 37–71.

Welsome, Eileen. *The Plutonium Files: America's Secret Medical Experiments in the Cold War.* New York: Dell, 2000.

Wolfe, Sidney M., and Peter Lurie. "Science, Ethics, and Future of Research into Maternal-Infant Transmission of HIV-1." *Lancet* 353, no. 9155 (1999): 1878–1879.

World Health Organization, United Nations Program on HIV/AIDS, and United Nations Children's Fund. *HIV and Infant Feeding: A UNAIDS/UNICEF/WHO Policy Statement.* Geneva, Switzerland: UNAIDS, 1997.

World Medical Association. "Principles for Those in Research and Experimentation." 1954. http://ethics.iit.edu/ecodes/node/5057.

World Medical Association. WMA Declaration of Helsinki. 1964. http://www.wma.net/en/30publications/10policies/b3/.

## FILM AND LITERATURE

*The Constant Gardener.* Dir. Fernando Meirelles. 2005. Focus Features. Based on the novel by John le Carré (New York: Simon and Schuster, 2001).

*Experimenter.* Dir. Michael Almereyda. 2015. Magnolia Pictures.

*Miss Evers' Boys.* Dir. Joseph Sargent. 1997. HBO. Based on the 1992 play by David Feldshuh.

*The Stanford Prison Experiment.* Dir. Kyle Patrick Alvarez. 2015. IFC Films. Based on Philip Zimbardo's book *The Lucifer Effect* (New York: Random House, 2008).

CHAPTER 16

# *Public Health Ethics*

**Daniel Goldberg**
*Assistant Professor, Department of Bioethics and Interdisciplinary Studies*
*Brody School of Medicine, East Carolina University, Greenville, NC*

**Craig M. Klugman**
*Professor of Bioethics and Health Sciences*
*DePaul University, Chicago, IL*

Beth Emhoff is a business executive who has returned home to Minneapolis from a business trip in China. She seems to have a cold. Two days later she is rushed to the hospital, where she dies. The virus quickly spreads into a pandemic, infecting nearly 10 percent of the world's population and killing almost 30 percent of the sick. Epidemiology surveillance officers from the Centers for Disease Control and Prevention (CDC) and from the World Health Organization (WHO) work to find the source of the outbreak and to isolate the virus in hopes of creating a cure or vaccine. As civil order breaks down, martial law is declared. When a vaccine is finally developed, decisions about who receives the limited amount of available serum cause controversy and tough choices. By the end, twenty-six million people have died. This scenario is the plot for the 2011 film *Contagion*, which depicts a worldwide pandemic and the public health response to contain it.

This chapter deals with public health ethics. People who are not familiar with the field presume that public health ethics is simply a version of medical ethics applied to larger populations that emphasizes justice over autonomy. This chapter explains what public health is and then describes public health ethics. Understanding what makes public health unique is essential to understanding how ethics functions in this area of health.

## WHAT IS PUBLIC HEALTH?

As defined by the WHO, public health "refers to all organized measures (whether public or private) to prevent disease, promote health, and prolong life among the population as a whole." In many countries, there is no distinction between public health activities and the delivery of medical care. But in the United States, medicine professionalized at the dawn of the twentieth century and left many activities outside of its sphere of practice. Thus, public health arose to take on such issues as sanitation, safety and prevention, and health promotion.

361

**Comparison of Medicine and Public Health**

| Category | Medicine | Public Health |
|---|---|---|
| What is it? | "Diagnosis, treatment, relief of suffering, and rehabilitation." (Mann 1999, 84) | "Public health is what we, as a society, do collectively to assure the conditions for people to be healthy." (Institute of Medicine 1988, 19) |
| Where practiced? | Clinics, hospitals, doctors' offices | Everywhere—environment, community, clinics |
| Who practices? | MD, RN, DO, other health-related providers | MPH, DrPH, PhD |
| Acts on | Individual patients | Communities and populations |
| Orientation | Downstream | Upstream |
| How funded? | Insurance, Medicare, Medicaid, private funds | Tax dollars, grants |
| How it operates? | You go to medicine | Public health comes to you |
| What is health? | Absence of disease | Maximizing longevity and years lived in a state of health |
| Therapeutic relationships | Physician–patient | Government–community |

**Table 16.1.** *Comparison of Medicine and Public Health.*

Most of us are familiar with medicine. We go to the doctor for a checkup, to get a diagnosis and treatment when ill, or to a hospital when we need surgery or have an accident. Fewer people are familiar with public health, even though it has a greater effect on our everyday life. Table 16.1 compares some of the differences between medicine and public health.

Although both medicine and public health are concerned with human health, they approach that goal from distinctly different perspectives. In general, medicine deals with "downstream" activities—that is, helping people once they are already sick. For example, for a person with cancer, medicine offers chemotherapy, radiation, and surgery as treatment. In the film *50/50* (2011), Adam Lerner is diagnosed with schwannoma neurofibrosarcoma, a type of cancer. He undergoes chemotherapy and surgery for his treatment, which puts his cancer in remission. Like medicine, the focus of the film is on one individual patient (and his or her family).

In contrast, public health works largely in "upstream" activities—creating conditions that prevent illness and disease. Public health would try to prevent cancer by monitoring the environment for toxins, regulating exposure to carcinogens, and legislating limits on dumping industrial waste. In the film *Erin Brockovich* (2000), a community is found to have a cancer cluster—a higher frequency of cancer diagnoses in the community than should statistically exist. The film follows the legal fight to prove that a local power company illegally dumped chromium in the ground in this community, which has been the cause of the high rate of cancer. The law firm wants to get compensation for the victims, as well as force the company to admit fault and pay for cleanup to prevent future cancers. Like public health, the focus of the film is on the whole population of the community, not an individual.

To be sure, there is a lot of overlap between medicine and public health, such as when a physician gives vaccinations or informs patients about the value of healthy eating and exercise. In addition, many physicians are employed in public health work, such as staffing free clinics to provide care to the underserved.

## FUNCTIONS OF PUBLIC HEALTH

In practice, public health has three main functions:

1. Ensure access to care
2. Assess and monitor
3. Create public policy

### ENSURE ACCESS TO CARE

The first function of public health is ensuring access to care. This can include running clinics that provide medical care to people with low socioeconomic means, performing free health screenings in schools, and providing financial assistance to help pay for medical expenses (Medicare, Medicaid) or nutritious food (Special Supplemental Nutrition Program for Women, Infants, and Children [WIC]; Temporary Assistance for Needy Families [TANF]). The notion is that people are due (i.e., as a matter of justice—a topic discussed later in this chapter) a certain level of basic medical services, and if people cannot access those services on their own, then the government has a limited obligation to make them available.

### ASSESS AND MONITOR

Public health is responsible for such activities as tracking disease patterns and outbreaks, as dramatized in *Contagion*. Public health professionals also monitor the air and water for cleanliness (as in *Erin Brockovich*), as well as plants and animals so that they are safe to eat, and public health professionals even perform health inspections of restaurants. These efforts ensure our health in ways that we could not do as individuals.

For example, when you awoke this morning and turned on the tap to brush your teeth, did you check the water for levels of lead, insecticides, bacteria, viruses, and chlorine? Before you walked outside and took a breath of air, did you check it for particulate levels, ozone, sulfur dioxide, or nitrogen dioxide? When you were making your breakfast, did you run a test to make sure your eggs did not have salmonella?

Most likely, the answer to all these questions is "no." It is beyond the knowledge and ability of any one person to make sure that we have clean water, air, and safe food. Ensuring that these things are safe is the work of public health departments in every city, county, and state, and in the US federal government. When there is a problem, public health gives a warning to people—stay indoors, boil your water—and then finds the source of the problem and works to correct it.

### CREATE PUBLIC POLICY

Unlike any other area of health, public health has regulatory and enforcement powers. That is, public health departments can draft regulations and then have police power to enforce them. For example, restaurant refrigerators must be kept below a certain temperature to ensure food safety. Public health will perform inspections to make sure that these rules are followed. When the rules are violated, public health will issue a citation for corrections to be made, may close the business until the corrections are made, and will inform the public. Public health officials can also work with legislators to draft laws to regulate practices that can affect health, such as requiring the installation of air bags in cars or the vaccination of children before they go to public school.

# THE GOALS OF PUBLIC HEALTH

These functions enable public health to reach its goals. The goal is not to ensure the health and well-being of every individual person, but rather to guarantee that the population as a whole is healthy. In other words, public health is concerned with reducing morbidity (injury/disease) and mortality (death) in the community. In medicine, health is measured by a patient getting well or having test values like cholesterol that fall inside a certain range.

Because of its interest in groups, public health relies heavily on statistics to demonstrate and measure health. For example, commonly cited measures include life expectancy, infant mortality, and causes of death. Nations, states, counties, cities, and even neighborhoods are often ranked on these factors. Internationally, in 2015 the United States ranked forty-third in life expectancy, with an average person at birth expected to live until age 79.68 (CIA 2015). The highest-ranking country is Monaco at 89.52 years, followed by Japan at 84.64 years. These data do not mean that each person in Japan will live to 84.64 years, but rather that the average age at death of all people is 84.64 years. The group is what matters, not necessarily the individual person.

This emphasis on demographics (i.e., characteristics describing a population) and statistical calculations of health and illness in populations is known as *epidemiology*. *Epi* is from the Greek meaning "on" or "upon," *demos* means "people," and *logos* is "the study." Thus, "Epidemiology is the *study* of the *distribution* and *determinants* of *health-related states or events* in *specified populations*, and the *application* of this study to the control of health problems" (Last 2001, 61; emphasis added). In short, epidemiology is the science of public health.

Epidemiologists are concerned not only with rates of illness in a given population, but also with disease patterns. Are some groups more likely to get sick than others? Do some groups have worse outcomes when they do get sick? Which ones? Why? These group-level differences are often termed *inequalities*, and they are central both to any theory of justice and to public health ethics. Although many population health inequalities strike people as intuitively unfair, the issue is often more complicated than it seems. For example, there are stark gender-based inequalities in prostate cancer screening. The same is true for breast cancer screening. The reason is simply that women lack a prostate and men have much less breast tissue.

Thomas McKeown (1912–1988) was a physician and a trained demographer who studied the single-largest recorded gain in life expectancy in Western history. Between approximately 1580 and 1940, life expectancy in England nearly doubled. Such an increase is, in epidemiologic terms, an astonishingly large gain in a relatively short period of time (fewer than four centuries). But what caused this gain? Was it improvements in medicine and medical technologies?

It was not. The first truly effective modern pharmaceuticals (the sulfa drugs, an early class of antibiotics) did not come into production until the 1930s. Yet McKeown and his colleagues showed that all of the major killers of the nineteenth century were in substantial decline well before the sulfa drugs were discovered. If medicine was not all that effective on the population level, then it could simply not be the cause of the single largest gain in life expectancy in Western history. McKeown argued instead that rising standards of living and improved nutrition were largely responsible for the remarkable gain in life expectancy (Szreter 2004). The factor that increased life spans was public health.

One might think that was the case until 1940 when penicillin became available. Is it possible that medical services have transformed into the paramount determinant of population health in the interim? The best answer is "probably not." A veritable mountain of epidemiologic evidence confirms McKeown's general point: "The stark fact is that the vast majority of disease on the planet is a product of the social conditions in which people live and work" (Stonington, Holmes, and *PLoS Medicine* Editors 2006). Of course, this does not mean that medicine and health-care services are unimportant to health outcomes; nor does it mean that they are morally insignificant. It simply means that where myriad factors outside of access to medicine and health-care services are prime determinants of health and its distribution, the emphasis in public health ethics on what we owe each other (justice) must address these nonmedical determinants of health. Indeed, if such nonmedical determinants are responsible for the lion's share of health outcomes, then arguably public health ethics must devote a corresponding share of its own resources and analysis to such determinants as well.

The prime determinants of health and its distribution in human populations turn out to be the social and economic conditions in which people live, work, and play. Public health is concerned with creating opportunities for health, such as disease surveillance as portrayed in *Contagion*. It is also interested in how cities are built for walking and for providing parks for physical activity. These are examples of addressing the *social determinants of health*. These determinants include:

- Neighborhood and built environment
- Health and heath care
- Social and community context
- Education
- Economic stability

Thus, public policy needs to address more than providing access to care; it is also concerned with improving neighborhoods, ensuring a health environment, and creating opportunities for businesses to flourish and provide jobs, as well as having schools that provide a good education. Healthy people require a healthy community and a group effort because it is beyond the ability of any one person to do all of this for himself or herself.

When a person lives in an area with a deficiency in one of the determinants of health, say economic stability, she or he tends to have deficiencies in multiple determinants. Thus, a person belonging to a group that experiences low socioeconomic status is more likely to have low educational attainment, be food insecure, live in substandard housing, and/or be exposed to health risks such as violence, racism, and other forms of discrimination. In other words, disadvantage tends to cluster socially. Of course, this clustering is a group-level phenomenon. Individual members of these groups may well escape some of these disadvantages. But because the disadvantages cluster at the group level, individual members of the multiple-disadvantaged group are more likely to experience several of these disadvantages than members of comparatively advantaged groups.

The clustering of disadvantage has obvious implications for population health. If social and economic conditions are the prime determinants of health and its distribution, the clustering of conditions that may be severely adverse to good health is a major, perhaps *the* major, public health problem. Moreover, the clustering of disadvantage has profound ethical ramifications as well. Some commentators actually make it the core of their entire account in public health ethics (Powers and Faden 2006). Although the existence of health inequalities between and within groups is of paramount importance in public health ethics, prioritizing inequalities for public health action is extremely difficult. How do we know which inequalities matter most?

Philosophers Madison Powers and Ruth Faden (2006) argue that the answer to this question actually turns on the clustering of disadvantage. Powers and Faden refer to this clustering via a helpful metaphor, as "densely woven patterns of disadvantage" (2006, 71). Various social disadvantages intertwine densely, ensnaring members of disadvantaged groups in complex webs from which escape is extremely difficult. Factors that intensify or sustain such densely woven patterns of disadvantage are therefore the top priority for public health action.

According to Powers and Faden, these factors tend to drive many population health inequalities, thereby expanding health gaps between the poor and the affluent to a morally impermissible extent. For example, the high rates of incarceration of African American men in the United States almost certainly qualify as a factor that drives densely woven patterns of disadvantage. Incarceration is profoundly socially disadvantaging and is powerfully linked to poverty, low socioeconomic status, unemployment or underemployment, low educational attainment, and a host of other drawbacks (Western and Pettit 2010). In turn, these disadvantages are strongly correlated with worse health outcomes (WHO 2008). This fact makes incarceration itself a significant determinant of race-based health inequalities between African Americans and whites in the United States today.

Once one identifies the most vulnerable populations (the elderly and children, and likely poorer subgroups within these populations), which public health interventions should be prioritized?

Although the temptation might be simply to prioritize the given intervention that is likely to be most effective, the issue quickly becomes more complicated. Public health is fundamentally public in both its object and its implementation. That is, it is not merely groups or publics who are the target of the intervention. It is the public that is widely charged with enacting public health; thus, public health at its core implicates state action.

This does not mean that private actors are irrelevant in implementing public health—quite the contrary, in fact. But even where private actors can have pronounced effects on public health for good or for ill, the vast majority of those effects are mediated through government mechanisms, whether through laws and regulations, or through public-private partnerships (which are often seen in the arenas of sanitation and water policy). Thus, for example, maintaining safe air and water standards is a task few would leave entirely to the private oil and gas industry, which can have an enormous impact on the safety of our air and water. It is for this reason that state entities such as the federal Environmental Protection Agency (EPA) are charged with implementing and enforcing rules and regulations designed to ensure safe air and water.

## PUBLIC HEALTH ETHICS

As was described in the Introduction to this volume, medical ethics and much of bioethics developed based on the medical model—the idea of a sole actor. Thus, principlism, as described in Chapter 1, emphasizes the mid-level principles for moral deliberation of autonomy rather than the principles of beneficence, nonmaleficence, and justice. In early discussions of what a public health ethics should comprise, it was suggested that principlism still held, but the emphasis shifted from autonomy to justice. Justice is roughly understood as giving people what they are owed. If we think people are entitled to some measure of health, then satisfying that "measure" requires much more than ensuring access to health-care services but, rather, working within the social determinants of health to improve the conditions in which health can flourish. Thus, there is widespread agreement in public health ethics that justice—in its emphasis on groups and on what we owe each other as a society—is of central importance and that thinking about justice and public health requires that we move far beyond a conception of justice that ties it to access to health-care services.

Although Western medical ethics has not ignored justice concerns, the scope of these concerns has been narrow, focusing almost exclusively on the paradigm of physician-patient relationships (the health-care "system"). The challenge is that principlism is biased toward individual patients (and their families) with their individual care providers. Because of this bias, the principlist framework has limited use for public health issues.

There are a wide variety of competing conceptions of justice. For example, Aristotle in *The Nicomachean Ethics* (fourth century BCE) describes three types of justice: (1) distribution of resources (distributive justice); reparation, rectification, and punishment (criminal justice); and treatment of "likes" alike and "different" differently (social justice). Social justice is at the core of public health. One way to conceive of this concept is as *equity*, which philosopher Albert Jonsen (1931–), physician-ethicist Mark Siegler (1941–), and health law ethicist William Winslade (1941–) define as "the ethics of fair and equitable distribution of burdens and benefits within a community" (2006, 160). An example would be if every household in a city pays taxes to support a hospital, which is then built in an upper socioeconomic part of town to which people in less affluent areas have little access. In this case, although the burden is shared by all, the benefit belongs to the few, who already have social and economic advantages. Building the hospital in a more central location or where there is the greatest need would be more *equitable*.

Bioethicists Powers and Faden (2006) offer a more public health–oriented approach. They argue that social justice is defined by health sufficiency, or the idea that everyone is owed a minimum level of resources across six essential dimensions of well-being: (1) health; (2) personal security; (3) reasoning; (4) respect; (5) attachment; and (6) self-determination. Taken together, these six dimensions are the foundation of human flourishing. We can evaluate public health policies, laws, and interventions based on the extent to which they guarantee the sufficiency of these dimensions for a given population.

A simplistic notion of public health ethics looks at justice as balancing the needs of the community against the rights of the individual. This approach suggests that there can only be one winner—the individual or the community. Thus, early presentations of public health ethics suggested that anything done for the group had to justify any limitation on the individual. Bioethicist Nancy Kass offers six questions that should be asked of any public health proposal to make sure that it does not unduly step on individual rights.

1. What are the public health goals of the proposed program?
2. How effective is the program in achieving its stated goals?
3. What are the known or potential burdens of the program?
4. Can burdens be minimized? Are there alternative approaches?
5. Is the program implemented fairly?
6. How can the benefits and burdens of a program be fairly balanced? (Kass 2001)

The problem with this approach is that it ignores the so-called prevention paradox. For example, in 2015 California passed a law requiring all schoolchildren to be vaccinated even if the parent objected. The parent (and therefore child) lost the liberty to refuse vaccination. The result is that the community is better protected against the disease and less likely to be infected. That also means this child (and parent) are protected and less likely to become ill with that particular disease. But here's the paradox: it's not simply giving up a right because the individual benefits from the group protection. A society is made up of a group of individuals, which means that if something benefits the society, it benefits most individuals as well.

Bioethicist Bruce Jennings has proposed that a theory of public health ethics must have a group or outcomes basis. He offers three potential theoretical sources for public health ethics.

- *Utilitarianism* is the idea that the goal of action should be to maximize a utility (often pleasure or happiness). For public health, we could say the utility would be health. This theory focuses on outcomes and consequences, thus making it a good match for public health with its emphasis on improving epidemiologic measures of health. One challenge to this theory is that it tends to treat everyone the same and can ignore human rights and individual needs.

- *Contractarianism* holds that a group of individuals comes together and relinquishes some of their freedom to an authority (such as a government) in exchange for safety and security. For instance, as discussed above, there are some goods that we as individuals cannot provide for ourselves, such as clean water and air. One might give up the freedom to dump toxic waste anywhere in exchange for the security that an authority will make sure no one can dump toxic waste, thus keeping the environment safe. One criticism of this theory is that it tends to view the individuals as unconnected to one another except by a contractual agreement and that such individuals are in constant competition with one another. Public health assumes that collaboration is required to protect group health.

- *Communitarian* theories hold that the group comes before the individual. These theories presume that the individual lives as part of a network of relationships that connect one person to another—none of us truly exists as a separate entity. Thus, a communitarian approach prioritizes the group and the importance of the rich relationships between people. Public health assumes that people are social and interdependent.

## PRINCIPLES OF THE ETHICAL PRACTICE OF PUBLIC HEALTH

In 2002, the Public Health Leadership Society of the American Public Health Association published a list of principles for public health (see Table 16.2). The authors stated that public health is an inherently moral enterprise and thus should be guided by ethical precepts. Until this list was published, ethics in public health was assumed but not specifically stated. These principles are supposed to define the values of public health, describe the expected behaviors of public health professionals, and be used to assist in making decisions.

As useful as this list is for teaching and for reflecting on what it means to act in public health, its bulkiness limits its usefulness in decision making. One advantage of the four principles of biomedical ethics presented in the next section is that they are an efficient shorthand for much more complicated philosophical concepts.

## PUBLIC HEALTH PRINCIPLISM

Drawing on the advantages of mid-level principles in the four-principles approach to biomedical ethics, Craig Klugman (2007) has developed a separate list of four public health principles. For public health, however, the principles need to spring from a communitarian foundation rather than be presented as an individual one. The four public health principles are *solidarity, efficacy, integrity,* and *dignity* (Klugman 2007).

- *Solidarity* is the notion that public health is a community activity that brings all people together for a common good—reducing morbidity, mortality, and inequity. This principle refers to Public Health Leadership principles 1, 7, and 9 (see Table 16.2), which reflect on acting to improve health and outcomes, acting promptly, and improving the whole health environment. This communitarian perspective looks to improve the group's health and opportunity for health. In *Erin Brockovich,* solidarity would hold that the toxic chromium must be cleaned up.

- *Efficacy* asks whether the program is scientifically based and socially feasible (Klugman 2007). Is a proposed plan of action scientifically sound, supported by data? This principle also asks if there is political, cultural, religious, and social support for enacting the proposal. This idea reflects Public Health Leadership principles 4, 5, 11, and 12 (in Table 16.2), which focus on empowering communities, working with communities, and being experts in this work. For example, in *Contagion,* the decision as to whom to treat first with the limited amount of vaccine available could have been

### Principles of the Ethical Practice of Public Health

1. Public health should address principally the fundamental causes of disease and requirements for health, aiming to prevent adverse health outcomes.
2. Public health should achieve community health in a way that respects the rights of individuals in the community.
3. Public health policies, programs, and priorities should be developed and evaluated through processes that ensure an opportunity for input from community members.
4. Public health should advocate and work for the empowerment of disenfranchised community members, aiming to ensure that the basic resources and conditions necessary for health are accessible to all.
5. Public health should seek the information needed to implement effective policies and programs that protect and promote health.
6. Public health institutions should provide communities with the information they have that is needed for decisions on policies or programs and should obtain the community's consent for their implementation.
7. Public health institutions should act in a timely manner on the information they have within the resources and the mandate given to them by the public.
8. Public health programs and policies should incorporate a variety of approaches that anticipate and respect diverse values, beliefs, and cultures in the community.
9. Public health programs and policies should be implemented in a manner that most enhances the physical and social environment.
10. Public health institutions should protect the confidentiality of information that can bring harm to an individual or community if made public. Exceptions must be justified on the basis of the high likelihood of significant harm to the individual or others.
11. Public health institutions should ensure the professional competence of their employees.
12. Public health institutions and their employees should engage in collaborations and affiliations in ways that build the public's trust and the institution's effectiveness.

SOURCE: Public Health Leadership Society 2002, 4

***Table 16.2.*** *Principles of the Ethical Practice of Public Health.*

to treat the wealthiest first, or the most politically connected first, or those at greatest risk first. But in real-life pandemic scenarios, first responders have stated that they will prioritize their own people for receiving services first. The idea behind this thinking is that a first responder, having put her or his life on the line to help others and being part of a social contract, is owed priority care. Thus, in *Contagion,* it is understandable that an emergency medical technician would be given vaccines before an at-risk sick twelve-year-old girl. This is an example of social expediency—sometimes what will work is what the society and the culture allow.

- *Integrity* says that public health should "preserve the nature and character of a cultural community" (Klugman 2007, 9). Integrity obligates the public health practitioner "to not fundamentally change a local way of life if at all possible" (10). This principle can be thought of as community autonomy in that public health planning should include members of the community who are being targeted and should be explained in terms of local knowledge—language and experience commonly used. Community leaders should be informed and have an opportunity to decide whether their group will participate. This concept is reflected in Public Health Leadership principles 3, 6, 8, and 10 (Table 16.2), all of which focus on working with a community respectfully, protectively, and as an equal partner with public health bureaus.

- An example of integrity comes from the 1992 play and 1997 film *Miss Evers' Boys*, based on the true story of the US Public Health Service Tuskegee Syphilis Study, begun in 1932 in Tuskegee, Alabama. In this story, a community in rural Alabama becomes part of an experiment on the natural progression of syphilis. Men in the study are told they are receiving "treatment" for their disease when, in fact, there is no treatment and they are only being monitored. Even after a cure is developed, the men are denied treatment so that the study can continue. This study went on for forty years, even though for the last thirty years of the study a cure was available. The integrity of this community was violated because members of the town were not part of the planning and did not have a say in what would happen. Nor was the project explained in terms that they would understand. In fact, they were lied to. While men in surrounding towns and not in the study went off to fight in World War II, these men could not (because they would have been given treatment by the army): the nature of their community was changed. Thus, a corollary to integrity is the *least destructive alternative*—when choosing among options, choose the one that best preserves the community and its way of life.

- *Dignity* is the principle that recognizes the vulnerability of human life. Thus, this idea is that people's human rights should be protected. That does not mean that human rights can override a proposal that follows solidarity, efficacy, and integrity. Rather, it dictates that human rights should be protected wherever possible. This principle reflects Public Health Leadership principles 2 and 10 (Table 16.2), which speak to protecting the rights of individuals and having good reasons to override them.

A corollary to the principle of dignity is the *least restrictive alternative*—one should choose the option that preserves people's individual liberty. In *Contagion*, Beth is separated from other people against her will in order to protect the population from infection. This action is known as *quarantine*, and it limits a person's freedom of movement. Beth's husband and child, however, voluntarily choose to remain at home to avoid coming into contact with infected people. The voluntary choice to remain separate (whether to avoid getting the disease or to avoid having the infected person pass it on to others) is known as *isolation*. Isolation is a choice to limit one's movement, whereas quarantine is a police order. Though both achieve the same aim, one preserves liberty and one overrides it. Isolation is the least restrictive alternative, though if one violates isolation, quarantine may be imposed.

## BALANCING AUTONOMY VERSUS PATERNALISM

In a society that values autonomy above all else, public health poses another philosophical challenge—it is inherently paternalistic. As asked in an earlier scenario, while you may not know what the safe levels of lead in drinking water or soil are, a public health expert does. We rely on people in public health to know more than we do and to take action to keep us safe. Public health is paternalistic because it has more information than we do and is required to act on that information to protect us. Paternalism can be defined as "interfering with the liberty of action of a person, against her will, to protect or promote her welfare" (Faden and Shebaya 2015). Unlike in medicine, where informed consent is needed before a diagnostic test or treatment can be administered, public health requires no such consent—it has the police powers to act on our collective behalf. Where it does try to preserve autonomy is in making all of its reports, studies, records, and actions available to the public.

Indeed, the vast majority of commentators working on concepts and theories of public health maintain that the tension between collective action and individual rights is the most significant prism for understanding public health and its limits. Lawrence Gostin (1949–), who is widely recognized as one of the founders of public health law as a field of study, frames the entire field in terms of this debate (2008). Often, the tension is characterized as one between paternalism and individual rights.

The paternalism/individual rights framing, however, may not be particularly useful because public health is fundamentally parental (Gostin and Gostin 2009). This is literally the case; public health action is generally an exercise of the government's *parens patriae* power. The Latin *parens patriae* translates as "parent to the nation" and is often taken to refer to the government's power to defend those who are unable to defend themselves (Gostin 2008). But because the vast majority of public health interventions require state authority and investment, a great deal of public health action can arguably be seen as invoking *parens patriae*. How, for example, is an individual resident or family supposed to compel a nearby factory to cease dumping industrial waste into the local water supply as happened in *Erin Brockovich*? The family could file a lawsuit, but such a lawsuit makes use of the state via the government's courts and judicial processes. Moreover, state actors, such as the EPA, are in a vastly superior position relative to private citizens in their capacity to enforce regulations against pollution.

There are unquestionably myriad examples of public health officials exercising their paternal powers in ethically questionable ways. For example, between 1900 and about 1975, at least sixty thousand women, many of whom were poor and African American, were involuntarily sterilized in the United States. The justification for taking this action revolved around eugenicist concerns regarding so-called defective heredity, but also involved anxieties about "gender norms, female sexuality," and of course race (Stern 2008).

Although forced sterilization arguably violates universal ethical norms, the fact that individualism and individual rights occupy such an important place in the political culture of the United States also matters. Consider, for example, a more communitarian-focused nation, such as Cuba. In the 1980s, the AIDS epidemic exploded, and some of Cuba's very close neighbors, such as Haiti and Jamaica, experienced astonishingly high rates of HIV/AIDS. Given patterns of sexually transmitted disease and the various social, political, and economic relationships between nations, one would predict that the prevalence of AIDS in Cuba would rise significantly over time. Yet, this did not happen. Rates of HIV/AIDS in Cuba remained surprisingly low. In fact, the rates are still among the lowest in the Western Hemisphere (Anderson 2009). The WHO even certified that Cuba had eradicated maternal-fetal HIV transmission there (McNeil 2015).

How did this happen? First, even in the face of scarce resources, Cuba maintains a strong public health and health system infrastructure. Second, Cuba's communist rule enabled an extremely active and strong government—individual rights in many cases became subservient to the state's interpretation of collective needs. Facing a looming pandemic, Cuban public health officials were ordered to conduct extremely aggressive disease surveillance. When persons who tested positive for HIV were located, they were forcibly removed, isolated, and quarantined indefinitely (Hoffman 2004).

Obviously, such methods are highly intrusive and coercive, as well as in violation of the least restrictive alternative corollary. They might well be illegal under US law, and even if they were not, they would be untenable in a US political culture that lionizes individual liberty. However, the draconian policies seem to have worked. Although such interventions were not the only reason HIV/AIDS prevalence remained so much lower in Cuba than in its neighboring countries, such policies almost certainly reduced the impact of the disease in Cuba.

These examples show that public health actions can and do infringe on individual rights. Moreover, efficacy alone is not necessarily a sufficient grounding for ethical public health action. Even where the Cuban response to the AIDS epidemic was at least somewhat effective, such results were only achieved through a significant trespass on people's individual rights (*dignity*). Whether such a trespass was morally justifiable given the consequences is debatable, which demonstrates that the ethical inquiry requires more analysis than simply finding "what works" and implementing it.

In 1348, as a response to the outbreak of the Black Death, the government of the Italian city of Milan ordered three houses sealed up with their living occupants still inside (Carmichael 1991). Unlike most of its neighbors, Milan escaped the ravages of plague, although the extent to which its escape was the result of its drastic action is uncertain. The point is that, even presuming a direct causal link between its public health action and the salutary consequences (a less severe outbreak), the trespass of individual rights (ignoring dignity or at least not looking at the *least restrictive alternative*) may be too significant to pass ethical muster (when balancing solidarity, efficacy, and dignity).

Although state action taken in the name of public health may be morally problematic if it violates individual rights, the issue is obviously one of degree. It cannot be the case that every time a public health action imposes on an individual right, the latter prevails and the public health action is deemed impermissible. A very large number of public health interventions impose at least some restrictions on individual rights and liberties. For example, quarantine to prevent the spread of disease was discussed in relation to *Contagion*. Or, as shown in *Erin Brockovich*, environmental laws prevent companies from dumping whatever substances they like in rivers and lakes. Mandatory reporting laws require health-care providers to notify public health officials of the positive diagnoses of certain communicable diseases for surveillance and monitoring purposes.

If public health action in general was limited to those activities that do not circumscribe individual rights, there would be little public health action at all. The question is always one of extent—what kinds of restrictions on individual liberty are permissible in the name of public health? This is obviously a context-dependent, fact-specific question. Gostin (2008) has posited that resolution of the tension, at least from a legal perspective, requires a balancing test between the substantial protections for individual rights enshrined in US law and the also-substantial police powers that US states wield to regulate for the health, safety, and welfare of their citizens.

# ISSUES IN PUBLIC HEALTH

### DISASTER AND CRISIS MANAGEMENT

The 2012 film *The Impossible* was based on the true story of a family vacationing on a beach in Thailand in 2004 who became caught up in an epic disaster. After one of the strongest earthquakes ever recorded, a tsunami devastated Thailand's most popular beach resorts. This "killer wave" had the power of twenty megatons of TNT and killed nearly 8,150 people. Increasingly, preparing for mass disasters whether from a natural event or a human-made one (terrorism, climate change), is becoming a focus of public health activities.

The genesis of organized, centralized public health action in the United States began in earnest in the nineteenth century. Although the incipient New York Metropolitan Board of Health initiated some important public health activities in the 1850s, the US Civil War irrevocably changed public health in the United States. Violence and war often present myriad acute health emergencies (including but going far beyond the infliction of actual war wounds), and the US Civil War was certainly no exception. Two out of every three soldiers who died during the war succumbed to disease, and the organization and capacity of the federal Sanitary Corps supplemented the already-rising tide in support of organized, centralized public health action. In a very real sense, then, the beginnings of modern public health in the United States were forged in the fires of disaster and tragedy (i.e., war). And so a crucial task for public health ethics is preparing for and responding to disasters and crises of various types.

As in *The Impossible*, public health is interested in not only reacting to disasters but in planning responses to them. Earthquakes, tidal waves, and tropical cyclones do in fact occur, and their happening is not within human control. Yet the severity of the consequences of these events is most assuredly within our control. For example, in 2010 a major earthquake struck Haiti, the most impoverished country in the Western Hemisphere. Over 250,000 people died from the earthquake and its immediate aftermath. In 2011, a major earthquake and tsunami struck Japan. Approximately 20,000 people died in the Japanese event. Any loss of life is of course tragic. Nevertheless, since an obvious goal of public health action is to minimize loss of life in a disaster scenario, the fact that ten times fewer people died as a result of the 2011 Japan earthquake than in the Haiti earthquake just a year earlier is important.

Why did so many more people die in Haiti in 2010 than in Japan in 2011? Although the events themselves were of course different, at least one principal factor was the relative state of infrastructure and development of the two countries, including each nation's disaster preparedness (Farmer 2011). Both Haiti and Japan are disaster-prone, with each perennially experiencing significant risks from earthquakes, tidal waves, floods, and tropical cyclones. Yet Japan is a wealthy nation, whereas Haiti is poor. Japan is widely recognized as the most disaster-prepared country on the planet; Haiti is not. Thus, as important as it is to recognize the acute dilemmas that arise in the face of public health crises, it is equally crucial not to lose sight of the forest for the trees.

There are reasons why some communities are more able to prepare for disasters and to respond to them than others. Such inequalities are themselves an important object of public health ethics analysis, as we have seen. Which is most important? Should public health actors focus on improving social and economic conditions in a given community, thereby strengthening infrastructure to facilitate disaster preparedness? Or is the best means of intervention to check individual buildings for adherence to fire safety protocols and to implement rapid response teams to disasters when they occur? Should we protect and sustain the building or improve the water pressure?

Of course, nothing stops us from working both on the structural, systematic problems that diminish public health and on the acute emergencies to which public health actors are called to respond. Arguing that we are forced to choose one path or the other is an instance of what is called the "false-choice fallacy," which is exactly what it sounds like. However, note that while answering "both" is legitimate, it is never by itself a sufficient answer to the difficult questions of priority-setting that help define the field of public health ethics. This is because even if we can try to do A, B, C, and D, in a world of scarce resources, we are unlikely to be able to invest equal levels of resources and attention to all of the worthy public health programs and policies that should be implemented. Policy is inevitably contested space (Stone 2002), so even if we are free to support a number of public health policies simultaneously, we are nevertheless called upon to make difficult choices as to which public health intervention is more important than others.

As to acute disaster preparedness and response, important and difficult moral quandaries still arise. First, because such activities obviously affect human life and health, they have significant ethical implications. Second, as Jennings notes, "emergency preparedness planning requires ethical analysis and scrutiny because it is an activity conducted under the auspices of the state that involves the use of power, and potentially the use of coercion. It has an impact, not only on the health and safety of individuals, but also on their liberty, autonomy, civil and human rights, property, and other fundamental interests" (2008, 42).

Third, disaster preparedness raises important concerns regarding paternalism. Such concerns tend to be common ones as to public health action in general. They are arguably even more applicable to questions of crisis and disaster preparedness and management, given the potential acuity and severity of the public health problem (i.e., the disaster!).

In addition, there are profound issues related both to the unequal distribution of risks from an impending disaster and the allocation of resources devoted to preparing for and responding to the disaster when it occurs. For example, it is well known that heat waves disproportionately affect elderly populations in much of the world (including the United States). There are multiple reasons for this impact, including the fact that the elderly poor may lack access to air-conditioning and the increased risk of social isolation that affects elderly populations in the United States. Given that elderly people as a population bear disproportionate burdens of the health risks posed by heat waves, perhaps preparedness plans (i.e., plans for community cooling centers, check-in programs to reduce the risks of isolation) ought to prioritize such vulnerable populations.

## SURVEILLANCE, QUARANTINE, AND STIGMA

As described earlier, two of the most effective public health tools are surveillance and quarantine. Surveillance is a critical public health intervention inasmuch as prevention and management of communicable disease is impossible without it. Consider that every state has mandatory reporting laws for certain diseases and conditions so that the public health professionals can track diseases. For example, in every state, a positive HIV test must be reported to the relevant county or state public health agency. The agency is then often empowered to employ contact tracing—that is, contacting previous sex partners to inform them of possible exposure to the HIV virus. Naturally, all of these actions trespass on the individual's right to privacy, let alone a person's right to autonomy (i.e., whether to disclose private and sensitive medical information).

Note also the power of disclosure that is frequently granted to public health officials to contact *past* sexual partners of the individual who has tested positive for HIV. Officials may make this contact even where those partners are no longer involved in a sexual relationship with the individual, and hence are not in immediate danger of further exposure. Public health officials will typically attempt to shield the individual who tested positive by refusing to divulge his or her identity to any sexual partners contacted, but, obviously, this is no guarantee that the individual's identity will remain unknown to said partners.

The point is that public health authorities possess considerable and necessary surveillance powers. The scope of that power often trespasses on individual rights—to privacy, confidentiality, and autonomy—and can result in stigma against disadvantaged individuals and groups. And yet it is critical to effective disease management. Although the harm in question is often less urgent with regard to noncommunicable disease, here, too, ethical issues have arisen.

Faced with an alarming growth in the incidence and prevalence of type 2 diabetes and an extremely limited budget for diabetes surveillance and management, in 2005 the New York City Board of Health made blood sugar levels (HbA1C, or hemoglobin A1C) subject to mandatory reporting requirements. The creation of the ensuing diabetes registry provoked a firestorm of controversy (Mello and Gostin 2009). Opponents of the requirements argued that the harm to be avoided was so much less imminent than that faced with registries dealing with communicable disease rendered the trespass on privacy and confidentiality unethical. Moreover, while it is inarguable that knowledge of blood sugar levels is essential to good control of diabetes on both individual and population levels, such knowledge is obviously insufficient to prevent and manage type 2 diabetes effectively. In contrast, the evidence that tight surveillance of dangerous communicable diseases improves population health outcomes is significantly more robust. Thus, opponents of the New York City efforts argued, quite plausibly, that the evidence of benefit flowing from the registry was simply inadequate to justify the trespass on rights or privacy and confidentiality.

As the example of the Cuban response to the HIV/AIDS epidemic suggests, quarantine often follows on the heels of surveillance. We have already discussed quarantine and the extent of its restrictions on movement, fraternization, and liberty. But the consequences for those quarantined and/or isolated can be severe. Consider the infamous case of Mary Mallon, an Irish immigrant who lived in New York City at the dawn of the twentieth century and was the subject of a PBS docudrama (Porter 2004). Although most know her by the epithet bestowed upon her by the popular press, "Typhoid Mary," it is ethically dubious to knowingly refer to her as such. Why?

Like thousands of other New Yorkers of the time, Mallon was a healthy carrier of typhoid fever (Leavitt 1997). That is, she harbored the typhoid fever bacillus in her body but was not actively ill. This facilitated transmission, as did Mallon's job as a cook and domestic servant. After municipal public health officials traced several infections to Mallon, they quarantined her, demanded stool samples—at a time in which the germ theory of disease was still novel and extremely unlikely to be understood and assimilated by laypeople—and eventually freed her only after three years and litigation undertaken on her behalf. As a condition of her release, Mallon was required to forswear her occupation as a cook and servant, even though this was the only work for which she had trained and performed in her adult life (Leavitt 1997).

Mallon disobeyed the board of health's requirements that she inform the board if she moved, and she changed her name, presumably to avoid the board's scrutiny. Although she tried to subsist as a laundress for a while, Mallon faced limited opportunities given her

***Mary Mallon (1869–1938), an Irish immigrant living in New York City at the dawn of the twentieth century, became vilified in the popular press as "Typhoid Mary."*** *Mallon was healthy but was also a carrier (as were many others at the time) of the pathogen associated with typhoid fever. Mallon worked as a cook and domestic servant until municipal public health officials traced several typhoid infections to her, ultimately subjecting Mallon to quarantine for the better part of the last three decades of her life.* **MARY EVANS PICTURE LIBRARY/ALAMY.**

socioeconomic precarity, as well as her immigrant status in the early 1900s. Eventually, Mallon returned to cooking, subsequent to which more people contracted typhoid fever, several of whom died. The public health officials traced the cases in 1915 to Mallon, captured her, and incarcerated her on North Brother Island, New York, for the remainder of her natural life. Mallon died in 1938 after spending more than three decades of her life in quarantine.

As historian Judith Walzer Leavitt (1940–) explains (1997), the ethics of what happened to Mallon are vastly more complicated than that for which simplistic narratives typically allow. For example, although many public health practitioners point to the negative consequences of Mallon's behavior, the very idea that a person could be a healthy carrier was unlikely to sound plausible to most people in Mallon's position. Moreover, there were unquestionably thousands of healthy carriers of typhoid fever in New York City alone at the time. There were also documented and publicized cases of other people in the New York area involved in food handling and preparation who had likely communicated typhoid fever to others (Leavitt 1997). Yet, no one else was treated as Mallon was: only she spent the last twenty-five years of her life incarcerated on an island in New York Harbor. Why municipal public health authorities singled Mallon out remains an open question, although there seems little doubt that Mallon's existence as a poor Irish immigrant woman (each an independent social disadvantage at the time) rendered her socially vulnerable and more likely to be a target of state action in the name of public health (Leavitt 1997).

Although contemporary actors are not empowered to remedy whatever wrongs were done to Mallon in the name of public health, how we remember her does have ethical content and is within our control. The popular press of the time vilified Mallon as a merchant of death, all the while playing on gendered and nativist tropes that facilitated the creation of a symbol: Typhoid Mary. "Typhoid Mary" is a symbol that does no justice whatsoever to the complexity of the ethical issues that surround policies of surveillance and quarantine. However necessary such policies may be to public health, they are invested with significant state powers and have historically been likely to be disproportionately wielded against stigmatized and vulnerable groups.

The case studies of the New York City diabetes registry and Mallon are juxtaposed here for a reason. Modern public health in the West is founded on the crucible of the great infectious diseases of the nineteenth century. Although dreaded epidemic diseases, such as cholera, yellow fever, and typhoid fever, earn the lion's share of the publicity, the fact of the matter is that diarrheal diseases were the major killers of the time (Grob 2002). Such diseases killed the young and the old in droves, and the great sanitary reform movements of the nineteenth century were at least partly a response to the horrifying mortality costs of such illnesses (as well as the other primary killer, tuberculosis, which remains a disease connected with substandard sanitary and living conditions).

As suggested earlier, the majority of the illnesses that affected Civil War soldiers were infectious in nature. Therefore, officials dealing with increasingly urgent urban public health problems and the immense disease burden of the Civil War had to grapple primarily with the needs of the communicably ill in terms of both acute disease management and, of course, with prevention of such illnesses. The advent of the so-called bacteriological revolution—the ability to see bacteria under microscopes and to link them to all manner of infectious diseases—in the late nineteenth to early twentieth century fueled this emphasis on communicable disease. To some extent, the type of diseases that dominate a particular population have something to do with its relative state of economic development.

Consider that less economically developed populations tend to experience higher burdens of communicable disease than more economically developed communities. In the city of Chicago alone, someone living in a wealthy North Side neighborhood may have a life expectancy that is thirty years longer than someone living a few miles away in a poorer South Side neighborhood.

As the industrialization and urbanization of the late nineteenth and early twentieth centuries took hold in the United States, it also led to what many people term an epidemiologic or a health transition. As burdens of communicable disease decreased, the disease footprint of chronic, noncommunicable disease (NCD) in the United States increased dramatically (Bodenheimer, Chen, and Bennett 2009) (see Chapter 7 to see how causes of death have varied by time and place). This process, which is again a somewhat typical feature of economies transitioning to higher states of development, has accelerated to the point where at least 60 to 80 percent of the disease burden in the United States is chronic NCD. Of course, these changed proportions of disease type do not imply that infectious disease is unimportant to public and population health. Nothing could be further from the truth.

Nevertheless, as the disease footprint in the United States has shifted to chronic NCDs, a public health tradition literally founded on the need to manage and prevent infectious disease has had to adapt its methods and approaches to an entirely different class of illnesses that present many different challenges. Many of these challenges raise ethical problems with which public health practitioners must grapple.

## HEALTH BEHAVIOR CHANGE

In taking an upstream approach to reducing morbidity and mortality, public health seeks to change behaviors that are detrimental to good health. Recall that in public health, *health* means increased longevity and living more years of life absent infirmity or disease. Disease and chronic health conditions are caused by the social determinants of health on the larger scale. On the personal scale, health is an interplay of three factors: (1) genetics, (2) environmental exposures, and (3) behavior. Genetics is discussed in Chapters 4 and 5, and currently there is not much that we can do to change our genes. Environment includes ecology, where one lives, exposure to toxins and chemicals in the built environment, the availability of fresh food and outdoor space for exercise, as well as safety in one's home and area. If one has the means, then one can move to a neighborhood that allows greater opportunities for health. Many people in low-socioeconomic conditions do not have that luxury. Also consider that toxins and pollutants in the environment are beyond an individual's control. That leaves behavior as the one component of health over which the individual has control. In this arena, public health encourages behavior change for all of us to adopt healthier habits: getting more exercise, eating more nutritious foods, using seat belts, and not smoking.

Many public health leaders maintain that the health transition from a society dominated by concerns of infectious disease to one grappling mostly with NCD initiates new challenges for public health actors. For example, public health officials have extraordinary powers to restrict individual liberty in the case of epidemic disease. Yet, preventing NCDs seems to require very different interventions from those needed to prevent the spread of infectious disease.

If tobacco consumption is a risk factor for a variety of NCDs included but not limited to cancer, coronary artery disease (CAD), and type 2 diabetes, then one appropriate class of public health interventions might be those devoted to changing consumption behaviors. Efforts to change behaviors, and the larger structures of which they are a part, are widely viewed as quite different from the public health interventions commonly applied in the face of infectious disease (e.g., pathogen tracing and surveillance, food inspection, clinical laboratory services, and, if necessary, quarantine and isolation).

**Smoking**. The film *The Insider* (1999) is based on the true story of Jeffrey Wigand, who was a whistle-blower against the tobacco industry. Despite the industry's decades-long avowal that smoking tobacco was not bad for health, Wigand exposed buried studies conducted by tobacco companies that clearly showed a link between smoking and cancer, diabetes, and heart disease.

Smoking has been the primary cause of preventable disease in the United States for decades. Reducing the incidence, that is, the number of new cases of smoking, is therefore almost universally regarded as a top public health priority (*solidarity*). Numerous programs and interventions have been directed toward this end, and they seem to have had at least some effect, as incidence has slowly but steadily declined since the late 1990s (*efficacy*). However, programs to stop smoking are campaigns to convince people to choose to stop smoking, rather than making all tobacco illegal (*dignity—least restrictive alternative*). At the same time that incidence has decreased, the distribution of smoking has also changed in many Western countries (Capewell and Graham 2010). Increasingly, it is affluent people who smoke less than poor people. Therefore, although overall incidence has decreased, poor people are smoking more than affluent people, a situation that has increased existing inequalities in smoking-related diseases. So while the overall population health has improved, inequalities in smoking-related diseases between the affluent and the poor have expanded.

The fact that public health efforts to reduce smoking incidence have increased existing health inequalities obviously does not mean that such efforts are unethical. But it does suggest that we might prefer approaches that promise to reduce incidence and to decrease health inequalities at the same time. What might such approaches look like? Consider the possibility of intensive investment in early childhood development.

Epidemiologists have long pointed out that early childhood (age zero to two) is a sentinel period for the development of health across the life span. Experiences during early childhood are extraordinarily accurate predictors of health many decades later. Indeed, early childhood is so powerful a determinant of health that epidemiologists can predict the health of the *next generation* simply by knowing the economic and living conditions that the parents experienced in their early childhood (Liu, Jones, and Glymour 2010). Early childhood can therefore affect health intergenerationally (although the correlations are unsurprisingly weaker, they remain statistically significant in predicting the later-life health of *grandchildren* from the early childhood experiences of the grandparents) (Osler et al. 2005). Therefore, antismoking efforts aimed at children are most likely to have the best long-term success in preventing new smokers.

**Nutrition**. Public health has also focused on changing the way we eat. In the United States, food that is high in fats and low in nutritional carbohydrates is cheap and readily available. Healthful food tends to be more readily available in higher socioeconomic areas than in lower socioeconomic areas. The effect of this unhealthy diet is demonstrated in the documentary *Super Size Me* (2004), in which filmmaker Morgan Spurlock puts his life in danger by consuming nothing but McDonald's cuisine for an entire month. Encouraging stores to carry a larger array of more healthful food has long been an effort of public health. This effort has ranged from having pharmacies offer fresh fruit next to candy and First Lady Michelle Obama's efforts to not only increase children's amount of exercise but also to change the food that is available to them in schools.

To improve nutrition (*solidarity*) in New York City, Mayor Michael Bloomberg decided to ban the sale of sugar-sweetened soft drinks larger than sixteen ounces (Grynbaum 2014). Vocal opposition to the move arose from a variety of corners, but especially from those who viewed the intervention as an unwarranted intrusion on the freedom of consumers to control their own consumption of sugar-sweetened beverages (*efficacy—is it socially possible?*). The ban undoubtedly sought to limit a particular kind of behavior deemed risky to public health, even where that behavior only exposed the individual to risk. The individual's behavior did not expose others to risks in the same way that, for example, parental refusal to vaccinate children or secondhand smoke does.

It is well-settled law in the United States that states can enact compulsory vaccination laws and require parents to have their children vaccinated with only extremely narrow exemptions permitted. This legal power is often justified on moral grounds because the freedom to refuse vaccinations on behalf of one's children exposes others to significant risks of harm from infectious childhood diseases. In contrast, the decision to consume a twenty-two-ounce sugar-sweetened soft drink seemingly does not expose others to the same risk of harm. Therefore, Mayor Bloomberg's decision to restrict the freedom to purchase beverages in such sizes was deemed an unreasonable intrusion on individual liberty (*dignity*). Pointing to the rising burden of NCDs, such as type 2 diabetes, coronary artery disease, cerebrovascular disease, and their correlation with patterns of food and sugar consumption, proponents of the mayor's policy argued that the ubiquitous consumption of sugar-sweetened beverages does impose significant costs on others and can be likened to an epidemic.

Proponents also pointed out that environmental structures strongly shape consumption behaviors. This fact is well known to major food and beverage producers (and is harnessed to develop marketing strategies to encourage or discourage consumption of certain products). Therefore, simply providing more information to consumers, such as by

***Subway advertisement from the New York City Department of Health in 2014, urging parents not to let their children drink sugary beverages.*** *Prior to leaving office, New York Mayor Michael Bloomberg attempted to prohibit food establishments licensed by the city from selling high-calorie drinks, such as cola, in containers larger than sixteen ounces. Vocal opposition to the move arose from a variety of corners, but especially from those who viewed the intervention as an unwarranted intrusion on the freedom of consumers to control their own consumption of sugar-sweetened beverages.* **RICHARD LEVINE/ ALAMY.**

requiring that restaurants disclose the amount of calories in a given menu item, is unlikely to change consumption behaviors. Rather, argue the supporters of the mayor's policy, what is needed are structural changes to the environment in which consumption is patterned.

For example, some dentists have called for the elimination of the screw cap from bottles of sugar-sweetened soft drinks precisely because they tend to increase consumption of such beverages. Eliminating such screw caps might well change people's consumption behavior without restricting their ability to purchase whatever size of beverage they wish. The argument is that while outright bans on the consumption of such beverages is too significant a restriction on individual liberty, altering the environment in which such liberties are exercised is warranted and appropriate as a means of reducing the burden of NCD in the United States.

## Summary

The responsibilities of public health are vast, and its resources are thin. Public health initiatives account for only 3.1 percent of the US budget and only 8 percent of the nation's gross domestic product (GDP). Thus, a major ethical dilemma faced by every public health department is where to spend its money—maternal-child health, infectious disease surveillance and monitoring, crisis and disaster management, health of the environment, health education, free (or subsidized clinics), epidemiologic analysis, drug and medical device safety testing (US Food and Drug Administration), public safety, and research, to name a few. Should a local health department prioritize maternal and child health or HIV screening and surveillance? How far upstream the causal pathway of disease should local public health officials go? Should they seek to intervene on root social and economic conditions? Or is it more feasible and of greater impact to intervene proximally or subsequent to the onset of disease itself, through such tools as screening, point-of-contact behavioral interventions, and acute disease management (i.e., quarantine and isolation)?

Even within these activities, public health needs to decide where to prioritize spending among different communities, ethnicities, age groups, and socioeconomic groups. We have seen that these questions are extremely complex and that simple answers such as "do what is most effective" accomplish nothing so much as raise additional difficult questions (Effective for whom? Which groups matter most? What is our measure of effectiveness? Do inequalities matter, or just improvements in absolute population health?). Grappling with these issues requires tools of public health ethics that are fundamentally distinct from medical ethics. The unit of analysis in medical ethics is typically the individual patient, which tends to promote an emphasis on the principle of autonomy or self-determination. In contrast, public health ethics focuses on groups and group-level phenomena, which tends to result in an emphasis on the principle of justice, or questions of what we owe each other in society.

Moreover, we cannot simply move our analysis from individual patients to groups without falling afoul of the fallacy of division. This fallacy occurs when we reason that because all the members of a particular group have a particular property, all the members of the group must have the same property. Thus, we cannot say that because all the parts of the machine are small, the machine must be small (maybe its casing is large!).

Division is also seen in the notion of the *ecological fallacy*. This is the statistical idea that correlations at one level of analysis (say groups) are not necessarily true for other levels of analysis (say individuals). For example, the life expectancy of a baby born today in the United States is 79.68 years. That is a group-level measure. This does not mean that any one person can expect (or be predicted) to live that many years. In another example, if the average family in the United States has 2.5 children, that does not mean that every individual family will have 2.5 children. Applying a group-level statistic to an individual is a fallacy in logical thinking. In terms of ethics, this idea holds that what is right or wrong for the group may not be right or wrong for any particular individual. For our purposes, what matters here is the idea that groups require different ways of moral thinking than do individual units.

Armed with tools suited to the kinds of moral problems that arise in public health contexts, we can move on to consider any number of such problems, including but not limited to disaster and crisis management, allocation and scarcity, surveillance and quarantine, and stigma. Any reasonable conception of public health ethics must include within its ambit questions related to inequalities. These questions flow from the basic epidemiologic fact that patterns of disease are not generally distributed equally in human populations; illness, like most other kinds of social disadvantage, tends to cluster. Although not all health inequalities are unjust, many rightly strike us as morally questionable, and there is ample reason to conclude that compressing them is a crucial ethical goal for public health practice.

Questions of priority setting, of inequalities, and of justice are central to public health ethics. Especially because public health ethics requires us first to understand the basic causes of ill health in human populations, it offers a powerful perspective for thinking through difficult moral problems related to human flourishing and well-being.

## Bibliography

Allebeck, Peter. "The Prevention Paradox or the Inequality Paradox." *European Journal of Public Health* 18, no. 3 (2008): 215.

Anderson, Tim. "HIV/AIDS in Cuba: A Rights-Based Analysis." *Health and Human Rights Journal* 11, no. 1 (2009): 93–104. http://cdn2.sph.harvard.edu/wp-content/uploads/sites/13/2013/07/10-Anderson.pdf.

Beauchamp, Tom L., and James F. Childress. *Principles of Biomedical Ethics*. 7th ed. New York: Oxford University Press, 2013.

Blackburn, Henry. "Geoffrey Rose's Prevention Paradox." University of Minnesota. http://www.epi.umn.edu/cvdepi/essay/geoffrey-roses-prevention-paradox.

Bodenheimer, Thomas, Ellen Chen, and Heather D. Bennett. "Confronting the Growing Burden of Chronic Disease: Can the U.S. Health Care Workforce Do the Job?" *Health Affairs* 28, no. 1 (2009): 64–74.

Braveman, Paula, and Colleen Barclay. "Health Disparities Beginning in Childhood: A Life-Course Perspective." *Pediatrics* 124, Suppl. 3 (2009): 5163–5175.

Burris, Scott. "Disease Stigma in U.S. Public Health Law." *Journal of Law, Medicine, and Ethics* 30, no. 2 (2002): 179–190.

Capewell, Simon, and Hilary Graham. "Will Cardiovascular Disease Prevention Widen Health Inequalities?" *PLoS Medicine* 7, no. 8 (2010): e1000320. doi: 10.1371/journal.pmed.1000320.

Carmichael, Ann G. "Contagion Theory and Contagion Practice in Fifteenth-Century Milan." *Renaissance Quarterly* 44, no. 2 (1991): 213–256.

Central Intelligence Agency (CIA). *The World Factbook*. Accessed December 7, 2015, via https://www.cia.gov/library/publications/the-world-factbook/.

Colgrove, James. "The McKeown Thesis: A Historical Controversy and Its Enduring Influence." *American Journal of Public Health* 92, no. 5 (2002): 725–729.

Faden, Ruth, and Sirine Shebaya. "Public Health Ethics." In *The Stanford Encyclopedia of Philosophy*, edited by Edward N. Zalta. Spring 2015. http://plato.stanford.edu/archives/spr2015/entries/publichealth-ethics/.

Farmer, Paul. *Haiti after the Earthquake*. Philadelphia: PublicAffairs, 2011.

Goldberg, Daniel S. "The Implications of Fundamental Cause Theory for Priority Setting." *American Journal of Public Health* 104, no. 10 (2014): 1839–1843.

Goldberg, Daniel S. "Social Justice, Health Inequalities, and Methodological Individualism in U.S. Health Promotion." *Public Health Ethics* 5, no. 2 (2012): 104–115.

Gostin, Lawrence O. *Public Health Law: Power, Duty, Restraint*. 2nd ed. Berkeley: University of California Press, 2008.

Gostin, Lawrence O., and K. G. Gostin. "A Broader Liberty: J. S. Mill, Paternalism, and the Public's Health." *Public Health* 123, no. 3 (2009): 214–221.

Grob, Gerald N. *The Deadly Truth: A History of Disease in America*. Cambridge, MA: Harvard University Press, 2002.

Grynbaum, Michael M. "New York's Ban on Big Sodas Is Rejected by Final Court." *New York Times*, June 26, 2014. http://www.nytimes.com/2014/06/27/nyregion/city-loses-final-appeal-on-limiting-sales-of-large-sodas.html.

Guyer, Bernard, et al. "Early Childhood Health Promotion and Its Life Course Health Consequences." *Academic Pediatrics* 9, no. 3 (2009): 142–149.

Hatzenbuehler, Mark L., Jo C. Phelan, and Bruce G. Link. "Stigma as a Fundamental Cause of Population Health Inequalities." *American Journal of Public Health* 103, no. 5 (2013): 813–821.

Hoffman, Sarah Z. "HIV/AIDS in Cuba: A Model for Care or an Ethical Dilemma?" *African Health Sciences* 4, no. 3 (2004): 208–209.

Institute of Medicine. *The Future of Public Health in the 21st Century*. Washington, DC: National Academies Press, 1988.

Jennings, Bruce. "Disaster Planning and Public Health." In *From Birth to Death and Bench to Clinic: The Hastings Center Bioethics Briefing Book for Journalists, Policymakers, and Campaigns*, edited by Mary Crowley, 41–44. Garrison, NY: The Hastings Center, 2008.

Jennings, Bruce. "Frameworks for Ethics in Public Health." *Acta Bioethica* 9, no. 2 (2001): 165–176.

Jonsen, Albert, Mark Siegler, and William J. Winslade. *Clinical Ethics: A Practical Approach to Ethical Decisions in Clinical Medicine.* 6th ed. New York: McGraw Hill, 2006.

Kass, Nancy E. "An Ethics Framework for Public Health." *American Journal of Public Health* 91, no. 11 (2001): 1776–1782.

Klugman, Craig M. "Public Health Principlism." *Online Journal of Health Ethics* 4, no. 1 (2007): 1–13. http://aquila.usm.edu/ojhe/vol4/iss1/4.

Kraut, Alan M. *Silent Travelers: Germs, Genes, and the Immigrant Menace.* Baltimore: Johns Hopkins University Press, 1995.

Last, J. M., ed. *Dictionary of Epidemiology.* 4th ed. New York: Oxford University Press, 2001.

Leavitt, Judith Walzer. *Typhoid Mary: Captive to the Public's Health.* Boston: Beacon Press, 1997.

Liu, Sze, Richard N. Jones, and M. Maria Glymour. "Implications of Lifecourse Epidemiology for Research on Determinants of Adult Disease." *Public Health Reviews* 32, no. 2 (2010): 489–511.

Mann, J. "Medicine and Public Health, Ethics, and Human Rights." In *New Ethics for the Public's Health,* edited by Dan E. Beauchamp and Bonnie Steinbock, 83–93. New York: Oxford University Press, 1999.

McNeil, Donald G., Jr. "Cuba Wins W.H.O. Certification It Ended Mother-to-Child H.I.V. Transmission." *New York Times,* June 30, 2015. http://www.nytimes.com/2015/07/01/health/who-certifies-end-of-mother-to-child-transmission-of-hiv-in-cuba.html?_r=0.

Mello, Michelle M., and Lawrence O. Gostin. "Commentary: A Legal Perspective on Diabetes Surveillance—Privacy and the Police Power." *Milbank Quarterly* 87, no. 3 (2009): 575–580.

The Nizkor Project. "Fallacy: Division." http://www.nizkor.org/features/fallacies/division.html.

Osler, Merete, et al. "Effect of Grandparent's and Parent's Socioeconomic Position on Mortality among Danish Men Born in 1953." *European Journal of Public Health* 15, no. 6 (2005): 647–651.

Powers, Madison, and Ruth Faden. *Social Justice: The Moral Foundations of Public Health and Health Policy.* New York: Oxford University Press, 2006.

Powers, Madison, and Ruth Faden. "Social Practices, Public Health and the Twin Aims of Justice: Responses to Comments." *Public Health Ethics* 6, no. 1 (2013): 45–49.

Public Health Leadership Society. *Principles of the Ethical Practice of Public Health.* Accessed December 8, 2002, via http://phls.org/CMSuploads/Principles-of-the-Ethical-Practice-of-PH-Version-2.2-68496.pdf.

Puhl, Rebecca M., and Chelsea A. Heuer. "Obesity Stigma: Important Considerations for Public Health." *American Journal of Public Health* 100, no. 6 (2010): 1019–1028.

Rose, Geoffrey. "Sick Individuals and Sick Populations." *International Journal of Epidemiology* 14, no. 1 (1985): 32–38.

Rose, Geoffrey. *The Strategy of Preventive Medicine.* New York: Oxford University Press, 1992.

Secretary's Advisory Committee on Health Promotion and Disease Prevention Objectives for 2020. *Healthy People 2020: An Opportunity to Address the Societal Determinants of Health in the United States.* July 26, 2010. http://www.healthypeople.gov/2010/hp2020/advisory/SocietalDeterminantsHealth.htm.

Stern, Alexandra Minna. *Eugenic Nation: Faults and Frontiers of Better Breeding in America.* Berkeley: University of California Press, 2008.

Stone, Deborah. *Policy Paradox: The Art of Political Decision Making.* Rev. ed. New York: Norton, 2002.

Stonington, Scott, Scott M. Holmes, and The *PLoS Medicine* Editors. "Social Medicine in the Twenty-First Century." *PLoS Medicine* 3, no. 10 (2006): e445. doi: 10.1371/journal.pmed.0030445.

Szreter, Simon. *Health and Wealth: Studies in History and Policy.* Rochester, NY: University of Rochester Press, 2004.

Venkatapuram, Sridhar. *Health Justice: An Argument from the Capabilities Approach.* Bristol, UK: Polity Press, 2011.

Western, Bruce, and Becky Pettit. "Incarceration and Social Inequality." *Daedalus* 139, no. 3 (Summer 2010): 8–19. https://www.amacad.org/content/publications/pubContent.aspx?d=808.

Wolff, Jonathan, and Avner de-Shalit. *Disadvantage.* New York: Oxford University Press, 2007.

World Health Organization (WHO). "Public Health." 2016. http://www.who.int/trade/glossary/story076/en.

World Health Organization (WHO), Commission on Social Determinants of Health. Final Report. *Closing the Gap in a Generation: Health Equity through Action on the Social Determinants of Health.* Geneva, Switzerland: Author, 2008. http://www.who.int/social_determinants/the commission/finalreport/en.

**FILM**

*Contagion.* Dir. Steven Soderbergh. 2011. Warner Brothers.

*Erin Brockovich.* Dir. Steven Soderbergh. 2000. Universal Studios.

*50/50.* Dir. Jonathan Levine. 2011. Summit Entertainment.

*The Impossible*. Dir. J. A. Bayonna. 2012. Warner Brothers.

*The Insider*. Dir. Michael Mann. 1999. Touchstone Pictures.

*Miss Evers' Boys*. Dir. Joseph Sargent. 1997. HBO. Based on the 1992 play by David Feldshuh.

*Nova*. "The Most Dangerous Woman in America." Dir. Nancy Porter. Season 32, episode 5, 2004. PBS.

*Super Size Me*. Dir. Morgan Spurlock. 2004. Samuel Goldwyn Films.

# *Glossary*

## A

**ABO compatibility.** The need for the blood type of a donor to be favorable to the recipient so that the recipient's body does not reject the donation.

**abortion.** The deliberate termination of a human pregnancy; in the United States, each state regulates the laws related to abortion rights. *See also* selective abortion.

**adenoviruses.** Viruses containing double-stranded DNA that infect a variety of vertebrate hosts; in humans, symptoms of infection by these viruses range from none to life threatening. The most studied adenovirus is the common cold. *See also* vector.

**advance care planning.** Having conversations about a person's desires for medical treatment or nontreatment in the event that future medical decisions must be made and the individual is incapable of making or conveying his or her choices.

**advance directives.** Documents that (1) assign a surrogate decision maker to a person in the event that he or she is unable to make and state choices and (2) contain a living will that dictates what medical treatments a patient would choose in the event that he or she has a terminal illness or condition and lacks capacity to make decisions.

**allele.** Two forms of a gene found at the same point on homologous chromosomes; an individual can have two variations of the same allele (e.g., one for brown eyes and one for blue) or two of the same variations. *See also* DNA.

**altruism.** The principle of concern for the welfare of others without gain for the individual, associated with the idea of selflessness.

**altruistic unbalanced paired kidney exchange (AUPKE).** Program that matches incompatible donor/recipient pairs with another incompatible pair so that each donor and recipient receives a compatible match.

**assent.** The nonlegal approval of or agreement with proposed medical intervention; agreement to understanding of the treatment, which does not necessarily give permission to complete the intervention. *See also* consent.

**assisted reproductive technology (ART).** A variety of technologies used to achieve a pregnancy in otherwise infertile individuals; these treatments include fertility medications, artificial insemination, in vitro fertilization, and surrogacy. *See also* in vitro fertilization (IVF).

**assisted suicide.** The intention to end one's own life with the aid of another person. Often this person is a health-care provider, in which case the event is known as provider-assisted or physician-assisted suicide, but family members or friends have been known to aid this process by providing life-ending medications and other forms of assistance that directly lead to the death of the individual. *See also* physician-assisted suicide, provider-assisted suicide.

**autonomy.** The right of a rational, competent, capacitated individual to self-governance free of coercion, particularly in terms of health-care decisions. One of the four founding principles of bioethics. *See also* capacity, coercion, competence.

## B

**Baby Doe rules.** One of the amendments of the US Child Abuse Amendments of 1984 that identifies criteria and guidelines for the treatment of seriously ill and disabled newborns. The amendment requires mandated reporting of child abuse if any child that is not either irreversibly comatose or terminally ill has medical care withheld for any reason, including assessments of the child's quality of life or the wishes of the guardian.

***Belmont Report.*** Subtitled *Ethical Principles and Guidelines for the Protection of Human Subjects of Research.* A report generated by the National Commission for the Protection of Human Subjects of Biomedical and Behavioral Research in 1979. Summarizes ethical principles and guidelines for research involving human subjects. The core principles of this report include respect for persons, beneficence, and justice. *See also* beneficence, justice.

**beneficence.** In medicine, the concept that medical providers have the obligation to provide benefit to a patient in addition to taking action to prevent harm. In research, the obligation to do no harm and to minimize possible harms. *See also* nonmaleficence.

**biobank.** A facility that provides long-term storage of biological samples, such as semen, ova, blood, tissue, and urine.

**bioethics.** The study and discussion of innovative, controversial, or ambiguous ethical issues related to advancement in the fields of biology and medicine. *See also* clinical ethics.

**biomarkers.** Indicators of the presence or severity of a condition, disease, physiologic state, or genetic tendency in an individual. Biomarkers can be created by the individual or introduced into the body as a means of examining an aspect of health status (e.g., organ function).

**blastocyst.** The spherical mass of developing embryonic cells during the period from approximately five days postconception to two weeks postfertilization.

**boundary crossing.** A clinician's action or behavior that deviates from expected activity but poses no harm or threat to the patient. *See also* boundary violation.

**boundary violation.** A clinician's action or behavior that crosses the boundary of appropriate professional behavior. The action is either directly harmful or has the potential to cause harm to a patient. *See also* boundary crossing.

**BRAIN Initiative.** Brain Research through Advancing Innovative Neurotechnologies. A collaboration between the US government and private researchers with the goal of supporting the development and application of innovative technologies to generate a deeper and more dynamic understanding of brain function.

*BRCA1* **and** *BRCA2*. Tumor suppressor genes found in all humans that are involved in the repair of damaged DNA. Mutations of these genes substantially increase an individual's risk for developing breast cancer. Genetic testing can be completed to determine the presence of mutation. *See also* genetic testing.

# C

**capacity.** A clinical term referring to the power of an individual to make a decision regarding his or her health care. This determination is made by a provider and can be specific to the task, meaning that an individual may have the capacity to make some decisions without the capacity to make others. *See also* competence.

**cardiocirculatory death.** Cessation of cardiovascular function, including the heart, blood, and vessels. Differentiated from brain death by the fact that the heart has stopped beating; if organs are being donated, transplantation must occur imminently after this type of death has occurred. *See also* death by neurological criteria/brain death.

**carrier testing.** A type of genetic testing used to determine whether individuals planning to parent together are carriers of specific autosomal recessive conditions that could lead to harmful outcomes in their offspring. *See also* genetic testing.

**casuistry.** Ethical reasoning based on referring to previous cases in which a similar moral dilemma was encountered. The resolution to the previous dilemmas provides guidance to the current situation.

**clinical ethics.** The determination and application of ethical principles to health-care settings.

**clinical ethics consultants.** Individuals or groups of trained individuals who listen to complex cases, identify ethical concerns, and make recommendations about decision making and ethically appropriate care.

**clustered, regularly interspaced, short palindromic repeat (CRISPR).** Segments of prokaryotic DNA that are being used experimentally to edit the human genome. Use of these fragments offers the potential to create genetically modified or cloned human beings once the technology has been perfected.

**coercion.** The act of physically or psychologically forcing an individual to take certain actions or make particular decisions. Actions made with such force violate autonomy and free will. In health care, coercion can be perpetrated by providers, family members, and other health-care staff. *See also* autonomy.

**cognitive liberty.** The ability and right of an individual to have control over his or her thoughts, mental processes, and consciousness.

**coma.** A particular state of unconsciousness wherein an individual cannot be awakened; makes no visible attempts at voluntary movements; has abnormal or absent responses to pain, light, or sound; and lacks a normal sleep-wake cycle.

**comfort care.** Health care focused on relieving symptoms and optimizing the patient's comfort rather than curing or treating the underlying condition. *See also* palliative care.

**Common Rule.** A federal policy (United States Code, Department of Health and Human Services 45 CFR part A) that protects human research subjects. The rule applies to seventeen federal agencies and the research that they fund. Includes the requirements for informed consent, institutional compliance with regulations, and institutional review board functions. Parts B–D of the rule protect vulnerable populations, including children, prisoners, pregnant women, and fetuses from exploitation by research.

**competence.** A legal term referring to an individual's ability to make decisions. Competence is presumed to be present in each adult individual unless a court has ruled otherwise. *See also* capacity.

**confidentiality.** A promise between individuals or a set of rules put in place by an institution that ensures the protection and keeping of secret information, and limits access of this information to particular individuals. Confidentially allows for open and honest communication between health-care provider and patient.

**conflict of interest.** A situation in which an individual owes fealty to more than one party and this dual loyalty may affect obligations to always act in the patient's interest.

**consent.** An active process of giving permission for a particular event, such as a procedure or medication administration, to occur. *See also* informed consent.

**CRISPR.** *See* clustered, regularly interspaced, short palindromic repeat (CRISPR).

**cryopreservation.** The process by which cells, tissues, or any other live samples are preserved for later use by cooling them to subzero temperatures, at which point cellular activity is effectively stopped. *See also* biobank.

**culture.** (1) A broad term referring to the way that a defined group of people share a way of life, including customs, beliefs, traditions, activities, and worldviews, and pass this view on to future generations. (2) A medium in which cells are grown in a glass plate in a laboratory.

# D

*de facto.* "In practice"; things that are done based on tradition, evidence, or the majority opinion.

*de jure.* "In law"; ideas or practices that are rooted in law.

**dead donor rule (DDR).** States that vital organs (organs required for life) should be taken only from persons who are dead and that individuals should not be killed for their organs. This theory was the original premise for the ethics of organ transplantation.

**death anxiety.** Feelings of excessive stress, dread, or fear when an individual thinks about the process of dying or "ceasing to be."

**death by neurological criteria/brain death.** The complete and irreversible cessation of the function of the brain, including involuntary functions such as independent breathing.

**deception.** The intentional withholding or provision of false information to an individual; usually occurs when providers withhold information from patients.

**Declaration of Geneva.** A statement adopted by the World Medical Association in Geneva in 1948 and frequently revised. A covenant of physicians to dedicate medical practice objectives to the humanitarian goals of medicine.

**Declaration of Helsinki.** A statement of the World Medical Association pertaining to research principles created to protect human subjects; emphasizes an individual's right to self-determination, autonomy, and informed decision making.

**diagnostic testing.** Different tools used by health-care providers to identify the cause of a condition, including computed tomography (CT) and X-ray imaging, as well as blood and urine testing.

**disclosure.** (1) Making previously unknown, sometimes sensitive, information about oneself known; such as conflicts of interest, sexual orientation, gender identity, or disease status (such as a test result). (2) A legal requirement of a professional to explain certain ideas, facts, or concepts to a potential patient or research subject.

**DNA.** Deoxyribonucleic acid (DNA) is the basic hereditary material in human cells that is passed from one generation to the next. This double strand of amino acid nucleotides is arranged in a double helix and consists of base pairs matched as the purine adenine with the pyrimidine thymine and the purine guanine with the pyrimidine cytosine. DNA is the blueprint for all life.

**DNR, DNAR, or AND.** Abbreviations for do not resuscitate, do not attempt resuscitation, and allow natural death. Traditionally known as a do not resuscitate order, this document applies inside the hospital setting and states that the individual does not wish to receive cardiopulmonary resuscitation (CPR) if his or her heart stops or breathing ceases.

**durable power of attorney for health care.** A legal document associated with end-of-life preparation that names a family member or friend as the medical decision maker should the individual not be capable of making his or her own decisions.

# E

**EEG.** Electroencephalography. A method of monitoring electrical activity in the brain using sensors that are placed on specific areas of the scalp.

**embryo.** A developing offspring during the early stages of development. Extends from two weeks postconception until the tenth week, at which point the fetal period begins.

**end-stage kidney disease.** The last stage of chronic kidney disease, at which point the kidneys are no longer able to filter blood and function on a level needed for day-to-day life, making dialysis treatment or kidney transplant necessary for survival.

**enhancement.** Improving the effectiveness, value, quality, or extent of an idea, action, or individual. In genetics and neuroscience, the process of modifying a human being (or human DNA) to give the person capabilities that surpass what is typical of humans.

**epigenetics.** Changes to the expression of genetic material (DNA) that are caused by external factors such as the environment and lifestyle choices of an individual. *See also* DNA.

**equipoise.** The ethical concept that human subjects may be given experimental treatments only if the medical community has a genuine uncertainty as to whether the experimental treatment will be beneficial.

**ethics committee.** A group of individuals with varying experiences and expertise, brought together by an institution to protect the interests of patients and to address moral issues in the health-care setting. Usually charged with ethics education, developing ethics-related policies, and consulting on ethical dilemmas.

**ethics consultation.** A hospital referral service that provides a process for ethical deliberation, insight, and recommendations in navigating moral questions in the health-care delivery arena.

**eugenics.** Ideals and beliefs guided toward improving the genetic quality of the human population, usually through controlled breeding or genetic engineering.

**euthanasia.** The act of taking direct action to end the life of another human being with the intent of relieving pain or suffering.

**extraordinary care.** A type of treatment that is distinguished from "ordinary care" by the fact that it places a significant burden on the patient or community. This differentiation is important in the moral view of Catholicism because agreeing to receive ordinary health-care treatment is obligatory under Catholic law whereas one is not obligate to accept extraordinary treatment. *See also* ordinary care.

# F

**fetal rights.** The moral or legal rights of an unborn offspring.

**fiduciary.** Generally, an individual who has been entrusted with private, special, or sensitive information.

**fMRI.** Functional magnetic resonance imaging (fMRI) is a method of measuring and making a map of brain activity by observing blood flow to different areas when an individual thinks, acts, or feels.

**forensic testing.** The use of genetic testing to identify individuals by characteristics of their DNA.

**fragile X syndrome.** A genetic syndrome characterized by a range of learning disabilities and cognitive impairment issues that can be detected using genetic testing. Individuals can be tested for this genetic abnormality before having children to assess their risk. *See also* genetic testing.

**frailty.** The general feeling or appearance of being weak or fragile that is commonly seen in older adults.

**futility.** The point at which medical intervention will provide no more measureable physiological or psychological improvement in health outcomes, as determined by the health-care provider.

# G

**gamete.** A cell containing half of the genetic material required for life, commonly known as sperm and egg cells; cells created by the male or female reproductive system that, when combined under the right circumstances, can produce life.

**gene.** (1) In general, the sequence of nucleotides that code for characteristics that can be transmitted to an offspring. (2) Specifically, a segment of DNA that codes for a particular protein.

**genetic counseling.** A process in which a professional assists individuals in understanding their risk of developing or giving birth to offspring with certain genetic conditions assessed via genetic testing. Individuals or couples are counseled on the nature of the disorder, the consequences of its course, and the probability of their offspring contracting the condition, and given options for management and family planning.

**genetic determinism.** The belief that DNA defines not only physiology but also psychology and behavior of an individual while minimizing the effect of environment and culture.

**genetic engineering.** The act of directly changing an organism's genetic material (DNA) intentionally to produce new functions, substances, or expression of characteristics.

**genetic enhancement.** The use of genetic engineering to endow a person with capabilities and characteristics that surpass what is typical of human beings. *See also* genetic therapy.

**Genetic Information Nondiscrimination Act (GINA).** A 2008 federal act that prohibits the use of genetic information in health insurance and employment decisions.

**genetic interventions.** A wide range of biotechnology and scientific methods used to modify or alter genetic makeup and expression.

**genetic testing.** The use of biotechnology to identify possible genetic risk factors and mutations that put an individual (and his or her future offspring) at higher risk for certain diseases and conditions. *See also* genetic counseling.

**genetic therapy.** The use of DNA alteration or changes in expression to prevent or treat disease. *See also* genetic enhancement.

**genome.** The complete genetic makeup of an individual that includes both the genes and noncoding segments of the DNA.

**germ-line gene therapy.** The process of modifying the genetic material of gametes by replacing nonfunctional or dysfunctional DNA with function genes. *See also* gamete, genetic therapy.

**gestational surrogacy.** A reproductive treatment process in which an individual or couple contracts with a woman to gestate an embryo to bring it to term. The egg may or may not be hers. The fertilization process occurs outside of the womb via in vitro fertilization. *See also* in vitro fertilization (IVF).

**GINA.** *See* Genetic Information Nondiscrimination Act (GINA).

**global health ethics.** A division of bioethics focused on addressing controversial or moral issues related to health care around the world.

**Good Samaritan obligations.** The general obligation of all capable individuals in a society to provide appropriate care and treatment to those in need. In countries that practice English common law, legal protection protects from liability those who act in good faith to give reasonable assistance to those they believe to be in need or in danger.

**graft.** The transplantation of living tissue from one organism to another, or from one location on an individual to another.

**Groningen Protocol.** Guidelines created by physicians, lawyers, and parents in the Netherlands containing directives for providers to actively end the life of infant who has a condition incompatible with life, without legal prosecution. *See also* euthanasia.

# H

**harm principle.** The idea that the government may limit a person's actions to prevent injury, pain, trauma, or any form of impairment to others.

**Health Insurance Portability and Accountability Act (HIPAA).** A US federal law enacted in 1996 and amended in 2013 that restricts access to private health information to health-care providers and prevents discrimination in health insurance.

**higher-ordered multiple pregnancies (HOMPs).** Pregnancies with three or more fetuses. These type of pregnancies are often the result of in vitro fertilization.

**HIPAA.** *See* Health Insurance Portability and Accountability Act (HIPAA).

**Hippocratic Oath.** Written by the Pythagorean physicians in ancient Greece, the oath details professional thought and behavior of physicians, including obligation to do no harm, protect patient privacy, and to act in the patient's best interest.

**HOMPs.** *See* higher-ordered multiple pregnancies (HOMPs).

**hospice.** A holistic philosophy of care for those at the end of life, typically six months or less without medical interventions as determined by two providers, that emphasizes symptom relief and rejects curative interventions. *See also* comfort care, palliative care.

**Human Genome Project.** Completed in 2003, the project was an international scientific research endeavor with the goal of mapping all of the genes of the human genome by determining the sequence of DNA that makes up each gene. *See also* DNA, genome.

**human leukocyte antigen.** A gene complex that encodes for proteins that allow the human body to recognize its cells as self rather than as foreign cells.

**Huntington's disease.** An autosomal dominant degenerative neurological disease symptoms of which usually appear after the age of 35 years. Individuals in families with the genetic mutation that leads to this disease may choose to undergo genetic testing to determine whether they have the mutation.

**hysterectomy.** The surgical removal of a female's uterus and accessory structures. Hysterectomy renders the female unable to become pregnant.

# I

**impaired drivers.** Individuals who, based on physical impairments or cognitive deficits, are no longer capable of operating a motor vehicle safely.

*in utero.* A Latin term meaning "in the womb" used to describe an embryo or fetus while it is inside of the uterus.

**in vitro fertilization (IVF).** The process of fertilizing an egg outside of the body that includes the act of removing an egg from a woman's body and retrieving sperm from a man and combining them in a laboratory. The resulting embryo is then transferred into a woman's uterus for gestation.

*in vivo.* A Latin term meaning "within the living" used to describe the gene therapy method in which genes are modified while still in the body.

**informational privacy.** The legal, political, and ethical issues surrounding the collection, protection, and dissemination of health-care data.

**informed consent.** The process of obtaining an individual's legal approval to complete an action (medical test, treatment, or being a research subject) only after ensuring that the consent has been given based upon a clear understanding of the facts, implications, risks, alternatives, and consequences of that action.

**institutional review board (IRB).** A committee tasked with reviewing research involving human subjects at a particular institution.

**instrumental.** Something that is of importance because of its value to the functioning, integrity, or structure of another process.

**intensive care unit (ICU).** A particular department within a health-care institution, which caters to patients with severe and life-threatening illness that requires close monitoring.

**intracytoplasmic sperm injection (ICS).** The process of injecting a single sperm directly into an egg.

**intrinsic.** A characteristic that is inherent, or naturally occurs within an individual or group. Having value simply for its own sake, not because of any outside factor, involvement, or relationship.

**IVF.** *See* in vitro fertilization (IVF).

# J

**justice.** *What is due.* (1) The ethical principle that one should consider the availability and allocation of medical resources when determining who should receive them. (2) Treating likes alike and avoiding discrimination based on arbitrary characteristics. (3) Fairness.

# L

**living will.** A legal document that allows an individual to specify which actions should and should not be taken for their health should they have a fatal illness or terminal condition and be unable to articulate their wishes.

# M

**magnetic resonance imaging.** *See* MRI.

**mandatory reporting laws.** Laws that dictate the requirements for individuals working with vulnerable populations to report suspected crimes against children, disabled persons, and senior citizens.

**maternal rights.** The rights of women to make choices regarding their bodies and their children.

**mature minor.** A judicial determination that emancipates minors who possess the maturity and capacity to understand and make decisions for themselves.

**medical ethics.** The study of moral issues and controversial ideas and advancements in the area of the life sciences.

**medical tourism.** The action of traveling to a particular location to receive medical treatment specifically because it is illegal or impossible to receive such treatment in the individual's home country or because the treatment is significantly better or less expensive at the destination.

***mens rea.*** The idea that an individual must have knowledge of wrongdoing to be guilty of a crime.

**metabolomics.** The study of metabolites, or the chemical products that cellular activity processes leave behind.

**minimally conscious state (MCS).** A term used to describe the condition of a mostly unresponsive individual who has barely detectable levels of consciousness that may be inconsistent but sometimes shows reproducible signs of awareness.

**minor.** A term used to describe an individual younger than the age of legal responsibility for a particular action or privilege. In the United States, generally under eighteen years of age.

**molecular medicine.** The field of research that utilizes biological, chemical, and physical techniques to identify genetic errors and develops molecular interventions to help correct them.

**moral status.** A characteristic endowed by humans to other entities to indicate that they matter for purposes of moral decision making and ethical consideration.

**MRI.** Magnetic resonance imaging (MRI). A technique used in medical diagnosis to image the anatomy and physiological structures of the human body.

**mRNA.** A type of genetic material (molecular RNA) that assists in translating DNA into proteins.

# N

**National Organ Transplant Act.** A US federal law that makes buying, selling, or exchanging goods for organs illegal throughout the United States.

**National Research Act.** A 1974 US federal law that called into being the National Commission for the Protection of Human Subjects of Biomedical and Behavioral Research. The commission wrote the *Belmont Report.*

**neurodeterminism, neural determinism.** The concept that the brain determines our behaviors, actions, and character without our conscious awareness; along the lines of "my brain made me do it" as a criminal defense.

**neuroethics.** A distinct subcategory within bioethics that focuses on the consequences of treatment and research particular to the human brain, including the ethics of neuroscience and the neuroscience of ethics.

**neuroimaging.** The ability to produce images of the structure and activity of the brain, spinal cord, and peripheral nervous system using biotechnology. *See also* fMRI.

**neuroinformatics.** The use of analytical tools and computational models to organize neuroscience research data.

**neurolaw.** The study of the effect of neuroscientific discoveries on legal rules and standards. For example, the extent to which individuals with brain tumors can be charged for crimes.

**neuromarketing.** A subfield of marketing research dealing with individuals' sensory, cognitive, emotional, and motor response to marketing cues.

**neurophilosophy.** The interdisciplinary integration of philosophy and neuroscience that seeks to apply neuroscientific research to ideas traditionally identified as philosophic theories.

**neuroprivacy.** The protection of an individual's thoughts from outside listening and influence.

**neuroscience.** The scientific study of the brain, spinal cord, and peripheral nervous system.

**neurotechnology.** Technological equipment whose results have an impact on the understanding and function of the human brain.

**neurotheology.** The study that attempts to explain religious experiences in the context and terminology of neuroscience.

**newborn screening.** The series of tests completed on a newborn just after birth to identify conditions likely to affect the long-term development, health, comfort, or survival of the infant.

**nonidentity problem.** A situation in which a person appears to be harmed by an action that is also imperative in the formation of their own existence.

**nonmaleficence.** The ethical obligation to do no harm.

**Nuremberg Code.** A list of ten principles written in response to the human subjects research atrocities committed in Nazi Germany; this ethical code provides principles for the ethical treatment of humans in experimental processes.

# O

**open fracture.** A specific type of bone break in which the bone penetrates the skin and is exposed to the external environment.

**opt in.** A situation in which individuals must choose to become involved, otherwise they will not be included.

**opt out.** A situation in which individuals must choose not to be included, otherwise they will be involved.

**ordinary care.** A moral theory of medical treatment derived from Catholic ideals that requires individuals to accept treatment considered minimally burdensome to the patient or community. *See also* extraordinary care.

**organ donation.** The removal of an organ or biological tissue from one individual (living or deceased) for the purpose of surgically implanting it into a living recipient.

**organ donor.** An individual, living or deceased, from whom an organ or biological tissue is taken with the intention of being placed in another human being for continued function.

**organ recipient.** An individual who receives an organ transplant.

**organ trafficking.** An international crime that involves the harvesting and sale of organs from unwilling donors or donors coerced into the sale.

**organ transplant.** The implantation of an organ from one organism to another with the intent that the recipient will continue to use the function of that organ.

**out-of-hospital DNR.** A legal document signed by a physician that states a person does not want cardiopulmonary resuscitation in a nonhospital environment. This document is not available in all states.

# P

**palliative care.** A medical specialty with a focus on symptom relief and pain management; patients receiving this type of treatment need not be terminally ill, as opposed to those receiving hospice care.

**Parkinson's disease.** A degenerative disease of the nervous system that first affects motor movement but progresses to affect thinking and behavioral processes.

**paternalism.** The concept that an individual, organization, state, or institution limits the freedom or autonomy of another individual for what is perceived as for that individual's own good; this principle drove medical care until the introduction of bioethical awareness.

**patient-centered care.** The idea that patients should be actively involved in their care plan, treatment decisions, and health-care experience.

**persistent vegetative state (PVS).** A state in which higher brain function is absent but lower brain function, such as blinking, sleep-wake cycles, and heartbeat, still appears. Patients may open their eyes and exhibit reflexes to stimuli. Usually declared when an individual has been unresponsive for more than one month.

**personalized medicine.** A medical model that organizes patients into groups based on their relative risk for certain conditions and personalizes individuals' health care based on their predicted response or risk. *See also* precision medicine.

**personhood.** The status of being a person that includes innate rights, protections, and privileges unique to the human experience.

**PET scan.** Position emission tomography (PET). An imaging test that uses radioactive tracers to identify disease in the body.

**physician-assisted suicide, provider-assisted suicide.** The process by which a health-care provider supplies an individual with the means to end his or her own life. The health-care provider does not aid the individual in administration of the medication. *See also* euthanasia, suicide.

**placebo-controlled trial.** A research experiment in which a group of subjects receives the experimental treatment and another group receives a treatment specifically designed to have no real effect, also known as a placebo.

**POLST.** An acronym for physician/provider order for life-sustaining treatment. Available in only some states, a POLST allows terminally ill or extremely elderly individuals to indicate desired medical interventions, refuse resuscitation efforts, and name a designated decision maker. Unlike an out-of-hospital DNR, this document is in force in all environments and follows the patient, not the medical record. Permits emergency medical personnel to withhold or cease resuscitative efforts.

**precision medicine.** A medical theory in which treatment, practices, and products are customized to the individual patient.

**predictive testing.** Genetic testing used to detect gene mutations associated with conditions or diseases whose symptoms appear later in life, such as Huntington's disease. *See also* genetic testing.

**preimplantation testing.** Genetic testing completed on embryos of in vitro fertilization to ensure that harmful defects or disorders are not present in the genetic material of the embryo. *See also* genetic testing.

**prenatal testing.** Screening for disease or defects in fetuses to establish the medical condition of the child and the child's potential effect on the mother before birth.

**presymptomatic testing.** *See* predictive testing.

*prima facie* **principle.** A moral requirement that can be superseded by another moral requirement.

**principlism.** A process of moral deliberation based on the four principles of autonomy, beneficence, nonmaleficence, and justice.

**privacy.** The state or condition of being free from observation by unwanted sources.

**probate.** A legal process by which a deceased individual's will is proved valid in a court of law.

**procreative beneficence.** The moral obligation of parents choosing in vitro–fertilized embryos to implant those expected to have the greatest chance for success in life based on the genetic information provided.

**procreative liberty.** The right of an individual to have control of his or her reproductive activities without interference or coercion.

**professionalism.** The basis of a field's contract with the individuals they serve, grounded in ideas of competence, altruism, knowledge, and professional conduct.

**proteomics.** The study of the structure and function of proteins in the human body, the external environment, and their interactions.

**public health ethics.** The use of ethical and moral principles to prioritize and justify courses of public health intervention and action.

## R

**randomized clinical trial (RCT).** A research method, focused on minimizing bias, in which participants are arbitrarily placed in their treatment group.

**rejection.** An unwanted outcome of organ transplantation in which the recipient's body does not accept the donated organ and it is unable to function.

**research ethics.** The application of ethical and moral concepts to (1) protecting human research subjects and (2) the design, operation, and analysis of scientific research.

**resuscitation.** The restoration of consciousness or other signs of life to an individual using medical intervention focused on returning normal vital organ function such as cardiopulmonary resuscitation (CPR).

## S

**selective abortion.** In a pregnancy with multiple embryos, the intentional removal of one or more embryos with the intent of providing a better chance of survival for the remaining embryos.

**social Darwinism.** A discredited theory that holds to the idea that principles of natural selection apply to social concepts such as politics, wealth, and success.

**somatic gene therapy.** The delivery of new genetic material into a defective component of a regular type of body cell rather than into a gamete. *See also* gamete.

**standard of care.** The minimum degree of caution required to be taken by medical professionals when providing treatment to individuals. Breaking this standard puts the individual being cared for at risk for harm.

**stem cell.** Unique cells of the human body—either embryonic or adult—that are undifferentiated, and thus have the ability to become any type of body cell. These types of cells are particularly important in genetic research. Stem cells can derive from totipotent embryonic cells or can be found as partially differentiated adult cells.

**steroids.** An organic molecule of four carbon atoms arranged in hexagonal rings. Steroids naturally occur in the human body where they are a component of the cell wall (such as cholesterol) and act to signal certain receptors. Corticosteroids are naturally occurring hormones that can also be artificially synthesized and are used to reduce inflammation. Anabolic steroids are synthesized hormones that trigger the body to increase male characteristics such as larger muscles, facial hair growth, and male-pattern baldness, among other secondary characteristics. Anabolic steroids have the potential to be abused by individuals, particularly athletes, for their enhancement of physical performance.

**substituted judgment.** In situations in which an individual is unable to communicate his or her wishes and has no documentation of desires, a surrogate decision maker (such as a health-care proxy, family members, friends, or care provider) makes the medical decisions that that individual would have made.

**suffering.** The subjective experiences of sadness, anger, frustration, and hopelessness that occur either independently of or concurrently with pain.

**suicide.** The act of intentionally ending one's own life.

**surrogacy.** *See* gestational surrogacy.

# T

**therapeutic obligation.** The idea that providers have a duty to provide individuals with what they believe to be the most effective, or "best," treatment available.

**transnational surrogacy.** A form of medical tourism in which individuals in one country, typically one of higher socioeconomic status, seek out a woman from another country to gestate their embryo to birth for an agreed price.

**transplant tourism.** The act of traveling to another country where one has determined or been told that one is more likely to receive or purchase an organ for transplant.

**treatment.** The application of drugs, surgeries, diet, and other interventions for the management and care of an individual's health and wellness needs by a health-care provider.

**truth-telling.** The obligation of medical professional to provide accurate, authentic information to their patients.

# U

**Uniform Determination of Death Act.** A model law drafted in 1980 by the National Conference of Commissioners on Uniform State Laws. This model legislation provides a legal definition of death as (1) the traditional definition of cardiopulmonary death and (2) a new definition of death by neurological criteria, also known as brain death. *See also* death by neurological criteria/brain death.

**United Nations Universal Declaration of Human Rights.** A seminal 1947 document that sets standards for international fundamental human rights to be universally protected.

# V

**vector.** A means, usually a living organism such as an insect, by which disease is transferred.

**ventilator.** A machine designed to artificially move air into and out of the lungs for patients who are unable to do so in the long term or have insufficient capability for a short time.

**vivisection.** Surgery completed on living organisms, typically animals, with central nervous systems, for research or educational purposes.

# W

**withdrawing treatment.** The decision to discontinue or remove methods of medical intervention that have already been put into effect on an individual, usually because these interventions are seen as futile efforts. *See also* futility, withholding treatment.

**withholding treatment.** The decision not to begin treatment believed to be futile by the provide or patient. *See also* futility, withdrawing treatment.

# *Index*

The index is alphabetized in word-by-word order. Page references in *italics* indicate illustrations. Page numbers followed by *t* refer to tables.

## A

ABO compatibility, 385
Abortion, 41–67
  Arizona disclosure law, 219
  bodily autonomy arguments, 52–57
  conscientious objector physicians, 57–60
  defined, 385
  fetal vs. maternal rights, 51–52, 64
  moral status of the fetus, 44–51, 62, 64
  overview, 41–42
  partial-birth, 43
  selective, 36, 58, 60–62, *61*, 393
  shared values of opponents and supporters, 62–65
  vilification of opposing views, 42–44, 51
Access to care, 363, 365
  *See also* Allocation of resources
Accommodation strategy, for conflicts of interest, 269
Act utilitarianism, 8–9
  *See also* Utilitarianism
ACTG 076 clinical trials, 349, 350
Active listening, in ethics facilitation, 289
ADD (attention deficit disorder), stimulants for, 138
Adenoviruses
  defined, 385
  as gene therapy vectors, 100, 103
Adolescents
  assent to treatment, 247, 248–249

confidentiality concerns, 237–239, 241
  genetic testing, 82–83
  organ donation, 315–317
  pregnancy and abortion issues, 63, 64
Adoption
  contested parentage guidance for genetic testing, 86
  of embryos, 20, 21, 77
Adult stem cells, 76
  *See also* Stem cell research
Advance care planning
  cultural aspects, 215
  defined, 385
  need for, 169–175, 177–178
  physician-assisted suicide concerns, 192–193, 197
Advance directives, 170–175, 193, 385
Advanced paternal age, 36
Advanced reproductive age, 18, 19, 36
Adverse events, conflicts of interest in disclosure of, 218, 263, 264, 268
Advisory Committee on Human Radiation Experiments, 340
Affordable Care Act (2010), 79, 92, 239, 274
African Americans
  health inequalities in, 366
  incarceration rates and race-based health ineqalities, 366
  negative eugenics, 117, 118, 371
  organ allocation concerns, 320–321, 323
  sickle-cell trait, 87–88
  Tuskegee Syphilis Study, 243, *251*, 252, 332, 340, 341–342, 354, 370
*Afterparty* (Gregory), 132

Age
  advanced reproductive age, 18, 19, 36
  assent vs. consent to treatment, 248–249
  capacity and, 247–248
  correlation with desire for medical intervention, 172
Age of majority, 247
Age of the City, views of death, 160
Agency, neuroethical concerns, 140–143, 145
Aging. *See* Elderly
AIDS. *See* HIV/AIDS
Alcohol abuse. *See* Substance abuse
Alexander, Shana, 320
Alleles, defined, 385
Allocation of resources
  fairness concerns, 99–100, 105–108
  futility of care considerations, 176
  organs for transplantation, 6–7, 319–325
  public health role, 374, 380–381
  utilitarianism perspective, 8
Allow natural death (AND) orders, 174, 388
Altruism
  in deception spectrum, 209, *209*
  defined, 385
  in egg donation, 23, 25
  in germ-line gene therapy, 104
  in gestational surrogacy, 30, 32, 35
  in organ donation, 312–313, 314–315, 318, 323
  paradox with self-interest, 261, 275
Altruistic unbalanced paired kidney exchange (AUPKE), 385
Alzheimer's disease, 158, 212, 236

American Academy of Pediatrics, 82, 307, 316

American Civil Liberties Union, 52

American College of Medical Genetics and Genomics, 82, 85

American College of Physicians, 240

*American College of Physicians Ethics Manual*, 189, 190

American Medical Association
  code of ethics, 71, 227–228
  on life-sustaining treatment, 163
  Nazi Doctors' Trial, observation of, 335–336
  prohibition on assisted suicide and euthanasia, 190–191
  research ethics development, 336

American Nurses Association Code of Ethics, 2–3, 228

American Pharmacists Association, 228

American Public Health Association, 228, 368

American Society for Bioethics and Humanities (ASBH), 287, 288–289

American Society for Reproductive Medicine (ASRM), 24, 26, 28, 81

Americans with Disabilities Act (1990), 92

Amygdala, role in brain function, 133

Ancillary care, in medical research, 346, 353

AND (allow natural death) orders, 174, 388

Anencephaly, moral status arguments, 50

Animal research, human research and, 332, 334–335, 336

Antiretroviral therapy (ART), allocation concerns, 8

Anxiety, about death, 162, 165, 170, 178, 387

Aristotle, 9, 131, 346, 367

Arizona abortion law, 219

*Arizona Board of Regents, Havasupai Tribe of Havasupai Reservation v.* (2008), 75–76, 355

Arizona State University, 74–76, 355

ART. *See* Antiretroviral therapy (ART), allocation concerns; Assisted reproductive technologies

Arthur, Joyce, 58, 59

Artificial insemination
  gestational surrogacy, 30, 86
  intrauterine insemination, 61

Artificial nutrition
  advance directive wishes, 171, 193
  right to refuse, 167–168, 169, 185, 187
  VSED vs. NSED, 195–196
  withholding vs. withdrawing treatment, 175

ASBH (American Society for Bioethics and Humanities), 287, 288–289

ASRM (American Society for Reproductive Medicine), 24, 26, 28, 81

Assent, 247, 248–249, 316, 385

Assessing and monitoring, public health role, 363

Assisted reproductive technologies (ARTs), 15–40
  defined, 385
  egg donation, 21, 23–27, 57
  egg freezing, 27–29, *28*, 38–39
  embryo creation and destruction, 19–21
  in vitro fertilization, 16–19, *17*, 38
  increased multiple pregnancy from, 36, 58, 60–61
  overview, 15
  procreative liberty concerns, 36–38, 41, 393
  sperm donation, 15, 21–22, *21*, 57
  surrogacy, 29–36

Assisted suicide, 183, 184, 385
  *See also* Physician-assisted suicide

*Association for Molecular Pathology v. Myriad Genetics* (2013), 79

Aston, Carla, 286

Atkins, Nevaeh, 51, 58

Attention deficit disorder (ADD), stimulants for, 138

Aulisio, Mark, 283, 284

AUPKE (altruistic unbalanced paired kidney exchange), 385

Australia
  cultural safeguards for truth-telling, 215, 216
  genetic discrimination concerns, 91
  surrogacy prohibition, 34

Autism spectrum, paternal age risks, 36

Autonomy
  abortion rights, 51, 52–58
  advance care planning, 170
  assent, 247, 248–249

confidentiality concerns, 227
defined, 385
in defining death, 158
egg donation concerns, 25
end-of-life decisions, 165–169, 170
germ-line gene therapy, 104
informed consent, 244, 245–246
Kant, Immanuel, on, 4
neuroethical concerns, 126
organ donation, 305–306, 308, 312, 319, 322
physician-assisted suicide, 181, 185, 189–190, 191, 198–200
procreative, 37–38, 110–111
public health ethics, 366, 370–372, 374–375
role in principlism, 5–6
truth-telling considerations, 208
utilitarianism views, 8
*See also* Free will

Awareness
  in virtuous actions, 9
  volitional movement research, 131

AZT (zidovudine), 349, 350

## B

Babies. *See* Infants

Baby Doe regulations, 385

Baby M case, 30, 31, 86

*Baby Mama* (film), 15, 28, 29, 31, 32, 33, 38

Baby selling, 29, 31–32

Bad news, difficulty discussing, 258

*Baird, Eisenstadt v.* (1972), 41

Baker, Robert, 339

*Ballastexistenzen* (dead-weight existences), 335

Bangladesh, organ trafficking in, 317

Bartlet, Jed (television character), 280–281

Bases, in DNA, 97–98

*Bearder et al. v. State of Minnesota, et al.* (2009), 82–83

Beauchamp, Thomas, 5, 158

Beckwith, Francis, 46, 62

Beecher, Henry, 72, 338, 339, 341

Begos, Kevin, 71

Behavior
  brain damage effects, 142
  criminal, 140–143
  health behavior changes, 377–380, *380*
  neuromarketing studies, 143

Behavioral genetics, 88–90, 98
*Beleno v. Lakey* (2009), 83
Belgium
    physician-assisted suicide legalization, 184, 192, 193
    universal health care, 201
*Bell, Buck v.* (1927), 71
*Belmont Report*, 72, 332, 344–347, 351, 356, 385–386
Beneficence
    in *Belmont* principles, 344–346, 351, 356
    defined, 386
    in defining death, 158
    in exploring physician-assisted suicide, 189, 191
    futility of care considerations, 175–176
    procreative, 110, 111, 393
    role in principlism, 6
Benny, Jack, 70
Bentham, Jeremy, 7
*Bereitschaftspotential* (readiness potential), 131
Bernard, Claude, 71–72
Best interest standard, 173
    *See also* Interest perspective
Beta-blockers, standard of care, 348
*Beth Israel Deaconess Hospital, Culliton v.* (Massachusetts 2001), 86
Better and worse, in ethics, 281
Biblical views of death, 159
*The Big C* (television show), 175, 213
Binding, Karl, 70
Biobanks
    consent challenges, 353, 355
    defined, 386
    disclosure of research results and, 79
    genetic research tissue samples, 73
Bioethics, 1–2, 386
    *See also* Medical ethics
Bioethics mediation, 289
Biological death, 154–156
    *See also* Death
Biomarkers, defined, 386
Birch, Samuel, 306
Birth control, 47
    *See also* Abortion; Contraception
Birth defects
    assisted reproductive technology risks, 19, 36
    Thalidomide-related, 42
Black Death, 372

Blastocysts, 16, 43, 386
Blinding, in research, 252
Blindness, potential somatic gene therapy, 102
Blocked fallopian tubes, 18
Blood donation, bodily autonomy concerns, 54
Blood testing
    newborn blood screenings, 82–83
    organ donation, 313
Blood transfusions, Jehovah's Witnesses refusal, 247–248, 255
Bloomberg, Michael, 379
Body donation, advance directive documentation, 174–175
Body-sustaining treatment. *See* Life-sustaining treatment
Bone marrow transplantation, bodily autonomy concerns, 52, 54, 55
Boonin, David, 57
Bosnian immigrants, cultural aspects of truth-telling, 215, 217
*Botsford, Union Pacific Railway v.* (1891), 166
Boundary crossings and violations, 271–272, *271*, 274, 386
*The Boys from Brazil* (Levin), 88
BRAIN (Brain Research through Advancing Innovative Neuro-technologies) Initiative, 123–124, 125, 386
Brain damage
    effects on personality and behavior, 142
    ethics consultation case study, 290–291, 293–295, 297
Brain death. *See* Neurological determination of death
Brain imaging. *See* Neuroimaging
Brain-machine interfaces, 139–140
Brain research
    advances in, 121–122, 123–125
    personal vs. impersonal dilemmas, 129–130
    research and clinical neuroethics, 125–127
Brain-training games, 144
Brandeis, Louis, 69, 90
Brandt, Karl, 333, *334*
Brazil, presumed consent for organ donation, 309
*BRCA1* and *BRCA2* genes, 79, 386
Breast cancer, patent litigation, 79–80

Breast-feeding, HIV prevention and, 350
Brennan, William, 41
Breslin, Abigail, *81*
Britain. *See* United Kingdom
British Medical Association, 339
British Medical Research Council, 339
Brody, Howard, 351–352
Brown, Lesley, 17, *17*, 18
Brown, Louise, 17, *17*, 20
*Bubble Boy* (film), 101
*Buck v. Bell* (1927), 71
*Burwell v. Hobby Lobby* (2014), 47
Bush, Jeb, 168
Buxtun, Peter, 342

## C

*Cake* (film), 165
California
    advance directive legislation, 170
    physician-assisted suicide legalization, 184
    vaccination law, 368
California Natural Death Act (1977), 170
*Calvert, Johnson v.* (California 1993), 86
Canada
    cultural safeguards for truth-telling, 215
    egg donation regulation, 24
    genetic discrimination concerns, 91
    physician-assisted suicide legalization, 184
    surrogacy prohibition, 34
Cancer
    false diagnosis and treatment case, 212
    fetal vs. maternal rights, 52
    gene therapy link, 102
    gonadotoxic therapies, 18
    hospice care, 163–164
    palliative care, 165
    terminal sedation considerations, 6
    truth-telling in diagnosis, 210
    unethical research on, 341
Cannold, Leslie, 62–63
*Can't We Talk about Something More Pleasant* (Chast), 169
Canterbury, Jerry, 244

*Canterbury v. Spence* (1972), 244, 246, 249
Capability, 166
Capacity
    in adolescents, 247–248, 316
    competence vs., 246–247
    defined, 386
    for health-care decision making, 166
    neuroethical concerns, 140–143
    Nuremberg Code requirements, 337
    role in informed consent, 246–248, 311, 345
    truth-telling considerations, 212–213
Capital punishment, organ donation concerns, 310, 318
*Captain America: The First Avenger* (film), 97, *98*, 99
Carder, Angela, 52
Cardiocirculatory death, 306–308, 325, 386
Cardozo, Benjamin, 243
Carrier testing, definition, 386
Cartesian dualism, 131, 157
Case-based reasoning. *See* Casuistry
Case studies
    conflicts of interest, 261–263, 331
    ethics consultation, 287–288, 290–291, 293–295, 297
    research ethics, 331–332
CASES method of ethics consultation, 290
*Casey, Planned Parenthood v.* (1992), 41
Casper, Monica, 51
Casuistry, 10, 386
*Catalona, Washington University v.* (2007), 73
Catalona, William, 73
Catholic Church
    embryo disposal concerns, 20
    extraordinary vs. ordinary means, 167
CDC. *See* US Centers for Disease Control and Prevention
cDNA (complementary DNA), 80
Ceftriaxone, 262, 331
Cell division, 76
Cell lines
    HeLa cells, 74, 354, 355
    Mo cells, 72
Cellular death, 155
Certainty, in Hedonistic Calculus, 7

Certificate-of-need laws, 273
Cesarean section, forced, 52
*Chakrabarty, Diamond v.* (1980), 79
Character
    in ethics consultation, 295
    as part of ethics, 281, 282
    in virtuous actions, 9
Chast, Roz, 169
Chatterjee, Anjan, 137, 138
Child abuse, reporting of, 238
Children
    ART health risks, 22, 36–38, 60, 61
    assent to treatment, 247, 248–249
    deception from providers during treatment, 212–213
    designer children, 82, 110–111, 113–114
    euthanasia legalization, 184
    genetic testing, 82–83, 85
    moral development, 130
    organ donation by, 315–317
    organ transplantation in, 324
    smoking prevention initiatives, 378–379
    *See also* Adolescents; Infants
Childress, James, 5, 158
Chimerism, 108–109
China
    cultural aspects of truth-telling, 217–218
    germ-line gene therapy research, 104
    organ donation from executed prisoners, 310, 318
Chromosomal abnormalities, assisted reproductive technology association, 19, 36
Chronic, noncommunicable diseases, increase in, 377, 378
Civil War (1861–1865), public health development, 373, 377
Claims, in ethics consultation, 296–297
Clear and convincing standard, for medical wishes, 168
Climate change, genetic intervention, potential benefits on human behavior, 111–112
Clinical equipoise, 351–352
Clinical ethics, 386
Clinical ethics consultants, 386
Clinical ethics consultation, 279–300

    case studies, 287–288, 290–291, 293–295, 297
    defined, 284–286, 386
    models of, 288–290
    multiple senses of medical ethics, 280–282
    overview, 279–280
    process of, 290–297
    purpose of, 282–284, 286–288, 299
    scope of practice, 294–295, 298
    types of consultations, 285–286
Clinical relevance, in disclosure of research, 78
Clinical trials
    *Belmont* principles, 344–347, 356
    placebo-controlled, 252, 345, 351–352, 393
    randomized, 252, 331, 348, 349, 351, 352, 393
    standard of care argument, 348–350
    therapeutic obligation and clinical equipoise, 350–352
    Trovan controversy, 262, 331
Clinton, Bill, 340
Clinton, Hillary, 340
Cloning
    fictional depictions of, 88, 310
    stem cell research ethics, 76, 77
Clooney, George, 170
Clustered, regularly interspaced, short palindromic repeat (CRISPR), 104, 386
Clustering of disadvantage, 365–366
Codes of ethics
    American Medical Association, 71, 227–228
    American Nurses Association, 2–3
    confidentiality aspects, 226, 227–228
    historical overview, 71–72
Coercion
    in boundary violations, 271–272
    brain imaging concerns, 134
    defined, 386
    in egg donation, 24–25
    in gestational surrogacy, 35
    informed consent concerns, 245, 345
    in organ donation, 311, 312, 313, 316

Cognitive enhancement. *See* Neurological enhancement

Cognitive liberty, defined, 386

Collaboration
  in ethics of care, 2
  in industry-sponsored research, 268, 270
  in patient-physician relationship, 209, 210

*College Holiday* (film), 70

Collins, Angela, 22, 26, 27

Collins, Francis, 123, *124*

Colombia, physician-assisted suicide legalization, 184

Coma, defined, 387
  *See also* Persistent vegetative state

Coma dépassé, 305

Comfort care, 387
  *See also* Palliative care

Commercial surrogacy, 30–31
  *See also* Gestational surrogacy

Commercialization
  genetic research, 79–80
  neurotechnologies, 143–145

Commodification
  of eggs, 26–27
  of organ donation, 318, 319
  of surrogacy, 31, 32

Common Rule, 333, 353, 355, 387

Communicable diseases
  mandatory reporting laws, 223–224, 230–231, 240
  surveillance and quarantine concerns, 374–377

Communication
  in ethics consultation, 298
  in ethics of care, 2
  euthanasia and physician-assisted suicide, language considerations, 183–184, 184t, 258–259
  *See also* Consent; Truth-telling in health care

Communitarianism, in public health ethics, 368, 369

Compassion
  in end-of-life care, 190, 199, 202
  in ethics of care, 2, 3

*Compassion in Dying v. Washington* (9th Cir. 1996), 188

Competence
  assent to treatment and, 248–249
  brain imaging role in determining, 141
  capacity vs., 246–247

defined, 387
  for health-care decision making, 166
  role in informed consent, 246–248

Complementary DNA (cDNA), 80

Complexity, in conflicts of interest, 269

Composite transplants, 303

Computer-brain interfaces, 139–140

Conception, beginning of life arguments, 45, 47

Conclusions, in ethics consultation, 296–297

Conditional organ donation, 322–324

Confidentiality, 223–242
  adolescent patients, 237–239, 241
  defined, 387
  ethical basis of, 226–227
  genetic testing concerns, 84–85, 90–92
  HIPAA protections, 228–230, 240
  informational privacy concerns, 228–231, 239–240, 241
  legal-ethical dilemmas, 224, 231–236, 240–241
  mandatory reporting laws, 223–224, 230–231, 234, 235, 374–375
  oaths and codes, 227–228
  overview, 223–224
  privacy vs., 224–226, 240
  public health surveillance powers vs., 374–375
  truth-telling considerations, 208, 238
  *See also* Privacy

Conflicts of interest, 261–277
  boundary crossings and boundary violations, 271–272, *271*, 274
  case studies, 261–263, 331
  defined, 387
  descriptive and performative aspects, 265–266, 265t
  difficulties in defining, 264–265
  donation after cardiocirculatory death, 307
  levels of the problem, 269–271, 275
  overview, 261
  proposed solutions, 268–269, 270–271, 274–275

self-referral, 272–274
  social arrangements in, 264–267, 265t, *267*, 270, 274
  support for industry viewpoint, 268

*Conn v. U.S.* (2011), 86

*Connecticut, Griswold v.* (1965), 41

Conscientious objection to abortion, 57–60

Consciousness
  brain death determination, 157
  in the fetus, 49, 50
  *See also* Disorders of consciousness

Consensus/facilitation model of ethics consultation, 288–289

Consent, 243–260
  by adolescents, 238, 241
  assent to treatment, 247, 248–249
  competence and capacity in, 246–248
  cultural aspects, 257–259
  for deceased organ donation, 308–309
  defined, 244–245, 387
  emergency, 253t, 255
  health information disclosure, 228–230
  implied, 229, 253–255, 253t
  information vs. understanding, 249–251
  moral importance of, 245–246
  Nuremberg Code requirements, 332, 337
  overview, 243–245, 245t
  presumed, 253t, 255–257, *256*, 308–309
  role in research, 251–253, *251*
  surrogate, 337
  types of, 253t
  *See also* Informed consent

Consequential considerations
  conditional organ donation, 323
  in ethics consultation, 295

Consequentialism. *See* Utilitarianism

*The Constant Gardener* (book and film), 261–262, 331

Consumer behavior, neuromarketing studies, 143

Consumption behaviors, public health initiatives, 377–380, *380*

Contact tracing, 374–375, *376*

*Contagion* (film), 231, 361, 363, 365, 369, 370, 371
Contagious diseases. *See* Communicable diseases
Context dependence
  assisted reproductive technology concerns, 38–39
  ethics of care, 2
Contraception
  emergency, 47
  sanctity of life viewpoint, 47
  Supreme Court decisions, 41
Contractarianism, 368
Contribution-based distribution of resources, 301
Controlled donation after cardiocirculatory death, 306–308
Convention for the Protection of Human Rights and Dignity of the Human Being with Regard to the Application of Biology and Medicine (Council of Europe) (1997), 336
Conversation Project, 170
*Conviction* (film), 89
Cosmetic neurology, 137
Cosmopolitan Age of Death, 160
Costs. *See* Economic considerations
Council of Europe Convention for the Protection of Human Rights and Dignity of the Human Being with Regard to the Application of Biology and Medicine (1997), 336
Council of the Transplantation Society, 316
Cranford, Ronald, 122
Crick, Francis H. C., 97
Crime
  genetic testing implications, 88–90
  neuroethical concerns, 140–143
Crisis and disaster management, 372–374
CRISPR (clustered, regularly interspaced, short palindromic repeat), 104, 386
Cruzan, Nancy, 167–168, 187
*Cruzan v. Director, Missouri Dept. of Health* (1990), 187
Cryopreservation
  defined, 387
  eggs, 27–29
  embryos, 19–20, *28*
Cuba, response to AIDS, 371–372

*Culliton v. Beth Israel Deaconess Hospital* (Massachusetts 2001), 86
Cultural considerations
  consent, 257–259
  truth-telling, 214–218, 220
Culture, defined, 387
Cutler, John Charles, 354

**D**

Dana Foundation, 122
Daniels, Norman, 99–100
Darwin, Charles, 70
Data management
  brain-training game data collection, 144
  in ethics consultation, 296–297
  neuroethical concerns, 126–127
DCD (donation after cardiocirculatory death), 306–308, 325
DDR. *See* Dead donor rule
*De facto*, as term, 387
*De facto* vs. *de jure* standard of care, 348–350
*De jure*, as term, 387
Dead donor rule (DDR)
  defined, 387
  donation after cardiocirculatory death, 306–308, 325
  neurological determination of death, 304–306, 325
Dead-weight existences (*Ballastexistenzen*), 335
Death
  cardiocirculatory, 306–308, 325, 386
  definitions of, 154–159, *155*, 157*t*, 177
  historical perspective, 159–162, *160, 161*
  informational privacy after, 225
  managed, 160, 162
  maternal mortality, 55
  in organ donors, 312
  top causes of, *160,* 161, *161*
  *See also* End-of-life preparation; Euthanasia; Neurological determination of death; Physician-assisted suicide
Death anxiety, 162, 165, 170, 178, 387
Death by neurological criteria. *See* Neurological determination of death
Death certificates, 156

*The Death of Ivan Ilyich* (Tolstoy), 162, 207
*Death on a Pale Horse* (engraving), 153, *154*
Death over Dinner program, 170
Deceased organ donation, 304–310
  consent for, 308–309
  defining death, 304–306, 325
  directed, 322–324
  donation after cardiocirculatory death, 306–308
  neurological determination of death, 156, 304–306
  by prisoners, 310
Deception, 211, 387
  *See also* Truth-telling in health care
Deception spectrum, *209*
Decision making
  by adolescents, 238, 241
  assent to treatment, 247, 248–249
  brain imaging research, 133
  capacity for, 247–248
  end-of-life concerns, 165–169
  information vs. understanding, 249–251
  informed consent role in, 244–245
  role of family in, 257–258
  surrogate decision makers, 171, 172–173, 248, 337
  truth-telling considerations, 208, 209–211
Decisional privacy, 224–225
  *See also* Privacy
Declaration of Geneva (1948), 228, 333, 336, 387
Declaration of Helsinki (1964), 333, 336, 338, 339, 343, 387
Declaration of Istanbul on Organ Trafficking and Transplant Tourism (2008), 317
deCODE Genetics, Inc., 87
Deep brain stimulation, 126, 135, 136–137, *136*
*A Defense of Abortion* (essay), 53
Delmonico, Francis, 316, 318
Dementia
  Alzheimer's disease, 158, 212, 236
  impaired driving concerns, 235
  moral status arguments, 48
Democritus, 130–131
Denial, of conflicts of interest, 269

Denmark, research conflicts of interest, 269–270
Deontology
    confidentiality concerns, 226, 227, 240
    primer on, 3–4
    in trolleyology, 4, 128–129, 130
Departments of motor vehicles (DMVs), 235
Depression
    deep brain stimulation therapy, 136
    Havasupai Indian tribe unethical research, 75
    physician-assisted suicide concerns, 190, 193
    tDCS treatment claims, 144
Descartes, René, 131, 157
The Descendants (film), 170, 175, 176
Desert-based distribution of resources, 301
Designer children
    genetic engineering concerns, 110–111, 113–114
    genetic testing concerns, 82
Designing for the Sexes (television show), 279, 286
Determinants of health, 365
Developing countries
    local vs. global standard of care, 348–350
    research ethics concerns, 346, 347, 353
Developmentally disabled people, access to organ transplantation, 321
Dewey, John, 282
Diabetes
    genetic testing group harm, 74–76, 75
    public health surveillance concerns, 375
Diagnostic testing, defined, 387
Diamond v. Chakrabarty (1980), 79
Dignity, in public health ethics, 370, 371, 378, 379
Dilemmas, personal vs. impersonal, 128, 129–130
Direct-to-consumer genetic testing, 83
Directed organ donation, 312–315, 322–324
Directive for mental illness, 173
Directives to physician and family (living wills), 171–172, 390–391

See also Advance care planning
Director, Missouri Dept. of Health, Cruzan v. (1990), 187
Dirty Dancing (film), 59
Dirty Pretty Things (film), 317
Disabilities
    abortion concerns, 45–46, 47
    brain death vs., 168, 169
    discrimination concerns, 92
    genetic intervention concerns, 116–117, 118
Disaster and crisis management, 372–374
Disclosure
    of conflicts of interest, 269
    deaths in genetic research, 103
    defined, 387
    of errors, 218
    genetic research results, 77–79
    genetic testing results, 82, 84, 86–87
    See also Truth-telling in health care
Discrimination
    in conditional organ donation, 323
    disability, 92, 116–117, 118
    genetic testing concerns, 90–92, 236
    HIV/AIDS, 234
    neuroethical concerns, 126
    physician-assisted suicide access, 200
    pregnancy, 52
Disease. See Communicable diseases; specific diseases
Disorders of consciousness, 135–136
    See also Minimally conscious state; Persistent vegetative state
Distribution of resources. See Allocation of resources
Distributive justice, 346, 347, 367
Diversity, genetic intervention concerns, 114, 115–116, 117
DMVs (departments of motor vehicles), 235
DNA, 97–98, 99, 388
DNA identification, 80, 89
DNR (do-not-resuscitate) orders, 173–174, 177, 388
Do-it-yourself neurostimulation devices, 144–145
Do no harm. See Nonmaleficence

Do-not-resuscitate (DNR) orders, 173–174, 177
Do You Really Want to Know? (documentary), 80
Doctor-patient relationship. See Patient-physician relationship
The Doctor's Word (short story), 207–208
Doe v. Marselle (1996), 84
Dolan, Christopher, 155
Donation after cardiocirculatory death (DCD), 306–308, 325, 386
Doré, Gustave, 153
Double effect
    natural law and, 4–5
    primer on, 4–5
    role in physician-assisted suicide, 188–189, 194–195
Double-effect sedation, 195
Double helix structure of DNA, 97
Down syndrome, genetic intervention concerns, 117
Dresser, Rebecca, 172
Dried blood spots, genetic testing, 82–83
Driverless cars, casuistry views, 10
Drug abuse. See Substance abuse
Dualism. See Cartesian dualism
Due process clause
    abortion arguments, 41
    right to die aspects, 187, 188
Dugan, Brian, 140, 141
Durable power of attorney for health care, 171, 172–173, 388
Duration, in Hedonistic Calculus, 7
Duty
    in deontology, 3–4
    in ending life, 181–182
    as part of ethics, 281, 282
    to truth-telling, 211
    to warn/protect third parties, 224, 231–233, 240–241, 374–375
Duty-based ethics, 4
    See also Deontology
Duty of rescue, 353
Dworkin, Ronald, 172
Dying
    active vs. passive, 154
    historical perspective, 159–162, 160, 161
    See also Death

# E

East Asian cultures, health disclosure customs, 215

Ebola outbreak (2014–2015), 177

Ecological fallacy, 381

Economic considerations
deception to obtain insurance coverage, 211, 212
egg cryopreservation, 29
egg donation compensation, 23–27
genetic interventions, 116
genetic testing, 80
in vitro fertilization, 19
organ sales and incentives for donation, 317–319
pharmaceutical industry funding of research, 268, 269–271
pharmaceutical industry marketing, 262
pharmaceutical industry payments to providers, 263, 264–265, 266–267
surrogacy, 29, 30–31, 33–36
*See also* Allocation of resources

Economic inequality. *See* Socioeconomic inequality

Edson, Margaret, 153

Education
commercial neurotechnology aids, 143–145
as determinant of health, 365
in medical ethics, 283–284, 285
teaching hospitals, 254–255

Edwards, Robert, 17, *17*, 20

EEG. *See* Electroencephalography

EEOC (US Equal Employment Opportunity Commission), 92

Efficacy, in public health ethics, 369, 371, 378, 379

Eggs (human)
cryopreservation of, 29
donation of, 21, 23–27, 57
germ-line gene therapy, 103–104
in vitro fertilization, 16, 19, 20–21, 23

Eighteen, as age of majority, 247

*Eisenstadt v. Baird* (1972), 41

Ejiofor, Chiwetel, 317

Elderly
heat wave risks, 374
impaired driving concerns, 235
physician-assisted suicide and euthanasia concerns, 181–182, 195, 197, 199, 202

Electroencephalography (EEG)
brain-machine interfaces, 140
consciousness detection, 135, 136
defined, 388
neuromarketing application, 143
volitional movement research, 131

Electronic health records, 239, 241

Embryonic vs. nonembryonic stem cells, 76–77

Embryos
adoption of, 20, 21, 77
cryopreservation of, 19–20, 28
defined, 388
disposal of, 19, 20
donation of, 19–20
embryonic vs. nonembryonic stem cells, 76
germ-line gene therapy, 103–104
in vitro fertilization, 16–17
moral status of, 19, 20, 76–77
stem cell research, 76–77

Emergency consent, 253t, 255

Emergency contraception, 47

Emergency preparedness, 372–374

Employment discrimination
genetic testing concerns, 91–92
pregnancy, 52

End-of-Life Clinic (Netherlands), 192

End-of-life preparation, 153–179
advance care planning, 169–175, 177–178
autonomy considerations, 165–169
cultural aspects, 215
definitions of death, 154–159, *155*, 157t, 177
double effect of morphine administration, 5
history of death and dying, 159–162, *160*, *161*
overview, 153–154, *154*
physician-assisted suicide concerns, 182, 196–198, 200–201, 202
provider issues, 175–177
terminal sedation considerations, 6
ways of dying, 162–165

End-stage kidney disease, 388

Ends (goods), 282, 311

England. *See* United Kingdom

Enhancement, 388

*See also* Genetic enhancement; Neurological enhancement

Enhancement/therapy distinction. *See* Therapy/enhancement distinction

Environmental justice, 90

Epicurus, 131

Epidemiology, 364

Epigenetics, 69, 90, 99, 388

Epilepsy, 132, 216

Equal protection clause, 188

Equipoise, 351–352, 388

Equity, 6, 7, 301, 367
*See also* Fairness; Social justice

Erde, Edmund, 264, 274

*Erin Brockovich* (film), 362, 363, 369, 371

Errors, disclosure of, 218

*Estate of Pack, Safer v.* (New Jersey 1996), 84–85, 236

*The Eternal Sunshine of the Spotless Mind* (film), 138

Ethical theories, 1–2
*See also specific theories*

Ethics committees, 282, 284–286, 388
*See also* Clinical ethics consultation

Ethics consultation. *See* Clinical ethics consultation

Ethics facilitation, 289

Ethics of care, 2–3

Eudaimōnia, 9

Eugenics
defined, 388
forced sterilizations, 27, 71, 335, 371
genetic determinism underpinnings, 27
genetic intervention concerns, 117–118
historical overview, 70–71

Eugenics Committee of the United States, 71

Eugenics laws, 71

Europe
brain research initiatives, 124–125
germ-line gene intervention prohibition, 104
gestational surrogacy prohibition, 34
physician-assisted suicide concerns, 200
presumed consent for organ donation, 256
*See also specific countries*

Euthanasia
abortion argument parallels, 45, 46
autonomy considerations, 185, 191
defined, 388
double effect concerns, 194–195
killing vs. allowing to die, 185–187
language considerations, 183–184, 184*t*
legalization efforts, 184, 201–202
Nazi atrocities, 27, 70, 333, 335
under negative eugenics, 27, 70
overview, 181–183
passive, 174
physician-assisted suicide vs., 183–184, 184*t*
principlism views, 189–191
pro and con arguments, 198–201
slippery-slope arguments, 192–194, 201
terminal sedation vs., 6, 195
*See also* Physician-assisted suicide
*Evangelium Vitae* (papal encyclical), 43
Evidence, in ethics consultation, 296–297
*Ex Machina* (film), 44, *44*
Ex vivo somatic gene therapy, 101
Existential distress, 165
Exoneration of crimes, with genetic testing, 89
*Experimenter* (film), 340
Experiments on Obedience to Authority, 340
Expressed sequence tags, 79
Extent, in Hedonistic Calculus, 8
Extraordinary care, defined, 388
Extraordinary vs. ordinary means, 167
*See also* Life-sustaining treatment
*Extreme Measures* (film), 256, *256*

**F**
Fabre, John, 309
Fadiman, Anne, 216, 258
Fairness
allocation of organs, 319–325
distribution of genetic intervention resources, 105–108, 113, 115
distribution of health care resources, 99–100, 301
performance-enhancing substances in sports, 106–108
role in justice, 6, 7
SSRI effects on behavior, 139
*See also* Equity; Justice
Fallacy of division, 381
False choice fallacy, 374
Family
assisted reproductive technology changes, 38, 39
cultural aspects, 215, 216, 217–218, 257–258
genetic testing implications, 86–88
genetic testing results, 84–85
organ donation consent, 308, 309, 312–313, 314
Farah, Martha, 123
*The Farewell Party* (film), 182–183
*The Fault in Our Stars* (Green), 2
FDA (US Food and Drug Administration), 80
Fecundity, in Hedonistic Calculus, 8
Federal Trade Commission, 144
Federation of State Medical Boards, 240
Feeding tubes. *See* Artificial nutrition
Fertility drugs, 16, 60–61, 168
Fetal development
abnormalities, 42, 45–46
capacity for consciousness, 49–50
health care delivery, 51–52
Fetal reduction. *See* Selective abortion
Fetal rights, 51–52, 388
Fetal screening, 80–82
Fetal viability, 41
Fey, Tina, 15
Fiala, Christian, 58, 59
Fiduciary, defined, 388
Fiduciary relationships, 205, 264
*See also* Conflicts of interest; Truth-telling in health care
Fiennes, Ralph, 331
*50/50* (film), 362
Film. *See specific films*
*Final Destination* (film series), 162
Final Rule (organ donation), 322
Financial considerations. *See* Economic considerations
Finkbine, Sherri, 42
Five Wishes advance directive form, 170
fMRI (functional magnetic resonance imaging), 133–134, 135, 140, 388
Footbridge Dilemma, 128–130, 139
Forensic testing, 388
Foster, David, 308
Fourth Amendment, DNA identification concerns, 89–90
Fox, Renee, 307
Fragile X syndrome, 85, 388
Frailty, defined, 388
France
egg donation regulation, 24
sperm donation limitations, 22
Francke, Linda Bird, 44–45
Franklin, Rosalind, 97
Free will
autonomy connection, 165
criminal culpability, 88–89
neuroethical concerns, 130–131, 140–143
*See also* Autonomy
Freedman, Benjamin, 217, 351, 352
Freedman, Lori, 58–59
Freedom. *See* Liberty
Freedom of conscience, 59
Freezing of embryos and eggs. *See* Cryopreservation
Friedlander, Henry, 70
Frustaci septuplets, 60, 61
Full committee ethics consultations, 285
Functional magnetic resonance imaging (fMRI), 133–134, 135, 140, 388
Futility, defined, 389
Futility of care, 175–177
Future generations
genetic engineering concerns, 113
germ-line gene therapy effects, 103–104

**G**
Galton, Francis, 70
Gametes, defined, 389
*See also* Eggs (human); Sperm
GAO (US Government Accountability Office), 83
Garland-Thomson, Rosemarie, 117
*Gattaca* (film), 70, 71, 236, *237*
Gelsinger, Jesse, 102–103
Gene therapy. *See* Genetic therapy
Genes
deactivated, 99
defined, 97, 389
functioning of, 97–98

Genesis, book of, on death, 159

Genetic counseling, 82, 85–86, 389

Genetic determinism, 27, 389

Genetic disorders
abortion arguments, 45–46
assisted reproductive technology risks, 36
confidentiality concerns, 235–236
duty to warn/protect third parties, 224

Genetic engineering
arguments against enhancement uses, 112–115
chimerism, 108–109
defined, 389
designing children, 110–111
disabilities implications, 116–117
eugenics concerns, 117–118
inequality concerns, 115–116
policy making implications, 108–109, 112
potential climate change benefits, 111–112

Genetic enhancement
arguments against, 112–115
chimerism, 108–109
defined, 389
distinction from gene therapy, 104–108, *107*
genetic engineering implications, 108, 109
overview, 99

Genetic Information Nondiscrimination Act (GINA) (2008), 90, 92, 389

Genetic interventions, 97–120
arguments against enhancement uses, 112–115
chimerism, 108–109
climate change, potential for benefits, 111–112
defined, 389
designing children, 110–111
disabilities implications, 116–117
eugenics concerns, 117–118
germ-line gene therapy, 103–104, 109
inequality concerns, 115–116
overview, 97–99, *98*
policy making implications, 109–110, 112
somatic gene therapy, 99–103, *100*, 108

therapy/enhancement distinction, 104–108, *107*
types of, 109t

Genetic perspective
moral status of fetuses, 45–47
objections to violinist example, 57

Genetic research
disclosure of deaths, 103
genetic engineering concerns, 109–110
genetic therapy trials, 101–103
research ethics concerns, 72
stored tissue samples, 72–74
Universal Declaration on the Human Genome and Human Rights, 109

Genetic testing, 69–96
in clinical care, 83–86
confidentiality concerns, 235–236, *237*
defined, 389
disclosure of research results, 77–79
group harms from, 74–76, *75*
for health-care decision making, 80–83, *81*
historical aspects, 70–72
implications for parentage and families, 86–88
intellectual property concerns, 72–73, 79–80
in law enforcement, 88–90
overview, 69–70
privacy and discrimination concerns, 69, 90–92, 236
research supporting, 71–74
stem cell research, 76–77

Genetic therapy
defined, 389
distinction from genetic enhancement, 104–108, *107*
germ-line, 103–104, 109
overview, 98–99
somatic, 99–103, *100*, 108, 394

Genetics, defined, 69

Genetics Institute, 72–73

Geneva Declaration (1948), 228, 333, 336, 387

Genome
defined, 97, 389
editing, 104
genetic engineering concerns, 109–110

Human Genome Project, 72, 91, 390

Genova, Lisa, 80

George Washington University, 52

Germ-line gene therapy, 103–104, 109, 389

Germany
egg donation prohibition, 24
research ethics, 333–335
*See also* Nazi regime

Gestational surrogacy
Baby M case, 30, 31, 86
baby selling concerns, 29, 31–32
commercial surrogacy, 30–31
defined, 389
exploitation concerns, 29, 32–35
genetic vs. legal parentage, 86
overview, 29–30
transnational surrogacy, 33–36, 394

Gey, George Otto, 354

Gibson, William, 139

Gilligan, Carol, 2

GINA (Genetic Information Nondiscrimination Act) (2008), 90, 92, 389

GiNo's DicE method of ethics consultation, 290

Global health ethics, defined, 389

Global vs. local standard of care, 348–350

*Glucksberg, Washington v.* (1997), 188–189

God committees, 320

Golde, David, 72–73

Gonadotoxic therapies, 18

Good and bad, in ethics, 281, 282

Good Samaritan obligations, 353, 389

Gordon, Elisa J., 320

Gosselin family, 60, 61

Gostin, Lawrence, 371

GRACE method of ethics consultation, 293–295

Graded-risk model of boundary crossings, 271–272, *271*

Graft, defined, 389
*See also* Organ transplantation

*Gramley, Stewart v.* (1997), 88

*Grandma* (film), 51, 65

*Gray Matters* (reports), 124

Greatest happiness principle. *See* Utilitarianism

Greek mythology views of death, 159

Greely, Henry, 74

Green, John, 2
Gregory, Daryl, 132
*Grey's Anatomy* (television show), 211, 223, 257–258
*Grimes v. Kennedy Krieger Institute (2001)*, 77–78
*Griswold v. Connecticut* (1965), 41
Groningen Protocol, 184, 389
Group harm, 74–76, *75*
    *See also* Harm principle
Guatemala, Sexually Transmitted Diseases Inoculation Study, 340, 354–355
Gundersen Health System, 170
Guyer, Bernard, 60
Gyges the Lydian, 298–299
Gyllenhaal, Jake, 101, *267*

**H**

Habits, in ethics consultation, 291–292
Hackman, Gene, 256, *256*
Haiti earthquake (2010), 373
*Hamlet* (play), 153
Hammond, Karen, 60
Hanson, Margaret, 22, 26, 27
Happiness
    eudaimōnia concept, 9
    in utilitarianism, 7–9
*Hard Sell* (Reidy), 266, *267*
Harm, avoiding risk of. *See* Nonmaleficence
Harm principle
    allowing vs. inflicting harm, 128
    assisted reproductive technology risks, 36–38
    in *Belmont* principles, 345
    defined, 389
    egg donation, 25
    genetic testing, 74–76, *75*
    genetic testing confidentiality, 84–85
    group harm, 74–76, *75*
*Harnicher v. University of Utah Medical Center* (1998), 82
Harrelson, Woody, *314*
Harvard Medical School, 157, 305, 338
Havasupai Indian tribe, 74–76, *75*, 355
*Havasupai Tribe of Havasupai Reservation v. Arizona Board of Regents* (2008), 75–76, 355
Health behaviors, difficulty of changing, 377–380, *380*

Health-care ethics committees, 282, 284–286
    *See also* Clinical ethics consultation
Health-care professionals
    duty to warn/protect third parties, 224, 232–233
    responsibilities of, 279–280
    *See also* Mental health professionals; Physicians
Health history. *See* Medical history
Health inequalities
    genetic intervention concerns, 115–116
    public health role, 364, 365–366, 381–382
    *See also* Socioeconomic inequality
Health insurance
    deception from providers to ensure coverage, 211, 212
    genetic discrimination concerns, 91–92
    HIPAA privacy protections, 229
    in vitro fertilization coverage, 19
Health Insurance Portability and Accountability Act (HIPAA) (1996)
    confidentiality concerns, 225, 228–230, 239, 240
    defined, 389
    electronic health records management, 239
    genetic discrimination protections, 92
Hearing loss, as social death, 158
Heart attack patients, beta-blocker treatment, 348
Heart transplantation, 303
Hedonistic Calculus, 7–8
HeLa cell line, 74, 354, 355
Held, Virginia, 2
Heller, Jean, 341, 342
Helsinki Declaration (1964), 333, 336, 338, 339, 343, 387
Hemophilia, somatic gene therapy, 101–102
Herd immunity, 8
Higher-ordered multiple pregnancies (HOMPs), 58, 390
    *See also* Multiple gestation and births
HIPAA. *See* Health Insurance Portability and Accountability Act
Hippocratic Corpus, 6
Hippocratic Oath

confidentiality aspects, 227
    defined, 390
    nonmaleficence in, 6, 71
    prohibition on assisted suicide and euthanasia, 190
    therapeutic obligation, 350–351
HIV/AIDS
    ACTG 076 clinical trials, 349, 350
    confidentiality concerns, 226–227
    Cuba public health response, 371–372
    duty to warn/protect third parties, 224, 234, 374–375
Hmong cultural beliefs, 257–258
*Hobby Lobby, Burwell v.* (2014), 47
Hoche, Alfred, 70
Homicide, defined, 185
HOMPs (higher-ordered multiple pregnancies), 58, 390
    *See also* Multiple gestation and births
Hospice care
    defined, 390
    end-of-life planning, 163–164, 177
    physician-assisted suicide concerns, 196–198, 200–201, 202
Hospitalization
    death during, 161, 162–163, 177
    implied consent concerns, 229, 254–255
*House M.D.* (television show), 207, 208–209
*HTT* gene, 80, 81, 86–87
Huard, Patrick, *21*, 22
Human Brain Project (European Commission), 124–125
Human Genome Project, 72, 91, 390
Human leukocyte antigen, 390
Human Radiation Experiments, 340
Huntington's disease
    confidentiality concerns, 236
    consent in diagnosis, 254
    defined, 390
    genetic testing concerns, 80, 86–87, 91
Hysterectomy, defined, 390

**I**

*I Am Legend* (film), 97, 99
Iceland, national genetic database, 86, 87

ICSI (intracytoplasmic sperm injection), 16, 19, 36, 390
ICUs (intensive care units), 162–163, 177, 390
Identity
brain-machine interfaces, 140
genetic testing implications, 83, 87–88
neuroethical concerns, 121, 127
nonidentity problem, 37, 392
Imaging, brain. *See* Neuroimaging
*The Immortal Life of Henrietta Lacks* (Skloot), 74, 355
Immunizations. *See* Vaccines
Immunosuppressants, 303
Impaired drivers, 224, 235, 390
Impersonal vs. personal dilemmas, 128, 129–130
Implantation, embryo
abortion arguments, 47
physical process, 16, 17
Implied consent, 229, 253–255, 253t
*The Impossible* (film), 372, 373
In utero, defined, 390
In vitro fertilization (IVF)
defined, 390
with donor eggs, 23
history, 16–19, *17*
with patient eggs, 23
potential harm from, 36
for surrogacy, 30
In vivo, defined, 390
In vivo somatic gene therapy, 101
Incidental findings, 78, 127
India, transnational surrogacy, 33–34
Induced pluripotent stem cells (IPSCs), 76
*See also* Stem cell research
Inequality. *See* Equity; Fairness; Health inequalities; Socioeconomic inequality
Infants
ethics consultation case study, 287–288
euthanasia legalization, 184
genetic testing, 82–83
HIV prevention, 349, 350
moral development, 130
newborn screening, 82–83, 392
Infectious and contagious diseases. *See* Communicable diseases
Infertility, causes of, 18
Infertility treatment. *See* Assisted reproductive technologies
Informal consultation, 225

Information vs. understanding, in informed consent, 249–251
Informational privacy, 224–225, 390
*See also* Confidentiality; Privacy
Informed, as term, 245
Informed consent
in *Belmont* principles, 344–345
Common Rule, 333, 353, 355, 387
competence and capacity in, 246–248, 311 —
cultural aspects, 257–259
deep brain stimulation therapy, 136
defined, 244, 253t, 390
disclosure of research controversy, 78
genetic testing and research, 72, 73, 74–76, 87
information vs. understanding, 249–251
moral importance of, 245–246
neuroscience research, 126
newborn blood screenings, 82–83
Nuremberg Code requirements, 332, 337
organ donation, 311
overview, 244–245, 245t
patients with disorders of consciousness, 135
recency of concept, 244
role in research, 251–253, *251*, 338–339
therapeutic research exemption, 338–339
truth-telling considerations, 208, 210–211
Tuskegee Syphilis Study, 342, 343
*See also* Consent
InFuse (recombinant human bone morphogenic protein-2), 262–263, 264, 274–275
Innocence Project, 89
*Inside the O'Briens* (Genova), 80
*The Insider* (film), 378
Institute of Medicine, 165, 196, 354
Institutional review boards (IRBs)
Common Rule revisions, 355
defined, 390
establishment of, 252, 332, 343, 344, 356

in Netherlands, 337–338
Instrumental, defined, 390
Insurance. *See* Health insurance
Integrity, in public health ethics, 369–370
Intellectual property, genetic research, 72–73, 74, 79–80
Intensity, in Hedonistic Calculus, 7
Intensive care units (ICUs), 162–163, 177, 390
Intention
brain imaging role in determining, 142–143
killing vs. allowing to die, 185–187
law enforcement implications, 142–143
neuroethical concerns, 128
Interest perspective
moral status of fetuses, 48–50
role in informed consent, 244, 246
*See also* Conflicts of interest
International Federation of Gynecology and Obstetrics, 47
Intracytoplasmic sperm injection (ICSI), 16, 19, 36, 390
Intrauterine insemination, 61
Intrinsic, defined, 390
IPSCs (induced pluripotent stem cells), 76
*See also* Stem cell research
Iran, legal sale of organs, 317, 319
IRBs. *See* Institutional review boards
Irreversible coma criteria, 157, 157t, 305
Ishiguro, Kazuo, 310
*The Island of Dr. Moreau* (Wells), 109
Isolation, social, 158, 160, 161, 162, 374
Isolation vs. quarantine, 370
Israel, surrogacy prohibition, 34
Italy, egg donation prohibition, 24
IVF. *See* In vitro fertilization
Ivy, Andrew, 335–336

## J

Japan earthquake and tsunami (2011), 373
Jargon, avoiding, 250
Jefferson, Thomas, 71
Jehovah's Witnesses, consent and, 247–248

Jewish Chronic Disease Hospital Study, 332, 340, 341
John Paul II (pope), 43, 45, 46
Johns Hopkins University, 74
Johnson & Johnson, 52
*Johnson v. Calvert* (California 1993), 86
Joint Commission, 285, 307
*Jon and Kate Plus 8* (television show), 60
Jonsen, Albert, 10, 261, 367
Judgment, substituted, 173, 394
*Juno* (film), 43
Justice
    in *Belmont* principles, 344–345, 346–347, 351, 356
    defined, 390
    in defining death, 158
    futility of care considerations, 176–177
    in organ donation, 322–324
    in public health ethics, 367, 381–382
    public health role in, 363, 365
    role in principlism, 6–7
    in standard of care argument, 350
    *See also* Fairness
Justification
    in ethics consultation, 293
    in medical ethics, 284

**K**

Kaczor, Christopher, 47, 57, 307
Kamrava, Michael, 60
Kant, Immanuel, 3, 4, 165, 311
Kantian ethics, 4, 84
    *See also* Deontology
Kass, Leon, 112–113, 114, 115
Kass, Nancy, 367
*Kate Plus 8* (television show), 60
Katz, Jay, 84
Kennedy, Edward, 343
*Kennedy Institute of Ethics Journal*, 306
Kennedy Krieger Institute, 77–78
*Kennedy Krieger Institute, Grimes v.* (2001), 77–78
Kevorkian, Jack, 182, 183
Kidney disease
    dialysis access, 320
    end-stage, 320, 388
    in kidney donors, 311–312, 316
Kidney transplantation
    allocation of organs, 320, 324

donation after cardiocirculatory death, 306
    living donation, 311–312, 317
    as most common transplanted organ, 303
    organ allocation concerns, 321
Kilgour, David, 318
Killing vs. allowing to die, 185–187, 195–196
King, Alonzo, 89
*King, Maryland v.* (2013), 89
Kissling, Frances, 62, 63
Krumholz, Harlan, 263

**L**

La Crosse, Wisconsin, advance directives participation, 170
Lacks, Henrietta, 74, *354*, 355
*Lakey, Beleno v.* (2009), 83
Language considerations
    physician-assisted suicide and euthanasia, 183–184, 184*t*
    translation services, 258–259
*Lawrence Berkeley Laboratory, Norman-Bloodsaw v.* (Ninth Circuit 1998), 91
Laws. *See* Legal considerations; *specific laws*
le Carré, John, 261–262, 331
Lead paint abatement, 77–78
Learning. *See* Education
Least destructive alternative, 370
Least restrictive alternative, 370, 371, 378
Legal considerations
    compulsory vaccination laws, 8, 368, 379
    confidentiality, 228–236, 240
    egg donation, 23–24
    genetic testing role, 88–90
    genetic vs. legal parentage, 86
    gestational surrogacy, 34
    neuroethical concerns, 140–143
    organ trafficking, 317–318
    physician-assisted suicide legalization, 184, 201–202
    *See also* Mandatory reporting laws; Policy making; *specific court cases*; *specific laws*
Legal death, 156
    *See also* Death
*Leland Stanford Jr. University Board of Trustees, Salgo v.* (154 Cal. App. 2d 1957), 244

Leonard, John, 106, 107
Leukemia, somatic gene therapy-related, 101
Levin, Ira, 88
Levonorgestrel, 47
LGBT concerns, truth-telling to providers, 213–214
Liberty
    genetic intervention objections, 113
    harm principle, 25
    least restrictive alternative concept, 370, 371, 378
    procreative, 36–38, 41, 393
    soft-drink consumption restrictions, 379–380
Libet, Benjamin, 131
Lies. *See* Lying
Life expectancy, increase in, 364–365
Life insurance, genetic discrimination concerns, 92
Life support. *See* Life-sustaining treatment
Life-sustaining treatment
    donation after cardiocirculatory death concerns, 306
    emergency consent, 255
    living will expression of desires, 171–172
    neurological determination of death concerns, 304–305
    physician/provider orders for, 174, 393
    right to refuse, 163, 167, 185–187, 202
    withholding or withdrawing, 175, 183, 185–187, 188
*Limitless* (film), 121
Lindemann Nelson, Hilde, 10
Liposomes, as gene therapy vectors, 100
Live Organ Donor Consensus Group, 316
Liver transplantation
    alcohol use prohibition, 319, 320
    frequency of, 303
    living donation, 311, 312, 317
    organ allocation concerns, 320
Living nondirected donors, 314–315
Living organ donation, 310–319
    balancing risks and benefits, 311–312, 325
    directed, 312–315, 322–324
    financial considerations, 317–319
    by minors, 315–317

Living wills, 171–172, 390–391

Local vs. global standard of care, 348–350

London, Alex John, 348

Louisville, Kentucky, Teenage Parents Program, 64

*Love & Other Drugs* (film), 266, *267*

Ludmerer, Kenneth, 71

Luminosity, 144

Lung transplantation, 303, 311, 324

Luxembourg, physician-assisted suicide legalization, 184

Lying
    brain imaging research, 134
    deception spectrum, *209*
    deception vs., 211
    reasons for, 209
    *See also* Truth-telling in health care

## M

Magnetic resonance imaging (MRI)
    defined, 391
    for determination of death, 157
    functional magnetic resonance imaging, 133–134, 135, 140, 388
    neuroethical studies, 1
    in physician-owned facilities, 273

*The Making of the Unborn Patient* (Casper), 51

*Malcolm in the Middle* (television show), 173, 175

Mallon, Mary ("Typhoid Mary"), 375–376, *376*

Managed death, 160, 162

Mandatory reporting laws
    child abuse, 238
    communicable diseases, 223–224, 230–231, 240, 372
    confidentiality concerns, 230–231
    defined, 391
    diabetes, 375
    HIV/AIDS, 224, 234, 374–375
    impaired drivers, 235
    physician-assisted suicide, 193
    surveillance and quarantine powers, 374–375

Manslaughter, defined, 186

Marginalized groups, truth-telling considerations, 213–214

Marquis, Don, 45, 46, 351

*Marselle, Doe v.* (1996), 84

Marshall, Henry Rutgers, 127

Martinez, Richard, 272

*Maryland v. King* (2013), 89

Matas, Arthur, 318

Matas, David, 318

Maternal mortality, 55

Maternal rights, 51–52, 391

Matesanz, Rafael, 309

*The Matrix* (film series), 127

Mature minors, 247, 391

Maxims, defined, 4

Maynard, Brittany, 182

Mayo Clinic, 55

McCaughey septuplets, 60, 61

McFall, Robert, 54

*McFall v. Shimp* (1978), 54

McKeown, Thomas, 364, 365

McMath, Jahi, 155–156, *155*, 158

MCS (minimally conscious state), 135–136, 391

Meat consumption, contribution to climate change, 111–112

Meat intolerance, through genetic intervention, 112

Mecca, Jensen T., 268–269

Medical death, 156–158
    *See also* Death

Medical ethics
    defined, 391
    empirical and normative aspects, 1–2
    multiple senses of, 280–282

Medical excuses in organ donation, 313

Medical history
    confidentiality concerns, 226, 229
    electronic health records management, 239
    sperm donation concerns, 22
    truth-telling considerations, 27

Medical power of attorney, 171, 172–173

Medical technology. *See* Assisted reproductive technologies; Genetic interventions; Life-sustaining treatment; Neurotechnology

Medical tourism
    defined, 391
    transnational surrogacy, 33–36
    transplant tourism, 317–318, 394

Medicare
    end-of-life care, 170, 197
    physician-owned facility procedures, 273

Medicine vs. public health, 361–362, 362t

Medtronic, 262–263, 264, 274–275

*Meet Joe Black* (film), 153

Memory-enhancing substances, 137–139

Mendel, Gregor, 69

Mengele, Josef, 333

*Mens rea* principle, 142, 391

Mental disabilities, moral status arguments, 48

Mental health professionals
    boundary crossings and boundary violations, 272
    duty to warn/protect third parties, 224, 232–233

Mental illness
    brain imaging research, 140–141
    deception in treatment, 212, 220
    deep brain stimulation therapy, 136
    directive for, 173
    HIPAA privacy protections, 230
    law enforcement implications, 140–141
    organ transplantation concerns, 319
    physician-assisted suicide concerns, 193

Merit-based distribution of resources, 301

Metabolomics, 391

Methyl groups, 69, 90

Metrodin, 60

Milan, Italy, Black Death response, 371

Milgram, Stanley, 340

Military research ethics, 338–339

Mill, John Stuart, 7, 25, 245

Miller, Franklin, 305, 351–352

Mind-body problem, neuroethical concerns, 127

Mind reading, neuroethical concerns, 132–134

Minimally conscious state (MCS), 135–136, 391

*Minority Report* (film), 143

Minors, defined, 391
    *See also* Adolescents; Children

Miscarriage, moral status of fetus concerns, 47, 51

*Miss Evers' Boys* (play and film), 342, 370

Mo cell line, 72

Modafinil, for performance enhancement, 121
Molecular medicine, defined, 391
Moll, Albert, 333
Moniruzzaman, Monir, 317
Montana, physician-assisted suicide ruling, 184
Moon, Brandon, 89
Moore, Francis, 311
Moore, John, 72–73
*Moore v. Regents of the University of California* (1990), 72, 73
Moral argumentation, in ethics consultation, 296–297
Moral brain, 128–130, *129*
Moral case deliberations, 289
Moral considerations, in ethics consultation, 293–295
Moral evaluation, in ethics consultation, 292–293
Moral guidance
    designer children, 110–111
    informed consent, 245–246
    therapy/enhancement distinction, 105–108
Moral instrumentation, in ethics consultation, 295–296
Moral law, 3–4
Moral philosophy
    ethics of care approach, 2
    neuroethical concerns, 128–130, *129*
Moral psychology, as discipline, 128
Moral reasoning
    in ethics of care, 2
    SSRI effects on behavior, 139
Moral reflection, in ethics consultation, 291
Moral responsibility. *See* Responsibility
Moral rights
    conscientious objection to abortion, 57–60
    fetal vs. maternal rights, 51–52, 64
    fetuses, 44–51
Moral status
    defined, 391
    of embryos, 19, 20, 76–77
    of fetuses, 44–51, 62, 64
Moral value
    of assent, 249
    of autonomy, 245
Moral virtue, 9

Morality
    habit of, 291–292
    neuroscience of, 128
Morning-after pill. *See* Emergency contraception
Morphine administration, 5, 164, 185
Morrison sextuplets, 60–61
Mortality. *See* Death
Motivation
    in conflicts of interest, 265–266, 265*t*, 270, 274
    in deception spectrum, 209, *209*
    neuroethical concerns, 128
    organ donation, 311, 314–315
Mourning rituals, 159–160
MRI. *See* Magnetic resonance imaging
mRNA, defined, 391
Multiple discussions, need for, 251
Multiple gestation and births
    health risks from, 60, 61–62
    IVF risks, 36
    selective abortion concerns, 58, 60–62, *61*
Murder, defined, 185–186
Murphy, Paul, 309
Muscular dystrophy, gene therapy potential, 108
*My Sister's Keeper* (book and film), 52–53, 81–82, *81*, 238, 315
Myriad Genetics, 79–80
*Myriad Genetics, Association for Molecular Pathology v.* (2013), 79
Mythological views of death, 159

**N**

Narayan, R. K., 207–208
Narrative ethics, in virtue ethics, 10–11
National Bioethics Advisory Commission, 73
National Commission for the Protection of Human Subjects of Biomedical and Behavioral Research, 72, 332, 333, 343–344
National Human Genome Research Institute, 80, 102
National Institutes of Health (NIH)
    ACTG 076 clinical trials, 349–350
    call for new research oversight division, 270–271
    gene therapy concerns, 102
    genetic research funding, 72
    neuroethics workgroup, 124

    research ethics development, 339, 341
    stem cell research guidelines, 76, 77
National Organ Transplant Act, 317, 391
National priority purposes, disclosure of information, 230
National Research Act (1974), 72, 332, 343, 391
National Socialist German Workers' Party (Nazi Party), 335
National Socialist Physicians' League, 70
Native Americans
    forced sterilizations, 117
    Havasupai Indian tribe, 74–76, *75*, 355
    Navajo health disclosure customs, 215
    views of death, 159
Natural law, 4–5
Naturally stopping eating and drinking (NSED), 195–196
Nature-nurture debate, 69, 88, 118
Navajo people, health disclosure customs, 215
Nazi Doctors' Trial, 332, 333–336, *334*
Nazi Party (National Socialist German Workers' Party), 335
Nazi regime
    negative eugenics, 27, 70, 117, 333
    unethical research, 332–336, *334*, 338, 341
Need-based distribution of resources, 301
Negative eugenics, 27, 71, 117, 118, 371
Nelson, Hilde Lindemann, 10
Netherlands
    moral case deliberations, 289
    physician-assisted suicide and euthanasia practices, 184, 192, 195
    research ethics, 337–338
    universal health care, 201
Neurodeterminism, 391
Neuroethics, 121–151
    commercial applications, 143–145
    defined, 122–123, 391
    health and enhancement applications, 135–140, *136*
    historical overview, 121–125

Neuroethics, *continued*
    law and policy applications,
        140–143
    mind reading applications,
        132–134
    research and clinical questions,
        125–127
    theoretical questions, 127–132,
        *129*
Neuroethics: Mapping the Field
    conference (2002), 122
Neuroimaging
    defined, 391
    for determination of death, 157
    for disorders of consciousness,
        135–136
    law enforcement implications,
        140–143
    lie detection applications,
        133–134
    mind reading concerns, 133–134
Neuroinformatics, defined, 391
Neurolaw, defined, 391
Neurological determination of death
    criteria for, 157, 157*t*, 305
    defined, 387
    McMath, Jahi, case, *155*,
        155–156
    need for legal definition, 156
    organ donation considerations,
        156, 304–306, 325
    questions of humanness in, 169
Neurological enhancement
    commercial neurotechnology
        aids, 143–145
    neuroethical concerns, 137–140
*Neuromancer* (Gibson), 139
Neuromarketing, 134, 143, 391
Neuromaterialism, 132
Neurophilosophy, defined, 391
Neuroprivacy, 127, 391
Neurorealism, 125
Neuroscience
    advances in, 121–122,
        123–125
    defined, 391
    free will concerns, 131
    neuroethical concerns, 125–127,
        137–140
Neurotechnology
    advances in, 121–122, 123–125
    clinical applications, 135–137
    defined, 392
    neuroethical concerns, 125–127,
        137–140

neurological enhancement appli-
    cations, 137–140, 143–145
Neurotheology, 131–132, 392
*Never Let Me Go* (book and film),
    310
New Jersey, death declaration laws,
    156, 305
New York, death declaration laws,
    156, 305
New York City Department of
    Health, 375, 380
New York Metropolitan Board of
    Health, 373
New Zealand, cultural safeguards for
    truth-telling, 215
Newborn screening, 82–83, 392
    *See also* Infants
Nicarico, Jeanine, 140
Nicolelis, Miguel, 140
Nigeria, clinical trial controversy, 331
NIH BRAIN Neuroethics Work-
    group, 124
Nocebo effect, 216
Noddings, Nel, 2
Noncommercial surrogacy, 30, 32
Noncommunicable diseases, chronic,
    increase in, 377, 378
Nondirected organ donation,
    313–315
Nonidentity problem, 37, 392
Nonmaleficence
    in *Belmont* principles, 345
    cultural safeguards for truth-tell-
        ing, 215
    defined, 392
    in defining death, 158
    futility of care considerations,
        176
    in organ donation, 304, 306,
        318
    physician-assisted suicide con-
        cerns, 189, 191
    in principlism, 6, 7, 158
Noonan, John T., 50
NOPP (Notice of Privacy Practices),
    229
Normal functioning, difficulty defin-
    ing, 137
*Norman-Bloodsaw v. Lawrence Berke-
    ley Laboratory* (Ninth Circuit
    1998), 91
Normative fallacy, 130
Normative medical ethics, 1–2
Notice of Privacy Practices (NOPP),
    229

NSED (naturally stopping eating and
    drinking), 195–196
Nuffield Council principles,
    347–348
Nuremberg Code, 332–336, *334*,
    338, 392
Nuremberg war crimes trials,
    332–336, *334*
Nursing, ethics of care approach, 2–3
Nurture-nature debate. *See* Nature-
    nurture debate
Nutrition, public health initiatives,
    379–380, *380*
NZT (fictional pill), 121

## O

Obama, Barack, 123–124, *124*,
    354
Obama, Michelle, 379
Obligations. *See* Responsibility
O'Connor, Sandra Day, 188–189
"Octomom" (Nadya Suleman), 60
O'Donnell, Christy, 181
*Of the Epidemics* (Hippocrates), 6
Office for Civil Rights, 230
Office of Science and Technology
    Policy (OSTP), 355
Office of the Surgeon General,
    338–339
O'Leary, Hazel, 340
Open fracture, defined, 392
Opt in, defined, 392
Opt-in model of consent for deceased
    organ donation, 308–309
Opt out, defined, 392
Opt-out model of consent for
    deceased organ donation,
    308–309
OPTN (Organ Procurement and
    Transplantation Network), 303,
    323
Ordinary care, defined, 392
Ordinary vs. extraordinary means,
    167
    *See also* Life-sustaining treatment
Oregon, physician-assisted suicide
    legalization, 184, 193, 199
Oregon Death with Dignity Act
    (1997), 184, 193
Organ donation
    advance directive documentation,
        174–175
    after cardiocirculatory death,
        306–308

deceased donation, 156, 304–310

defined, 392

justice in distribution, 6–7

presumed consent for, 255–257

Organ donor, defined, 392

Organ Procurement and Transplantation Network (OPTN), 303, 323

Organ recipient, defined, 392

Organ trafficking, 317–318, 392

Organ transplantation, 303–329

allocation system questions, 319–325

deceased donation, 156, 304–310, 325

defined, 392

living donation, 310–319, 325

need for legal definition of death, 156

overview, 303–304

Ornithine transcarbamylase deficiency (OTC), 102–103

Osler, William, 72

OSTP (Office of Science and Technology Policy), 355

OTC (ornithine transcarbamylase deficiency), 102–103

Ought implies can principle, 350, 352

Out-of-hospital DNR, 174, 392

Ovarian hyperstimulation syndrome, 23

Ovarian torsion, 23

Overreach, in ethics consultation, 294

Oversight committees. *See* Institutional review boards

Ovulation

contraception effects, 47

in vitro fertilization, 16, 23

Oxytocin, neuroethical concerns, 139

**P**

Pack, George, 85

Pain

beneficence recognition of, 6

epidemic of, 165

suffering vs., 165

Pain management

hospice care, 163–164

need for, 165

palliative care, 164–165

physician-assisted suicide concerns, 194, 197, 198–199

Palliative care

defined, 392

end-of-life planning, 164–165

physician-assisted suicide concerns, 196–198, 200–201, 202

Pan American Sanitary Bureau, 354

Pancreas transplantation, 303

Pappworth, Maurice, 339, 341

*Parens patriae* power, 371

Parentage

genetic testing implications, 86–88

incidental findings, 78

Parkinson's disease

deep brain stimulation therapy, 126, 136

defined, 392

as social death, 158

somatic gene therapy, 101

Partial-birth abortion, 43

Partial-Birth Abortion Ban Act of 2003, 43

Passive euthanasia, 174

Pastoral Age of death, 159–160

*Pate v. Threlkel* (Florida 1995), 84

Patents, genetic testing and research, 72–73, 79–80

Paternal age, advanced, 36

Paternalism

autonomy vs., 6, 370–372

defined, 392

egg donation concerns, 25

Mill, John Stuart, on, 245

in organ donation approval, 312

in pediatric care, 212

in public health ethics, 370–372

surrogacy concerns, 35

truth-telling considerations, 208, 209, 212

Paternity

genetic testing implications, 86–88

incidental findings, 78

Patient-centered care

defined, 392

ethics of care approach, 3

truth-telling considerations, 218–219, 220

Patient history. *See* Medical history

Patient information

electronic health records management, 239

HIPAA protections, 228–230

Patient-physician privilege, 226

Patient-physician relationship

boundary crossings and boundary violations, 271–272, *271*

confidentiality concerns, 224, 225, 226, 240

cultural aspects, 214–218

genetic testing concerns, 83–86

physician-assisted suicide concerns, 181, 182, 189–190, 193, 197, 199, 200, 202

truth-telling considerations, 208, 210–211, 214–220

Patient Protection and Affordable Care Act (2010), 79, 92, 239, 274

Patient Self-Determination Act (1990), 170–171

Patric, Jason, *81*

Pavone, Frank, 42

Payne, Michael, 279, 286

PCSBI (Presidential Commission for the Study of Bioethical Issues), 124, 354–355

Peabody, Francis, 83–84

Pediatric care. *See* Adolescents; Children

Peer review, 338, 341, 343

Pellegrino, Edmund, 59, 283

Penicillin, Tuskegee Syphilis Study concerns, 342–343, 365

Percival, Thomas, 71

Perfection, impossibility of, 113, 115

Performance-enhancing substances

fairness concerns, 106–108

neuroethical concerns, 121, 137–139

*See also* Neurological enhancement

Pergonal, 60

Persinger, Michael, 132

Persistent vegetative state (PVS)

Cruzan, Nancy, case, 167–168, 187

defined, 392

determination of death and, 157

moral status arguments, 50

neuroethical concerns, 135–136

organ donation concerns, 306

Quinlan, Karen Ann, case, 166–167, 187

Schiavo, Terri, case, 158, 168–169

Personal vs. impersonal dilemmas, 128, 129–130

Personality
brain damage effects, 142
neuroethical concerns, 126, 133
Personalized medicine, 76, 392
Personhood
bodily autonomy arguments,
53–55
defined, 392
moral status of embryos, 19, 20
moral status of fetuses, 44–51
PET (positron emission tomography)
scans, 157, 392
Petchesky, Rosalind, 63
Pfizer, 262, 331
Pharmaceutical industry conflicts of
interest
case studies, 261–263, 331
descriptive and performative
aspects, 265–266, 265*t*
industry-friendly views, 268
levels of the problem, 269–271,
275
proposed solutions, 268–269
social arrangements in, 264–267,
265*t*, *267*
*Philadelphia* (film), 226, 234
Philosophy of mind, neuroethical
concerns, 127
Physical privacy, 224–225
*See also* Privacy
Physician-assisted suicide, 181–204
autonomy considerations, 181,
185, 191
court cases, 181, 187–189
defined, 393
double effect concerns,
194–195
end-of-life care considerations,
182, 196–198, 202
euthanasia vs., 183–184, 184*t*
killing vs. allowing to die,
185–187, 195–196
language considerations,
183–184, 184*t*
legalization efforts, 184, 201–202
overview, 181–183
principlism views, 189–191
pro and con arguments, 198–201
slippery-slope arguments,
192–194, 201
*See also* Euthanasia
Physician-owned facilities, 272–274
Physician-patient privilege, 226
Physician-patient relationship. *See*
Patient-physician relationship

Physician/provider orders for life-
sustaining treatment (POLST),
174, 393
Physicians
conscientious objection to abortion, 57–60
duty to warn/protect third parties, 224, 231–233, 240–241
participation in negative eugenics, 70
payment of, 266
sphere of duty for genetic disclosure, 84–85
in teaching hospitals, 254–255
training in truth-telling, 218–219
*See also* Conflicts of interest;
Patient-physician relationship;
Physician-assisted suicide
Picoult, Jodi, 52–53, 315
Pinker, Steven, 132
Pitt, Brad, 153
Pittsburgh Protocol, 306, 307
Placebo-controlled trials, 252, 345,
351–352, 393
*Planned Parenthood of Arizona v.*
*Terry Goddard* (Arizona 2009), 58
*Planned Parenthood v. Casey* (1992),
41
Platt, Oliver, *267*
Plutonium experiments on humans,
340
Poddar, Prosenjit, 232–233, *232*
Poehler, Amy, 29
Policy making
ethics committee role, 285
genetic interventions, 109–110,
112
neuroethical concerns, 140–143
public health role, 363, 365
POLST (physician/provider orders
for life-sustaining treatment), 174,
393
Pontius, Anneliese A., 122
Positive eugenics, 27
*See also* Eugenics
Positron emission tomography (PET)
scans, 157, 392
Post-traumatic stress disorder, pro-
pranolol treatment, 139
Potential for personhood, abortion
arguments, 50
Power of attorney for health care,
172–173, 388
Precision medicine, 76, 393
Predictive testing, defined, 393

Pregnancy
burdens of, 55
fetal vs. maternal rights, 51–52
health risks from multiple pregnancy, 60, 61–62
underreporting of risky behavior,
214
Pregnancy discrimination, 52
Preimplantation testing, 80–82, 87,
393
Premises, in ethics consultation,
296–297
Prenatal testing, 80–82, 86–87,
393
Presidential Commission for the
Study of Bioethical Issues (PCSBI),
124, 354–355
President's Commission for the Study
of Ethical Problems in Medicine
and Biomedical and Behavioral
Research, 285
President's Council on Bioethics, 20,
306
Presumed consent, 253*t*, 255–257,
*256*, 308–309
Presymptomatic (predictive) testing,
393
Pretty, Helen, 54, 56
Pretty, Simon, 54
*Prima facie* duties
abortion arguments, 62
confidentiality, 223, 231, 240
organ donation to family members, 312
in principlism, 5
truth-telling, 211, 219
*Prima facie* principle, 92, 393
Principles for Those in Research and
Experimentation (World Medical
Association) (1954), 337–338, 339
Principlism
defined, 393
in defining death, 158–159
in ethics consultation, 296
in exploring physician-assisted
suicide, 189–191
primer on, 5–7
in public health ethics, 366–367
Prison experiment, Stanford University, 340
Prisoners
deceased organ donation by, 310,
318
health inequalities in, 366
unethical research on, 340, 341

Privacy
abortion and contraception court decisions, 41
brain imaging concerns, 134
brain-training game data, 144
confidentiality vs., 224–226, 240
defined, 393
genetic testing concerns, 69, 74–76, 87, 90–92
neuroethical concerns, 126–127
neuromarketing concerns, 143
newborn blood screenings, 82–83
public health surveillance powers vs., 374–375
truth-telling considerations, 208
See also Confidentiality
Probate, defined, 393
Pro-choice vs. pro-life viewpoints
shared values, 62–65
vilification of opposition, 42–44, 51
See also Abortion
Procreative autonomy, 37–38, 110–111
Procreative beneficence, 110, 111, 393
Procreative liberty, 36–38, 41, 393
Professionalism, defined, 393
Property rights
body parts and tissues, 73, 74
genetic research, 79–80
Propranolol, neuroethical concerns, 138–139
Proprietary privacy, 224
See also Privacy
Protected health information, 229, 230
Protection of third parties. See Third parties, duty to warn/protect
Proteomics, defined, 393
Providers. See Health care professionals
Proximity, in Hedonistic Calculus, 8
Psychiatric disorders. See Mental illness
Psychopathology, brain imaging role in diagnosis, 140–141
Public Health Council (Netherlands), 337–338
Public health ethics, 361–384
balancing autonomy and paternalism, 370–372
confidentiality concerns, 226–227
defined, 393

definition of public health, 361–362, 362t
disaster and crisis management, 361, 372–374
distribution of resources, 380–382
efforts to change health behaviors, 377–380, 380
functions of public health, 363
goals of public health, 364–366
individual rights vs., 69
mandatory reporting laws, 223–224, 230–231, 240, 374–375
newborn blood screenings, 82–83
overview, 366–368
principles of, 368–370, 369t
surveillance and quarantine, 370, 371, 374–377, 376
utilitarianism in, 8
Public Health Leadership Society principles, 368, 369t, 370
Public Health Service
research ethics development, 339, 341
Tuskegee Syphilis Study, 342, 343, 370
Public solicitation of organ donation, 323–324
Pure facilitation/pure consensus model of ethics consultation, 288–289
Purity, in Hedonistic Calculus, 8
PVS (persistent vegetative state). See Persistent vegetative state (PVS)

Q
Quality of life
abortion arguments, 46
in end-of-life planning, 164, 172, 196
neuroethical concerns, 135
Quarantine, 370, 371, 374–377, 376
Quill, Vacco v. (1997), 188
Quill v. Vacco (2nd Cir. 1996), 188
Quinlan, Karen Ann, 166–167, 187

R
Racial considerations
brain imaging research, 133
conditional organ donation, 322–323
genetic testing and identity, 87–88

health inequalities, 366
negative eugenics, 27, 71, 117, 118, 371
organ allocation concerns, 320–321
Radiation experiments on humans, 340
Ramsey, Paul, 114
Randomized clinical trials (RCTs)
consent, 252
defined, 393
research ethics, 331, 348, 349, 351, 352
Rape. See Sexual assault
Rapp, Emily, 46
Readiness potential, 131
Reasoning
for finding moral law, 4
in medical ethics, 284
moral, 2, 139
natural law views, 5
Reciprocal justice, in research ethics, 346
Recognition of complexity, in conflicts of interest, 269
Recombinant human bone morphogenic protein-2 (InFuse), 262–263, 264, 274–275
Reese, Peter, 312
Refusing medical treatment. See Right to refuse medical treatment
Regan, Donald, 55
Regents of the University of California, Moore v. (1990), 72, 73
Regents of the University of California, Tarasoff v. (Calif. 1974, 1976), 232–233
Rehabilitation Act (1973), 92
Reidy, Jamie, 266
Rejection (organ transplantation), 393
Relationships
directed organ donation concerns, 315, 323, 324
in ethics, 282
in ethics of care, 2, 3
violinist example objections, 56–57
See also Family; Patient-physician relationship
Release and Destruction of Lives Not Worth Living (Hoche and Binding), 70
Religion
consent aspects, 247–248

Religion, *continued*
    neurotheological approach,
        131–132
    objections to declaration of death,
        156
    views of death, 159
Repeated discussions, need for, 251
*Report of the Public Responsibility in
    Medicine and Research (PRIM&R)
    Human Tissue/Specimen Banking
    Working Group*, 74
Reporting laws. *See* Mandatory
    reporting laws
Repositories for biological samples.
    *See* Biobanks
Reproductive technologies. *See*
    Assisted reproductive technologies
Repugnance argument for organ
    donation incentives, 318
Rescue, duty of, 353
Research, defined, 71
Research ethics, 331–359
    assent to participation, 248–249
    *Belmont* principles, 344–347, 356
    confidentiality concerns, 225
    conflicts of interest, 263,
        264–265, 269–271
    defined, 393
    genetic research, 72
    genetic testing, 71–74
    Good Samaritan obligations and
        duty of rescue, 353
    history of research abuses,
        339–342, 356
    informed consent, 72, 73, 74–76,
        87, 126, 251–253, *251*,
        338–339
    Nuffield Council principles,
        347–348
    Nuremberg Code, 332–336,
        *334*, 338, 392
    overview, 71–72, 331–332
    post-*Belmont* questions, 353–355
    post-Nuremberg regulations,
        336–339
    rise of regulatory oversight,
        341–344
    standard of care argument,
        348–350
    stem cell research, 77
    therapeutic obligation and clini-
        cal equipoise, 350–352
Resource distribution. *See* Allocation
    of resources
Respect for persons

in *Belmont* principles, 332,
    344–345, 356
disclosure of research controversy,
    78
in Nuffield Council principles,
    347
Respecting Choices program, 170
Responsibility
    in ethics consultation, 294
    neuroethical concerns, 140–143
    violinist example objections, 56
Resuscitation, 173–174, 393
    *See also* Do-not-resuscitate
        (DNR) orders; Life-sustaining
        treatment
Revoked implied consent, 254
rhBMP-2 (recombinant human bone
    morphogenic protein-2), 262–263,
    264, 274–275
Right to refuse medical treatment
    autonomy considerations,
        165–169
    right to die aspects, 181, 182,
        185, 188, 202
Rightness of action, 3–4, 281
Ring of Gyges, 298–299
Rodwin, Marc, 270, 271
*Roe v. Wade* (1973), 41, 42
Rofecoxib (Vioxx), 268
Role modeling, in virtue ethics, 10
Roles, in ethics, 281, 282
Roskies, Adina, 122
Ross, Lainie, 313, 314
Roth, Rachel, 51–52
Rothman, David, 338
Royal Society of London, 122
Rudy, Kathy, 64
Rule-based ethics. *See* Deontology
Rule utilitarianism, 8–9

**S**

Safer, Donna, 84–85, 235–236
*Safer v. Estate of Pack* (New Jersey
    1996), 84–85, 236
Safety concerns
    adverse events and conflicts of
        interest, 218, 263, 264, 268
    genetic interventions, 102, 103,
        108, 113, 118
    public health ethics, 363, 366,
        368, 370
    research ethics, 344, 345, 352,
        353
    tDCS devices, 145

*See also* Nonmaleficence
Safire, William, 122
*Salgo v. Leland Stanford Jr. University
    Board of Trustees* (154 Cal. App. 2d
    1957), 244
Saliva genetic testing, 83
Sampedro, Ramón, 183
Sanctity of life viewpoint, 45
Sandel, Michael, 113–114, 115
Sanitary Corps, 373
Saunders, Cicely, 163–164
Savulescu, Julian, 110
Sawyer, Allan, 51, 58, 59
Scalia, Antonin, 89
Scheper-Hughes, Nancy, 317
Schiavo, Michael, 168
Schiavo, Terri, 158, 168–169
Schizophrenia
    Havasupai Indian tribe unethical
        research, 75
    paternal age risks, 36
    tDCS treatment claims, 144
Schloendorff, Mary, 166, 243
*Schloendorff v. Society of New York
    Hospital* (1914), 166, 243, 256
SCID (severe combined immune
    deficiency), 101
Science-fiction film, 44, *44*, 46, 48
    *See also specific films*
SCNT (somatic cell nuclear transfer),
    77
Scope of practice, 294–295, 298
Screw cap proposed restrictions,
    380
*Scrubs* (television show), 311, 314,
    319
*The Sea Inside* (film), 183
Sebelius, Kathleen, 340
*Sebelius, Sherley v.* (DC Circuit Court
    2011), 77
Sedation to death. *See* Terminal
    sedation
Selective abortion, 36, 58, 60–62, *61*,
    393
Selective serotonin reuptake inhibi-
    tors (SSRIs), 139
Self-determination
    right to die aspects, 185, 187,
        199–200
    truth-telling considerations, 208
    *See also* Autonomy
Self-driving cars, casuistry views, 10
Self-interest, paradox with altruism,
    261, 275
*Selfless* (film), 153, 162

Self-referral conflicts of interest, 272–274

Self-removal, as solution for conflicts of interest, 269

Sentience, moral status of fetus concerns, 48, 49–50

*Seven Pounds* (film), 313–314, *314*, 315

Severe combined immune deficiency (SCID), 101

Sex selection, through genetic testing, 81

Sexual assault
    abortion arguments, 46–47
    DNA identification concerns, 89

Sexual orientation, truth-telling to providers, 213–214

Sexually Transmitted Diseases Inoculation Study, 340

Shakespeare, William, 153

Shame, truth-telling considerations, 213, 214, 218

Shameful death, 160, 162

Shemie, Sam, 307

Shepard, Dax, 29

*Sherley v. Sebelius* (D.C. Circuit Court 2011), 77

Shimp, David, 54, 55, 56

*Shimp, McFall v.* (1978), 54

Sickle-cell trait, 87–88

Siegler, Mark, 367

Simmerling, Mary, 313

*The Simpsons* (television show), 108–109

Singer, Peter, 50, 62

Singular ethics consultants, 285

Situation dependence. *See* Context dependence

Skloot, Rebecca, 74, 355

Slepian, Barnett, 42

Slippery-slope arguments
    boundary crossings and boundary violations, 272
    physician-assisted suicide, 192–194, 201

Small bowel transplantation, 303

Small team ethics consultations, 285

Smith, Will, 313, *314*

Smoking, prevention efforts, 378–379

"Snowflake" (embryo) adoption, 20

Social arrangements, in conflicts of interest, 264–267, 265*t*, *267*, 270, 274

Social Darwinism, 70, 393

Social death, 158
    *See also* Death

Social determinants of health, 365

Social justice
    in exploring physician-assisted suicide, 189–190, 191, 199
    overview, 301
    in public health ethics, 367–368

Social media, confidentiality concerns, 239–240, 241

Social workers, hospice care, 164

*Society of New York Hospital, Schloendorff v.* (1914), 166, 243, 256

Socioeconomic inequality
    abortion access concerns, 58, 63–64
    assisted reproductive technology concerns, 38–39
    disaster and crisis management concerns, 373–374
    egg cryopreservation concerns, 29
    genetic intervention concerns, 116
    health inequalities from, 364, 365–366, 381–382
    local vs. global standard of care, 348–350
    organ allocation concerns, 320–322
    research ethics concerns, 347, 353
    smoking-related diseases and, 378
    surrogacy concerns, 29–30, 31, 32–36
    surveillance and quarantine concerns, 376, 377

Soft-drink consumption restrictions, 379–380, *380*

Solidarity, in public health ethics, 369, 378, 379

Somatic cell nuclear transfer (SCNT), 77

Somatic gene therapy, 99–103, *100*, 108, 394

Somatic stem cells, 76

Southam, Chester, 341

Spain, opt-out model of consent for organ donation, 308, 309

Specimen repositories. *See* Biobanks

*Spence, Canterbury v.* (1972), 244, 246, 249

Spence, William, 244

Spencer, Herbert, 70

Sperm
    donation of, 15, 21–22, *21*, 57
    germ-line gene therapy, 103–104

Sperm banks, 22

Spinal fusion surgery, 262–263

*Spine Journal*, 262–263

*The Spirit Catches You and You Fall Down* (Fadiman), 216, 258

Spital, Aaron, 313

Spitz, Don, 42

Sports, genetic intervention concerns, 106–107, *107*, 108

Spurlock, Morgan, 379

SSRIs (selective serotonin reuptake inhibitors), 139

Standard of care, defined, 394

Standard of care research ethics framework, 348–350

*The Stanford Prison Experiment* (film), 340

Stanford University, 122, 340

Stansel sextuplets, 61

*Starbuck* (film), 15, *21*, 22, 38

Stark law, 273

*State of Minnesota, et al., Bearder et al. v.* (2009), 82–83

Stateville Penitentiary Malaria Study, 340

*Steel Magnolias* (film), 162, 163, 175

Steinbock, Bonnie, 48, 49, 50

Stell, Lance, 268

Stem cell, defined, 394

Stem cell research, 76–77

Steptoe, Patrick, 17, 20

Sterilization, forced, 27, 71, 335, 371

Stern, Elizabeth, 30

Stern, William, 30, 31

Steroids, defined, 394

*Stewart v. Gramley* (1997), 88

Stigmatization
    abortion providers, 58
    disabilities, 116, 117
    genetic testing concerns, 74–76, 91
    public health ethics, 375, 376

*Still Alice* (film), 236

Stimulants, neuroethical concerns, 138

Stone Age of death, 159

Stossel, Thomas, 268

Strong model of consent for organ donation, 309

*Studio One in Hollywood* (television show), 288

Substance abuse
    effects on personality and behavior, 142
    organ donation concerns, 319, 320
Substituted judgment, 173, 394
Suffering
    defined, 394
    pain vs., 165
    physician-assisted suicide concerns, 190, 192–193, 198–199
Suicide
    assisted, 183, 184, 385
    defined, 183, 394
    physician-assisted suicide vs., 198
    *See also* Physician-assisted suicide
Suleman, Nadya ("Octomom"), 60, *61*
Sulfa drugs, introduction of, 364
Sumner, L. W., 49
*Super Size Me* (film), 379
Superovulation, 16, 23
SUPPORT (Study to Understand Prognoses and Preferences for Outcomes and Risks of Treatment), 196
Surrogacy. *See* Gestational surrogacy
Surrogate consent, 337
Surrogate decision makers
    consent and assent issues, 248, 337
    medical power of attorney, 171, 172–173
Surveillance, public health, 370, 371, 374–377, *376*
Sweden, sperm donation limitations, 22
Switzerland, physician-assisted suicide legalization, 184
Syphilis
    Guatemala study, 340, 354–355
    Tuskegee study, 243, *251*, 252, 332, 340, 341–342, 354, 370

**T**

Takahashi, Kazutoshi, 76
Tarasoff, Tatiana, 232–233, *232*
*Tarasoff v. Regents of the University of California* (Calif. 1974, 1976), 232–233
Tatou, Audrey, 317
Tay-Sachs disease, abortion arguments, 45–46

tDCS (transcranial direct current stimulation), 144–145
Teach-back method, 250–251
Teaching hospitals, consent for treatment by students, 254–255
Technological imperative, 13
Technology. *See* Assisted reproductive technologies; Genetic interventions; Life-sustaining treatment; Neurotechnology
Teenage Parents Program (Louisville, Kentucky), 64
Teenagers. *See* Adolescents
Terminal illness
    deception in sharing diagnosis, 207–208
    hospice care, 163–164
    *See also* End-of-life preparation
Terminal sedation
    beneficence recognition of, 6
    double-effect sedation vs., 194–195
    *See also* Physician-assisted suicide
Terri's Law, 168
*Terry Goddard, Planned Parenthood of Arizona v.* (Arizona 2009), 58
Test-tube babies. *See* In vitro fertilization (IVF)
Texas Advance Directive Act (1999), 176
Thalidomide, 42
Theoretical neuroethics, 127–132, *129*
Theories, ethical, 1–2
    *See also specific theories*
Therapeutic obligation, 350–352, 394
Therapeutic research, informed consent exceptions, 338–339
Therapeutic use exemptions, 108
Therapy, defined, 99
    *See also specific types*
Therapy/enhancement distinction
    genetic interventions, 104–108, *107*
    neuroethical concerns, 137–140
Third parties, duty to warn/protect, 224, 231–233, 240–241, 374–375
Thomas Aquinas, 4, 5
Thompson, Hunter S., 158
Thomson, Judith Jarvis, 52, 53, 55–57
*Threlkel, Pate v.* (Florida 1995), 84
Tilousium, Rex, *75*

Tissue samples
    cell lines from, 72, 74, 354, 355
    genetic research ethics concerns, 72–74
TMS (transcranial magnetic stimulation), 132, 140
Tolstoy, Leo, 162, 207
Tooley, Michael, 62
Totipotent cells, 76
Toulmin, Stephen, 10
Tourette's syndrome, 88
Tracy, Steve, 63, 64
Trans PULSE project, 214
Transcendence, neurotheological research, 132
Transcranial direct current stimulation (tDCS), 144–145
Transcranial magnetic stimulation (TMS), 132, 140
Transfer effect, 144
Transhumanism, 110
Translators, 258–259
Transnational surrogacy, 33–36, 394
Transplant tourism, 317–318, 394
Transplantation Society, 324
Treatment, defined, 394
Trolley Car Dilemma
    deontological perspective, 4, 128–129, 130
    double effect perspective, 5
    ethics of care perspective, 3
    neuroethical concerns, 128–130, *129*
    principlism perspective, 7
    SSRI effects on behavior, 139
    summary, 2
    utilitarianism perspective, 8–9, 128, 130
    virtue ethics perspective, 10–11
Trovafloxacin (Trovan), 262, 331
Truog, Robert, 305
Trust
    disclosure of research controversy, 78
    organ donation consent, 309
    oxytocin potential effects, 139
    *See also* Conflicts of interest; Truth-telling in health care
Truth-telling in health care, 207–222
    confidentiality concerns, 208, 238
    cultural aspects, 214–218, 220
    defined, 394
    deontological approach, 4
    disclosure of errors, 218

historical perspective, 208–210, *209*

informed consent and, 210–211

medical excuses in organ donation, 313

overview, 207–208

patient-centered framework, 218–219

patient role, 213–214, 220

provider role, 211–213, 219–220

*See also* Trust

Tucci, Stanley, *98*

Tuskegee Study of Untreated Syphilis in the Negro Male

film depiction of, 370

Guatemala study vs., 354

lack of informed consent, 243, *251*, 252

research ethics concerns, 332, 340, 341–342

Tuskegee Syphilis Study Ad Hoc Advisory Panel, 342–343

"Twelve Angry Men" (*Studio One* episode), 288

"Typhoid Mary" (Mary Mallon), 375–376, *376*

**U**

*Unborn in the U.S.A.* (documentary), 42

Uncontrolled donation after cardiocirculatory death, 306

Understanding vs. information, in informed consent, 249–251

Undocumented immigrants, access to organ transplantation, 321

Undue inducement

egg donation, 25

gestational surrogacy, 29, 32–33, 34, 35

Uniform Determination of Death Act (1981), 156, 157, 177, 305, 394

Unilateral DNR orders, 177

*Union Pacific Railway v. Botsford* (1891), 166

United Kingdom

egg donation regulation, 24

embryo storage regulation, 20

sperm donation limitations, 22

United Nations, 109

United Nations Universal Declaration of Human Rights (1948), 317, 333, 336, 394

United Network for Organ Sharing (UNOS), 6–7, 309, 310, 320

Universal Declaration on the Human Genome and Human Rights, 109

Universal laws, 3–4

Universalizability test, 4

University of California, Los Angeles, 72

University of Oklahoma, 268–269

University of Pennsylvania, 122

*University of Utah Medical Center, Harnicher v.* (1998), 82

UNOS (United Network for Organ Sharing), 6–7, 309, 310, 320

Unreasonable search and seizure

DNA identification concerns, 89–90

dried blood spot screening, 83

*U.S., Conn v.* (2011), 86

US Army, 338–339

US Centers for Disease Control and Prevention (CDC)

ACTG 076 clinical trials, 349

film depiction of, 231, 361

mandatory reporting laws, 230–231

Tuskegee Syphilis Study, 342, 343

US Conference of Catholic Bishops, 63

US Department of Health, Education, and Welfare (DHEW), 342–343, 344

US Department of Health and Human Services, 355

US Equal Employment Opportunity Commission (EEOC), 92

US Food and Drug Administration (FDA), 80

US Government Accountability Office (GAO), 83

US Public Health Service, 252

US Supreme Court

abortion and contraception decisions, 41, 42

compulsory sterilization case, 71

DNA identification case, 89

gene patent ruling, 79

physician-assisted suicide cases, 187–189

Utilitarianism

act vs. rule, 8–9

confidentiality concerns, 226–227, 240

primer on, 7–9

in public health ethics, 368

in trolleyology, 8–9, 128, 130

**V**

Vaccines

compulsory vaccination laws, 8, 368, 379

Nazi regime experimentation, 335

utilitarianism views, 8

*Vacco, Quill v.* (2nd Cir. 1996), 188

*Vacco v. Quill* (1997), 188

Values

in donation after cardiocirculatory death, 307

in ethics consultation, 287–288, 289, 294

as part of ethics, 281, 282, 284

Vanderford, Marsha, 42–43

Vásquez Aldana, Carmen Guadalupe, 47

Vassilieva, Sofia, *81*

Vectors

defined, 394

in gene therapy, 100–101, *100*, 102, 103, 104

Vegetative state, 135–136

*See also* Persistent vegetative state

Ventilators

brain death determination and, 305

defined, 394

neurological determination of death concerns, 304–305

Quinlan, Karen Ann, case, 167, 187

Vermont, physician-assisted suicide legalization, 184

Veterans Administration, 290

Viagra, conflicts of interest in selling, 266

Vigils, hospice, 164

Vikander, Alicia, *44*

Violinist example, 53–57

Vioxx (Rofecoxib), 268

Virtue ethics, 9–11

Virtuous actions, 9

Viruses, as gene therapy vectors, 100–101, *100*, 102, 103, 104

Vision loss, as social death, 158

Vitrification, 28

Vivisection, 334, 335, 394

Volitional movement, neuroscience research, 131

Voluntarily stopping of eating and drinking (VSED), 187, 195–196

Voluntary choice, in virtuous actions, 9

Voluntary palliated starvation, 196
VSED (voluntarily stopping of eating and drinking), 187, 195–196
Vulnerable research subjects, as term, 345

# W

*Wade, Roe v.* (1973), 41, 42
Wadmann, Sarah, 269–270
War Crimes Tribunal, US, 332
Warning third parties. *See* Third parties, duty to warn/protect
Warrant, in ethics consultation, 297
Warren, Mary Anne, 47–48, 62
Warren, Samuel, 69, 90
*Washington, Compassion in Dying v.* (9th Cir. 1996), 188
Washington State, physician-assisted suicide legalization, 184
Washington University, 73
*Washington University v. Catalona* (2007), 73
*Washington v. Glucksberg* (1997), 188–189
Watson, James D., 97
Weak model of consent for organ donation, 309

Weaver, Sigourney, 29
Weber, Michael, 268
Wells, H. G., 109
Welsome, Eileen, 340
*The West Wing* (television show), 280–281
Whitehead, Mary Beth, 30, 31
Whitehouse, Peter, 172
WHO (World Health Organization), 231, 361, 371
Whole brain death, 157
Wicklund, Susan, 62
Wigand, Jeffrey, 378
Wilcox, John T., 56, 57
Wilkinson, Timothy, 308
Willowbrook Study of Infectious Hepatitis, 252, 332, 340
Winslade, William, 367
*Wit* (play), 153, 163, 173–174
Withdrawing treatment, 175, 185, 187, 188, 394
Withholding treatment, 175, 185, 187, 188, 342–343, 394
Wolf, Naomi, 62
Wolf, Susan M., 78
Wolpe, Paul Root, 123
World Health Organization (WHO), 231, 361, 371

World Medical Association Declaration of Geneva (1948), 228, 333, 336, 387
World Medical Association Declaration of Helsinki (1964), 333, 336, 338, 339, 343, 387
World Medical Association International Code of Medical Ethics (1949), 333
World Medical Association Principles for Those in Research and Experimentation (1954), 337–338, 339
World War II aftermath, Nuremberg Code development, 332–336, *334*
Wright, Joseph, 63

# Y

Yale University, 263
Ye Shiwen, 106–107, *107*
*You Don't Know Jack* (film), 183

# Z

Zidovudine (AZT), 349, 350
Zimbardo, Phil, 340
Zone of privacy, 224